THE AUSTRO-HUNGARI
THE FIRST WORL

This is a definitive account of the Austro-Hungarian Royal and Imperial Army during the First World War. Graydon A. Tunstall shows how Austria-Hungary entered the war woefully unprepared for the ordeal it would endure. When the war commenced, the Habsburg Army proved grossly understrength relative to trained officers and manpower, possessing obsolete weapons and equipment, and with the vast majority of its troops proved inadequately trained for modern warfare. Well over one million Habsburg troops mobilized, creating an enormous logistical challenge of forging an army from the diverse cultures, languages, economic and educational backgrounds of the empire's peoples. Tunstall shows how the army suffered from poor strategic direction and outdated tactics, while launching a two-front offensive against both Russia and Serbia. He charts the army's performance on the battlefields of Galicia, Serbia, Romania, the Middle East and Italy through to its ultimate collapse in 1918.

GRAYDON A. TUNSTALL was formerly Professor of History at the University of South Florida. His previous publications include *Planning for War against Russia and Serbia: Austro-Hungarian and German Military Strategies, 1871–1914* (1993), *Blood on the Snow: The Carpathian Winter War of 1915* (2010) and *Written in Blood: The Battles for Fortress Przemyśl in WWI* (2016).

This is a major new series of studies of the armies of the major combatants in the First World War for publication during the war's centenary. The books are written by leading military historians and set operations and strategy within the broader context of foreign-policy aims and allied strategic relations, national mobilisation and domestic social, political and economic effects.

Titles in the series include:

The American Army and the First World War by David Woodward

The Austro-Hungarian Army and the First World War by Graydon A. Tunstall

The British Army and the First World War by Ian Beckett, Timothy Bowman and Mark Connelly

The French Army and the First World War by Elizabeth Greenhalgh

The German Army and the First World War by Robert Foley

The Italian Army and the First World War by John Gooch

The Russian Army and the First World War by Bruce W. Menning

THE AUSTRO-HUNGARIAN ARMY AND THE FIRST WORLD WAR

GRAYDON A. TUNSTALL

University of South Florida

CAMBRIDGE
UNIVERSITY PRESS

University Printing House, Cambridge CB2 8BS, United Kingdom

One Liberty Plaza, 20th Floor, New York, NY 10006, USA

477 Williamstown Road, Port Melbourne, VIC 3207, Australia

314–321, 3rd Floor, Plot 3, Splendor Forum, Jasola District Centre, New Delhi – 110025, India

103 Penang Road, #05–06/07, Visioncrest Commercial, Singapore 238467

Cambridge University Press is part of the University of Cambridge.

It furthers the University's mission by disseminating knowledge in the pursuit of
education, learning, and research at the highest international levels of excellence.

www.cambridge.org
Information on this title: www.cambridge.org/9780521199346
DOI: 10.1017/9781139043342

© Graydon A. Tunstall 2021

First published 2021

A catalogue record for this publication is available from the British Library.

Library of Congress Cataloging-in-Publication Data
Names: Tunstall, Graydon A. (Graydon Allen), author.
Title: The Austro-Hungarian Army and the First World War / Graydon A. Tunstall,
University of South Florida.
Description: Cambridge, United Kingdom ; New York, NY : Cambridge University Press, 2021. |
Series: Armies of the Great War | Includes bibliographical references and index.
Identifiers: LCCN 2021026868 (print) | LCCN 2021026869 (ebook) | ISBN 9780521199346
(hardback) | ISBN 9780521181242 (paperback) | ISBN 9781139043342 (epub)
Subjects: LCSH: Austro-Hungarian Monarchy. Heer–History–World War, 1914-1918. |
Austro-Hungarian Monarchy. Heer–Operational readiness. | World War, 1914-1918–
Campaigns–Eastern Front. | World War, 1914-1918–Austria. | BISAC: HISTORY /
Modern / 20th Century | HISTORY / Modern / 20th Century
Classification: LCC D539 .T86 2021 (print) | LCC D539 (ebook) | DDC 940.4/25–dc23
LC record available at https://lccn.loc.gov/2021026868
LC ebook record available at https://lccn.loc.gov/2021026869

ISBN 978-0-521-19934-6 Hardback
ISBN 978-0-521-18124-2 Paperback

To my soulmate, Wendy, for her endless patience and encouragement and to Jessica, Giovanna and Donato with love as you embark on your promising future.

CONTENTS

FIGURES

MAPS

ACKNOWLEDGMENTS

I owe an enormous debt to my friend and mentor, the late Dennis Showalter, who encouraged me to return to research and teaching after a twenty-seven-year hiatus in university administration. His friendship, support and valuable feedback will be sorely missed. My dissertation advisor, renowned Habsburg historian, the late Robert Kann, left a profound impact on my research interests to this day. I am proud to have been his last student of note.

This work would not have been possible without the help of several important people. In particular, I would like to thank Judy Drawdy who spent untold hours typing revisions; Charles Harris, a former graduate assistant of mine at the University of South Florida, who assisted in proofreading and copyediting; as well as John Northrup who provided constructive insights. I also wish to thank Cassidy Simpson for his valuable assistance in finalizing the manuscript and preparing the maps and Index.

I am grateful to the staff at the Vienna War Archives, who assisted me over many years, particularly my very dear friend, the late archival librarian Herr Moser. In the USA, I especially want to thank Sandra Law, Interlibrary Loan specialist at the University of South Florida, for her patience and assistance.

~

Introduction

Austria-Hungary entered the First World War totally unprepared to conduct a prolonged economic and military conflict. Its army had suffered decades of insufficient funding because of Hungarian obstructionist policies, placing it at a great disadvantage to the other European great powers that had been arming during the multiple years' arms race, particularly after 1911. Its industrial base proved inadequate to fight a long war. The Entente naval blockade prevented the Dual Monarchy from receiving crucial raw materials and food supplies, producing starvation and misery and retarding industrial development. Internally, the Czech and South Slavic peoples increasingly demanded autonomy while the nationality issue affected both internal and external affairs. During 1914, 5,100 businesses closed with the mobilization and the basic economy suffered from the unemployment caused by the call-up of millions of soldiers.[1]

Throughout the war Germany provided raw materials and financial assistance of a hundred million marks per month until late 1918, purchases having to be for German goods. The Germans also supplied submarines for the Adriatic Sea and airplanes for reconnaissance purposes. They also provided seventy planes in 1914 and ten a month throughout the conflict. The ally consistently reacted to Habsburg appeals for military assistance, when it ultimately depended on the Western front military situation for its survival. The Central Power alliance became fatal in 1918, when the Entente determined that no separate peace could be consummated with Austria-Hungary following Emperor Karl's "Canossa" at the May 12, 1918 meeting at the German headquarters at Spa.

As the war continued the overall economic situation steadily worsened, while the railroads began to deteriorate during 1916. The lack of raw materials eventually caused factories to fail to meet their quotas and, by 1918, many had to close because of the lack of coal and oil as well as the necessary materiel.

When the war commenced, the Habsburg Army proved grossly under-strength relative to trained officers and manpower, possessing obsolete weapons and equipment, and the vast majority of troops proved inadequately trained for modern warfare. Only 414,000, a quarter of the mobilized troops, were trained professional soldiers. Well over a million Habsburg troops mobilized, many not having had any military training for years, if any, particularly the older *Landsturm* troops. Some literally had had none.

In the initial 1914 military campaigns the Habsburg Army suffered embarrassing defeats and enormous casualties on both the Balkan and Russian fronts. The army, unprepared and incapable of conducting a two-front war, was probably capable of only defeating Serbia. General Conrad von Hötzendorf, chief of the Austro-Hungarian General Staff, altered his 1914 mobilization plans just before the Habsburg mobilization. This resulted in disaster and catastrophic casualties, particularly in the professional officer and troop ranks, which could never be replaced. Attacking Habsburg infantry received inadequate artillery support, if they received any, and artillery shells were rapidly expended early in the war. The early embarrassing battlefield defeats forced General Conrad to approach his German ally for immediate assistance, and each year the Germans had to turn their attention from the critical Western front to aid their lackluster ally on the Eastern.

A major problem resulted from General Conrad's adherence to the cult of the offensive. This proved catastrophic with the two early devastating Lemberg battles and resulting retreat. Conrad continued to launch offensives against numerically superior enemy forces. The Habsburg artillery branch proved grossly inadequate when it failed to support infantry attacks in the repeated Conrad offensive formations against numerically superior enemy forces. The fact that the Habsburg Army had no defensive doctrine, or training, because of Conrad's belief in the offensive, resulted in the unanticipated September 1914 retreat proving an absolute chaotic disaster.

The Dual Monarchy was also the only European great power that did not possess a reserve army; its railroad system proved inadequate to conduct a one-front war, let alone a multiple-front conflict. Poor annual harvests worsened the Homeland food situation, resulting in annual food crises early in the war. During 1914 food rationing commenced. Meanwhile, the enormous battlefield casualties eroded troop and civilian morale, and war weariness escalated as the Habsburg economic situation steadily worsened. As the war dragged on, people desired peace as Dual Monarchy cemeteries filled to capacity.

Anti-military and dynastic episodes had occurred before the war erupted, particularly in Bohemia during the 1912–1913 Balkan Wars. With the two fateful 1914 Lemberg battles, the defeated troops retreated 150 kilometers into the Carpathian Mountains. Then, after the catastrophic failure of the Carpathian Mountain Winter War campaign, Italy declared war on May 23, 1915. The Dual Monarchy became mired in a three-front war for which it was totally unprepared. Russian numerical superiority and its numerically superior artillery overpowered the Habsburg Army numerous times, while in the three 1914 Balkan campaigns a serious underestimation of Serbian troop capabilities and failed strategy rapidly proved disastrous. The German High Command did not comprehend the depth of Dual Monarchy nationality problems, while in September 1914 Conrad was not informed that General Moltke had been removed as chief of the German General Staff and replaced by General Eric Falkenhayn, the war minister. Allied command friction commenced almost immediately.

Austria-Hungary represented the exception in an age of extreme nationalism as the Dual Monarchy consisted of eleven major nationalities.[2] The Habsburg nationality issue extended back to Empress Maria Theresa (r. 1740–1780), crowned Queen of Bohemia and her son Joseph II (r. 1780–1790), who decreed that the German language be that of the empire. Matters remained fairly quiescent until the nineteenth century, when the 1848 revolutions reopened the nationalism question and the first serious national and political stirrings of the Dual Monarchy's various peoples.

The Dual Monarchy possessed a majority Slavic population particularly when the provinces of Bosnia-Herzegovina were annexed in 1908. When the war erupted, the Slavic peoples did not enthusiastically support fighting against fellow Slavic Russians and Serbians. Many Slavs also opposed the German alliance. Reputed Slavic troop desertions and surrendering to the enemy on the Russian and Serbian fronts led to charges of treason against them, but all Slavic troops fought well against the hated Italians who were perceived as seeking to seize South Slav lands, when Italy declared war on May 23, 1915.

The failure of the Habsburg central government to alleviate the multitude of problems that arose during the war, or provide adequate alternatives – particularly for food shortages and hunger – proved disastrous. The steadily worsening economic situation following the multiple Habsburg battlefield defeats ultimately destroyed the empire during October 1918. The masses eventually turned to revolutionary activity, even creating national councils. The central government quickly proved it could not resolve the accelerating economic and nationality problems. Government corruption became rampant, accelerated by the lack of coordination between Vienna and Budapest. The unresolvable economic situation gradually awakened the festering nationality question. By 1918 the government had been paralyzed, as attention turned to the anticipated German Western front offensive victory. The multiple Habsburg military defeats culminated in the catastrophic June 1918 offensive disaster. German Western front defeats and the September 1918 collapse of the Bulgarian front resulted in ultimate defeat and the almost bloodless Austrian revolution as the various nationalities established their own sovereign states. The Bulgarian debacle opened the Balkan front to eventual Serbian invasion of Hungary and accelerated the end of the war. It also persuaded German Generals Hindenburg and Ludendorff that the end was approaching.

During 1917 indications abounded that the government had become helpless, but by 1918 it had failed to resolve the nationality issue because of the lack of any positive action with battle defeat on the Italian front, which resulted in the collapse of the entire Habsburg edifice. The German alliance allowed the Habsburg central government to avoid any earnest attempt to resolve the nationality issues until it proved too late.

Common people, suffering war weariness and malnutrition, desired peace at any price. The government's failure to also resolve the multiplying domestic problems proved fatal. During January 1918 hunger strikes added political dimensions to the numerous monarchy problems. Many obstacles prevented resolving critically necessary Dual Monarchy reforms. The few attempts before the war collapsed and the failure of Habsburg leadership to agree upon, or attempt, to find a wartime solution proved deadly. This caused Vienna to increasingly depend upon a German Western front military victory to justify the lack of resolution to solve the deadly nationality issue.

Economic difficulties commenced with the early rationing measures resulting chiefly from the Entente blockade of food and raw materials in 1914.[3] The blockade resulted in shortages of all forms of food, producing starvation in the general population, and the loss of raw materials increasingly retarded industrial production; by 1918 it dwindled catastrophically.

A major factor in the ultimate fate of the Dual Monarchy resulted from the Germans and Hungarians vociferously fighting to maintain their special privileged positions in their respective halves of the empire, a result of the 1867 *Ausgleich*, the agreement to create the Austro-Hungarian Empire. In Austria the Germans enjoyed cultural leadership and fought to maintain it, while in Hungary any attempt to change the status quo, particularly relative to the numerous nationalities, was vociferously opposed and considered a violation of Hungarian rights. The Magyarization policy prevented a solution to the increasingly fatal nationality policy.

The *Reichsrat*, the Habsburg parliament, had been dissolved in March 1914 because of the vociferous Czech-German nationalistic obstruction tactics that precluded smoothly conducting the empire's political affairs. When resurrected during 1917 it provided the opportunity to again obstruct business while increasing nationalist claims and opposition. Prior to 1914 various national delegates had attempted to force the government to support their specific programs, negatively affecting the conduct of regular business. This eliminated any possibility of compromise as the common people increasingly became malnourished, grew war weary and desired peace. Increased disillusionment targeted the ineffective and inefficient central government. Meanwhile, in the 1917 resurrected *Reichsrat* Czech passive resistance accelerated against the German liberal parties. This encouraged South Slav agitation commencing in late 1917 that steadily increased because the central government failed to provide assistance for famine conditions in the southern areas of the Dual Monarchy. The South Slavs in the Yugoslav Club, particularly Slovene Catholic leaders, became concerned about potential Italian or

German intentions for their territories. The significant May 1917 Declaration progressively produced radical solutions to perceived South Slavic problems. The May Declaration increasingly unleashed nationalistic demands for some form of South Slavic unity, originally without Serbian leadership. The movement gained support as it spread from Slovenia to other South Slavic provinces.

By 1918 the nationality question proved fatal combined with the horrendous general conditions created by the war. Complicating the situation, all the main eleven nationalities were in different phases of political, cultural and economic development. In addition, several, such as the Slovaks, Serbians, Slovenes, Romanians and Ruthenians, did not possess a national history. They had to be created. The various nationalities had become members of the Dual Monarchy through Habsburg dynastic ties, marriage and war, but the question became whether they could adjust and survive in this age of rampant nationalism.[4]

The German and Hungarian populations represented less than one-half in their respective portions of the empire. In the Austrian section Germans represented only 35 percent of the population, Slavic peoples 65 percent, but the Germans predominated culturally as their language remained the official one and they represented almost 70 percent of the army's officer corps. However, during the prewar period, opposition steadily increased toward such privileged positions. During the war, a serious lack of sufficient numbers of officers speaking the various ethnic languages became a significant factor when many of the original officers and noncommissioned officer corps perished on the 1914 battlefields. The reserve officers that replaced them, in addition to many displaying inferior leadership skills, could not speak or understand their troops' languages. Professional officers had to be conversant with any national group that comprised 20 percent of unit manpower.

The Hungarians represented only 48 percent of their country's population but dominated all aspects of government and society. The post-1867 *Ausgleich* period resulted in the introduction of a Magyarization policy, or cultural and social supremacy, against the non-Magyar nationalities. All attempts at empire-wide reform failed because the Hungarians refused to compromise their privileged positions to the various nationalities. (Power rested with the landed aristocracy not the people.) Any attempt to fulfill Slavic efforts toward an altruistic creation of separate Slavic entities failed because of determined Hungarian resistance to losing any power or influence.

The South Slavic (Croats, Slovenes, Serbians) problem became irreversibly intertwined with the Great Serbia nationalistic movement outside of Austria-Hungary, particularly after the Habsburgs formally annexed Bosnia-Herzegovina during the 1908–1909 crisis. These provinces became the center of Serbian agitation within the Dual Monarchy. During the Bosnian Crisis the South Slav question became a dominant factor for the Habsburg regime, remaining unresolved until the demise of the Dual Monarchy in 1918, because Habsburg leadership failed to provide a solution to the cancerous problem. Following the 1912–1913 Balkan Wars, Serbia became a magnet for South Slavs seeking leadership, while the Dual Monarchy's positions in the Balkan Peninsula suffered. The South Slav question became an internal and external Habsburg matter, because the Slavs would become a vast majority within Hungary if it annexed Bosnia-Herzegovina, thus the provinces became a separate administrative unit within the Habsburg territories. They increasingly became a hotbed for Serbian propaganda in that they represented the majority of the population. Later wartime conditions and the central government's failure to alleviate the people's plight slowly eroded South Slav loyalty to the state.

The festering question could not be settled partially because of Russian protection of Serbia that made it a major foreign policy issue. South Slavic unrest resulted from opposition to the Magyars' privileged position and their Magyarization policies. Following the March 3, 1918 Treaty of Brest-Litovsk, South Slavic *Reichsrat* deputies formed a Yugoslav committee that demanded independence and the creation of a separate South Slavic state within the Monarchy. Meanwhile, during July 1917, exiled Slavic compatriots formed a Yugoslav committee. Eventually they accepted that the Serbian government would create a Slavic state regardless of the problem of various religious, cultural and language differences.[5] Unlike the Czechs and Poles, the South Slavs did not possess an independent military force fighting on the Entente side (only the Serbians at Salonica). The revitalized *Reichsrat* Yugoslav Club began attacking the lack of central government support as the economic, particularly food, situation worsened in the South Slav territories. During October 1918, as the Dual Monarchy disintegrated, Slovene and Croat representatives met in Zagreb. They proclaimed the creation of a new state consisting of Croatia, Slovenia, Dalmatia and Bosnia, intending to prevent an Italian occupation of the Dalmatian coast and Istria. Serbian military crushing of the bandit green cadres helped bring the Croatians and Slovenes into Belgrade's orbit as their cities and the countryside became estranged.

South Slavic political influence was partially handicapped because the Slavic population lived in both portions of the Dual Monarchy, but the connection between northern and southern Slavs was maintained through religion and language ties. The resolution of the South Slav problem would be decided in 1918 when the Entente Powers determined to destroy the Austro-Hungarian monarchy after they accepted that Vienna had become irrevocably subservient to the German alliance after the May 12, 1918 meeting at the Spa military headquarters when Emperor Karl approved closer ties to Germany. This followed Emperor Karl's disastrous Sixtus Affair fiasco, an attempt to negotiate peace with the French, to be explained in detail in Chapter 9.

The Croats, 9 percent of the population in Hungary, enjoyed some autonomy having been the Kingdom of Croatia-Slavonia in the eleventh century and battling the Turks earlier at the Habsburg frontier for centuries. During the decade preceding the war, but particularly in 1917, the Croats became major players in the South Slavic unification issue. During the nineteenth century, Zagreb became the center for the attempt to achieve cultural independence vis-à-vis the Hungarians. Croatian leaders also desired a trialist Austria-Hungary with them serving in the Slavic leadership role. The failure of the central government to alleviate the deteriorating wartime economic situation in South Slavic lands resulted in the Croats joining the Slovenes to support their May 30, 1917 May Declaration. The Croats' favorable position resulted from their 1868 agreement with the Hungarian government, which reputedly guaranteed them specific rights.

The Croats and the other South Slavic peoples became bellicose when the terms of the 1915 Entente Treaty of London with Italy became known; they recognized that if Italy won the war it would seize Croatian and other Slavic territory. Ultimately, on October 29, 1918, in order to preclude Italian occupation of the territories and fearing German hegemony, the Zagreb Sabor [parliament] proclaimed Croatia, Slavonia and Dalmatia a sovereign state. Serbian troops invaded the territories, in the process, as mentioned, eliminating the green cadres – former Habsburg soldiers that had become powerful, fully armed renegades particularly in South Slavic regions. Their suppression by Serbian military forces became a major factor in creating the new "Yugoslav" state with obvious Serbian dominance.

Turning to the Czechs, it was claimed that during the opening 1914 Serbian campaign Czech troops deserted their units, causing multiple battlefield defeats. Often these accusations camouflaged command mistakes and continued throughout the conflagration. A prewar prejudice against Slavic troops escalated during the conflict that increased Czech resentment toward the Habsburg regime. Also, many inadequately trained Czech *Ersatz* troops often became cannon fodder.

Oppressive central governmental and military measures in the Czech lands of Bohemia, Moravia and Silesia produced internal opposition as several national leaders were arrested, including leading radicals, such as Kramar, arrested in September 1914. Emperor Karl eventually released him and other Czech leaders accused of treason with his 1917 amnesty act that backfired because Czech *Reichsrat* deputies increasingly demanded the creation of a Czech state. The emperor's amnesty produced extreme opposition in Habsburg military leadership and civilian circles.

The Czech region contained the most advanced industrialized area within the Austrian portion of the Dual Monarchy. Before the war Czech leaders sought autonomy within the Austro-Hungarian Monarchy, having become part of it after the battle of Mohacs in 1526. The continued struggle over the administrative language question in regional education and administration matters developed into one of the major if not the most significant nationality problem haunting the Habsburg establishment until the late October 1918 collapse. The language question fueled the Czech-German struggle that intensified between 1879 and 1909. The Czech question had remained dormant until the 1815 Congress of Vienna following the Napoleonic Wars. Czech leaders demanded the acceptance of their *Staatsrecht* dating back to the 1620 Pragmatic Sanction after the fatal lost Thirty Years Wars 1618–1648 battle of White Mountain when they lost their independence.

A Czech-Slovak National Council was eventually established in Paris but the émigré leaders such as Tomáš Masaryk and Edvard Beneš had little influence in the Homeland until late in the war. In the Czech lands a *Mafie*, an underground organization of loyal supporters of Masaryk, helped spur passive resistance toward the Habsburg central government, even perpetuating sabotage activities. Coordination between Czech émigrés and leaders at home only became significant late in the war as living conditions continued to decline and the Habsburg Army collapsed after the fatal June 1918 battle. Earlier in 1848, a turning point in the nationality question, the "Old Czech" party was gradually replaced by the "Young Czech" in the late 1880s *Reichsrat*. The Czech passive resistance strategy against the Germans in the *Reichsrat* was later utilized by the Poles, Romanians, Slovenes, even Italians. One of the major factors in the evolution of Czech nationalism evolved from the 1867 *Ausgleich*, which ignored Czech nationality strivings. For seven decades until 1918 Bohemia remained the classic nationality battleground for Austria with continuing unresolved Czech-German hostilities.

Many Czechs proclaimed loyalty to the Habsburg regime early in the war, but in time these proclamations became insecure pledges of support. In 1914 many Czechs still accepted that Austria-Hungary prevented German and Russian expansion, so appeals for national separatism were temporarily subdued. Nevertheless, the Czechs enjoyed greater political autonomy than other nationalities, gaining experience governing themselves. This proved critical during late October 1918, when the existing Habsburg bureaucracy personnel simply reverted to governing the new nation, Czechoslovakia. The Hungarian Slovak population, on the other hand, did not experience any self-government.

During the war the Paris Czech National Committee had the advantage of developing a strong diplomatic position with the Entente, while the creation of the Czech Legion in Russia made it part of Allied military forces. Secret negotiations, a result of Habsburg peace feelers, between March 1917 and April 1918, made the Entente leadership reluctant to commit to the Czechs. The November 1917 Bolshevik coup and Lenin peace decree changed the situation, as did the Russo-German Austro-Hungarian Brest-Litovsk Armistice on March 3, 1918 and the belated US declaration of war against Austria-Hungary. During 1918 the Czech Legion fought its way across Siberia to redeploy to the Western front to fight the Germans, but became embroiled in the Russian Civil War in 1918 as it traveled eastward on the one-track Trans-Siberian railroad.

After the fateful Emperor Karl Sixtus Affair and resulting Habsburg Canossa meeting at the German headquarters at Spa in May, US Secretary of State Lansing informed President Wilson that the Habsburg monarchy had become an irrevocable instrument for German domination of Southeastern Europe. Secretary of State Lansing insisted that a defeated Dual Monarchy be divided into national components. Not completely comprehending the significance of the situation, on May 29, 1918 President Wilson encouraged Czech-Slovak and South Slavic national aspirations. Britain and France followed suit on June 3. On June 28 an American position statement declared that all Slavic peoples should be freed from the German-Austrian yoke. Then on September 3 the USA recognized the Czech National Council in Paris as the de facto Czech government. Seeking permanent political change became the Czech objective, particularly after the Entente allies rejected a final Austrian appeal on September 14, 1918 for nonbinding discussions to establish peace terms. Even though the Habsburg government had acted independently of the Germans, the overture was rejected. President Wilson eventually agreed that the Dual Monarchy should be divided into its various national parts, which proved disastrous for Austria-Hungary during the historical October 1918 events. On October 28 a Czech-Slovak republic was proclaimed and, on November 13, a provisional assembly created a provisional national assembly. The Czechoslovakian state was recognized in the St. Germain (Austria) and Trianon (Hungary) Versailles treaties.

The Slovaks, 9.4 percent of the population in Hungary, suffered because they had lived only in that country. Even with the possibility of joining the Czechs in the Austrian portion of the empire, the Slovaks feared not being accepted as an equal partner, which actually proved fatal later. Czechs and Slovaks also possessed significant linguistic and literary distinctions. During the century after the 1815 Congress of Vienna, the Slovaks remained the most severely suppressed national group in the Dual Monarchy, a result of Hungarian Magyarization policies. Their population spread over large areas east of the Carpathian Mountains, but they possessed no independent political history because of the thousand-year Magyar domination. They also possessed no sizable intellectual class and few middle-class or industrial elements. To their detriment, the Czech leader Tomáš Masaryk made "equality" promises during the war to the Slovaks if they joined the new Czechoslovakian state that never occurred, the promises never being fulfilled.

The question of Italian irredentism in the Habsburg Trentino province and 1915 Treaty of London presented a major roadblock to Austria-Hungary's attempts to establish a separate peace with the Entente. Italian demands for the Tyrol and Habsburg maritime crown lands (the Adriatic Sea area) stiffened

Habsburg and Slav resistance during the war. The Italian territorial demands extending to the northern Brenner Pass represented a crass negation of Wilson's self-determination principle. The Italians and Yugoslavs clashed over claims to the Adriatic coast possessions during the early postwar period.

Italians represented the smallest national group in the Dual Monarchy, but increasingly looked across the frontier, particularly after the 1861 and 1870–1871 Italian unification. During the July 1914 crisis, the Italians declared neutrality on the basis of the Triple Alliance Treaty Article VII, that the war was not a defensive one. The Italians then awaited what they considered the most opportune moment to declare war on their former ally. This transpired on May 23, 1915, influenced by the earlier disastrous Habsburg Carpathian Mountain Winter War campaign. Unfortunately for the Italians the Germans launched the successful Gorlice–Tarnow offensive just before the declaration of war. After multiple Central Power Russian front victories, significant Habsburg troops were redeployed to the Italian theater. During the November 1918 armistice negotiations with the Italians, Rome's actions were influenced by the intent to seize all the irredentist lands promised to it in the 1915 Treaty of London, as well as grasp additional territory in the Adriatic Sea region. Italy received numerous promises of compensation to declare war on Austria-Hungary. Because of the Entente's unfavorable military situation, its leaders felt they needed Italian assistance, but became disillusioned with the lack of successful Italian military efforts during the conflict.

War on the Italian front produced some of the most horrific battle conditions of the entire war, much of the fighting conducted on steep mountainous terrain. Winter mountain weather proved horrendous as Habsburg troops faced an enemy with an enormous superiority in troop and artillery piece numbers. Soldiers on both sides suffered from periodic avalanches, Habsburg troops losing 1,200 men in one day from one such disaster, 12,000 during one month. Lightning storms, frostbite, hypothermia and the "White Death" (freezing to death) also caused many noncombat deaths. Troops had to remain in their positions accompanied by dead, wounded and sick comrades as enemy artillery consistently blew body parts asunder numerous times, killing many soldiers. Habsburg defensive positions had to be dynamited or bored into the rocky mountain surfaces. By the 1917 Tenth and Eleventh Isonzo River offensives, the intensity of the battles and casualties matched those of Verdun and the Somme on the Western front, with the distinct difference that bloody battle never really halted on the Italian front. Italy then suffered the humiliating Caporetto defeat, but with British and French assistance the Italian military recovered for the Habsburg June 1918 battle and won the so-called Vittoria Veneto victory over diseased, starving and war-weary Austro-Hungarian troops.

The critical relationship between the Serbians and the Austro-Hungarian monarchy commenced with the 1875–1876 Bosnian uprisings against brutal

Turkish rule. This resulted in the 1877–1878 Russo-Turkish War, and the 1878 Treaty of San Stefano, which revealed Russia's increasing interest in expanding into the eastern Balkan Peninsula and produced Serbian independence. That same year Habsburg troops occupied the provinces of Bosnia-Herzegovina to administer them according to the San Stefano Treaty terms; however, Turkey retained sovereignty over the provinces. Then in 1881 the King of Serbia signed a secret treaty with Austria-Hungary and domiciled mainly in Vienna until the treaty expired in 1895. Vienna dominated Serbian foreign policy during this period. A Serbian-Bulgarian conflict was fought in 1885, and then in 1897 the Russian and Austro-Hungarian monarchies placed the "Balkans on ice" by treaty to cover the tsarist European flank while they expanded into Asia, commencing after the 1854–1856 Crimean War.

During 1903 the Serbian Royal couple was murdered, and immediately that country's policy reversed against the Dual Monarchy and radically shifted toward Slavic Russia and a "Great Serbia" program. This represented the early commencement of Serbia's attempt to become the leader of a South Slav independence movement. However, for the time being Russia and Austria-Hungary retained their 1897 "Balkans on ice" policy. The Serbian issue proved particularly complicated because the country's mostly peasant population resided in four separate Habsburg areas – Dalmatia, Hungary, Croatia-Slovenia and Bosnia-Herzegovina – as well as in Serbia.

The 1904–1905 Russo-Japanese War had a major effect on the Balkan Peninsula, Europe and the world. Russia refocused its major expansionist attention to Europe and the Balkan Peninsula after its disastrous Asian military defeat. A year earlier the 1903 "Pig War" economic struggle had erupted between the Dual Monarchy and Serbia, but backfired for Vienna as it ended Serbian economic dependence on the Dual Monarchy. It also exacerbated the mounting tension between the two countries. The major event that provided the initial step toward the world war resulted from the 1908–1909 Bosnian Crisis. Austria-Hungary formally annexed Bosnia-Herzegovina, releasing the two provinces from Turkish administrative control while presenting a serious challenge to Serbian national interests. Bosnia had a majority Serbian population, so it provided a perfect target for great Serbian propaganda. This also partially served as background to the creation of a Balkan League consisting of Serbia, Bulgaria, Greece and Montenegro that produced the 1912–1913 Balkan Wars aimed initially at Turkey.[6]

Serbia immediately mobilized troops following the Austro-Hungarian annexation proclamation followed by Russian and Austro-Hungarian partial mobilizations. But Russia remained hampered by its 1904–1905 Asian defeat and resultant serious destruction of its armed forces. Therefore, Serbia had to accept the 1909 situation. Soon the 1912–1913 Balkan Wars erupted, which readjusted the Balkan Peninsula balance of power to the Entente's favor. The major victor, Serbia, increased its population and territory by 50 percent.

However, once again Russia could not fully support Serbia because of its continued military weakness and had to back down again. Russian leaders determined that they could not do so a third time during the 1914 July crisis.

The Austro-Hungarian government sought to neutralize Serbia as a major threat internally and externally with the June 28, 1914 assassination of the Habsburg heir apparent Archduke Franz Ferdinand. The dramatic event appeared to offer an excellent opportunity to defeat the archenemy in a successful local war, which eventually resulted in the outbreak of the First World War. The following unanticipated three 1914 Serbian Balkan military victories not only destroyed Austro-Hungarian prestige in the Balkan Peninsula but accelerated Serbian irredenta actions and goals. In October 1915, however, a lightening Central Power military campaign, spearheaded by German troops, defeated Serbia. The remnants of its army ultimately sailed to Salonica, Greece, where they would participate in the September 1918 military collapse of Bulgaria, repossession of Serbia and then invasion of southern Hungary. Language, religion and cultural differences divided the Habsburg South Slavs from the Greater Serbian movement, but the Serbian Army, crushing the green cadre forces in those areas, pushed Croats and Slovenes into the Serbian orbit to create the future Yugoslavia with its discord.

The Hungarian possession of Transylvania entrapped three million Romanian peasants, because of Romania's adherence to the 1883 Triple Alliance Treaty that prevented strong irredentist activity. That treaty left the Transylvanian Romanians, the largest non-Magyar national group, to the fate of the Hungarians. Transylvania became part of Hungary in 1848. Lacking a separate or strong parliamentary group, the Romanian population possessed no political voice and suffered from the Magyarization policy, as did the other nationalities in that province and elsewhere.

By the 1883 treaty the Romanian Army accepted the obligation to protect the vital Habsburg right flank area if war with Russia ensued. It thus assumed a critical position in Habsburg military planning, involving a question of the Habsburg Army losing the aid of four hundred thousand troops if Romania earlier declared its neutrality, or eight hundred thousand if it fought against the Dual Monarchy. During the 1913 Balkan War, Romania allied with Serbia against Bulgaria, the Habsburg mortal enemy. Thus, Romania could no longer be considered a reliable ally, but, as long as Hohenzollern King Carol reigned, it could be assumed that Romania would not wage war against the Central Powers. Following Carol's death in October 1914 and Romania's earlier declaration of neutrality, his son and successor Ferdinand awaited a definitive Entente military victory before joining the Entente and declaring war on Austria-Hungary. Romania entered the war in late August 1916 because of the overwhelming successful Russian Brusilov offensive that almost destroyed the Austro-Hungarian Army, but that offensive had stalled by then. Nevertheless, on August 17, 1916, following long negotiations, the Entente promised Romania Transylvania, the Banat, the Bukovina and other frontier areas if it declared war on the seemingly critically weakened Austria-Hungary. The success of the Brusilov offensive overcame Romanian hesitancy to enter the war to receive its irredenta terrain.

Romania declared war on Austria-Hungary on August 27, 1916, which gravely threatened the Dual Monarchy, already seriously weakened by the disastrous Brusilov offensive. There were no significant Habsburg troops available to counter a Romanian invasion. Serbia had been conquered in late 1915 and the bloody attrition battles of Verdun, Somme and the Brusilov offensive caused Entente leadership to determine that it required Romanian military assistance. Earlier, the German government and military leadership had demanded Habsburg concessions be conceded to the Romanians in the Bukovina and Transylvania to prevent their entering the war. The Romanians should have committed themselves earlier, because the timing of their declaration of war proved fatal. Their army was quickly overwhelmed by rapid Central Power military action, partially because of its poor military leadership, which forced the Russians to extend their front two hundred kilometers and terminate their Brusilov offensive. The Romanian Army proved unprepared for the war, as it had made no improvements to its armed forces during the intervening time. The victorious Central Powers received a ninety-nine-year lease on Romanian grain, minerals and oil that helped them continue the war with those critical acquisitions. However, Romania reentered the war after it became evident that the Central Powers had been finally defeated in October 1918. The Versailles Treaty added Transylvania, the Bukovina and Banat to a greatly enlarged Romania.

Following the 1867 *Ausgleich*, nationalism was suppressed in the Carpathian Mountain area, particularly affecting the Ruthenian peasant population. When the war erupted in 1914 many Ruthenians (Ukrainians) were accused of disloyalty and treason, which resulted in mass arrests and executions. Many welcomed invading Russian soldiers and provided valuable military information to them during the various phases of the 1914 Eastern front campaigns. The Ruthenians had served as a political counterweight to the Polish leaders in the Habsburg divide-and-conquer strategy during the prewar period, but were severely oppressed by the Polish landowners. The March 3, 1918 Brest-Litovsk peace treaty with Russia gave Cholm and its surrounding territory to the Ruthenians. This produced an enormous spontaneous negative reaction among the Poles, as they terminated their support of the central government, having held important positions in the imperial government since 1873. Immediately following the war bloody clashes erupted between Poles and Ruthenians in Galicia, including Fortress Przemyśl. Then during 1919 the Ukrainian Republic proclaimed its independence to endure political and military upheaval for several years following the war. It also lost some territory to Czechoslovakia with the Versailles peace treaty.

The Ruthenians, the largest Slavic element in Austria, represented the majority population in eastern Galicia, consisting mostly of illiterate peasants. Many sought to join their thirty million kin in the Ukraine. In the Bukovina, by 1910, Ruthenians received autonomy along with six other nationalities, which proved quite successful contrary to events in other Habsburg lands. Both during the prewar period and early in the conflict pro-Russian propaganda flooded the Ruthenian sections of Galicia.

The Slovenes, the third-smallest Dual Monarchy population (only two million people or 4.4 percent of the population) represented the most advanced South Slavic group that also lived in a strategic area. The majority lived in Styria and parts of Austria and Dalmatia, but were scattered in six separate Habsburg crownlands. At the beginning of the war twenty-seven Catholic Slovene priests were arrested in Carinthia, which did not endear the general population to the Habsburg cause, particularly because the native Catholics were loyal to the Habsburg state. Many bloody battles witnessed Slovene troops dying, battling numerically superior Italian forces after Italy declared war on Austria-Hungary on May 23, 1915. The Slovenes and other Southern Slavs hated the Italians and often fought to the death defending their positions against them during the war. Then during 1917, but particularly in 1918, with starvation and famine conditions significantly worsening, combined with oppressive Habsburg governance, the Slovenes became more receptive to the concept of a separate South Slav state. This occurred particularly when their economic well-being was increasingly being ignored in Vienna. Then the earlier mentioned May 30, 1917 Declaration regarding South Slav aspirations increasingly gained adherents as it spread to Croatia and Bosnia. The Slovenes later joined the new Yugoslavia, although not enthusiastically. Serbian troops "conquered" the South Slav territories in 1918, eliminating the green cadre danger and neutralizing the Italian threat, but soon introduced decades of oppression in the nationalist Serbian Yugoslavia.

Unique to the other Habsburg nationalities, the Poles represented an international problem concerning Russia, Germany and Austria-Hungary. The Polish population enjoyed self-administrative rule and much autonomy in Galicia in that far-distant Habsburg province.[7] In 1846 a Galician peasant revolutionary uprising was crushed, which served as a warning to Polish overlords that if they desired to preserve their political and economic power, they had to prevent a social revolution from below. Accordingly, Polish leadership restrained from political revolutionary activity in the future. Late in the century conflict developed between major Polish landowners and the mostly peasant Ruthenians. Open hostility reappeared at the end of the war, as presented earlier.

Polish nationalism was also political; its ultimate goal to reestablish an independent nation. The Central Powers negotiated a potential Austro-

Polish solution, but Germany later refused to accept Habsburg control of Poland. On November 15, 1916 Emperors Wilhelm and Franz Joseph issued a proclamation announcing the creation of an independent Polish kingdom excluding Habsburg or German Polish territories. The proclamation failed to specify the exact territory of the future country, but German military leadership intended Poland to become a satellite in the expanding Eastern European German Reich. The Polish situation became critical as revolutionary events engulfed Russia. During August 1917 a Polish National Committee was established, quickly gaining support to launch an independent state following the February 1917 Russian Revolution. Poles no longer had to fear their old enemy Russia, while the French also established a Polish Army during June 1917. For decades the Polish Galician conservative government strongly supported the Vienna central government through the Polish club in the *Reichsrat*. The 1918 February treaty with the Ukraine and the March 3, 1918 Brest-Litovsk peace terms by which the Ruthenians received the district of Cholm reversed that support and opened the door to national conflict as the war wound down. Polish delegates to the *Reichsrat* left it during October 1918.

Earlier, two Polish prime ministers and a foreign minister served the Dual Monarchy government. The Central Power allies never negotiated a satisfactory solution to the Polish quagmire. The loss of Galicia, the Habsburg Polish province, during the September 1914 military campaigns proved devastating. In addition to Eastern Galicia being conquered, a large proportion of critical grain and oil supplies as well as a rich troop recruitment area had quickly been conquered. Russian troops occupied Galicia twice before the May 1915 Gorlice–Tarnow battle, during which they devastated the province, destroying farms, transportation centers and railroad junctions, while initiating a scorched-earth policy when they ultimately retreated from the province during summer 1915 with their Gorlice–Tarnow defeat. Russian occupation also created an enormous flood of refugees, which created a nationalist reaction against them when they migrated into the Austrian portion of the empire, particularly into Vienna, as starvation conditions progressively worsened throughout the empire. Ethnic hostilities increased with the accelerating war weariness and steadily worsening Dual Monarchy food situation. When German troops deployed in Galicia in mid-1915, they discovered an alien society, describing Galicia as dirty, backward and having many Jewish occupants. This would have an effect in 1939.

Last, but not least, the Jewish presence in the Dual Monarchy must be considered. The vast majority lived in Polish Galicia, but many settled in Vienna and Budapest. By 1910 they represented almost 9 percent of Vienna's population. During the last years of the nineteenth century they assumed major positions in banking, medicine, law, industry and journalism. Anti-Semitism became immersed in the national and racial struggle that exploded into the Second World War. During the First World War the

Jewish population suffered greatly from the anti-Semitism, particularly in Galicia, but spreading to other parts of the Austrian crown lands as well. Many Jews, meanwhile, served in the Habsburg Army during the war.

Food rationing in the Dual Monarchy had already commenced during 1914, and by 1915 had caused much human suffering that led to riots and unrest, exacerbated by the failure of crop yields that continued throughout the war. The Dual Monarchy's agricultural sector declined severely from the enormous number of farm workers and laborers drafted into the army, leaving only children, women and the elderly to tend the land. Many horses were requisitioned, and the necessary nitrates to feed the soil were utilized in ammunition production, further harming food production. The 1914 loss of Galicia cut more than a third of the Dual Monarchy's food supplies. Later in the war prisoners of war would be utilized in the countryside, industry and the army.

The increasingly devastating lack of food supplies and basic commodities resulted in further rationing, which later resulted in the radicalization of the masses, raising serious social issues. Riots erupted as early as 1915, but by January 1918 hunger revolts added political dimensions to the unresolvable economic problems as war weariness and the desire for peace evoked dangerous trends in the civilian population. The situation exploded out of control during the last year of the war as the nationality grievances, worsened social conditions and failure of the government to alleviate the disastrous situation brought chaos. This became significant because of the disastrous Habsburg military situation, particularly after the suicidal June 15, 1918 offensive.

The failure of the central government to alleviate the civilian and military situation, because of corruption, inaction and lack of coordination between Viennese and Budapest leaders, reawakened the nationality question. That circumstance, accelerated with the increasingly unbearable war weariness and continuing atrocious casualties, produced vociferous demands for peace. The population increasingly blamed the significantly worsening social ills, such as hunger and inflation, on the government, compounded by the expanding nationality issues that the government could not resolve. Attention was riveted on the Western front during spring 1918, until it had become obvious that the Central Powers could not win the war. During October 1918 several new states proclaimed their independence before the peace negotiations commenced in Paris.

As early as 1914 Habsburg unemployment skyrocketed because of the situation created by the July mobilization, such as the cited 5,100 businesses closing. The military seized control of the transportation system for much of the rest of the year and later for major military campaigns. Excessive printed paper money produced inflation, and steadily rising prices made basic life increasingly difficult for the masses. War bonds helped finance about 40 percent of the war costs, while Germany provided millions of gold marks to keep the Austro-Hungarian economy afloat. The ally also provided critical raw materials such as manganese, copper and metal until 1918 as well as war equipment, submarines and airplanes to buttress Habsburg military efforts. Each year German troops rescued their ally from military defeat on the Eastern front and in late 1917 on the Italian.

The increasing scarcity and lack of raw materials and food sources forced the utilization of *Ersatz*, or substitute materials, for weapon and ammunition production, as well as increasingly for food during the early and later war years. Because of the almost immediate scarcity of many critical raw materials, reliance increased for German imports as a result of the Entente blockade. A crisis also rapidly developed because of the lack of strategic nonferrous metals critical for armaments production. Prewar production had been satisfied by using aluminum, because of the lack of lead, zinc or copper. By 1915 demand for raw materials had been outstripped by serious scarcities, resulting in the frantic search for *Ersatz* materials.

The collapse of the Habsburg transportation system commencing in 1916 signified that available raw materials could not be shipped to the factories where needed most. This applied to coal and food shipments as those commodities became increasingly scarcer, particularly in cities such as Vienna during the cold winter seasons. The lack of maintenance, oil lubricants and raw materials, and the drafting of thirty-five thousand railroad workers in 1914, produced a deleterious effect on the railroad network. The drafted workers were replaced by untrained personnel, which lowered traffic efficiency.

A problem that was never satisfactorily resolved involved the Central Powers' failure to establish a unified Eastern front command system.[8] During the prewar correspondence between Generals Conrad and Moltke (chiefs of the General Staffs of Austria-Hungary and Germany), which commenced during the 1909 Bosnian Crisis, both misled the other on their ultimate military intentions. They never revealed specific details about their mobilization plans in their 1909–1914 correspondence. They also never discussed a unified Eastern front command. By the reputed prewar agreements General Conrad was to deploy forty infantry divisions against Russia in a war in the East, but in 1914 launched an invasion of Serbia with twenty of the Habsburg forty-eight divisions. This negated reputed prewar correspondence "commitments." Both Emperor Wilhelm and General Moltke pressured, unsuccessfully, that Serbia must be a secondary front as the less dangerous opponent. Conrad must deploy the mass of Habsburg troops against the obviously most dangerous opponent, Russia. Habsburg civilian and military leaders, however, had determined to initially invade Serbia, hoping to achieve a rapid localized victory. With the German July 2, 1914 "blank check" Vienna gambled on a war with tsarist Russia as well. The problem was that the strategic interests of both chiefs of the General Staff had changed since the 1879 alliance.

German Generals Hindenburg and Ludendorff won major military victories against the Russians in the opening August 1914 campaigns at Tannenberg and the Masurian Lakes in East Prussia. General Conrad's troops suffered disastrous defeat in the two calamitous and embarrassing Lemberg battles. On July 1, Conrad altered the 1914 deployment plans against Russia with his *Rückverlegung*, or drawing of the Habsburg deployment rearward to the Bug–Vistula River line, to permit a successful invasion of Serbia. This proved fatal. The Habsburg Army sacrificed many professional soldiers in the opening campaigns on both the Russian and Balkan fronts, which proved devastating, because they could never be replaced. The effectiveness of the 1914 army rapidly deteriorated as unprepared reserve officers replaced their fallen comrades. The army quickly became a militia force.

Attempts to create a unified command had been initiated in November 1914 at German suggestion. Habsburg Archduke Friedrich would have become the supreme commander with German General Erich Ludendorff his chief of the General Staff. The proposal would have given power to the German High Command. Senior German officers would not accept General Conrad or any other Habsburg generals commanding their troops. Although during 1914 the Germans initially deployed only their Eighth Army on the Eastern front, the Habsburgs sent twenty-eight then thirty-one infantry divisions against Russia. Conrad immediately threatened to resign because he would obviously have been reporting to the German command. Habsburg supporters for such a command structure argued that it would draw German attention to the Eastern front, particularly piquing Emperor Wilhelm's interest. Perhaps then German High Command would deploy more troops east to battle Russia. The question became who could replace Conrad, who had cashiered some potential candidates.

General Conrad vehemently defended his position as chief of the Austro-Hungarian General Staff throughout the war, fearing his loss of freedom of action if the Germans assumed command of Central Power armed forces. He utilized national, dynastic, political and operational grounds including his opposition to younger, more successful German generals assuming command, such as Eric Falkenhayn and later Ludendorff. He also questioned the problems that could arise with German command of Habsburg Slavic troops in his desperate efforts to protect his position and reputation that had suffered because of the multiple Habsburg battlefield defeats.

Commencing in September 1914 and during the October–December 1914 military campaigns, German forces had to rescue the Habsburg Army from defeat by sending troops. They again had to redeploy troops for the 1915 Gorlice–Tarnow offensive, following the disastrous Habsburg Carpathian Mountain Winter War campaign. There followed the embarrassing Rovno fall campaign and then the fateful Brusilov summer 1916 offensive. It became necessary to rescue the retreating Habsburg forces during the 1917 Kerensky offensive by launching a decisive counterattack on July 19, 1917, then command the fall Caporetto offensive against Italy. German commanders and troops were integrated into Habsburg units.

The devastating Brusilov offensive defeat finally convinced Viennese leaders to seek a unified Eastern front command. The numerous Habsburg battle defeats resulted in German commanders' loss of respect for General Conrad and his troops. The command agreement, consummated on September 6, 1916, proved short-lived because of Franz Joseph's death and his nephew Karl's accession to the throne. Karl designated himself as the commander of the Austro-Hungarian forces, and relieved Conrad and his entire Supreme Command staff in early 1917.

The Dual Monarchy rapidly became the Central Powers' junior partner. Its military forces proved incapable of repulsing numerically superior enemy attacks on multiple occasions, something German forces often achieved. Habsburg offensive actions invariably required German assistance to succeed. The Habsburg military also quickly became dependent upon Germany for economic and military aid to remain in the war.

The catastrophic 1916 Brusilov offensive, coupled with the death of Franz Joseph in November 1916 and subsequent crowning of the inexperienced Emperor Karl, led to the removal of Franz Joseph's bureaucrats and diplomats. General Conrad's replacement became the far more pliable General Arz. Emperor Karl concentrated on seeking peace, but the disastrous Sixtus Affair, to be explained in its context, led to distrust of the emperor by the Entente Powers and the loyal Dual Monarchy German and Hungarian elements. As a result of the Sixtus episode, Emperor Karl had to face his Canossa with the powerful German High Command at its headquarters in Spa on May 12, 1918. This resulted in closer Central Power military cohesion, which caused the Entente Powers to seek to defeat and encourage the various nationalities to obtain their independence from the Dual Monarchy. Entente leaders accepted that Austria-Hungary had fallen totally under German control.

When Italy declared war on Austria-Hungary on May 23, 1915, the Dual Monarchy was totally unprepared to conduct a three-front war, although the Gorlice–Tarnow campaign had already made incredible progress against rapidly retreating Russian forces. The month-long delay in launching an Italian offensive provided valuable time to establish primarily primitive defensive positions. Eleven Isonzo River offensives erupted through 1917 on extremely inhospitable mountain terrain, resulting in enormous casualties for both participants. Habsburg forces, however, were on their last legs; it was questionable whether another Italian attack could be halted. This resulted in the German decision to launch the October 1917 Caporetto offensive that it commanded.

A summary is necessary about the Dual Monarchy's navy and air power.[9] The Habsburg Navy had increased in size during the prewar period with Archduke Franz Ferdinand's strong support, but then the continental arms race heated up by 1910 and money went primarily to the army. When war erupted, the Habsburg naval strategy became to preserve the fleet in the Adriatic Sea in case Italy declared war on Austria-Hungary. The navy's mission included protecting 6,300 miles of frontier. It was rapidly determined that the fleet would not undertake any major risks, resulting in only minor encounters with enemy fleets.

The bulk of Habsburg naval forces were concentrated in the northern Adriatic Sea. In 1914 the navy possessed three dreadnoughts, adding another in 1915. It also possessed three Radetsky class semi-dreadnoughts, nine pre-dreadnoughts as well as coastal defense ships. In addition, the fleet contained seven cruisers (with two more under construction), nineteen destroyers, around fifty seafaring torpedo boats, forty coastal torpedo boats and seven submarines. The navy participated on four separated fronts during the war: the Adriatic Sea, Danube River, Black and Mediterranean Seas.

One Habsburg dreadnought was sunk in the Otranto Straits, another in late 1918 when the navy was transferred to the South Slav National Council. The fleet consisted of four squadrons, each with three capital ships and large torpedo boats. Attached to these was a cruiser section with two torpedo flotillas of destroyers supporting local coastal defense squadrons of smaller torpedo boats and obsolescent warships.

The Entente naval forces' overwhelming superiority prevented any major Habsburg naval battle victory. The Adriatic Sea Otranto Straits became the main theater for the Austro-Hungarian fleet. After its declaration of war Italy and its allies attempted to block Central Power access to the Mediterranean Sea by setting up a defensive structure composed of trawlers with nets (termed drifters) in an attempt to prevent German and Austro-Hungarian submarines from passing through the narrow sixty-mile stretch of the Otranto Straits to the Mediterranean Sea. German submarines transported by railroad and reconstructed in Habsburg territory sailed from Pola into the Adriatic and Mediterranean Seas. By the end of October 1914, eleven German submarines flew the Habsburg flag because Germany and Italy were not at war. Three additional submarines were railroad transported from Germany and reassembled on the coastline. During fall 1915 a separate submarine flotilla command was established at Cattaro. Twenty-seven, mostly smaller, models, were constructed during the war. Germany also donated seventy airplanes to Austria-Hungary during 1914, then ten a month until the late November collapse of the Habsburg monarchy.

The major Austro-Hungarian naval effort against Italy occurred on the first day of war, May 23, 1915, when the fleet sailed to interrupt Italian mobilization efforts by firing salvos at coastal cities, railroads and other military targets. Action in the Otranto Straits witnessed minor activity from May 31 through July 9, 1916, when a few drifters were sunk. The main Otranto Straits battle occurred on May 15, 1917, the largest naval encounter since the 1915 opening naval action. Habsburg ships sank fourteen of the forty-seven drifters, while damaging four others, three seriously. The Habsburg fleet, however, remained in port except for hit-and-run raids as the two enemies occasionally unleashed excursions into the Straits. Habsburg naval forces successfully protected their Adriatic coastline.

The 1914 Habsburg Navy's Danube fleet consisted of six monitors. The Danube fleet had multiple war missions, including reconnaissance efforts, supporting the army's 1915 Serbian invasion and 1916 Romanian campaigns. The fleet protected the transport of supplies and troops across rivers and the shelling of enemy positions to support army operations. During 1918 some ships protected boats transporting grain from the Ukraine and Romania to the Homeland.

The first Central Power submarine success occurred on June 5, 1915, while in late May some Italian dirigibles were destroyed during a lightning raid. The Habsburg Navy also possessed forty-three airplanes that briefly provided them aerial superiority against the Italians, but the situation reversed after 1916. The Italians also sustained staggering ship losses during the first three months of the conflict, which included two armored cruisers, a destroyer, three torpedo boats, four submarines and two airships. During June naval raids continued on a much smaller scale than that of May 23, as Entente naval superiority rapidly proved overwhelming. The much larger Italian Navy and its allies blocked the Otranto Straits south of Pola.

Central Power submarines patrolled the Adriatic Sea area while German vessels proved successful in the Mediterranean Sea. However, during late 1915 the British established anti-submarine nets at the Otranto Straits to prevent Central Power submarines from entering the Mediterranean Sea from the Adriatic. Adriatic Sea naval actions slackened considerably during 1918, but the submarines could not be halted.

During July 1915 a revolutionary event erupted at the Pola naval station. Though resolved peacefully, officers continued to receive more and better-quality food and far more leave time than the sailors. As the year progressed rationing became stricter and uniforms and shoes became more difficult to obtain or maintain even for officers. War weariness, food shortages and the receptiveness to peace over time also lowered the sailors' morale and led to the naval revolt at the Cattaro Naval Base on February 2, 1917. This social revolution resulted from enlisted sailors being served inferior food, sometime even rancid portions. They also received far less leave time than officers and had to continually execute monotonous daily duty, for what purpose? War weariness and ongoing Brest-Litovsk negotiations caused great consternation to the general population as well.

Switching to airpower, Austria-Hungary did not become a major player, because of the lack of industrial-base and raw materials compounded by consistently worsening economic conditions. Germany constructed 44,000 airplanes, Habsburg industry only 4,300, a mere 10 percent of their ally. The maximum Habsburg airplane strength became 550 airplanes. Both the army and navy would be hampered throughout the war by the lack of adequate equipment and military hardware. The Entente blockade, which prevented the flow of raw materials, and the deterioration of the Habsburg railroad system had a major negative effect by 1918 on the fledgling Habsburg aircraft industry.

The Habsburg Air Force eventually established thirteen flight (FLIK) companies, often with fewer than the allotted airplanes. Austria-Hungary had inadequate domestic production facilities, and constructed some aircraft with German aviation firm cooperation. Air reconnaissance flights proved valuable during the Russian, Romanian and Balkan campaigns although hindered by weather and mechanical issues. On the Italian front the enemy enjoyed an enormous aircraft numerical advantage until German air power swung the balance during the 1917 Caporetto campaign. The Italians regained the advantage during 1918, with the removal of German forces from the Italian Peninsula.

Habsburg 1914 aerial activity consisted mainly of reconnaissance flights on the Eastern and Balkan fronts. The few available aircraft, faulty equipment and inclement weather conditions prevented major aerial successes on both fronts. During 1914 Habsburg reconnaissance aircraft failed to locate major Russian troop deployments on the Habsburg Eastern flank, which ultimately proved disastrous in the opening campaign on that front. Such efforts proved more beneficial on the northern First Army front.

The major Habsburg aerial activity occurred on the Italian front. The Dual Monarchy maintained aerial supremacy in that theater between 1914 and 1916, then Italy gained dominance that continued until the late October 1917 battle of Caporetto. Italian Caproni bombing raids regularly struck Habsburg forces. The German Air Force provided Central Power aerial supremacy during the October 1917 Caporetto campaign as it did during the 1915 Gorlice–Tarnow operation. The Germans deployed eight aviation companies and three fighter units as well as a bomber squadron for the Caporetto campaign. During late 1915 the Central Power invasion of Serbia reconnaissance efforts were negatively affected by inclement weather and mountainous terrain conditions.

Habsburg pilots had significant problems to overcome on their various fronts. The Eastern front extended vast distances with enormous stretches of flat terrain, mountains, forests and swamps. During winter snowstorms it proved extremely difficult to pinpoint one's own or the enemy's exact location. Maps, inaccurate and often outdated, proved of little value. Long flights tested a pilot's physical endurance, as winter wind and cold froze him and his machine gun. Fortunately, most Russian planes, though outnumbering particularly Habsburg aircraft, proved obsolete. Supplying and moving the squadrons was difficult because of the underdeveloped railroad lineage and vast miles of the front. Horses and oxen often transported disassembled aircraft across often rugged and mountainous terrain.

Similar conditions were encountered on the Italian, Romanian and Serbian mountain fronts as well as in the Carpathian chain. Wind currents, altitude and other considerations made flying extremely dangerous. Such problems worsened as the fronts expanded, in other words Ukraine (1917–1918). In Serbia 1915 the terrain presented difficulties for logistics, particularly relative to aircraft. German aircraft provided aerial supremacy for such Allied campaigns as Gorlice–Tarnow in 1915, the 1917 Kerensky offensive and the late 1917 Caporetto campaign against Italy. Godwin Barnowski, Austria-Hungary's most successful air "ace," had thirty-five kills. Luis Arigi achieved thirty-two and Benno Fiala twenty-eight victories.

In Chapter 1 we will describe the *k.u.k.* Austro-Hungarian Army.

1

The Austro-Hungarian Army

> To fully understand the battles in the Carpathians with their interchange
> of success and failure ... one must take into account the condition of the
> most important component of the War Machine, the infantry, and the
> conditions under which they were forced to perform ...
>
> Colonel Georg Veith

The Austro-Hungarian Royal and Imperial Army (*k.u.k.* [*kaiserlich und
königlich*] *Armee*) entered its last great battle woefully unprepared for the
ordeal it would endure. Habsburg armed forces were, quite simply, incapable
of conducting modern warfare on the level of the 1914 conflict, as they would
shortly experience. As one prominent Austrian commander would later admit,
General Conrad's armies suffered from poor strategic direction and outdated
tactics and equipment.[1] Indeed, several noted historians have concluded that
the 1914 army was only capable of defeating Serbia alone; it was certainly not
capable of simultaneously launching a two-front offensive against both Russia
and Serbia. Nevertheless, and to the surprise of many at the time, the army
muddled through multiple battlefield defeats until the end of October 1918,
only weeks before the cessation of hostilities. Thus, despite the multiple
inadequacies and poor battle results, the army remained battle-worthy until
almost the end of the conflict.

The Austro-Hungarian Army that mobilized for the First World War
proved far from resilient for the hardships it would encounter on the battlefields of Galicia, Serbia, Romania, the Middle East and Italy. The opening
1914 battles essentially destroyed the once proud professional *k.u.k.* peacetime
army, transforming it into a *Miliz*, or militia, by the end of the year and for the
remainder of the war. By the end of the opening campaign, Habsburg fighting
forces were suffering from their inherent frailties, even exhibiting some signs
of disintegration.

Throughout the prewar period, the Dual Monarchy consistently lagged
behind other European powers in the accelerating armaments race. Its population had increased more than 40 percent in the fifty years leading up to the
conflict; in Europe this level of increase placed the empire third, trailing only
Russia and Germany. However, military expenditures and improvements in

weapons had not kept pace. Expenditures on military forces equaled only 25 percent of Germany and Russia and one-third of Great Britain and France; even Italy outspent it. Between 1906 and 1914, the monarchy's military budget increased some 64 percent (during the 1912–1913 Balkan Wars the increase was 123 percent), yet even this proved insufficient, despite consuming 21 percent of the total fiscal budget.

Adding to the fiscal woes, the Habsburg Army seriously lacked organizational uniformity, having three separate and parallel structures. Following the 1866 Austro-Prussian War defeat, the 1867 *Ausgleich* – an agreement between Austria and Hungary that created the Austro-Hungarian monarchy – also produced a joint army, although the Hungarian and Austrian units each maintained separate identities. In addition, Austrian second-line *Landwehr* units and Hungarian *Honvéd* units, although essentially independent territorial military forces, became integrated into the Common Imperial and Royal Army with the war, and would be designated as first-line units as early as the 1914 mobilization, although the regular army would provide requisite support troops as well as General Staff functions. On mobilization, each Austro-Hungarian corps would be comprised of two regular army divisions and one of either the *Honvéd* or *Landwehr* divisions.

The diversity of cultures, languages and economic and educational backgrounds of the empire's peoples were represented in the army's recruiting classes, creating additional organizational challenges, even at the level of basic ability to communicate with each other. The attendant difficulties of troop integration were particularly acute between the two largest empire ethnic identities, namely the German-speaking Austrians and the Hungarians. This situation was interrupted by the introduction of military conscription, which essentially destroyed the old professional long-term service army that had been the backbone of the Habsburg military establishment. In 1868 all fit male subjects faced twelve years of military service. At twenty years of age, each potential conscript drew a lot; if selected, he was required to serve three years' active duty, seven in the reserves and two in either a *Landwehr* or *Honvéd* unit. Short-term citizen soldiers replaced long-serving professional troops, introducing politics and disruptive nationalistic elements into barracks life.

Compounding these problems, the Hungarian parliament proved unwilling to increase appropriations for the *k.u.k.* Common Army, but willingly approved funding for *Honvéd* units. In 1898 the joint war ministry requested a minor increase in conscription levels, but Hungarian parliamentary obstruction tactics blocked passage of the request. This issue resurfaced in 1903, when the common war minister requested the approval of the Hungarian parliament to approve an increase in funding, as well as a rise in conscription above levels mandated in 1889. (The 1889 law called for a total conscription of 103,000, of which 19,970 would report to the *Landwehr* and 12,500 to the *Honvéd*.)

Finally, in 1907 approval allowed the increase in the number of conscripts by 23,000; however, resulting from repeated financial shortfalls many conscripts served only two years' active duty rather than the mandated three, thus effectively vitiating the increases.

Insufficient funding also limited reserve troop training to a two-week period, while *Landsturm* units had none. The lack of financial support assured that the Dual Monarchy would field too few and insufficiently trained soldiers in 1914. As many as 30 percent of conscripts joined the ready reserve units as *Ersatz* replacement troops. Only one of every eight eligible men actually underwent military training. Thus, despite an 1890 population of forty million, and fifty-two million in 1910, effective troop levels did not increase. As a result, the *k.u.k.* Army was comprised of an insufficient number of active military units. Moreover, the majority of soldiers received inadequate and varied levels of training and many reservists had none whatsoever. Despite the fact that all political parties agreed that the existing conscription laws needed revision, the Hungarians employed political tactics as leverage to gain concessions favoring their national interests, particularly funding for *Honvéd* units. They also consistently demanded a greater usage of the Hungarian language and that their soldiers wear their own identifying insignia, even in *k.u.k.* units. The Hungarians also demanded that *Honvéd* units be transformed into first-line forces equal to the Common Army after they received artillery units in 1913.

Tensions reached such a boiling point that the General Staff actually prepared a War Case "*Ung*" (Hungary) in the summer of 1905, but the constitutional question was eventually resolved. As part of this resolution, and to appease Hungarian nationalists' demands, artillery units joined *Honvéd* formations in 1913; thus, they evolved into the desired de facto first-line units. The Hungarian negotiating position was not without its weaknesses. The threat of introducing universal suffrage prompted the Hungarian compromise on the issue, because of the land magnates' dread of losing their political dominance to the large blocs of minorities that populated Hungarian territory who would possibly be enfranchised.

Between 1908 and 1912 minor increases in defense spending greatly benefited the navy, championed by Archduke Franz Ferdinand and his entourage. Spending for shipbuilding doubled, as an Austro-Hungarian-Italian naval race developed to contest control of the Adriatic Sea. Unfortunately for the army, the increase in defense spending was almost totally consumed by the naval buildup, meaning army spending barely rose. When war broke out the army desperately needed modern weapons and sufficient numbers of well-trained troops. Thus, the armed forces had not been prepared for the expansive land war that exploded in 1914.

A 1912 army law, a result of the 1911 Italian-Tripoli War and the 1912–1913 Balkan Wars crises, finally provided for raising army manpower numbers and funding. During the last year of peace the army conscripted a record 227,000 troops, 66,670 of which reported to the *k.u.k. Landwehr* and 24,717 to the *k.u.k. Honvéds*. The law called for 236,000 recruits by 1918, which would provide a reserve force of 450,000 troops by 1924. Unfortunately, this law only went into effect in the winter of 1913, too late for it to have a major consequence on preparedness in the summer of 1914. Additionally, while the law called for new technical formations, some heavy-artillery and mountain batteries, machine-gun sections and telegraph troop formations, these formations came at the cost of infantry troop numbers, which were already too few.[2]

The Austrian delegation funded *Landwehr* (*k.u.k.*) units, a first-line reserve army formed in its crown lands; seven *Landwehr* infantry divisions fought on the Russian front during the opening battles of the war. Like the Common Army, *Landwehr* units were divided among nine military districts, with eight districts each producing one infantry division. The ninth district, in addition to raising two army regiments, raised naval personnel for the Habsburg Navy. *Landwehr* and *Honvéd* formations, low on the priority list for supplies and armaments, were severely shortchanged on manpower, weapons and equipment, and had virtually no indigenous artillery formations. The net effect of the law meant that *Landwehr* units were beginning to receive more modern weapons, but the decades of accumulated neglect in conscription meant that the army possessed no major second-line forces, in striking contrast to other European powers.

The Hungarian National Army, the *Honvéd* (Defenders of the Country), termed Royal Hungarian or *königlich-ungarisch* (*k.u.*) units, provided six army corps to the Common Army (*k.u.k.*). Eight *Honvéd* infantry divisions fought on the Eastern front until the early 1915 Carpathian Winter War campaign.[3]

Peacetime *Honvéd* infantry companies averaged fifty-five soldiers and formed eighty-two battalions, four of which consisted of entirely Croatian troops. The 1912 army reorganization law reduced the number of battalions per regiment to three, resulting in the creation of thirty-two new field regiments. *Landwehr* and *Honvéd* units bore the name of their home district. A Magyar delegation voted on funding of Hungarian units and a separate Hungarian minister of defense oversaw the *Honvéd* units.

In 1887 *Landsturm* units were designated as second-line Austrian units to defend the various provinces. In 1914 many would be deployed on the Eastern front, though their weapons and training remained far inferior to that of regular troops. Such units, issued the obsolete M90 rifle or the single-shot Wendle rifles, also lacked machine-gun and artillery attachments. The often-unwieldy formations, created to increase troop numbers, proved of little combat worth and merely raised casualty numbers as the troops quickly became cannon fodder. These losses meant that by late 1914 many companies only had one professional noncommissioned officer, and by 1915 many battalion-level formations had only a single commissioned officer. It quickly became commonplace for reserve lieutenants to command battalions and *gendarme* officers companies as the quality of the troops declined.

A typical *Landsturm* unit's travails during the early phases of the war included language difficulties, inadequate leadership and lack of modern weapons. Other factors compounded these woes. *Landsturm* soldiers wore outdated blue uniforms, revealing themselves to the enemy as lesser-quality soldiers. Age also played a role. Prior to the First World War *Landsturm* troops' age range spanned from nineteen to forty-two. A younger age group, including troops who had recently received regular army military training, included nineteen- to thirty-four-year-olds. The older group, obviously unversed in modern warfare techniques, ranged between thirty-three and forty-two years old. In spite of such problems and unnecessary casualties, during the war several *Landsturm* regiments distinguished themselves by their exceptional service.

During August and September 1914 both *Landsturm* levies were called to duty. The army originally intended to utilize the older troops for only non-combat duty. However, in 1914, military necessity dictated that they immediately be deployed beside first-line formations in an attempt to counter the enemy's significant numerical superiority and the unexpectedly large casualties Habsburg troops sustained in the opening battles. The older *Landsturm* levy formed into seventeen *k.u.k. Landsturm* territorial brigades (130 battalions) and nine *k.u. Landsturm Etappen* brigades.

As the war progressed and casualties mounted precipitously with battlefield defeats, an increasingly large number of poorly trained replacement troops and reservists were deployed to the front as first-line troops. The escalating casualties gradually transformed the Habsburg Army into a *Landsturm* army. While this phenomenon would occur in all the armies participating in the war, the problem was particularly acute for the Habsburgs, since they had substantially fewer surviving professional cadres to draw on. Additionally, *Landsturm* units did not receive replacement troops as frequently as did regular army units. On October 15, 1914 the first *Landsturm* March battalions (replacement troops) designated for the *k.u. Landsturm* infantry regiments prepared for deployment. These March units included wounded soldiers returning to front-line service as well as the older and inadequately trained troops.

This rather confusing military organization reflected a similarly enigmatic form of government that consisted of three parliaments. Separate Austrian and Hungarian assemblies conferred with a joint delegation. The joint Austro-Hungarian federated government, linked under the aegis of the Habsburg dynasty and Emperor Franz Joseph, possessed a common foreign ministry, finance minister and military organization.

One bright spot for the army was the elite *k.u.k.* Officer Corps, one of the major props of the Dual Monarchy, which considered itself to transcend ethnic divisions within the empire. A Habsburg officer had to master multiple languages to be capable of conducting simple conversations with his soldiers and to relate to the troops under his command. Such language skills helped assure the maintenance of discipline among the multinational troops and increased confidence in the military leadership while fostering troop loyalty. However, drill language varied – German for the Austrian side of the monarchy, Hungarian on their side (except for the few Croatian units that had earned the right to use their own language for their service against the Turks centuries earlier). The uniform command language consisted of a vocabulary of eighty German, Hungarian and Croat words. A service language pertained to mainly written communication, and the regimental language for daily unit discourse. However, many Austro-Hungarian officers, of all ranks, lacked necessary command qualities, received low pay and, like all troops, remained concerned about their families and troops.

The Austro-Hungarian Army, essentially a microcosm of the empire, served as an indissoluble support to the Habsburg dynasty, one of its three pillars, the others being the Catholic Church and the aristocracy. The Habsburg Officer Corps was unique in Europe in its concept of service and loyalty. In an age of nationalism, the officer corps acted without the ethnic and regional prejudices affecting other societies, including its own, on the eve of the twentieth century. A socially diverse group, its membership during the decades before the war witnessed a decline in hereditary nobility to the extent that between 1866 and 1918 not one of the chiefs of the General Staff claimed noble blood – the vast majority of General Staff officers actually rose from the lower ranks of society.[4] Unfortunately, this bright spot would quickly dim as less capable reserve officers replaced the professional casualties during the initial campaign. This also resulted in nationality issues entering the ranks and leading to disturbances and indiscipline.

This thinning of officer ranks became all the more dire with a law enacted in 1868 stating that no soldier could rise from the enlisted ranks to become an officer, another manifestation of the 1867 *Ausgleich*. This lack of upward mobility for worthy noncommissioned officers (NCOs) proved to be a major determent to the army during the war. Habsburg reserve officers represented a small minority compared to German reserve officers in the regular 1914 officer corps. An earlier problem with the officer corps was its ethnic composition: Although they considered themselves trans-ethnic in the sense of being able to work with minorities, in 1906 about 60 percent of reserve officers were German, 26 percent Hungarian, almost 10 percent Czech and the remainder from the other seven major nationalities. Romanian, Polish, Ruthenian and Croat reserve officer numbers, grossly underrepresented earlier, increased sharply after 1907. The officer corps became a unifying force for both the regular and reserve officers regardless of religious, social or ethnic background. The keystone element was loyalty to the throne and dynasty. Upon receiving their commissions all swore an oath of loyalty to the monarch and House of Habsburg. By 1900 Emperor Franz Joseph had commissioned all officers, realizing that the monarchy's survival depended on its army, as demonstrated during the bloody 1848–1849 revolutions. The officer corps, the only unquestionably loyal Habsburg element, represented a nonnational group, the last vestige of a feudal loyalty to a supreme warlord, whose code had not changed for centuries.

Reserve officers often shared such sentiments, but not as enthusiastically as those of the regular army. Not only had their military experience been much briefer than regular officers, but they remained closely tied to their civilian lives and their ethnic identity. Middle-class reserve officers often brought ideology, such as ethnic nationalism, and even socialist ideas, into their ranks, while regular army officers clearly opposed such tendencies. No mention of nationality appeared on officer qualification lists, making any effort to dissect the ethnic composition of the Habsburg Officer Corps an almost impossible task to achieve. Unlike regular officers, Habsburg reserve officers spent a year in active service as reserve noncommissioned officers, becoming reserve lieutenants within three years. They chiefly emanated from the professional and commercial classes and many had a university education, which helped assimilate the middle classes into the army ranks.

In spite of these differences, both active and reserve officers shared a highly rigid sense of honor, common code and identity, using the more informal *du* regardless of rank or position, unique in European armies. Many also held an almost medieval fascination with honor and chivalry rooted in ancient customs. Most reserve officer candidates absorbed regular officer corps values because the middle classes tended to mimic them. On a negative note, the officer corps had a slow process of promotion as well as relatively modest pay, the exception being the General Staff, a small elite group. Membership brought prestige and more rapid advancement, but overwhelming officer numbers were relegated to long-serving career captains and majors, who spent most of their time as company and battalion commanders. Regardless, all officers recognized the army's many limitations and deficiencies.

Religion also provided a mainstay of the Habsburg dynasty. The majority of the Dual Monarchy inhabitants were Roman Catholic, and Austria-Hungary represented the preeminent Catholic empire in Europe. Indeed, army chaplains fostered Habsburg dynastic loyalty among their troops as they stressed the moral and loyal aspects of the soldiers' duties. The Catholic Church helped establish legitimacy for the monarchy and army for many soldiers. This dedication to Christianity was not confined to Roman Catholicism, and in fact was a most critical element for the monarchy's Orthodox Christians in Bosnia, Croatia and Transylvania as well, especially when confronted with the Ottoman alternative.

The admixture of various national and social groups shared common experiences vis-à-vis the more than one hundred Common Army regiments. The army regimental system had introduced Habsburg soldiers to proper social and political attitudes for three centuries. In 1914 the regiment remained the basic Common Army, *Landwehr*, *Honvéd* and *Landsturm* tactical formation. Each regiment contained four infantry battalions of four companies, each divided into four platoons. Each Common Army infantry company had to contain at least 25 percent active-duty soldiers. No more than one-sixth of the ranks could consist of *k.u.k.* reserve troops, with the remaining troop numbers serving as local reservists. Prewar regulations, however, had stipulated that only 20 percent of a war stand of any unit should be inadequately trained *Ersatz* reservists. These regulations, however, rapidly became unenforceable due to the enormous casualties suffered in the opening campaign battles.

An infantry division consisted of two brigades that contained two regiments consisting of four battalions of four companies. A peacetime infantry company contained 99 officers and men, but its wartime strength allocation called for it to expand to a total of 240 troops of all ranks. A regiment contained 4,041 rifles and 8 machine guns. Full regimental combat strength came to a total of 4,200–4,600 officers and men. The full Common Army consisted of 112 regiments and an additional 32 battalions of elite *Feldjäger* troops.[5] These light elite infantry formations, *Jäger* and *Kaiserjäger*, emanated from mountainous geographic regions such as the Tyrol, and were composed of German and Italian troops. Unfortunately, many of these elite formations were decimated on the Galician plains or in Serbia, well before their unique skills could be put to use on the mountainous Italian front after Italy declared war on Austria-Hungary on May 23, 1915.

Traditionally, the recruitment and training of all soldiers was effected in specific containment districts, assuring that every regiment developed into a distinct entity with its own traditions, battle honors, formations and language. Thus, the legacy regimental system promoted close bonds between the troops and their regional and ethnic heritage. However, by 1914 this cohesion had been undermined by the passage of the 1912 military law, which reduced the active-duty commitment from three years to two, and no longer assigned conscripts to a local regiment. This eventually produced a significant breakdown in communication among the multiethnic troops and encouraged nationalist and particularistic affairs, in spite of the army's previous attempts to equitably accommodate its language diversity.

An infantry regiment required four trainloads of troops for railroad transport. Regular rail passenger carriages transported officers, while the troops rode in converted "cattle" cars (forty to a car). On foot, the maximum daily march distance was not to exceed fifty kilometers. Once the war commenced, however, commanders were quickly forced to ignore peacetime guidelines. In spite of such demands from superiors, the infantry, particularly reserve or *Ersatz* troops, often proved physically incapable of carrying sixty-pound backpacks long distances and quickly became exhausted from the long, tiring marches well before encountering a combat situation. Soldiers often abandoned equipment along march routes, particularly during the initial deployment in the 1914 summer heat, although this continued throughout the war.

The Dual Monarchy was divided into sixteen military territorial districts, each one fielding one corps, containing either *Landwehr* or *Honvéd* and *Landsturm* troop formations. One hundred twelve *Ergänzung* (supplementary) districts were also scattered throughout the Dual Monarchy. Hungary possessed forty-seven, Bosnia-Herzegovina four, with the remaining sixty-one in the Austrian portion of the empire. These districts strengthened troop formations, as well as morale, by providing replacement troops from the same recruitment area. Unfortunately, during the 1915 Carpathian Winter War campaign and later, because of reputed treason by various national group troops and units, the system was drastically altered to replenish field units with replacement troops from other, more loyal areas, regardless of the ethnicity of the receiving formation. The situation worsened drastically when national units considered unreliable were garrisoned in reliable monarchy areas, loyal units in unreliable regions, with the mandated exchange of Czech and Hungarian units presenting a major example.[6]

The levels of social, economic, educational and political development varied greatly from one Austro-Hungarian region to another. Austrian, Czech and some Hungarian areas were as advanced as in any part of Europe. However, in large sections of the empire, particularly rural Hungary and South Slav lands, the people lived in extreme poverty and backward conditions. Many recruits from these areas could not read or write. Illiteracy rates reached 60 percent in Galicia, almost 65 percent in Bosnia-Herzegovina and 64 percent in the South Slav provinces. The existence of such diverse cultures obviously made it very difficult to form cohesive national units in the army. With the varied languages, cultures and social classes, how could one develop a common heritage or generate Habsburg patriotism?

Nationalistic outbursts and agitation raised fears about the loyalty of specific ethnic groups, particularly among Slavic troops who were fighting a war against fellow Slavic Russians and Serbians. The entire Ruthenian (Ukrainian) population, immediately considered unreliable, made up a great portion of the frontier Galician XI Corps troop stand, as well as the Fortress Przemyśl garrison on the San River protecting entrance to the Carpathian Mountain ranges. Postwar Austrian historiography addressed the sensitive nationality issue by asserting that the best Habsburg combat troops emanated from German, Magyar and South Slavic (Croat and Orthodox Serb) areas. Throughout the war, field commanders deployed such troops at the most critical or endangered front areas. As casualties rapidly mounted, however, field commanders had to accept replacement troops from throughout the monarchy rather than their own region of origin. A serious negative result of this practice was the strained relationship between officers and troops – even factoring out ethnic rivalries, a basic inability to communicate meant increased inefficiency and stress between leadership and the soldiery. The sheer diversity of languages spoken within individual units further exacerbated the situation. Interestingly, Slavic soldiers fought well with German Army officers during the Gorlice–Tarnow and Caporetto offensives.

The severe losses sustained by the professional officer corps, noncommissioned officer ranks and professional soldiers during the opening battles of the war had a devastating effect on the cohesiveness of the Habsburg Army. Increasing numbers of reserve officers, besides being unfamiliar with modern warfare tactics and not physically prepared for the rigors of combat, replaced professional officer casualties. These officers often neither spoke their troops' language nor had much commonality with which to create any meaningful bonds of trust. As the official Austrian history of the war emphasized, when officers could no longer effectively communicate with their soldiers, a certain measure of confidence, security, influence and comradery was sacrificed. In the heat of battle communication often collapsed, with fatal consequences for all concerned. Soldiers frequently misunderstood orders, which at critical moments in battle could mean the difference between life or death, victory or defeat. With ten major languages spoken within the ranks, as well as other minor ones, it is not hard to imagine the difficulties in communication between various troops.

Although these difficulties are hard to overstress, there was one factor that partially mitigated the language barrier. Few unit stands spoke only one language; in 142 of the infantry regiments deployed in 1914 most were bilingual and 24 had 3 distinct languages. Troops in several regiments spoke 4–5 different languages. To appreciate the average language diversity, the typical Habsburg infantry unit consisted of 25 Germans, 23 Magyars, 13 Czechs, 9 Serbs or Croats, 8 Poles, 8 Ruthenians, 7 Romanians, 2 Slovenes and 1 Italian.[7]

Of the regiments, only fifteen had at least 90 percent of a single ethnic group within its ranks in 1914. k.u.k. Landwehr consisted of only nineteen regiments where a single language was spoken, forty-four with two languages, and one with three. It is noteworthy that the army went to great lengths to assure linguistic diversity within its ranks. Mobilization posters in 1914 appeared in fifteen different languages. When a soldier was buried, his regiment number was engraved on the tombstone. A special regimental day, separate troop colors, songs, even marches differentiated the various units.

The prewar national composition of the professional officer corps consisted of, on average, 1,000 professional officers, comprised of 761 Germans, 107 Magyars, 52 Czech, 27 Polish and 27 Serbians or Croatians. The decimation of the Habsburg professional officer corps in 1914 forced a widening of this ethnic composition; German officers would still remain in the majority. As the war progressed, of 1,000 reserve officers, on average 568 were German, 245 Magyar, 106 Czech, 33 Polish and 19 Serbian or Croatian.

German soldiers comprised 25% of Habsburg troop numbers, while of the remaining ranks, 18% were Magyar, 13% Czech, 11% Serbo-Croatian, 9% Polish, 9% Ruthenian, 6% Romanian, 4% Slovak, 2% Slovenian, 2% Italian and 1% diverse. At the outbreak of the war, the Dual Monarchy population had reached 51.5 million, of which 13.0 million were German, 9.3 million Magyar, 6.8 million Czech-Slovak, 5.6 million Serbo-Croatian, 4.7 million Polish, 4.4 million Ruthenian, 3.0 million Romanian, 2.0 million Slovak, 1.3 million Slovene, 0.9 million Italian and 0.5 million diverse.

Perceived differences between various peoples and cultures inevitably compounded language and ethnic difficulties. Though Habsburg soldiers represented a multitude of unique cultural heritages, the Viennese government prided itself on its ability to maintain unity in the polyglot empire. The army itself was drawn primarily from the peasant class. Romanian, Ruthenian, Slovak and South Slavs provided the majority of infantry troops. Within Bosnia-Herzegovina, a separate administrative entity within the Dual Monarchy, the most famous units, designated the *Bosniakan*, proved ferocious and excellent soldiers; their ranks consisted of Croatians, Serbs and Muslims. In addition, the Croatians possessed their own infantry division, the 42. *Honvéd* Division, nicknamed the Devils Division. Ethnic antagonisms, however, often resulted in strained relationships within the ranks. Romanians against Hungarians, Germans against Czechs, Poles against Ruthenians provide examples of the most extreme ethnic conflicts, but many others existed as well.

Outside factors contributed to ethnic unrest within the army, particularly as conscripts and reservists began to replace the long-term professional casualties. Powerful neighbors, such as Russia, and lesser ones, such as Italy, Serbia and Romania, coveted portions of the Dual Monarchy lands as irredenta territory, and their desires could potentially stoke up support among Habsburg troops sympathetic to their respective causes. Prewar anti-Habsburg and anti-military propaganda began to seriously influence Czechs, Serbs in Bosnia-Herzegovina (influenced by Russian Pan-Slavism), the Romanians in Transylvania and the Bukovina, and the Ruthenians in Galicia. During the war it increasingly influenced troops at the front as well. Internal political bickering and the government's inefficiency and failure to respond to deteriorating economic conditions weakened efforts to fight such machinations. Central government weakness and ineffectiveness resulted in increased economic distress, ethnic conflict and army–civilian resentment that erupted into revolution in October 1918.

As the war dragged on morale suffered owing to the many battlefield defeats. Low morale was universal, especially in the rear echelons. Reserve units became breeding grounds for nationalistic fervor and in 1918 evolved into revolutionary activity. During the war Slavic soldiers tended to desert on the Russian and Balkan fronts, but not on the Italian, because Slavic troops recognized Italian desire to seize their territory.

Reports of reputed troop treasonous activity, particularly from Czech and Ruthenian infantry regiments, increased as the war progressed. In the initial 1914 battles, Slavic units could generally be regarded as loyal and battleworthy. The one notable exception, the 21. *Landwehr* Infantry Division, fought in the August 1914 Balkan campaign. This predominantly Czech division was accused of causing the original Balkan military defeat. However, as the short-war illusion dissipated, physical and psychological stereotypes attributed to various ethnic groups increasingly became associated with battlefield setbacks, at a time when growing disaffection among the troops intensified. By the fall 1914 campaigns, allegations of reputed front-line Slavic troops' desertions became widespread. In early 1915, the battleworthiness of various units, particularly predominantly Slavic ones, came into question. However, recent research has demonstrated that nationalistic problems only rose to a fatal level during 1918, when the Dual Monarchy began to implode.[8] Multiple factors such as disease, increasing lack of food supplies, years of persistent battlefield defeats, lack of maintenance of and procurement of weapons, the disastrous June 1918 offensive and frequent inclement weather conditions produced the circumstances for the collapse of the Habsburg Army in October 1918. The lack of effective professional officers and noncommissioned officers, increasing lack of equipment and inadequate logistical services that remained a most serious problem throughout the conflict became additional factors influencing the armed forces.

However, already by September 1914 troublesome excesses accumulated during the preparations for and railroad transport of Czech March formations. The Dual Monarchy's alliance with the German Empire and fighting against Russia and Serbia raised resentment in Slavic troops, which posed serious problems. Prewar anti-dynastic and anti-military propaganda intensified, spreading into the Czech working-class sections, such as Prague, and increasingly influenced troops deployed to the front. Discipline within Czech ranks suffered, particularly upon the arrival of replacement units from homefront city regions. Italian, Romanian, Serbian and Ruthenian troops also often proved unreliable in combat situations and deserted. These were compounded by frustration over the horrendous battlefield conditions, enormous casualties and numerous defeats. Such factors certainly affected various ethnic group troops' morale. Also, inadequate and irregular food deliveries that decreased in amounts as well as problems with the delivery of ammunition and artillery shells, or their total absence, constantly aggravated combat situations and lowered troop morale as well as their physical condition (malnutrition in the latter phases of the conflict in Italy). There was prejudice in the officer corps particularly against Czech troops. Many soldiers were not trained sufficiently, and officers covered up command mistakes and blamed others for their predicaments.

In his memoirs, General Conrad accused Czech soldiers of treason and malfeasance. He wrote that on November 27, 1914 an estimated 5,500 IX Corps (Bohemia) Czech soldiers abandoned their front-line positions and deserted to the enemy. According to Russian sources, between December 20 and 24, 1914, 49,000 Habsburg prisoners of war were captured.[9] In early April 1915, the infamous Czech Infantry Regiment 28 (discussed in Chapter 6) reputedly shrank from 2,000 to 150 men within a few hours, without a single shot being fired. On January 21, 1915, Czech soldiers of Infantry Regiment 81 fraternized with Russian prisoners of war at a railroad station. Numerous other incidents occurred, particularly involving Czech Infantry Regiments 11 and 36.

Each battalion in an infantry division received a monthly allotment of March battalion replacement units from the hinterland. Initially, these replacement troops were deployed after undergoing two months of basic training, but military necessity because of the enormous casualties meant that as the war progressed they were deployed to the front with a dangerously short training period. *Ersatz* formations consisted of third-line troops that in 1914 received only eight weeks of basic training (later four then by necessity two weeks). March battalion units, unprepared for the ardors of modern combat, often were hurriedly and haphazardly deployed as combat entities in difficult battle zones without proper artillery, machine guns, signal units or other equipment and weapons. The shorter the troops' training period, the greater their casualty numbers, a vicious cycle that continued throughout the war. Commanders blatantly ignored repeated directives forbidding the deployment of such unseasoned troops into combat situations, but what alternative existed under the dire battlefield circumstances? The results, nevertheless, produced mountains of corpses, and wounded and physically disabled soldiers.

The swift and profound deterioration through battle losses at the tactical level of junior rank command structure (lieutenants and non-commissioned officers) soon proved of significant consequence. Older, physically unfit reserve officers, unschooled in modern warfare techniques and sometimes increasingly influenced by nationalistic anti-Habsburg propaganda, received command positions, commencing during the 1915 Carpathian Mountain Winter War campaign and increasing during later operations.

The Habsburg Army's battlefield effectiveness eventually hinged upon the quality of its replacement troops, but the inability to maintain a steady flow of disciplined, adequately trained and armed troops throughout the war became one of the most debilitating army deficiencies. Replacement troops often also lacked proper moral and physical fortitude. Their deployment into front lines during inclement weather and unfavorable terrain conditions accelerated their process of decline. The deployment of potentially politically unreliable troops from Czech, Romanian, Ruthenian and Italian recruiting areas often exacerbated the situation. Habsburg Supreme Command grew increasingly paranoid about the influx of replacement soldiers from specific regions of the monarchy, but the seriousness of the military situation meant that the failing system had to be continued.

Replacement troops neither adequately replaced the staggering losses, provided the necessary defensive strength to halt enemy offensives nor gave the impetus to launch a successful offensive. Subaltern officers, officer candidates and previously passed-over one-year volunteers had to be rapidly deployed to offset the accelerating shortage of professional officers, but most proved incapable of adequately fulfilling their duties.[10]

Following insufficiently brief training, recruits and *Landsturm* soldiers were placed into March formations. March replacement companies contained 266 and March battalions 1,101 soldiers. Each infantry division received one March battalion and each corps a March brigade usually monthly to replace its casualties. A March brigade originally contained seven March battalions consisting of 7,300 troops and 150 cavalry troopers. Already on August 3, 1914, a second installment of March formations had become necessary. On August 13, the third had already formed, then on September 23 the fourth and fifth were authorized. Officers and enlisted soldiers who had recovered from wounds or illness joined these formations. The mounting losses, however, became increasingly difficult to replace. As early as 1915, the Carpathian Mountain Winter War campaign forced a new major influx of replacement troops. In four months, 927,091 men and 19,756 officers were transported to the Carpathian Mountain front by rail transport. Some 435,000 sick and wounded troops returned to the home front, the numerical difference amounting to 511,847 soldiers.[11]

Two months later, the Seventh and Eighth March battalions had to be trained, but not surprisingly, field commanders reported that the Seventh March Battalion troops proved unprepared for combat and lacked proper weapons and field training. The army could not satisfy the increasing demand for replacement troops, nor could it satisfy their enormous need for equipment. The most elemental piece of equipment for any soldier is his rifle but the loss of so many on the battlefield required replacements; however, not enough standardized rifles could be issued, resulting in each Habsburg battalion having two or three different models.

The *k.u.k.* Army nationality problem has long been the subject of historical debate. Although troops of every nationality at one time or another abandoned their positions, retreated or deserted, Conrad's attention focused primarily on Slavic troops: Czechs, Slovaks, South Slavs (Serbs, Croats, Slovenes) and Ruthenians. It was Conrad's and his commanders' tactical mistakes that resulted in battlefield defeat, not the conduct of Slavic soldiers.

Other critical factors undermined the confidence and effectiveness of the Habsburg Army during the opening and subsequent campaigns that helped explain incidences of desertions. Persistent exposure to the overwhelmingly superior tsarist and Italian troop numbers and their numerically far superior artillery had a major negative effect. Tsarist battlefield tactics and tenacity in battle, particularly during retrograde movements, took their toll in casualties, but also on Habsburg troop morale. Furthermore, the Habsburg Supreme Command's frequent disregard of severe inclement weather and unfavorable terrain conditions when launching offensives, and often aimless and excessively long marches, also took their toll. Major operations commenced too hastily without sufficient planning preparation, enough troop numbers for success or an adequately functioning logistical system. Designated attack units often arrived after the offensive had been launched, dissipating the initial attacking strength. Inadequate artillery support produced unnecessary losses, and shells were often in short supply so had to be spared. However, with competent officers, proper training and equipment and regular food supply, Czech, Serbian and other ethnic soldiers performed well on the battlefield. Unfortunately, this often proved to be the exception rather than the rule. The official Austrian history of the war concedes that the escalating Slavic problem stemmed from the increasingly unreasonable demands placed upon the troops and their horrific battlefield conditions. In addition, the troops had to improvise throughout the war, fighting often with obsolete equipment, held up by inadequate or no artillery support. Also, late in the war, they had to suffer declining production and quality of military necessities, including at the end of the conflict defective and obsolete gas shells. The multiple difficulties and often inhumane field conditions suggest that perhaps desperation, not dishonor, drove many soldiers of all nationalities to retreat or desert to the enemy. Most tellingly, Austria-Hungary had far more troops captured by the enemy than any of the war's other combatants.

Mobilization plans were predicated on the necessity to rapidly seize the initiative to counter the obvious tsarist troop numerical advantage. The army had to assemble and deploy troops as quickly as possible against an anticipated slower mobilizing tsarist army. Conrad thought that he possessed a two-week window of opportunity to launch an offensive to defeat the separately deploying tsarist units before they had completed their mobilization. Habsburg cavalry forces had to be march-ready on the third mobilization day, their immediate mission to provide protection for the deployment of the main army, while simultaneously conducting reconnaissance missions to locate deploying enemy units and ascertain their strength and intentions. Mobile Habsburg artillery units, to be march-ready on the fifth mobilization day, would support the lightly armed cavalry units.

Common Army infantry and field cannon batteries had to be combat-ready by the seventh mobilization day, while other artillery units, such as howitzer-, mountain- and heavy-artillery batteries would be operational between the eighth and tenth days of mobilization. *Landwehr/Honvéd*, March and *Ersatz* formations had to be action-ready by the tenth day.[12]

Cavalry forces proved totally unprepared for war. The initial strategic reconnaissance effort launched on August 15, covering a several-hundred-kilometer front, quickly made the horses unsuitable for duty when newly issued saddles produced deep sores on the animals' backs. Moreover, the colorful uniforms made the cavalry troopers easy targets for Russian sharpshooters. Tsarist cavalry forces, protected by infantry units' firepower, prevented any meaningful Habsburg reconnaissance results regarding the Russian deployment. Air reconnaissance on the Habsburg extreme right flank also failed, partially because invading Russian soldiers marched at night, and partially due to the mechanical problems experienced on the few available Habsburg airplanes.

Obsolete tactics also explained the cavalry's failure to fulfill its mission. The army applied sweeping and unrealistic peacetime maneuver tactics to the battlefields, with little success. Like many of their artillery and infantry counterparts, senior cavalry officers resisted implementing recent improvements in armaments and training, demonstrated in the recent 1904–1905 Russo-Japanese and 1912–1913 Balkan Wars. Personal trooper weapons consisted of only a heavy saber, a carbine without bayonet and fifty rounds of ammunition, totally unsuitable for modern battle.

Enemy artillery, machine-gun and infantry fire quickly rendered Habsburg cavalry forces helpless. Exploding artillery shells frightened the inexperienced troops and their mounts, causing many to panic, particularly during the early phases of the war. Mass hysteria often ensued. One *Honvéd* cavalry division fled sixty kilometers after one of the first 1914 encounters.

In fairness, too much was demanded of the cavalry troops. Fatigue, irregular supply of feed and inclement weather took an enormous toll on soldiers and horses, ultimately producing larger casualty figures than incurred in battle. The losses during the first weeks of the war drastically reduced cavalry troop numbers. Soon the shortage of quality horses, trench warfare, the shock effects of modern warfare and the excessive loss of officers necessitated the transformation of many mounted cavalry troops into dismounted infantry.

Airpower, in its infancy, had to be expanded in terms of production of both aircraft and trained pilots. In 1914 the army possessed thirty-nine planes. By the end of the year this had increased to ninety-one, an insufficient rise, and the few new factories faced material shortages slowing production because of the blockade. As the war dragged on, the transportation system collapsed and raw materials became even scarcer. By 1918 the army had to improvise because of lack of equipment. The troops had to fight with obsolete and inferior equipment and weapons, particularly later on the Italian front.

Upon the 1914 mobilization, 1,100 infantry battalions and 400 *Landsturm* and March formations were deployed. The peacetime army of 414,000 professional soldiers expanded to 3,350,000 mobilized troops, with 2,080,000 troops deployed to the battlefield and the remaining 1,270,000 assigned to Homeland duty. Regardless of unit size, the majority of each infantry company or battalion consisted of unprepared reservist soldiers. During the mobilization period, so many reservists and *Ersatz* soldiers reported for duty that insufficient weapons, uniforms and other necessities became available for distribution. Food, shelter and barracks also proved insufficient.[13] Thousands of excess personnel crowded army locations.

March Brigade and *Landsturm* units became integrated into the three separate mobilization groupings. The first, the A-Group, would always be deployed against Russia. It consisted of twenty-eight and a half infantry and ten cavalry divisions, as well as twenty-one *Landsturm* and March brigades. The second mobilization force, the B-Group (representing a swing force) would provide the offensive punch on either the Russian or Balkan front depending on the situation at mobilization. It consisted of twelve infantry divisions and one cavalry division, with six *Landsturm* and March brigades. The third formation, Minimal Group Balkan, the defensive group against Serbia-Montenegro, was comprised of eight infantry divisions and an additional seven *Landsturm* and March brigade units.

The military initially consisted of six armies and sixteen corps numbered in sequence. The corps contained divisions of all three types of military formations: Common Army, *Landwehr* and *Honvéd*. All untrained twenty-one-year-olds were immediately mobilized and assigned to reserve formations. Older trained troops became members of *Landsturm* regiments. On July 26 all 1914 recruits and *Ersatz* reserve units (born in 1893) were called to duty.

The number of Habsburg units deployed against Russia in August 1914 encompassed 819 infantry battalions, 384 cavalry squadrons and 380 artillery batteries, with 2,082 artillery pieces.[14] In October, following the disastrous opening August–September campaign defeats and subsequent retreat, those numbers sank to 693 infantry battalions (156 *Landsturm*), 352 cavalry squadrons and 291 artillery batteries now consisting of only 1,650 artillery pieces. At least temporarily, sufficient replacement troop numbers covered the staggering losses. However, enormous quantities of equipment and armaments had also been lost, destroyed or abandoned, negatively affecting the battered army's future performance. The continuing enormous casualty numbers became increasingly difficult to replace.

As the enormous first campaign casualty numbers became public, particularly in Vienna, the general August 1914 enthusiasm quickly turned to pessimism. As the official Austrian history admits, the enormous loss of infantry troops could initially be replaced; however, the professional army ranks and troops' physical preparedness and morale for future combat could not. The hot August weather was soon replaced by the fall rainy season, with its consequent effects during the retreat movement on troop morale and physical endurance. Weather, inhospitable terrain conditions and combat situations produced inhumane conditions, particularly during the 1915 Carpathian Mountain Winter campaign and mountain battle during the eleven Isonzo campaigns and *Straf* (punishment) expedition on the Italian front. This resulted in enormous casualties and untold soldier suffering.

Conrad consistently ignored a cardinal rule of military campaigning: To fight effectively, troops must have adequate rest and preparation for their mission. Conrad's lack of concern for his troops' welfare had a negative effect on them and resulted in countless unnecessary casualties. That and immediate battle casualties also produced lack of respect for the Habsburg Supreme Command, exacerbated by its lack of experience in modern warfare methodology: Conrad and his commanders had only experienced combat some forty years earlier, during subjection of Bosnia-Herzegovina in the 1870s and early 1880s. Compounding this problem, army commanders and chiefs of staff received their command responsibilities first during the mobilization period, thus lacked familiarity with their units, and their units with them. Further problems resulted from incompetent royal family army commanders, such as Joseph Ferdinand, who commanded Fourth Army at the 1914 Komarov battle, until he was removed at German command demand during the 1916 Brusilov offensive. Russian officers and troops had gained sobering combat experience during the 1904–1905 Russo-Japanese War and Serbians the 1912–1913 Balkan Wars. This provided them great advantage during the initial 1914 campaigns and afterwards.

Habsburg Supreme Command's inexperience quickly became evident. Contradictory orders, excessive march goals and too hastily prepared offensive operations produced chaos on the battlefield. The lack of artillery–infantry cooperation resulted in numerous early battlefield defeats and enormous casualties. Confusion was not limited to the tactical level; during the initial deployment against Serbia, the vast majority of Second Army (B-Group) was railroad transported to the Balkan theater, then on August 18 many units were ordered to redeploy to the Russian front. They arrived too late to avoid defeat and their redeployment contributed to the disastrous Balkan front defeats, where an ill-prepared and rushed Fifth Army, with its northern flank protection gravely weakened by Second Army's redeployment to the Russian front, launched its tardy offensive effort. The troops' excessive exhaustion from long, arduous marches, an inadequately functioning logistical system and command errors help explain the failure of the three 1914 Balkan and Galician operations and later campaign results explained in the narrative. Emperor Karl's 1917 cashiering of Conrad's Habsburg Supreme Command and its staff, replacing Conrad with the pliable General Arz, also had negative effects.

Following the often interrupted and delayed railroad retransport to the Russian war theater, B-Group forces disembarked from their trains to be immediately hurled into battle in a belated attempt to halt the unexpected and irresistibly strong Russian offensive launched from the Galician eastern flank area. Second Army XII Corps, deployed in this area (where the B-Group Second Army and allied Romanian troops should have been deployed in a War Case "R" [Russia]), was force-marched toward the endangered and exposed northern Third Army's eastern flank positions. Quickly fatigued XII

Corps troops could attain neither their extensive march goals, nor the necessary combat effectiveness in battle. The troops of 10. Cavalry Division, after a five-day train ride, rode eighty-five kilometers in twenty-two hours in the August heat. The weary unit then experienced two periods of panic when the troops, many of whose horses had been driven to death, finally encountered the superior enemy.

Conrad's July 1, 1914 decision for a rearward Habsburg deployment to the San–Dniester River line placed his units far rearward of their originally planned Galician frontier positions. Consequently, the troops had to endure long marches in the August heat to attain the originally specified lines determined in prewar Railroad Bureau planning. The troops became exhausted well before launching their offensive.

After a short recovery following its long September retreat, the army somewhat surprisingly participated in three subsequent fall 1914 campaigns, one each month, alternating offensive and defensive actions, but paying dearly in blood for their efforts.[15] Embarrassing retrograde movements occurring during deteriorating inclement weather conditions followed each other in rapid succession. The troops' esprit de corps and confidence in military leadership suffered accordingly. In late December 1914, Third Army sustained further losses defending against the enemy's powerful Carpathian Mountain assaults toward the Hungarian frontier commencing on December 20. Thus, the army entered 1915 severely weakened, and desperately requiring rehabilitation. Yet, Conrad designated that army as the main offensive force for the initial January Carpathian Mountain Winter War campaign that eventually destroyed the Habsburg Army again as in the opening and three fall campaigns. New armies had to be mustered also after the disastrous 1916 Brusilov offensive. German military assistance became necessary with a concomitant extension into Habsburg command positions.

During a series of campaigns each side conducted offensives and retreats, but with no decisive results. Russian troops conducted successful large-scale retreats to the San River line in early October 1914, in December 1914 after the Limanova–Lapanov battle, as well as during the early 1915 Carpathian Mountain Winter War and subsequent Gorlice–Tarnow campaigns. However, tsarist retrograde movements, in contrast to those of the Habsburgs, resulted in insignificant loss of war materiel.

The outbreak of panic that ensued during the humiliating Habsburg September retreat can, to a large extent, be attributed to the soldiers' inexperience. Only the failure of Russian commanders to rapidly pursue the badly shaken Austro-Hungarian Army saved it from annihilation. During the 1914 Serbian campaigns, the troops were mindlessly driven until they collapsed exhausted, particularly during their disastrous November/December 1914 defeat. The seriously inadequate functioning supply system, neglect for the troop welfare and faulty strategy ultimately cost 273,000 Habsburg casualties and enormous quantities of equipment, although three-quarters of these casualties reputedly returned to duty.

The combination of the 1914 military setbacks and the Russian occupation of Galicia and Bukovina created a panic atmosphere in Habsburg Supreme Command headquarters. The defeats also significantly increased the possibility that Italy and Romania could enter the conflict against the Habsburgs. A declaration of war by either, or both, could create an untenable military situation; in particular, the May 23, 1915 Italian declaration of war opened a major third front, further stretching the demand for the dwindling available resources. The role of European neutrals remained significant throughout the war, for all warring countries.

Fighting a multiple-front war signified that military units often had to be redeployed as military necessity dictated. Units might be positioned for an offensive or to strengthen a weak defensive line. Often inadequate attention was paid to the toll these actions took on the troops. Numerous veterans' diaries repeatedly complained about the unnecessary and self-defeating effects of *hin und her* (back and forth) marching and the repeated repositioning of artillery pieces when not necessary. These often-pointless efforts merely produced physical and mental fatigue. Often such overexertion of the soldiers' physical capabilities continued into the night, not allowing time for adequate and necessary rest.[16]

Excessive movement was due, in part, to expectations created by prewar military exercises that had been based on unrealistic conditions and experiences. During prewar maneuvers, troops marched at breakneck speed to achieve success. However, all activity halted at nightfall. The excessive marches could not be sustained under combat conditions, particularly by reserve formations, a lesson that commanders failed to learn.

Also lacking was adequate consideration of the difficulty in maneuvering troops through mountainous terrain. The peacetime mountain exercises occurred during favorable spring and summer weather. Thus, when serious battle commenced in the Carpathian Mountains after the September Habsburg 1914 retreat, and Italian front after 1915, many soldiers had inadequate or no training and no lessons or past experience to draw upon. On the Italian front troops had to be retrained for weeks before they could be inserted into combat.

Tactical training drew primarily from the 1866 Austro-Prussian War, the 1870–1871 Franco-Prussian War and the 1878–1879 and 1881–1882 experiences of the Bosnian occupation campaigns. Flanking and envelopment movements received emphasis. Similar to French methods, the offensive dominated military theory and training, as exemplified by Conrad to whom morale and willpower could overcome the new rapid-fire weapons. His prewar penchant for the cult of the offensive is critical to understanding the catastrophic results of the initial 1914 offensives. Immediate frontal attacks failed to heed the major changes wrought by the late-nineteenth-century introduction of modern weapons, including machine guns and much improved rapid-fire artillery with recoil mechanisms, producing the dominance of the defense due to the new massed and rapid firepower. The effectiveness of such weapons in defense was demonstrated during the Boer War (1899–1902) and the Russo-Japanese War (1904–1905); however, military circles largely ignored these advances, thinking them to be aberrations associated with colonial warfare.[17] Conrad's extensive writings on tactics included fewer than two pages devoted to defensive warfare. Thus, launching mass frontal assaults with little, if any, artillery support was tantamount to criminal negligence, producing multiple unnecessary bloodbaths, defeats and the loss of hundreds of thousands of troops. Nevertheless, Conrad continued to launch unsuccessful offensives in an attempt to maintain the initiative against a vast tsarist numerical superiority.

Conrad believed that by assuming a defensive stance one surrendered the initiative to the enemy, thus his outnumbered forces had to continually attack the numerically superior tsarist forces. Compounding his error, Conrad's 1911 field regulations emphasized infantry advancing in close echelon formation. His strategic and tactical ideas thus contained several major flaws, not the least of which included his lack of appreciation for infantry–artillery coordination and the virtual ignoring of combined arms preparation before launching an attack.

His mismanagement of the 1914 two-front deployment and offensive actions exacerbated the Eastern front troop number ratios. The chaos produced by altering preplanned Railroad Bureau timetables a month before the war erupted resulted in the already boggled redeployment of troops from the Balkan to the Russian front, leaving multiple B-Group divisions in the Balkan theater. Thus, only twenty-eight divisions initially deployed against the tsarist enemy, and the Balkan front defeat resulted from removal of some of the B-Group forces for redeployment to the Northern front. This exposed Fifth Army flanks in the initial Balkan campaign, resulting in defeat. Second Army troops arrived on the Eastern front to be hurled into a disastrous battlefield.

The Dual Monarchy remained at a major disadvantage compared to the other European great powers because the three million plus soldiers mobilized in 1914 possessed a bewilderingly varied level of training, each corps defining its own conception of it. The 1912 Army Law could not improve the army's many shortcomings before the war erupted.

Liaison officers often lacked effective leadership qualities. Conrad and his senior commanders consistently had little first-hand knowledge of the actual battlefield conditions. Conrad never visited the front during the 1915 Carpathian Mountain Winter War or Italian *Straf* offensive and only three times during 1914 campaigns. Following his marriage to the much younger Gina von Reininghaus in October 1915, headquarters evolved into a society of wives, which rankled the senior German liaison officer. Conrad spent much of his days with his new wife.

Field troops and officers quickly realized that higher-echelon commanders harbored little appreciation or knowledge of the persistent horrific conditions at the front and that Conrad too often failed to accurately assess his army's capabilities or employ effective military tactics. Field commanders often realized they lacked the necessary means and troop numbers to achieve this mission, a result of the impossibility of complying with Conrad's orders. Several army commanders sought to transfer offensive missions to fellow commanders. Before the first January 1915 Carpathian Mountain offensive, the Third Army commander General Boroević attempted to transfer the main attack mission to Army Group Pflanzer-Baltin. Prior to the second February 1915 Carpathian Mountain offensive, the Second Army commander, General Böhm-Ermolli, did likewise. Troop numbers consistently remained inadequate for their missions, inclement weather conditions worsened and terrain proved unsuitable for most operational success. Conrad placed no limit on Habsburg casualty ratios, emphasizing the importance of achieving an offensive battlefield victory at any cost. His prewar proclivity to repeatedly demand preventive wars against Italy and Serbia before it was too late and the Dual Monarchy would have to face more powerful opponents in a multifront war interestingly had some objectivity.

Adding to soldiers' woes, the hot 1914 summer weather created conditions ripe for the outbreak of epidemics, while the damp and colder autumn weather brought cholera and typhus. In the late fall 1914 campaign many troops succumbed to cholera until an immunization program was established, often resisted by higher commanders. Winter weather suppressed infectious diseases, but frigid conditions produced cold-related illnesses, such as lung and intestinal disease, as well as frostbite. Tens of thousands of soldiers froze to death or lost limbs in the Italian Alps and Carpathian Mountains. Poor personal hygiene resulted from the troops' squalid conditions. Troops wore the same uniforms for weeks, even months, which encouraged the outbreak of such infectious diseases as typhus. Fortunately for the troops such outbreaks proved sporadic in nature. Lice quickly became a major problem on both the Eastern and Balkan fronts. Significant troop numbers succumbed to typhus before its connection to lice was discovered.

By fall 1918 troops lacked full uniforms, literally existing in rags that in combination with severe malnutrition spread illness through the ranks. Such conditions persisted since at least 1917, seriously hurting the last vestige of troop morale. Soldiers dug up the graves of fallen soldiers from the early war years to gain possession of proper uniforms. An interesting report by a *Landsturm* unit surgeon claimed that frostbite had already posed a major problem during the fall 1914 campaigns; cases of gangrene became numerous and amputation was the immediate solution. Reports of frostbite cases appeared as early as October 1914, even before freezing nighttime temperatures became the norm. Damp boots, undernourishment, overexhaustion and failure to change footwear regularly caused gangrene.

The medical prognosis for exhausted and wounded soldiers generally proved bleak. Many died quickly, often within a quarter hour, even when the wounds were not life-threatening. Many soldiers simply succumbed, particularly in the 1915 Carpathian Mountain Winter War campaign and the 1915 Italian front mountain warfare. In high terrain, if wounded troops could not move or be moved, they faced freezing to death. Many wounded troops died on the bumpy wagon transport down the mountain terrain, or simply froze to death. Losses from battle and illness skyrocketed. Many soldiers also committed suicide or self-mutilation to escape the horrible conditions they had to endure.

Tsarist forces did not just outnumber Habsburg units in troop strength and artillery guns. They also initially possessed a substantial superiority in machine guns of thirty-two per infantry division, compared to the Habsburg twenty-four. According to one Austrian military historian, the Russians initially possessed a 60–70 percent advantage in infantry troop numbers, a 90 percent surplus in light-artillery guns and 23 percent in heavy artillery.[18] Habsburg forces received more modern artillery pieces during 1915, but artillery performance, except on rare occurrences, remained inadequate. The lack of raw materials and fuel resulting from the Entente blockade retarded industrial production of necessary weapons and equipment.

A new emphasis on indirect artillery fire (weapons hidden by terrain features, emplaced well behind the front lines) appeared during the 1904–1905 Russo-Japanese War, and was quickly adopted during the World War. This was accompanied by increased firing range, the greater lethality of high explosive shells and increased rate of fire because of the introduction of recoil mechanisms and steel barrels replacing bronze and iron ones. The development of the field telephone also produced a potential revolution in artillery efficiency, but truly effective radio communication did not appear until after the war when it influenced the development of German Panzer divisions. Meanwhile, aerial reconnaissance gained importance on the Eastern front, particularly during and after the 1915 Gorlice–Tarnow campaign. It also proved critical on the Italian and Romanian fronts.

The modern machine gun evolved between 1885 and 1900, with the American Maxim's improved model adding a substantial lethality to European arsenals. Many strategists failed to recognize its future battlefield significance. Increased firepower was not limited to automatic crew-served weapons. By 1900, single-shot rifles had evolved with multiround magazines. The new .30 caliber cartridges traveled at twice the velocity of earlier rounds, struck with much greater force and caused much greater bodily injury. The new bolt-action chamber-feeding mechanisms greatly increased the speed of reloading a weapon and multiplied the rate of fire, thus killing power.

The enormous 1914 Habsburg casualties forced the creation of a new Austro-Hungarian army in early 1915, the "picket fence," *Landsturm* or

Miliz army. However, critical shortage of rifles hindered replacement formation training. Many wounded soldiers abandoned their weapons on the battlefield, requiring troop details to recover them, a problem not limited to Habsburg forces. Major troop formations were soon armed with captured enemy rifles, artillery and shells. Following the disastrous fall 1915 Rovno campaign the Russians armed two complete corps with recovered Habsburg weapons. The shortage of appropriate field uniforms meant that many troops had to fight the fall and winter campaigns in lightweight summer uniforms.[19] The Entente blockade compounded this problem, causing a serious disruption in the Habsburg textile industry. By 1918 uniforms could not be manufactured to supply needs. The quality had also declined sharply, with paper serving as a substitute to cloth. Many troops had to fight in part of uniforms, troops having to borrow portions for special formations for dignitaries.

Artillery units also had to endure a steep learning curve, as prewar doctrine had to be scrapped and new accommodations made for advancements in technology or tactics. Artillery barrages did not support dense infantry formation advances, which produced catastrophic losses that the army could ill afford. Many lives were sacrificed until the army converted to high-explosive from shrapnel shells, to neutralize enemy entrenchments. Shrapnel shells proved effective against infantry formations on open terrain, but once soldiers dug covered fortified trenches for protection, high-explosive shells that could penetrate such positions became critical. A shell crisis developed until high-explosive rounds could be manufactured in sufficient quantity, which remained a dire issue throughout the war. By 1917–1918 industry could not meet the army's needs. During 1918 industry collapsed because of the lack of raw materials and due to the transportation (rail) system failures. Permanent trench lines converted artillery from a highly maneuverable weapon into a stationary one, that required far more shells than had been anticipated during the prewar period. Industry could not produce sufficient amounts of shells due to the growing shortage of raw materials and the decline in processes, yet another manifestation of the Entente blockade. Later in the war gas shells often proved defective, regular ones duds and gun barrels worn out or exploded.

The Dual Monarchy concentrated much of its limited military resources on artillery expansion, increasing its number of heavy batteries more than tenfold during the war. During 1914 a division field artillery brigade contained about seven batteries of six to eight mainly obsolete guns. Early 1915 artillery units were improved with the addition of new and higher-caliber guns.

Austro-Hungarian infantry divisions in 1914 each possessed five field cannon and two 10-cm field howitzer batteries, three batteries fewer than their tsarist opponents. In 1914, a Habsburg division possessed less firepower than any other European great power, a most serious disadvantage and indication of its unpreparedness to wage a major war. However, by 1917–1918 Habsburg troops had become battle-hardened, and possessed adequate quality weapons, although still lacking in sufficient numbers as industry production eventually declined. During the eleven Italian Isonzo River campaigns the vast enemy artillery superiority hurt Habsburg troop morale, as well as causing enormous casualties.

The failure of many offensive operations underscored the lack of artillery effectiveness, as well as inadequate training. Field commanders recognized that artillery had failed them, particularly during the early war. The army lacked sufficient medium- and heavy-artillery pieces throughout the war. Conrad, again, failed to recognize the critical need for artillery–infantry cooperation, and the troops paid the bloody price. During the 1915 Carpathian Mountain Winter campaign many batteries remained behind mountain ridges because it proved exceedingly difficult to emplace guns off the few roads and trails in the snow- and ice-covered terrain, as later also occurred in the Italian mountain campaigns. Often artillery pieces could not be retrieved if a retreat ensued. Declining pack animal numbers and proper equipment led to a great reliance on "improvisation." During the Italian Isonzo River campaigns, only a third of the horses remained to move artillery pieces, severely limiting maneuverability. Throughout the war untold hundreds of thousands of animals perished from starvation, the harsh elements and extreme exhaustion.

In the 1914 battles artillery batteries were deployed at the front lines to provide direct fire support for attacking troops, but could not be moved quickly if the infantry achieved success or rearward if a retreat ensued. Inevitably the artillery proved incapable of directing accurate indirect fire against entrenched enemy positions. Tsarist artillery performed far more effectively and outranged Habsburg guns. The modern field artillery pieces' range increased to almost seven kilometers and rapid-fire field cannons significantly increased the effectiveness and destructiveness of artillery fire. The enhanced effect of artillery forced changes in infantry tactics and necessitated closer cooperation between the two armies.

By fall 1914 the Habsburg Army conducted campaigns on mountain terrain, revealing the importance of more mobile mountain artillery pieces, and their transport requirements. Conrad had appealed for reorganizing and provisioning mountain-artillery units prior to the war, but in 1914, the few mountain batteries proved ineffective in battle. Only ten and a half regiments existed, each of six batteries, four equipped with the obsolete 7-cm M99 mountain-artillery guns. The M99 gun had a range of 6,600 yards and a six rounds per minute rate of fire.

The 1908–1909 Bosnian Crisis brought new pleas for additional modern artillery and demands for deployment of new mountain-artillery units, particularly in Bosnia-Herzegovina. The new M08/09 gun began to replace older models, but by 1914 stocks proved inadequate. In combat, inferior artillery pieces and rapid shell shortages placed Habsburg troops at a severe disadvantage throughout the war. Tsarist and Italian artillery pulverized Habsburg positions and decimated attack formations. Shell shortages frequently prevented troops from completing their missions or, worse, resulted in their defeat. On the eve of the war, Habsburg shell stocks were dangerously low, and industry proved incapable of producing the number other major combatants achieved throughout the conflict. Lack of shell production often forced Habsburg artillery units to conserve their supplies to the fatal infantry disadvantage.

Materiel deficiencies and obsolete doctrine were not the only issues facing Habsburg gunners. Another serious problem involved the inadequacy of artillery field training. Only 50 practice rounds per gun were provided annually during the prewar period, whereas Germany allowed 650 and Russia 500–600. Critically, artillery observers often lacked field experience. Many had never fired or even observed an artillery shell land.[20]

Effective artillery fire boosted troop morale. However, infantry quickly realized that its support lacked effectiveness, while tsarist batteries continually neutralized Austro-Hungarian gunfire from further than a thousand meters' distance. This deficiency extended to the Italian front between 1915 and 1918, although on multiple occasions effective Habsburg artillery support halted massed enemy attacks.

Other equipment deficiencies plagued the army. Inferior quality saddles caused sores on cavalry horses' backs, as mentioned. Cavalry units often could not accompany infantry over rough terrain. A shortage of trucks (many lost in Serbia in 1914) and the accelerating loss of horses and other pack animals sacrificed to battle, sickness, injury, starvation and overexertion further lessened military maneuverability, preventing a regular flow of desperately required supplies, food and ammunition to the front. Even when ample ammunition stores were available, shipping them to the designated units proved a major logistical challenge. Forty-five different gun models existed, each requiring its own specific shells. Many antiquated bronze gun barrels remained in service, which proved far less durable than those constructed of steel. Nor were most artillery pieces equipped with recoil mechanisms or protective shields as the Russians' were. The incessant utilization of artillery left numerous guns requiring repair early in the fall 1914 campaigns, particularly replacement of gun barrels. Excessive short rounds soon became a danger, compounded by numerous deficient artillery rounds as the war continued and worker productivity declined.[21]

Transportation became a significant problem. Already during the September 1914 retreat thousands of wagons and horses, locomotives and railroad cars had been abandoned to the enemy. Many of the heavy wagons, built in the mid-century, proved too cumbersome for travel on the precarious Polish and Serbian roads and trails. Lighter local Polish wagons and smaller *ponja* horses were pressed into service as substitute transport.

Artillery effectiveness was also severely compromised by doctrinal conflict relative to the advantages of direct versus indirect fire. Most senior officers distrusted the "new doctrines" and continued to support the standard tactics. Worse, inadequately trained artillery reserve officers lacked knowledge of modern tactics and the proper utilization of weapons. In contrast, tsarist gunners enjoyed a major advantage by applying the Russo-Japanese lessons such as utilizing indirect fire tactics, enabling them to quickly establish artillery dominance on the Galician battlefields.[22] The Habsburg Army obtained a few new field howitzer batteries during 1914 from undelivered ordinance ordered by the Chinese and Turkish governments. These modern steel barreled M14s eventually replaced obsolete M99 guns, but remained limited in quantity.

Relative to Fortress Przemyśl's surrender on March 22, 1915, of the nearly one thousand fortress artillery pieces, the vast majority consisted of obsolete guns. The M61 guns circa 1861 fired black powder through bronze barrels and possessed only short-range capabilities. They comprised one-third of the citadel armaments. The second enemy fortress siege tightened in late December 1914 and forced the slaughter of thousands of horses to provide troop sustenance, which resulted in a corresponding loss of maneuvering for fortress artillery and the transport of shells to endangered citadel areas.

Another critical military disadvantage involved the paucity of railroad lines servicing major operational areas. The overburdened Hungarian rail system to Galicia, extending like a spiderweb from Budapest, created critical problems at the beginning of the war. Increases in troop transport numbers caused an interruption in reinforcements and war materiel traffic, often adversely affecting the tactical situation. Civilian traffic was halted for military purposes for the opening campaign, as well as other major operations, such as the June 1918 military disaster. Toward the end of the war, for example, before the fatal June 1918 offensive, priority went to army needs, shipping of coal and consumer goods to cities terminated for months at a time.

The railroad situation proved extremely significant throughout the war. Successful offensives depended upon timely, rapid and regular transport of troops, supplies, ammunition, artillery and shells. The Carpathian Mountains, for example, encompassed a four-hundred-kilometer-wide battle area, with extremely limited railroad capacity on four inadequate rail lines that extended to the rearward mountain slopes. These few lines could not efficiently and rapidly transport large troop contingents, supplies and equipment. Serious delays and stoppages became a regular occurrence, often negatively affected by inclement weather conditions. The railroad situation proved inadequate even before the July 1914 mobilization. The prewar Russian railroad construction program, the 1913 Grand Program supported by French investments, presented St. Petersburg with at least a two-to-one daily troop transport capacities advantage by 1914. Each day 360 Tsarist trains rolled, contrasting with the

Habsburg Army's relatively meager 153, a vital Russian advantage accentuated by that country's overwhelming troop numbers. Habsburg rail limitations proved disastrous when the Russians commenced mobilization measures a week earlier during the July 1914 crisis. This provided the Russians a five-day mobilization advantage. On July 29 twelve tsarist corps mobilized in the four military districts of Warsaw, Kiev, Odessa and Kasa, deploying 1.1 million troops (fifty-five infantry divisions) on the Austro-Hungarian front. The tsarist military had initiated mobilization measures on July 25, 1914.

The surprisingly rapid Russian deployment forced Conrad to deploy military forces before all troop railroad deployments had been concluded. Meanwhile, an increasing stream of rolling stock clogged the few Eastern Galician rail lines from the opposite direction of travel. Railroad cars transporting wounded soldiers, the many fleeing refugees and empty trains became intermingled. Equipment and troop transport trains attempting to travel forward were caught in the chaos of major stoppages and delays. Similar occurrences would plague later campaigns, particularly on the Italian front.

In 1914, troop rail movement was also seriously impeded because Railroad Bureau planners limited deployment traffic to 50-car, 100-axle trains, ignoring the usage of 150–200-axle trains on the same lines operating regularly during peacetime. The use of 100-axle train units suited military planners as it made convenient transport of individual infantry battalions, artillery batteries or a cavalry squadron on one train; that convenience meant unnecessarily slow deployment of the army mass, another example of how army railroad planning proved grossly inadequate.

Several other factors proved detrimental to the mobilization and deployment. The Galician railroad system lacked sufficient numbers and large enough unloading ramps, and a satisfactory number of railroad stations. Moreover, mobilization trains traveled at eighteen kilometers per hour, requiring too much time to reach the front. Trains traveled at the slowest train's speed (i.e., on mountain lines). The Third Army commander's rail time required three times the typical peacetime duration on the same route. One could have ridden a bicycle that distance during the same time.[23]

Incredibly, only one railroad line ran from Budapest to the Bosnian frontier. Prewar attempts to add a second track to this critical line failed due to internal politics, which negatively affected B-Group rail transport invasion forces to the Balkan War theater, then further seriously delayed its rerouting to the Russian front commencing on August 18, 1914. The tardy transfer of Second Army troops from the Balkan War theater resulted in multiple train stoppages, further delaying arrival on the Northern front. Numerous C-echelon deployment trains (supplies, equipment) were also delayed because of the overcrowded and chaotic rail traffic.

Attempts to establish and maintain a regular flow of supplies to the Galician front during September 1914 failed. Third Army troops raided Fortress

Przemyśl warehouses of food, artillery, shells and other equipment when they liberated the citadel after October 10. At the same time, bridges and railroad tracks destroyed by earlier enemy action prevented a full resupply of the fortress warehouses before Russian troops besieged it for a second time in early November. This raises the question of whether the fortress would have had to capitulate on March 22, 1915 if the field armies had not cannibalized its stores of food and ammunition. Additionally, the inadequate railroad system toward the extreme eastern Carpathian Mountain front proved fatal to Conrad's strategic planning for his 1915 Carpathian Mountain Winter campaign strategy. This applied to the late January 1915 Third Army offensive as well as the subsequent Second Army operation in late February and the needless V Corps attempts after March 15 to liberate Fortress Przemyśl.

Galician roadways were vastly inferior to Central and Western Europe; the routes were intended for light Polish wagons. Upper road surfaces had been constructed for local traffic usage; long columns of artillery units and heavy supply wagons quickly damaged the few roads beyond repair. Heavy rains created deep potholes, substantially worsening road conditions and significantly retarding all traffic movement. Frontline troops often had to perform the work of dead or injured draft animals by pulling sleds loaded with machine guns, extricating artillery pieces from snow drifts and assisting transporting ammunition, food and battle gear to the front lines. Dogs were also pressed into service. Frequent rain or snow conditions transformed long roadway stretches to a quagmire of mud or ice later on the Italian Alpine mountain front as well. In all theaters, deserted wagons and horse carcasses littered travel routes. The grossly overworked horses and other draft animals died in huge numbers, their corpses often pushed into the muddy mire in an attempt to assist forward movement. Insurmountable difficulties also occurred in caring for and feeding the huge number of horses and heavier pack animals, particularly the transporting of feed into mountainous terrain. Secondary passage conditions also rapidly deteriorated because of the excessive utilization by long march and supply columns. A shortage of gravel led to multiple substitutes being utilized to attempt to fill the potholes and to provide traction.

Supply personnel and combat troops rapidly became exhausted attempting to maintain a steady supply transport in mountain terrain, as occurred in the 1915 Carpathian Mountain Winter campaigns, 1914–1915 Serbian, 1916 Romanian and multiple Italian campaigns. Mountain columns often had to wend their way over pathless ridges and steep slopes. Winter weather conditions seriously delayed supply efforts, while troops did not receive winter uniforms or equipment, because they had not been planned for a winter campaign.

Persistent icy winter winds lashed soldiers' eyes, producing a painful ice crust over their eyelids. Their faces registered shock and apathy, their hopeless expressions displayed despair and resignation because of physical exhaustion.

Many soldiers committed suicide to end their misery, while tens of thousands succumbed to the extreme weather conditions, either the "White Death," or the frostbite endemic on the Carpathian, Serbian, Italian or Romanian mountain terrain.

Another major hindrance resulted from the shortage of technical troops and military labor units to repair, or maintain, existing supply lines. The number of engineering units for bridge and road construction proved insufficient. Labor units encountered the described difficult road maintenance conditions. Steep icy ridges and deep snow combined to create difficult accessibility and horrendous working conditions for the typically understrength units.

During summer months, mountain ridges could be traversed in just a few minutes, but during winter it required hours to traverse the same terrain. Blizzard conditions left the few travel routes coated in ice, thus unusable until late morning sunlight effected a partial melt, seriously delaying logistical efforts. Maintaining the long mountain supply lines to the fronts in Italy, Galicia, Serbia and Romania assumed growing significance for military operations, consuming more and more resources that could thus not be employed elsewhere where required. Mountain terrain proved problematic in other respects. It often proved impossible to launch a successful offensive in the few main traversable passes until defenders had been driven from the high terrain peaks and ridges along the valleys. During the October 1917 Caporetto offensive, German troops triumphantly attacked through valleys, contrary to Habsburg tactics that emphasized initially seizing the high terrain.

Mountain regions also posed severe obstacles for a retreating army. Communication possibilities were rare. If the enemy neutralized a communication or logistical center, it easily forced the withdrawal of major units. Retreating troops, artillery and supply trains quickly created mass chaos and panic along the few valley roads. The 1917 Caporetto campaign provided an excellent example with the disastrous Italian retreat.

Emperor Franz Joseph, an octogenarian, epitomized his role as the irrefutable first soldier. He symbolized the unity of the diverse realm until his death in November 1916 after sixty-eight years of rule, maintaining the basic Dual Monarchy territorial structure. He alone could declare war, conclude peace and appoint or dismiss senior military commanders. Franz Joseph accepted as his first duty the security of his disparate realms; defense and foreign policy embodied two of his most crucial functions. The army always remained his first concern because it bound the disparate lands, producing a feudal type of devotion to the monarch. Keenly aware that the army played a vital role as the cornerstone of his monarchy, he also realized that patriotism based on a nation-state was impossible, because at least ten different nationalities filled army ranks. (The 1914 mobilization order was published in fifteen different languages.) The creation of a nineteenth-century secular nation-state proved beyond the ability of the unique Austro-Hungarian monarchy. Under such circumstances, the army had to maintain its soldiers' loyalty to it and the emperor (king in Hungary). During basic training, indoctrination focused on the army's unique cultural and historical mission. Franz Joseph, as a beloved figure, held the realms together, providing stability. His death created a vacuum that unleashed the forces that ultimately destroyed the Dual Monarchy in October 1918, as his nephew Karl proved unprepared to rule and incapable of obtaining peace for a war-weary Dual Monarchy, to a great extent due to the inability to break free from the German alliance.

In spite of his obsession with the military, Franz Joseph had not been successful in warfare. In 1859 Habsburg armed forces lost a war against France, although they soundly defeated the allied Italian forces. Defeat during the 1866 Austro-Prussian War proved particularly fateful for the patriarch. The Prussian victory drove the Habsburgs out of "Germany" after almost six hundred years of rule as Holy Roman emperors. This fatefully transferred Vienna's attention to the Balkan Peninsula, because Russia blocked expansion to the east, Germany to the north and Italy to the south. This shift of strategic focus later embroiled Austria-Hungary in the First World War.

The 1867 *Ausgleich*, or compromise, also forced a transformation of the Austrian Empire into the Austro-Hungarian monarchy, an immediate result of the Austro-Prussian War defeat. During the 1878 Congress of Berlin, Franz Joseph obtained the right to garrison troops in Bosnia-Herzegovina, and in 1908 annexed the two provinces, initiating an assertive foreign policy until 1914. Tragically, the events relating to these two provinces, particularly after the 1908–1909 Bosnian Crisis and 1912–1913 Balkan Wars, exploded into the World War. The alliance with Germany remained the main focus of the emperor's foreign policy.

The 1867 *Ausgleich* created two semi-independent states that shared a common monarch, who commanded the armed forces and conducted foreign affairs to maintain its Great Power status. During the World War tensions exploded between the two entities, Austria and Hungary, particularly as the effects of the Entente blockade and four years of poor harvests resulted in starvation conditions in Austria, with the Hungarians not initially cooperating to relieve the situation. The Hungarians shipped surplus grain to Germany, but often refused to aid their neighbor. By 1914, meanwhile, it had become questionable whether the Dual Monarchy remained a Balkan power, even a great power.

Franz Joseph's death had been anticipated for a long time, but his passing became a turning point in the history of the monarchy. Because of the assassination of Archduke Franz Ferdinand, the new emperor Karl became the unfortunate successor to the aged emperor. Karl had not been trained to rule, but he immediately recognized that the Dual Monarchy required peace. Tragically, his actions to obtain that result proved unsuccessful, particularly during the Sixtus Affair that will be described in Chapter 9. Karl also sought unsuccessfully to improve the Austro-Hungarian position relative to the German alliance. Once in power, he ordered a new Habsburg Supreme Command structure, cashiering Conrad and his staff. His choice of successor, a sycophant to the emperor, proved fatal as did his July 2, 1917 general amnesty that undermined his military command authority in time. His untimely October Manifesto infuriated his German and Hungarian supporters and opened the door for the Czechs and South Slavs to declare their independence.

The new emperor Karl had some military experience and training but proved a disastrous war commander, his actions too often counterproductive. A major mistake involved his assuming command of the army when totally unqualified for the post. This action ensured that any mistakes or battle defeats would be identified with him, as with Tsar Nicholas.

A major Karl misjudgment resulted from selecting an unqualified chief of the General Staff to replace Conrad. This position proved far above his choice's capabilities. Disastrously, he always deferred to Emperor Karl and lacked the strength of character to contradict him. He also had to command Generals Boroević and Conrad who had much more leadership experience than him. General Arz also proved indecisive at times and he and his chief of staff were chiefly responsible for the June 15, 1918 offensive defeat. That battle assured the military demise of the Dual Monarchy; then General Arz badly mishandled the armistice, as we shall see in Chapter 10.

With the 1918 collapse of the Austro-Hungarian monarchy Emperor Karl twice unsuccessfully attempted to reclaim the Hungarian crown in 1921. His wife Zita and his children were originally exiled to Switzerland. Following the two abortive attempts to reacquire the throne of Hungary the family was exiled to the island of Madeira where Karl died of pneumonia in 1922.

Chief of the General Staff (1906–1911, 1912–1917) Franz Conrad von Hötzendorf attempted to modernize the rapidly declining army during the prewar years. This produced numerous clashes with the common war minister over military budget matters and Foreign Minister Alois Aehrenthal over diplomacy, particularly relative to Italy, until Aehrenthal's death in 1911. All three were appointed to their positions during the change of guard in 1906, because of Archduke Franz Ferdinand's increasing influence in Habsburg governance matters as Emperor Franz Joseph grew older.

Conrad, often labeled a warmonger, repeatedly demanded the launching of preventive wars against the perceived enemies Italy and Serbia. He insisted that only military force could halt the destructive forces of nationalism within the multinational empire. Being a Social Darwinist partially accounts for his pressure to launch preventive wars, which he believed would save the monarchy from internal collapse and prevent future multiple-front wars.

Conrad demanded a war against Serbia as early as 1907 and continued to do so until the outbreak of war. An Italophobe, he viewed Italy's actions as perfidious and demanded war against it in 1907, 1908, 1910 and 1911.

His conflict with Foreign Minister Aehrenthal, who strongly supported proper allied relations with Rome, led to his removal as chief of the General Staff in 1911 resulting from his demand for war against Italy after the outbreak of the Tripoli War. He was reinstated because of the critical situation raised by the 1912–1913 Balkan Wars, and removed by Emperor Karl in 1917 when Karl also dismissed Franz Joseph's senior officials.

Although informal military agreements had been concluded with Germany in 1882, relations between the two monarchies at times had been less than cordial, particularly during General Alfred von Schlieffen's tenure in office (1891–1905). The 1909 Conrad/Moltke meeting and then renewed correspondence during the 1908–1909 Bosnian Crisis, following the Schlieffen-era hiatus, did not produce strategic coordination and definitive mutual war planning. Unfortunately, the strategic goals of the two allies proved incompatible. While invading Serbia in 1914 Conrad had committed his ally to launch a major offensive with forty infantry divisions against Russia regardless of events in the Balkan theater. Reputedly anticipating a supporting German offensive into Russian Poland, Conrad launched a series of offensives on both fronts despite the fact that Russian forces had deployed five days earlier and greatly outnumbered his troops. Second Army, intended to anchor the Galician right flank against the tsarist foe, was dispatched to the Balkan front to participate in that invasion. Throughout the war Conrad failed miserably to understand the capabilities of his army, a cardinal sin for a commander. Nor did he grasp the full significance of the army's lack of modern equipment and weaponry and inadequately trained troops.

Following the war, former General Staff officers wrote in legendary, almost mythical terms honoring and idealizing their former commander, in spite of his numerous command mistakes and lack of judgment. He was extolled as "the greatest soldier in Austrian history since Prince Eugene." In a very extensive biography, Oscar Regele, the chief administrator of the Austrian war archives after the Second World War, concealed his multiple weaknesses and failures through hundreds of pages. Recently, Lawrence Sondhaus has written an excellent account of Conrad's life and career.[24]

Conrad, pivotal in the training of the 1914 Austro-Hungarian Army, wrote the Habsburg tactics manuals published and republished until the war. His major deficiencies as a military commander were the failure to understand his army's capabilities and his poor planning and leadership. This occurred in the two 1914 Lemberg battles, 1915 Carpathian Mountain Winter War, fall 1915 Rovno campaign, the 1916 *Straf* expedition against Italy and his role in the fatal June 1918 offensive as a front commander.

At best Conrad was a tactician, not a strategist. During major battles he wrote thousands of pages of letters to the twenty-eight-year-younger Gina, mother of six children, that he met in 1907. When they married at Supreme Command headquarters Conrad spent too much time with her.

Rarely traveling to the front to grasp the actual military situation, he ignored the horrendous conditions his troops suffered throughout the war. Conrad fatally altered the Habsburg deployment plans on July 1, 1914, and then unrealistically attempted to rapidly crush Serbia before countering the far more dangerous Russian Army. His simultaneous offensives against both powers, with insufficient forces on both fronts, ensured failure on each. Conrad also committed critical command errors during the opening campaign, which continued to negatively affect the army's performance throughout the war. He hurriedly launched offensives before all troops had been assembled, and often ignored such critical factors as weather conditions, terrain, logistical necessities or the quality of soldier training.

Conrad nurtured grandiose strategic plans, including his beloved double envelopment, German troops launching an offensive from the north into the Polish sack while Habsburg troops, separated by almost four hundred kilometers, advanced northward. He believed in the offensive at any cost, which resulted in too many unnecessary deaths of soldiers. He neither grasped the importance of combined artillery–infantry battlefield cooperation nor comprehended the enormous impact of machine guns or new rapid-fire artillery weapons in the early war years.

Conrad always blamed others for his multiple command mistakes. For example, he chastised the Germans and his own diplomatic corps for the serious military disaster resulting from his faulty August mobilization and deployment and the fall 1914 operational failures. He repeatedly claimed that General Moltke had promised to launch an offensive into Poland to support his troops, a major misstatement. In actuality, German military leaders promised to bind significant Russian forces, succeeding to a far greater extent than anyone could have imagined. Moltke informed his counterpart on August 10 that he would not launch an offensive into Poland in the initial 1914 campaign, because tsarist forces had rapidly invaded Prussia. Also, documents from the Vienna War Archives Military Intelligence Bureau disprove Conrad's claim that he did not know the size of the Russian armies, their intended deployment locations and speed of the mobilization in the event of war.

Conrad assumed a major role in the July crisis and outbreak of the war, and his strategic decisions and plans proved fateful. His undeserved postwar fame has been overshadowed by many present historians examining his role as chief of the General Staff in much greater detail.

2

July 1914 Crisis

By June 1914, Russia and Serbia posed an increasingly dangerous threat to Austria-Hungary. The Dual Monarchy's statesmen and military leaders remembered the Russian role in the 1908–1909 Bosnian Crisis and the 1912–1913 Balkan Wars, as well as the significant growth of potential Serbian power as a result of that country's victories in the latter conflict. Adding synergy to these dual threats, since the assassination of the royal Serbian family in 1903, Russian influence and anti-Habsburg policies had flourished in Belgrade, creating an even greater threat of the two Slavic countries acting in concert.

In addition, a more forceful Russian foreign policy challenged Austria-Hungary on several fronts. Fear of the increasing Russian threat pressured Vienna's leaders to consider immediate military action following the June 28, 1914 assassination of Archduke Franz Ferdinand, particularly because of the tsarist Grand Program initiated at the end of the Balkan Wars. This would have increased Russian military power significantly. By the completion of the program in 1917, the Russian Army would be larger than the combined German/Austro-Hungarian forces, while Britain and France also had to be considered in military calculations. Its artillery complement increased 25 percent. Its railroad deployment capabilities would also increase significantly, while in 1914 the tsarist mobilization would send 360 trains daily, the Habsburg 154. Under Russia's umbrella, Serbia became increasingly antagonistic to the Habsburg Empire, while the German ally appeared not to fully appreciate the Serbian threat to Vienna during the Balkan Wars.

Generals Conrad and Moltke met at Carlsbad on May 12, 1914, where Moltke withheld any promise of additional German military aid in a campaign against Russia and continued to emphasize the Western front as the initial major German battlefield in Schlieffen fashion (whereby 90 percent of the German Army would be fielded in the west). Both recognized that one could not be successful without the other's cooperation. Austria-Hungary must deter Russian forces on its own, at least until Germany's Schlieffen Plan obtained victory in the west, allowing it to then transfer major troop contingents to the Eastern front.

Considering the accusation that the Central Powers started the war because of expanding Entente military potential prowess, Austria-Hungary and

Germany did not launch preventive wars when they had much better opportunities for success. That included the following 1904–1905 Russo-Japanese War, the 1908–1909 Bosnian Crisis, 1911 Tripoli War and 1912–1913 Balkan Wars.

As a result of the Turkish defeat in the Balkan Wars, Vienna's attention turned to Romania and Bulgaria as possible counterweights to the enlarged Serbia. However, the Balkan Wars had completely transformed the balance of power in the region, when Romania allied with Serbia against Bulgaria in the 1913 Second Balkan War. The question of Bulgaria and Turkey serving as counterbalances to Serbia became a major factor in Habsburg military calculations, while a Romanian alliance with Russia or neutrality in a Balkan war would compromise the Habsburg military strategic position on its extreme eastern flank in the event of a war. During June 1914, Emperor Wilhelm visited Archduke Franz Ferdinand, both convinced of the inevitability of war.[1] That meeting had a serious effect on Wilhelm during the ensuing July crisis following the archduke's assassination.

The June 28 Franz Ferdinand assassination radically altered the Habsburg power structure. The archduke's death presented an atmosphere that appeared favorable for Austria-Hungary to strike Serbia before its opponent's military advantage became threatening. Delay could make the German and Austro-Hungarian military situation more untenable because of the 1913 Russian Grand Program.

The archduke's assassination occurred on the 350-year anniversary of the Battle of the Blackbirds, when Turkish troops slaughtered 50,000 Serbians on the battlefield. The assassination provided a pretext for Habsburg leadership to initiate a final reckoning with Serbia. When news of the murder reached Vienna, Count Berchtold and Emperor Franz Joseph returned to the city. General Conrad returned from Bosnian maneuvers the next day.

Conrad, a pessimist and Social Darwinist, believed that the Dual Monarchy faced a life-or-death struggle for its survival. Earlier, he had advocated an aggressive preventative war policy in the Balkan Peninsula as well as against Italy. His incessant demands for a war against Serbia during the 1912–1913 Balkan Wars increased the bellicose atmosphere in Vienna. Conrad wrote, "It will be a hopeless fight, nevertheless, it must be waged, since an old monarchy and its glorious army must not perish without glory."[2] He immediately demanded immediate mobilization and invasion of Serbia without any preceding diplomatic overtures. On that historic day, not a single important German leader could be found in Berlin. One week later, the most powerful, among them the emperor and prime minister, issued the infamous "blank check" to Austria-Hungary on July 5 that would swing the diplomatic initiative to Vienna for the duration of the July crisis.

On June 28, Habsburg officials began meeting to determine their future course of action, the assumption being that the Serbian government was responsible at least partially for the assassination. Habsburg leadership assumed that monarchical solidarity would prevent Russia from supporting Serbia in this matter. It also recognized German support was essential to counter Russia, even for a war solely directed against Serbia. The consensus, however, was not unanimous; during the discussions between June 28 and early July, Hungarian Minister President Graf Istvan Tisza opposed launching an immediate war.

Multiple Habsburg leaders believed that Franz Ferdinand's assassination offered the last opportunity to resolve their South Slav problem because Russia had just commenced its great armaments program, and Serbia had not had sufficient time to absorb its new conquered Balkan Wars territories. The Russian rearmament program greatly concerned German and Austro-Hungarian military officials. War in 1914 would preclude a Russian military advantage that the Russians would have accomplished at the completion of their rearmament program, expected to be completed sometime between 1916 and 1917.

Habsburg leaders were convinced that the tsarist regime was attempting to create a new Balkan alliance against the Dual Monarchy. Fear and distrust of Russia had increased dramatically since the 1908–1909 Bosnian Crisis and 1912–1913 Balkan Wars.

Unfortunately for Vienna leadership, the 1914 diplomatic situation differed significantly from the 1908–1909 and 1912–1913 events, particularly due to the perceived new St. Petersburg aggressive policy. During those two events, Russia had backed down to Berlin's threats because of its military unpreparedness resulting from the 1904–1905 Russo-Japanese War destruction of its armed forces; such a reaction now could hardly be guaranteed, especially due to Russian embarrassment and loss of face during those crises because of its limited support of Serbia. Habsburg military leadership had anticipated a war with the tsarist colossus since the 1908–1909 Bosnian Crisis.

Franz Ferdinand's death created circumstances that made a military solution to the Serbian problem likely. For example, the archduke had been expected to remove Conrad as chief of the Austro-Hungarian General Staff in 1914. Instead, Conrad's bellicosity now faced no serious opposition. The assassination also allowed Foreign Minister Berchtold to exert his bellicose influence during the early July crisis deliberations. The archduke had been committed to a peace policy during the 1912–1914 crisis periods, which checked Conrad's demands for a preventative war. The assassination not only removed that calming and influential voice, but also galvanized many Habsburg diplomatic and military leaders who now believed that any action short of war would produce a loss of credibility and place the Dual Monarchy in jeopardy of collapse and loss of great power status. If the Dual Monarchy defeated Serbia it would raise Habsburg prestige and perhaps open Turkey to economic penetration. The close connection between Habsburg domestic and external matters remained critical, because of the Dual Monarchy's multi-national population and several neighboring states' irredentist claims. By June 1914, Viennese leaders had determined that they had to seize the initiative in the Balkan Peninsula, which included the complete isolation of Serbia.

Berchtold initially faced several critical policy issues. Foremost, the Habsburg diplomatic position for a showdown with Serbia had to be established, which required German support for Austria-Hungary's new aggressive Balkan policy. The Balkan Wars, however, had recently illustrated the serious deviation between the two allies' policies in the region. This helps explain the significance of the Matscheko Memorandum and then revised version (see below in this chapter), and the early July 1914 Hoyos mission to Berlin. German support became critical because the Dual Monarchy could not fight Russia alone.

The Matscheko Memorandum emphasized the new aggressive Russian Balkan policy, and the necessity to maintain Romania as an ally. During the 1913 Second Balkan War, Romania had allied with the implacable enemy Serbia. This reinforced the fear of a new Balkan alliance. Austria-Hungary sponsored the memorandum as a last attempt to clarify the Romanian position to the Triple Alliance. Serbia did not receive mention because its hostility was taken for granted.

Although Franz Ferdinand was not a popular figure in the Dual Monarchy, his assassination stunned Habsburg diplomats, politicians and military figures, many on holiday at the time. The opinion of the hastily returning leaders, this still affected by the recent unfavorable Balkan Peninsula events, was best expressed by Conrad, who termed the assassination, "Serbia's declaration of war on Austria-Hungary – the only possible response to it [was] war."[3] As a result of the monarchy's dwindling Great Power and Balkan status and the anticipated potential effect of the assassination upon its South Slav people, it quickly became accepted that to maintain credibility, there must be war. To Berchtold, the time had come for a "fundamental and final reckoning with Serbia"; there could be no doubt as to who was responsible for the assassination. Habsburg leadership felt the Dual Monarchy to be in mortal danger. Serbia had to be punished, or the monarchy would not only forfeit its Great Power status, but potentially disintegrate from inner turmoil.

These considerations led to a revision of the June 24 Matscheko Memorandum. The author, Baron Franz von Matscheko, advised a more aggressive diplomatic policy in the Balkan region.[4] His original document for Franz Joseph, Franz Ferdinand, Tisza and the German allies sought their support for new urgent Balkan policies. The memo emphasized Russia's more active and assertive foreign policies, particularly in the Balkans. It emphasized that as the Russian threat significantly increased, action must be taken now, rather than later. Matscheko emphasized that Russia had diplomatically encircled Austria-Hungary, and demanded immediate action to counter this threat.

Bulgaria and Romania had become vital factors as well, but interestingly, Serbia was not the focus of the memo, Russia and Italy were.

The "Young Turks" in foreign office, Graf Janos Forgach and Matscheko, upon news of Franz Ferdinand's assassination, rewrote the earlier 1914 memorandum. The revised document demanded a more aggressive Dual Monarchy diplomatic policy and a militant solution to the Serbian problem, while stressing the increasingly urgent necessity for Berlin's support. A private letter written by Franz Joseph to Wilhelm accompanied the memorandum to Berlin with the Hoyos mission, which blamed the assassination on Russian and Serbian Pan-Slavic policies and asserted that "the band of criminals should not go unpunished."[5] This earliest phase of the July crisis began on the day of the assassination, and ended with the dispatch of the Austrian ultimatum to Belgrade on July 23.

Vienna could no longer rely on Romania's support in a war against Russia. Both versions of the Matscheko Memorandum sought to define a united Austro-Hungarian-German Balkan policy based upon common interests. The revised version, however, offered a short-term solution that had been drastically altered as a result of the archduke's assassination.

Several Hungarian nobles occupied major positions in the Habsburg Foreign Service. For example, Section Chief Graf Janos Forgach had earlier been ambassador to Belgrade, while Count László Szögyény, Count Friedrich Szápáry and Johann von Pallavicinci had served as ambassadors in Berlin, Paris, St. Petersburg and Constantinople. These "Young Turks" exercised an enormous influence on Berchtold, who sought to dispel his earlier reputation for weakness during the Balkan Wars. The cabinet chief of the Foreign Ministry, Alek Hoyos, played a significant role in the July 5 Germany "blank check" mission. All supported an anti-Serbian policy.

All-important decision makers had returned to Vienna by June 29. Berchtold progressively assumed a strong stance, particularly after it became clear that Franz Joseph and Conrad favored action. His only problem became to neutralize Tisza, minister president of Hungary, who was worried about Russia. Tisza preferred a severe diplomatic punishment, not war. His main concern as a Hungarian was Transylvania.

Emperor Franz Joseph became the pivotal figure during the July crisis, which explains why both Berchtold and Tisza had to convince him that their positions were the correct ones to initiate. Berchtold rushed to Bad Ischl to discuss the situation with the emperor to block Tisza, who sought a more prudent position.[6]

On June 30, Berchtold and the emperor agreed to ascertain Berlin's position relative to supporting a Habsburg war against Serbia, because a localized Serbian conflict could explode into a European-wide war. The potential problem arose from Romanov support of Serbia during the 1908–1909 Bosnian and 1912–1913 Balkan War crises. Would Russia acquiesce a third time and lose prestige with

Habsburg Slavic people? Count Tisza, in contrast to his fellow Hungarians in the Foreign Service, opposed an immediate military action against Serbia when he pressed for a strong diplomatic response and further probe of the June 28 murder.[7] Thus, Berchtold and Franz Joseph determined to launch an investigation into the assassination and seek German support.

During a Conrad–Berchtold evening meeting on June 30, Conrad insisted on a swift mobilization and attack on Serbia without any diplomatic negotiations. Berchtold summarized Conrad's position as "War!" Conrad withdrew his preplanned 1914 deployment in Galicia against Russia (the *Rückverlegung*), on July 1. He transferred railroad detraining stations to allow more time to launch a Serbian offensive to ensure its success.[8] To reach the Galician frontier, Habsburg troops would now have to march for days in the summer heat whereas before they would be transported by rail.

On July 1 Berchtold instructed Conrad to prepare a memorandum to be dispatched to Berlin detailing the military consequences if Romania failed to fulfill its alliance obligations. On the next day Conrad emphasized the dangers of a Romanian-Serbian alliance that would present a major threat to the Dual Monarchy.

A somber mood prevailed in the capital where the feeling of "that's it, enough is enough" combined with anxiety, anger and frustration. In the past, Serbia had never fulfilled its treaties or promises, contributing to the sense that it was now time for action. Berchtold, Austrian Minister President Stürgkh, Common Finance Minister Leo Ritter von Bilinski and War Minister Alexander von Krobatin of the Common Ministerial Council supported launching a war. Conrad stated that a surprise military action would produce a rapid defeat of Serbia. With only one narrow-gauge railroad leading to a critical part of the Serbian frontier, the Habsburg deployment would require a minimum of sixteen days, signifying that military action could not commence until August 12 at the earliest. Conrad intentionally concealed very important information from the Common Ministerial Council meeting he attended on July 7. He provided an inaccurate assessment of the monarchy's military capabilities and the dangers inherent in his war-planning scenario. This proved to be a most fateful and tragic omission.

The German journalist Victor Naumann claimed that both the German government and public would support a Habsburg war against Serbia, contrary to Berlin's stance during much of the 1912–1913 Balkan Wars period. Naumann also stated that German leaders believed the moment propitious for Vienna to act and claimed that Emperor Wilhelm would approve the war against Serbia, provided he was approached correctly.[9]

That same day, General Alberto Pollio, chief of the Italian General Staff, suddenly died, removing a loyal Italian military commander to the Triple Alliance. Italy soon became a major actor during the July crisis, its new chief of the General Staff soon opposing any Habsburg approaches.

On July 2, Franz Joseph dispatched Count Alexander Hoyos with the revised Matscheko Memorandum and a letter to Wilhelm to ascertain Germany's position relative to supporting the Dual Monarchy. Hoyos was a well-known entity in German diplomatic circles, having been a senior liaison officer during the Bosnian Crisis of 1908–1909. He was also one of the Foreign Office's most bellicose members. Berchtold instructed his *chef de cabinet* that it was imperative to convince German leaders to support a Habsburg military action against Serbia to eliminate it as a political factor in the Balkans. When Berchtold met with the German ambassador, he learned that Berlin encouraged Vienna to initiate vigorous action against Serbia. By July 2 and 3, the majority of Habsburg leadership, with the significant and important exception of Tisza, approved an attack against Belgrade.[10] The psychological adjustment from forceful diplomacy to a war stance came easily to Viennese decision makers, as any other policy appeared less likely to provide success.[11]

Because of the Balkan War experiences, the Habsburg government determined that the Great Powers should be presented with a fait accompli concerning Vienna's response to the assassination. The words "now or never" were emphasized in a dispatch from Berlin to the German ambassador in Vienna.[12] Then on July 2, King Carol of Romania announced that his country would not fulfill its treaty obligations to the Triple Alliance; it would remain neutral. Conrad calculated that Romanian neutrality would signify the loss of four hundred thousand soldiers in a war against Russia. If Romanian troops deployed against Austria-Hungary, the troop losses would rise to four to eight hundred thousand. The three Russian corps deployed on the extreme Habsburg right flank would now be free for action against Habsburg forces.

Conrad remained convinced that Romania's role in an Eastern front war remained essential. To him, if Romania and Serbia became Habsburg opponents it would threaten any possibility of a military victory over Russia. Meanwhile, Hoyos carried the message to Berlin's leaders that the precarious Balkan situation could only be rectified "if Serbia, which presently formed the pivot of Russian Pan Slavic policy, was eliminated as a political power factor in the Balkans."[13]

Also, on July 2, at a Potsdam meeting in Germany, General Falkenhayn, Prussian war minister, stated that the German Army was prepared for any eventuality.[14] The German High Command then deliberately went on vacation in an attempt to hide the gravity of the situation, while Wilhelm commenced his traditional summer naval cruise. German leadership had meanwhile agreed that Austria-Hungary should attack Serbia as soon as possible, also realizing that Russia could intervene.

Interrogation of the Bosnian Serb conspirators on July 2 revealed that links did connect Serbia to the assassination plot. The nineteen-year-old assassin, Bosnian nationalist Gavrilo Princip, had received weapons and bombs in Belgrade, reputedly with the complicity of several members of the Serbian military and intelligence branches. However, no evidence could be found that the government was involved in the assassination.

By July 3 Franz Joseph, incensed by previous Serbian actions as well as the assassination, accepted a military solution to the Serbian threat. In a July 3 meeting, Berchtold informed German ambassador Heinrich Leonard von Tschirschky of the necessity for "a final and fundamental reckoning" with Serbia. The German ambassador, however, reacted with great caution. In contrast, General Oskar Potiorek, governor general of Bosnia, argued that Serbia had to be punished because of what he claimed to be alarming and persuasive "unrest" in the Dual Monarchy South Slav region, a major exaggeration. The Austro-Hungarian ambassador to Germany, Graf László Szögyény, received instructions to request interviews with Wilhelm and Chancellor Bethmann Hollweg. In the meantime, the German press launched a campaign against the Serbians.[15]

Upon his arrival in Berlin Hoyos initially met with Habsburg ambassador Szögyény, then visited German Foreign Office Undersecretary Arthur Zimmermann. During the afternoon he met with Wilhelm, Bethmann Hollweg, State Secretary of the Foreign Office von Jagow, then Zimmermann again.

The German ambassador to Vienna, Tschirschky, as mentioned, at first acted cautiously in relaying his communications from the Berlin Foreign Office, but received instructions to become more forceful and forthright. The German position maintained that Vienna had to act to remain a worthwhile ally. Bethmann Hollweg informed the Habsburg Foreign Office that a military attack against Serbia would be the "best and most radical solution" to its Balkan problems, and pressed for Vienna to take immediate action. In effect, the German emperor and chancellor advised that Germany would support Vienna. With German backup secured, Berchtold took the initiative with the next Habsburg measures and deflected any German interference.

When the Habsburg delegation met with the German emperor on the afternoon of July 5, Wilhelm declared that he had no reservations in supporting Vienna's aggressive position regarding Serbia. Hoyos met with the German chancellor later the same day, where Bethmann Hollweg, in contrast to Berlin's stance during the Balkan Wars, stated that Germany would support Vienna, its only loyal ally, "come what may." On the same day, Ambassador Tschirschky reported that the German emperor promised full support to the Dual Monarchy in defending its vital Balkan interests, with the important proviso that Vienna formulate a concrete plan that Berlin could support and not delay initiating action. After the Berlin meetings, Conrad met with Franz Joseph and inquired, "if the answer runs that Germany will stand by our side, then will we make war with Serbia?" The emperor replied, "in that case, yes."[16]

Berlin thus offered its backing to Vienna in the event of a military showdown with Serbia. This presumably signified that German armies would cover the Dual Monarchy's flank against Russia in a Balkan war. However, would they be able to accomplish this in light of the Schlieffen Plan that initially targeted France?

The critical point early in the July 1914 crisis – the decision to resolve the Serbian problem by war – emanated from Vienna. Once Germany issued its infamous "blank check," assuring Austria-Hungary's protection against Russia, Vienna assumed the driver's seat, Germany having surrendered the initiative, and determined the timing and manner of future July crisis measures. This eliminated any options appearing unsatisfactory to Vienna.

The Habsburg disclosure that Romania had become an unreliable ally shocked German leadership, although its support for Vienna did not waiver. The German chancellor declared that his country would not interfere, or provide advice relative to Serbia, but that Vienna could be assured that its ally would fulfill its alliance duty. Berlin placed increasing pressure on Vienna to commence immediate action; the chancellor added that now was better than later. Earlier, Wilhelm repeated the same message to Habsburg ambassador Szögyény, that this favorable moment should not be left unused. Wilhelm agreed that Vienna should take rapid and forceful action against its pesky Balkan neighbor, fully recognizing that Russia might intervene against Austria-Hungary, which could unleash a general European war.

It was also claimed that the South Slavs and Romanians would interpret it as a sign of Habsburg weakness if the Franz Ferdinand assassination remained unpunished and might encourage them to support Serbia. Meanwhile, the possibility of Russian intervention was underestimated in Vienna, although, as mentioned, military leaders had anticipated it in a Habsburg war against Belgrade since the Bosnian Crisis. Habsburg leaders believed that a diplomatic action had to produce war with Serbia; thus, an ultimatum to that troublesome neighbor must be worded so that Belgrade could not accept the terms. Emperor Wilhelm again emphasized that the international situation would now be more favorable than later.[17] Berchtold utilized the German reply to neutralize Tisza.

The July 5 Hoyos mission to Berlin, the first event in the chain of critical events that fateful July, served the July 7 Habsburg Common Ministerial Council's purpose to isolate the one dissenting voice among them, Tisza. Berchtold proposed that Austria-Hungary launch a surprise offensive against Serbia. Securing Germany's assurance of assistance helped Berchtold neutralize Tisza's opposition to initiating Balkan military action. Yet, for weeks, Vienna took no definitive diplomatic or military action. On July 5, Conrad and the war minister, encouraged by Berchtold, departed for vacation on July 7.

Returning to Vienna on July 6, Berlin's fateful "blank check" in hand, Hoyos met secretly with Berchtold, the two minister presidents, Stürgkh and Tisza, and German ambassador Tschirschky. Bethmann Hollweg repeated on the same day that he deemed the present moment more suitable for action than a later occasion. Ambassador Tschirschky also encouraged his Viennese counterparts to press for action, adding that if Austria-Hungary proved unable to solve the Serbian problem, it could lose esteem as a German ally.

Before departing on holiday, Conrad realized that he could not launch an immediate attack against Serbia because seven of the sixteen corps troops designated for deployment had been scattered across the monarchy on annual harvest leave that had just commenced. Six of his corps would return from harvest to duty between July 19 and 23. A sudden recall of these troops would have produced chaos, disrupted the harvest, overburdened key railroad lines and alerted Europe to possible Habsburg intentions, thus compromising any chance of diplomatic and military surprise. All troops did not return to active duty until July 25.

On July 6, Wilhelm dispatched a telegram that after the war became critical to the "war guilt" issue. He wrote that he anticipated Vienna would initiate immediate measures against Serbia, and Germany would provide its full support. Since Russia was presumed not prepared for war, the action should commence immediately.[18] Wilhelm also dropped his earlier opposition to a Bulgarian affiliation with the Triple Alliance, with the proviso that Sophia bear no aggressive intent toward Romania. The Habsburg diplomats departing Berlin were convinced that the German government supported an immediate offensive action against Serbia, also realizing that this could inevitably produce a major war.

Berchtold, with the assurances of German support, had already accepted Conrad's demand for a military showdown against Serbia. Senior Habsburg officials, with the exception of Franz Joseph, attended the subsequent lengthy all-day Common Ministerial Council meeting on July 7. The Council had already debated whether the monarchy should go to war three times during the past twenty months during the 1912–1913 Balkan Wars, but at this meeting the stakes had increased substantially.[19] Yet Tisza declined the demand for war, seeking a diplomatic solution, fearing a Romanian invasion of unprotected Transylvania. Council participants recognized that military action would probably result from their decisions, particularly after the 1912–1913 Balkan Crisis. Berchtold, as stated, received support for rapid action from Conrad, the war minister, the Austrian minister president and the Habsburg common finance minister. All agreed that Habsburg control of Bosnia-Herzegovina could only be retained if Serbia was defeated on the battlefield. A diplomatic success would not halt Serbian transgressions and maintain South Slav loyalty to the Dual Monarchy.

During this critical meeting, Conrad was queried as to whether it would be possible to mobilize against Serbia, and simultaneously against Russia. Conrad replied affirmatively. The army could be partially mobilized for a Balkan war, but it would have to be determined by the fifth mobilization day whether Russia intended to intervene, otherwise deployment plans could be disrupted.[20] Much of Conrad's testimony was not recorded in the official minutes because of its sensitivity, but the question of the fifth mobilization day became critical because of potential railroad technical problems during mobilization against both Russia and Serbia. August 1 became the deadline for a possible reversal of the priority from a Serbian campaign, redirecting the key swing B deployment group to the Russian front against the far more dangerous military opponent. Because of Conrad's prewar promise to launch a forty-division offensive force against Russia in the event of a war, it became critical to ascertain as soon as possible when St. Petersburg would intervene in a Balkan war. In his memoirs Conrad claimed that he would have preferred to have had a full mobilization. This would have relegated the Serbia war effort to a secondary action, but he claimed it would have been impossible to act merely because of suspicion of Russian intervention. This and multiple memoir entries should be taken with a grain of salt, although for decades they were accepted as factual by historians.[21]

In a July 7 afternoon Council of Ministers session, Conrad insisted to immediately commence preparations for a Serbian military conflict. His various military variants included the possibility of tsarist military intervention, but he minimized such risks. He emphasized that a decision relative to the fifth mobilization day was imperative to avoid confusion and not disturb fixed railroad Balkan deployment timetables once in motion. This decision would preclude significant loss of time for mobilization and deployment on the Russian front. If Russia declared war, it obviously would become the main opponent.[22]

Tisza did not support launching an immediate war because he believed that Russia would probably intervene; additionally, if Romania allied with Russia and Serbia, it could prove disastrous for Austria-Hungary. Acting too precipitously could produce a European war. Berchtold, buttressed by the German assurances, pushed for action, despite Tisza's opposition. Tisza also feared Habsburg South Slav reaction, which would be particularly dangerous after a successful war in which the Serbian territory was annexed.

German support throughout the July crisis proved pivotal in Vienna's decision-making process, providing a false sense of security relative to Russian response to the German actions. German leadership had reversed its position to Vienna during the Balkan War crises, partly because of growing concern relative to Russia's expanding military power. Berlin also wanted to maintain its only major ally and its Great Power status. German leaders thus encouraged a military solution against Serbia.[23] The German government learned of Vienna's intentions to present a harsh ultimatum to the Serbian government, which would make "evasion or concession" almost impossible. This would hide Vienna's true intentions to crush Serbia. However, because of its provocative nature, the Germans anticipated a rapid Habsburg action, to provide a fait accompli. To Berlin's extreme displeasure, no such rapid action occurred. Habsburg decision makers delayed action for weeks, ultimately to great disadvantage.

During the crucial July 7 Common Ministerial meeting the prevailing discussion revolved around determining the suitable course of action against Serbia. With prodding from Berchtold and István Burian (Tisza's liaison to Vienna) Tisza became firmly convinced that in the case of a successful war, partitioning of Serbia would be the only manner in which the monarchy could resolve its South Slav problem. The Ministerial Council yielded to Tisza pressure, determining that an initial diplomatic approach to Serbia had to be instituted. If it failed, the military could act. Tisza's divergent viewpoint, the only dissenting Council voice, precluded attaining a unanimous consensus. Thus, the participants agreed to prepare a strongly worded ultimatum that Belgrade would reject to justify launching a localized war. However, crops had to be harvested first. Tisza's delay may have caused a greater conflagration as the European powers gained additional time to prepare their diplomatic and military positions.

On July 8, German leaders reaffirmed Vienna taking rapid and decisive action; otherwise, they warned that the situation would become hopeless. Tisza's hesitancy waned between July 8 and 14. On July 8, Burian attempted to influence Tisza, but a July 9 King Carol letter assured Romanian neutrality in the event of a war. This relieved much of Tisza's concern about Romania and Transylvania. One of Tisza's main reasons for opposing an immediate war was fear of a Romanian invasion of that province.

Following the Council meeting, Berchtold traveled immediately to Bad Ischl to obtain Franz Joseph's support for the decisions and then begin a vacation. His proactive meeting with the emperor outmaneuvered Tisza, who, following the meeting, wrote a letter to the emperor to explain his position.

Concurrently, Habsburg leaders launched an investigation into the Sarajevo assassination, producing a dossier that delineated the actions of the anti-Habsburg Great Serbia movement, as well as Belgrade's hostile actions. During the first half of July 1914, no conclusive decision was formulated for action nor was adequate information relative to any direct Serbian government involvement discovered. In the meantime, Berchtold, as mentioned, advised Conrad and War Minister Krobatin to proceed with their summer vacations to camouflage the seriousness of the situation. By July 10, Tisza would reverse his stance, and become more closely aligned to that of the Common Ministerial Council, but he did not officially cooperate with them until July 14.

On July 11, a serious breach of security occurred when German Foreign Secretary Jagow informed the German ambassador in Rome of Vienna's "general" intentions. The German ambassador subsequently revealed the substance of the information to Italian statesman San Guiliana, who immediately forwarded it to Italian embassies in Vienna, Belgrade and St. Petersburg.

Vienna learned of the incident because Habsburg intelligence had broken the Italian diplomatic code.

During a July 12 meeting Franz Joseph attempted to persuade Burian to convince Tisza to reconsider his position. According to Burian, the monarch supported a military showdown with Serbia, because he believed the situation would not improve.

On July 13 Conrad officially ordered the rearward deployment (*Rückverlegung*) of Habsburg troops on the Russian front, fearing advanced tsarist military preparations and the dangerous situation that would develop if Romania did not mobilize on the Dual Monarchy's right flank in a War Case "R" (Russia).[24] This momentous decision proved fatal.

In seeking Tisza's support, Berchtold stressed the strong German support for action against Serbia, but, perhaps more effectively, emphasized the possibility of a Serbian-Romanian alliance against Austro-Hungary relative to Transylvania. Three million mostly Romanian peasants lived under harsh Magyar rule without serious political representation and suffered from Budapest's Magyarization policies.

During a July 14 Common Ministerial Council meeting, agreement was attained relative to the ultimatum content and structure to be delivered to Belgrade, presenting the Serbs a short forty-eight-hour time limit for reply. Tisza accepted the harsh ultimatum terms and short deadline, but only after posing two major conditions: Serbia could not be annexed in the event of a Habsburg military victory, and defensive measures had to be immediately initiated along the Transylvanian frontier to Romania.[25] Tisza opposed an armed conflict that not only threatened the existence of the Dual Monarchy, but, most importantly to him, Magyar preeminence in Hungary. On July 14, he was convinced that Serbia must be neutralized. Berchtold anticipated that Serbian leaders would be humiliated if they had to accept the ultimatum, and that Russia, if it had to capitulate a third time to the Triple Alliance as during the Bosnian Crisis and Balkan Wars, would also be humiliated.

The next day, the German government learned that Austria-Hungary intended to initiate War Case "B" (Balkan), deploying six army corps against its Balkan neighbor. No military action would be initiated in Galicia, but everyone understood that if Russia intervened, they would have to react immediately. The German General Staff and Foreign Office became concerned about the significant number of Habsburg corps to be deployed against Serbia, if Russia intervened. The Balkan mobilization, comprised of 40 percent of the Dual Monarchy's armed forces, would launch an attack against a nation of a few million people, while Russia consisted of a hundred million residents.

During the next few days, a veritable calm before the storm atmosphere prevailed throughout Europe. On July 16, Forgach dispatched a letter to Ambassador Merey in Rome, which revealed that Vienna's leaders had finally achieved unity of opinion relative to their course of action against Serbia, a most serious indiscretion. Some Viennese leaders feared that Serbia might accept the ultimatum terms, precluding the possibility of a war. If so, it would significantly worsen their situation because the Great Serbian movement would continue to exist. On July 18 Serbia began mobilizing its army reservists, and Sergei Sasonov, the Russian minister of foreign affairs, warned that any action against Serbia's independence would not be permitted. Count Szápáry, the Habsburg ambassador in St. Petersburg, momentarily appeased Sasonov's concerns about the projected action against Serbia.

Habsburg legal expert Friedrich von Wiesner's efforts relative to the assassination events proved fruitless and embarrassing to Vienna. His investigation caused further delay in initiating military action against Serbia, as it was anticipated that the investigation would confirm allegations that the Serbian Army trained the Bosnian Serb group of teenage assassins, providing justification for a military campaign. Unfortunately, the results embarrassingly proved inconclusive. On July 9 Wiesner traveled to Sarajevo instructed to find conclusive evidence relative to the assassination. The report had to be completed by July 13 because the next day the two Habsburg minister presidents would have their initial meeting. However, Wiesner found no evidence to prove the complicity of the Serbian government.

As time quickly slipped away, Viennese officials had neither reacted rapidly nor decisively as German leaders had demanded. They continued to procrastinate and delay action. Official European opinion temporarily remained sympathetic to the Habsburg situation, but in time such sympathy proved ephemeral. On July 16, Conrad, aware of the Dual Monarchy's potential military weakness, determined that Romania's official position had to be ascertained before he could launch the military operation against Serbia.[26]

At a secret Common Ministerial Council meeting on July 19 at Berchtold's private residence, the attendees discussed territorial changes relative to Serbia. Tisza, concerned about a loss of Hungarian plurality, insisted that once Serbia had been defeated none of its territory or population should be annexed. Hungarian support for the war hinged on the condition that no Serbian territory be acquired except perhaps strategic frontier adjustments for military security.[27] Berchtold suggested that large portions of conquered Serbian territory be divided among Albania, Bulgaria and Greece, possibly even Romania. Serbia might also have to be temporarily occupied. Foreign powers would have to be informed that no Serbian territory would be annexed.

The members reviewed and determined the terminology of the ultimatum to Serbia. It would be delivered on July 23 at 5 p.m., with the forty-eight-hour expiration date having a reply deadline of 5 p.m., July 25. Delivery had to be delayed to preclude any Franco-Russian collusion, as French President Raymond Poincaré and Foreign Minister Viviani were visiting St. Petersburg between July 20 and 23. The timing of the ultimatum transmission would be dictated by Poincaré and Viviani's departure from the Russian capital.

Unfortunately, the French and Russians had knowledge of Habsburg machinations because of successful code-breaking and they planned accordingly to agree on a course of action; the net result of the delay further squandered any advantage between Habsburg and Russian mobilization.

During the proceedings Conrad demanded speedy action against Serbia, because a swift offensive appeared favorable for military success.[28] Tisza insisted that Council members unanimously accept his motion that Vienna would not annex any Serbian territory, otherwise he believed that Russia would intervene. The Council accepted Tisza's motion.

General Conrad, questioned about what would occur if a Balkan mobilization commenced and Russia intervened, replied positively relative to action against Serbia, but qualified his answer concerning how any tsarist action would be dealt with. If Russia mobilized, Conrad incorrectly assumed that he had a two-week period free relative to the Russian threat, because of its reputed slower mobilization timetables. However, Russian mobilization measures, commencing as early as July 25, negated much of this advantage before hostilities commenced. The military lost an entire week of advantage to Russia.

Berchtold realized that Berlin officials were becoming increasingly nervous about the lack of timely action, and that the Italians knew through the mentioned indiscretions of the plans to dispatch an ultimatum to Serbia.

The ultimatum demanded that the Serbian government denounce the "Great Serbian" movement and publicize it in official newspapers. It also mandated that the national organization, Nardna Odbrana, be dissolved; however, the secret Black Hand society, actually involved in both the assassination plot and arming of the young Bosnian Serbs, received no mention. Most problematic, the Habsburg government demanded to participate in an investigation on Serbian terrain, a challenge to its sovereignty.

On July 20 Conrad informed the Army Railroad Bureau commander that the ultimatum would to be delivered to Serbia on July 23. When it was dispatched, Conrad ordered all railroad line commanders and traffic officials back to military duty. The Railroad Bureau received instructions to prepare train cars for War Case "B" (Balkan) alarm transport.[29] Security precautions (particularly with regard to railroads) and preparations commenced for a Balkan campaign three days before the ultimatum was delivered to Belgrade.

That same day, Franz Joseph read and accepted the ultimatum text because it was now obvious that Russia would not stand aside.[30] Rumors of an impending Habsburg *démarche* to Belgrade began to circulate through European capitals. On July 21 Russian diplomats began questioning whether the aging Habsburg monarch and reputedly weak foreign minister were capable of halting any aggressive actions. Russia would not accept another Serbian humiliation, much less it being invaded. Meanwhile, a sealed copy of the ultimatum arrived in Belgrade.

The final version was dispatched to Berlin on July 22, but provided virtually no notification of Habsburg intentions to German leadership. Ambassador Wladimir Giesl delivered the note to the Serbian government at 6 p.m. the following evening. Serbia had commenced mobilization measures three hours earlier, and Sasonov, extremely agitated after learning about the ultimatum, exclaimed, "this means European war."

On Thursday July 23, three and a half weeks after the assassination, the relative calm for many European leaders ended, as news of Vienna's ultimatum circulated through European capitals. Due to the earlier coordination with the French during their visit, St. Petersburg initiated military action on July 25, fewer than forty-eight hours after delivery of the ultimatum.

Berchtold purposely did not inform the Italian government of his diplomatic actions, to present Rome with a fait accompli. Habsburg diplomatic maneuvers produced a major shift in Italian official public opinion toward Vienna and the invasion of Serbia. The Italian government declared its neutrality.

The Austro-Hungarian ultimatum resulted in the convening of a Russian Council of Ministers special meeting the next day. This resulted in the order to mobilize the four military districts bordering the Dual Monarchy's frontiers, but none bordering Germany. This raised the critical question whether the tsarist partial mobilization would disturb plans for a general mobilization if it became necessary. The key involved the Warsaw Military District that bordered the German frontier. If the four reserve divisions designated for the Habsburg front stationed in that district mobilized, German High Command could consider it a provocative act. A tsarist partial mobilization against the Dual Monarchy would likely result in eventual German intervention, while creating chaos for the Russians if they had to switch from a partial to a general mobilization. Were the Russians bluffing by ordering partial mobilization measures?

Grand Duke Nicholas and War Minister Vladimir Sukhomlinov demanded a general mobilization, arguing that a partial one would be disastrous if further military measures suddenly became necessary. Germany, unlike Austria-Hungary, *could* mobilize faster than Russia; therefore, they argued that a full mobilization should immediately be proclaimed. German leaders continued to pressure Vienna to launch an immediate attack against Serbia to present a fait accompli before any great power could intervene. Berchtold asked Conrad why an immediate declaration of war could not be announced. Conrad replied that military operations on the Serbian front could not commence until August 12. The horrified Foreign Ministry warned him that the diplomatic situation could not hold that long.

Serbian mobilization measures were followed by preparations for a general mobilization. Reports of those actions arrived in Vienna on July 24 and 25. Although the harvest season had begun, full Serbian mobilization could be completed within four days. The Russian government's secret partial mobilization provided both Russia and Serbia valuable time advantage in their military measures, to Habsburg severe misfortune.

On July 25 the Serbian government in a conciliatory reply accepted most of the ultimatum conditions, except for an internal Habsburg investigation into the assassination conspiracy, which would infringe on basic Serbian sovereignty. When the "unsatisfactory" Serbian answer was received, Vienna immediately severed diplomatic relations, and its ambassador departed Belgrade by train soon thereafter. A few hours later, Emperor Franz Joseph signed the mobilization order for War Case "Balkan." This encompassed the defensive Minimal Group Balkan and swing B-Group (basically Second Army), a total of twenty-three infantry divisions, later reduced to twenty.[31]

According to Samuel Williamson, Viennese leaders now engaged in a "policy of deception" to "lull Europe," suggesting that no exceptional measures would be taken against Serbia.[32] The Habsburg press momentarily curtailed its negative commentaries about Serbia to allay possible fears of the impending war.

During the evening of July 25, the July crisis entered its decisive phase. A Russian imperial council meeting ordered a partial mobilization and the "period preparatory for war" in an attempt to prevent Habsburg forces from invading Serbia. This entailed the mobilization of the Kiev, Odessa, Moscow and Kazan military districts adjacent to Austria-Hungary. Russian military officials ordered troops to return to their permanent duty stations to influence Austro-Hungarian decision-making. Tsarist leaders, hoping to dissuade Austria-Hungary from initiating military action against Serbia, deceptively informed their German and Austro-Hungarian counterparts that no tsarist military measures had been initiated, despite multiplying intelligence reports indicating otherwise.

No Habsburg military action was initiated in Galicia to avoid provoking a Russian reaction, and troops not mobilized for War Case "Balkan" were ordered to return to their garrisons. Because it appeared that Russia had begun to mobilize, "Alarm" orders for War Case "R" (Russia) were delivered to the I, X and XI frontier corps commanders in Galicia. Conrad, however, hoped to achieve a rapid military victory over Serbia before Russian intervention could become dangerous.

General Dobrorolski, chief of the Russian mobilization section, pressed to extend tsarist military measures to the Warsaw District that bordered both Germany and Austria-Hungary, but without antagonizing the Germans.[33] How this could be accomplished was questionable, because both Berlin and Vienna soon learned the Russians had ordered a partial mobilization at the Austro-Hungarian frontier. Tsarist troop movements were almost immediately detected. Conrad, coordinating with his Operations Bureau chief during the afternoon of July 25, queried of the possibility of a simultaneous alarm transport for War Case "Russia" despite the current "B" (Balkan) deployment. Colonel Straub, Railroad Bureau commander, informed Conrad that he opposed any further adjustments to the planned "B" mobilization measures because of the additional wastage of time. At 9:23 p.m. on July 28, the Austro-Hungarians' Balkan mobilization was ordered. This signified the loss of two days for preparations for military action, but that day became a free day for Habsburg reservists to get their private affairs in order. Although mobilization had been ordered for July 28, not until July 29 did the general concentration of forces commence. This loss of several days resulted in serious Habsburg disadvantage, while simultaneously providing invaluable time to Russia and Serbia to advance their military measures. Meanwhile, the Serbian army commander, Vojvode Radomir Putnik, was arrested in Budapest on July 26 while taking mineral waters at a spa. In a perhaps archaic display of chivalry, Emperor Franz Joseph ordered his release, as no war existed between the two countries at the time of his arrest. This proved to be a monumental error.

On July 26, Foreign Minister Sasonov informed the German ambassador that the "rumors" of Russian military measures were inaccurate; not one horse or reservist had been called up.[34] Sasonov, perhaps bluffing, had ordered military measures to possibly cause Vienna to cease and desist on its threatened war on Serbia. The same day, War Minister Sukhomlinov gave his word of honor to the German military attaché that Russia had not issued a mobilization order for the four tsarist military districts bordering Austria-Hungary. He also warned that if troops crossed the Serbian frontier, the tsarist military districts bordering Habsburg territories would immediately be mobilized. He assured the attaché that no military measures had been ordered at the German frontier. The Habsburg military attaché, however, reported that the tsarist military districts bordering Dual Monarchy territory had been mobilized, and possibly elsewhere as well. The German military attaché reported that Russian military measures had become extensive.[35] Additional dispatches confirmed his reports.

Learning of tsarist military measures, Bethmann Hollweg dispatched an urgent telegram to Sasonov at 7:15 p.m., informing him that the alleged Russian military measures could force Germany to commence countermeasures, perhaps including a mobilization, which he emphasized meant war for Germany. This represented an attempt to localize a Habsburg-Serbian War and preclude a more generalized conflict that would engulf Russia and, by extension, Germany. Unfortunately, to the tsarist leaders, the Balkan balance of power had become vital to Russian interests, and could not be disturbed. Meanwhile, reports of Russian military measures continued to accumulate.

Russia thus became the first great power to initiate mobilization measures, and, over the next three days, the possibility of a localized war against Serbia rapidly dissipated. Conrad fatefully continued to hope for a decisive rapid battlefield victory against Serbia before Russia could seriously intervene. Alternatively a rapid victory could perhaps induce neutral Balkan states, even Turkey and Italy, to join the Habsburg cause. That would provide additional troops for deployment on the Russian front. Should other powers become involved, Russian forces would have to counter additional troops, but also deploy along a broader front.

During the evening of July 27, Conrad demanded that Berchtold notify St. Petersburg that its military measures would result in German countermeasures.[36] Germany increased pressure on Vienna to initiate its military action against Serbia. Berchtold replied that Vienna would issue an official declaration of war no later than July 29, to forestall any efforts at diplomatic mediation. The German ambassador to St. Petersburg warned Sasonov that military measures against Germany would result in German mobilization, which meant war. This July 26 warning was repeated on July 29.[37] Conrad had to ascertain Russia's intended reaction to the war against Serbia by August 4 or 5. He also realized the initial weakness of Habsburg forces countering Russia should that country enter the war, because of the priority for War Case "B" (Serbia).

The Serbian Army had been reorganized, adding five regiments to its original twenty-five. Additionally, the older class of trained troops were added to the mix, creating six additional regiments. First-line Serbian troops totaled five infantry and one combined division, while the second-line units added an additional five infantry divisions.

Wilhelm and his military entourage had meanwhile returned from vacation and met in Potsdam at 3:10 p.m. with Bethmann Hollweg and Undersecretary of State Jagow. The chancellor, seeking to blame German mobilization on St. Petersburg, insisted that Moltke delay initiating military action until the Russians provided suitable excuse for it. Bethmann Hollweg persuaded Wilhelm to dispatch a telegram portending to maintain peace, which could be used to depict the Russians as the aggressors in the evolving crisis. At least thirteen separate reports indicated Russian military measures along the German frontier.

Sasonov, angered by the Habsburg declaration of war against Serbia, ordered the chief of the General Staff to prepare two *Ukases* (plans) for the tsar's signature, one for a general mobilization, the other a partial one. The tsarist ambassador to Vienna declared that Russia would not remain idle if Habsburg troops crossed the Serbian frontier. This signified that if Austro-Hungarian forces could not launch the offensive into Serbia before August 12, the Habsburg declaration of war could become a terrible blunder.

British Foreign Secretary Sir Edward Grey introduced mediation proposals, recommending the convening of a four-power conference, but a precondition required that Vienna halt any military action. Grey declared that the Serbian reply to the ultimatum could provide the basis for negotiations to achieve a peaceful solution. Vienna rejected the proposal, no longer trusting the concert of Europe since 1912–1913 for unbiased negotiations and results.

On July 28 war was declared against Serbia. Conrad pressed Berchtold for confirmation whether there would be war against Russia, emphasizing that he had to know by August 1, because by then all transports would be rolling south according to War Case "B" (Balkan) plans.[38] Railroad deployment movement commenced on July 30, including the swing group of B-*Staffel* formations. Of forty-eight infantry divisions, twenty comprised the War Case "B" invasion force that headed south.

In the meantime, the Russians announced their mobilization, and the German government increased pressure on Vienna to act. While St. Petersburg also reputedly encouraged direct talks with Vienna, Russian leadership also insisted that Serbian sovereignty not be disturbed. Vienna declined both negotiation proposals.

On July 29, Austro-Hungarian artillery and gunboats bombarded Belgrade and the initial rail traffic prepared to roll to the Balkan front. Additional reports of Russian military activities arrived in both Vienna and Berlin, although after ordering general mobilization, the tsar countermanded his order when he received Wilhelm's telegram (the one pressed upon him by Bethmann Hollweg, the infamous Willy–Nicky telegram exchanges). Russian diplomatic and military leaders immediately pressured to reinstate general mobilization. Germany attempted to gain British neutrality for the rapidly approaching confrontation, as Britain's intentions loomed large in Berlin's plans, particularly regarding Belgian neutrality, as well as possible war at sea.

Moltke on July 28 dispatched a memorandum to Bethmann Hollweg, delivered July 29, declaring that a Russian attack against the Habsburg ally would produce the *casus foederis* for Germany. It had become imperative that Russia clarify its intentions so that the German decision could be made to immediately mobilize or delay such a drastic action. Bethmann Hollweg withheld the mobilization order over the objections of Generals Falkenhayn and Moltke, to blame Russia for the initial great power mobilization.[39] In the interim, Wilhelm proposed his "Halt in Belgrade" that called for Austro-Hungarian troops to invade Serbia, occupy its capital, then announce Habsburg demands without further military action.

In St. Petersburg Sasonov fulfilled Bethmann-Hollweg's wish that there could not be further delay proclaiming the Russian general mobilization. Sasonov announced that because of the Habsburg declaration of war, the four tsarist military districts bordering on it would be mobilized on July 29. That day coincided with the first Habsburg Railroad Balkan War mobilization. The Russian ambassador in Vienna notified Berchtold that Russia intended to mobilize those military districts.[40] That night, Conrad learned that tsarist mobilization had occurred, although the Habsburg A-Group (Russian) mobilization would be delayed until August 31.[41]

The German government demanded that Russia immediately cease all mobilization measures, while Austria-Hungary ordered general mobilization for August 6. Britain rebuffed German overtures for its neutrality. Moltke urged Conrad to not station troops at the Italian frontier and reiterated that "Germany is with you unconditionally." Moltke's communications with Conrad raised the serious question of whether he had usurped the chancellor's powers by contacting his military counterpart without going through civilian channels. Nevertheless, on July 30, Moltke notified Conrad that:

> Russia's partial mobilization is not yet a reason for [German] mobilization. Not until a state of war exists between the Monarchy and Russia. In contrast to the mobilizations and demobilizations which have been customary in Russia, Germany's mobilization would unconditionally lead to war. Do not declare war on Russia, but await its [Russia's] attack.[42]

Conrad replied, "We will not declare war on Russia and not begin a war."[43] However, he seems to have misinterpreted the intent of Moltke's telegram. He believed that Moltke insisted that a Russian mobilization did not provide a basis for Austro-Hungarian mobilization. In actuality, Moltke had simply predicated a German mobilization upon Russia's general mobilization.

Moltke telegraphed Conrad on July 30, dispatched the following morning: "Stand firm against Russian mobilization. Austria-Hungary must be preserved. Mobilize at once against Russia. Germany will mobilize. Bring Italy, by compensation, to her alliance obligations."[44] With this telegram, Moltke had exceeded his authority by transmitting the above advice to Conrad without Bethmann Hollweg's approval. Moltke demanded a third confirmation of the Russian general mobilization before ordering a German counteraction. On July 30, when Conrad met with Franz Joseph, he explained that a Russian attack on Austria-Hungary would cause Germany to order general mobilization, but, before any decisive action commenced in Galicia, a victory over Serbia must be obtained. Conrad again insisted that a Russian mobilization would be slow and providing sufficient time to defeat Serbia before Russia presented a serious military threat.

At 11 p.m. at a July 30 meeting, in reply to a Conrad question about when a first mobilization day against Russia could be ordered, Colonel Straub, head of the Railroad Bureau, requested twenty-four hours to study the matter, suggesting that the first mobilization day could not occur before August 4. The first alarm day would be August 2. At 10:30 p.m., July 31, Colonel Straub announced that the War Case "R" (Russian) first mobilization day would be August 4. Railroad Bureau officers, however, could not guarantee a timely redeployment of major forces from the Balkan theater to the Russian.[45] Meanwhile, the Russian mobilization of the military districts bordering Austria-Hungary involved far more troops than the entire peacetime Habsburg Army.

At 12:23 a.m., Vienna proclaimed its general mobilization, and at 12:30 a.m. instructions were dispatched to railroad line commanders. War Case "Russia" would run simultaneously with the Balkan deployment. Meanwhile, Conrad continued to calculate that the intervening time could be utilized to chastise Serbia. This was a most serious miscalculation, because the three Galician army corps commanders had already confirmed Russian mobilization. On the same day, Tsar Nicholas wired Wilhelm that "Russia stands behind Serbia." An invasion of Serbian territory would provide the *casus belli* for Russia. Addressing the diplomatic efforts to head off a generalized war, General Conrad insisted: "Berchtold can open discussions preliminary to negotiations as much as he wants, but operations against Serbia must not be held up by them. Any delay can only worsen the military position of Austria-Hungary."[46] Habsburg military leaders had resolved to crush Serbia regardless of the consequences, even if Russia intervened during the invasion of that pesky neighbor.

A crucial link in the chain of events leading to war resulted from Berlin's dispatch of two ultimatums on July 31. The first, to St. Petersburg, demanded that the Russian mobilization be terminated within twelve hours because of the extent of Russian military measures. The second ultimatum was dispatched to Paris, insisting on its neutrality in the event of a Russo-German war and demanding a reply within eighteen hours. While these two telegrams sped to their destinations, the German Foreign Office prepared the declarations of war.

In the meantime, the "Willy–Nicky" telegrams from Emperor Wilhelm and Tsar Nicholas crisscrossed the wires between Berlin and St. Petersburg. The tsar stated: "It is impossible to halt our military preparations because of Austria's mobilization. As long as the negotiations with Austria-Hungary in regard to Serbia continue, my troops shall not initiate any provocative action." Wilhelm's responding telegram countered: "Responsibility for the safety of my Empire forces upon me preventative defensive measures."[47]

At 7 a.m., Moltke ordered his Polish frontier corps commander to reconfirm Russian mobilization. Before he received a reply, a telegram arrived from St. Petersburg revealing that: "General Mobilization army and navy ordered. First day of mobilization 31 July."[48] The telegram arrived as Bethmann Hollweg conferred with Generals Moltke and Falkenhayn, resulting in the 1 p.m. German proclamation of "imminent danger of war," with German mobilization to occur within twenty-four hours.[49] During the night of July 31, irrefutable confirming reports arrived of Russian mobilization measures at the German frontier. The Russian mobilization measures left no time to lose because, according to the Schlieffen Plan (which, it should be noted, was Germany's only mobilization plan), during 1913 the *Gross Ost* mobilization had been discarded. German war timetables could not be compromised. Regardless, Moltke met with Bethmann Hollweg twice before the final decision fell.

Bethmann Hollweg then wired the German ambassador in Vienna that the Russian general mobilization forced Germany's proclamation of "imminent danger of war," presumably to be followed by mobilization. "This inevitably means war. We expect from Austria-Hungary immediate active participation in the war against Russia."[50] During the afternoon and evening, Moltke telegraphed Conrad, while Wilhelm wired the same message to Franz Joseph.

When Conrad read Moltke's telegrams to Berchtold, he responded, "who runs the government, Moltke or Bethmann Hollweg?" The decision to request Franz Joseph's signature on a general mobilization order followed the Berchtold–Conrad meeting. The aged emperor signed the order at 12:23 p. m. on July 31. Conrad, in a subsequent audience with the emperor, suggested that the following telegram be transmitted to Berlin: "[W]ar against Serbia shall be waged ... mobilize remainder of army and concentrate it in Galicia. General Mobilization will be ordered on August 1, with August 4 as the first day of mobilization. Request notification of your first mobilization ..."[51] Conrad penned that telegram at 7:30 p.m. on July 30, but did not dispatch it until 8 a.m. July 31, which suggests that he either was not anxious that Moltke learn the extent of the continuing military efforts against Serbia or that he was awaiting Franz Joseph's approval for its dispatch.

Moltke desperately wanted Austria-Hungary's main forces deployed against Russia, the far more powerful and dangerous military opponent, making Serbia a secondary front. In spite of Moltke's request, Franz Joseph cabled Wilhelm: "The action of my army against Serbia now proceeding can suffer no interruption from the threatening and challenging attitude of Russia."[52] Conrad continued to reputedly maintain that the Russian mobilization could be a bluff and, even if not, there would be sufficient time to complete a military campaign against Serbia before Russia presented a serious military challenge. Berchtold also made clear to his German colleagues that "War Case B" could not be retarded or halted regardless of any actions initiated by St. Petersburg.[53] Wilhelm then telegraphed Franz Joseph at 4:05 p.m., July 31:

> In this difficult struggle it is of the greatest importance that Austria-Hungary employ her main forces against Russia and not divide it by a [simultaneous] offensive against Serbia. This is even more important because a large portion of my army will be bound by France. In the gigantic struggle ... Serbia plays a secondary role, requiring only the most necessary defensive measures. Success in the war ... can only be expected if we meet the powerful enemy with our total forces.[54]

He also requested that Vienna attempt to gain Italy as a participating ally. The substance of the telegram was quite explicit. To Germany, Russia had to be Austria-Hungary's major opponent, and Italian support could prove critical. Every possible Habsburg soldier needed to launch an offensive to bind the Russian armies at Germany's eastern flank, while the vast majority of German forces smashed into France. At 4:15 p.m., a follow-up telegram was dispatched from Conrad to Moltke: "The Austro-Hungarian mobilization against Russia is provoked only by the Russian mobilization. It had only the purpose to guard against a Russian attack without the intention to declare war."[55] Moltke replied at 7 p.m.: "Chief of the General Staff had received a message from Conrad that Austria-Hungary does not intend to wage war against Russia. Germany will proclaim mobilization of entire military force probably August 2 and open hostilities against Russia and France. Will Austria-Hungary leave her in the lurch?"[56]

Moltke's greatest fear was that if Vienna delayed its mobilization against Russia, the weak German forces deployed in East Prussia would be overwhelmed by the onslaught of vastly numerically superior Russian troops. Conrad wired the following reply to the above telegram: "Today the information arrived about the German intention to immediately begin war against France and Russia. Request return statement whether this is the correct interpretation of German intent, so our action is coordinated accordingly."[57]

The Habsburg military attaché in Berlin telegraphed July 31 (3 p.m.) that Germany would soon mobilize its entire army, which meant war would be launched against Russia and France, as per the Schlieffen Plan. The telegram concluded with the words, "Germany stands solidly with Austria-Hungary." Moltke again demanded that all available Habsburg forces be deployed against Russia and that the Serbian offensive be relegated to a secondary action.

Austro-Hungarian general mobilization followed on July 31. However, the first "R" mobilization day was not until August 4 because of the confused railroad situation created by the dual war case deployment: against Serbia, then War Case "R," which should have included the swing B-Group that was already mobilizing for War Case "B." August 4 proved to be too late to effect a viable and successful deployment against the tsarist enemy. While the Dual Monarchy's general mobilization followed Russia's by only eighteen hours, four precious days had been sacrificed to ensure a smooth-flowing Balkan railroad deployment. The Vienna and Berlin governments began to exert pressure on potential allies.

During the evening of July 31 to August 1, Conrad conferred with his Railroad Bureau commander, and questioned whether War Case "B" railroad traffic could be reversed to retransport the B-Group north for deployment against Russia; the reply was negative. Colonel Straub claimed that railroad technical difficulties created in attempting to redeploy B-Group forces to the Russian theater would produce chaos; therefore, full War Case "B" had to be retained. Apparently, Conrad did not question his subordinate's position, leading one to speculate that he remained determined to quickly defeat Serbia regardless of the military situation against Russia. When Conrad finally determined that he must reverse the major military effort to the Russian front following strong German pressure, the results proved fatal on both fronts resulting in resounding Habsburg military defeats throughout the war.

France, meanwhile, refused to bow to German demands for its neutrality on August 1. Therefore, both countries mobilized and Germany declared war on Russia. The first German Alarm day for war against Russia commenced the next day. However, the Habsburg War Case "B" movement continued while German mobilization commenced, troops invading Luxembourg as a preliminary to the invasion of France in the west. Italy declared its neutrality on the grounds that the Triple Alliance Treaty was a defensive agreement, but, citing Article VII of the document, demanded compensation in the Balkans if Serbian territory should be conquered. Germany invaded Belgium and declared war on France on August 3, while Britain declared war on Germany because of the violation of neutral Belgian territory. To gain precious additional time for its invasion of Serbia and preclude railroad difficulties, Austria-Hungary did not declare war on Russia until August 6, completing the cycle. Europe commenced its civil war.

The contradiction of Habsburg and German planning is worth noting. In spite of the constant stream of communications between Franz Joseph, Berchtold and Conrad on one hand, and Wilhelm, Bethmann Hollweg and Moltke (as well as all the lesser officials of both empires), a common military strategy was never discussed nor developed in the prewar period. Each created war plans that relied on its alliance partner to counter a possible Russian military threat, while each power pursued its own war plans considered advantageous to them. Depending on Germany to neutralize the Russian threat while Conrad dealt with Serbia in the south, and only after Serbia's defeat, would Conrad deploy the swing B-Group to the Eastern front to counter the Russian colossus. Germany depended upon Austro-Hungarian troops to absorb the shock of the majority of attacking tsarist troops, allowing German forces to initially crush France, and only then redeploy significant troop numbers to deal with the Slavic foe. Neither power attained its initial goals and the Russian threat survived until the Treaty of Brest-Litovsk, consummated on March 3, 1918. Conrad's priority for the war against Serbia in conjunction with the inflexible German Schlieffen Plan to initially deal with France resulted in disaster on both Habsburg fronts. The Austro-Hungarian Army never really recovered from the fateful battlefield defeats incurred on the 1914 Russian and Balkan fronts.

We must now turn to those initial campaigns.

Galicia, August–September 1914

At the beginning of August 1914, Germany and France had both mobilized, and Germany had declared war on Russia on August 1. Austria-Hungary, however, did not formally declare war on Russia until August 6 due to perceived logistical complications relative to its preoccupation with the invasion of Serbia. Although Russia obviously became the main Habsburg opponent for the coming war, the demands of completing a successful Serbian campaign made it impossible to execute the planned War Case "R" deployment during early August. This proved fatal.

Because of this delay, Austria-Hungary had already sacrificed several days to tsarist military advantage to assure that it continued to achieve a smooth railroad deployment against Serbia. In the interim German troops invaded Luxembourg, while Italy declared its neutrality on the grounds that the Triple Alliance was a defensive alliance and therefore Rome had no obligation to mobilize under Article VII of the treaty. The Italians also demanded Balkan territorial compensation if Serbia was conquered, as stipulated by the earlier treaty. Germany invaded Belgium and declared war on France on August 3.

General Conrad briefly met with his army commanders on August 2, but did not provide any detailed instructions concerning mobilization measures, only their deployment areas, nor had he established a coherent strategic goal relative to the Russian front. Although Austria-Hungary began mobilizing against Russia on August 4, it did not officially declare war until August 6. Mobilization could not commence in earnest before that date because Habsburg planners feared that shifting their limited logistical resources to the Russian front might disrupt the planned Serbian campaign. The delay in declaring war provided the Russian military an additional week to complete its mobilization measures in preparation to invade Galicia. It also destroyed the anticipated time advantage for the Habsburg Supreme Command. Conrad's

Rückverlegung, or withdrawing his deployment rearward from the Galician frontier to the San–Dniester River line, nullified launching a rapid offensive from that province and provided his tsarist enemy the valuable additional time to deploy its troops to launch an offensive. It also signified that his armies must march through the August heat to reach the original deployment area. The exhausted troops of the twenty-eight infantry divisions, earlier planned to be forty divisions, initially encountered overwhelming enemy troop numbers. Instead of the originally planned thirteen corps only eight were available for the original Habsburg offensive because Second Army troops had been deployed against Serbia.

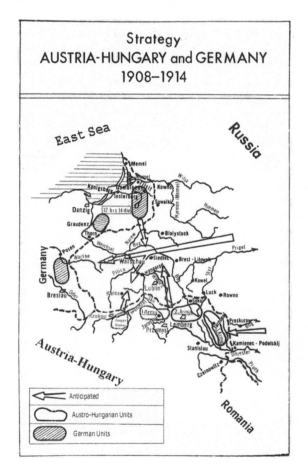

Map 1   *1908–1914 strategy*

1914 Austro-Hungarian Army

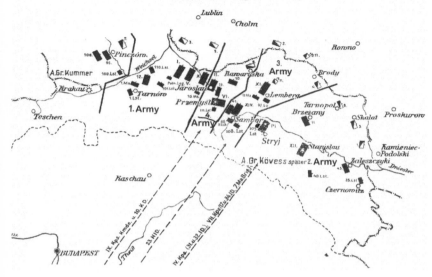

Map 2   *Austro-Hungarian deployment*

On August 6 the Russian High Command (*Stavka*) learned from intelligence reports that the majority of German troops had been transferred from East Prussia and had commenced railroad transport to the Western front. In the meantime, the Russian First and Second armies invaded East Prussia during mid-August, and at the same time had launched their Third, Fourth, Fifth and Eighth armies against Austria-Hungary. The Russians mobilized their Sixth and Seventh armies at the Black Sea coast and Romanian frontier, and prepared military security measures for St. Petersburg and Finland.

Upon completion of mobilization, the tsarist army consisted of 30 corps consisting of 59 active, 12 *Schutzen*, 31 reserve infantry divisions, 23 cavalry and about 12 Cossack divisions. This totaled 2.7 million soldiers while another 900,000 *Landsturm* troops served as fortress garrison and replacement troops. In sum, mobilized troops comprised the equivalent of 96 infantry and 37 cavalry divisions totaling 1,830 battalions, 1,250 squadrons, 6,725 guns and 5 million soldiers, while in Turkestan five and a half Siberian army corps prepared to be transferred west.[1]

A Russian infantry division consisted of sixteen battalions, six cavalry squadrons and forty-eight artillery pieces. Corps- and army-level artillery units in each division provided a further ten guns, most heavy caliber. A Russian reserve division had an equal number of troops as an active unit, but without the corps artillery.

Between August 7 and 10, the Russians mobilized two armies in the area of Warsaw: the Ninth and Tenth armies, each consisting of three corps. *Stavka* deployed two armies of six corps to invade Germany. In addition, III Caucasian Corps provided flank security for Fortress Ivangorod, a key tsarist Vistula River crossing point from which to attack Habsburg forces.

The Habsburg Army launched its initial offensive against Serbia on August 12, 1914, hoping to achieve a rapid Balkan victory before Russia could seriously intervene in the war. Vienna leaders hoped to convince Romania and Bulgaria to join the Habsburg campaign against Serbia to release some of their own soldiers for the fighting on the Russian front. However, between August 16 and 25, General Oskar Potiorek's Balkan troops suffered an embarrassing defeat against veteran battle-tested Serbian soldiers from the 1912–1913 Balkan Wars. On August 16, the Serbs launched a counterattack, driving the invaders back across the frontiers. The Habsburg Balkan front commander responded by launching a second offensive against strong Serbian positions during September, which ended in another defeat by mid-month. In November, a third Habsburg offensive commenced, which finally resulted in the capture of the capital city of Belgrade during early December. Potiorek mercilessly pressed forward his Habsburg troops by ignoring logistical necessities, the unfavorable terrain, inclement weather conditions and the resulting troops' terrible conditions. A December Serbian counteroffensive hurled the invaders back after their lines became severely overextended, producing a third very humiliating military defeat. During the three Balkan offensives, the Habsburg troops suffered 273,000 casualties while failing to attract Bulgaria and Romania as allies. However, the Serbian Army also sustained serious losses, including many soldiers to disease, effectively crippling its future offensive capabilities. The Serbian Army, not completely recovered from the 1912–1913 Balkan Wars, had suffered shortages in every major material category, effectively hamstringing their offensive capabilities.[2]

On August 15 the Austro-Hungarian Army unleashed its fifteen cavalry divisions across the Galician frontier to conduct distance reconnaissance on a 144-kilometer-deep and 400-kilometer-wide front in a vain attempt to locate Russian deployment areas and troop concentrations. However, tsarist infantry units supporting the cavalry forces stymied Habsburg attempts to pierce the opposing defensive lines because of the Habsburg troops' severe lack of firepower. The failed reconnaissance missions did not justify the enormous casualties in men and horses. Air reconnaissance also failed to locate the two Russian armies invading into the Habsburg Eastern Galician flank area. Thus, General Conrad had no indication of where tsarist troops were maneuvering on his northern or eastern front. He continued to ignore any intelligence reports that contradicted his plans to launch an offensive northward between the Bug and Vistula Rivers.

Multiple cavalry divisions proved unserviceable for a long time because of the enormous loss of horses and human casualties. New saddles, issued just before deployment, unfortunately crippled many horses. Within days, the saddles caused sores on the horses' backs, sometimes down to the bone, and effectively halted the cavalry forces' maneuverability.[3] Air reconnaissance also proved unreliable because of the poor mechanical condition of Habsburg airplanes, the inclement weather conditions and the unknown presence of the Russian Eighth and Third armies on the eastern Galician flanks. These Russian divisions had marched at night taking cover in villages and forests during the day. Thus, there was yet no indication of the major tsarist military units advancing toward the exposed Habsburg eastern flank. Consular reports, however, provided accurate information relative to Russian troop numbers and locations as reports as early as July 20, 1914 indicated that major Russian troop masses would approach the Habsburg eastern flank area. General Conrad ignored such information because it did not fit into his plans to launch a major offensive on the northern Galician front.

On August 14, the French pressured the Russians to immediately launch an offensive against Germany, which they did before their troops were battle-ready. In East Prussia, the Russian First Army advanced from the Nieman River area on August 17, then two days later the tsarist Second Army marched from the Narev River region to invade German territory. On the 450-kilometer-wide tsarist southwestern front, the Russians deployed four armies against Austria-Hungary that marched toward the bow-shaped Galician frontiers threatening to encircle Habsburg forces by merely advancing forward. Russian strategists sought to prevent a Habsburg retreat westward toward Fortress Krakow or south behind the Dniester River to the Habsburg homeland. The tsarist Fourth Army, consisting of nine and a half infantry and four and a half cavalry divisions, deployed its main units north of the San River in the Lublin area. The tsarist Fifth Army, deployed northwest of Lemberg, could intervene in the battle of either of its neighboring armies and against Fortress Przemyśl on the San River protecting access into the Carpathian Mountains. The Russian Third Army, consisting of thirteen infantry and five cavalry divisions, had the mission to seize Lemberg, provincial capital of Galicia, while Eighth Army deployed between Lemberg and the Dniester River would provide flank protection for the other tsarist armies against Habsburg relief efforts to liberate Fortress Przemyśl once it was besieged.

General Conrad believed that the best chance for a rapid Habsburg military success against Russia would result from an Austro-Hungarian-German offensive launched toward Siedlce in Poland near Brest-Litovsk. If, however, Germany did not participate in such a campaign, there was no justification for it to occur. Yet, Conrad retained that strategy. He originally intended to deploy his armies at the Galician frontier, but altered his planning, as mentioned, drawing his deployment area back west to the San–Dniester River line, the so-called *Rückverlegung*. This would allow time to conduct an invasion of Serbia. He also reinforced his main attack forces, the First and Fourth armies, to attack northward to clear the Habsburg left flank area between the Bug and Vistula Rivers and then if victorious swing east reputably with allied German forces.[4] His altered deployment plans caused a disruption in tsarist war planning, as well as his own. The Russian High Command miscalculated as the Habsburg armies launched their offensive northward, forcing a major change in tsarist strategic planning.[5] The tsarist assumption that the major Habsburg concentration of troops would be deployed at the east Galician frontier forward of the San River proved incorrect. Thus, the Russian Third and Eighth armies would defend in depth. Its Fourth and Fifth armies would launch an offensive southward from Poland, the objective to sever Krakow from the Habsburg Army then seize Lemberg and Fortress Przemyśl. As a result, the advancing tsarist Third and Eighth armies did not immediately make contact with the Habsburg forces at the eastern Galician frontier as anticipated in tsarist prewar planning.

Stavka planned to launch a double envelopment offensive with its four armies assisted by the flat terrain and bow-shaped Eastern Galician frontier. By merely advancing, tsarist forces could encircle and defeat Habsburg forces in the area of Lemberg. When General Conrad altered his deployment plans, it prevented the early planned tsarist envelopment of his northern offensive operations. The initial Habsburg–Romanov military encounters consisted of frontal offensives. General Ivanov, tsarist southwest front commander, divided his forces almost evenly between the northern and eastern Galician fronts, which negatively affected any Russian possibility of achieving a major decision on either one. The fact that the Russians initially overwhelmed Habsburg right flank forces with superior numbers resulted more from General Conrad's tactical miscalculations than tsarist battle plans.

For the Russians speed was important for victory on both the German and Austro-Hungarian fronts. Tsarist forces had the advantage of a good railroad network to the Habsburg frontier and could transport more than double the number of trains than the Habsburg military could. Two major factors influenced tsarist planning. First, the Austro-Hungarian armies might launch an offensive earlier than the completion of their mobilization to disrupt Russian troop concentrations. Second, the desire to achieve an initial victory in the opening campaign had a major effect on the timing of tsarist military activities.

The tsarist Eighth Army advanced toward the Habsburg eastern Galician frontier on August 18; Third Army followed the next day without its supply system completely established. Soon after the launch of their two-army invasion of East Prussia, the Russians learned that the opposing Habsburg forces were numerically weaker than they had anticipated because of their invasion of Serbia. That weakness would be utilized to advance rapidly, partially to reduce enemy pressure against their northern Fourth and Fifth armies. The tsarist armies' fronts extended some 200 kilometers with a 120-kilometer gap between them. The two eastern flank armies encountered no serious Habsburg defensive resistance for a week, as their twenty-one divisions advanced against an unsuspecting enemy. Conrad continued to refuse to believe that a major tsarist military action would be launched against his eastern flank deployment.

The Habsburg Third and Second Army troops not deployed to the Serbian front (B-Group) had the mission to protect the Habsburg eastern Galician right flank positions, while the main Austro-Hungarian offensive was launched to the north between the Bug and Vistula Rivers. Conrad's Third Army troops were generally deployed along the San–Dniester River line in mid-August to advance toward Lemberg, the Galician capital. Meanwhile, Third Army's XIV Corps was transferred to Fourth Army for its offensive operation. As the opening military campaign evolved, XIV Corps was transferred from one army to another four times, to the detriment of both Third and Fourth initial army campaigns.

During the initial military campaign, two major bloody battles raged in Galicia, the first between August 18 and September 3, 1914 in the areas of Lublin and Cholm on the Northern front. To the southeast on August 18 the tsarist Eighth Army crossed the frontier at the Zbrucz River, half its troops advancing toward Lemberg. The Habsburg First and Fourth armies attacked the tsarist Fourth and Fifth armies on the Northern front. Later the newly formed tsarist Ninth Army, initially designated for deployment on the German front, intervened against the Habsburg armies. The first of two decisive Lemberg battles raged between the Habsburg Third Army and available Second Army XII Corps units versus the full-strength Russian Third and Eighth armies. The Lemberg area terrain favored a defensive stance against an enemy advancing from the east. Habsburg forces eventually utilized the three rivers flowing north to south with interspersed valleys and hilly terrain for defensive purposes when their initial offensive efforts collapsed. The major portion of Second Army had been deployed in Serbia to encourage Bulgarian and Romanian military support of the Dual Monarchy's war against the South Slavic neighbor. If either of these two countries joined battle against Serbia, some Habsburg troops could have been redeployed against the more dangerous and numerically superior Russian enemy on the Galician front.

General Conrad's initial strategy entailed deploying his First and Fourth armies to attack northward between the Vistula and Bug Rivers to advance toward Lublin and Cholm. However, his strategy proved faulty. His first major miscalculation resulted from his reputed belief that the German Army would launch an offensive southward from East Prussia, crossing the Narev River to join his forces to simultaneously attack toward Siedlce in the Polish sack. He claimed that it had been mutually agreed upon in prewar correspondence with General Moltke. This ignored the fact that the weak German Eighth Army had to contend with the invasion of East Prussia by two tsarist armies. General Moltke had notified Conrad on August 10 that the Germans would not launch that offensive into Poland. Thus Conrad's strategy was based on false premises. Another miscalculation that cost the Austro-Hungarian Army dearly resulted from Conrad's determined refusal to consider that the Russians would deploy major forces east of Lemberg. Thus, only Third Army and the small available portion of his Second Army (XII Corps) were designated to protect the First and Fourth armies' northern offensive operations' right flank positions. If the Russians fielded major forces at the eastern flank area, the insufficient Habsburg troop numbers countering them could not overcome the threat. This problem compounded when Second Army initially fielded only its XII Corps to protect the extreme Habsburg right flank position when its main forces deployed on the Serbian front. That single corps' numerical strength was grossly inadequate to perform its mission to halt an enemy invasion on the Habsburg extreme flank. Prewar planning had Romanian troops protecting that specific area.

During the next several days tsarist units deployed along the Bug River stretch, near the flank positions of the Habsburg First and Fourth armies' offensive forces. Major concerns soon arose relative to the eastern Galician right flank area, where the Russians deployed Third and Eighth armies, unbeknownst to Habsburg Supreme Command intelligence. Fatally, the danger was too long ignored.

Habsburg Fourth Army received orders on August 18 to prepare to launch an offensive operation to the northeast and east and establish its positions by August 21. Meanwhile, Third Army received orders to advance toward Lemberg to protect Habsburg First and Fourth armies' right flank and rear echelon positions. Second Army XII Corps had to protect the extreme Habsburg right flank positions by advancing to the Dniester River, where it had originally planned to be deployed.[6]

One Second Army Corps remained on the Balkan front for a long time; two others would reputedly arrive on the Russian front by August 28. Tragically, they did not until later in September. General Conrad's decision not to mobilize rapidly against Russia proved disastrous, because only twenty-eight divisions were initially deployed on that front. This number increased to thirty-seven, but Conrad's insistence on launching a rapid campaign against Serbia before countering Russia ensured that his northern forces would be grossly outnumbered in the initial battles.

On the Habsburg northern front on August 20, First Army collided with tsarist Fourth Army formations about thirty kilometers southwest of Lublin. On the eastern Galician front there was yet no indication of a major enemy offensive effort, but increasing intelligence reports indicated major tsarist railroad activity in that area. Negative air reconnaissance reports encouraged General Conrad to assume that no significant tsarist forces had been deployed at the Dniester River, Tarnopol or Proskorov areas. Thus, when he ordered Third Army to advance to the north, it exposed its flanks to tsarist attack. Then, the tsarist Third and Eighth armies crossed the frontier on the Habsburg right flank. On August 20 Russian Fifth Army (eight infantry divisions) moved southwest, attempting to envelop Habsburg First Army's rear echelon positions. Habsburg Fourth Army's ten and a half divisions and First Army forces initially outnumbered tsarist Fourth and Fifth Army contingents, which momentarily halted them at the battles of Krasnik and Komarov, whereupon tsarist forces briefly shifted to a defensive posture to protect the critical railroad line between Lublin and Cholm.[7]

Meanwhile, the numerically superior Russian Third and Eighth armies collided with Habsburg Third Army units about sixty kilometers east of Lemberg in the two battles of Zlota Lipa and Gnila Lipa between August 26 and 29. Third Army was caught by surprise by an onslaught of twenty-one tsarist divisions that ultimately resulted in the loss of Lemberg and created the critical necessity of rapidly withdrawing increasing numbers of troops from the Balkan front to attempt to neutralize the evolving Habsburg Russian front crisis. This naturally weakened the Habsburg Balkan front, ultimately resulting in disaster there.

Also on August 20, Habsburg intelligence reports finally indicated that strong tsarist forces had crossed the eastern Galician frontier, advancing less than ten kilometers a day. Thus, they reputedly could attain the area of the upper Bug and Zlota Lipa Rivers by August 25, posing a serious threat to the attacking Habsburg First and Fourth armies' flank and rear areas. Conrad ordered his eastern flank forces (Third Army and Second Army XII Corps) to attack the enemy forces advancing from the east, but he still failed to recognize the extent of the escalating threat to his weak eastern flank forces, although he received the first indications of a major enemy threat from that direction.

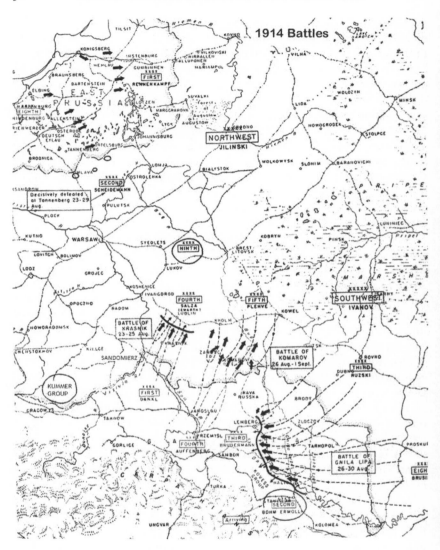

Map 3 *First Battles Eastern Front*
Map courtesy of the United States Military Academy Department of History

Meanwhile, on the Habsburg left flank offensive front on August 21 Russian troops retreated, with Habsburg First Army units in pursuit following the August 21–23 battle at Krasnik. Two Russian corps attacked the First Army X Corps flank, resulting in heavy battle. Further south Second Army XII Corps courted disaster, while other Second Army units still deployed in Serbia incurred casualties before their delayed transport to the Russian theater. Meanwhile, multiple intelligence reports indicated that the tsarist army was receiving numerous reinforcements at Lublin.

On August 22, General Conrad ordered First and Fourth armies to launch offensives toward Lublin and Cholm to secure the province of Galicia and neutralize any enemy attacks. The partially assembled tsarist Fifth Army and other formations marched south between the Bug and Vistula Rivers on a collision course with Habsburg forces. On August 23, *Stavka* ordered the rapid commencement of operations on its northern front to draw Habsburg attention from its developing eastern flank operation, where Third and Eighth armies prepared to launch offensives. The lack of clarity regarding the enemy's intentions and its strength in the area between the Dniester and Bug Rivers became a fateful Habsburg problem.

Russian Eighth Army (VII, XII and III Corps) had crossed the Zbrucz River at the upper Bug River frontier on August 18. Nevertheless, Conrad ordered his Fourth and First armies to advance northward, while Third Army protected the Habsburg right flank area by launching an offensive to bind any opposing tsarist formations. General Conrad's northern operation, however, could have little effect unless the Germans attacked from East Prussia as reputedly promised in prewar Conrad–Moltke correspondence. Regretfully for Conrad, that did not transpire, and he had been informed that it would not.

Habsburg First Army launched its attack toward Lublin on August 22. When that army achieved the early victory at Krasnik east of the San River, the enemy retreated in a northeasterly direction, but quickly reestablished defensive positions to protect the approaches to Lublin. As First Army advanced, its flank positions became exposed to potential tsarist attacks as the enemy increased its troop numbers.

The Russian Fourth and Fifth armies maneuvered toward the Habsburg First and Fourth armies, threatening the flanks of the major Habsburg northern offensive operation. If the Russians launched a major operation south of Lemberg, they could potentially envelop all Habsburg forces deployed between the San River and Carpathian Mountains. Continually unaware of tsarist intentions, General Conrad remained clueless to the enormous impending danger, although a map discovered on a dead Russian officer revealed that the tsarist Eighth Army had deployed in the Proskurov area. Conrad, however, continued his northern offensive operation, refusing to believe any intelligence reports that contradicted his plan to launch an offensive between the Bug and Vistula Rivers.[8]

Early on August 23, the Russian Third and Eighth armies entered eastern Galicia, while tsarist Fourth Army forces advanced on a broad front against Habsburg First Army, maneuvering toward Lublin. Habsburg First Army concentrated its left flank positions against the tsarist XXIV Corps, which after battle withdrew toward Lublin to avoid encirclement. In the process that retreat endangered its two neighboring corps, which joined the retrograde movement. Meanwhile, Russian Fifth Army brushed past Habsburg Fourth Army as it advanced toward the Habsburg First Army. Savage back-and-forth battle occurred between August 23 and 25 when the Habsburg First Army encircled the Russian Fourth Army right flank forces and compelled them to retreat toward Lublin. First Army suffered enormous casualties as attacking troops received little or no artillery support. After this victory, First Army continued its advance toward Lublin, which briefly presented Conrad with the initiative in the most significant sector of his northern offensive operation. The problem was that the offensive exposed the weak center forces and the divergent objectives diluted the chance of mass, presenting the tsarist enemy the opportunity to advance into the expanding gaps between the Habsburg First and Fourth armies.

As battle intensified on the multikilometer front, Habsburg troops rarely enjoyed the necessary artillery support as division supply trains and artillery columns lagged far behind the advancing troops. Tsarist artillery proved very accurate and terrorized the attacking troops. Using obsolete tactics and totally lacking the necessary training, troops attacked in dense formations into murderous machine-gun and artillery crossfire. Officer losses were atrocious as they could easily be spotted with their swords. Losses rapidly increased.

First Army's Krasnik victory caused *Stavka* to reverse its orders for the newly formed tsarist Ninth Army (eight divisions) originally intended to invade Germany. Instead that army now redeployed to the endangered tsarist position between the Bug and Vistula Rivers to assist in countering the unanticipated Krasnik defeat. Although later rescinded, an ensuing tsarist Fourth Army retreat brought a temporary order to transfer additional Habsburg Third Army forces to Fourth Army (XIV Corps).

Meanwhile, General Conrad ordered Third Army to rapidly march north to defend the provincial capital, Lemberg, as well as Fourth Army's exposed flank position. Meanwhile, Habsburg intelligence reports increasingly indicated significant enemy infantry and cavalry troop activity in eastern Galicia. On August 23 Conrad anticipated that eight to ten tsarist divisions had deployed on the Habsburg northern front between the Bug and Vistula Rivers. That information proved inaccurate, because by September 1 thirty-five or more tsarist divisions had become operational on his front. The few available Second Army units (XII Corps) on the Habsburg right flank received orders to originally concentrate at Stanislau, located seventy kilometers south of Lemberg. Their mission became to protect Third Army southern flank positions, but both of its flanks were threatened. Third Army III Corps received orders to prepare defensive positions near Lemberg in the area of Przemyślany. Second Army had to await the arrival of the remainder of its army units in transit from the Balkan front now trickling into the Stanislau area, to provide an effective fighting force. As Third Army formations marched northward, reports increasingly indicated that major enemy forces had mobilized to the east of that army.

Habsburg Third Army's nine infantry and four cavalry divisions had the mission to protect the Habsburg right flank deployment area east and north of Lemberg. Third Army covered a front of more than a hundred kilometers. Its XI Corps advanced to the Lemberg area, while XIV Corps marched northward. During the next few days, XIV Corps received contradictory orders to report to two separate armies (Third and Fourth) at different times. The shuttling of the corps resulted in its absence at critical moments in the ensuing major battles for both northern armies. Meanwhile, Second Army XII Corps troops marched ninety kilometers in three days; the exhausted troops requiring a rest day as overwhelming tsarist Third and Eighth troop numbers unexpectedly smashed into Habsburg right flank troop formations.

As the northern Habsburg First and Fourth armies advanced on August 23, increasing concern shifted to the threatened Third and Second Army XII Corps situation in eastern Galicia. Increasing pressure on Emperor Franz Joseph demanded a more rapid retransport of Second Army troops originally designated for the Galician theater in a War Case "R," but of which multiple units had become embroiled in the Serbian campaign. Arguments for quickly redeploying the critically needed forces to the Russian front emphasized that the main war decision now had to be attained against the major enemy, Russia, whose overpowering forces presently battled the northern First and Fourth armies; the German ally, reputedly contrary to prewar agreement, had fielded only nine infantry divisions on the Eastern front. Reports of the unanticipated early deployment of Siberian Corps on the Habsburg front threatened to aggravate the already increasingly unfavorable military situation; and numerous Russian forces had deployed against Habsburg units because of Romania's early declaration of neutrality. Most significantly, however, the unanticipated, overwhelming and dangerous Russian numerical superiority in the Habsburg right flank area necessitated the immediate strengthening of Habsburg forces southeast of Lemberg, where major battle began to erupt.

On the basis of these arguments, Emperor Franz Joseph accepted the transfer of the Second Army IV Corps to Galicia with the stipulation that the Balkan front Sava–Danube River line be adequately defended. That army's VII Corps, which boarded trains on August 22, did not begin to arrive at Galician railroad terminals until August 31, after the initial battles had been decided. IV Corps troops boarded trains for transport on August 30 and 31, but did not reach Galicia until September 18, well after the disastrous Lemberg battles, soon to be described. Thus, Habsburg forces lacked mass on the front and sought divergent objectives, which increasingly separated the armies. The result was that Second Army left the Balkan front, opening a flank to Serbian attack, and its units arrived on the Galician front too late to prevent a catastrophic defeat there. Second Army received orders to concentrate its troops as soon as more units arrived from the Balkan theater and to reach Stanislau, seventy kilometers south of Lemberg.

On August 24 Third Army received orders to deploy XII and available XI Corps units west of Przemyślany to force the advancing enemy out of eastern Galicia. XIII and III Corps troops had to advance to a line west of Dunajov by August 25. That army's commander remained unaware that superior enemy troop numbers had already occupied that area. Third Army received orders to attack and defeat the reputedly weak opposing enemy forces before their superior numbers could be united on the battlefield. Enemy numbers, however, had been grossly underestimated in this critical flank area.

Habsburg Fourth Army, deployed east of First Army, launched an offensive on a sixty-kilometer front toward Cholm also against "weak enemy forces." This, however, seriously altered the original Habsburg offensive plan, which had designated First Army to be the major driving force in the northern offensive operation area along the Vistula River. First Army continued to advance toward Lublin in heavy battle on a forty-kilometer front, unaware of the significant enemy reinforcements approaching its front, the enemy Fourth and Ninth armies. The tsarist Fourth and Fifth armies prepared to battle Habsburg First Army east of the San River. Fourth Army's advance direction increasingly separated it from First Army, creating a dangerous gap between the two armies, as well as the Fourth Army right flank area, from it to Third Army; thus, there existed two separate offensive actions. The unanticipated dangerous tsarist threat to the Habsburg eastern flank positions soon counterbalanced the favorable battle reports emanating from the northern First and Fourth Army fronts, where tsarist forces retreated from Krasnik. First Army launched frontal assaults against the Russian Fourth Army to drive it back to Lublin, sustaining serious officer and manpower losses.

Third Army finally launched its offensive, assuming it to be attacking an isolated tsarist corps (two to three divisions). This produced the first heavy fighting at the Zlota Lipa defensive line southeast of Lemberg. This caused Conrad to order XIV Corps to march back from Fourth Army to Third Army, its second redeployment during the initial actions. Third Army had to secure the Habsburg eastern flank frontier, while Second Army XII Corps held the terrain further south at the Dniester River area.

In the interim, First Army air reconnaissance pinpointed large Russian troop concentrations along the Vistula River advancing toward its flank and rear areas. Russian Fifth Army now attempted to turn the Habsburg First Army flank. Habsburg Fourth Army lacked reserves and reinforcements as its battle intensified against the tsarist Fourth Army. That army's troops had become exhausted from several days of battle in the heat, and their lack of food and water. Supplies of every type had been expended, logistical functions failing to rapidly resupply the advancing troops, while Russian and Austro-Hungarian forces both sustained heavy losses.

Casualties proved so enormous that often attacking troops could not exploit potential victories. Overpowering Russian artillery continued to exact a heavy toll on Habsburg troops because of its deadly accuracy, numerical superiority and lack of effective Habsburg counterartillery support or indirect fire. Faulty Habsburg tactics and attacking in thick formations also took an enormous toll of lives as tsarist Third Army troops approached Lemberg from the northeast.

On August 25, the extreme right flank Habsburg XII Corps units received the mission to halt any enemy excursions across the Zbrucz River; therefore, they had to consolidate their forces as rapidly as possible. Further north, Third Army launched its offensive in the general line from Lemberg to Zloczóv to halt the enemy incursions against the lower Zlota Lipa and Dniester Rivers (lines north toward Rava Russka), to provide its own flank security. By evening, the Second Army commander was expected to arrive with additional units from the Balkan front.[9] A major concern arose relative to security measures south of the Dniester River, where only the Second Army's 35. *Landsturm* Infantry Brigade had been deployed and could not be expected to have a major military effect.

Habsburg efforts to force further Russian retreat in the northern theater continued; then tsarist forces launched an unsuccessful attack against First Army while steadily increasing pressure against that army's right flank positions, causing fifteen thousand Habsburg losses. Russian Fourth Army, after initially retreating, established defensive positions south of Lublin. Russian Fifth Army received orders to assist Fourth Army at Lublin by launching an assault attempting to turn the attacking Habsburg right flank area. Tsarist artillery continually greatly outnumbered Habsburg guns. That front area had expanded enormously as tsarist Fifth Army shifted toward Komarov at the Habsburg Fourth Army flank.

The First Army advance initiated the confrontation at Zloczóv, which resulted in the disastrous first of the two decisive battles of Lemberg, while vastly numerically superior tsarist forces began to advance steadily against the Habsburg eastern Galician flank Dniester River positions. Thus, the Habsburg Zlota Lipa River defensive lines became critical. When General Conrad finally recognized the dangerous threat to his right flank forces, he telegraphed General Moltke demanding that German troops immediately be transferred to the Habsburg Eastern front. Conrad, however, failed to inform his German counterpart that his Second Army, contrary to prewar battle plans to be deployed against Russia if it went to war, had instead been deployed to the Balkan front in the attempt to rapidly defeat Serbia before its redeployment could occur to counter the far larger and far more dangerous tsarist armies. Moltke replied that ten Russian corps had attacked German Eighth Army in East Prussia. The mass of available German forces had commenced a desperate effort to encircle the five-corps-strong Russian Second Army that had crossed the East Prussian frontier on August 15. Thus, General Conrad could not anticipate immediate relief for his seriously outnumbered troops.

Conrad, in the interim, learned that Third Army had not yet deployed its troops onto high terrain as he had ordered. Third Army retained the mission to halt enemy troops from reaching Lemberg, while First and Fourth armies continued their successful offensives toward Lublin and Cholm. Third Army commenced movement to the east and southeast.

As an unknown number of Russian forces approached the Zlota Lipa River Habsburg defensive lines, Conrad ordered Third Army to attack them. Intelligence reports indicated the presence of five to six tsarist divisions. Third Army had to prevent those enemy troops from intervening against Fourth Army offensive efforts. Third Army continued to advance hurriedly toward Zloczóv, anticipating encountering three separate but weak deploying Russian troop concentrations before they had time to consolidate their troops.

The Habsburg military situation suddenly and unexpectedly worsened when Third Army and XII Corps troops had to retreat southeast of Lemberg, because of increasingly strong enemy pressure and being grossly outnumbered while sustaining horrendous losses. On August 26 Third Army withdrew from its Zlota Lipa defensive lines along the sixty-kilometer-wide front to north and east of the salient just outside of Lemberg at the Gnila Lipa River line. It had failed to halt the tsarist advance to Lemberg. Its troops advanced in close formation, becoming easy targets for enemy artillery. Tsarist numerical strength had proven far greater than anticipated and Habsburg losses far exceeded expectations. Russian artillery dominance and accurate barrages proved devastating to attacking Third Army troops, which began to flee toward Lemberg.

The Russian success could have been much greater, but the troops only cautiously pursued their defeated foe because of its own sizable casualties and logistical problems, partly a result of the different gauge railroad tracks on each side of the Galicia frontier. Nevertheless, the debacle commenced for Third Army as its front lines began to cave in.

Unseen tsarist machine guns mowed down the hapless attackers at point-blank range. The numerically superior enemy forces, particularly artillery units, caused enormous Habsburg casualties. Multiple regiments sustained unacceptable losses, specifically of professional soldiers. At noon a retreat commenced, more a panicked rout, after enemy artillery consistently halted attacks before advancing Habsburg troops reached tsarist defense lines. Inadequately trained reserve units suffered grievous losses to the precise pre-sighted Russian artillery fire. An ensuing ten-mile retreat resulted in an improvised Habsburg defensive line twenty-five miles from Lemberg.

In the interim, the sparse Second Army (XII Corps) forces assembling on the extreme right flank and the units arriving from the Balkan front received orders to launch an offensive across the Dniester River at Stanislau then advance northward to east of Lemberg. Victory, however, depended upon Third Army battle success further north at Lemberg. As First and Fourth armies continued advancing northward, the enemy inserted three to four divisions into the expanding gap between the two armies. First Army's right flank position became increasingly threatened while tsarist divisions approached Fourth Army's rear echelon area. Air reconnaissance reported large enemy formations advancing toward that army. Further south Russian Fifth Army attempted to cover the open breach with its Fourth Army countering the Habsburg First Army. Tsarist Fifth Army units unexpectedly collided with the Habsburg Fourth Army. Tsarist troops then retreated to Zamosc, with horrendous causalities sustained on both sides.

As Fourth Army commenced the battle of Komarov (August 26–September 2), its nine infantry and two cavalry divisions opposed approximately six to seven Fifth Army infantry and two to three cavalry divisions. The redeployment of XIV Corps to assist Fourth Army's right flank advance toward Komarov seriously weakened Third Army numbers, as that army suddenly encountered vastly superior enemy troops. Third Army supply trains could not keep pace with their rapidly moving troops. On August 26 Third Army launched its mentioned fateful, uncoordinated offensive before its deployment had been completed and without sufficient artillery support against vastly superior enemy formations. Its attack rapidly faltered. Tsarist troops commenced their own offensive operation within hours on the same day. Instead of attacking an assumed isolated Russian corps, multiple tsarist Eighth and Third Army corps (twenty-one infantry divisions) attacked Third Army's two and a half corps. The reputed isolated corps was the tsarist Eighth Army with three times the numerical strength of the attacking forces. Third Army's III Corps sustained severe losses at Przemyslany, many units losing two-thirds of their soldiers as they began to retreat. Significant Russian troop numerical superiority unexpectedly threatened to encircle Third Army's extreme right flank positions because Second Army units lacked sufficient troop numbers to halt a powerful tsarist assault against that army. Habsburg thickly massed attackers, particularly officers, became easy targets for the very accurate heavy enemy artillery barrages. The tsarist Third and Eighth armies advanced cautiously toward Lemberg and its favorable defensive terrain. General Conrad had ordered Second Army XII Corps units to close the sixty-to-seventy-kilometer gap separating it from Third Army, while simultaneously a hundred-kilometer gap opened between Third and Fourth Habsburg armies. Russian units rapidly poured into these dangerously exposed areas, while inflicting heavy casualties on August 26 and 27.

As General Conrad repeatedly demanded that German troops be deployed to the Habsburg front, his aerial reconnaissance efforts revealed that the tsarist Third Army had changed its march direction. Conrad then ordered that Second and Third Army forces halt tsarist egress at the Vereszyca River.

Fourth Army must change its advance direction to strike tsarist flank positions at Rava Russka to relieve the deadly pressure on the suddenly hapless Third Army. The Fourth Army's difficult situation eventually resulted in disaster.

On the northern theater serious First Army casualties and the arrival of Russian reinforcements quickly threatened that army's right flank positions. As Russian pressure steadily increased, it forced First Army troops to retreat on August 30. Meanwhile, Russian Fifth Army's effective retreat tactics exhausted attacking Habsburg Fourth Army forces, thus these units failed to achieve a rapid pursuit of the enemy.

On August 27 Habsburg First Army and tsarist troops continued to probe each other's positions, trying to determine their enemy's main troop location. Meanwhile, Russian Fifth Army units struck Habsburg First Army flank positions; the Habsburg commander unaware of the escalating threat of his troops being enveloped.

As overwhelming Russian forces had swung north to attack Third Army formations, III Corps in particular sustained enormous losses. Disaster quickly appeared imminent at Third Army's endangered flank position. Superior tsarist troop numbers and accurate artillery support forced Third Army units to initially halt then ultimately retreat, without orders. When five enemy corps and six cavalry divisions smashed into Habsburg positions, the front lines began to collapse as retreat to the new Gnila Lipa lines soon occurred.

On August 27 and 28 tsarist forces stabilized their retreat lines near Lublin then launched counterattacks that halted Habsburg First Army's progress. Tsarist forces also overwhelmed Habsburg Third Army flank forces northeast of Lemberg. Tsarist troops then halted to regroup before again advancing toward their ultimate objective, Lemberg, provincial capital of Galicia. Yet General Conrad continued to order Habsburg offensive operations. Superior tsarist firepower halted every Third Army attempt, often creating panic in that army's lines. Then enemy troops enveloped the Habsburg flanks. General Conrad now realized that while his First and Fourth armies had "victoriously" advanced, the success of the campaign depended upon the outcome of the Third Army battle raging around Lemberg.

Russian forces had seized Tarnopol and Halicz at their extreme western flank position against weak Second Army resistance, enabling them to reverse their front northward against Habsburg Third Army's seriously endangered flank positions. Enormous quantities of Habsburg food, equipment and ammunition were either destroyed or abandoned, because they could not be evacuated in a timely manner during the ensuing rapid retreat movements. The southernmost Habsburg XII Corps' mission remained to halt the enemy offensive operation south of Brzezány and prevent enemy attacks against Third Army's southern flank positions in the Lemberg area. Significant portions of Second Army, including IV and VII Corps, remained deployed on the Balkan front and in battle at Sabac.

The serious Third Army defeats caused General Conrad to consider halting Fourth Army's successful operation to change its advance direction 180° south toward Lemberg to support the seriously threatened Third Army. This maneuver, however, would create a seventy-mile gap between the northern First and Fourth armies. The reputedly defeated tsarist Fifth Army promptly advanced into that gap. Conrad's efforts to halt enemy progress toward Lemberg at any cost resulted in colossal Habsburg casualties during the first battle days. Attacking Third Army formations were annihilated by well-positioned and accurate Russian artillery units while Habsburg guns failed to support their troops' attack.

Fourth Army troops seized Zamosc on August 27 as that army attempted to envelop the tsarist flank as it advanced northeastward toward Cholm. However, air reconnaissance units reported that enemy troops were rapidly approaching Fourth Army's eastern flank area (tsarist Third Army).

A race ensued between Austro-Hungarian cavalry units attempting to fill the threatening gaps between their armies and Russian cavalry attempting to penetrate them, but Russian troops advanced into the open terrain between the First and Fourth, and Third and Fourth Habsburg armies. As the Habsburg military situation steadily deteriorated, General Conrad increasingly expressed his disgust at the German military "successes" reputedly earned at the Dual Monarchy's expense. In an attempt to disguise his own serious planning blunders, Conrad argued that of the one hundred operational German divisions, a paltry nine regular and three National Guard divisions had been deployed in East Prussia. Thus, Habsburg forces had to bear the overpowering brunt of the initial Russian onslaught that created the present perilous Habsburg military situation. However, that was the fault of the misinterpretations from the reputed Conrad–Moltke prewar correspondence agreements that did not include a detailed plan or mention of an Allied command structure.

Conrad, however, conveniently ignored the fact that his German counterpart notified him on August 10 that he would not launch an offensive into the Polish sack because of the unexpectedly rapid Russian invasion of East Prussia.[10] Nevertheless, in a letter to General Bolfras (the emperor's chief of the Military Chancellery), Conrad rehashed General Moltke's reputed prewar promise to deploy at least twelve divisions east of the lower Vistula River to attack toward Siedlce in Poland to support Habsburg offensive efforts.

Meanwhile, XIV Corps troops wasted valuable time and manpower marching back and forth between Third and Fourth armies as General Conrad vacillated on his intentions for that unit. On the morning of August 27, Conrad inaccurately surmised that Third Army's situation might not be as serious as it had appeared earlier, so he ordered XIV Corps be returned to Fourth Army to allow it to join the advance toward Komarov in the attempt to achieve a major battlefield victory. His judgment relative to Third Army proved disastrously incorrect.

In the meantime, Habsburg First Army troops had to rest and also rectify serious supply problems. Tsarist Fifth Army's seven infantry divisions now attacked First Army flank positions, but Conrad had to also focus increasing attention on the tense military situation in the Lemberg area.

The fact that Italy and Romania had not fulfilled their Triple Alliance Treaty obligations drastically worsened the Habsburg military situation. The early August Italian declaration of neutrality canceled five Italian divisions being railroad transported to East Prussia, releasing German troops to cooperate with Habsburg forces. Although General Moltke eventually transferred two German corps to Prussia from the Western front, their vanguard units did not arrive before September 1, or after the overwhelming Tannenberg victory and eve of the first Habsburg Lemberg disaster. Their redeployment, however, weakened the Schlieffen right flank attack against France at a critical time.

As Russian forces advanced on all fronts they continued to receive substantial reinforcements. Habsburg feeble counterattacks proved too few and isolated to have any serious effect, except to substantially increase casualties. Third Army repeatedly launched frontal assaults over the difficult terrain for two days, but tsarist artillery fire tore up the advancing Habsburg troops. All attacks were repulsed with heavy losses as Russian counterattacks eventually forced the Habsburg forces into a chaotic retreat so rapid that tsarist troops could not keep pace with them. Fortunately for Conrad, the Russians did not quickly pursue the defeated troops because of their own logistical problems and casualties.

With disaster threatening the Third Army flank positions and the entire Habsburg campaign, General Conrad underestimated the enemy strength crossing the Zlota Lipa River line. By evening, the battered Third Army received orders to "unconditionally hold their positions," while Fourth Army was to repel strong enemy cavalry incursions against it. The extended Habsburg supply lines and communication links became increasingly threatened as the week of vicious fighting exhausted troops on both sides. Habsburg logistical support proved totally ineffective.

During the last week of August, General Conrad continued to urge General Moltke to attack toward Siedlce to assist his troops battling toward Lublin and to support his sorely pressed Third Army forces east of Lemberg. In the interim, the Russian Third and Eighth Army attack had forced the grossly outnumbered Third Army troops to retreat, sustaining further heavy losses. Devastatingly accurate Russian artillery barrages battered both Third Army flank positions. This caused General Conrad to order the preparation of the new defensive line at the Gnila Lipa River, twenty-five kilometers west of the

Zlota Lipa River. This represented the next possible defensive position for his retreating troops. However, the reeling Third Army lacked sufficient troop numbers to occupy and defend the designated wide front with its decimated and seriously demoralized troops. Thus, the army failed to establish effective defensive positions before Russian troops attacked. Fourth Army again transferred XIV Corps units to the imperiled Third Army front to attempt to halt the incursion of strong advancing enemy cavalry forces. The continued shifting of XIV Corps between the two armies exhausted the soldiers, exposing them to enemy attack, and ensured the corps was not available at critical times, while also weakening the armies they had been transferred from.

On August 29 tsarist troops defeated Third Army III Corps troops north of the Gnila Lipa line near the town of Przemyslany. That army sustained critical losses, particularly officers. Overpowering Russian troop numbers broke through the Third Army front east of Lemberg in a two-day battle.

The Habsburg armies initially mobilized thirty-one divisions, thirty-seven by September 4 for the Eastern front, while awaiting Second Army units transport from the Balkan front. The Russians mobilized forty-five infantry and eighteen cavalry divisions in Galicia by the thirtieth mobilization day. Prewar Habsburg calculations assumed only twenty-four tsarist divisions could be deployed by that date. Five Russian armies ultimately launched an offensive into Galicia along a three-hundred-mile front.

At dawn on August 30, the Russians continued their relentless westward drive, as the consistently battered Habsburg forces retreated in disarray and panic to Lemberg. Second Army, where tsarist troops smashed a fifteen-kilometer gap in its lines, received orders to retire behind the Dniester River to await the arrival of IV Corps, anticipated to arrive from the Serbian front on September 1. However, it did not arrive until September 8, too late to affect the ongoing battle.

When First Army relaunched its offensive effort, it sustained enormous casualties as the enemy increasingly threatened its flank positions. On August 29 and 30 Conrad ordered the launching of additional offensives at the Gnila Lipa River line, as Habsburg troops were forced into a confined space that placed them in danger of being outflanked. Further south the Habsburg VII Corps flank became threatened while troops discarded enormous amounts of machine guns, wagons, equipment and prisoners of war. Conrad transferred his few remaining troops to bolster his left flank offensive operation, thereby exposing Lemberg to enemy attack. Between August 29 and 31, a three-day battle ensued, with the Russian Eighth Army breaking through Habsburg positions southeast of Lemberg. Habsburg armies could not halt the enemy advance, with Lemberg falling to the Russians on September 1. Second Army (now enlarged to six infantry and two cavalry divisions) was ordered to halt enemy forces that threatened Third Army's eastern flank positions. When

Conrad ordered Fourth Army to reverse its front to attack the enemy pressuring the faltering Third Army, it encountered tsarist Third Army troops as they also changed front to the southwest to attack Habsburg Fourth Army.

The Russian Fifth Army, meanwhile, had retreated about fifty kilometers from its previous positions, pursued by the Habsburg Fourth Army. General Conrad worried whether northern operational success could be achieved before suffering serious defeat on the eastern flank. The tsarist Third and Eighth armies' irresistible advance continued. By the end of August, nine to ten Second Army divisions had arrived on the Eastern front, but at least two corps still remained in the Balkan theater. The exhausted Habsburg Fourth Army troops could not rapidly pursue retreating enemy Fifth Army forces, while Third Army's retreat increasingly endangered Fourth Army's flank positions.

The failure of Second Army to relieve the overwhelming pressure on Third Army positions resulted in the retreat of Third Army's right flank troops. The Russians battered the mentioned fifteen-kilometer wedge into the Habsburg XII Corps lines, while their cavalry forces raided Habsburg supply lines and attacked hapless retreating Habsburg troops. Third Army troops had to withdraw from the Gnila Lipa River line after enemy troops broke through their lines to next prepare new defensive positions at the Vereszyca River. Third Army command calculated that they could better defend positions there, but desperately required reinforcements to replace their enormous casualties to enable them to counter the enormous tsarist numerical supremacy.

Although Third Army suffered complete defeat and Second Army right flank units collapsed, Conrad nevertheless continued to press First and Fourth Army commanders to achieve victory to reverse Third and Second armies' precarious situations and finally achieve an alignment of Second, Third and Fourth armies on one contiguous front. A strong four-division Habsburg cavalry corps deployed into the territory between Third and Fourth armies as did enemy troops. The spotlight now focused on Fourth Army's attempts to defeat the tsarist Fifth Army forces, the time factor becoming increasingly important. By August 30, the arrival of new Russian units and reinforcements, particularly the Siberian Corps, convinced Conrad that a less extensive victory than he had envisioned would have to suffice. Meanwhile, battered Habsburg forces desperately required reinforcements, because few reserve units remained due to using *Ersatz* and March battalions in combat as cannon fodder, a horrific loss of life, necessitated by the need to attempt to halt the irresistible enemy advances. Surviving troops were exhausted from the many long and arduous marches, lack of rest, battle and oftentimes ensuing chaos and panic. Enormous amounts of irreplaceable equipment and weapons were deserted in the hasty retreat movements, as tsarist artillery consistently took a heavy toll on retreating soldiers.

Yet, incredulously, General Conrad considered the Habsburg military situation not that serious, so he ordered Third and Second armies to hold the Lemberg–Mikolajov line and only in the "most serious" circumstances retreat behind the Vereszycz River where further battle erupted between September 3 and 11. As Fourth Army offensive units continued to attempt to encircle retreating Russian forces, the Third Army crisis situation forced it to withdraw its eastern flank position to Rava Russka. It became obvious that Third Army was approaching complete collapse as many of its troops fled the battlefield after being attacked by overwhelming enemy troop numbers. Fourth Army received orders to defend the high terrain west of Lemberg while its troops joined Third and Second armies' battle against the Russian onslaught against that city. Overwhelming enemy pressure on August 31 forced Third Army to withdraw multiple kilometers further west toward the San River.

Second Battle of Lemberg
September 2–11, 1914

■ Austro-Hungarian
▭ Russian

Map 4   *Second Battle of Lemberg*

Habsburg problems continued, to the troops' detriment, including poor leadership extending from Habsburg Supreme Command through its multiple command structure. The army's obsolete tactics, its poorly functioning logistical system, lack of infantry–artillery cooperation and sinking troop morale resulted in massive casualties, many thousands completely unnecessary.

There was no confidence that Third Army could halt the enemy at the Vereszyca River twenty-five kilometers west of Lemberg. At the same time XII Corps could not halt enemy progress toward Lemberg from the south. In the interim, Fourth Army troops advanced southward toward Lemberg to attempt to prevent complete defeat. The army was to strike the Russian forces crushing Third Army, but it proved to be too little too late.

Tsarist forces continued their relentless offensive efforts on both the northern and eastern Habsburg fronts. Habsburg First Army forces became threatened with encirclement on both flanks. The gap widened between northern Third Army troops and neighboring Fourth Army. As Conrad sat in his headquarters, a comfortable distance from the front, multiple Habsburg units retreated as soon as tsarist artillery commenced firing.

As the Galician campaign rapidly approached its decisive stage, intelligence sources cited that Russian forces stood at forty to forty-three infantry divisions while six additional tsarist corps could also be deployed on that front. Weak Second Army units continued to retreat from Halicz due to strong enemy pressure. Exhausted Habsburg troops continued to surrender in droves. The lack of medical assistance and personnel resulted in the death of untold thousands of wounded soldiers as casualties continued to increase grotesquely. There were far too few medical personnel. Panic and chaos permeated supply columns as discipline collapsed. Many troops abandoned their guns. The tsarist advantage in troop numbers became six to one on some portions of the battlefield. Irreplaceable railroad equipment fell into Russian hands as well, including a thousand irreplaceable locomotives and fifteen thousand railroad cars as well as the significant Lemberg railroad facilities. Habsburg troops lacked troop numbers as well as every battlefield necessity.

Finally, Fourth Army's seven-day battle at Komarov terminated when tsarist Fifth Army initiated a rapid retreat. However, that tsarist army had neither been encircled nor annihilated, because of insufficient Habsburg troop numbers and lack of sufficient time to complete the operation. Conrad divided Fourth Army's units, leaving weak troops (XIV Corps) to guard against the reputedly defeated and retreating tsarist Fifth Army, while three corps reversed their front and advanced south to strike the enemy forces attacking Third Army's northern flank. At the same time, the Russians realigned large troop formations to attack Habsburg Fourth Army.

In the meantime, the reputedly defeated Russian Fifth Army received reinforcements to replace its significant casualties sustained during the Komarov campaign. The army now could either march to the west to strike the Habsburg First Army's rear flank, or attack south against its former adversary, Habsburg Fourth Army. Tsarist Fifth Army launched two corps southward, threatening to overpower the Habsburg Fourth Army XIV Corps rear echelon guard. Battle expanded beyond Rava Russka.

The next day, September 2, as Russian troops massed to launch a massive counterattack against First and Fourth armies' inner flanks, Third Army surrendered Lemberg without battle, retreating twenty miles to the Grodek heights key to defending the terrain behind the Vereszyca River.[11] Russian troops occupied the provincial capital on September 3, delaying entry for two days while the Habsburg Third Army withdrew to regroup and attempt to restore its disastrous troop morale. Habsburg Third Army's critical situation forced Conrad to halt First and Fourth armies' offensive operations because the Lemberg defeat raised the threat of the enemy encircling those armies' flanks.[12] Third Army's catastrophic defeat made it impossible for its decimated troops to recover and rehabilitate on its present battlefield. Desperately necessary reinforcements did not exist, while the untrained *Ersatz* troops were killed in large numbers. The last option appeared to be to abandon Lemberg and attempt to defend the Vereszyca River line, but the vast enemy numerical superiority prevented effective Third Army resistance. Complete defeat loomed. XII Corps established a defensive position on the river line, but Third Army forced a Second Army retreat as XII Corps troops panicked and fled the battlefield. Entire Third Army battalions fled, as well as XII Corps troops in full panic. The collapse of the 23. Habsburg Infantry division opened the northern approach to Lemberg.

Meanwhile, the far-left flank *Landwehr* Group Kummer crossed to the eastern bank of the Vistula River to assist First Army's battle, but that army's right flank forces had already buckled by September 2. The seriously threatened First Army X Corps troops had to retreat, followed shortly by the remainder of the army.

A panicked General Conrad again contacted his German counterpart Moltke, requesting that at least two German corps be deployed to the Fortress Przemyśl area and that Archduke Friedrich, nominal commander of Austro-Hungarian forces, contact German emperor Wilhelm, stressing the pressing necessity for immediate Allied assistance. Conrad continued to charge that Berlin had reputedly not adhered to its prewar agreements. Friedrich wrote to Emperor Wilhelm, "now, it is decisive for the crushing of Russia that an energetic assault be launched in the direction of Siedlce."[13]

Emperor Wilhelm replied to Friedrich's communication: "Our small army in East Prussia had drawn twelve enemy corps against it and destroyed one-half and battled one-half, thus facilitating the Austro-Hungarian offensive entirely in keeping with the agreements. More than this could not be demanded of them."[14] Meanwhile, Habsburg Second Army's uncoordinated southern flank forces advanced northward toward Lemberg to attempt to relieve some enemy pressure on the already badly mauled Third Army. Third and Second armies had to defend the Dniester River line and prevent

Russian forces from crossing the Vereszyca River. Habsburg Fourth Army had to hold the Rava Russka front while Third Army attacked south of Lemberg. However, in the interim enemy forces suddenly appeared at the Fourth Army's flank and new rear echelon positions. Both sides sustained heavy losses in the resulting battle. Tsarist Fourth and Fifth armies' troop numbers increased significantly with their steady flow of reinforcements. The tsarist Fourth, Fifth and Ninth armies launched a general offensive against Habsburg First and Fourth armies. Russian Fifth Army had halted its earlier retreat movement and reversed its direction to advance against the previously victorious Habsburg Fourth Army. The tsarist Eighth Army advanced past the Vereszyca River to the line of lakes at Grodek west of Lemberg, where Third Army had rapidly prepared defensive positions. If the Russians seized Grodek it would open the way to the San River as the Russian Third Army moved to the northwest toward Rava Russka.

The Russian military position improved enormously after the capture of Lemberg, providing the opportunity to attempt to roll up all Habsburg right flank positions. Irresistible tsarist battlefield successes also negatively affected First and Fourth armies' situations. Further Habsburg attempts to advance, however, had become pointless and extremely dangerous once Third and Second Army offensive efforts terminated, and they had to retreat rapidly.

Four Russian corps entered the fifty-kilometer gap that formed when tsarist Third Army troops smashed into Habsburg Third Army forces as they attempted to close the gap between it and their Fourth Army. The Habsburg military situation had become untenable, while its logistical system failed miserably to deliver sufficient ammunition and supplies to restore the army's fighting power. Infantry efforts lacked critical artillery support while tsarist artillery continued to dominate the battlefield. Russian Third Army now launched major forces toward the Jaroslau bridgehead, which defended the approach to the San River Fortress Przemyśl bastion. Tsarist Eighth Army units supported these efforts by forcing Habsburg forces out of their Grodek defensive positions, resulting in rapid retreat. Fortress Przemyśl stood in the path of the advancing enemy forces, protecting egress into the Carpathian Mountains toward the Hungarian plains.

The Russians renewed their westward advance on September 4 on a wide front. Having gained the initiative, tsarist command possessed the terrain advantage, because few decent defensive positions existed for the hapless retreating Habsburg forces. Major enemy troop locations remained an enigma to Habsburg commanders. During this critical time, Habsburg reconnaissance efforts failed. The pummeled and demoralized Habsburg Third Army required multiple days of rehabilitation at the Vereszyca River line where it had retreated. Its battered and exhausted troops appeared incapable of providing effective resistance to any renewed enemy assault, forcing further retreat.

Further north, tsarist forces crushed both Habsburg First Army flank positions, particularly X Corps units on the army's eastern flank. They simultaneously rushed Russian XX Corps troops into the gap between First and Fourth armies. First Army's mission reverted to preventing an enemy breakthrough and halting enemy forces attacking Fourth Army's rear echelon areas. Reinforced tsarist units advanced cautiously against the outnumbered Habsburg defenders, who reputedly launched several local but futile counterattacks. Whether those orders were complied with remains questionable because of the horrendous troop conditions. Habsburg troops continued to surrender in large numbers and rapidly retreated in utter panic, abandoning inestimable amounts of weapons and supplies.

By September 5, First Army's hard-pressed right flank troops had been forced rearward. Estimating that thirteen enemy divisions opposed his forces, General Dankl reported that his troops could only momentarily maintain their present positions, while desperately requiring nonexistent reinforcements. At this critical moment German High Command announced that as soon as its Eighth Army forces had defeated the invading Russian troops in East Prussia, it would deploy a four-corps army to the Habsburg front. Meanwhile, German forces defended against eleven and a half infantry and five and a half cavalry divisions in East Prussia. Although the Habsburg military situation had become desperate, Conrad determined to launch a bold, but highly questionable, new double encirclement offensive operation to attempt to recover Habsburg military fortunes. Battered and exhausted Third and Second Army troops would launch an offensive to recapture Lemberg. To secure Fourth Army's rear echelon area the often transferred and exhausted XIV Corps troops deployed between the Bug and Vieprz Rivers to close that gap in the lines; however, tsarist Fifth Army troops attacked that group's rear echelon positions. Russian Third Army and Fifth Army units threatened XIV Corps and Fourth Army positions.

Second Army, still anxiously awaiting the arrival of its IV Corps still in railroad transit from the Balkans, prepared to launch an attack. At the same time, fifty thousand tsarist Fifth and Ninth Army troops advanced into the sixty-kilometer gap between Habsburg First and Fourth armies, while two Russian corps deployed at First Army's eastern flank area and attacked Fourth Army's rear echelon positions, exposed after Fourth Army's drastic and sudden change of front direction to assist the embattled Third Army. Russian forces threatened First Army with encirclement. Fourth Army was attacked by the tsarist Fifth Army that it wrongly believed it had defeated at the Battle of Komorav. By September 5, the Russian Third and Eighth armies had reached the Habsburg defensive positions west of Lemberg along the Vereszyca River. Battle raged along most of the front as both sides attempted to outflank the other north of Rava Russka, northwest of Lemberg, as tsarist military pressure dramatically increased. Meanwhile, tsarist Third and Eighth armies repelled repeated Habsburg attempted attacks along the Dniester River front between September 6 and 11. In the interim, General Boroević, earlier commander of Third Army VI Corps, became the commander of the luckless

Third Army. Its initial commander was cashiered. Boroević restored discipline to the unfortunate army.[15]

General Conrad, as so often during the war, failed to recognize his troops' horrendous physical and morale condition or their seriously decreased battlefield effectiveness. He unrealistically anticipated that his exhausted and demoralized Third and Second Army troops had sufficiently rehabilitated after the September 2 Lemberg battle. Unfortunately, his troops' conditions precluded launching a successful major counterattack or even initiating a major offensive. The Russian menace forced Conrad to contemplate having to defend the Carpathian Mountain passes against enemy attempts to traverse the mountains to gain egress onto the Hungarian plains to knock Austria-Hungary out of the war. Fortress Przemyśl, the Habsburgs' San River bulwark protecting against egress into the Carpathian Mountains, now assumed a critical role in the Dual Monarchy's military fate. Citadel troops had the mission to delay, or bind, as many advancing tsarist forces as possible, even if encircled, to relieve pressure from the reeling field armies.[16]

Russian forces conquered Zamosc on September 6 as the increasingly outnumbered Habsburg First Army right flank troops recoiled from enormous enemy pressure. After First Army's X Corps lines were pierced, tsarist Ninth and Fourth armies prepared to hurl that army back across the Galician frontier in early September. Further east, the bulk of the reputedly defeated tsarist Fifth Army crushed the weak Habsburg Fourth Army XIV Corps defensive screen in the Komarov area, then rapidly advanced against the now exposed Habsburg Fourth Army's rear echelon positions. Fourth Army flanks had become vulnerable when its troops shifted south to assist the imperiled Third Army.

On September 7, Conrad ordered Second Army to launch an offensive south of Lemberg, leaving a two-corps defensive force to protect its eastern flank ranks below the Dniester River. Meanwhile, as Fourth Army units retreated, they lost half their officer corps and one-quarter of their troop numbers, while the army's movements expanded the gap to seventy kilometers between it and First Army. Nevertheless, Fourth, Third, and Second Habsburg armies had finally established a consolidated front as the Russians unleashed a major onslaught between Rava Russka and the high terrain east of the Vereszyca River.

In the interim, Foreign Minister Berchtold contacted Conrad relative to his allegations that General Moltke failed to fulfill German prewar "obligations," thus Habsburg forces received the brunt of Russian offensive efforts. This had resulted in severe casualties and evacuation of East Galicia, the Bukovina and the loss of Lemberg. Conrad insisted that early Habsburg victories were sacrificed when First and Fourth armies had to retreat to the San River line, tsarist armies in hot pursuit. Hungarian Minister President Tisza also supported Conrad's claim of alleged lack of Allied cooperation on the Habsburg front.

Fourth Army, instead of striking the anticipated exposed Russian flank positions, launched what became a frontal assault. Second Army units also attacked south of Lemberg, on terrain perfectly suited for tsarist defensive action. Meanwhile, Russian Third Army and Habsburg Fourth Army continued their increasingly bloody stalemate. Ultimately, Fourth Army was almost surrounded, while further north two Russian armies threatened to crush Habsburg First Army forces between them.

On September 8 brutal battle continued as Habsburg troops desperately attempted to stem Russian assaults, but First Army had to initiate a retreat toward the San River, with Russian Fourth and Ninth armies in hot pursuit. Tsarist troops also continued their advance into the expanding gap between First and Fourth armies. Russian Eighth Army units now threatened to encircle Third and Second Army forces, while Russian Third and Fifth armies continued pressuring the Habsburg Fourth Army.

In his memoirs, Conrad claimed that on September 8 his Fourth, Third and Second armies had successfully launched an offensive in the Lemberg area to relieve the enemy pressure against Habsburg First and Fourth armies. He blamed the campaign's subsequent failure on various scapegoats, including the demoralized and battle-weary troops that could not deliver the victory he so desperately sought. Conrad ignored the fact that his offensive plans did not fit either the military situation or the horrendous conditions that the soldiers suffered. Not understanding his troops' capabilities became a major Conrad weakness throughout the war.

During the August and September 1914 chaotic fighting both Russian and Austro-Hungarian troops repeatedly plundered Galician villages. Horses, cows and birds were either requisitioned or stolen. Troops from both sides ransacked deserted and occupied homes. Habsburg troops discarded their equipment to lessen the weight they had to bear and ravaged vegetable fields for food to satisfy their hunger as their supply system failed to maintain food deliveries.

Also during the Habsburg retreat, some 250,000–300,000 refugees fled Galicia and the Bukovina before Russian troops arrived. Habsburg military units, in a desperate attempt to halt the enemy advance, burned farms and destroyed railroads and crops to deprive the enemy of supplies. The Russians removed people, machinery, grain and cattle and destroyed bridges, railroad locomotives and oil wells as they retreated during 1915. While the Western front settled into trench warfare, on the much larger and fluid Eastern front millions of people became exposed to the movement of troops. Military forces dominated the conquered territories initiating economic exploitation, which eventually destroyed popular goodwill toward both antagonists.

On September 9, the mistakenly believed defeated Russian Fifth Army recaptured Komarov, seriously threatening Fourth Army's exposed left flank positions and moved into the gap between Habsburg First and Fourth armies. Tsarist Fourth and Ninth armies continued their methodical and irresistible advance against Habsburg First Army positions, which forced that isolated army to retreat rapidly to south of Krasnik, scene of its earlier triumph. The retreating troops abandoned artillery pieces, the wounded and many prisoners of war in the hasty retreat, as the entire front threatened to collapse. This also created a large gap to the main Habsburg forces, negatively impacting other Habsburg army actions. The threatened envelopment of Third Army near Rava Russka, and Fourth Army shift toward that location, and the increasing threat to Fourth Army rear echelon positions finally convinced Conrad that further Habsburg offensive efforts would be pointless. All four Habsburg armies faced the threat of being outflanked, while many units reported the loss of three-quarters of their troop strength while desperately short of supplies. Frontal attacks in dense formations encountered devastating artillery and machine-gun fire, halting all attempts to advance.

In the interim, tsarist forces smashed into Fourth Army's II Corps, reducing its troop stand from fifty thousand to ten thousand troops, and severed First Army's supply lines and potential retreat routes to the San River encircling that army's flank positions. A decoded Russian radio broadcast alerted Fourth Army command to its potential mortal threat.[17] Simultaneously, Russian pressure intensified along the Carpathian Mountain foothills and Fortress Przemyśl. Fourth Army shifted its movement toward Rava Russka, but meanwhile a seventy-four-kilometer gap appeared between Fourth Army's left flank units and First Army. This threatened the Habsburg retreat to the San River, but there were no troops to insert into this area. In the meantime, Russian Ninth Army entered the battle during the second week of September, tilting the balance in favor of the Russians.

Nevertheless, by the evening of September 9, Second and Third armies and a major portion of Fourth Army had commenced a slow advance toward Lemberg, but the effort collapsed within twelve miles of its objective. The exhausted troops could do no more. Meanwhile, the unanticipated First Army left flank retreat placed all four Habsburg armies in a critical situation. However, the Habsburg Second Army attack surprisingly forced a tsarist Eight Army retreat, enabling the attacking army to briefly advance toward Lemberg. However, Second and Third Army operations lacked necessary and critical coordination, while Third Army's futile frontal attacks merely produced additional casualties as the enemy crushed Habsburg efforts piecemeal. Habsburg infantry forces again did not receive vital artillery support, which increased their casualties from enemy artillery fire. The troops' demoralization continued as they had long lost faith in their higher commanders.

Tsarist Fifth Army units now penetrated between the two northern Habsburg armies. Overpowering tsarist firepower easily repulsed Fourth Army counterattacks, until Russian troops enveloped Fourth Army's flank and rear echelon positions, resulting in the decisive second battle of Lemberg in the area of Rava Russka.

By September 10, General Conrad finally acknowledged that his offensive effort to reconquer Lemberg had failed. Overwhelming Russian troops continued to threaten to encircle First Army's left flank positions and cut off the army's main retreat route to Fortress Krakow. When First Army troops retreated, the second Lemberg battle terminated. The Russians pursued the defeated First Army. First and Fourth armies, threatened by the tsarist advance between the two armies, retreated to the San River. Fourth Army troops had to defend against enemy vanguard units as they fought their way back to the San River and anticipated safety. The Russian Third Army renewed its offensive in the Rava Russka area. Meanwhile, Conrad had ordered First Army to retreat its forces distant from the major battles occurring at Lemberg. His Fourth, Third and Second armies suffered from extreme supply difficulties.

Habsburg officer, noncommissioned officer and professional soldier casualties had been catastrophic, while most reserve officers that replaced them proved incapable of fulfilling their duties. The professional officer and troop losses could not be adequately or rapidly replaced nor restore the effectiveness of the original army. Several mixed nationality units were accused of not fulfilling their duty in battle, while some soldiers were executed for dereliction of duty. Multiple Ruthenian civilians were hanged for reputedly aiding the enemy, including many innocent people. A mayor who had brutalized wounded Habsburg soldiers was also executed. As a result of the enormous casualties, Habsburg regimental troop stands now averaged the equivalent of two weak battalions (normally 1,000 soldiers). Some regiment troop numbers dropped to 1,400, 800, 400 and even fewer troops out of the original 4,000-plus complements. All infantry units desperately required reinforcements, while diseases such as dysentery and cholera decimated the ranks.[18] Diarrhea became a major problem after soldiers drank unsanitary water.

On September 10, Conrad prepared a telegram to the German High Command pleading for the deployment of troops to the Galician war theater as soon as they became available. He never transmitted the message, to avoid revealing the terrible condition of his army. Brusilov's forces moved toward the Grodek–Vereszyca line, but the Russians encountered serious difficulties with logistics; as mentioned, this related to the difference in railroad track gauges between Russia and Austria-Hungary. The Russians had to utilize the captured Habsburg railroad materials for supply purposes.

On the morning of September 11, the Habsburg military situation worsened even further, because tsarist pressure forced First and Fourth armies to continue to retreat. The Russians threatened to break through their front lines and into their rear echelon positions. Thus, the decisive seventeen-day battle in Galicia terminated. Aerial reconnaissance revealed the threat of a vast tsarist encirclement maneuver, forcing Fourth Army to rapidly retreat further. Lacking training for retrograde movement as Habsburg troops began to retreat, entire units were torn to ribbons, adding multiple casualties. Almost all infantry companies were either half strength or less.

Habsburg troops had travailed for two weeks under terrible conditions along the thirty-mile front extending between Grodek and Rava Russka. All armies and supply columns were forced onto the few available roads while being hotly pursued by tsarist forces. Fourth Army, suddenly recoiling from the threat of being enveloped, destroyed huge amounts of food, supplies and ammunition in the Rava Russka area before retreating. The army troop stand had dropped to ten thousand soldiers. Half of the officers and a majority of troops had either become casualties or surrendered to the enemy. Morale had collapsed; the troops were now apathetic and despondent.

Conrad noted in his memoirs during late afternoon September 11:

> The advance of the Second and Third armies had brought no effective decision. On the contrary, the risk of a breakthrough ... behind the left wing of the Fourth Army threatened to place it in a catastrophic situation ... In the circumstances there was only one course of action to be taken with all speed, break off the battle and draw all the armies behind the San River.[19]

The transport of wounded troops and refugees blocked the few available roads, while the last-moment retreat prevented a catastrophe particularly for Habsburg Fourth Army. If the Russians had attempted, they could easily have broken through the Habsburg front because the battered army possessed no reserve forces. The rainy weather conditions made the situation even more hazardous for the retreating troops.

The demoralized troops, however, could not defend the San River line once they reached it, because they desperately required rehabilitation following the long 150-kilometer retrograde movement during persistent inclement weather conditions and enemy pressure. The high San River water levels saved the Habsburg Army from possible immediate destruction, allowing it to continue its retrograde movement and ultimately to establish tenable defensive positions. As Austro-Hungarian units retreated, the army desperately required immediate German support. The pursuing Russian forces, however, were also exhausted and their supply lines had become greatly overextended. Both armies' units had to be reorganized, resupplied and reinforced to fill the seriously depleted ranks before launching new offensive operations.

Unbeknownst to Conrad, on September 11, the Germans suffered their fateful and shattering defeat at the Battle of the Marne, destroying the fulfillment of a rapid German "Schlieffen Plan" victory. That historic defeat signified that major German Army units could not be transferred soon to the Eastern theater to assist the battered Habsburg troops. Unaware of the debacle, General Conrad telegraphed German headquarters emphasizing that he had to retreat to the San River line because of the serious threat to his northern flank positions and supply lines. Since his earlier request for two army corps to deploy to the Fortress Przemyśl area had been denied, he now requested that such units be transported to the Fortress Krakow area, because it was much too late for the former. He also complained again that if his ally had deployed the promised troop support during the initial campaign, a major Eastern front victory could have been achieved. He further asserted that when the German Eighth Army redeployed to counter the second invading Russian force at the Masurian Lakes following the Tannenberg battle, it allowed *Stavka* to deploy additional forces against Austro-Hungarian troops. He claimed this forced the Habsburg retreat to the San River. When notified that the Russian First Army had almost been destroyed at the Masurian Lakes, General Conrad desperately hoped that German forces would finally assist his reeling army. Fourth Army retreated southward toward the San River from the Rava Russka battlefield. Conrad's order for the retreat was issued at 5:30 p.m. that day. The Russians did not detect the beginning of the Habsburg rearward movement while they destroyed bridges over the river as they retreated.

The decisive Habsburg battle defeat resulted in the loss of most of Galicia, part of the Bukovina and many professional soldiers, which could never be qualitatively replaced. During their hasty retreat, Habsburg forces also destroyed or abandoned irreplaceable troops, horses, railroad rolling stock, ammunition, food supplies and artillery pieces.

As Habsburg troops rapidly retreated on September 12, tsarist Third Army units began to approach the Fortress Przemyśl environs. Russian units initially only attacked the eastern fortress group to divert Habsburg attention and cause the redeployment of citadel reserve units to that specific area. Simultaneously, tsarist forces began to encircle the forty-eight-kilometer fortress circumference. Habsburg Third Army's mission became to prevent tsarist attacks against the fortress and its Jaroslau and Sienava defensive bridgeheads, while First and Fourth armies were to prevent a major tsarist crossing of the San River. Second Army redeployed in the southern Fortress Przemyśl area. Meanwhile, German High Command notified Conrad that German troops would soon be transported to the Fortress Krakow area. The Habsburg defeat in Galicia raised German concern because industrial Silesia could now be outflanked from the south.

Enormous potholes wrecked supply wagons, and overexertion, the lack of feed and being overworked led to the death of tens of thousands of horses. On many occasions, supplies were either deserted or captured by the enemy. Meanwhile, battle rapidly exhausted the troops as morale spiraled downward due to the devastation of the Habsburg formations.

Commencing in mid-September, four weeks of steady rain battered troops on both sides and disease took a heavy toll on civilians and troops alike. Dysentery, typhoid, fever and flu struck as famine became a major problem because of the lack of farmworkers and destroyed farmlands in the formerly rich Galician agricultural areas. The number of orphans skyrocketed as fathers died in battle and mothers succumbed to disease.

As inclement weather conditions continued, on September 13 supply trains deployed in the middle of retreat movements created chaos. Retreating, exhausted and starving, Fourth Army troops were rendered incapable of battle. The next day, the Germans announced that they would deploy their newly formed nine-division-strong Ninth Army near Fortress Krakow. German command feared the increasing possibility of the collapse of the Habsburg armies and the potential major threat to the German industrial province of Silesia.

The question of Allied command relations quickly arose as to whether the supporting German forces would be under Habsburg command, since they represented the vast majority of Central Power Eastern front forces. General Hindenburg, commander of German Eastern front operations, outranked both General Conrad and nominal Habsburg commander Archduke Friedrich. Hindenburg had also become an overnight German hero because of the victories at Tannenberg and the Masurian Lakes, while Habsburg forces had been soundly defeated in their opening Lemberg campaigns. General Hindenburg's superior rank and sudden popularity ensured that the German Army retained its autonomy on the Eastern front. The Austro-Hungarian attempt to place German troops under Habsburg authority failed, a most costly mistake for the Central Powers.

Russian troops had crossed the lower San River area on September 14, again threatening to encircle First Army forces because of the extensive riverfront length the Habsburg Army had to defend and its rapidly declining troop numbers. Tsarist troops, meanwhile, pressed relentlessly westward until they reached the Carpathian Mountain chain.

Most retreating Austro-Hungarian troops, slogging through rain and mud, had retired behind the San River by September 15. Chaos continued in Fourth Army ranks with multiple units lacking officers and the troops described as walking skeletons. Supply trains often could not move because of the terrible road conditions and multiplying dead horses. The inclement weather and cold temperatures demoralized the troops as well as increased sick calls as sharp criticism of Conrad's leadership escalated in the army and Vienna.

When the armies retreated over the Dunajec River, forty-five March battalions replaced a portion of the enormous casualties. These replacement troops were of far lesser quality. The Imperial Army had been destroyed while Fourth Army lost 70 percent of its officer corps. As early as September 1914, the Habsburg Army was described as a people's militia commanded by multiple incompetent generals.

Tsarist frontlines stabilized east of the Dunajec River and along the Carpathian Mountain foothills. Eleven Russian Third Army infantry divisions besieged Fortress Przemyśl late in the month, while Eighth Army deployed into the Carpathian Mountains. Soon a new tsarist Eleventh Army, second- and third-line soldiers with some territorial troops, assumed the siege effort.

As Habsburg Third Army units attained the Fortress Przemyśl vicinity after some troops panicked on September 16, Conrad ordered his troops to avoid decisive battle until reinforcing German troops arrived. The weary troops must establish a solid defensive front line, but under no condition could First Army be pressed further south. The Habsburg armies had retreated into the narrow area between the Vistula River and Carpathian Mountains, while some troops retreated to the Dunajec River area with enemy cavalry forces in close pursuit.

General Eric Falkenhayn, new chief of the German General Staff, notified Conrad that four corps and one cavalry division would be ready for transfer to his front within a week. Habsburg armies therefore withdrew to the proximity of the area where the German troops would deploy. The threat of a Russian invasion into Hungary drew Berlin's attention to the potentially disastrous situation relative to Romania. German diplomats suggested that their ally cede the Transylvanian region of Suczava to obtain active Romanian cooperation in the war effort. As General Moltke's replacement after his collapse during the Marne battle, General Falkenhayn stated:

> The direct cooperation of Germany in the Austro-Hungarian-Russian war is now in force. The intervention of German forces could ensue after a decision in the west is gained. It is most significant, however, to obtain a great decision as soon as possible to preserve Hungary and Transylvania before a Russian intervention. To achieve this before winter requires active Rumanian cooperation. Thence all must be done to achieve this.[20]

Romanian troops could easily invade Transylvania without encountering resistance, because few Habsburg troops were available to halt them. Conrad also had to accept the fact that Bulgaria and Romania refrained from intervening as allies because of the continuing Russian battlefield successes against Habsburg forces.

General Conrad realized that only decisive battlefield success against Russia could encourage Romanian military cooperation, but if tsarist troops continued their impressive battlefield successes, that country could enter the war against Austria-Hungary. By mid-September, as Habsburg troops retreated and the Romanians learned of the German Marne defeat, Conrad insisted that Foreign Minister Berchtold clarify the diplomatic situation with Bucharest, while he continued to attempt to obtain Romanian armed assistance. On September 17, as two tsarist armies harassed the retreating First Army, Russian troops constructed bridges over the San River, which threatened any chance of the Habsburg Army establishing a solid defensive stand along that waterway. That forced General Conrad to order further retreat.

On September 18, 1914 the first serious meeting commenced between Austro-Hungarian and German military commanders. Generals Conrad and Eric Ludendorff initially disagreed on the next potential joint offensive operation as Habsburg troops had withdrawn into the Carpathian Mountains. General Falkenhayn continued to insist that a major military effort on the Eastern front had to await a decision in the Western theater because of the Ypres campaign (the "Race to the Sea").

German diplomats maintained pressure on Vienna, proclaiming that Romania's assistance could produce victory over Russia; therefore, Vienna should make territorial sacrifices to obtain that result. However, the Habsburg special envoy in Bucharest, Count Ottokar Czernin, reported that the Russian military successes discouraged Romania from siding with the Habsburgs. In fact, Romanian public opinion now demanded war against the Dual Monarchy. Envoy Czernin advised Vienna to offer a portion of the Bukovina province to Romania, and immediately announce extensive Hungarian political concessions to the three million Transylvanian Romanians under Hungarian rule. These concessions might influence the former ally to join the Central Powers. However, if such concessions were not initiated, the Romanians would grow increasingly hostile, but the Dual Monarchy military attaché in Bucharest reported that any offer of territorial concessions would be construed as Habsburg military weakness.

The overwhelming Russian victory in Galicia provided a sorely needed tsarist morale boost to counterbalance the East Prussian battlefield disasters at Tannenberg and the Masurian Lakes. German leaders continued to deplore Vienna's failure to cede territory to Romania, but Viennese diplomats focused their attention on Bulgaria since it appeared increasingly unlikely that either Italy or Romania would actively join the Central Powers. Meanwhile, General Ludendorff refuted Conrad's charges of the lack of German military assistance, arguing that German forces could not have attacked toward Siedlce with two Russian armies, composed of twenty-nine infantry divisions, assaulting their flank positions. He acknowledged that General Moltke had promised to deploy twelve regular infantry divisions and five reserve divisions in East Prussia, but the five reserve units could not be deployed when Italy failed to fulfill its Triple Alliance obligations.

On September 21, Conrad ordered his troops to continue their retrograde movement to the Dunajec River. The retreating troops abandoned many artillery pieces, rifles and other critical equipment. In three weeks, the Habsburgs had lost many of their best officers, noncommissioned officers and regular soldiers that could not be replaced in quality. Casualties reached 100,000 dead, 220,000 wounded, 120,000 prisoners of war, as well as 400 artillery pieces surrendered. Many units had fallen to 50–75 percent of their original strength, a deadly blow to Habsburg arms.

On September 28 German Ninth Army troops reached the Vistula River, marching on roads in terrible condition. Supply wagons and artillery pieces sank to their axles; the troops exhausted after marching 120 miles in nine days.

The first phase of the war had ended on the Austro-Hungarian front. The Western front Marne battle, the two battles of Lemberg and the German victories at Tannenberg and the Masurian Lakes terminated that phase at almost the same time. Suffering the two Lemberg battle defeats, Habsburg forces could not launch an offensive without German assistance. The next phase of the 1914 campaigns rapidly approached! But first we must visit the Serbian front for those events.

Serbian Campaigns 1914

During the 1880s and 1890s the Habsburg General Staff did not consider Serbia a serious military threat to the Dual Monarchy. In 1891 General Oskar Potiorek planned a defensive strategy to be implemented along the Serbian frontiers and rivers, while a Habsburg offensive would conquer the capital Belgrade, and then troops would advance into the strategic Morava Valley to attempt to encircle the Serbian armed forces from the north and west between the Drina River and that significant valley. This two-edged strategy entailed the defense of Habsburg territorial possessions, and a rapid defeat of Serbia.[1]

Austro-Hungarian Great Power prestige played a paramount role in 1890s military planning. Serbia continued to be regarded as an insignificant military opponent during the final decades of the century, nor was Russia considered a serious threat. Its latter nineteenth-century expansion into the Far East appeared to present no major necessity for revising earlier planning for a War Case "Russia." The result was that the Habsburg military focus remained on War Case "Serbia," to which twelve divisions would be mobilized in three strategic deployment areas, encompassing the frontier along the Sava and Danube Rivers, to seize Belgrade.[2]

In an 1894 *Denkschrift* (memorandum), Habsburg Intelligence Bureau officers assumed that in a military conflict Serbian forces would invade Bosnia or defend against a Habsburg attack. The Serbians could mobilize seven infantry divisions and a separate brigade. Habsburg forces would deploy rapidly, because it was anticipated that the Serbians could mobilize their forces in two weeks. The Habsburg General Staff considered its own training, armaments and morale far superior to the potential enemy forces. Additional planning resulted in one infantry division protecting against unrest in Bosnia-Herzegovina, and another protecting that frontier. The Habsburg deployment was planned along the Drina River frontier about 170 kilometers from the Sava River and 160 kilometers from Belgrade. Habsburg forces would rapidly cross the Danube River, but if Russia intervened, it would automatically become the major opponent. Russia, however, remained involved in its imperialistic endeavors in Asia, thus 1897 and 1898 plans for a War Case "Russia" remained the basis for planning until 1906, while shifting the major Habsburg deployment to eastern Galicia in a conflict with the tsarist regime.

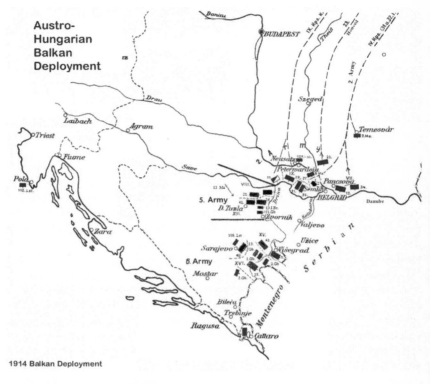

1914 Balkan Deployment

Map 5   *1914 Balkan deployment*

In a Balkan war, the main Habsburg offensive force would attack across the Sava and Danube Rivers, while a secondary group advanced over the Sava and Drina Rivers in the area of Visegrad. The invading force had to be powerful enough to achieve rapid victory. But one major question continued to haunt Habsburg Operations Bureau planners: What would happen if an invasion commenced against Serbia, then Russia intervened? That never-to-be-resolved critical question involved the timing of a tsarist intervention in a Habsburg conflict against Serbia. When that scenario occurred in August 1914 the Habsburg campaign ended in disaster, as will be described.

In 1906 the Habsburg Operations Bureau began to contemplate launching a Balkan offensive over the Drina River, replacing the earlier planned Sava–Danube River crossings. This entailed serious disadvantages relative to the difficulties to be encountered crossing the Drina River banks. Habsburg operational planners still paid scant attention to the possibility of Italy or Russia intervening in a Balkan conflict. Russia's disastrous defeat in the

1904–1905 Russo-Japanese War signified that, at least temporarily, it would not be a major threat to Germany and Austria-Hungary.

Conrad's 1908 military plans called for the advancement of Habsburg forces into Serbia from the west at the Sava and Danube Rivers. Having crossed the rivers troops would advance through the Jadar region to Valjevo. At the end of 1909, during the post 1908–1909 Bosnian Crisis, war planning anticipated a maximum War Case "Balkan," while between 1909 and 1912, it again could be assumed that neither Italy nor Russia would intervene if Austria-Hungary invaded Serbia. Between 1909 and 1914 planning increasingly emphasized invading Serbia from the west rather than through Belgrade, the historical direction. However, in 1911/1912 the question became whether Habsburg troops could rapidly seize the key Morava Valley, thus attention reverted to invading Serbia from two different directions, between the Drina and Morava Valleys to attempt to encircle the main Serbian troop concentrations. Ten infantry divisions and one cavalry division were deemed necessary to achieve a rapid and successful Balkan campaign. If Russia intervened, only minimal troops would be deployed against Serbia; major forces had to be concentrated against the far more powerful tsarist forces. It remained critical for the Dual Monarchy to maintain its prestige as a Balkan and great European power, so it continued planning for launching a rapid campaign to defeat Serbia before Russia could decisively intervene in a conflict. A military confrontation with Serbia became increasingly possible after the 1912–1913 Balkan Wars. Belgrade continued to attract attention as a military objective because of its political and strategic significance. Once the capital was captured, Habsburg forces could rapidly advance into the strategic Morava Valley. Habsburg operational planning, however, continued to emphasize the advantages of encircling Serbian forces from the north and west, launching an offensive across the Drina River to rapidly defeat Serbian forces deployed there.

Habsburg Second Army, the powerful Habsburg swing force, would attack across the Sava and Danube Rivers, while Fifth Army crossed the rivers between the two waterways. Sixth Army would deploy along the Bosnia-Herzegovina frontier area from Visegrad to the Bay of Cattaro. Remaining Habsburg troops would deploy in the Sarajevo and Mostar areas.[3] Sixth Army had the mission to secure and defend Bosnia-Herzegovina, and neutralize enemy forces as far east of Sarajevo as possible.

A 1913 Habsburg war school study emphasized that an offensive should be launched through Belgrade to achieve a rapid success, as strongly advocated by multiple military leaders in 1914. Three potential invasion routes existed into the Serbian interior. Advancing east of Belgrade Habsburg troops could advance to the Morava Valley, or to the west and south of Belgrade, to the Kolubara River toward Valjevo. The third would occur from the northwest quarter of Serbia to cross the Sava River to Sabac to converge on Valjevo from the opposite direction. The Serbian military might not defend its capital, instead concentrating further south, or retreat to Nis thus prolonging the campaign and extending Habsburg lines of communication. This scenario would be disastrous if Russia entered the war.

In 1914, General Potiorek's Balkan campaign plan, War Case "Balkan," ignored several major factors. First, the rugged and mountainous terrain to be traversed lacked sufficient roads for successful logistical purposes, a most significant potential problem. Further, Fifth and Sixth armies, critical for military success, were deployed over seventy miles apart, thus at critical times in battle they could not support each other. This also limited the mission of Second Army, basically the swing B-Group, the most powerful force to be deployed on the Serbian front, and lessened the chances of achieving military success. The plan also ignored the Serbian troops' 1912–1913 Balkan Wars combat experience, and that they would vigorously defend their territory. Thus, General Potiorek's plans contained elements that raised the serious possibility of failure from the beginning.

To the military advantage of the Serbians they had learned from the early Balkan Wars mistakes, something Habsburg commanders did not initially consider with their own troops, resulting in many casualties. Also important was that the Serbian Army had been weakened by having to occupy its newly conquered territories after its Balkan War casualties and loss of significant amounts of ammunition and equipment, particularly rifles.

On the Habsburg side the multiple 1914 Austro-Hungarian Army deficiencies again included lack of critical firepower, because most artillery pieces were obsolete and numerically inadequate, while the Serbians possessed some modern rapid-fire French medium-artillery guns. All Habsburg field-artillery weapons, except the M80-mm pieces, were outmoded. Deficient tactical training and doctrine and the general lack of artillery and infantry cooperation would spell disaster in the 1914 Balkan campaigns.[4] As the German liaison officer at Habsburg Supreme Command headquarters later stated, Habsburg armed forces were adequate for a Balkan campaign, but not to fight a great power like Russia.[5]

The final 1914 Habsburg War Case "Balkan" plan had Fifth Army launching an offensive over the lower Drina River, its major objective still to attain Valjevo. The swing B-Group (basically the Second Army) would cross the Sava River and launch an offensive in conjunction with Fifth Army. Sixth Army, leaving minimal forces to prevent a Montenegrin invasion, had to defend Bosnia-Herzegovina, then advance toward Uzice. Other troop formations would cross the Drina and Sava Rivers to crush enemy resistance advancing into the Belgrade–Valjevo–Uzice area. Combined Habsburg forces would then drive into the heart of Serbia.

The Second and Fifth armies' initial objective to envelop opposing enemy forces required conquering northwest Serbia, extending to Kolubara. Second Army, eleven infantry divisions and five brigades, would cross the Danube

River to deploy along the entire length of the Sava and Danube Rivers.[6] Sixth Army would support them by advancing toward Uzice, eventually the Banat, to then occupy the Morava Valley. The three Habsburg armies would be separated by three major rivers, so they had to rapidly overcome multiple terrain impediments. Sixth Army, based in southeast Bosnia-Herzegovina, required more time to be deployed, because of its inadequate railroad situation and extensive deployment area. This became a critical factor in the initial 1914 Balkan campaign. Habsburg Supreme Command initially anticipated that Romania and Italy would mobilize, according to prewar treaty obligations.

Fifth Army concentrated its troops along the Drina River between Zvornik and the Sava River. The majority of its VIII Corps troops originated from the South Slavic regions of the Dual Monarchy. XIII Corps, considered one of the Habsburgs' premier units, was based in Croatia. The army consisted of seventy-nine thousand troops.

Sixth Army was composed of the XV and XVI Corps mountain troops and five mountain brigades. Second Army's VII Corps, with 42,000 soldiers, provided the largest invasion troop contingent;[7] the total troop numbers reached 240,000 soldiers. Second Army would launch a diversionary effort to support Fifth Army efforts. Lesser-combat-prepared *Landsturm* and March formations added 114,000 additional troops to the invasion force.

Three major battles were fought during the opening Balkan campaign on Mount Cer, along the Drina River, and in the Kolubara region. Fifth and Sixth Army troops invaded across the rivers into extremely rugged terrain, but Sixth Army deployed too many of its troops to defend Bosnia-Herzegovina. The mountainous terrain provided excellent defensive positions for the combat-experienced Serbian defenders, and General Putnik utilized it advantageously.

Only three railroad lines extended to Serbia's western frontier, seriously compounding the logistical situation. Horses and wagons had to transport supplies inland. A far better plan would have been to attack north through Belgrade, the historical route, directly toward the Morava Valley. This would have placed Habsburg troops on fairly level terrain before they reached much more difficult areas. Eight railroad lines led to the Serbian frontiers at the Sava and Danube Rivers; one traversed the entire stretch of the vital Morava Valley. The Habsburg strategy not utilized during the 1914 campaigns produced military success during the Central Power October 1915 invasion of Serbia.

Serbian armed forces consisted of three armies and one army group; the main force, the First and Second armies, deployed eight infantry divisions and one cavalry division in the country's central area between the Morava and Kolubara Valleys. Initially some units provided frontier security at the Danube–Sava River fronts. The Serbian Third Army, two infantry divisions and smaller weak groups deployed at the Sava–Drina River front where the waterways connected. One infantry division and three smaller detachments deployed at Uzice and then extended their lines to the Montenegrin frontier.

This encompassed six first-line divisions consisting of ninety-six thousand troops, six second-level divisions of seventy-six thousand soldiers and a third levy of six divisions with a hundred thousand troops. Allied Montenegrin forces added forty thousand troops of questionable value.

Although historical argument has evolved about the topic, in some ways the Serbian Army was not prepared for the 1914 war, because it suffered from internal chaos, major casualty numbers and the significant loss of many weapons and ammunition that had to be replaced as a result of the 1912 and 1913 Balkan Wars. Shortages included rifles, machine guns and ammunition/artillery shells. Serbia possessed some superior medium-artillery pieces purchased from France. Belgrade depended upon France and Russia for military aid. The initially levied 180,000 main troops increased to 350,000 on mobilization with the call-up of reservists.[8]

Having mobilized several times during the recent previous years, the Serbian Army mission became to bind as many Habsburg forces as possible to weaken their troop numbers deployed against Russia in the event of a two-front war. If Habsburg forces launched an offensive into Serbia, a defensive stance would be maintained until the opportunity arose to counterattack either into Bosnia or Syrmia. Also, the Montenegrin Army lacked sufficient troop numbers to obtain a decision in Herzegovina, thus two-thirds of its soldiers would deploy in the Sandžak area and with forces in the Uzice region advance on Sarajevo.

Habsburg War Case "Balkan" fielded "Minimal Group Balkan" and "B Group," or seven corps, for the invasion into Serbia.[9] Fifth and Sixth armies concentrated in Bosnia-Herzegovina along the west Drina River branch, to advance to the Morava River Valley. Once Habsburg troops crossed the Drina River they advanced through marshy and mountainous terrain. Muddy roads in the area rendered the area nearly impassable, providing easily defensible mountain terrain for Serbian defenders.

The Balkan front troops' first mission was to defend the frontier and secure against an enemy attack. Frontier fortresses and the Sarajevo garrison must be defended, while the only railroad, a small-gauge one, provided the only logistical artery into Bosnia-Herzegovina–Dalmatia. Sixth Army's main operation direction became Visegrad–Uzice and through the Lim area. The Herzegovina and south Dalmatia fortresses would also help defend those areas.

Serbian strategy initially was defensive. General Putnik, with his thorough knowledge and familiarity of Serbian topography, understood his strategic goal was to protect the Morava–Jadar corridor. He masterfully adjusted to General Potiorek's plans and countered them accordingly during the three 1914 Balkan campaigns. He initially deployed all three Serbian armies far from the frontiers.

On July 23 Archduke Friedrich received command of the Balkan forces. On July 25 Second, Fifth and Sixth armies mobilized, consisting of eight corps or twenty-two infantry divisions, including mountain-trained troops.[10]

On July 24 the first reports of Serbian mobilization arrived. The following day the Serbians refused to accept all the terms of the Habsburg ultimatum, although they presented a conciliatory response. On July 25 Serbia fully mobilized and three days later its troops destroyed bridges across the Danube and Sava Rivers.

At midnight on July 26 Austro-Hungarian mobilization commenced. War was declared on July 28, as Emperor Wilhelm and General Moltke plaintively pleaded that Serbia be a secondary front and the main Habsburg military effort should be against Russia. Significantly, the Russians and Serbians gained a four-day advantage in mobilization and deployment times, which they utilized to their advantage. The next day Habsburg artillery fired on Belgrade. Then, on July 31, Conrad placed priority on the Balkan troop railroad transport versus a Russian deployment, when that country declared war; a fatal error. Conrad met with the Railroad Bureau commander later that night (July 31) to attempt to reverse War Case "B" to a War Case "R & B."

In the interim on July 27 Alarm Instructions took effect in Bosnia-Herzegovina–Dalmatia. Sixth Army received the mission to block the most important invasion routes, particularly the one through northeast Bosnia. This encompassed the 220-kilometer area south of the Sava River, which was protected by fifty-seven Habsburg infantry battalions and twenty artillery battalions.

Count Berchtold, Hungarian Minister President Tisza and General Potiorek desired a rapid victory against Serbia to gain Bulgaria, Romania, Italy or Turkey as allies. Conrad considered immediate Bulgarian participation vital, but its army had been seriously weakened during the 1912–1913 Balkan Wars. Berchtold demanded the greatest possible troop numbers deployed on the Balkan front, even if Russia became an opponent. On August 22, as military action commenced against Russia, Berchtold pressured Emperor Franz Joseph for General Potiorek to receive sole Balkan front command. Berchtold consistently opposed any weakening of troop numbers on that front, because of the potential political and military consequences for which he refused to accept responsibility. He understood that the Serbian threat to invade Bosnia-Herzegovina presented a potentially critical problem.

On July 31 War Case "Russia" became official, but orders remained to complete the Balkan deployment for a rapid defeat of Serbia. However, Serbian defeat depended upon neutral power assistance, particularly Bulgaria, which did not transpire. Second Army troops deployed to the Balkan front had been designated for the extreme eastern flank against Russia in a War Case "R." Its Balkan deployment essentially bared the Habsburg extreme right flank front, resulting in catastrophe as described in Chapter 3.

Conrad sought to end the Serbian campaign before the Russians became a serious threat. He was concerned about the potential effect on the morale of the monarchy's South Slavic populace. Thus Conrad initially refused to halt or diminish troop strengths for the Balkan front offensive operation until the situation on the Russian front became critical and disastrous defeat loomed.

General Potiorek's strategy encompassed defeating Serbian groups separately, as Conrad did on the Russian front. Potiorek anticipated Serbian troops would be deployed in the Belgrade area, northwest Serbia and in the Uzice and Lim area. Four to six Serbian divisions could be anticipated to be deployed in the Sarajevo area. Potiorek feared that the Serbians would attempt to seize Sarajevo and instigate a South Slav uprising that would create serious morale as well as material effects in the region and the overall war effort.

Habsburg Balkan forces must prevent the invasion of the monarchy and defend Bosnia-Herzegovina. Conrad and Potiorek agreed that this required a rapid offensive operation.

Only limited military actions transpired during the first week of the war, mostly in the Sandžak region along the southern border of Serbia and Montenegro. On August 1 Conrad reversed full War Case "Balkan" to War Case "Russia and Balkan," which should have signified that only Minimal Group Balkan forces would be deployed against Serbia. When that did not occur, it resulted in catastrophic military defeat on both fronts. Despite War Case "Russia," both Conrad and Potiorek attempted a rapid defeat of Serbia before the Second Army B-Group had to be redeployed to Galicia to counter Russia. Second Army received orders on August 6 (the day war was declared on Russia) to redeploy its forces to that front on August 18 when the railroad lines would be more favorable for troop transport. Only Conrad could approve Second Army Balkan front offensive action, thus General Potiorek immediately employed his connections with the emperor and his military chancellery to gain command of Second Army while its troops remained on the Balkan front. The removal of Second Army units drastically weakened Balkan front forces, and critically exposed Fifth Army's northern flank positions, resulting in disaster.

Italy declared its neutrality on August 3, while on August 6 Austria-Hungary declared war on Russia with troop transports commencing for "War Case B" on the tenth and thirteenth mobilization days. Troops defending Bosnia-Herzegovina had the mission to halt any threat emanating from the east or attempts to seize Sarajevo, but sufficient troop numbers also had to be available to launch a counterattack.

Sixth Army XV Corps deployed one infantry division toward Visegrad, while XVI Corps deployed five mountain brigades around Sarajevo, as well as the 18. Infantry Division. Then, on August 4, General Potiorek informed Conrad that the Sixth Army's main forces could not reach the Sarajevo front before August 13. The troops then required five days of marching to reach the Drina River, a fatal factor in the forthcoming campaign.

On August 3, three Serbian battalions crossed the Drina River into Bosnia-Herzegovina, capturing several towns near Visegrad. On the same day General Potiorek presented his campaign plans to Conrad, scheduled to commence on August 12, a catastrophic delay relative to military action against both Russia and Serbia.

Conrad originally planned that Second Army would prevent a Serbian invasion of Habsburg territory, but then Russia declared war. General Potiorek intended to utilize Second Army troops until their ordered redeployment to the Eastern front on August 18. Some troops disastrously became involved in battle, but received orders not to cross the Danube River. Generals Conrad and Potiorek's multiple counterproductive commands to Second Army created confusion during the campaign, partially motivated by personal and professional jealousy. However, the news that Second Army troops had to prepare to redeploy from the Balkan front by August 18 lessened the chances for Second and Fifth armies' cooperation.

Second Army redeployment to the Russian front significantly reduced the chances of a rapid military success against Serbia. When General Conrad rejected Potiorek's numerous requests to utilize Second Army forces in his campaign, Potiorek determined to launch the Balkan offensive as soon as possible. On August 6, General Böhm-Ermolli, the Second Army commander, learned of Potiorek's intention to seize Belgrade by August 10. He suggested launching a powerful demonstration, so his army did not remain idle during the initial Serbian invasion, confusing the already chaotic Balkan command situation. Conrad planned to send untrained *Landsturm* and March formation troops to replace Second Army units redeployed to the Northern front, while General Potiorek ordered bridge-crossing equipment and technical troops, rushed to the Second Army front. Some Second Army units crossed the river and attacked enemy positions at Sabac.

On August 5 Montenegro declared war on Austria-Hungary and commenced firing artillery barrages from Mount Lovćen against the key Bay of Cattaro naval station. The following day, Serbian and Montenegrin troops skirmished at towns inside Bosnia-Herzegovina, but because the entire Sixth Army was stationed in the provinces, they achieved little.

Until mid-August, Habsburg artillery consistently bombarded Serbian towns and cities. Between August 9 and 11, small Habsburg military units attempted to cross the lower Drina River under protective artillery fire to reconnoiter Serbian defensive positions.

General Potiorek assumed command of Fifth and Sixth armies on August 6 and received permission for Second Army diversionary military actions across the Sava River. On August 9, the Second Army commander telegraphed Conrad that he could not remain idle, because the entire Balkan campaign depended upon his army's active participation – that army's support was critical. Conrad permitted Second Army's diversionary activities west of

Sabac, but specifically ordered the Second Army commander not to launch an offensive action, because his forces had to soon be redeployed north.

Defensive operations commenced on the future Italian front on August 8, while indications abounded that Serbian and Montenegrin troops would attack against Sarajevo, which must be prevented. By August 10 the Serbians had deployed their main troops defensively in depth, planning to launch a counterattack when possible. Three Serbian armies concentrated in northern Serbia to counter an enemy threat from the west, with a group deployed at Uzice to protect their rear echelon positions from possible attack and to coordinate with the Montenegrin ally to invade Bosnia-Herzegovina. The reinforced Serbian Second Army would counter any Habsburg attack emanating from the north or west, while Third Army defended the Drina River line.

The role of neutral nations became critical between August 8 and 11. Habsburg leaders anticipated that Bulgaria would mobilize within a few days as Conrad considered it had to participate in the Balkan campaign for it to be successful. However, when the August 12 offensive was launched, both Conrad and Potiorek knew that Bulgaria would not participate in the operation.

When Habsburg troops crossed the Drina River, heavy fighting ensued. Potiorek ordered an offensive launched toward Visegrad and Sarajevo as a diversionary tactic, but the military situation remained murky as Habsburg troops crossed the Drina and Sava Rivers at several locations.

Habsburg Fifth Army advanced eastward toward Valjevo and the Jadar Valley. Then Fifth and Sixth armies were to attack toward Kragujevac in central Serbia to destroy the anticipated major enemy forces there. General Potiorek, however, failed to consider the rough mountainous terrain, the lack of usable roads and that the further his troops advanced the more difficult logistics would become. Cooperation between Second and Fifth armies remained critical as Second Army IV Corps units were drawn into battle at Sabac, a Serbian command and logistical center.

Fifth Army VIII Corps troops crossed the Drina River, advancing across marshy terrain. Its 9. Infantry Division quickly encountered Serbian infantry and artillery fire that delayed its advance. Its sister 21. *Landwehr* Infantry Division met stiff opposition as well, but could not cross until early evening. The troops were hampered by man-high cornfields and trees that camouflaged enemy infantry and artillery positions. *Cetniks*, Serbian irregular forces, often not wearing military uniforms, delayed movements and logistical support. Marshy terrain impeded movement, while Habsburg air reconnaissance missions failed because the terrain camouflaged Serbian positions.

Searing temperatures and lack of water supplies took a heavy toll on Habsburg troops as the supply system functioned inadequately. By nightfall 9. Infantry Division troops had advanced two kilometers, but 21. *Landwehr* Infantry Division remained on the riverbanks. Further north Second Army's IV Corps attempted to divert Serbian attention from the Drina River main

Habsburg operation by attacking Sabac, which achieved the only significant but unsatisfactory progress that day.

Sixth Army continued to concentrate its forces, but, as mentioned, could not cooperate with Fifth Army action for multiple days, being separated by some seventy miles. Logistical efforts proved overwhelming.

To summarize August 12–13 Balkan front events, Fifth Army units had not attained their starting positions, while Sixth Army remained unprepared for battle. Fifth Army fought an isolated battle, but attempts to reach Valjevo, the center of Serbian defenses in western Serbia, quickly stalled. Sixth Army belatedly prepared to launch an offensive toward distant Visegrad, across difficult mountain terrain. Neither army could rapidly assist the other, the assumption being that Second Army would bind the main Serbian force critical to achieving offensive success.

Three Habsburg armies crossed the Danube, Sava and Drina Rivers on August 12 in a semicircle configuration southeast, south and southwest of Belgrade. Second Army troops crossed the Sava and Drina Rivers and quickly seized Sabac, while further south some Sixth Army troops advanced against Montenegrin forces invading Bosnia and Herzegovina, traversing ridges and rugged terrain that lacked roads and railroads. Fifth and Sixth armies had not yet completed their assembly or established their logistical systems when they were ordered to advance in column formations through thick vegetation and two-meter-high cornfields. Bridge-crossing materials were available at only one site. Heavy Serbian artillery fire immediately struck them, as conflicting and counter-orders confused the Habsburg situation.

Fifth Army's right flank 42. Infantry Division crossed the Drina River at Zvornik against slight enemy opposition, then penetrated northeast through mountainous terrain toward the Serbian Third Army's exposed left flank positions, intending to swing north into the Jadar Valley. Malfunctioning telephones created serious communication problems. Serbian High Command was initially uncertain where the main Habsburg offensive would be launched, so Putnik did not commit the main Serbian forces.

Both sides' strategies quickly became evident. Potiorek prepared a pincer movement to attempt to encircle Serbian forces at Valjevo, sweeping through the Macvac Valley, right flank forces advancing into the Jader Valley. In the center of the advance line Mount Cer separated two Habsburg corps. Potiorek determined to seize Mount Cer to facilitate further progress. Serbian First Army units and 21. *Landwehr* Infantry Division rushed toward that location. Putnik realized that the main Habsburg attack would be launched by Fifth Army, with Second Army serving as a secondary front.

Putnik determined that the main Habsburg offensive effort would be toward Valjevo, thus he deployed his main forces accordingly, realizing that Habsburg Second Army Sabac front did not present a serious threat.

On August 14, Habsburg Fifth Army troops approached Valjevo in the Morava Valley, entering an area twelve miles long by four miles wide. Mount Cer, situated along the shortest advance route, dominated the Drina and Jadar Valleys' hills and ridges. Advancing troops, particularly *Landsturm* units, quickly became exhausted from the difficult uphill marches in stifling heat burdened with full field packs. The Habsburg troops' logistical situation steadily worsened the further they advanced; they increasingly lacked water, food and ammunition supplies. Meanwhile, Potiorek continued to utilize his connections to the emperor's military chancellery to make his Balkan command independent from Conrad.

Many Habsburg troops, particularly Fifth Army, lacked necessary mountain training, were ill-equipped and were armed with obsolete weapons. The lack of regular food and water supplies quickly manifested itself in the 95° heat because of the insurmountable logistical problems. Supply columns were often halted or delayed by Serbian irregular forces requiring additional security formations for protection.

The Habsburg offensive operation failed to achieve sufficient progress; its troops finding it difficult to advance through the man-high maize and trees. On August 16 Serbian troops successfully counterattacked Habsburg forces at Sabac, resulting in the August 16–19 Battle of the Jadar. The encounter did not affect the overall situation, except for heavy losses. On August 15 Habsburg troops reached the Jadar Valley and key Cer Planina, a range of hills along the Jadar Valley.

On August 20 Serbian Second and Third armies unexpectedly drove Fifth Army XIII Corps troops back across the Drina River. A surprised Potiorek learned that Fifth Army suddenly was in a critical situation. Serbian forces had attacked the army's center positions, initiating a life-and-death struggle, while a 29. Infantry Division setback at Sabac forced IV Corps to withdraw after being attacked in high maize, its troops suddenly caught in a crossfire.

Fifth Army troops had attempted to attain their key objective, Valjevo, by August 18, when Second Army had to redeploy units to the Russian front. Sixth Army troops finally arrived at the ordered upper Drina River area on August 20 to launch their offensive operation, but before all troops had reached their deployment area. On August 15, Fifth Army's 21. *Landwehr* Infantry Division, composed mostly of Czech troops and the only *Landwehr* division in the Balkan invasion forces, advanced up Mount Cer that dominated the surrounding Macva Plain and Jadar Valley. The inexperienced and exhausted troops were briefly halted by a fierce rainstorm during their long hot marches. The troops had received no food or water for two days when Serbian troops attacked them.

The next day, August 16, after a sixteen-kilometer march, Serbian forces attacked the division during a dark rainy night, while many of its soldiers slept. The exhausted troops had failed to establish listening posts, or initiate security measures, thus Serbian forces struck them unawares. Chaotic firefights erupted at point-blank range, Czech troops caught in a crossfire. Concentrated Serbian fire caused horrendous casualties as the hapless Czech soldiers were quickly overwhelmed, with chaos ensuing. Both sides sustained serious casualties, but particularly Habsburg officer ranks.

Two Serbian artillery batteries fired over open sights at close range, decimating the opposing helpless Czech troops. Habsburg artillery could not participate because its guns remained in rear echelon areas, or had been neutralized by enemy artillery fire. *Cetnik* forces harassed Habsburg troops when they began to retreat.

Lack of Habsburg infantry–artillery cooperation, continuing well into the war, worsened the ensuing confusion. Mutual exhaustion ultimately terminated the battle. Habsburg Infantry Regiment 28 positions rapidly collapsed as most officers succumbed to direct Serbian machine-gun fire. 21. *Landwehr* Infantry Division remnants, having sustained enormous casualty numbers, often in hand-to-hand combat, commenced a panicked retreat from the mountain. Neighboring 9. Infantry Division had to join the retrograde movement, which forced the entire Fifth Army to follow suit.

The demoralized 21. *Landwehr* Infantry Division soldiers retreated in disorder, lacking the necessary ammunition and supplies to fight an extended battle. Serbian troops and irregular formations pursued the retreating troops on August 17, resulting in further bloody battle. The 21. *Landwehr* Infantry Division had not been trained for its mission, consisting of many younger and middle-aged soldiers, mostly reservists, the majority not physically prepared for the hardships they encountered.

This first failed Balkan campaign had an enormous effect on Habsburg domestic politics. The plan that "War Case B" be successfully achieved before "War Case R" became effective resulted in the overhasty launching of the Fifth Army offensive to cover the distance that separated it from Sixth Army. That also affected the failure of the belated Sixth Army offensive. Its slow advance allowed the Serbians to hurl additional forces against Fifth Army, creating a difficult military situation for it. Sixth Army could not advance until August 20, but on August 12 Fifth Army had advanced.

Also on August 17, Habsburg Second Army right flank units were forced back toward Sabac. Sixth Army, after finally launching its offensive over its difficult terrain, also encountered problems during battle at Visegrad after some initial success. This forced that army to retreat over the Drina River on August 24. Potiorek had deployed only eight of his available nineteen divisions in the initial invasion attempt. Fifth Army's eighty thousand original troops suffered one-quarter casualties as General Potiorek blamed this initial Balkan front defeat on the failure of significant Second Army support. Specifically, the excessive loss of regular company and battalion-level officers could never be replaced. The Mount Cer disaster unsurprisingly damaged troop morale and cohesion.

Between August 18 and September 2 Montenegrin troops had to be driven out of Herzegovina. On August 20 Serbian Sandžak Army forces crossed the Drina River into Bosnia, while the Uzice Group crossed at Visegrad. Their mission was to reach Sarajevo and encourage a South Slav uprising.

In analyzing the disastrous initial Balkan operation, Habsburg troops rushed to attack regardless of the tactical situation. Contradictory orders and counterorders followed in rapid succession, negatively affecting the outcome of the battle. Troops, consisting of many ill-prepared *Landsturm* reserve formations, not prepared or intended to be utilized in combat, were hurled into battle, accelerating casualty figures. Nor had an efficient supply system been established. The offensive, launched in searing August heat, had failed to achieve significant progress when the Serbians launched a counterattack against Second Army troops at Sabac. A major factor resulted from the grievous Habsburg underestimation of the Serbian foe.[11]

On August 21 renewed battle at Sabac resulted in IV Corps remaining on the Balkan front, crossing the Sava River on August 23. Corps troops advancing in close column formation were struck by enemy crossfire, causing heavy losses, panic in the ranks and a serious decline in morale. Eventually Emperor Franz Joseph approved the transfer of IV Corps to the Russian front. When Second Army troops redeployed from the Balkan front it provided the enemy numerical superiority. Serbian troops forced a Habsburg retreat from Sabac, which terminated Potiorek's offensive efforts, it becoming a military and political catastrophe.

On August 20, Potiorek had demanded command of all remaining Second Army forces as one-third of its corps troops commenced transport to the Russian front. He insisted that if Second and Sixth armies did not immediately launch offensives it would result in catastrophic battlefield defeat. It could also negatively affect the monarchy's South Slavic peoples' allegiance. Conrad, however, refused Potiorek's request for further utilization of IV Corps and 29. Infantry Division to launch another attack. Conrad now did not possess full authority over the Balkan front command, because of General Potiorek's excellent connections to the imperial court.

On August 21, Potiorek persuaded General Bolfras, head of Franz Joseph's military chancellery, that his command become independent. The tragic results of this manifested itself quickly on the Eastern front where disaster struck in the two fateful battles of Lemberg. Potiorek's supporters, however, argued that a Habsburg defeat on the Balkan front would negatively affect neutral Bulgaria, Romania, possibly even Italy, thus, they would not ally to fight Serbia. Second Army forces, nevertheless, were also vitally necessary to counter the numerically superior tsarist armies invading Galicia.

Arguments for retaining troops in the Balkan theater included that if that campaign failed, Romania might attempt to seize Transylvania and the Bukovina from Hungary. Also, if Serbia could not be rapidly defeated,

Bulgaria, a critical factor, would not become a Habsburg ally. Turkey, meanwhile, desperately required ammunition and weapons to fight Russia when it entered the war. Romania blocked Danube River traffic, preventing delivery of military assistance to the Porte.

Two Second Army VII Corps divisions did not participate in the decisive Lemberg battles because of late arrival in Galicia, while their departure from the Balkan front assisted the Serbian victory. Fifth Army deserted the battlefield after its ten-day campaign without pressing necessity, partially from a result of the failed command structure. Potiorek, supported by Foreign Minister Berchtold and the emperor's military chancellery, continued to demand that Second Army leave troops in the Balkan theater. The argument also included that maintaining troop numbers would also prevent the military situation from worsening after the initial Balkan defeat. Berchtold claimed that his diplomatic maneuvering relative to Bulgaria had been compromised by the recent Balkan military setbacks.

By mid-August General Conrad realized his disastrous military mistakes during the mobilization and deployment period, particularly deploying Second Army to the Balkan theater. While he initially blindly concentrated on the Serbian campaign, the Russians launched a four-army offensive into Galicia that resulted eventually in defeat on that front. Conrad could not escape the dangerous dilemma. He had demanded a rapid operation against Serbia, but because of the ensuing fateful defeat on that front, Bulgaria and Romania did not ally with the Dual Monarchy. Then the seriously outnumbered troops on the Russian front were overwhelmed at the end of August and mid-September 1914 at the two Lemberg battles.

On August 19, as the hapless 21. *Landwehr* Infantry Division troops prepared to recross the Drina River, Conrad and Potiorek enjoined heated disputes through letters to the emperor's chancellery. Fifth Army's unanticipated retreat and Sixth Army's failure to rapidly advance resulted in Habsburg forces withdrawing completely from Serbia.

No Habsburg units remained on Serbian soil by August 24. The first Balkan offensive had ended in disaster and humiliation: Austria-Hungary's army had been soundly defeated by the small Balkan nation's combat-experienced forces. Although Potiorek should have been relieved of command, instead he commenced an immediate search for scapegoats. Potiorek retained his command because of his close relationship with Viennese leaders. To camouflage their own tactical mistakes, Conrad and Habsburg field commanders quickly blamed the Czech 21. *Landwehr* Infantry Division for the disastrous campaign. Actual guilt belonged to the inadequate training of the physically unprepared reserve troops, their lack of modern equipment, the lack of infantry and artillery cooperation, an inadequate logistical support and incompetent leadership.[12]

During the prewar period, many officers had developed an inherent prejudice against Czech soldiers, so it became easy to blame them for the Balkan debacle. General Potiorek demanded an official investigation of the division because of reputed tactical errors that resulted in the Fifth Army defeat and retreat. Such accusations, however, contradicted the facts. The division did not receive reserve formations rapidly enough to replace its enormous casualties, resulting in escalating troop demoralization and indiscipline in the ranks. Being blamed for the battlefield defeat alienated VIII Corps Czech soldiers (particularly in the 21. *Landwehr* Infantry Division). Many Czech soldiers also became disillusioned by the continued accusations and resented their treatment. The question of Czech troop loyalty remained a decisive factor throughout the war.

After the first Russian front Lemberg battle commenced on August 27, Conrad requested a unified Habsburg command (Conrad–Potiorek) because vitally necessary cooperation was lacking between Habsburg diplomatic and military leaders for the two-front war. Foreign Office personnel demanded emphasis on the Balkan front, but Russia obviously posed a much more significant military threat. The divisive struggle by the advocates of a major military effort on the Eastern or Balkan front helped produce the catastrophe that evolved on both fronts.

Major command mistakes seriously affected the first Serbian campaign results. General Potiorek's obsolete tactics and his launching numerous attacks without artillery support resulted in tremendous bloodshed. Soldiers advancing in mass formations produced heavy losses to defensive firepower. Also, Fifth Army launched its offensive before Sixth Army had become operational. The armies did not coordinate their operations, but Fifth Army bore the brunt of Serbian attacks. Thus, when Sixth and Second armies (to the north and south of Fifth Army) commenced their advances, it was too late. The Fifth Army front collapsed, forcing its retreat.

Conrad also attempted to disguise his disastrous military mistakes by blaming others, particularly the Habsburg diplomats and German military leaders for their reputed lack of support to prevent the catastrophic battlefield defeats.[13] He specifically blamed Foreign Minister Berchtold, because he claimed that the diplomats had failed to gain allies against Serbia; also, Italy and Romania did not fulfill their alliance agreements and Bulgaria did not become an ally. Military assistance against Serbia was critical, because as many troops as possible had to be deployed on the main Russian front, to counter the vastly numerical tsarist troop masses. This dilemma continued until Russia withdrew from the war after its two 1917 revolutions.

After the failed initial Serbian campaign Potiorek still possessed sufficient troop strength to halt a Serbian invasion, but, determining to revenge his failed campaign, he sought to launch a second offensive. Emperor Franz Joseph and his military chancellery immediately supported Potiorek's plan to again invade Serbia. The main military objective remained Valjevo. However, as preparations commenced to launch the operation, Serbian troops invaded the Banat, but soon were hurled back across the frontiers.

Multiple Habsburg political leaders blamed Conrad for the faulty and tragic military planning that proved fatal on both fronts. Conrad and Berchtold had disagreed on the army's priority goals, although both desired a rapid initial victory over Serbia. No Habsburg leaders had calculated on a rapid Balkan military defeat or the Russian front disastrous results.

Humiliated by the disastrous outcome of the anticipated rapid victorious Serbian campaign, Potiorek insisted that the negative diplomatic and political results of the defeat could only be nullified by his launching a new offensive to prevent a potential Serbian invasion of the Dual Monarchy. Conrad initially warned Potiorek not to risk another military failure, but the Balkan commander used his royal connections to complain that Conrad limited his command action freedom. With Hungarian Minister President Tisza, General Bolfras and Foreign Minister Berchtold's support Potiorek received imperial approval for the creation of a separate command structure for the Balkan theater, thus he no longer had to worry about Conrad's interference. His supporters now anticipated that he would achieve that rapid victory over Serbia.

General Potiorek's plans encompassed Fifth and Sixth armies crossing the northern Drina–Sava and lower Drina Rivers. Fifth Army would cross the Sava River to invade the Macva area, then strike Serbian flank and rear echelon positions, with the major objective remaining Valjevo.

On the Russian front First Army achieved victory at Krasnik between August 23 and 25, Fourth Army reputedly at Komarov August 26–September 2, and then the fateful second battle of Lemberg occurred between September 6 and 11. The latter was fought without the multiple Second Army troops that remained engaged on the Balkan front.

This time, Habsburg invasion forces launched a coordinated offense over the Drina and Sava Rivers. Sixth Army forces deployed along the Drina River from its confluence with the Sava as far south as Zvornik. Habsburg troops outnumbered their foe by nearly two to one, were well equipped with artillery and their units were back to full strength.[14] Potiorek believed that the Serbian Army was in poor condition. However, it had been resupplied with new rifles and ammunition from Russia, but its artillery units suffered from an acute shortage of artillery shells, preventing it from countering Habsburg artillery barrages except to repel attacks.

During the September 1914 campaign, Potiorek summarily cashiered multiple field commanders as attacking Habsburg troops quickly became mired in the muddy terrain following several days of steady rainfall in the Macva area. Troop exhaustion resulted from traversing the inhospitable mountain ranges along the Bosnian frontier, while Serbian forces stubbornly defended every meter of ground. Casualties mounted as supporting artillery fire did not assist the attacking troops because they too lacked shells.

France and Russia, meanwhile, pressured Serbia to launch an offensive into Bosnia. On September 3 the Serbian Uzice Group and Montenegrin forces invaded to attempt to seize Sarajevo, which also threatened the flank and rear echelon of the attacking Habsburg forces, but they were halted at Metrovica. On September 5 Habsburg Fifth and Sixth armies crossed the Drina River. The next day Serbian units crossed the Sava and Danube Rivers, and on September 7 Second Army units crossed the Sava River to advance to Belgrade. Heavy rainfall and the resultant extreme terrain conditions seriously retarded movement, particularly supply columns.

On September 6 the news of the Serbian First Army invasion of Bosnia and the capture of a Hungarian village, on the heels of the earlier Habsburg defeat, produced great embarrassment in Vienna. Realizing that weaker Serbian defensive forces had been deployed along the Drina River, Potiorek determined to counter the enemy invasion by supporting the Macva operation. Intelligence reports indicated that Serbian troops were exhausted from long forced marches and inadequate rations, artillery shells and serviceable equipment, thus they were incapable of initiating serious offensive action. This proved to be faulty intelligence and had a major effect with what transpired.

When Serbian troops crossed the Sava River near Metrovica on September 6, initiating several battles, Habsburg 29. Infantry Division counterattacked, destroying the *Timok* Division at Sabac with coordinated artillery and infantry support although strong Serbian forces crossed the river and effectively halted the Fifth Army offensive action toward Macva. South of Uzice, Serbian and Montenegrin forces – forty battalions and thousands of irregular troops – maneuvered behind Sixth Army troops and advanced toward Sarajevo to attempt to incite an uprising against Habsburg rule in Bosnia, an area with a large Serbian population. Many Fifth Army troops failed to cross the river. Sixth Army, forty miles to the south, encountered much weaker opposition, forcing the Serbians to halt their offensive toward Visegrad. Serbian Second and Third armies prevented the Habsburg attempts to cross the Drina River, while Serbian invasion troop numbers proved insufficient to cross to Metrovica but nevertheless battle continued through the month. The invaders reached to within twenty miles of Sarajevo.[15]

The Habsburg offensive utilized the August 1914 invasion route. The main Fifth Army offensive force deployed along the Drina River from its confluence with the Sava to as far south of Dvornik. Following a day-long artillery bombardment Fifth Army invaded the Macva region supported by Sixth Army that deployed further south along the Drina River. Fifth Army's 29. Infantry Division crossed the Sava River at Sabac, while Sixth Army's right flank XVI Corps attacked on the other flank. Fifth Army, however, had launched its offensive before being fully operational, after its exhausted troops had endured long railroad rides.

After daylong September 8 artillery barrages, the Serbian Second Army attacked Habsburg Fifth Army VIII Corp troops as they crossed the Sava River into the far northwestern sections of Serbia in marshy terrain where the

Sava and Danube Rivers met. The now infamous 21. *Landwehr* Infantry Division defended against Serbian assaults while its neighboring 9. Infantry Division troops crossed the lower Drina River near its mouth. Further south Habsburg XIII Corps advanced to the northeast of Lonick, unsupported by artillery fire. Serbian Second Army then counterattacked, hurling all Habsburg units back across the rivers.

On September 9 the 21. *Landwehr* Infantry Division again attempted to cross the Drina River to advance toward the Morava Peninsula. Following a multikilometer forced march, a surprise Serbian assault rebuffed the division with severe losses, forcing it to retreat. Serbian troops could not exploit their victory because many units became disoriented in the swampy terrain that enabled 21. *Landwehr* Infantry Division to escape across the river albeit abandoning large quantities of supplies and materiel. 9. Infantry Division efforts were repulsed by Serbian artillery fire. When Potiorek learned of these events, he ordered Fifth Army to again cross the Drina River, but the enormous Fifth Army casualties forced termination of offensive operations on September 13. Ten days of vicious fighting had exhausted both combatants. On September 13 Serbian artillery continued to dominate the battlefields from its well-placed position as Habsburg batteries conserved shells, resulting in lack of support for any attacks.

Between September 10 and 30 Sixth Army fought on the difficult terrain around Sarajevo, then occupied the Jadar Valley as the Serbian Third Army finally retreated. On September 10 invading Serbian troops advanced another twenty miles. Inclement weather conditions continued to interrupt supply activities so Habsburg troops often received no food, ammunition or equipment.

On September 11, Sixth Army pushed Serbian Third Army across the Drina River to the main mountain peaks in the Drina Valley, but meanwhile Putnik had correctly assumed that Sixth Army's mission remained to seize Valjevo. If that army succeeded it would encircle Serbian forces in the Macva area from the south. The coordinated attacks across the Drina and Sava Rivers assumed that the Serbian Army had suffered more than the Habsburg, a major mistake.

Fifth Army again failed to achieve its goals; its troops becoming mired in the swampy Macva area terrain following several days of steady rainfall and horrendous conditions. Then its exhausted soldiers attempted to advance through the Bosnian Mountains. The Serbians had meanwhile consolidated their defensive positions and fought fiercely for every foot of their terrain, while Habsburg soldiers relied on their artillery fire to provide advantage in the battle.

After regrouping, Fifth Army resumed its offensive across the Sava River on September 14, while the Serbian First Army advanced into the eastern portion of Syrmien in an area forty kilometers wide and twenty deep, but then had to evacuate the conquered terrain and recross the Sava River.

Serbian strategy to disturb the Habsburg invasion succeeded. During the battle at Macva Kamen, attacking troops sustained heavy losses, as battle became segmented into narrow terrain areas. Large troop formations had to be deployed into confined areas, exposing them to devastating enemy artillery fire. This battle became the bloodiest and costliest to date on the Balkan front. Many Sixth Army troops collapsed from exhaustion and sustained thirty thousand casualties within two weeks. Some Habsburg troops surrendered to Serbian forces to escape the terrible weather, terrain, supply conditions and bloodshed.

On September 15, 21. *Landwehr* Infantry Division, unable to maneuver, attacked frontally in mass formations. Unfortunately, artillery support was not coordinated, resulting in enormous casualties. Most infantry companies had only one surviving officer, some units none.

On September 16 Habsburg Fifth Army's Combined Corps crossed the Sava River, threatening Serbian Second Army positions. The marshy terrain continued to delay forward progress. Well-entrenched Serbian Second Army troops counterattacked, inflicting heavy casualties, and forced Habsburg units to again retreat across the Drina and Sava Rivers.

The Serbians also attacked Sixth Army southern flank positions, while overpowering troop numbers crossed the Drina River at Visegrad, creating a new Fifth Army crisis on September 15. The invaders sustained many casualties crossing the river.

Habsburg 42. *Honvéd* Infantry Division repeatedly launched attacks between September 3 and 15, sacrificing forty officers and two thousand men. Serbian artillery attempted to prevent crossing the Drina River, but twelve battalions finally gained access to the opponent's shore.

A September 19 Serbian counterattack cost its attacking *Timok* Division almost two thousand casualties and lowered Serbian Second Army's *esprit de corps*. Yet, victorious Habsburg Fifth Army troops quickly got bogged down in the marshy soil. Later in the month, trench warfare commenced. Habsburg Sixth Army troop exhaustion required rehabilitation time, thus Fifth and Sixth armies terminated their campaigns and an interlude in battle ensued.

Serbian First Army crossed the Sava River into Habsburg territory on September 16, but, meanwhile, its Third Army's situation had become serious. Fifth Army troops had crossed the Sava River at Macva when Serbian forces attacked them. Rainy weather since September 13 in the northern Macva Valley resulted in serious flooding because of nontraversable swampy areas. Combined Corps lost 50 percent of its *Landsturm* troops during its operation.

On September 24 the many poorly trained Habsburg officers and reserve troops were hurled into battle, but the attempted crossing of the Sava River failed the next day. The horrendous loss of professional officers and non-commissioned officers had an enormous negative effect on the Habsburg Army. Serbian troops advanced east of Sarajevo and by the end of the month

Uzice Group forces, after multiple attacks, had seized much of the province. Sixth Army, losing enormous amounts of supplies and equipment, suddenly was threatened with encirclement. The Habsburg Army feared a general uprising in Bosnia. Thus, if Serbian troops captured Sarajevo, it would create immense political embarrassment, lost Balkan Peninsula prestige and the threat of the creation of an enlarged Serbian state at Dual Monarchy expense. This forced Conrad to divert part of the Habsburg strategic reserve units – although sorely needed on the Russian front – as well as newly deployed units on the Italian frontier to reinforce the battered Sixth Army. Most XVI Corps troops crossed the Drina River to relieve the pressure against the Sixth Army rear echelon positions, eventually stabilizing the situation.

In the interim, Danube fleet monitors destroyed Serbian bridges over the Sava River, severing their supply route and forcing them to retreat. Forty infantry battalions, supported by thousands of irregular troops, had invaded Bosnia, causing panic but no uprising to support the Serbians. Defending Habsburg troops proved more tenacious than the Serbians had anticipated. Nevertheless, it required much of September to drive enemy soldiers out of Bosnia; they actually reached within twenty kilometers of Sarajevo.[16]

By the end of September both antagonist troops suffered from exhaustion, sustained severe officer casualties and low ammunition, that led to trench warfare that continued until the end of October. During the lull in battle both sides replenished their forces and prepared for further battle. At the same time, the weather had turned cold, roads had become impassable and serious illness had spread out in the ranks. Cholera arrived, transmitted by Habsburg troops redeployed from the Russian front. That and typhus took a heavy toll on Serbian soldiers and civilians. Only one large-scale Serbian action occurred by the end of October. In the Macva area Serbian troops were deployed on flat marshy terrain, which provided little natural cover. Devastating Habsburg artillery fire decimated their ranks.[17] On September 28 Serbian troops crossed the Sava River to attempt to halt Habsburg shelling of Belgrade, retaking a village, otherwise the temporary lull descended on the front.

The Habsburg invasion momentum slackened at the end of September. Attacking in mass columns produced enormous casualties; troop numbers had been drastically reduced. The troops sustained forty thousand casualties while failing to seize serious territorial gain. On September 29 Uzice Group troops had reached the zenith of their success, having encountered scant Habsburg resistance. Habsburg troops then attacked the invaders' flank positions and forced them into a defensive stance as winter weather arrived.

Soldiers suffered through the inclement weather conditions during September. The rainy conditions and cold as well as the early arrival of snow caused enormous misery compounded by the inadequate supply conditions. The health of many soldiers declined on both sides of the front.

On September 26 Fifth Army's VIII Corps ended its twelve-day offensive. Well-camouflaged Serbian artillery units deployed in isolated positions caused enormous Habsburg casualties. On October 4 Potiorek ordered XIII and XV Corps to launch an offensive as the Western front "Race to the Sea" was occurring. But by October 5, Habsburg forces lacked sufficient troop numbers to continue their efforts, thus they reverted to a defensive stance. Inclement weather conditions and water-filled trenches sapped troop morale; nevertheless, Potiorek deployed all available troop formations to southeast Bosnia to halt the Serbian invasion. The Drina and Sava River fronts then settled into trench warfare as between October 18 and 21 the battle at Sarajevo raged.

From mid-October General Potiorek labored under inaccurate intelligence reports that negatively affected Habsburg offensive activity during the last third of October. The need to preserve what little Habsburg prestige remained precluded not launching further offensive actions.[18]

Between October 22 and 30 Habsburg troops rapidly advanced to the Drina River to prevent the Serbian troops from having sufficient time to dig trenches. Potiorek also commenced planning for launching a major November 6 offensive over the Upper Drina River line. His troops suffered from inhumane demands forced upon them. Autumn rains transformed roads into muddy swamps, negatively affecting the movement of artillery pieces and supply wagons transporting food and equipment.

Habsburg Fifth Army would advance toward Valjevo then, if successful, the Kolubara River. Sixth Army again received the mission to outflank the Serbian Kolubara River line from the south. If the two-pronged attack succeeded, Serbian forces would be separated and their main ammunition factories in Kragujevac would be threatened. Inclement weather conditions had worsened, inundating the valleys, while snowfall commenced in the mountainous terrain. Wounded soldiers could not be evacuated, and supply transport almost ceased. Meanwhile, a typhus epidemic swept through Serbia.

Habsburg Fifth Amy troops crossed the Drina and Sava Rivers to advance east and south. After crossing the Drina River, XIII Corps conquered the already bloodied Mount Cer and accompanying high plateau. Sixth Army XV and XVI Corps troops crossed the Drina River further south.

On October 23–24 Serbian troops withdrew over the Drina River, terminating the Serbian-Montenegrin forays into Bosnia-Herzegovina, but that diversion served to delay the next Habsburg offensive effort toward Valjevo launched on October 24 after a two-hour artillery barrage. Serbian First and Third armies regrouped and received reinforcements. The last strategic reserve troops deployed from the Russian front improved the Habsburg military situation. On October 24 Habsburg Fifth Army attacked the Serbian Second Army, battle continuing through October 26–27. On October 26 Potiorek planned to commence decisive battle to conquer the Kolubara area then seize the railroad line that connected Obrenovic to Valjevo, vital for Habsburg logistical support. When he diverted troops to the northeast after the capture of Kolubara it overextended Habsburg Fifth and Sixth armies' lines.

When Danube River traffic remained blocked by the Romanians, General Falkenhayn renewed his requests to launch another offensive against Serbia to enable transport of weapons and material to the Turkish ally.[19] On October 28, after Habsburg troops cleared eastern Bosnia of enemy troops, German High Command again requested another campaign into Serbia.

Commencing on November 6, superior Habsburg troop numbers crossed the lower Drina and marshy Sava Rivers, their first coordinated attack supported by heavy-artillery fire. This enabled troops to finally advance into the Kolubara Valley. Potiorek ordered Fifth Army to advance from Sabac toward Valjevo to attempt to encircle Serbian Second Army right flank positions. XVI Corps maneuvered toward Valjevo to encircle Serbian First Army left flank positions. Remaining Fifth and Sixth Army forces would frontally attack Serbian Third Army. This pincer movement would meet at Valjevo to attempt to envelop the enemy Second and Third armies at the Jadar Valley and Macva. This would introduce the third Balkan offensive.

On November 5 Habsburg divisions crossed the Sava River southwest of Belgrade, encountering enemy forces reduced by desertion, disease, casualties and short of ammunition, particularly artillery shells. Serbian troop numbers had diminished to two hundred thousand soldiers. While Serbian forces focused on defending Belgrade, Habsburg troops seized Valjevo by November 15 and advanced toward the Kolubara River. The Habsburg armies had finally achieved their four-month-earlier initial objective.

The next day Habsburg Fifth Army drove south from the Sava–Drina River triangle while Sixth Army pushed across the Drina River, despite heavy rainfall advancing into rugged terrain. Potiorek, however, had driven his troops, still in summer uniforms, through muddy valleys and mountain snow while food and ammunition supplies halted because they could often not be transported to the front. Weather conditions hindered Serbian retreat movements as casualties increased from the inclement weather conditions and battle.

On November 6 Habsburg artillery commenced a two-hour barrage, but the next day Serbian troops briefly halted the assaults. Their Second and Third armies then retreated, which left Mount Cer and the Jadar Valley open to invasion. The Habsburg offensive continued unabated on November 8, then on November 9–10 Serbian forces retreated to defend Valjevo and the important small-spur Obrenovic railroad terminal that would be critical for logistical purposes if Habsburg forces advanced further into Serbian territory.

The continued lack of sound Habsburg combat experience resulted in multiple problems occurring on the railroad and supply routes, similar to simultaneous Russian front experiences. Sixth Army had to capture the small-spur Obrenovic railroad line to ensure supply functions in the Kolubara Valley. The unfolding Drina battle did not achieve the anticipated early

November encirclement of Serbian forces. Continuing battle evolved into frontal pressure against the enemy. The Habsburg offensive operation ultimately failed because of the lack of reserve forces, the difficulties encountered on the mountain terrain south of the Loznica–Valjevo line and very effective Serbian defensive efforts.

Potiorek's attempts to drive Serbian forces back to Valjevo and Kolubara resulted from his belief that enemy troops were close to collapse. However, indications abounded that Putnik would not surrender Valjevo without serious resistance, while maintaining the Kolubara defensive line.

By mid-November Habsburg troops desperately required rehabilitation after two months of almost uninterrupted battle, a failing logistical system and serious collapse of troop morale. Weather conditions changed as winter approached.

On November 10 Habsburg offensive efforts shifted toward Belgrade supported by Danube River monitors, which helped establish a foothold on the other side of the river. A Serbian counteroffensive initially stymied the effort, but Potiorek's troops rapidly advanced toward Valjevo, while Fifth Army troops, after crossing the Kolubara River, seized the key Obrenovic railroad necessary to alleviate its logistical difficulties.

Serbian forces, meanwhile, faced the threat of encirclement by the Habsburg Fifth and Sixth armies. The lack of artillery shells negatively affected Serbian troop morale while desertion rates skyrocketed. General Putnik prepared to withdraw his troops at the Kolubara and Ljig Rivers, or approximately twenty-five to thirty kilometers, where he would establish a new defensive line. On November 13 Habsburg troops seized the Morava trench region, as defeated Serbian forces desperately required reinforcements and ammunition stocks, but they had just surrendered their critical supply railroad line that connected to the Morava–Vardar trench.

On November 16 the Habsburg advance was delayed by unfavorable climatic conditions, thus the troops could not keep pace with retreating enemy forces. The Macva and Jadar Valleys, now muddy quagmires, enabled the Serbian Second and Third armies to escape intact across the Kolubara–Ljig Rivers and establish defensive positions. Habsburg XVI Corps seized Valjevo, while Fifth Army had finally reached Kolubara.

The ensuing Kolubara battle, when the Habsburg Fifth and Sixth armies finally captured Valjevo between November 16 and 25, covered an immense area of 110 kilometers. The northern Kolubara battle area encompassed the area between the Danube and Sava Rivers, west to Kolubara, and then southwest into the Morava Valley. Habsburg forces had sustained 130,000 casualties since early September while Sixth Army did not possess one traversable road because of the horrendous mud conditions. The delayed advance finally encountered serious Serbian resistance, until the Serbians retreated forty miles in five days toward Kragujevac and Arangjelovac between the Kolubara and

Morava Valleys. This severe defeat caused Putnik to order his Second Army to retreat toward Kragujevac, surrendering Belgrade. The Serbians established a mountain defensive line extending fifty to sixty kilometers deep, which created a major barrier between the Danube, Sava, Kolubara and greater Morava Rivers. The flooding and constant rain in the Kolubara and Ljig Rivers areas neutralized all Habsburg military advantages, particularly the perpetual supply difficulties. Serbian troop morale continued to sink, because there were no reserve forces. The battle area lacked traversable roads during the terrible winter conditions, which separated the Macva Plain and the Kolubara River from western Serbia. Dead soldiers were often thrown into deep ditches and left to rot.[20] Both sides lacked trained reinforcements. Habsburg March battalions were hurled into combat as soon as they arrived at the front because of the horrendous casualties, merely adding to the casualty lists.

Habsburg Fifth and Sixth armies advanced into the western Morava Valley after conquering Valjevo. The two armies intended to drive deep into the heart of Serbia with XV Corps but Habsburg troops continued to endure horrendous conditions. The troops outran their logistical support, thus they lacked food, ammunition and other necessities. Accurate enemy artillery fire caused misery and many casualties.

The exhausted Habsburg forces could not defeat retreating Serbian formations on November 16. General Potiorek again seriously underestimated Serbian resistance abilities, accurate enemy troop numbers and their combat effectiveness while he overestimated his own situation. Assuming falsely that the Serbian Army had begun to implode, he determined that one last major offensive operation could produce the desperately sought Habsburg victory.

Serbian forces continued to sustain unacceptable casualty numbers as war weariness swept through their ranks then expanded into the hinterland. Troop desertions increased, while ammunition supplies evaporated, causing Serbian resistance capabilities to decline.

Habsburg troops encountered stiff Serbian resistance on November 18 at the Kolubara River line, but nevertheless they launched an attack the next day. On November 22 Fifth Army troops advanced toward Belgrade while XV and XVI Corps continued their forward progress.

On November 21 Serbian Third Army launched an offensive against XV and XVI Corps, but the next day the two Habsburg corps forced Serbian First Army to retreat, while Second Army continued battle with Habsburg Fifth Army's VIII Corps along the Kolubara River. Habsburg Fifth Army troops wheeled toward Belgrade, which capitulated on November 30, then turned south to the Morava Valley. Heavily involved in battle since November 8, Habsburg troops paid a high human price in the terrible weather conditions and fierce enemy resistance. As Fifth and Sixth Army troops advanced the more they distanced themselves from their logistical support. During late November food shortages appeared throughout the Dual Monarchy while cold weather conditions and disease became a serious problem for both Balkan antagonists. Sixth Army XV Corps had 500–600 soldiers a day report to sick call.

Fifth and Sixth armies launched simultaneous attacks on November 23 and 24 as much of the Kolubara Valley remained underwater so troops could not advance without sustaining heavy casualties. Frostbite also became a serious problem for the troops. On November 25 the Habsburg forces unleashed their most concentrated heavy-artillery barrages to date, which enabled VIII Corps to cross the Kolubara River and defeat defending Serbian troops. The next day, Habsburg XV Corp troops forced Serbian Second and Third Army forces to retreat between the Kolubara and west Morava watersheds, which opened Belgrade to attack.

Heavy fighting continued on November 27, but the Serbian First Army being unable to defend the mountain terrain dividing the Kolubara and west Morava watershed convinced General Putnik to abandon Belgrade. During the night of November 29–30 Serbian forces began retreating to the new defensive lines fifty kilometers from Belgrade.

Although General Potiorek anticipated that Sixth Army XV and XVI Corps troops would not encounter serious enemy opposition, they in fact encountered multiple difficulties in the treacherous mountain terrain. Elsewhere, strong Serbian resistance, high water levels in the valleys and the swampy Kolubara River terrain prevented Habsburg use of the captured Obrenovic–Valjevo railroad supply line. Fifth Army's advance took it further into the inhospitable mountain terrain where already difficult supply conditions worsened.

By the end of November Habsburg troops had occupied northwestern Serbia, but Serbian forces again crossed the Drina River, threatening Sarajevo. General Potiorek continued to ruthlessly push his troops although some units no longer received food and ammunition and uniforms had become mere rags. During late November, Serbian forces meanwhile abandoned several key cities without serious resistance.

Then Putnik ordered his Second and Third armies to spearhead a counterattack against the weakened Habsburg Sixth Army. Accurately assessing the military situation and unfavorable weather conditions that made roads and supply efforts almost impossible, Putnik assembled nearly all his reserve formations and raw recruits for the counterstroke. When General Potiorek ordered Fifth Army to swing toward Belgrade, more a political than a military objective, it provided Serbian forces an advantage that Putnik quickly utilized. General Potiorek's plans and expectations proved far beyond his troops' capabilities.

A shipment of desperately needed ammunition, particularly artillery shells from France and Russia, allowed General Putnik to deploy troop mass by denuding all other positions for deployment at the decisive battle point, something Potiorek consistently failed to do. Taking a major strategic gamble, General Putnik decisively defeated his enemy's forces.[21] Conquered Belgrade had to be abandoned by December 15. Casualties were horrendous.

During the first week of December Habsburg troops advanced north along the valley barrier of the lower Drina and Sava Rivers into the Kolubara Valley. On December 2 Habsburg Fifth Army troops entered an abandoned Belgrade captured on the sixty-sixth anniversary of Emperor Franz Joseph's reign. Habsburg troops still wore summer uniforms in high mountain altitudes in snow conditions, and multiple units continued not to receive food and ammunition. Suddenly the Serbian armies halted their retreat movements, thus the Habsburg Fifth and Sixth armies unexpectedly found themselves in serious battle. Putnik utilized the fact that they had been delayed by mountain snow and valley rain, seriously impeding supply efforts because of the impassable roads.

As his exhausted, starving and sick troops continued their inhumane existence attempting to maintain their forward progress, Potiorek extended his already too extensive front sending Fifth Army left flank units toward Belgrade. Terrain conditions remained grossly unfavorable.

Belgrade was conquered for a very brief time; nevertheless, Potiorek's reputation was restored and he became a hero until the city had to be abandoned. On December 2 Putnik ordered his First and Third armies to reconquer Valjevo. The Serbian Second Army attacked Obrenovic.

On December 3, during battle Serbian forces rapidly pierced Sixth Army's southern flank forces, exposing another corps to attack, forcing it to also retreat. Serbian forces recaptured Valjevo between December 5 and 8, as Habsburg Fifth Army's predicament increasingly became critical. XVI Corps was literally annihilated by Serbian attacks on December 5; its troops fled the battlefield in disarray, opening a gap in Habsburg lines. Serbian troops threatened their rear echelon areas. Potiorek had to immediately request reinforcements, but because of the Limanova–Lapanov battle none could be provided.

Potiorek responded to the suddenly worsening military situation on December 6, ordering Sixth Army to retreat to Kolubara to prevent it from being routed. On December 7, Serbian forces attacked Habsburg units between Valjevo and the western Morava area. Surviving Habsburg Corps troops retreated from Belgrade in panic. On December 8 Serbian forces crossed the Kolubara River, smashing the remaining defensive positions at Valjevo.

Then Serbian troops forced Habsburg Fifth and Sixth armies apart on December 9 – Fifth Army at Belgrade and Sixth Army at Sabac at the Drina and Sava Rivers, forcing a general retreat to Sabac. In a few days, both armies retreated behind the Drina–Danube Rivers. For the next four days defeated Sixth Army troops crossed the Sava River, while Fifth Army narrowly averted catastrophe, attempting to halt Serbian attacks at Sabac before it retreated.[22]

Fifth Army rearguard units evacuated Belgrade on December 15 after blowing up the Danube River Bridge and abandoning enormous amounts of equipment, food and prisoners of war. Its troops retreated sixty miles behind the Drina River. Serbian troops triumphantly reentered their capital. General Potiorek's fateful November offensive operation failed to achieve any of its major objectives, particularly knocking Serbia out of the war and inducing Bulgaria and Romania to assist the Central Powers. The Habsburg Balkan Army lost half of its original troop numbers. Of 273,000 casualties, 28,000 died, 122,000 were wounded and 79,000 were captured as prisoners of war; 100,000 became permanent losses. "The Serbian defeat constituted a politically serious diminution of the Dual Monarchy's prestige and self-confidence."[23]

The losses of Habsburg Fifth and Sixth armies proved so overwhelming that the two entities had to be combined. Many units had well over 100 percent casualties even after receiving reinforcements during the campaigns. Multiple units were annihilated and required constant *Ersatz* and March units. The army now recruited men found unfit years earlier. On the Russian front 170 tsarist divisions countered only 60 Habsburg units.

On December 22, Archduke Eugene replaced the disgraced General Potiorek as commander of the Balkan forces. The Fifth Army commander was also relieved of his duty. A day earlier, Conrad reported that the best professional soldiers had been killed or wounded and replacement troops were inferior to those deployed during the first campaign. He emphasized that the army could not survive a war of attrition, because of the Russians' enormous numerical superiority. Nevertheless, the first significant military victory over Russian forces transpired at Limanova–Lapanov between December 2 and 12 that partially restored Habsburg military honor after its embarrassing Balkan defeats. The three Balkan and Russian campaigns destroyed Habsburg military prestige in the Balkan Peninsula, and seriously weakened its reputation with its German ally.

The Serbian Army also sustained enormous casualties – twenty-two thousand dead, ninety-one thousand wounded and nineteen thousand captured or missing. Dysentery, cholera and typhus ravaged both armies. The Serbians, however, could not replace their human or equipment losses, so they became incapable of launching a major offensive. The 1914 Balkan campaigns destroyed Serbian military power.

Serbian cannons, rifles, field equipment and uniforms became scarce. Much had been damaged or destroyed. The Serbian forces had been so badly mauled that in January 1915 General Conrad could transfer VIII and XIII Corps from the Balkan front for his January Carpathian Mountain Winter War offensive, and XV and XVI Corps to the Isonzo River front after Italy declared war on May 23, 1915. Multiple factors explain the three Habsburg 1914 Balkan campaign failures. The failure to deploy troop mass at the decisive attack points, as well as inadequate artillery support for infantry attacks, had a major effect. Insufficient troop numbers and unresolved logistical problems plagued Habsburg military operations throughout the three campaigns, as well as later campaigns.

Inadequate Habsburg troop training, unfavorable weather and terrain conditions and only a minority of troops as regular soldiers produced disastrous results. Most *Landsturm* and replacement troops lacked proper physical conditioning and were not prepared for the deplorable battlefield conditions they encountered. Obsolete tactical doctrine also proved lacking against a combat-experienced enemy.

Reconnaissance efforts failed on both the Russian and Balkans fronts. Thus, the Serbians launched multiple surprise attacks. The lack of regular army officers, noncommissioned officers and soldiers because of the enormous casualty numbers fatally affected outcomes in both war theaters. The horrific losses could not be replaced by adequately trained personnel, as new reserve officers generally were in poor physical condition and could not speak their troops' language. *Landsturm* and March units, middle-aged and nineteen-year-old recruits, as cited, had few regular army officers, were armed with obsolete rifles and often had no machine guns or field-artillery support. By the end of 1914 many newly deployed lacked rifles, because even obsolete models were no longer available. Growing indiscipline in the ranks and many self-inflicted wounds to avoid combat became a problem, particularly with the grotesque losses and battlefield defeats.

Potiorek's faulty leadership caused the ultimate failure of the Balkan campaigns, but lack of his concern for his troops' welfare was a major factor. Having captured the strategic Valjevo area during mid-November, Potiorek ignored reports that his troops desperately required rehabilitation as morale rapidly collapsed. By focusing on the capture of Belgrade in December 1914, he drove his soldiers to their physical breaking point. Despite numerical and material superiority during the third Balkan campaign, the troops sustained an embarrassing defeat.

The defeats also portrayed the Habsburg Army's multiple weaknesses in 1914. The invading armies lacked coordination and were deployed too distant from each other on both fronts. The two-front war and tragic faulty division of forces ensured the failure of both the Russian and Serbian campaigns. These results had a severe psychological effect on troop and officer corps morale. Many supply wagons were damaged or destroyed and the army lacked sufficient numbers of horses because of their excessive losses from exhaustion and lack of fodder during the 1914 military campaigns.

Much postwar historical criticism has focused on the Habsburg Balkan war plans. The most often cited emphasized that Habsburg troops should have invaded Serbia through Belgrade, the historical route. Also, too many troops were deployed to protect Bosnia-Herzegovina–Dalmatia against insurgency, partly because of the long Adriatic coastline and fleet deployed there.

Austrian historians also blame the 1914 defeats on the lack of prewar readiness and decades of insufficient expenditures for the army. Some critics claimed that the Serbian Army was better equipped and supplied, and that the Habsburg Army had been ill-prepared for the war, as emphasized, its training inadequate, its artillery and weapons obsolete, while the rapid shortage of artillery shells seriously affected effectiveness during the battle.

A serious problem was that only one small-spur railroad serviced Bosnia and Herzegovina, thus launching the offensive across the Drina River created enormous logistical problems. After the three Balkan defeats, sufficient troop numbers remained to protect the Balkan provinces from invasion. If Bulgaria had immediately allied with Vienna, Serbia might have been quickly crushed, but that did not occur.

Turning to Italy, the Italian front is often ignored when studying the First World War as most people concentrate their attention on the Western front. However, well over one million soldiers, mostly Italians, died during the war years of 1915–1918. The Italian war witnessed the largest-scale mountain warfare in history during which combat raged in extremely high terrain, dangerous to animals and men alike. Poor weather conditions, rugged terrain, disease and avalanches resulted in more than ten thousand deaths during 1917.

Major battles occurred along the Isonzo River in the rugged mountainous Carso and Bainsizza Plateaus, producing eleven bloody and ferocious battles. The postwar Versailles Treaty and poor economic conditions in Italy at the end of the war enabled Benito Mussolini's fascists to seize power. The Second World War resulted. Significantly the Italian *fasciti* heavily recruited its troops from the veteran population, but many troops could not recover from their experiences and comfortably adjust back to civilian life.

Although Italian troops fought in the 1911 Libyan war they did not gain the experience required for their 1915 war against Austria-Hungary. On July 1, 1914, the pro-Triple Alliance chief of the Italian General Staff, General Pollio, unexpectedly died, replaced by General Cadorna. On August 1 Conrad contacted Cadorna hoping to continue the negotiations initiated with Pollio, relative to Allied strategy. Conrad requested the number of Italian troops to be deployed with Triple Alliance forces, while on August 2, Cadorna requested information relative to the three army corps that Italy promised to deploy to the German-French front according to the Triple Alliance Treaty. On July 31, however, Italy proclaimed its neutrality, repeated on August 3.

The question of Italian neutrality immediately became a major focus in all Habsburg military planning. In 1914 the Italian government declared the Austro-Hungarian war against Serbia an aggressive act, not defensive as called for in Article VII of the Triple Alliance Treaty. German Emperor Wilhelm wrote to Italian King Victor Emmanuel on July 31; Victor Emmanuel's reply emphasized that there was no *casus foederis* requiring his country to go to war.

On August 1 Emperor Franz Joseph's letter to Rome received a similar answer. The Allied leaders agreed that it must be ensured that Italy maintain its neutrality. Simultaneously, German leaders pressured their ally to surrender territory to obtain Italy's intervention in the war. Meanwhile, the Russian government offered Italy territory if it did not ally with the Triple Alliance.

During August 1914, preparatory military measures commenced for a War Case "Italy." On August 13, General Franz von Rohr was ordered to monitor the Italian border situation and prepare plans for a rapid mobilization if it became necessary. On August 8, directives were issued for the security and defense of Tyrol against invasion. *Landsturm* and *Ersatz* battalions were formed from the regional *Kaiserjäger* and *Landesschützen* formations. Some 18,000 of 32,400 *Standesschützen* (*Landsturm*) troops rapidly deployed to the Isonzo front. Forty-four infantry battalions and twenty-three *Standesschützen* infantry companies mustered in Tyrol and Vorarlberg. In Carinthia 10,000 volunteers (*Freiwillige*) formed four regiments (25,000 troops) to be immediately available to defend the frontier. These troop units mainly contained second-line *Landsturm*, March and *Ersatz* battalions; many soldiers were physically unfit for combat duty so they could not be expected to halt a major Italian invasion. Major regional combat units (*Kaiserjäger* and XIV Corps) were deployed to the Galician front against Russia.

On August 6 Italian leaders demanded the Trentino province to maintain neutrality, but both Conrad and Berchtold declared that territory could only be surrendered if Italy allied with Austria-Hungary. Meanwhile, the Italians called up three reserve units, which caused Conrad to mobilize forty thousand *Landsturm* troops in the Trentino area, and another twenty thousand troops to resist an Italian invasion. The native *Standesschützen* troops predominated in the small initial Habsburg defensive force.

On August 11, General Dankl received command of the Tyrolean forces, General Rohr the Carinthian territories. By mid-August 1914 the first military crisis loomed on both the Russian and Serbian fronts. On August 21 soundly defeated Habsburg troops retreated from the Serbian front. Italy, Romania and Bulgaria awaited a major battlefield success to determine the winning coalition before they declared war.

The Habsburg military attaché in Rome reported on September 2 that Italy had initiated preparations for war. During the next several months the question of surrendering South Tyrol to Italy gained increasing significance. Conrad vehemently opposed any territory being surrendered to the perfidious enemy.

After the December Serbian military victory, Conrad realized that he desperately required German military assistance, but he also requested that German troops be deployed to the Italian frontier, which he felt would have a major effect on Italian conduct.

During the last prewar years several strong Habsburg fortifications had been constructed to secure troop deployments to invade Italy if a war erupted.

Invasion routes on the Isonzo River front between the Massiv Krn and the Adriatic Sea encompassed a front of fifty-five kilometers, much of it consisting of difficult terrain. Initially defensive positions were established some distance from the frontier, because of the enemy's enormous numerical superiority.

During August 1914 Cadorna intensified planning for a potential war against Austria-Hungary, improvements commenced on Italian frontier fortifications and military units were deployed to the frontier. Eventually almost 150,000 Italian troops mobilized. During January 1915, mobile Italian militia units became activated, while multiple troop units redeployed to frontier areas. On April 23, 1915 the first field army force mobilized, attaining a strength of six corps by May. Thus, the May 23, 1915 Italian declaration of war was a mere formality.

Only seventeen Habsburg infantry battalions and twelve mobile guns became available for defensive purposes in September 1914. During autumn 1914, the Italian High Command planned to launch three major offensives in the event of war. The first objective became Tyrol, the second Vienna and the third the city of Gorizia that blocked the Italians from their major objective of Trieste. The province of Tyrol consisted of significant mountainous terrain, forming a salient jutting into Italian territory. Gorizia became a major Italian target because it could be attacked after a successful assault across the Isonzo River. Much blood spilled during the Isonzo River campaigns to seize Gorizia until its capture as part of the 1916 Sixth Isonzo offensive.

Until 1917, Italy served as a secondary military theater for Habsburg military efforts, which ensured that the enemy possessed significant numerical superiority in troop numbers, artillery, shells and airplanes. The 1915 Carpathian Mountain Winter War and Russian front Gorlice–Tarnow campaigns resulted in the loss of thousands of professional officers, noncommissioned officers and soldiers, while regional *Kaiserjäger* and *Kaiserschützen* units from the Italian front region bled to death on those fronts. In December 1914, as the Russians advanced against the Austro-Hungarian armies in the Carpathian Mountains, General Cadorna accelerated war planning against Austria-Hungary. When the Carpathian Winter campaign became an obvious major Habsburg defeat, Italy prepared to enter the war to ensure its major territorial expansion.

Habsburg military commanders realized that the best invasion route toward Vienna was through the Isonzo River Valley and, less favorably, the Julian Alps mountains, with their poor road network, but these areas also provided ideal defensive terrain. General Boroević commanded the late 1914 and early 1915 major troop units that fought the Carpathian Mountain campaigns' defensive battles.

During 1915 the Italian front became the scene of some of the most brutal fighting of the entire war, comparative to the Verdun and Somme blood battles, but we must return to the bloody Eastern front for the commencement of 1914 warfare in the Carpathian Mountains.

Galicia, October–December 1914

By September 14 German High Command realized that the Habsburg Army's collapse threatened its Silesian industrial center. Therefore, it had to rescue its ally; a new army was deployed to the Eastern front. Meanwhile, Russian High Command determined to launch a major offensive to capture Silesia, then drive to Berlin. German Eastern High Command, Generals Hindenburg and Ludendorff, also determined to launch a campaign across the Narev River toward Warsaw. The disadvantage for all was the lateness of the season and the fact that the Russians purposely had not constructed major railroads or roads from Warsaw to the western frontier.

In less than a month the devastating Lemberg battlefield defeats and three traumatic setbacks against Serbia had transpired. Following the disastrous 1914 opening campaign defeats against Russia and Serbia General Conrad had to await the arrival of reinforcing German troops to shore up his defeated and demoralized forces.[1] As his forces resupplied and refilled their ranks, October 1914 introduced a very eventful period for the obsolete San River Fortress Przemyśl, the citadel defending the entrance to the Carpathian Mountains protecting Hungary from invasion. After besieging the citadel in late September, Russian forces sought to capture it before a Habsburg relief attempt could be initiated. Bloody storm assaults against the citadel during October 5–7 failed, and eventually Russian troops retreated from all but the eastern bulwark perimeter areas. Fortress Przemyśl extended over forty-eight kilometers of partly hilly and partly flat land. Following the earlier Habsburg retreat, it was garrisoned with 131,000 troops, but only the 23. *Honvéd* Infantry Division, ravaged during the Lemberg battles, served as the major offensive unit. Overwhelming supply challenges and terrain difficulties made Habsburg efforts to liberate the fortress exceedingly difficult. Heavy supply wagon traffic and weeks of inclement weather rendered the inadequate Galician mountain roadways nearly impassable, thwarting Habsburg Third Army attempts to rapidly relieve the fortress. The ensuing October, late November and December campaigns to recapture the citadel revealed how difficult it became to wage war on winter mountain terrain.

Fortress Przemyśl was briefly liberated on October 9, although numerous vital railroad bridges required immediate repair before sufficient food supplies could be transported to replenish the partially empty fortress food stores. Habsburg offensive efforts to relieve the fortress resulted in having to extend the Third Army front about ninety miles from its major railroad depot, thus its troops often lacked sufficient food or ammunition as they advanced toward the fortress. The appalling weather conditions also resulted in widespread cholera, dysentery and typhus, killing hundreds of soldiers.

Conrad hastily launched the fortress relief operation because he feared that it would be incapable of repulsing mass tsarist attacks and it had suddenly become a major prestige factor. To the north, German troops simultaneously advanced to Fortress Krakow, reaching the San–Vistula River line to assist their battered ally.

Between October 1 and 10 Habsburg troops purged the wooded Carpathian Mountain region of enemy troops. By October 4, an advancing Second Army had reached the key Dukla Pass, bringing the war to the Carpathian Mountain foothills and closer to the Romanian frontier. Between October 2 and 7, Second Army deployed strong forces into the mountainous terrain south of Fortress Przemyśl.

Russian Third Army initiated the siege of the fortress on October 1. The renewed Habsburg offensive to recapture the citadel depended upon German forces protecting their northern flank position and relieving enemy pressure. The Russians attempted to capture the fortress before it could be rescued. They planned to attack the strongest VI Defensive District (Siedliska), a series of six forts, while simultaneously launching diversionary attacks. Initial tsarist efforts attempted to draw citadel reserve forces from the intended target, Siedliska, the major offensive effort.[2]

Both combatants had destroyed railroad lines and bridges during previous offensive and retrograde maneuvers, negatively affecting supply lines crucial for Third Army's offensive operation to devastate the bastion. The month of constant heavy rainfall and congested wagon traffic also ruined the few poorly constructed roads, making Third Army supply lines almost impossible to traverse.

Russian forces hastened their attack against the fortress after receiving inaccurate intelligence reports that some garrison units had become unreliable. Tsarist artillery barrages commenced destroying the citadel's defensive barbed-wire emplacements, but powerful defensive artillery fire halted enemy infantry attacks. Following each attack Habsburg troops could not remove Russian corpses before the citadel walls to prevent the spread of disease because of harassing tsarist artillery fire.

The failure of the Schlieffen Plan after the battle of the Marne signified a German military debacle, compounded by the fact that the Austro-Hungarian Army required immediate assistance to prevent its collapse. Habsburg forces had suffered a more serious defeat than German High Command had originally thought, so German troops were deployed north of Fortress Krakow to support the reeling ally. The new German Ninth Army marched to the Vistula River area to deflect enemy attention from the battered Habsburg forces after an eleven-day train ride (450 miles).

The German advance into Poland, commencing on September 29, reached the area east of Lodz, forcing the enemy to shift major troop contingents from the Habsburg to the northern Vistula River front to counter the new threat. This relieved tsarist pressure from the Habsburg front proved critical to the October 9 liberation of Fortress Przemyśl.[3] The Germans advanced to within twelve miles of Warsaw before being forced to retreat on October 17.

In early October, Habsburg Fourth Army approached the San River north of Fortress Przemyśl. Conrad planned for Second and Third armies to launch an offensive through the mountains to attempt to envelop the tsarist extreme left flank positions and force their troop concentrations away from the fortress area. Fortress troops could then join Third Army's battle. Supplying the advancing field armies with food, artillery shells and other vital equipment forced the citadel garrison to transfer a significant portion of its food stores and ammunition (particularly artillery shells) to the field armies once liberated on October 9, 1914.[4] Terrain and weather conditions continued to hinder supplying Third Army, thus once inside the bulwark the army commandeered many lighter fortress supply wagons to replace its heavier, obsolete (fifty-year-old) models, to transport fortress grain supplies and artillery shells to its field units.

On October 5 tsarist forces attempted to storm the citadel, but the siege forces lacked the necessary heavy artillery to be effective. Nine and a half infantry and two cavalry divisions (150 battalions, 48 cavalry squadrons and 800 artillery pieces) launched increasingly powerful attacks against the fortress Siedliska Defensive District VI. Constant bloody battle raged between October 6 and 9, producing horrendous casualties for both sides. Russian artillery shells, fused for contact, exploded too rapidly to seriously damage the old fortification walls, providing the garrison protection from severe damage.

Tsarist artillery barrages nevertheless largely destroyed defensive infantry positions that had no overhead protective cover, as well as most barbed-wire emplacements and trenches located between various interval fortifications. Telephone communication quickly broke down, while thick clouds often prevented air reconnaissance missions.

By October 3, tsarist Eleventh Army second- and third-line troops replaced regular Third Army soldiers at the siege lines.[5] The enemy intensified artillery fire against the key VI Defensive District (Siedliska) fortifications in preparation to launch a major attack. The citadel commander launched a twelve-infantry battalion sortie to prevent tsarist troops from withdrawing from the bulwark area, while Habsburg Third Army troops encountered no serious enemy opposition as they approached the fortress.

Serious battle commenced on October 4, with artillery exchanges, which intensified during the night to October 5, followed by powerful tsarist infantry assaults against the VI Defensive District forts.[6] Tsarist infantry divisions with a thousand officers and ninety-two thousand troops initiated seventy-two hours of bloody battle as the Russians stormed and attempted to capture the citadel. Inclement weather and terrain conditions continued to frustrate efforts to liberate it. Advancing Habsburg infantry had no artillery support because their guns lagged far behind in the mountain terrain, while inadequate replacement troop training resulted in enormous casualties on the battlefield. Between October 5 and 7 Habsburg Third Army units slowly approached the citadel, the sound of their gunfire signaling to the garrison that relief would soon arrive.

The major tsarist attack launched against the Siedliska defensive fortress works, and intensifying artillery support, failed to suppress defensive artillery fire. Realizing the serious threat to the fortress bulwarks, eleven Habsburg infantry battalions were reinforced with 350 artillery pieces (twenty-five batteries).[7]

Destroyed railroad lines and bridges continued to present a significant hindrance to Habsburg offensive efforts to relieve and then resupply the citadel; it required three weeks to repair the railroad bridges after liberation of the fortress. Meanwhile, wagon supply trains attempted to transport Third Army's eight-hundred-ton-per-day supply requirements along the few and eroded roadways.

Supply issues continued even after the railroad bridges had been repaired. When the bridges became operational during late October, railroad resupply efforts had to be extended to the distant northern and southern fortress flank areas since no rail line connected to the central area. This critical shortcoming also hampered troop mobility as well as logistical services, producing a disastrous negative effect on resupply efforts.[8] Temperatures dropped as snowstorms commenced, adding to the supply woes and troop conditions. Then seven Second Army divisions, advancing south of the fortress, entered a narrow pass at Chyrov where it proved almost impossible to maneuver. There, the troops unexpectedly made contact with the entire Russian Eighth Army.

The Russians resumed offensive efforts against the fortress during the night of October 8 despite their earlier failed attempts. Habsburg field armies finally approached the fortress environs. Thousands of dead and seriously wounded troops lay before the VI Defensive District walls. Russian casualties included 4,000 dead, and three times more probably wounded or captured. The tsarist 19. Infantry Division alone sacrificed forty-four officers and 3,400 soldiers, 25 percent of its original stand.

Conrad planned to launch a double envelopment offensive operation against tsarist forces to roll up Russian lines from south of the fortress. On October 8 and 9, Third and Fourth Army forces advanced to the San River, while on the next day Second Army troops approached the fortress perimeter. The rain-drenched terrain continued to retard movement.

As major relieving forces approached the fortress environs, the besieging enemy army withdrew to just east of the citadel into the old Habsburg defensive positions. The withdrawal was also dictated by the German offensive effort at Warsaw–Ivangorod, which briefly threatened the tsarist northern front positions. Tsarist Fourth, Fifth and Ninth armies consequently redeployed to the Vistula River line south of Warsaw to counter the sudden German threat. This action seriously reduced their troop numbers on the Habsburg front. The German advance into Poland succeeded in relieving pressure against the Austro-Hungarian forces.

The tsarist attacks against Fortress Przemyśl failed for multiple reasons. The exhausted assault troops had endured long approach marches during the inclement weather conditions, only arriving immediately prior to launching their assaults. A lack of experienced combat officers and serious supply difficulties stemming from the unfavorable weather and hazardous terrain conditions also took their toll. The hastily prepared offensive plans proved flawed. Faulty intelligence also negatively affected the operation, while no reconnaissance missions preceded the attack. Tsarist artillery failed to adequately support attacking infantry troops by neglecting to neutralize fortress artillery fire. Devastating fortress defensive fire proved decisive during the operation and the casualties wreaked havoc on the attacking troops' morale.[9]

A Habsburg cavalry patrol reached the outer perimeter of the western fortress walls, on October 9, while tsarist forces began establishing new strong defensive lines within artillery range of the fortress's eastern and southeastern perimeters. They also established a major stronghold on the Magiera Heights, soon to witness fierce, bloody battle.

Between October 10 and 23, battle expanded in the Carpathian Mountains as enemy resistance stiffened, halting any Habsburg efforts to advance eastward. On October 10, when Fourth Army units approached the San River, tsarist troops blocked their attempts to cross it.

Fortress Przemyśl suddenly became a very significant Eastern front bastion and remained a major factor until forced to capitulate again in early November 1914. The lack of adequate resupplying attempts became compounded by the necessity to support the relieving field army forces. Evacuation of sick and wounded soldiers could not be completed before the Russians recaptured the fortification. Seven thousand wounded troops were left behind, bringing the total number of wounded to fifteen thousand.

During the night to October 11, while tsarist rearguard units evacuated their fortress positions, Habsburg Fourth and Third Army forces briefly pursued the enemy. Twenty-two fortress infantry battalions and twenty-seven artillery batteries joined the field army advance until forced back into the citadel by tsarist counteractions.

Not previously revealed, on October 4, General Conrad ordered fortress bakeries to prepare a four-day bread supply to feed the equivalent of four field army divisions of fifty-six battalions, or 88,000 portions. This, unknowingly, became the initial factor toward the surrender of the 120,000-man garrison fortress on March 22, 1915. For the first time in history, a citadel besieged for weeks and now preparing for a new enemy attack received orders to bake bread for an approaching field army, instead of husbanding its resources.[10]

Upon entering the fortress, starving Third Army soldiers plundered the garrison's food stores. The fortress also provided further food supplies for the October 9–12 Third Army in its environs.[11] The citadel had unknowingly sealed its own fate by doing so. Fortress food supplies provided nineteen days of food and twenty-six of hay to the field armies. Given the extent of the plundering of the food stores, the total may have been significantly higher. One wonders whether the fortress would have had to surrender on March 22, 1915 if such quantities of supplies had not been removed during the October 1914 liberation.

To resupply its warehouses, the fortress desperately required the use of the destroyed railroad bridges leading to it that had to be repaired. On October 27, a key railroad line reopened, while October 28 brought some resupply services to the fortress following the repair of the critical Nizankovice railroad bridge. One hundred locomotives, hundreds of railroad cars, and railroad personnel participated during these short resupply efforts. Such attempts continued until November 4, when the field armies again retreated from the citadel. The resupply efforts lasted six days. On November 5, Russian troops again besieged the fortress.

On October 11 and 12, a fortress sortie was launched during unrelenting rain to cooperate with the Third Army operations. Conrad ordered Fourth Army to seize various Vistula River crossing points on October 14, an action that was delayed until October 17, because the troops could not penetrate the strong tsarist defensive artillery fire and vital bridge crossing equipment had not arrived. Heavy Russian artillery fire halted all attempts to cross the river, producing numerous casualties.

Habsburg First Army's approach routes to the San River consisted of groundless mud; nevertheless, it had to prepare to cross its river front on October 12. During October 11 through October 13, Second Army's VII and XII Corps were ordered to attack opposing Russian forces, resulting in severe fighting around Chyrov. Habsburg attacks continued through October, but the army could not break through tsarist flank positions. Inclement weather conditions and low supplies of ammunition affected the battle. Meanwhile, the war's first major mountain battle erupted at Magiera, one of the bloodiest encounters on the Eastern front. On October 17, Fourth Army was forced into a defensive stance when its attempt to cross the river failed against solid tsarist defensive action. The Battle of the San River raged from October 13 into November. The Habsburg Third Army suffered devastating casualties during the bloody battle of Magiera October 11–15, without sufficient artillery support, assaulting reinforced and well-constructed enemy positions. The enemy had besieged Fortress Przemyśl for three weeks, and although unsuccessful in capturing it nevertheless achieved its main mission of binding significant enemy forces.

On the German front between October 14 and 18 battle raged at Ivangorod. When the Habsburg First Army reached the San and Vistula River lines it attempted unsuccessfully to cross them. On October 15, the troops attacked Russian forces as they did cross the Vistula River at Ivangorod. Around Warsaw, the enormous Russian numerical superiority forced a German retreat on October 20, but the Vistula River operations succeeded in disrupting tsarist plans to launch a major invasion into Germany to conquer Silesia. Further south, an eighty-mile gap opened between the Habsburg Third and Fourth armies, while Second Army continued to battle enemy forces. The multiple attempts to cross the San River ended in failure. Fourth Army's lack of success on October 17 resulted in Russian units crossing, forcing Habsburg Third and Fourth armies into a defensive stance. The German retreat from Warsaw exposed Conrad's northern flank. Because shell shortages continued, artillery had to be utilized almost exclusively to defend against enemy attacks that the infantry could not repulse. This merely produced further unnecessary casualties. A major cause of the artillery shell shortage resulted from the Dual Monarchy's lack of industrial capacity and raw materials, a result of the Entente blockade. This resulted in the inability to produce vital military materiel in sufficient quantities. This situation would only worsen! The enormous loss of horses to starvation, death and overexertion also seriously affected maneuverability, while Fourth Army troops' low morale and physical condition hampered that army's effectiveness.

On the German front, German Ninth and Habsburg First Army right flank forces launched an attack along the Vistula River toward Warsaw on October 9. The Russians' resistance stiffened as their troops retreated to the forts protecting the city. The Central Powers pursuit did not press the retreating troops because of the major casualties they had sustained. The Russians then regrouped, preparing a sixty-division counterattack against the Germans, three armies drawn from the Habsburg front. When German troops withdrew from the Warsaw vicinity, Russian troops crossed the San River on the Habsburg front. After First Army's unlucky battle at Ivangorod, the tsarist Fourth and Ninth armies pursued battered Habsburg troops to Krakow and further to the Nida River line.

As German troops recoiled from their failed Warsaw campaign, the Russians launched an offensive into Galicia between October 17 and 19, forcing a general Habsburg retreat into the Carpathian Mountains. Conrad again had overestimated his armies' capabilities against superior Russian troop numbers, while tsarist artillery remained better in every category.

The tsarist Galician offensive smashed the badly shaken Habsburg First Army, whose failed Ivangorod offensive cost fifty thousand casualties, with the survivors forced to retreat to the Fortress Krakow area. The unanticipated German Warsaw area retreat movement exposed First Army positions to an enemy-flanking maneuver, endangering Habsburg positions on the Vistula River front and exposing Third and Second armies' flank positions at Fortress Przemyśl.

A Russian attack against First Army's left flank positions on October 25 threatened it with encirclement, resulting in a retreat, effectively neutralizing Conrad's plans. Meanwhile, Fourth Army troops managed to maintain their positions along the San River, south of Fortress Przemyśl.

Once entrenched north of Fortress Krakow, Habsburg First Army's mission became to defend its positions as long as possible to facilitate Fortress Przemyśl resupply efforts. Unrelenting Russian attacks, however, forced it to retreat, which threatened to compromise the entire San River defensive line and expose Fortress Przemyśl to enemy siege. The rapid Habsburg retreat from the fortress in late October and early November 1914 marked the second time that Conrad had allowed his military operations to be dictated by the fate of the fortress.

During early November, before the second Russian siege, Third Army commander and the fortress chief of staff recommended that the citadel be abandoned. Ignoring this advice resulted in multiple bloody futile attempts to terminate the second enemy siege and recover the fortress garrison. The Russian shift of emphasis to the German front removed one of Fortress Przemyśl's major *raisons d'être*, to bind significant tsarist troop numbers. Austro-Hungarian forces failed to defeat Russian forces even though the Russians redeployed four armies against Germany, leaving only three in Galicia.

When Russian units crossed the San River on November 2, they foiled Habsburg Second Army attempts to encircle Russian flank positions. Habsburg armies retreated into the Carpathian Mountains on November 3. The second Fortress Przemyśl siege commenced on November 4, as cold weather conditions exacerbated the Habsburg soldiers' physical situation. Tsarist forces continued to threaten to traverse the Carpathian Mountains and invade Hungary to end the war. Major battle erupted at Fortress Krakow and on the German front between November 16 and 20.

On the Western front outnumbered German troops participated in the "Race to the Sea," terminating at Ypres, leading to trench warfare. On the Eastern front Command concentrated troops in the Thorn area, as the Russians continued preparations for their planned major invasion of Germany.

In early November Conrad transferred major Second Army units to the German front to assist German protection of the Silesian industrial region and operations in Poland, weakening the Habsburg Carpathian Mountain defense. The Russians immediately took advantage of the new situation, thus, throughout early November, the Habsburg military crisis continued. Habsburg First and Fourth armies battled north of Fortress Krakow, Second and Third armies below the Vistula River line. Continuous battle produced enormous Third Army casualties. On October 29 tsarist Third and Eighth armies had launched an offensive along a front of more than a hundred miles, from Fortress Krakow to the Carpathian Mountains, their second attempt to cross the San River.

In spite of the advantage provided by intercepted Russian communications, by late September Habsburg units were forced back by the sheer weight of enemy numbers. The tsarist armies hurled seven corps against retreating Austro-Hungarian forces, with two to three corps alone striking First Army's left flank positions. That army, which had sustained the cited severe casualties at Ivangorod, lacked artillery shells to support its hard-pressed troops. Repeated attempts to liberate Fortress Przemyśl proved futile for five months with the renewed tsarist siege. The failed attempts merely produced enormous casualties and suffering for the fortress and field troops.

Commencing in early November, the Eastern front gained increasing significance in the overall war picture. The deteriorating Central Power Eastern front military situation, combined with the negative results of the first battle of Ypres in Flanders, forced General Falkenhayn to reassess his military options. He determined that the Russian advance north of the Vistula River had to be countered; meanwhile, Conrad established defensive positions in the Fortress Krakow area, to support a Fourth Army crossing of the Vistula River.

All Habsburg units desperately required reinforcements to replace the mounting casualties and replenish depleted ammunition stores, particularly artillery shells and damaged equipment. The exhausted troops also required rehabilitation as weather conditions continually worsened.

The Habsburg First and German Ninth armies' early November retreat from the Ivangorod front threatened to break contact between the Allied armies. Ninth Army returned to its original positions. Neither could overcome the enemy's numerical superiority, nor could the Germans provide reinforcements from the hotly contested Western front. The Allied retrograde movements also isolated Fortress Przemyśl, where fortress troops removed fifteen thousand bloated Russian corpses from the fortress perimeter.[12] Conrad hoped that the second citadel defense would be successful and that it could repel enemy attacks, as well as bind significant troop numbers from joining their numerically superior field troops.

Third Army's attempt to advance a day's march east of Fortress Przemyśl encountered strong Russian opposition, which forced its retreat to the Carpathian Mountain Dukla Pass region to block an invasion of northern Hungary. The troops had to surrender their San River defensive positions conquered earlier at such great human cost.

On the German front, when tsarist troops briefly paused their movement, Ninth Army hurled three rapidly transported corps toward Thorn to the southeast, to intercept advancing Russian Second and Fifth Army formations to attack their right flank forces. Uncoded Russian messages proved very valuable. Ninth Army deployed every available soldier extending from Thorn toward the tsarist Lodz–Warsaw positions, initiating a giant pincer movement on November 11 attempting to drive a wedge between the Russian First and Second armies near Lodz. Lodz was the starting point for a Russian major offensive against Germany. Advancing German troops struck tsarist First Army's northern flank positions then moved against Second Army. The tactically successful Ninth Army operation almost annihilated the tsarist First Army and then hurled the Second eighty miles back to Warsaw.

Conrad ordered Third and Fourth armies to assist First Army, but the Fourth commenced a retreat on November 4. When Conrad agreed to help defend Silesia and seal the dangerous 180-kilometer gap in the Central Powers front lines it opened a gap in his lines, where Second Army troops had been deployed, inviting a major Russian offensive thrust into the Carpathian Mountain region.

To seal the dangerous gap, remaining Second Army troops redeployed to key Carpathian Mountain ridge lines near Chyrov to thwart enemy forces from advancing west from the area south of Fortress Przemyśl. Southmost Army Group Pflanzer-Baltin's mission remained to defend the east Carpathian Mountain crossing points and Bukovina province near the Romanian frontier. Meanwhile, the third Balkan offensive commenced against Serbia, but the campaign ended in disaster in early December.

Persisting inclement weather conditions and continuing combat losses negatively affected Habsburg military fortunes, causing Conrad to again request German assistance, but denied because of the Western front "Race to the Sea" campaign. Three Russian armies pressed Habsburg forces from three different directions – across the San River line toward Fortress Krakow, Fortress Przemyśl and into the Carpathian Mountains. The fortress resupply efforts had to be terminated on November 4 because of tsarist military advances, leaving its ammunition magazines and food depots half full.

The retrograde movement halted at the main Carpathian Mountain ridges at the Dukla, Lupkov and Uzsok Passes in an attempt to block the key invasion routes into Hungary. Meanwhile, on November 4, as the fortress was again besieged, the question of a joint Eastern front command was raised. The German military chancellery recommended that Archduke Friedrich, nominal commander of the Habsburg Army, become the honorary Allied commander, while German General Eric Ludendorff assumed the duties of chief of the Allied General Staffs. Conrad would continue to command Austro-Hungarian forces, General Hindenburg the German. This infuriated Conrad, who threatened to resign, perceiving the attempt as a lack of confidence in his leadership, as well as a German attempt to destroy Habsburg military independence. This vital question of a unified Eastern front command structure would be resuscitated numerous times when this one failed, but remained unresolved until late 1916 following the Brusilov offensive disaster, and that one only briefly, as we shall learn. This failure to resolve this vital question proved fatal to Central Powers' efforts, particularly in 1916 when Falkenhayn unleased his Verdun operation and Conrad his *Straf* expedition.

On November 5, after almost a month of constant battle, Habsburg field armies began to withdraw from the Fortress Przemyśl area, a major blow to the army's and Conrad's prestige. The tsarist Third and Eighth armies' offensive across the San River resulted in the second fortress siege. The fortress proceeded to exert an increasing influence on Conrad's military strategy. As Habsburg troops withdrew from the citadel, tsarist forces continued to advance westward between the Vistula River and Carpathian Mountain forelands penetrating the major mountain ridgelines. This was despite Russian High Command prioritizing an invasion of Germany.

Habsburg Third Army's mission became to defend the main Carpathian Mountain invasion routes to the Hungarian plains. Horrendous weather and terrain conditions, poor communications and insufficient resources made the mission extremely difficult, but an invasion of Hungary had to be prevented at all costs. Third Army and remnants of Second Army had to defend the main mountain crossing points, which was much more difficult once Second Army transferred multiple divisions to the German Silesian front.

Third Army had to extend its front lines from the Carpathian Mountain forelands to slow the tsarist advance after the capitulation of Fortress Przemyśl, while Second Army units had to secure the critical crossing points between the Dukla and Uzsok Passes.[13] Habsburg troops' deteriorating physical, mental and material conditions worsened with the chronic lack of reserve formations, and raised serious concern about the declining troop morale and increasingly inadequate replacement troop training. Those troops were almost immediately deployed to the front as cannon fodder. The severe shortage of rifles resulted in wooden stocks replacing them during training. Troop preparedness had declined precipitously because basic training time continued to decrease as a result of the incessant necessity to replace the consistent severe battlefield casualties, particularly professional troops. They were being rendered *hors de combat* at an alarming rate.[14]

A Fortress Przemyśl sortie attempted to ascertain the composition of the enemy siege forces, while small excursion parties scrounged for equipment and food that the rapidly retreating field armies had discarded. By November, horses had to be slaughtered to provide food for the garrison troops, and the lack of straw and surrogate mixtures to feed remaining animals had rendered them little more than skin and bone. With the Habsburg retreat the fortress lay increasingly distant from the front lines, while Russian troops initiated a slow, systematic siege to starve the garrison into submission. The fortress's chief mission continued to bind as many troops as possible, but the situation proved far different from the first siege. The fortress no longer lay in the center of battle.

Further north, tsarist forces also attacked First Army positions, causing one-third casualties. When German High Command reported on November 6 that its troops protecting that army's left flank positions would be immediately transferred to protect the Silesian frontier, Conrad ordered First Army to retreat to Fortress Krakow and Fourth Army to rapidly deploy troops to that Vistula River area. He planned to launch an offensive, despite the army's increasingly weakened condition and horrendous troop situation.

Fourth Army's movement increased the threat of a Russian invasion into the Carpathian Mountains, because it removed troops to the Krakow area. Third Army forces established defensive positions to secure the key Uzsok Pass railroad connections and critical Mezölaborcz communication and rail-road center in the Laborcz Valley as its troops steadily retreated.

The encirclement of Fortress Przemyśl occurred between November 8 and 11, tsarist forces using the inclement weather conditions to assist their efforts to sever railroad and road access to the citadel. Siege troops remained gener-ally passive during the remainder of the month, satisfied with starving the garrison into submission. The new Eleventh Army, composed of second- and third-line forces, became the siege force. Massive defensive fortress artillery barrages temporarily thwarted Russian efforts to approach the bulwark perimeter.

Recent battle and disease had reduced the garrison combat strength by 20,000 troops, leaving a force of approximately 120,000 soldiers and 21,500 horses.[15] Approximately 30,000 civilians remained in the fortress, 18,000 of which the military had to feed, further depleting citadel food supplies. Why hadn't more been evacuated?

When the mass of tsarist Eighth and Third armies advanced into the Carpathian Mountains, Eighth Army forces seized several strategic passes, particularly the Dukla. Third Army pressed Habsburg Third Army west into other key passes and forelands between November 10 and 19. Conrad became increasingly desperate to restore his army's battered reputation, especially to neutral Italy and Romania, but he commanded a wounded army.

On November 11 a 23. *Honvéd* Infantry Division sortie was launched to disrupt Russian supply efforts as well as to pin down enemy siege forces, while garrison units scavenged for food outside the citadel's perimeter. Some fortress perimeter defensive areas were extended outward to provide additional future fortress foray maneuver room.

In the Carpathian Mountains, despite Habsburg Third Army troops having established protracted defensive lines, particularly at the Dukla and Uzsok

Passes, they failed to halt the irresistible enemy pressure that forced numerous retreats. Decoders intercepted numerous tsarist wireless messages, which revealed that they planned to launch a three-army offensive toward Fortress Krakow on November 15. Conrad's counterstrategy entailed launching a spoiling attack with First and Fourth armies to attempt to roll up the Russian front at that fortress. Meanwhile, winter weather settled into the mountainous terrain with a vengeance, heavy snowfall commencing on November 19. Frigid conditions ravaged the ill-provisioned soldiers, many still wearing summer issue uniforms, which severely increased cold-related illnesses and frostbite cases. From mid-November battle raged at Fortress Krakow, while in the Carpathian Mountains Russian offensive forces reached the Dukla Pass, simultaneously threatening nearby Lupkov and Uzsok Passes.

Fifteen days after its retreat from Warsaw, the German Ninth Army drove a wedge into the Russian left flank at Lodz, surprising an enemy four-army advance to attempt to invade Silesia. Faced with potential military disaster, *Stavka* eventually canceled plans to launch its offensive into Silesia. Instead, it had to transfer troops to relieve the battered First and Second armies, which retreated toward Lodz.[16] The German objective became to puncture the junction between Russian First Army defending the northern flank of the invasion force. The brunt of the attack struck the two corps between First and Second armies.

The Russians were caught completely by surprise. On November 11 and 12, General Mackensen's troops drove tsarist right flank forces back. Four German Ninth Army corps attacked to the north and east of Lodz until November 20 when enemy troops in turn attacked the Ninth Army's rear position, which forced an army retreat on November 25. Soon after, trench warfare began to settle on this front. Between November 16 and 22, German Ninth Army, in its turn, barely escaped defeat. Finally receiving reinforcements from the Western front, troops reached Lodz, but seven tsarist corps halted the German advance at the Russian defensive perimeter. Battle lasted until November 25, when the Germans faced encirclement.

Earlier, after heavy battle, tsarist Second Army extricated itself to the west and north where battle continued into early December. Both tsarist armies quickly retreated. The invading German troops were handicapped by having long supply lines.

Instead of supporting their ally's Lodz effort, Habsburg troops retreated toward Krakow pursued by enemy troops. Habsburg armies again teetered on the brink of disaster. On November 16, Russian Ninth Army pressed Habsburg Fourth Army troops back to the Fortress Krakow area, while other enemy forces advanced into the Bukovina. A gap of more than a hundred kilometers separated Habsburg Fourth and Third armies, as Russian troops threatened the mountain passes leading toward Hungary. Only Russian command ineptitude and the early December arrival of the full-strength German

47. Reserve Infantry Division eventually stemmed the seemingly unstoppable enemy tide.

Weakened Habsburg Third Army units, bloodied from months of offensive action, could not halt the tsarist Third and Eighth armies, compelling further retreat. Russian Eighth attacked toward the Dukla and Uzsok Passes on November 17, while Conrad launched his own surprise offensive as Fourth Army attacked enemy right flank positions at Fortress Krakow. As these events unfolded, Conrad became increasingly concerned about the enemy Eighth Army's advance through key mountain passes (Uzsok, Beskid and Dukla Passes). Those forces quickly seized main portions of the Lupkov and Dukla Passes, pressuring the isolated Habsburg Third Army that was frantically struggling to defend the main ridgelines. Fortunately, the Russians did not attempt to advance beyond the critical Dukla depression area because the farther west they progressed the more vulnerable their northern flank positions became to a German counterattack.

Fourth Army Group Roth (XIV Corps), reinforced by the newly arrived German 47. Reserve Infantry Division, launched an attack into the gap between the Russian Third and Eighth armies.[17] Meanwhile, good news arrived from the Balkan front, where the Serbians had retreated; Habsburg Fifth Army had finally attained some key offensive objectives. To follow up on this success, Falkenhayn pressured Conrad to launch an offensive into the northeast corner of Serbia to open the Danube River for ammunition supply transit to the Turkish ally. Conrad balked, claiming he lacked sufficient troop numbers, and feared that it would provide Romania an excuse to enter the war against the Central Powers.

At a *Stavka* meeting in Siedlice, General Ivanov, the Habsburg front commander, advocated launching a major offensive into the Carpathian Mountains; somewhat surprisingly considering that Germany had been designated the primary threat. *Stavka* reluctantly accepted his proposal.

By November 20, Fortress Przemyśl continued to hold, launching troops on one of the largest siege sorties, although little was achieved. The besieging Eleventh Army (only six infantry and one cavalry division) was composed almost entirely of reserve and territorial troops. Therefore, they did not pose an immediate threat to the garrison, but rather would starve it out. They proved sufficient to maintain the siege until the fortress's surrender on March 22, 1915. Assured that time was on his side, the tsarist siege commander remained passive during much of November. The increasing isolation of the fortress, and the Russian advance into the Carpathian Mountain passes, significantly diminished the value of the fortress. This allowed the Russians to maintain their leisurely investment, and redeploy combat troops elsewhere.

By November 21, Habsburg supply efforts continued to lag, as temperatures plummeted to −13°C and troops increasingly suffered from frostbite. At Fortress Krakow, increasing Russian pressure encountered little resistance as the Habsburg military situation deteriorated. Russian forces unleashed a major offensive in the Beskid Pass area between November 22 and December 2. Russian columns advanced in the key Dukla Pass area. Habsburg Third Army's front remained overextended and its troop stands continually decimated in battle.

Third Army retreated on November 23 as the military situation at Fortress Krakow heated up. Tsarist troops hurled weak Habsburg covering troops rearward. Between November 24 and 28, the critical Dukla, Lupkov and Beskid Passes were surrendered. Meanwhile, Fourth Army troops battled the eight-division tsarist Fourth Army and the fourteen-to-fifteen-division Ninth Army around Fortress Krakow. To the north, Habsburg First Army sustained further serious casualties. Falkenhayn reiterated his request to launch a Habsburg offensive against Serbia, but Conrad could not comply.

Tsarist forces had reached the vital Carpathian Mountain upper Laborcz River area, forcing defending VII Corps units toward the key Mezőlaborz transportation center. Enemy forces also attacked the Uzsok Pass on November 25, where fighting continued through December. Then Conrad launched a surprise attempt to envelop enemy positions, approaching Fortress Krakow with three Fourth Army divisions. First Army had to unconditionally defend its front northwest of the fortress to support the operation.

Fourth Army Group Roth (XIV Corps) expanded to eight infantry and three cavalry divisions for the major battle developing around Fortress Krakow during late November. During the night of November 27 two and a half Russian corps smashed into Third Army's weakened defensive lines, threatening to pierce that army's mountain front. Its exhausted troops sustained additional excessive casualties, while a severe shortage of ammunition, particularly artillery shells, winter uniforms and equipment added to the soldiers' misfortune.

Strong Russian forces also continued to attack Fortress Przemyśl positions, utilizing inclement weather conditions to achieve surprise. Fortress artillery barrages halted the attacks, while two days later fortress troops launched a counterattack, but by the end of the month the bulwark's situation had returned to normal.

As an example of the Habsburg soldiers' travail, Infantry Regiment 74 reported temperatures at $-15°C$, brutal winds battering its exhausted soldiers. The troops had not received food for four days, while battalion strengths had dropped as low as two hundred rifles instead of the usual thousand. The few remaining troops defended extended front lines while their sparse numbers prevented the creation of reserve formations and resulted in gaps opening in the front lines. The Russians skillfully utilized the unfavorable terrain and weather conditions to launch frequent night attacks against the regiment. One attack captured an entire regimental staff, resulting in further rapid retreat.[18]

The Austrian official history of the war complained that Czech replacement troops had been poisoned by anti-military and anti-dynastic propaganda and could not physically cope with winter mountain warfare. Many reputedly surrendered to the enemy without a struggle. Notwithstanding the horrendous conditions and the purported defection of Czech troops, Habsburg forces could no longer halt enemy attacks.

A major attack was launched against Habsburg forces in the Mezölaborcz area between November 28 and December 2, forcing Third Army's battered III, VII and IX Corps to retreat. Unrelenting tsarist attempts to seize the key mountain passes, combined with the weakness of Habsburg forces, secured the Russian flank positions for a major invasion into Silesia. Favorable Balkan theater battlefield reports, however, encouraged the reeling Habsburg troops to continue their efforts. Fortunately, the Russians did not pursue retreating Third Army units, but it remained questionable whether the sorely pressed troops, desperately needing reinforcements, could halt another attack. The incessant attacks in the mountain passes posed a critical threat.

By the end of November, the tsarist Third and Ninth armies had advanced to within twenty-five kilometers of Krakow. Fourth Army Group Roth (XIV Corps) launched an offensive at Fortress Krakow on December 2. Three and a half months of continuous fighting and marching had seriously weakened its forces. Division strengths had been reduced to two to three thousand from twelve to fifteen thousand soldiers.

Fortress Przemyśl artillery capabilities began to rapidly decline. Deteriorating gun tubes could not be replaced, meaning the guns' effective firing range dropped precipitously. Shells had to be conserved, while some caliber rounds were depleted, placing multiple guns out of action.[19] Conrad remained fixated on liberating Galicia and Fortress Przemyśl, despite the fact that the *k.u.k. Armee* had been destroyed on the bloody 1914 battlefields and his units were now reeling on both fronts.

Considering the deplorable battle and supply conditions and earlier transfer of significant Second Army units to the German front, the postponing of any major offensive efforts until spring seemed prudent. Conrad, however, desperately needed to secure a victory against the Russians to restore damaged Habsburg military reputation after the many battlefield defeats. Early December's disastrous Balkan front defeat, discussed in the last chapter, severely embarrassed Dual Monarchy leadership, and destroyed any remaining Habsburg prestige in the Balkan Peninsula. German military command pressured Conrad to rectify that inglorious defeat, but his primary motivation for launching an offensive in early December in Galicia stemmed from the threat of neutral Italy and Romania entering the war. Both craved irredentist lands but awaited definitive tsarist battlefield results to assure easy seizure of the desired territories.

A decisive change in the unfavorable Habsburg military situation appeared unlikely to occur during early December. The perilous gap in the front lines between Fortress Krakow and the Carpathian Mountain ranges continued to widen, while various portions of the fronts settled into a semi-trench line. The steadily declining fortress food supply and troop conditions demanded rapid action. An effective attempt to liberate the citadel could only be launched from the Carpathian Mountains, the front now some eighty kilometers from there.

December developed into an especially difficult and eventful month for Habsburg military fortunes. Costly Fortress Przemyśl sorties continued to be launched, while the battered and demoralized Third Army troops carried on defending the Carpathian Mountain terrain. The chronic shortage of troops and mounting casualties posed a major problem, while the lack of reinforcements and replacement troops only worsened the critical situation.

Pitched battle soon erupted at the strategic Carpathian Mountain Laborcz Valley railroad center at Mezölaborcz that continued unabated through early February 1915. The eventual loss of Mezölaborcz proved detrimental to efforts to liberate Fortress Przemyśl, because its two-track railroad line was critical for any operation to achieve that.

Habsburg troops suffered enormous hardships, fighting twenty-four-hour battles with little protection from enemy artillery fire, while lacking regular logistical support. The constant loss of professional officers and noncommissioned officers resulted in declining battlefield effectiveness and slackened discipline in the ranks. Accelerating physical exhaustion produced troop apathy and loss of morale.

The battle of Limanova–Lapanov (December 2 to 11) produced the first significant military victory over the previously undefeated tsarist forces. The offensive objective included driving tsarist troops across the Vistula River. During the ensuing bloody battle and fifty-kilometer enemy retreat, the Russian Eighth Army suffered 70 percent casualties, momentarily thwarting the threat of an invasion of Hungary. The Russians also had to abandon their efforts to invade Germany because of the threat to their right flank positions caused by their retreat. Habsburg forces temporarily regained the initiative.

Third Army III Corps had lost more than half its numbers. IX Corps' battleworthiness had been almost destroyed following eleven days of marching and thirty-five days of combat. Nevertheless, Third Army received orders to intervene in the ensuing Limanova–Lapanov battle. In their weakened physical condition, troops marched only fifteen kilometers a day toward the new battle front, but ultimately proved decisive in the battle outcome. Other Third Army contingents continued battle in the Carpathian Mountains.

The worsening food shortages prompted the slaughter of thousands of horses at Fortress Przemyśl to increase the meat supply and help alleviate the shortage of straw and hay. Troops continued to forage for food outside the fortress walls, while requisition commissions confiscated excess food from civilians within the bulwark. Horsemeat, originally a despised commodity, became a delicacy. Germ-infested water had to be boiled to prevent disease.

On December 1, strong tsarist assaults renewed against the critical fortress VI Defensive District Na Gorach perimeter position, but a timely sortie forced an enemy retreat. To bind siege troops during the Limanova–Lapanov battle, eighteen-and-three-quarter infantry battalions, supported by fourteen artillery batteries, launched a mission in coordination with the field army's latest offensive effort to liberate the citadel. The distance separating the fortress and field armies proved too extensive; all December attempts to liberate the citadel failed.[20] The Austro-Hungarian Limanova–Lapanov campaign involved thirteen infantry and four cavalry divisions (90,000 troops) attacking eleven to thirteen enemy infantry divisions (100,000 to 120,000 soldiers). On December 1 and 2, the Russians launched heavy forays against the Carpathian Beskid Pass, but Habsburg Third Army enjoyed a short rehabilitation period between December 2 and 7, because the Russians transferred at least three army corps to the German front.

The reinforced Fourth Army Group Roth on December 3 launched a three-infantry division offensive northward toward Limanova, a small village located at the Russian Third Army flank and rear positions. This struck the Russians' most vulnerable position: a sixty-kilometer gap between Third and Eighth armies, offering the chance for victory. Tsarist troops, however, quickly countered the initial offensive efforts, as the town of Neu Sandec became a magnet for both combatants.

By December 4 the Russians rapidly reinforced their threatened flank positions. Habsburg Fourth Army forces faced only weak tsarist cavalry forces, but enemy resistance steadily increased. The tsarist VIII and XXIV Corps approached the critical Neu Sandec area, threatening Habsburg flank positions. By December 5, XIV Corps required immediate reinforcements because it lacked sufficient reserve formations, while the enemy steadily received additional troops. Habsburg forces, encountering strong tsarist resistance, were repulsed everywhere. Tsarist forces advancing toward Neu Sandec had to be halted, a task assigned to the recuperating Third Army.[21] Conrad, on December 6, ordered Third Army to commence forced marches to reach the Fourth Army battle zone and prevent consolidation of the two tsarist Eighth Army corps. On the Balkan front, the capture of Belgrade on December 2 improved Habsburg morale, although it was short-lived. Following a Serbian counterattack, Belgrade had to be evacuated, a further major loss of Habsburg prestige in the Balkan Peninsula. Conrad worried that further military setbacks could sway Italy, Bulgaria and Romania to intervene against the Dual Monarchy.

German diplomatic and military leaders again urged Conrad to join in an offensive to conquer the Negotine (northeastern) sector of Serbia to restore Habsburg military honor, and open a secure supply route to Turkey. A Balkan victory might also convince Bulgaria to join the Central Powers, but his outnumbered troops were firmly tied to the Russian front, frantically battling the numerically superior enemy.[22]

Reconnaissance reports and radio intercepts revealed that strong enemy forces had maneuvered into the eighty-kilometer gap between Third Army and Group Roth's attack forces. Reinforcements were dispatched to the Neu Sandec area to secure Fourth Army's right flank positions.

On December 6 the Habsburg military situation worsened as the tsarist Fourth and its own Fourth Army battled while enemy Ninth Army troops forced back Habsburg Fourth Army units south of Fortress Krakow. Emperor Franz Joseph reputedly stated, "How on earth can we pursue even a tolerable foreign policy when we fight so badly?"

On the Third Army Carpathian Mountain front tsarist forces drove Habsburg troops back from their positions at Sanok and defeated Army Group Pflanzer-Baltin's forces further south. A seventy-kilometer gap had widened between Third and Fourth armies until Third Army troops slowly approached the Limanova–Lapanov battlefield.

The newly arrived, full-strength 47. German Reserve Infantry Division, its troops unaccustomed to winter mountain warfare and possessing no mountain equipment, nevertheless became critical. By December 6 thirteen First Army divisions battled fourteen to fifteen Russian Ninth Army divisions northwest of Fortress Krakow, while Russian Third Army troops began threatening Fourth Army units' flank positions at Neu Sandec. Habsburg Fourth Army launched a frontal assault toward Limanova.

As Group Roth continued its assault toward Neu Sandec, a two-corps Eighth Army enemy attack threatened its eastern flank and rear echelon positions. As sickness, battle and dwindling troop numbers weakened Fourth Army efforts, only Third Army could assure victory by preventing other Russian units from intervening in the battle. The accelerating tsarist pressure against Group Roth increased the necessity for Third Army to intervene in the battle as rapidly as possible.

The situation became critical on December 7 when Russian Eighth Army units advanced toward Limanova, where only minimal Fourth Army troops countered the strong enemy forces. Still-distant Third Army troops encountered serious delays marching through difficult wooded terrain, where many *Landsturm* troops collapsed from exhaustion. The lack of Habsburg reinforcements and adequate troop numbers intensified the crisis as fighting extended from Lapanov north to Limanova.

On December 9 tsarist XXIV Corps intervened in the battle as Habsburg Third Army units continued their advance to the battlefield. Meanwhile, the Habsburg Third Army units still deployed in the Carpathian Mountains attempted to liberate Fortress Przemyśl. A powerful citadel sortie was launched on December 9 (nineteen infantry battalions and fourteen artillery batteries) to hinder tsarist troop withdrawal of siege troops for use on other fronts. The sortie bound Russian troops on the bulwark's southeastern perimeter on December 9 and 10.

In an often-repeated scenario, fortress 23. *Honvéd* Infantry Division troops reached forward Russian positions, but lacked sufficient numbers to pierce the strong enemy lines. Additional efforts proved fruitless as the Russians rapidly neutralized each attempt. The notorious inaccuracy of Habsburg artillery fire, already noticeable during the first siege, continued. On December 10, the exhausted surviving sortie soldiers withdrew into the fortress, having achieved nothing for their effort.

Heavy battle between December 9 and 28 significantly reduced the garrison's offensive strength. Sorties, launched on December 13 and between 15 and 18, resulted in significant officer and veteran combat fortress troop casualties. The effort launched on December 15 consisted of between twenty-three and twenty-five infantry battalions, fifteen artillery batteries and eight and a half cavalry squadrons from the 23. *Honvéd* Infantry Division. Initially, the operation produced a string of successes, overcoming numerous strongly fortified enemy forward defensive lines. However, inadequate troop numbers, unfavorable terrain conditions and lack of effective artillery support prevented further breach of the enemy's main defensive positions.[23] Fortress troop and civilian morale plunged as the possibility of liberation appeared to dissipate by the end of 1914. Meanwhile, Third Army right flank forces, attempting to liberate the fortress, advanced to within fifty kilometers of the citadel, but then their efforts stalled.

The Russians continued to deploy reinforcements to the Fortress Krakow battle area, which succeeded in halting Habsburg Fourth Army progress. A reinforced tsarist Third Army counterattack regained the initiative, smashing into Group Roth's open flank position, forcing its troops rearward. Habsburg Third Army troops had meanwhile advanced to within twenty kilometers of Neu Sandec while five infantry and one cavalry division defended the high terrain at Limanova against the tsarist VIII Corps; these units had to deploy noncombat troops to fill their ranks. Troop numbers continued to shrink; to cite one example, by December 10 3. Infantry Division's effective numbers stood at only nine hundred troops.[24]

Inclement weather conditions interrupted Habsburg air reconnaissance efforts, which failed to discover significant tsarist troop movements. Delays in railroad traffic continued to hamper the arrival of reinforcements. Third Army troops, approaching Neu Sandec, finally compelled the enemy to retreat by decisively driving through the gap between the two tsarist armies, preventing them from combining forces. This action assured victory.

During the night to December 12 tsarist III and XXIV Corps troops began to retreat from the Neu Sandec area. Third Army units had advanced on December 8 to prevent tsarist Eighth and Third Army forces from uniting.

That army's troops attacked the enemy VIII Corps' rear echelon positions, then shifted toward Neu Sandec. The ultimate victory owed much to the full-strength German 47. Reserve Infantry Division, which possessed more troops than all the participating Habsburg divisions.

Excessive casualties and lack of reserve formations to replenish depleted Third Army ranks hindered a rapid pursuit of enemy forces following the significant victory. Overreliance on limited railroad capacity seriously retarded transport of troops and supplies, resulting in traffic chaos negatively affecting all efforts.

Conrad's forces had defeated numerically superior tsarist forces by skillfully using maneuver tactics and interior lines. Third Army units, some still fighting in the Carpathian Mountains, attempted to achieve a major victory on their right flank there by inserting X and XVIII Corps to attempt to encircle retreating enemy forces. Ice-covered roads severely hampered progress, and extreme troop exhaustion and excellent Russian retrograde tactics prevented major tsarist territorial losses and seriously hindered their pursuit.

The threat to Fortress Krakow ended temporarily and the front stabilized. Tsarist Eighth Army's slow retrograde movement delayed Habsburg Third Army pursuit near Fortress Przemyśl by destroying San River bridges as it withdrew. The effort allowed Eleventh Army to maintain its siege, and pre-vented garrison troops from advancing north of the fortress and Third Army eastern flank forces from liberating the citadel.

Conrad planned to capitalize on the Limanova–Lapanov victory by launching a relentless pursuit to attempt to encircle retreating enemy soldiers, but the Russians had commenced preparations to launch their own major offensive operation. They easily replaced casualties and speedily recovered from the Limanova–Lapanov battles. Sickness, extreme exhaus-tion and escalating casualties steadily decreased Habsburg and tsarist troop numbers as their declining physical condition and lack of equipment, artillery shells and food exacted an increasingly enormous toll. Habsburg Third Army pursuit efforts slackened between December 18 and 20; at the same time, the seemingly endless Russian reinforcements enabled them to launch a series of counteroffensives that ruptured weak Habsburg positions. Tsarist occupation of key mountain ridges provided continued security for the Fortress Przemyśl siege, while offering future opportunity to launch an offensive into Hungary. The enemy continued to enjoy its major advantage of shorter, direct railroad and road transport routes for the transport of supplies and reinforcements. Habsburg units, ensconced in higher moun-tain terrain, had to transport reinforcements over a much wider area, then march considerable distances over rugged terrain to reach their deployment area.

On December 17 an alarming internal fortress report indicated that the citadel could only sustain its food until early January 1915 because of rapidly depleting supplies. An alarmed fortress commander established a commission to investigate the matter.

Conrad's exhausted troops had been "pumped dry" after launching three major offensives against the Russians, each resulting in defeat and retreat, the army sustaining a million casualties. On December 21, Conrad reported that "the best officers and non-commissioned officers had died or been removed from service," then described replacement troops as "being of poor quality and partly young, partly older men." The field armies abandoned enormous amounts of irreplaceable equipment and food supplies during their multiple retreats. The first-year campaigns had almost eliminated the Habsburg Army as a viable fighting force. The casualty toll included 1.3 million troops: 189,000 dead, 500,000 wounded and 280,000 prisoners of war. Officer casualties numbered around 30,000 of which 4,800 had been killed, 12,000 were wounded, 11,200 were sick and 4,200 were prisoners of war or missing in action. In December 1914, only 303,000 troops remained to counter the numerically superior enemy. German liaison officers reported that Conrad had lost faith in his troops and that a dangerous fatalism permeated the Supreme Command, while he seethed at German expressions of superiority over his troops and their snide comments about Habsburg military capabilities.

Habsburg Supreme Command remained almost completely unaware of tsarist intentions, except for radio intercepts. In the meantime, unbeknownst to Conrad or his staff, the enemy amassed enormous troop numbers opposite the Third Army right flank area, which prevented any future attempts to liberate the fortress.

Between December 20 and 24, the Russians launched a decisive counter-offensive on the Galician front. Using the cover of heavy snowfall and fog, troops seized major ridgelines, neutralizing any potential Habsburg military threat from that direction. On December 20, the benumbed nine-division Third Army succumbed to a twelve-division Russian attack. The renewed tsarist military successes again raised the specter of Italy and Romania entering the war against the Central Powers. When Third Army had to retreat, it forced neighboring Fourth Army right flank units to also move rearwards. Habsburg III Corps' three divisions numbered only 10,200 troops, while IX Corps numbers were equally low.[25]

As battle continued to rage at Fortress Przemyśl, the newly convened Commission of Inquiry investigated the dwindling food supply and horse fodder reserves. The Commission concluded that the supply of horse feed would last until February 18, and fodder until March 7, 1915, providing the garrison several extra weeks of sustenance. To attain these goals, the commission demanded the immediate slaughter of ten thousand horses, to provide additional sustenance for the starving garrison troops. These commission findings proved misleading, as they grossly underestimated the number of garrison troops, horses and civilians in the fortress.[26]

On December 22, a major enemy assault threatened to pierce Third and Fourth armies' inner flank positions. Continuing drastic casualties raised the question whether the Habsburg Army could withstand further enemy pressure. Battle fatigue prevented Habsburg troops from offering serious resistance to enemy offensive efforts.

Meanwhile, Third Army attempted to execute Conrad's offensive plan, initially gaining considerable territory and striking a weak point in the enemy line (the Russians had concentrated their main efforts against the critical Dukla Pass). However, a tsarist counterattack pierced VII Corps lines on December 22, forcing the entire Habsburg front to buckle. Conrad lacked necessary troop numbers to halt what became a decisive tsarist offensive.

During the Christmas holidays, Fortress Przemyśl's future seemed hopeless to garrison troops as they contemplated continued battle, death or capture. By December 21, fortress inhabitants prepared for Christmas as some troops trudged into the woods outside the fortress and brought back trees to cheer up hospital patients. The garrison enjoyed a brief unexpected respite as tsarist artillery lay silent until the New Year. Undernourished and exhausted perimeter troops continued to suffer from the fluctuating bitter winter weather conditions without cover, warmth or adequate artillery protection, while others continued around-the-clock repair work on the citadel walls.

During the holiday season, Russian pilots halted bombing missions against the fortress. Opposing troops had developed a form of camaraderie, oftentimes discoursing by name across the front lines. Both sides honored the unofficial truce until after Christmas; the Russians naturally anticipated the same during their Orthodox holidays.

Apart from the fortress environs, no Christmas truce occurred on the Habsburg front. On Christmas Day, field armies commenced a general retreat to shorter defensive lines to await replacement troops and sorely needed artillery shells. This retreat coincided with a Russian attack on Third Army lines in the Dukla Pass area, creating renewed crisis. Retreating on muddy routes pushed the troops to the brink of physical and emotional breakdown.

Between December 25 and 27, the enemy seized the key Beskid Mountain roads and continued to advance, forcing defending troops back to the main Carpathian Mountain ridgelines. His armies again on the verge of collapse, Conrad urgently appealed for immediate German assistance to help maintain his tenuous mountain front, emphasizing the danger of the neutral powers intervening because of the increasingly unfavorable military situation.

The loss of Galicia to the enemy signified a major reduction in grain supplies, oil, horses and army recruits; the loss of much of the Bukovina raised the concern of Romania declaring war on Austria-Hungary. The loss of Galicia exacerbated a major economic disaster because of the mounting pressure from the Entente blockade. It also inflamed ethnic relations as hundreds of thousands of Galician refugees fled into the monarchy's interior, aggravating the deteriorating food situation.

The Habsburg mountain-front military situation worsened further between December 28 and 31 when Third Army troops withdrew along the important narrow-gauge Lupkov Pass railway following another Russian attack on the entire front. On December 28, battle raged at the Dukla, Uzsok and Lupkov Passes and other critically important areas. The Habsburg military situation had deteriorated so drastically that Conrad contemplated redeploying Second Army forces from the German theater to the gravely endangered mountain front.[27]

At year end in Fortress Przemyśl the combination of troop starvation and increasingly inclement weather conditions diminished garrison resistance to disease. Cases of petty crime, embezzlement and robbery increased. Harsh penalties no longer prevented crime since even military authorities had become complicit in the corruption. Wounded patients received little medical attention and many starved to death. Casualty numbers increased substantially with the launching of the multiple December fortress sorties. Extremely low morale in the hospital wards resulted partially because many nurses were untrained and unqualified for medical service. When adolescent girls became nurses, it created a life-threatening situation for many sick and wounded soldiers. Medical supplies rapidly depleted, although some were flown by plane into the citadel, while a thousand cases of cholera continued to require quarantine.[28]

The year thus ended poorly for the Austro-Hungarian Army. The three embarrassing Serbian defeats produced severe Habsburg losses, over quarter of a million, while the bloody battlefield setbacks on the Russian front were hardly mitigated by the brief Limanova–Lapanov victory. Conrad realized that he required a major victory to sway the wavering neutral countries, particularly Italy. With the increasing threat of an invasion of Hungary, the Habsburg Army had to defend the remaining Carpathian Mountain crossings albeit sustaining additional casualties during the recent battlefield encounters.

Conrad thus faced several major problems at the end of the year. The hemorrhaging troop losses required immediate replacement. The crushing end-of-December military defeats again opened the invasion routes though the Carpathian Mountains. The Russian objective remained to push Third Army forces out of the mountains, allowing the fortress to be starved into submission without serious threat of military interference. Moreover, the Russians had gained a favorable starting point to invade Hungary in 1915.

German officials continued to urge Conrad to cooperate with them to conquer the Negotine (northeastern) sector of Serbia to restore Habsburg military honor and prestige, while providing sorely needed ammunition to the Turkish ally. That operation might finally compel Bulgaria to join the Central Powers, but Falkenhayn also announced that no further German troops could be removed from the hotly contested Western front. Only a skeleton or *Miliz* Habsburg force remained, while the enormous casualties could only partially be replaced with inadequately trained reserve troops and officers.

For Fortress Przemyśl, rapidly dwindling food supplies would soon force the bulwark to capitulate. Conrad commenced planning to launch a major offensive in the Carpathian Mountains to defeat the Russian Army, protect Hungary, liberate Fortress Przemyśl and keep neutral countries out of the war. However, the Carpathian Mountain region was particularly unsuitable for such a major campaign that Conrad envisioned for early 1915. The rugged terrain and severe inclement weather conditions had already presented insurmountable obstacles to his armies during late 1914. Further, the sparse and inadequate Galician network of roads, trails and railroad lines would severely restrict movement of large army formations as well as assuring that a regular supply system would be almost impossible to achieve. Such a campaign would also severely jeopardize the troops' health conditions and place inhumane physical demands upon them. Ultimately, they had to launch deadly frontal attacks against strong tsarist defensive positions, because of the time constraints of liberating Fortress Przemyśl.

By the end of December 1914, only 45,000 infantry troops remained of the original 900,000 originally deployed during August 1914. Only 303,000 combat soldiers remained on the Russian front. Meanwhile, more than 690,000 March Brigade, or *Ersatz* replacement troops, had been deployed in the front lines, although they possessed no machine guns or artillery units and lacked adequate mountain equipment and training. Infantry losses amounted to 85 percent of the original 1914 mobilized troops. Dual Monarchy troops were now deployed behind the Dunajec River in the mountains, thirty-five miles from Fortress Krakow.

Continued failure to properly coordinate relief efforts of Fortress Przemyśl with the field army resulted in huge casualties for both entities. The Russians never had to withdraw substantial troop numbers from their siege lines to contain garrison breakout efforts, despite the fact that after November 1914 only second- and third-line units besieged the citadel.

Fortress sorties repeatedly sallied forth from the same location, with the same tactical units and the same objectives. These sortie missions proved far too ambitious considering the limited number of fortress troops deployed, as well as their lack of effective planning. Compounding the problem, the overemphasis on flank security reduced troop numbers that should have participated with the main attack efforts, which produced increased casualties. The Russians anticipated all fortress military operations, aided by Ruthenian spies within the fortress and the fact that they had, unbeknownst to the garrison, broken the Habsburg code.

Both opponents faced the prospect of mountain winter warfare and the necessity of winning a decisive battle to keep neutral countries out of the war, or gain them as allies. The only geographical area that Conrad considered advantageous to launch a major early 1915 offensive in became the inhospitable Carpathian Mountains. The next chapter focuses on the preparations for the Carpathian Mountain Winter War in January 1915, and assesses the condition of the participating troops. Was the Habsburg Army prepared to launch a major offensive in late January 1915? Were General Conrad's plans realistic? Could the field armies liberate Fortress Przemyśl before it had to surrender? Only time would tell.

Figure 1 Count Leopold Berchtold
(Photo by Hulton Archive/ Stringer via Getty Images)

Figure 2 Oskar Potiorek
(Photo by Universal Images Group via Getty Images)

178

Figure 3 Alexei Brusilov
(Photo by Fine Art Images /Heritage Images/ Hulton Archive via Getty Images)

Figure 4 Luigi Cadorna
(Photo by Mandadori Portfolio via Getty Images)

Figure 5   Conrad von Hötzendorf
(Photo by Print Collector/ Hulton Fine Art Collection via Getty Images)

Figure 6   Erich von Falkenhayn
(Photo by Time & Life Pictures/ The LIFE Picture Collection via Getty Images)

Figure 7 Franz Ferdinand
(Photo by Bettman via Getty Images)

Figure 8 Emperor Franz Joseph
(Photo by Atelier Carl Pietzner/ ullstein bild via Getty Images)

Figure 9 Paul von Hindenburg
(Photo by Estate of Emil Bieber/Klaus Niermann/ Hulton Archive via Getty Images)

Figure 10 Nikolai Ivanov
(Photo by the Print Collector/ Hulton Archive via Getty Images)

Figure 11   Erich Ludendorff
(Photo by Estate of Emil Bieber/ Klaus Niermann/ Hulton Archive via Getty Images)

Figure 12   Radomir Putnik
(Photo by Bettmann via Getty Images)

Figure 13 István Tisza
(Photo by Hulton Archive/ Stringer via Getty Images)

Figure 14 Emperor Karl I
(Photo by Hulton Archive/ Stringer via Getty Images)

Figure 15   Svetozar Boroević
(Photo by DEA/ A. DAGLI ORTI/ De Agostini via Getty Images)

Figure 16   August von Mackensen
(Photo by Corbis Historical via Getty Images)

6

1915

The year 1915 witnessed further massive Entente offensives on the Western front, while on the Eastern front the three Austro-Hungarian Carpathian Winter War offensives were launched between the end of January 1915 and mid-April. With the possible collapse of the Habsburg Army after the unsuccessful Carpathian Mountain campaign, and the Russians threatening to invade Hungary, the Germans launched the Gorlice–Tarnow offensive commencing on May 2, 1915. This produced the Central Powers' greatest victory during the war. After forcing the Russians hundreds of miles into their own territory, the Germans terminated the offensive. General Conrad then determined to gain some glory for Austro-Hungarian forces, by launching the ill-fated fall Rovno offensive. The year ended with a victorious Allied invasion of Serbia in October. In the meantime, a severe shortage of manpower resulted from the horrendous casualty numbers produced during the Carpathian Mountain Winter War campaign and the Gorlice–Tarnow operation. The victory over Serbia resulted in Central Power dominance in the Balkan Peninsula.[1]

The year also produced worsening economic news. The Habsburg economy began to decline, but somehow maintained itself through late 1917, to everyone's amazement. The results of the Entente blockade became the worst threat to Dual Monarchy civilian morale, because by spring 1915 food had become much more expensive and supplies scarcer while inflation continued to increase. The year's harvest was one-half of what was anticipated, mainly because of June and July drought conditions. During March flour was rationed, soon followed by butter, vegetables, milk, fruit and pork. This resulted in the first food riots exploding in Vienna, and their spread to other parts of the Dual Monarchy would accelerate during the next years.

The effect of the 1914 Russian occupation of Galicia also intensified, because one-third of Dual Monarchy cereal crops, significant manpower and oil supplies were surrendered; a very severe blow. The Russians caused immense devastation during their initial occupation, and when they retreated during the May and June 1915 Gorlice–Tarnow offensive they unleashed further destruction upon the province. Disease became prevalent; dysentery, typhoid fever and influenza filled cemeteries. The destruction of thousands of farms produced famine in Galicia. The battles and epidemics caused many soldiers' deaths, as well as children and women.[2]

Habsburg industry also began to suffer. The steel industry proved incapable of meeting rising demands for armaments and munitions. The increasing lack of essential raw materials became a key factor in declining war industry production, largely a result of the Entente blockade. Also, the deficit in nonferrous metals became obvious, particularly the copper and zinc essential for steel production. The railroad transportation system already could not fully meet wartime needs.

Italy declared war on Austria-Hungary on May 23, 1915, which quickly evolved into a war of attrition. The main 1915 Italian objectives, Gorizia and the Carso Plateau, witnessed battles fought during searing heat conditions, on inhospitable mountain terrain, and with an unbearable lack of water supplies. During autumn rain and mud predominated, then the bitter cold of winter arrived. During the year the Italians suffered more than two hundred thousand casualties, not counting the sick, thus infantry regiments lost two-thirds of their troop numbers for insignificant territorial gains. Fighting on this front became the deadliest of all Habsburg First World War campaigns.

January 1915 brought a pause in the fighting in the Carpathian Mountains, but this served merely as a prelude for the disastrous Carpathian Mountain Winter War campaign, January 23 to mid-April 1915.[3] This campaign introduced the first mountain warfare involving million-man armies. Conrad's location choice for the campaign proved disastrous. The mountain terrain lacked satisfactory railroads, good communication lines and the multiple resources necessary for maneuvering massive forces in this remote area. Huge Russian and Austro-Hungarian armies soon clashed in the inhospitable winter mountain terrain.

The Dual Monarchy found itself in a most unfavorable military situation by the end of 1914, after the disastrous opening campaigns and those launched with its German ally between October and December 1914. The result was the loss of much of Galicia and all of the Bukovina. Habsburg military leadership recognized that continued battlefield defeats, particularly with the disastrous August, September, November and December 1914 Balkan campaigns, would encourage neutral countries such as Italy and Romania to enter the war against the Central Powers during the forthcoming spring.

General Conrad focused his attention on the Carpathian Mountain region in mid-December 1914. That mountain range extends 300 kilometers in a southeastern direction. Its greatest width measures 120 kilometers, its narrowest 100. The area extends from present-day northern Slovakia and Poland southward to the borders of Transylvania, then part of Hungary, now Romania.

Transportation, particularly for supply and troop movements, proved most difficult, as only a half dozen mountain passes offered favorable road and railroad access from Galicia to the Hungarian plains. The main mountain passes for the 1915 military campaign were the Dukla, Lupkov and Uszok. These three critical passes witnessed particularly bloody battle. The most significant militarily, the Dukla Pass, provided the easiest access to either Galicia or in reverse Hungary and witnessed brutal battle throughout the three Carpathian Mountain Winter War campaigns.

The Dukla Pass, forty kilometers wide and sixty long, consisted of rolling hills possessing good road connections. It was most difficult to defend and provided the Russians the most favorable route to invade Hungary to knock Austria-Hungary out of the war. Tsarist General Ivanov selected this location for the major tsarist counterattacks once the Habsburg Carpathian War Mountain offensive operation commenced.

The second major pass, the Lupkov, is twenty kilometers southeast of the Dukla Pass. This much larger and higher pass gained its significance because its railroad connected the pass to Fortress Przemyśl that originally became important during the 1914 Habsburg retreat.

When tsarist forces captured the strategically important Uszok Pass, it enabled them to advance toward the Dukla Pass. As the New Year unfolded, Conrad had to resolve two serious problems. First, Hungary had to be protected from a Russian invasion, and second, Fortress Przemyśl had to be liberated. Political and military pressure to liberate the fortress caused Conrad to make the fortress the most important factor in his military planning. To rescue the fortress became a call to arms as well as a matter of honor for Habsburg soldiers. In addition, Emperor Franz Joseph demanded that the fortress not be allowed to capitulate to the Russians.

Adding to the crisis situation, a January 1915 Fortress Przemyśl report estimated that the bulwark food supplies would last only until mid-March 1915. Thus, each day became increasingly significant as the question arose of whether the fortress garrison could defend itself until it could be recaptured, particularly because food supplies were rapidly running short. This resulted in Conrad making the fortress's liberation the foremost consideration through-out fall 1914 and the three Carpathian Mountain Winter War campaigns until the fortress capitulated on March 22, 1915.

Launching a major offensive on the Carpathian Mountain terrain proved very difficult because only four railroad lines traversed the mountain front. These railroad lines, originating from Budapest, were snow-covered between November and April each year. Intermittently freezing weather and frequent warming periods produced flooding accelerated by periodic winter rain. After launching attacks, battle formations became easily separated in the narrow, wooded valleys, dividing large military units into smaller entities. Worse, there were no major railroad connections crisscrossing the mountains and valleys, seriously limiting maneuverability.

Anticipating a Russian attempt to invade Hungary and convinced that only a swift military action could provide victory and avert such a military disaster,

Conrad devised a complicated plan to launch an offensive operation on a broad mountain front. The bloodied and exhausted Third Army that had fought in all the 1914 campaigns became the major participant in the initial action. During early 1915, a simultaneous offensive would be launched by newly created South Army with some German units but composed mostly of Habsburg soldiers. The two armies would launch frontal offensives northward to envelop the extreme Russian left flank positions and liberate Fortress Przemyśl.

General Conrad requested Allied military support for his projected campaign. He rehashed his 1914 strategy, calling for a massive battle of encirclement with German troops attacking to the south and Austro-Hungarian troops advancing northward from the Carpathian Mountains; the Allies to converge in the middle of the Polish salient. General Falkenhayn replied negatively, insisting that the offensive could not produce a major victory because the Allied forces were separated by 375 kilometers and the Russian armies could simply retreat into their vast homeland to avoid major defeat. Worried about the Habsburg Army's poor performance to date, he informed Conrad that the best a Carpathian campaign could achieve would be a local victory. A compromise led to the creation of the three-division force, the South Army, to support the projected Third Army offensive. Major German strategic reserve units participated in the second Masurian Lake battle that commenced on February 7, 1915. The German Ninth Army during the Masurian campaign destroyed a portion of that enemy army. The bitter winter conditions helped prevent complete success as many tsarist troops managed to escape.

Conrad recognized that his Carpathian Mountain offensive could only succeed against a numerically superior enemy if he seized the initiative and achieved surprise. Much also depended on his troops' capabilities and he hoped that a rapid attack could preclude a long winter mountain campaign. He utilized the short battle pause in early January 1915 to prepare for his operation.

That favorable military outcome never occurred, because Conrad seriously underestimated the many obstacles his troops would encounter on the rugged mountain terrain and the effect of winter weather conditions. Transporting supplies and artillery into the mountains presented a logistical nightmare that was never resolved. The army lacked proper equipment, even winter uniforms, as well as sufficient artillery units and significant troop numbers to conduct a winter battle but also defeat a numerically superior foe. Tsarist troops proved better acclimated to the harsh winter weather and possessed superior equipment. On the Eastern front, the Russians deployed on high terrain, as the Germans had on the Western front, in well-constructed defensive positions close to their rear echelon railroad connections.[4] Habsburg troops would have to conduct their mountain campaign under extremely debilitating conditions that had never been recorded in previous military history.

Three offensive operations to liberate Fortress Przemyśl were launched during this campaign. The first, consisting of Third and South Army troops, was launched on January 23, 1915 and, proving unsuccessful, halted in February 1915. A second offensive, launched by the Habsburg Second Army redeployed from the German front, lasted from February 27 until March 14, 1915. A third feeble Habsburg attempt to liberate the fortress consisted only of reinforced V Corps troops that lasted from late March until mid-April 1915. A bloody 1915 Easter battle would be the last major Russian attempt to smash through the remaining mountain ridges to invade the Hungarian plains. Tsarist troops launched their last major offensive on March 20, a series of rapid mass assaults that immediately placed the defending Habsburg Second and Third armies in an untenable military predicament. The Carpathian Mountain winter offensive failed, with disastrous casualties.

For the initial operation, Habsburg Third Army, fifteen infantry and four and a half cavalry divisions and South Army's three infantry and two cavalry divisions totaled 175,000 combatants. These forces launched a frontal attack northward on a 160-kilometer front against weakly held left flank Russian positions. Third Army's main objective became to seize the major enemy railroad transportation junctions at Sanok and Stary Sambor. Neighboring South Army would attack Russian Third Army flank areas and, if successful, the two armies would envelop and roll up the enemies' extreme left flank positions.

The initial Third Army assault gained insignificant victories, although it advanced forty kilometers against numerically inferior enemy troops. Then winter storms struck and, combined with tsarist counterattacks, caused numerous casualties. Frostbite, sickness and freezing to death (the white death) also exacted a heavy toll. Attacking divisions were quickly reduced to regiment or brigade size numbers. The wide attack front quickly became too extensive for the number of available troops to even defend their positions. Troops also lacked sufficient reserve formations to continue their attacks. Troops had to remain in open exposed terrain for weeks at a time in inclement winter weather conditions with no chance for relief or rehabilitation.

Enemy troops were relieved every forty-eight hours with the constant arrival of reserve and reinforcement units on the road and railroad connections located directly behind their front lines. Weather conditions produced horrendous circumstances for the participating troops, for example, South Army commenced its attack during a raging snowstorm on rugged mountain terrain covered with meter-deep snow. Troops often struggled to advance through chest-deep snow drifts while having to shovel footpaths to attack. Because of the paucity of pack animals, and their excessive death rates in the extreme weather and mountain conditions without sufficient fodder, combat troops had to assist in transporting machine guns, ammunition and other supply materials to the front lines. They also had to place artillery pieces into

firing position. Frozen terrain prevented digging defensive positions or providing cover to protect the soldiers from the inclement weather conditions
when not in battle or under enemy fire. Many soldiers collapsed from exhaustion; some even fell asleep while talking. Often troops had to wade through
streams, then occupy their positions in frozen uniforms. Frigid winds and ice
crusted their eyelids while temperatures dropped as low as $-30°C$. The troops,
still in summer uniforms, received blankets and other cold-weather gear from
their families at home.

Habsburg battle casualties were rapidly outnumbered by noncombat causes.
By the end of the first campaign week, battle fatigue had become universal.
Some soldiers committed suicide to escape the harsh and inhumane conditions. Many wounded soldiers perished in the bumpy cart rides down the
mountain ridges and slopes, bled or froze to death, or were eaten by wolves in
no-man's land at night.

Tsarist troops often utilized the inclement weather conditions to launch
counterattacks, particularly at night. Attacking Austro-Hungarian troops often
did not receive artillery support as they attempted to advance through blinding
snowstorms in waist-deep snow, because multiple batteries had been left
behind at lower ridgelines or in rear echelon areas at least three days' march
from the combat zone. During the Second offensive, the main Second Army
attack group left twenty-seven artillery batteries several days' march from
the battlefield.

Enemy troops also often awaited a pause in Habsburg offensive actions to
launch swift powerful counterattacks against the benumbed forces. These
attacks on ice- and snow-covered mountain slopes resulted in many deaths.
Meanwhile, Habsburg Supreme Command headquarters remained a comfortable distance from the horrific scenes of combat.

Faulty tactical strategy did not help Habsburg efforts. Operations often lacked
coordination between attacking units, which proved advantageous to the
defending enemy troops. Repeatedly, attacking units concentrated on a single
enemy position, often awaiting neighboring units' battle success, but many
commanders ignored orders to attack, leaving participating units isolated.

Three days after commencement of the initial offensive, Third Army's
battlefront extended to between the Dukla and Uszok Passes. Fighting also
erupted in other mountain areas; however, unbeknownst to Habsburg field
commanders, the turning point of the offensive had already been reached. On
the fourth battle day the Russians unleashed a massive counterattack, striking
Habsburg Third Army middle and right flank positions, advancing to the
strategic Dukla Pass area. By early February the first Habsburg offensive failed
when the anticipated rapid victories never materialized, weather conditions
worsened and the enormous casualties could not be replaced.

The Russian Southwestern front army commander, General Ivanov, determined his next major military objective would be to occupy the critical

Laborcz Valley, specifically the key Mezölaborcz railroad junction. During the ensuing bitter bloody battles, three Habsburg corps were decimated. Russian commanders then committed an often-repeated error of not immediately pursuing the badly defeated Habsburg troops, preventing their catastrophic defeat. The Russians captured the critical Mezölaborcz–Lupkov rail junction following bitter hand-to-hand combat during a brutal snowstorm.

In reply to sharp Conrad criticism, Third Army commander General Boroević responded that "catastrophic snowfall" had halted all efforts to receive critical reinforcement units, and crippled regular supply efforts. He further argued that an insufficient number of militia labor and Sapper units ensured lack of maintenance for the inadequate supply roadways to the front lines and the severe weather conditions also made roads unusable. An infuriated Conrad ordered Third Army to halt its retreat movement and prepare to launch a new assault against the enemy, because of the mounting pressure to liberate Fortress Przemyśl.

Meanwhile, participating attack troops suffered from constant enemy artillery barrages, assaults during horrendous weather conditions and incessant combat fatigue that left troops apathetic. As Habsburg troops began to retreat, a new cold wave sent temperatures plummeting to −20°C. Third Army, lacking reserve formations, had to defend the 90-kilometer-wide front, while neighboring South Army maintained 113 kilometers of even harsher mountain terrain.

Compounding the armies' problems, chaos ensued on the sparse railroad lines. Traffic congestion often brought supply traffic to a complete halt. The low-capacity railroad lines became overburdened with the transport of replacement troops, the few available reinforcements, reserve units and supplies to the front lines. The lack of adequate loading ramps at railroad stations worsened the logistical nightmare. Ultimately, the entire support system ground to a halt.

For the second Carpathian Mountain offensive effort the combined Second Army, including units redeployed from the German front, and some Third Army units launched a frontal attack against some of the same strong Russian defensive positions that Third Army operations had unsuccessfully attempted to seize earlier. The Habsburg objective became to defeat the enemy forces blocking the most direct route to the besieged fortress on the Baligrod roads.

On February 25, the original offensive launch date, a warm spell produced flooding and muddy mountain terrain conditions, significantly delaying troop and supply movement along the few roadways to the front. Additional draft animals became necessary to move supplies forward over the treacherous terrain, which proved extremely tedious and time-consuming. For the Second Army offensive operation only one major railroad line supplied the four corps attack troops.

Just a few hours before commencement of the attack after unit dispositions had been prepared for distribution, rising temperatures had transformed the single supply artery into a sea of mud, making it impassable for traffic. At the very last minute the offensive had to be delayed for two days, or until February 27. Thousands of wagons had sunk to their axles in the mire, while many horses perished in their struggles to overcome the quagmire. Often their carcasses were thrown into the mud, attempting to improve forward movement. At critical locations flooding washed away important bridges. Too few vitally necessary military labor units were available to repair and maintain the single four corps emergency supply route. Combat troops had to assist the road crews in their attempts to maintain some flow of supplies to the frontline troops. Then, abruptly, the night before the rescheduled offensive was to launch, cold weather returned, adding an additional three and a half feet of snow in the mountains. Weather conditions again favored the defending tsarist army.

Second Army command requested that the offensive be postponed until weather conditions improved, but Conrad ordered that it commence because of the threat of the capture of Fortress Przemyśl. Reports claimed food provisions could last only until March 16. This substantially increased pressure to liberate the fortress before it had to surrender. Conrad could not allow the fortress to capitulate, partly because it would free additional tsarist mobile siege troops to deploy against the Second, Third and Army Group Pflanzer-Baltin's already outnumbered troops on the mountain front. The question of Italian and Romanian neutrality also played a major role in Conrad's order to immediately launch the offensive. However, he miscalculated relative to several major factors. He correctly assumed that for the first time attacking Habsburg troops would have the advantage of superior numbers, but failed to consider the troops' terrible condition, particularly frontline units. Many battled the enemy and harsh mountain climate conditions without being relieved or rehabilitated. General Conrad thus ignored the lessons of the ill-fated Third Army January offensive.

Conrad's demand for a rapid launching of the second offensive presented the Second Army commander little flexibility in operational planning. He had to launch the offensive along the most direct route and shortest distance to the citadel. But the narrow twelve-kilometer-wide front faced extremely well-fortified enemy defensive positions. Attacking troops required numerically superior troop numbers and effective artillery support, neither of which they received.

Because of the extreme time pressure, the offensive had to be launched before all the designated tactical units and necessary materiel had been assembled. Multiple critically necessary Habsburg artillery batteries remained one or two days' march behind the mountain ridges, because of the extreme difficulties encountered emplacing heavy-artillery pieces into position in the snow-covered rugged mountain terrain. The main offensive force left twenty-seven artillery batteries far from the battlefield, thus the strongly fortified enemy positions could not be neutralized by effective artillery fire. Attempts to transport heavy equipment had to utilize improvised methods, which resulted in the loss of thousands of horses and wagons. In addition, many Habsburg artillery pieces either malfunctioned, became totally inoperable or, when sent to rear echelon areas for repair, often returned to the front still not functional, to be discovered in the heat of battle.

Meanwhile, General Böhm-Ermolli, Second Army commander, harbored serious doubts about any prospect for his offensive's success, understanding the negative impact of severe mountain weather and terrain conditions from his previous 1914 Carpathian Mountain experiences, particularly the problem of routinely delivering reinforcements and supplies to frontline troops. He therefore suggested that any reinforcements be directed to Army Group Pflanzer-Baltin on the southernmost mountain front to launch the major offensive.

The offensive finally commenced on February 27, initially producing a surprisingly large number of enemy casualties, but the narrow attack front proved insufficient to achieve success. On March 2 tsarist forces launched an offensive against Habsburg Third Army left flank positions. Conrad responded by ordering a general offensive to be launched on March 5. Exhausted Second Army troops again hurled themselves against the impenetrable Russian positions, which by March 10 had been further strengthened. On the next day the Second Army offensive force was struck by a counterattack during extremely unfavorable weather conditions, crippling its operation.[5] On March 12 a new wave of bitter cold conditions struck as the Russian counterthrust completely halted any further Habsburg attack attempts. The "white death" also drastically reduced Habsburg troop ranks, while survivors were totally exhausted. On March 14 the offensive terminated. The next day the Russians advanced.

During the two-week period between March 1 and 15, Second Army suffered the loss of nearly one-third of its original troop numbers, the vast majority resulting from sickness and frostbite rather than battle.[6] Thousands of ill-equipped and unprepared soldiers perished in the horrendous conditions.

In March General Conrad launched the third final attempt to liberate the fortress. This bloody sacrificial fiasco destroyed whatever remaining Habsburg troop morale existed. Second Army's V Corps received inadequate support for its impossible mission to lift the siege of the fortress. Conrad had still not understood, after two failed offensives, that his troops remained too numerically weak to launch a successful offensive. The fortress still lay nearly a hundred kilometers as the crow flies from Habsburg front lines, and the offensive force consisted of only a reinforced corps, thus it had absolutely no chance of achieving success.

Inexplicably, Conrad never informed Second Army or V Corps command of an earlier failed March 19 fortress breakout attempt. Thus, the bloody sacrificial attempts to liberate their comrades on March 20 and 21 proved senseless. On March 22, the fortress garrison capitulated reputedly because the troops in the garrison were starving.[7] The remaining garrison of 117,000 soldiers and 2,000 officers became prisoners of war and were marched away into captivity.

Conrad, realizing that the fortress could not be liberated, ordered the fortress garrison to launch a desperate breakout attempt on March 19, 1915. The fortress offensive unit, the 23. *Honvéd* Infantry Division, sustained seventy percent casualties in this bloody effort to maintain the honor of the Austro-Hungarian Army. Hundreds of starving and exhausted troops dropped out of the ranks, many dying marching through the fortress to reach their assembly area to prepare to attack the tsarist siege lines. Meanwhile, the Russians learned of the Habsburg plan from decoding activity so they prepared their defensive positions ensuring that many garrison troops would be slaughtered in the doomed operation.

As an immediate result of the fortress capitulation, besieging tsarist Eleventh Army units rapidly redeployed to the Carpathian Mountain front. These additional troops aided the Russian March 20 offensive effort to cross the remaining Carpathian Mountain ridges to invade Hungary. The unanticipated overpowering enemy pressure forced Habsburg Second and Third Army flank units to retreat. By March 24 Habsburg troops were in an extremely precarious military situation.

The troops, in imminent danger of collapse, forced Conrad to dispatch his scant reinforcements there, while tsarist forces continually received additional troops. Conrad appealed to General Falkenhayn for assistance who swiftly transferred the understrength *Beskiden* Corps into the bitter battle zone. These three undermanned German divisions immediately halted Russian progress before their front and Habsburg Third Army lines. Meanwhile, Second Army troops had retreated behind the last Carpathian Mountain ridge lines, which shortened frontline positions, significantly improving their logistical support system and troop battle conditions. Thus, these troops defended their lines through April. The ensuing April Easter battle represented the last tsarist attempt to invade Hungary before the May 2 German Gorlice–Tarnow offensive was launched.

Neither the Austro-Hungarian nor Russian strategic objectives were achieved during the Carpathian Mountain Winter War campaign. Conrad's objectives – the decisive envelopment of the extreme tsarist left flank positions and liberation of Fortress Przemyśl – and General Ivanov's attempt to advance into Hungary to end the war failed. Meanwhile, four Russian armies had advanced deep into the Carpathian Mountains on the eve of the May 2,

1915 Gorlice–Tarnow offensive, which proved disastrous to them. The tsarist High Command (*Stavka*) eventually extricated the threatened four armies from the mountain front, but with enormous difficulty and multiple casualties. The Gorlice–Tarnow rapid success quickly threatened to outflank the tsarist forces ensconced in the high terrain. Conrad's Carpathian Mountain operations, influenced by his desire to liberate Fortress Przemyśl, fatefully had too strong an influence on Hapsburg military planning to the detriment of hundreds of thousands of field soldiers during early 1915. Habsburg losses have been calculated to be at least eight hundred thousand, the Russians ones well over one million.

The ensuing battle of Gorlice–Tarnow to extricate the Austro-Hungarian Army from its dire Carpathian Mountain straits became the greatest Central Power victory of the war and represented the apex of its coalition warfare. Successful German tactics of short, but massive artillery preparations followed by frontal infantry attacks became the norm for German offensive operations for the next two years. This reversed the Schlieffen strategy school of battles of encirclement. The offensive not only rescued the floundering ally in the Carpathian Mountains, but also ultimately prevented Romania from declaring war on Austria-Hungary.[8]

The Central Powers' early April 1915 Eastern front military situation appeared very unfavorable. On the Western front, the French and English had launched offensives with a numerical superiority of six hundred battalions. The outcome of these battles remained uncertain, but the Germans anticipated that the Entente armies would achieve only local victories because of their previous defensive successes. On the Eastern front, the Austro-Hungarian armies continued to retreat from incessant Russian attacks throughout spring 1915. General Conrad desperately requested German reinforcements to buttress the faltering mountain front and callously continued to pressure his battered troops, already bled white, to halt the enemy advance. By early spring, Austro-Hungarian forces had come perilously close to collapse, the threat increasing that Italy would enter the war against Austria-Hungary to gain its claimed irredenta territory. Conrad needed a major offensive success against Russia to prevent this, while the constant Russian advances toward the Hungarian Plains encouraged Romania to enter the war to seize Transylvania and the Bukovina. The Russians had suffered enormous casualties as had Dual Monarchy troops. Increasing war weariness was taking its toll on the troops and indications abounded that the army had begun to disintegrate. A noticeable decline in troop effectiveness became evident, especially in Czech, Romanian, Italian and South Slavic units. Predominantly Slavic units allegedly surrendered en masse to the enemy during the Carpathian Mountain campaign as did other nationality troops because of the inhumane battlefront conditions.

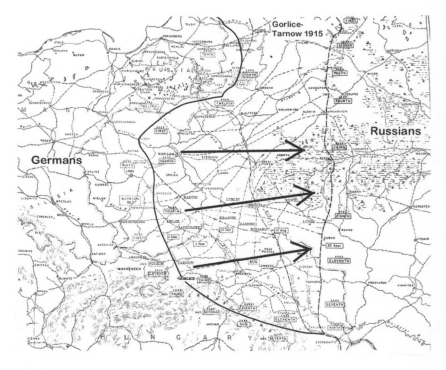

Map 6   *1915 Gorlice–Tarnow*
Map courtesy of the United States Military Academy Department of History

Tsarist forces advancing on the Habsburg front lacked necessary troop strength to fully exploit their victories by mid-April 1915. After its enormous losses, Russia had to deploy inadequately trained and armed troops, its forces now basically a peasant army. The Russians also increasingly suffered from ammunition shortage, particularly artillery shells, an acute weakness.

Elsewhere, the French and British Dardanelles Gallipoli campaign outcome remained unclear. The Entente sought to open the Straits to Russian trade benefit and possibly knock the Ottoman Empire out of the war. During January 1915, but throughout the Carpathian Winter War campaigns, Falkenhayn suggested that Conrad launch an offensive against the Serbians, but the Habsburgs lacked sufficient troop numbers. The Carpathian Mountain region proved so unfavorable for successful battle that Falkenhayn sought a more appropriate location to initiate a major rescue operation. The German *Beskiden* Corps halted further tsarist successes against the battered Habsburg Third Army X Corps, bringing immediate relief to the German ally.

On April 4, as battle raged in the Carpathian Mountains, Generals Conrad and Falkenhayn conferred in Berlin and agreed to maintain a defensive position on the Italian front should Italy declare war. Earlier, Falkenhayn had begun to consider launching an offensive in the area of Fortress Krakow to relieve pressure on the Habsburg mountain front. The ranking German liaison officer conferred with Habsburg Railroad Bureau personnel to investigate the feasibility of major German troop deployments to the region south of Fortress Krakow, determining that such a deployment would require eight days to complete. The initial operational objective became the Wisloka River near the Dukla Pass and Fortress Przemyśl. General Falkenhayn had to terminate his plans to launch a Western front offensive. Falkenhayn harbored two major concerns, that his invaluable reserves remain under his command, and that they should not fill gaps in the Habsburg lines.

Conrad approached Falkenhayn on April 6, requesting that seven German divisions be deployed to the Italian frontier and three to the Romanian to free Habsburg troops for the threatened Carpathian Mountain front. By April 10, Russian troops had crossed to the far side of the mountains while six tsarist Third Army divisions had been transferred to the Bukovina and deployed into the mountains, weakening that army's strength. Then, on April 13, Falkenhayn announced, without revealing specific details, that a new German Eleventh Army would be deployed to the Gorlice–Tarnow area where Habsburg Fourth Army had unsuccessfully battled in early March 1915. During that battle Fourth Army's VI Corps failed to conquer Gorlice because of grossly inadequate troop numbers, unfavorable winter weather conditions and strong enemy defensive positions on that important sector of the front. Conrad had realized the strategic significance of Gorlice, with its important railroad junctions. The attempts faltered in part due to snowstorms, but primarily due to insufficient troop numbers.

Multiple arguments supported a decision that an offensive could not be launched on the Carpathian Mountain front because the terrain prevented rapid movement and a sustainable logistical system. The Gorlice–Tarnow terrain, with its low rolling hills, would allow maneuver for a frontal attack. The Germans would enjoy a vast numerical superiority, particularly heavy-caliber artillery at the attack point. German troops, many Western front veterans, had superior training and higher morale than Habsburg troops. The troops would also not face a major river obstacle. The Germans utilized the recent Western front Soissons offensive lessons at Gorlice, ensuring mission secrecy and utilizing massed heavy artillery to destroy enemy trenches and emplacements.

Gorlice served as a crucial transportation center for the Russian Southwest front with its important railroad connections. On April 14, Conrad and Falkenhayn determined that German Eleventh Army would attack toward Zmigrod, Sanok, the Dukla Pass and Fortress Przemyśl. With Habsburg

Third and Fourth armies protecting its flanks, Eleventh Army would then assault tsarist Eighth Army positions at the Lupkov Pass. The Germans maintained command over the two Habsburg armies during the operation. Although irritated by the command structure, Conrad appreciated that Falkenhayn would intervene on the Carpathian Mountain front where Habsburg troops fought on the last mountain ridges before the Hungarian plains. The command question involved Habsburg prestige, a major factor. Habsburg Supreme Command would issue orders, but the German command made the important decisions.

The German and Habsburg forces would attempt to penetrate tsarist positions at the Lupkov Pass. Southern flank troops would pierce defensive lines along the Gorlice–Jaslo basin line. On April 21, the first German soldiers commenced railroad transport to the Galician front.

It was a controversy whether Conrad or Falkenhayn had conceived the original idea for the very successful Gorlice operation. Conrad had earlier recognized the Gorlice area's military significance. Falkenhayn, who also recognized its strategic importance, provided the necessary troop strength to achieve victory. Falkenhayn, aware of the Habsburg Army's earlier debilitating defeats, held little regard for the Dual Monarchy's military capabilities.

When Fortress Przemyśl capitulated in late March, the Russians occupied the citadel and began to improve defensive capabilities. Tsar Nicholas visited the compound between April 23 and 25, after which serious improvement work on the fortress commenced. Tsarist heavy-artillery pieces and numerous troop units converged on the desolate fortress.

By the end of April 1915, the Central Powers' military situation remained extremely unfavorable, maintaining military and political defensive posture on all fronts. If Italy entered the war against Austria-Hungary it could also bring Bulgaria and Romania into the conflagration. Indications abounded of major Allied offensive plans for the Western front, and, by April 25, the second phase of the Gallipoli campaign had commenced. General Falkenhayn questioned the possibility of launching an offensive against Serbia to open the Danube River and supplying necessary war materiel to the Ottoman ally to continue the war while relieving Allied pressure in the Balkan Peninsula. Central Power leadership sought to shift the Balkan Peninsula balance of power back to its favor. When major Entente offensives failed at Champagne and Artois on the Western front between February and March, German military leadership determined to strike in the East. General Falkenhayn sought to gain the strategic initiative against the tsarist foe.

By late April, one-third of a million Central Power troops had assembled to launch a surprise offensive against the unsuspecting Russian Third Army. German artillery included approximately 500 heavy- and light-artillery pieces, 96 trench mortars and 600 machine guns, the greatest concentration of artillery to date on the Eastern front. The Russians proved ill-prepared to counter the offensive. Tsarist Third Army possessed 675 light artillery pieces, 4 defective heavy-artillery guns, 600 machine guns and no trench mortars. Its trenches were only three feet deep while its front had been quiescent for weeks. In the interim German reconnaissance flights had flown far into the tsarist rear echelon to report whether the enemy had been alerted to the impending offensive and was moving reinforcements to buttress its front lines. Only minimal tsarist activity was reported. Surprise would be achieved.

Falkenhayn pressured Conrad to negotiate with Italy and demanded that Vienna meet Rome's recent territorial demands. He also urged his ally to negotiate with Bulgaria concerning an alliance against Serbia. Conrad responded that even if the Galician campaign produced a decisive victory and Italy remained neutral, a military campaign against Serbia was out of the question before the end of May. He refused Falkenhayn's request to divert forces from the Serbian front, because he feared a surprise enemy attack into Bosnia. Falkenhayn responded that the Serbians could not launch an offensive into Habsburg territory because of flooded rivers; therefore, Conrad could redeploy those troops.[9] General Conrad inquired about the strength of as well as when German military units would be deployed against Italy if it came to war against that perfidious ally. Conrad also pressured his foreign minister to keep Italy out of the war.

The Gorlice–Tarnow offensive was launched twenty-five miles just northeast of the key Lupkov Pass between the two locations. The attacking troops would pierce tsarist defensive lines, then swing south to pressure the Russian armies ensconced in the Carpathian Mountains. The first objective, breaking through the enemy front, would ensure that the Russian positions leading to the Lupkov Pass could not be maintained. The offensive evolved into two separate campaigns, one lasting from May 2 to June 3. The second, commencing on July 13, ended in September when the Allies drove the Russians out of Poland.

On May 1, 1915, German artillery registered its guns, then they fell silent at 3:00 a.m. to allow for reconnaissance missions. Then at 9:00 a.m. trench mortars fired their devastating rounds for one hour, destroying many shallow tsarist trenches and machine-gun nests. The artillery shifted its fire forward as the first German attack wave rapidly advanced. The German hurricane-artillery bombardment quickly pulverized enemy trenches and destroyed all communication links between the defending units. Large Russian troop numbers surrendered during the first breach of enemy positions; German artillery destroyed all tsarist obstacles and communications. A second tsarist defensive line was nonexistent despite an order on April 16 to establish one. Many Russian soldiers died or were wounded as they fled over open terrain. Of the 250,000-man Russian Third Army, 210,000 became casualties in one week (including 140,000 prisoners of war). Two tsarist corps had been destroyed (X and XXIV). A reconnaissance pilot of Habsburg Flight Company 10 witnessed the destruction.[10]

The offensive struck a very weak Russian position, the connecting point between the Romanov, German and Austro-Hungarian theaters (Russian North and Southwest fronts). Tsarist Third Army had deployed many troops for the Carpathian Mountain front offensive. Thus, when attacked, there was insufficient time to transfer reinforcements from the mountain front to the unexpectedly threatened army. Third Army, occupying its front for months, had not established effective defensive positions, including no definitive second or third positions.

The subsequent troop movements and battles created enormous devastation, the worst occurring during the six weeks before the Great Russian retreat that eventually extended three hundred miles into the enemy's interior. Artillery barrages, plundering troops or burning of villages resulted in fleeing civilians clogging roads, delaying both the progress of Central Power troops and hindering tsarist retreat efforts.

When Italy declared war on Austria-Hungary on May 23, 1915, Generals Conrad and Falkenhayn quickly agreed to maintain a defensive stance against the former ally and to continue the successful Gorlice offensive operation. Fortunately for the Dual Monarchy, the Italians wasted a month before launching the first Isonzo River campaign with overwhelming troop numbers at the end of June 1915. The initial attempted invasion of Austria-Hungary failed because the inexperienced Italian troops had to attack uphill against numerically inferior, but some combat-proven Habsburg defensive forces. Initially advancing Italian soldiers had little machine-gun or artillery support, while the small number of defenders gained sufficient time to rush reinforcements to maintain their lines.[11]

Conrad lacked the troop numbers to attempt launching an offensive because of the Gorlice–Tarnow operation. He initially had to depend on the defensive capabilities of the few local troops defending their home mountain terrain.

The more deeply Russian troops had penetrated into the Carpathian Mountains, the more problematic their circumstances became. As Gorlice offensive forces progressed east, increasingly those outflanked tsarist four armies became entrapped in the mountains. They had to retreat rapidly to prevent encirclement when advancing Central Power troops approached the San River.

The German Army reorganized, providing new formations for the Gorlice–Tarnow operation. Divisions reduced regiments from four to three, which added eight hundred soldiers or more and machine guns to each remaining one. This created eight new infantry divisions that General Falkenhayn originally intended to utilize on the Western front and for an offensive against Serbia. However, the extremely precarious Habsburg front situation forced his plans to be altered.

Well-supported military feints and demonstrations were launched in Courland and the Bukovina to conceal the assembly of soldiers and artillery for the Gorlice operation. General Falkenhayn also launched an offensive on the Flanders' Ypres front to camouflage the transfer of the eight German divisions to the Eastern front to participate in the offensive.

Attempts to create a Central Power Eastern front command structure had failed, which continued to plague the Allies during the present operations. The Habsburg Third and Fourth armies protected the German Eleventh Army flanks during the early Gorlice campaign, the first major Austro-Hungarian-German troops fighting under unified command. General August von Mackensen commanded the operation subject to German High Command orders and informal Conrad command. General Conrad grudgingly accepted the decision, forcing him into the background.

Falkenhayn's minimal objective encompassed crippling Russian military potential that time and his resources allowed, and to seize and maintain the initiative on the Eastern front. He remained wary of the inherent dangers and problems of conducting large-scale operations against tsarist Russia. His immediate objective of relieving the tsarist pressure on the Habsburg Carpathian Mountain front was accomplished, while tsarist battlefield weaknesses enabled further victories. During the initial attack the Russians could neither rapidly nor effectively reinforce their Third Army, which ultimately proved disastrous. Within forty hours that army had been shattered, and in three days its defensive positions overrun. This rapid defeat resulted partially from the fragmented *Stavka*.

By the end of the first battle day Central Power troops had advanced one and a half to three and a half miles, partially because tsarist Third Army lacked strength in depth. The majority of troops deployed in forward defensive lines were decimated by the preoffensive artillery bombardment. General Ivanov soon had to deploy the III Caucasus Corps, his reserve force, to replace the enormous casualties.

Multiple German aircraft flew reconnaissance missions during the morning of May 2 to assist directing artillery barrages and locate enemy artillery positions. On May 3, a fifteen-to-twenty-kilometer-wide breakthrough forced the enemy's eventual retreat to the San River. General Ivanov attempted to launch a III Caucasus Corps counterattack at the Dukla Pass, although his forces had sustained enormous numbers of prisoners of war, casualties and loss of huge quantities of weapons and equipment.

Tsarist forces fought and retreated over their vast terrain with an intact narrow-gauge railroad network and unlimited opportunities to continue withdrawing. Falkenhayn's main concern remained the Western front, but one of his major objectives involved continuing the Eastern front offensive to inflict unacceptable casualties and cripple the Russian Army, ultimately to force it to sign a separate peace treaty. Falkenhayn launched limited, but effective, offensive actions to paralyze Russia's offensive power. He did not seek to conquer enormous territorial acquisitions, because they could create major problems. He always protected his limited gains, cognizant of the dangers inherent in conducting large-scale operations in Russia. In early May his initial operational goal aimed to seize the road junction at Zmigrod and to sever the tsarist army's lateral communication in the Carpathian Mountains. Zmigrod fell on May 9. Thus, one week after the offensive commenced, Eleventh Army had achieved its objectives.[12]

The Gorlice–Tarnow operation enjoyed several advantages. Very successful aerial reconnaissance from rapidly achieved air superiority provided excellent information about Russian Third Army positions, particularly its artillery. Ground reconnaissance results and accurate maps proved invaluable for artillery targeting that allowed no guns preregistering to maintain operational secrecy and assure surprise for the commencement of the campaign.

Falkenhayn agreed that Habsburg Third Army should have the honor of reconquering Fortress Przemyśl, when Central Power troops approached the citadel. Third Army progress lagged because of strong enemy resistance. Falkenhayn determined that because of Habsburg Third Army's lack of progress, Eleventh Army must alter its attack direction and seize the fortress. The inadequate roads leading to the bulwark slowed supply movement and created difficult problems for the assault troops.

The rapid and overwhelming Gorlice–Tarnow offensive success kept Romania from entering the war, while tsarist military weakness caused the tsarist front to rapidly collapse in the Tarnow area as the German Eleventh and Habsburg Fourth armies advanced swiftly. Russian Eighth Army, entrapped in the Carpathian Mountains, retreated to the Lupkov Pass because of the increasing threat of encirclement. Effective German heavy-artillery fire played a major role throughout the campaign, proving indispensable in preparing the multiple short infantry attacks. As during much of the war, Habsburg artillery was described as ineffective and inadequate. The Russians claimed they did not have to move their artillery battery positions during the three Carpathian Mountain Winter War campaigns, because of the lack of effective Habsburg counterfire.[13]

German artillery forward observers proved extremely effective, particularly combined with air reconnaissance missions. They precisely charted Russian artillery positions, enabling German gunners to neutralize enemy defensive firepower with little artillery shell expenditure.

The Russian Army suffered from numerous disadvantages during the campaign, although it conducted its customary, effective rearguard and retreat actions. Tsarist forces suffered from materiel shortages, an increasing lack of weapons, particularly rifles, ammunition and artillery shells, while faulty Third Army troop dispositions made it impossible to halt the original German advance. Reinforcements were ineffectively and piecemeal dispersed, consuming them too rapidly when launching counterattacks into German artillery barrages.

Dispersed units of the tsarist III Caucasus Corps deployed far to the rear of the Gorlice battlefront as a reserve force; therefore, the corps could not immediately deploy on the battlefield following the May Central Power offensive. Its eventual intervention briefly delayed the Allied advance, but on May 4, German Eleventh Army's right flank forces pierced the Russian Third Army front, as III Caucasus Corps launched a counterattack. Tsarist Third Army units retreated behind the Wisloka and Wislok Rivers, a short distance from their present positions. The Wisloka River extended almost a hundred kilometers in a north–south direction fifty miles west of the San River. The Russians unsuccessfully attempted to achieve local military successes by launching counterattacks.

The Central Power advance toward the San River eventually trapped the four tsarist armies ensconced in the Carpathian Mountains. German troops, advancing ten miles a day, eventually forced the tsarist mountain armies to retreat to the San River to avoid encirclement and annihilation. Thousands of tsarist troops perished attempting to cross the river. During the next two weeks, Central Power troops attained the San River line, but encountered serious logistical and transportation problems because Eleventh Army's main railroad supply depot was more than fifty miles to the rear of the assault troops.

Air reconnaissance reports revealed that enemy troops were receiving reinforcements on the Carpathian Mountain front. German efforts forced a Russian retreat before the tsarist troops could prepare strong defensive positions; advancing forces achieved success on both flanks as Habsburg Third Army slowly approached Fortress Przemyśl from the west and south. German Eleventh Army shifted its main forces toward the San River.

Tsarist Third Army X Corps received the brunt of the initial German offensive thrust and had to retreat, opening an enormous gap in the Russian lines. That corps' numbers dropped to 1,500 men. The Central Powers' success forced the tsarist retreat to the Wisloka River area. General Ivanov wanted to continue the retreat to the San River line, but *Stavka* ordered that his retrograde movement halt at the Wisloka River, anticipating that Italy would soon declare war, which would immediately improve tsarist military fortunes. This condemned Russian Third Army, even though two divisions from the tsarist Northwest front reinforced its buckling front.

Between May 5 and 8, the advancing Central Power troops completed a series of successful short advances; the poor mountain roads and necessity of resupply, particularly of artillery shells, delayed Central Power operations somewhat, which enabled Russian troops to escape to the northeast. The Russians, however, failed to destroy the advancing enemy troops' pontoon bridges that enabled them to safely cross waterways. Meanwhile, at the Eleventh Army flank, Habsburg Third Army forced enemy troops out of the Dukla Pass then advanced through the Jaslo–Krosno–Sanok basins, which made the tsarist Lupkov Pass positions untenable.

On May 6 the German ambassador and military attaché in Rome recommended that the Dual Monarchy immediately submit its maximum concessions to Rome. Falkenhayn emphasized that "we stand at a crossroads," but agreed that the Allies could not launch an offensive against Serbia before the end of May, and that Bulgaria must become an ally. He strongly suggested that Habsburg diplomats avoid war with Italy "under any circumstances."[14] On May 4 Conrad pressured Foreign Minister Burian to keep Italy neutral and continue the ongoing Italian negotiations. Earlier, on April 28, Conrad had appealed to Emperor Franz Joseph to drop his opposition to initiating defensive measures along the Italian frontier.

The reeling Russian Third Army inserted its few remaining reserves (two infantry regiments) between Fortress Przemyśl and the Jaroslau bridgehead as its mountain front continued to collapse.

By May 6, Central Power troops had smashed the large gap in the Russian Third Army front, tsarist forces becoming totally disorganized. The May 5 seizure of the Lupkov Pass, the immediate geographic objective to exploit the Gorlice breakthrough, resulted in the victorious Allied troops continuing their advance to the San River as the Russian Carpathian Mountain front crumbled. German advances after heavy battle finally forced the tsarist mountain armies to retreat as quickly as possible to the San River to avoid their destruction.

On May 7 III Caucasus Corps launched a counterattack just as German forces commenced their assault across the Wislok River on May 7 and 8, to continue their advance to the San River. That troop stand numbered four to five thousand troops from its original thirty-four thousand after it launched its unsuccessful counterattacks. The four tsarist armies in the Carpathian Mountains rapidly retreated to the San River. The Germans rebuilt railroad lines and restored destroyed bridges as rapidly as possible to facilitate their progress. They also constructed bridgeheads, which proved of great assistance as they pushed further east, and expanded their maneuver room so that Eleventh Army could eventually shift its attack direction.

General Mackensen proposed that the offensive continue to force the retreating Russians behind the San River line as the operation rapidly developed into a strategic triumph. Then, on May 10, General Ivanov received orders to defend the San–Dniester River lines when his forces were deployed well forward of that line. Central Power reconnaissance flights confirmed tsarist rearward movement toward Fortress Przemyśl.

Meanwhile, three Central Power corps attempted to isolate Fortress Przemyśl from the north and east. Strong Russian defensive positions hindered Habsburg Third Army forward progress so it could not rapidly capture the citadel. In the interim Conrad requested that some German troops be deployed in the southern Carpathian Mountains because tsarist Ninth Army had launched a major attack in the Bukovina. Falkenhayn's reply emphasized that he could not spare additional German troops from the Western front, because an anticipated Anglo-French offensive had just commenced, binding all available German reserves units there.[15] He also believed that the "spearhead" of the Gorlice offensive should not be weakened for a secondary front.

Conrad and Falkenhayn agreed on the necessity to continue the Gorlice–Tarnow offensive, but momentarily failed to determine a further specific objective. To Falkenhayn it mattered little if the Habsburg Seventh Army had to retreat multiple kilometers in the Bukovina, but Conrad believed that if Seventh Army suffered a decisive defeat, it could reverse the favorable Gorlice offensive situation and create a major negative impression on neutral states. The Russian Ninth Army won a considerable but basically irrelevant success in that province, thus by mid-May the Habsburgs had lost much of the Bukovina.

Since long-distance personal exchanges proved inconclusive, Conrad and Falkenhayn required private meetings to determine such matters as the disposal of captured weapons, ammunition and equipment. The two exchanged a flurry of memoranda between May 9 and 12, until they finally met personally. On May 12, they agreed to continue the offensive to the San River. The broad attack objectives included liberating Fortress Przemyśl.

Falkenhayn also announced that the present offensive success would possibly facilitate the transfer of troops against Italy if necessary. He reminded Conrad that the new Anglo-French offensives made it impossible to divert any forces from the Western front, while the divisions promised by Generals Hindenburg and Ludendorff had not yet been freed for deployment. Conrad stressed that the Russians had to be prevented from constructing a strong San River defensive line, and informed his counterpart that the Russian major offensive against Seventh Army in the Bukovina forced him to dispatch two divisions to halt the tsarist advance.[16] Meanwhile, German High Command established new Eastern front headquarters, indicating that the main German war theater remained in the East at least for the near future.

The Russians attempted to establish defensive positions on the San River line, but not rapidly enough. Having sustained excessive casualties, they possessed few reserves. A May 9 Conrad telegraph to General Falkenhayn emphasized that the main goal of Habsburg diplomacy remained preventing war with Italy. At a May 7 conference at German headquarters, consensus had Italy soon declaring war on Austria-Hungary. German High Command promised solidarity with its ally; its contribution of military forces, however, would be dependent upon the momentary situation. Conrad believed that there was no chance of an agreement with Italy, thus studied various defensive measures to initiate on the potential new front. He continued to pressure Habsburg diplomats to avoid war with Italy under any circumstances and argued that the Gorlice offensive would likely facilitate troop transfers to the threatened Italian front.

On May 10 the tsarist Third Army center positions buckled as the severely weakened army had lost much of its fighting force. It had lost nearly 200 artillery pieces and 140,000 prisoners of war. From the original 200,000 Russian soldiers and 50,000 replacement troops hurled into the battered front lines, only 40,000 unwounded soldiers now defended the threatened San River line. The Russian losses proved so severe that two corps barely existed; one had lost 80 percent of its manpower, another stood at three-quarters of its original strength and one now consisted of only two thousand troops. This forced *Stavka* to reverse its earlier decision to not retreat to the San River. Grand Duke Nikolai stipulated that tsarist forces defend the San–Vistula River line and then prepare to launch an offensive. *Stavka*'s main concern became to not surrender Galicia. However, the tsarist Third Army retreat forced the entire Russian front to withdraw. The Gorlice–Tarnow operation rapidly developed into a strategic triumph, when General Ivanov had to defend the San–Dniester River line. If the river line was surrendered, all connections from the Carpathian Mountain front would be compromised.

Emperor Franz Joseph finally approved activating Habsburg military measures on the Italian front as the German government launched a diplomatic offensive in a last-ditch effort to prevent Italy from declaring war. Naturally, Habsburg concerns about a possible third military front and its dire implications also increased. General Conrad was convinced that Italian entry into the war could spell defeat for Austria-Hungary, thus the Central Powers.

The Russian Third and Eighth Army forces, trapped in the Carpathian Mountains, suffered major defeat when Central Power troops recovered the 130 kilometers of Galician terrain extending to the San River. During the next two weeks, carefully planned assault efforts were launched across the San River as German and Habsburg air reconnaissance reports provided accurate and valuable information on the movement of tsarist forces and artillery emplacements.[17] May 12 ended the first phase of the Gorlice–Tarnow campaign. Western Galicia had been recaptured and the tsarist front hurled back to the Nida River and Carpathian Mountain forelands. Depleted Habsburg morale resulting from the disastrous Carpathian Mountain Winter War campaign demoralized the army and civilians alike. However, Falkenhayn noticed a continuing disintegration of Habsburg units as significant tsarist reinforcements appeared on the battlefield. Conrad admitted that the military success resulted from German support and efforts.[18]

Offensive progress, when delayed, occurred more from logistical problems than serious Russian resistance. For the next two weeks German units advanced toward the San River, a major objective to construct bridgeheads to propel an Allied advance over that river and to provide maneuver space for the Eleventh Army to alter its offensive's direction if necessary. The most feverish activity, however, consisted of constructing railroad lines because the nearest major supply depot extended over sixty miles from the present front lines.

Meanwhile, Habsburg Third Army achieved only slow progress against the Russian Eighth Army defending the southern and western approaches to Fortress Przemyśl. The terrible condition of supply roads hindered all efforts to advance east of the Carpathian Mountains. Two German corps crossed the San River to establish blocking positions to protect Eleventh Army right flank positions. Three Habsburg corps swung to the south and southeast to isolate Fortress Przemyśl from the north and east.

On May 13 an interesting Central Power exchange occurred relative to the potential deployment of the German Alpine Corps on the Italian frontier. General Falkenhayn insisted that Conrad order his troops to avoid any activity that might influence an active Italian response. Falkenhayn stated that it was absolutely essential that Habsburg Southwest front deployment not disturb German diplomatic efforts in Rome at this critical moment.

Conrad and Falkenhayn again discussed the military situation, informing the Bulgarians that they must "immediately" prepare for a campaign against Serbia, but the threatening Italian situation caused Sofia to shy away.

Allied forces initiated another short advance along the northern San riverbank on May 13 as General Mackensen prepared to attack Fortress Przemyśl. The Jaroslau bridgehead provided a position for German XXXI Corps to neutralize Russian positions at Radymno before they attacked the fortress. That corps attacked the citadel from the northwest. However, serious Russian resistance initially retarded progress.

Slackened combat activity that day provided a welcome respite for Eleventh Army troops who had endured nine straight days of battle, partly pursuing retreating Russian forces. General Conrad suggested that the Allied offensive be halted at the San–Dniester River line to then construct strong defensive positions to free twenty infantry divisions to counter an Italian attack. Falkenhayn disagreed; the ongoing offensive took priority.

Air reconnaissance reports provided continually accurate and invaluable information to higher field commanders, finally revealing that tsarist troops had begun to retreat from the Fortress Przemyśl environs.[19] The question remained, did the enemy intend to defend Fortress Przemyśl? Throughout early May the Russians could not decide; thus, they prepared to transport troops and weapons out of the citadel. *Stavka* then suddenly reversed its decision to retreat and determined to defend the fortress. The German assumption that the enemy would attempt to avoid decisive battle at the San River line proved erroneous.

On May 14, a Habsburg and German corps seized the key tsarist defensive positions close to Jaroslau, having advanced eighty miles. The Russians hoped to utilize arriving reinforcements to defend Fortress Przemyśl and their lower San River defensive line. A tsarist counterattack failed.

Meanwhile, on May 11, Emperor Franz Joseph had finally approved the full activation of Habsburg forts on the Italian frontier as Habsburg leaders anticipated that Rome would soon declare war. The following day, Foreign Minister Burian agreed to the secession of nearly all territory inhabited by Italians, but would not surrender it until the end of the year. The Italian government rejected the offer.

Allied discussions commenced relative to appropriate military measures on the Italian front when that country finally declared war. On May 14 Emperor Franz Joseph approved initiating defensive measures at the frontier against an Italian attack after sanctioning the preparation of Habsburg fortifications for an Italian attack. General Falkenhayn again queried, relative to the probability that with German and Bulgarian troops the Allies could defeat Serbia.[20]

Meanwhile, the Eleventh Army offensive continued through inclement weather conditions, its right flank positions protected against a possible tsarist sortie launched from Fortress Przemyśl. The arrival of a critical resupply of artillery shells allowed renewal of the offensive, which ultimately drove some Russian troops across the San River between May 15 and 23. Air reconnaissance missions, however, confirmed that significant enemy forces remained ensconced west of the river.

The worsening shortage of artillery shells weakened Russian forces. On May 16 German units crossed the San River, forcing enemy troops protecting Jaroslau to capitulate, which negated any tsarist attempt to launch a major counterattack.[21] As the Allied advance continued, air reconnaissance units deployed forward to conduct long-range reconnaissance missions to pinpoint tsarist troop units and artillery positions.

Premature attacks against sections of Fortress Przemyśl failed because of insufficient artillery support. Tsarist resistance increased against Central Power forces as they retreated across the San–Dniester River line.

Falkenhayn stated that once Allied troops had secured the San–Dniester River line, that front could be maintained with thirty Habsburg divisions. Conrad suggested that this would free troops for deployment against both Italy and Serbia, freeing seventeen to eighteen Austro-Hungarian and seven German infantry divisions (excluding the Eleventh Army). Thus, twenty-four to twenty-five divisions would suffice for the Gorlice operation if the Russians continued to retreat. A combined German, Austro-Hungarian, Bulgarian and Turkish offensive could then be launched again Serbia.

As battle raged at the San River line, Central Powers forces successfully crossed. In the meantime, *Stavka* commanded General Ivanov to prevent the loss of Fortress Przemyśl at all costs. For six days Central Power preparations commenced for the next phase of the Allied operation, again requiring renewed stockpiling of artillery shells and awaiting the arrival of *Ersatz* troops to replace recent severe casualties.

By May 22 Central Power forces had advanced fifty-five miles in just three weeks, but the terrible mountain road conditions hampered Habsburg Third Army efforts to approach the fortress because heavy-artillery shells could not be transported over them. Continued slow progress against the tsarist forces defending the western and southern fortress approaches also delayed Third Army's planned assault. German Eleventh Army therefore shifted its advance direction to attack the citadel after a short battle pause. The operational break became necessary on May 19 to restock artillery shells and for supply trains to traverse the destroyed roadways, bridges and railroad lines that delayed the delivery of vitally needed equipment and food. Feverish repair work continued on damaged railroad lines. The Russians could no longer launch major counterattacks, although they stiffened defensive resistance. Conrad and Falkenhayn had continually to reassess the strategic situation, particularly because of the increasing Italian threat to enter the war.

As Habsburg and German forces prepared to liberate Fortress Przemyśl, the question of when Italy would declare war dominated Allied military discussions. Falkenhayn also raised serious concern about the protection of Bavaria and South Germany. Pressured Habsburg troop railroad transports to the Italian frontier continued as preparations commenced to prepare fortified defensive lines. Although Conrad wanted twenty Eastern front infantry divisions redeployed to launch a powerful offensive against Italy, two-thirds of forces on the Serbian front that could also participate were presently not capable of launching an effective offensive.

Falkenhayn continued to pressure Conrad to launch an Allied offensive against Serbia to attract Bulgaria as an ally, but the majority of his forces remained bound on the Russian front. The next major question concerned the troop numbers necessary to obtain military success against Serbia, particularly relative to potential Bulgarian and Turkish units. Falkenhayn pressed to attack before Austria-Hungary had to fight Italy. Lacking sufficient troop numbers to establish solid defensive positions, Conrad initially utilized guerrilla warfare tactics against a potential Italian invasion. Bulgaria announced that it would remain neutral during the invasion of Serbia.

Habsburg Fifth Army forces transferred from the Serbian front as a first echelon force to defend the Habsburg-Italian frontier. The numbers initially deployed proved pathetically low. *Standesschützen*, local *Landsturm* defense troops, protected the Italian frontier until the five designated infantry divisions could be deployed to that front. Falkenhayn in the interim calculated that the Italian Army would not be combat ready until late June.

On May 21 Falkenhayn informed Conrad that he doubted that the Italians would immediately launch an offensive when they declared war. He promised German units would be deployed to the Italian front, if they did not weaken the Eastern front. Conrad anticipated an immediate Italian invasion into the Dual Monarchy. He believed his defensive forces were too weak to launch even an effective counterattack, leaving the Italians free to march almost unopposed into Habsburg territory. Falkenhayn adamantly opposed deploying large German troop numbers against Italy.

While Falkenhayn's main attention remained focused on the Western front, he recognized the necessity of at least temporarily exploiting his Eastern military successes. His pressure on Conrad to launch an offensive against Serbia also had to be dismissed momentarily, because of the Bulgarian refusal to cooperate.

The failure of the Russians on the center of their front on May 19 and 20 resulted in preparations commencing for the May 24 to June 6 Central Power battle to conquer Fortress Przemyśl. Artillery shells had to be stockpiled while awaiting the arrival of replacement troops. The foremost concern involved the critical shortage of large-caliber artillery shells and the persisting problems of delayed logistical efforts because the closest major railhead depot lay almost ninety kilometers behind the front. In addition to the lack of motor vehicles, a shortage of fodder limited the use of horses. The few travel routes' terrible terrain and road conditions required the construction of railroads. Such logistical problems impeded offensive efforts more than enemy resistance.

On May 24, with two-hours preparatory artillery barrages, Allied forces approached Fortress Przemyśl. Conrad then turned his attention to the pressing matter of Italy with its May 23 Italian declaration of war. Allied troops crossed the San River and regrouped for the attack on the fortress.

Conrad remained concerned about Romanian intentions. If Romania intervened on the Habsburg side, he postulated that the Central Powers could win the war and that victory also remained possible if it simply remained neutral. But he remained convinced that if Romania attacked, defeat would be inevitable. Bulgaria and Romania remained pivotal factors in the Central Powers' diplomatic and political calculations.

On May 26, as Central Power forces advanced toward Fortress Przemyśl, fighting continued for days along the San River front. Then, on May 27, tsarist forces launched a powerful counterattack from the northern and northeastern fortress fronts against German Eleventh and Habsburg Fourth armies. *Stavka* determined to defend the fortress thus deployed reinforcements to it. On May 30, German heavy artillery commenced bombarding the citadel. The next day, two Habsburg infantry regiments stormed a northern fort position, but failed to capture it, because they lacked sufficient artillery support. Tsarist command became convinced that the enemy would not launch its major attack from the northern fortress perimeter; therefore, it considered the attack merely a demonstration. The mass of tsarist reserve-artillery pieces was transferred to the southwest fortress front where the Russian commanders now anticipated the main assault.

On May 31, at 11 a.m., heavy-artillery barrages, assisted by precise artillery observation, turned several of the citadel forts into rubble. A Bavarian division stormed several ruined fortress walls and seized the three northernmost positions. However, plans had to be postponed for any further assault until June 1, with anticipated delivery of heavy-artillery shells, but artillery barrages continued. Night artillery fire, including devastating 42-cm heavy mortar fire, leveled several of the forts into piles of rubble. Assault troops then stormed two fortress fronts. On June 1, German offensive units penetrated the defenses. Tsarist reinforcements arrived too late to affect the outcome of the battle.

In the early morning of June 2, the Russians launched a counterattack at one fortress defensive district, but Allied firepower halted the effort. Russian defensive positions quickly collapsed and those soldiers who could retreat did so. Remaining troops burned fortress supplies and destroyed the last bridge spanning the San River. Russian troops then attempted to establish a solid defensive stand north of Zuravica, but this also collapsed. The plan to launch a major assault against the fortress on June 3 proved unnecessary since the bulwark capitulated during the afternoon. German Eleventh Army troops occupied the citadel, capturing eight thousand prisoners of war. Estimates of Russian losses vary during the battle, but Central Power spoils proved insignificant.

The Central Power military situation became extremely complicated when Italy declared war on Austria-Hungary (but not Germany) on May 23, 1915. Habsburg Supreme Command had to immediately reinforce its thinly manned defensive lines along the Italian frontier, while Allied commanders adjusted to the new military situation. When Austro-Hungarian-German forces advanced east toward Lemberg, Fortress Przemyśl had no further major influence on Habsburg strategy and the military situation. Falkenhayn tactlessly offered the fortress to Emperor Franz Joseph, while Conrad had to accept the galling fact that German units liberated the fortress. The citadel capitulated in 4 days compared to the 137 it required the Russians to starve the garrison into surrender during their second siege in March 1915. The tsarist army had relinquished its most powerful defensive pivot on the San River front when it retreated from the citadel.

By June 21, 1915, Habsburg fortress troops had performed all the intended restoration work within the citadel with the construction of multiple new infantry defensive positions. Few artillery batteries were provided to support the garrison. Given the potential cost of reconstruction work and that the fortress had lost much of its military significance, it was not fully reconstructed. Habsburg *Landsturm* units and ten thousand Russian prisoners of war rebuilt the few redesignated infantry positions, while life returned to normal within the fortress city. Twenty Russian, five Polish and two Italian prisoner-of-war labor companies completed the few reconstruction projects.

In hindsight, the recapture of Fortress Przemyśl did not provide as significant a victory as is sometimes proclaimed in Austrian historiography. The conquering troops failed to capture the tsarist forces defending the fortress, which enabled them to evacuate the bulwark in a timely fashion.

The Central Power campaign also provided a diplomatic success, preventing Romania from entering the war. The Russian military collapse convinced Romanian leadership to maintain its neutrality. Then the German Eleventh and Habsburg Third armies had to assist the embattled Austro-Hungarian Fourth Army, which sustained some battlefield setbacks, compelling Falkenhayn to adjust his offensive plans. A Russian counterattack forced that army's southern flank units to retreat behind the San River, interrupting Third Army and South Army forward progress. By May 17 the tsarist armies had lost at least 412,000 troops, including 170,000 prisoners of war and huge quantities of war materiel.

The recapture of Fortress Przemyśl neutralized the four tsarist armies embroiled in the Carpathian Mountains by threatening their envelopment. Their rapid withdrawal ended the Russian threat to invade Hungary. By the end of June 1915, the Central Powers had regained most of the territory surrendered during the Carpathian Mountain Winter campaign. The Gorlice–Tarnow campaign continued throughout summer 1915 and into the fall. Russia lost at least a million prisoners of war and suffered a million combat casualties. The new German offensive methods continued with rapid, deep breakthrough movements supported by overpowering artillery support that produced a string of unbroken Eastern front victories.

The bloody failure of the French-British offensives on the Western front resulted in the transfer of three German divisions and two Hindenburg–Ludendorff forces to reinforce Eleventh Army. General Mackensen maintained command of the Habsburg Second and Fourth armies while Conrad's Third Army was disbanded and multiple units transferred to the Italian front.

After a short operational pause to bring up artillery units, a new attack on June 18 proceeded to seize the railroad line north of Lemberg to isolate that city. The tsarist Grodek defensive line quickly collapsed and the Russian Third Army retreated northward, the other tsarist armies east and south. On June 22 portions of Habsburg Second Army entered Lemberg. Meanwhile, German General Seeckt suggested that Army Group Mackensen turn north to advance into the southern side of the Russian Poland salient. After the recapture of Fortress Przemyśl, its garrison remained skeletal as major battle raged further to the east. Plans were finalized to continue the Gorlice–Tarnow offensive after a meeting at Pless; a ten-day operational pause allowed Eleventh Army to rebuild its stockpile of artillery shells and conduct thorough aerial reconnaissance of Russian defensive positions. The renewed objective became the railroad line located between Lemberg and Rava Russka. Eleventh and Fourth armies secured the San River crossings for all three armies to continue the offensive.

Following Italy's declaration of war, the question of the utilization of the German Alpine Corps became a bone of contention between Generals Conrad and Falkenhayn. Falkenhayn notified Conrad that he had learned that the

Alpine Corps had been ordered to be deployed in the Habsburg front lines, which placed them partially in Italian territory. He ordered that they not advance into Italy because that country had not declared war on Germany. If battle occurred between German and Italian troops on Tyrolean territory, the Italians had to appear to be the aggressors. An infuriated Conrad informed his counterpart that the orders to the German troops had been revised.

By June 13, Allied troops prepared to resume the offensive, collapsing Russian defensive positions within two days. Following a four-day advance Eleventh Army forces reached the chain of lakes and forests west of Lemberg that included the last tsarist defensive line around Grodek. After another brief pause the renewal of the attack pierced the Russian defensive positions. On June 18, with the seizure of its railroad line, Lemberg became isolated.

Demoralized Russian troops, fearing encirclement, quickly retreated from Lemberg, substantially raising Dual Monarchy troop and civilian morale. Only the tsarist Eighth, Ninth and Eleventh armies remained on the front as the badly mauled Third Army retreated to the Russian northwest front. The next logical option appeared to be to advance north into Russian Poland toward Brest- Litovsk, the hub of the Russian Polish railroad network. Its loss would be a serious blow to the Russians. Thus, an attack ensued northward against the southern portion of the Polish salient.

Conrad and Falkenhayn hoped that a successful Polish campaign would force Russia to conclude a separate peace. German Eleventh Army troops crossed the frontier into Russian Poland during June 28 and 29, encountering little enemy resistance except weak rearguard actions.

During the last week in June battle slackened, as weather conditions remained favorable, while much of the terrain contained flat areas and some swampy regions. The sandy roads turned into bottomless pits of mud after heavy rainfall. A problem resulted from the tsarist narrow-gauge railroad tracks once Central Power troops crossed the Russian frontier.

On July 1 Eleventh Army encountered a new Russian defensive position on both sides of the Wiep River. The Russian retreat, meanwhile, had created a much shorter and straight defensive front line along the southern portion of the tsarist Polish salient. The Russians launched a major counterattack against Eleventh Army's right flank positions on the Bug River. Although Eleventh Army forces neutralized this effort, German High Command determined that the Russians had concentrated major forces, at least four corps, in that area. Thus, Eleventh Army's right flank position required additional protection. A new army became designated the Bug Army.

On July 2 Generals Conrad and Falkenhayn determined that General Mackensen's forces would be supported by an attack from the Hindenburg–Ludendorff *Oberost* front in eleven days. By July 12 an army reached the Zlota Lipa River line, another the lower Bug River area. The two armies provided flank protection to the Seventh Army's left flank, and Eleventh

Army's right and rear flanks. Habsburg First Army units marched through Lemberg establishing new positions in Second Army's left flank area. These rearrangements facilitated the redeployment of Eleventh Army's front to the north for its next major operation.

On July 13 the offensive resumed. Twelfth Army attacked the edge of the Polish salient, while a major advance evolved from southwest of the Masurian Lakes toward Romania. Again, aerial reconnaissance played a major role as reinforcements arrived from the Western front. German Eastern forces also launched an offensive on July 13, but progress proved slow on both fronts because of tsarist defensive actions and swampy terrain. Army Group Mackensen, now consisting of the Habsburg First and Fourth armies, the German Eleventh and the newly created Bug Army, had to advance over extremely swampy terrain. The Russians launched several counterattacks against the Bug Army. Hindenburg's Eighth Army also found its progress hampered by the swampy Narev and Bobra Rivers terrain and the well-prepared Russian defensive actions, thus initially only slow forward progress occurred at the northern and southern sides of the Polish salient.

On July 15 First Army, supported by the Bug Army, attacked toward Vladimir-Volinsky into the large Russian salient in Poland. Eliminating the salient would shorten Central Power front lines, free numerous troop formations for deployment elsewhere and potentially cripple Russian offensive power for some time. The decision to continue the offensive witnessed a rare degree of unanimity among German High Command, Hindenburg–Ludendorff *Oberost* and Habsburg Supreme Command. The critical problem came with determining operational details.

General Falkenhayn's more cautious tactical concept, compared to that of Generals Hindenburg and Ludendorff, relied on the continuation of the methodical bludgeoning of enemy positions that had already proven so successful. Falkenhayn's plan proved tactically, operationally and logistically more suited to the 1915 military situation. The final decision relative to Falkenhayn's proposal for future operations received approval because the agenda had been prearranged for a July 2 Posen command meeting. Emperor Wilhelm and Generals Falkenhayn and Conrad agreed on the proposed strategy, negating General Hindenburg's more radical strategic concepts.

General Hindenburg suggested that a massive offensive be launched to encircle the Russian northern flank positions instead of Falkenhayn's proposed attack across the Narev and Bobra Rivers toward Brest-Litovsk. Hindenburg desired an attack against the obsolete Russian Kovno fortress on the Nieman River, whereby German Tenth Army, supported by the newly created Nieman Army, would swing southeast toward Vilna to advance 162 miles to the Minsk area. This, with the seizure of Brest-Litovsk, would reputedly trap the entire Russian northwest front armies. General Falkenhayn, however, proposed a severely truncated operation for *Oberost* forces. They should attack much further west across the Narev and Vistula Rivers at the western edge of Russian Poland to support his offensive operations further south.

The Russian July 22 retreat followed the 1812 tradition by executing a scorched earth policy. *Stavka* also made seriously flawed decisions determining to maintain large garrisons in its obsolete Vistula River fortresses, most notably that of Novogeorgievsk. After the previous weeks of military activity, General Mackensen commenced an operational pause to regroup his depleted forces and replenish artillery shells in preparation for the new offensive.

A week later he renewed the offensive, coinciding with the resumption of *Oberost*'s efforts in late July on the Narev and Vistula Rivers. Both operations commenced as the Russians accelerated their evacuation of Poland, thus by early August the enemy defenses had collapsed after two weeks of steady pressure.

Attacking troops conquered Lublin on July 31 and Cholm on August 1 (both major scenes of battle during the opening 1914 campaigns of the war). Crossing the Vistula River Central Power forces isolated Fortress Ivangorod, while a Habsburg corps reached the fortress on August 3. Central Power heavy artillery quickly crushed the tsarist network of fortresses in Poland, particularly Novogeorgievsk. By the end of August *Stavka* had determined to evacuate Poland, after Central Power troops crossed the Narev River.

The Russians abandoned Warsaw commencing August 4. German troops conquered Warsaw on August 5, then proceeded toward obsolete Fortress Novogeorgievsk constructed in the 1880s. Two corps, heavy-artillery units and accompanying siege trains encircled the citadel when on August 13 German heavy-artillery barrages rapidly destroyed the fortification works. Because of the progress of the offensive the next objective would be the major tsarist railroad junction at Brest-Litovsk. Army Group Mackensen would shift its operations to the northeast, while *Oberost* Tenth Army advanced against the obsolete Fortress Kovno. That fortress surrendered on August 19, supplying prisoners of war and vast amounts of war materiel. As a serious consequence of the tsarist retreat operations Grand Duke Nicholas was cashiered as *Stavka* commander and replaced by Tsar Nicholas II, assuming command on September 5; a fatal error by the tsar. Any further defeat would redound on him. During the remainder of August and early September Army Group Mackensen advanced to the northeast toward Brest-Litovsk.

That fortress capitulated on August 26, while Hindenburg's troops advanced into Lithuania. German High Command soon terminated the Eastern front campaign. Meanwhile, Falkenhayn transferred some of his victorious troops to the Western front, while Mackensen redeployed to the Serbian frontier for the next major Central Power operation. The Gorlice offensive terminated by the end of August 1915.

Meanwhile, *Oberost*'s attempted northern battle of encirclement was delayed by harsh weather conditions, its expectations proving grossly overoptimistic. Central Power efforts were greatly aided by Russian defensive tactics, which included launching immediate counterattacks to attempt to regain any lost terrain. The successful penetration of enemy lines usually achieved sufficient width and depth as each assault typically resulted in the enemy frontline positions collapsing. Examples of this included commencement of the battle of Gorlice–Tarnow, and the subsequent San River crossing operation.

Logistics played a major role during the entire operation. General Mackensen's forces repeatedly advanced miles from the nearest railroad supply depot location, which forced the battle pauses that usually lasted about a week. During this military inactivity, railroad lines were extended forward, and ammunition stocks, especially artillery shells, were replaced, reinforcements inserted into their proper units and heavy-artillery batteries deployed forward.

German aerial reconnaissance proved critical during the campaign, assisted by Central Power airpower superiority, which ensured little enemy opposition. In-depth photographic images of Russian defensive positions identified crucial targets for the artillery because every German artillery shell counted. Another factor was that the Russian primitive trench systems could not withstand the short German heavy-artillery barrages that continued for ninety minutes to about two hours.

The Gorlice–Tarnow operation produced the major Central Power victory of the war. It drove tsarist troops hundreds of miles into their own territory; however, the Russian Army remained intact. Many tsarist troops lacked rifles and artillery shells. Austria-Hungary had once again been rescued from probable defeat. Conrad's resentment against the German High Command success partly explains the next major Russian front campaign, the disastrous Habsburg Rovno fiasco. Meanwhile, the Gorlice–Tarnow campaign resulted in Bulgaria finally joining the Central Power invasion of Serbia.

Falkenhayn terminated the Gorlice–Tarnow campaign to prepare for an invasion of Serbia before approaching winter weather prevented any chance of success. Conrad, meanwhile, determined to launch an offensive to attempt to encircle twenty-five Russian divisions in what became known as the disastrous Black-Gold offensive. Conrad attempted to restore Habsburg troop morale and self-confidence in his leadership by launching an attack between the Russian West and Southwest fronts separated by the Pripet Marshes. Conrad sought to establish Habsburg independence from German High Command as Austria-Hungary progressively fell into a junior partnership in the alliance. The *Schwarzgelb* operation was also intended to free Eastern Galicia from Russian occupation and expand Habsburg power well into Russian territory.[22]

Conrad launched the offensive toward Rovno (in northwestern Ukraine), preferring to continue the Eastern front campaign before participating in an invasion of Serbia. Nevertheless, serious negotiations for a campaign against Serbia progressed. Falkenhayn, skeptical of Conrad's plans, hoped that the Rovno offensive would further weaken the battered tsarist armies and improve Habsburg military self-confidence. His attention focused on knocking Serbia out of the war so that desperately needed ammunition and supplies could be transported to the Turkish ally. By the end of 1915, General Falkenhayn had also abandoned his Western front offensive operations; his troops' mission became to defend their present lines. German High Command hoped that Russian offensive strength had been paralyzed for a long time. The successful completion of the forthcoming Serbian and Gorlice–Tarnow campaigns eliminated the danger of Romanian intervention against Austria-Hungary.

Habsburg First Army launched the initial Rovno offensive on August 26, a frontal assault against strong Russian defensive positions rather than encircling the enemy flank as specifically ordered. On August 31, its troops captured Lutsk, Russian troops conducting a skillful withdrawal behind the Styr River. Ultimately, fourteen Habsburg divisions could not defeat six opposing enemy units. When the Russians received further reinforcements, troops designated for the campaign against Serbia had to remain deployed on the Eastern front. This also signified that no reinforcements could be sent to the Italian front, where they were desperately needed.

Commanders displayed poor leadership although the opposing troops originally withdrew. Habsburg Army corps and division commanders ignored orders, displayed no initiative and failed to inspire their troops. Meanwhile, as the Russians initially retreated, they destroyed roads and bridges, which with inclement weather conditions delayed Habsburg pursuit.

On September 3 the Russians launched a surprise counterattack that immediately threatened two Habsburg Army positions. The Rovno operation would later be termed "among the most shameful" of the entire war as the Habsburg offensive was halted by two tsarist infantry brigades. An interesting note in the daily log of General Conrad's adjutant revealed that "without German forces we cannot advance and make progress."[23]

The devastating Rovno defeat could be blamed on poor command and tactics extending from Habsburg Supreme Command down to division level. The excessive professional officer casualties resulted in inadequately trained replacements that often proved unqualified for command positions. Once they had received reinforcements, Russian forces regrouped and attacked First and Fourth Habsburg armies, from the Rokitno marshes, normally considered unsuitable for large-scale military operations. The resulting tsarist breakthrough was also affected by Habsburg troop exhaustion.

By September 10 Conrad expressed serious concern about his troops' retrograde movement, which also upset his German counterpart. The Russians continued their attack against Habsburg First Army on the next day while Second and Fourth armies made no progress in their offensive efforts. As the Russians continued to advance, Conrad's adjutant recorded that the Germans would rescue them. Fourth Army offensive achieved only slow progress, because of swampy terrain.

The effect the Habsburg defeat would have on Romania became significant. Habsburg troop morale slipped drastically as troops had to remain on the tsarist front instead of being redeployed to the Serbian front as intended.

On September 16 Conrad learned that the Germans would replace Habsburg divisions for the approaching Serbian campaign, because of the serious Habsburg military East Galicia situation. Conrad acknowledged disappointment on having to depend upon German military assistance and its negative effect on Dual Monarchy prestige.

Meanwhile, Fourth Army continued its retreat, but the Russians halted their offensive because the Habsburg retreat occurred so rapidly. German divisions had to be deployed behind Fourth Army lines. Tsarist forces captured abandoned equipment sufficient to arm two army corps!

Emperor Franz Joseph expressed his displeasure about the recent Galician front setbacks. A great distinction existed between Habsburg division troop numbers and opposing tsarist divisions. Conrad complained that he could not plan any offensive operations with his troops, but again he had demanded too much of them and ignored the inclement weather conditions that turned the operational terrain into a quagmire. German reinforcements had to be rapidly redeployed to the Russian front, where they again successfully limited the Habsburg defeat. The disastrous Rovno campaign defeat resulted in multiple repercussions. The Habsburg reputation in the Balkan Peninsula in Bulgaria, but more significantly Romania, suffered. It also considerably weakened Habsburg Supreme Command and German High Command and Foreign Office relationships. The Balkan theater had become a German one, replacing the Habsburgs as the dominant power in that region.

It also produced a negative effect on the negotiations with Bulgaria relative to the projected Serbian campaign. Bulgarian and Turkish military leaders would only sign a military agreement with a German command.

Habsburg Army morale, particularly officers, sank as Conrad's forces sustained 230,000 casualties, including an embarrassing 100,000 prisoners of war during the Rovno campaign. Significantly, Slavic troops proved reliable under German command, although they comprised a large number of the numerous prisoners of war. Entire Czech and Polish battalions reputedly surrendered to the enemy without resistance. By late 1915 only 5.2 percent of German officers had been listed as missing or captured; the Habsburg Fourth Army percentage reached 32.9 percent. The enormous loss of Habsburg prestige resulted in the Young Turks in the Habsburg Operation Bureau designating the battle the "autumn swine" campaign.

Habsburg military leaders continued to be infuriated by German slights concerning their lack of battlefield achievements and their ally monopolizing credit for all Eastern front victories. Furthermore, personal tensions, disputes and mutual recriminations relative to the conduct of the war increased particularly between Conrad and Falkenhayn.

German leaders demanded that their ally provide territorial concessions to Romania in the Bukovina and Transylvania because of their increasing concerns about the competence of the Habsburg Army.[24] Many Habsburg troops panicked before Russian assaults were actually launched.

During early 1915, the first rumors surfaced of the Italians demanding additional territorial concessions from Vienna to simply maintain their neutrality. On January 1, 1915 Conrad telegraphed Falkenhayn his concerns about the Italian situation.[25] On January 5 it was learned that Italy and Romania had signed a formal agreement, thus to Generals Conrad and Falkenhayn a decisive early 1915 victory against Russia became an absolute necessity.

Conrad informed Falkenhayn on January 4 that negotiations concerning the territorial demands were being conducted, but reports of their movements at the frontier appeared to Conrad to be preparations for a general mobilization. He reiterated that the Central Power military situation would become hopeless if Italy entered the war. After one more decisive Habsburg military defeat, Italy would attack Austria-Hungary.

The new foreign minister Count Burian informed Conrad that Habsburg territories could not be surrendered, specifically the Isonzo area, Trieste, the Dalmatian Islands and Albania. Burian would attempt to continue negotiations, but surrendering territory to Italy could sacrifice Austria-Hungary's Great Power position.

On January 5, Conrad telegraphed Falkenhayn that to surrender territory to Italy would cause Romania to demand Transylvania and the Bukovina. If Italy went to war against the Dual Monarchy, Romania and Bulgaria would also. Conrad requested German troops be deployed at the Italian frontier to demonstrate German support. If the Italians invaded Habsburg territory, they would be resisted by both Habsburg and German troops. To Conrad, the mere appearance of German troops would have a major detrimental effect on the Italians.

On January 6 German leaders again pressured Vienna to surrender territory to Italy to keep it neutral, but Conrad repeated that he could not accept Italian demands. He again insisted that the situation on both the Eastern and Balkan fronts could only be resolved by obtaining a decisive victory against Russia. A major success over Serbia would be worthless if Russian forces had not been soundly defeated. On January 11, when Conrad and Falkenhayn conferred at Breslau, Falkenhayn pressed his counterpart to provide concessions to Rome to maintain its neutrality. Using the unfavorable Habsburg Eastern front military situation, the Italian government again raised the question of territorial compensation to maintain its neutrality.

On January 21 Falkenhayn telegraphed Conrad that an agreement with Italy must be concluded quickly, emphasizing that if Italy did declare war, Romania would follow suit. Conrad replied that no territory would be surrendered to Italy because negotiations would be worthless.[26] But with the first Carpathian Mountain Winter War offensive defeats in January and early February 1915 and the threat of the Dardanelles Gallipoli landing, German High Command again demanded that the Habsburgs provide compensation to Italy to maintain its neutrality and insisted that a decisive victory against Russia was necessary before German troops could be deployed against Italy.

Conrad announced on March 8 that he would only accept the surrender of the Trentino to Italy if absolutely necessary, but such an action would represent a severe sacrifice on both political and historical grounds.[27] The next day, Vienna accepted the surrender of some territory as a basis for further negotiations. On March 14 the very unfavorable Carpathian Mountain front military situation made further negotiations with Italy a necessary priority, but Conrad would only consider the surrender of territory extending to the language frontier for its neutrality. Falkenhayn increasingly pressured Conrad during April to immediately offer compensation to Italy; on April 1 the report of Italian troop movements and mobilization preparations caused Conrad to ponder whether Italy had commenced a general mobilization. This increased German foreign office pressure on Habsburg authorities to surrender territory.

On March 27, the Italian ambassador in Vienna announced that Italy demanded all the South Tyrol to maintain its neutrality. German pressure accelerated to avoid Italian intervention before a decisive military victory had been achieved over Russia. During April the Italians extended their demands to include the entire Brenner Pass area and Flitsch, which provided easy access to Villach, Gorizia and other sensitive Habsburg areas. Meanwhile, Berlin's military and political leaders continued pressure on Vienna to avoid war with Italy at all costs, which produced a temporary crisis between the Allies that only negotiations ended.

Conrad notified Burian on April 1 that if Italy entered the war the Dual Monarchy would be crushed by the overwhelming enemy numbers. This raised the question of seeking a separate peace with Russia, even sacrificing Galicia, to provide a free hand against Italy. Conrad preferred to surrender Galicia rather than the Tyrol.

Conrad approached Falkenhayn on April 6, inquiring whether seven German divisions could be redeployed from the Eastern front to establish an early defense force if Italy declared war. On April 9 Conrad repeated his request that seven German divisions be deployed to the Italian front. Falkenhayn strongly advised Conrad that the Habsburg Army must maintain the Carpathian Mountain front particularly after Fortress Przemyśl capitulated on March 22, 1915, releasing the tsarist siege army for transfer to the Carpathian Mountain front. Then on April 13 Allied negotiations commenced relative to German troops launching a major offensive in the area of Gorlice–Tarnow to relieve the Habsburg mountain front.

On April 10 Habsburg leaders recognized that the Italians sought acquisition of their conationals in the Dual Monarchy, but also strategic territorial advantage. Italian demands struck at the internal Dual Monarchy structure, thus for Italian neutrality Vienna would have to surrender Trieste, the Dalmatian coast and islands.

Habsburg leadership found itself in a quandary. It had to avoid presenting Italy any excuse to go to war, while initiating basic military defensive preparations at its frontier. During mid-April troop transports commenced to the Italian theater; armaments and troops to man the border forts on May 12.

The Italian government signed the London Protocol with the Entente Powers on April 26, promising them South Tyrol extending to the Brenner Pass, the cities of Trieste, Gorizia and Gradiska. They were also promised Istrian and northern and middle Dalmatian territory, in addition to important Adriatic Sea islands and would receive Albanian territory if they attacked Austria-Hungary within thirty days.

In the interim Habsburg leadership frantically requested that German leaders continue to energetically intervene for them in Rome with the Italian government. Foreign Minister Burian continued negotiations, increasingly necessary because of the unfavorable Carpathian Mountain military situation. Meanwhile, the Italians commenced a secret mobilization completing military preparations for war at the upper Isonzo River area by April 27. By mid-month, the first skeleton Habsburg military staff was transferred to the Italian frontier. By May 25, additional military personnel arrived in future battle zones.

At a Conrad–Falkenhayn meeting on April 24 Falkenhayn suggested seeking a separate peace with Russia so it could concentrate on defeating France and England. Bethmann-Hollweg argued that seeking a separate peace with the tsarist government would be regarded as a sign of weakness.

Unfortunately for Italy the Russians unexpectedly became bogged down with the Central Power Gorlice–Tarnow offensive, unleashed on May 2, 1915, which eliminated Russian offensive action to support an Italian offensive.

Emphasizing the successful Gorlice–Tarnow operation, Vienna attempted at the last minute to prevent Italy from declaring war, offering it the South Tyrol to the language frontiers, Trieste and autonomy for the western region of the Isonzo River region. Entente promises, however, offered far more to the territory-hungry Italians. On May 4 Italy denounced the Triple Alliance Treaty agreement, but on May 7 initiated negotiations with Vienna demanding South Tyrol as the price for neutrality although Italy had already signed the London Treaty with the Entente Powers.

During early May 1915, General Conrad could deploy only twenty-four weak *Landsturm* battalions on the Italian front, which had the difficult mission to prepare defensive positions on the rugged rocky mountain terrain already under Italian artillery barrages. On May 23, Carpathian Mountain campaign Third Army forces, now designated Fifth Army, arrived on the Italian front. The only battle-experienced troops available before Fifth Army's deployment consisted of three *Landsturm* infantry divisions. Unanticipated Italian military inactivity provided valuable time for Habsburg troops to erect a primitive defensive front, but so few available troops could not halt the large, reputedly well-trained Italian Army if it launched an early offensive. Conrad originally determined to abandon the critical Carso Plateau after the Italian declaration of war because of the Italians' vast troop numerical superiority. The lack of serious military activity from the Italians resulted in them not capturing the key bridges across the Isonzo River, and launching an initial rapid advance to the Carso Plateau. Italian forces sustained tens of thousands of casualties attempting to capture the critical Gorizia and Tolmein bridgeheads a month later.

The troops' first order on the new front demanded that the Isonzo River line be held to the last man. Meanwhile, troops being railroad transported to the new front suffered multiple stoppages and delays. Railroad lines to the Italian frontier became overwhelmed, halting the timely arrival of vital combat troops from the Balkan front when reassigned to Italy.

On May 10, Vienna transmitted its last peace proposal to Rome emphasizing the enormous Gorlice–Tarnow offensive initial successes. On May 11, Emperor Franz Joseph finally approved arming frontier forts and the deployment of troops along the Italian frontier. On May 19, the *Standesschützen* (local *Landsturm* troops) were called to duty in the Tyrol.

Conrad appealed to General Falkenhayn to deploy ten German divisions to the new front, because he lacked sufficient troop numbers to launch a counter-offensive against the anticipated Italian invasion. His counterpart, however, refused to weaken Eleventh Army, but because of the sensitivity of the Italian frontier area to Bavaria and Habsburg concerns, he promised to deploy the recently created Bavarian *Alpen Korps*, basically a reinforced brigade, for defensive purposes on that front. This disappointed Conrad, while early during the war thousands of Tyrolean and other mountain troops had perished on the Eastern front flatlands and mountains. Regardless, without the addition of significant German troop units, no offensive operation could be launched against Italy. Because Italy had declared war only on Austria-Hungary, not Germany, German High Command refused to deploy troops to fight on Italian soil. Instead, General Falkenhayn suggested that Conrad redeploy his Balkan front troops in Serbia to replace the requested ten divisions, which he did.

Conrad immediately transported any available troops from the Balkan and Russian fronts to defend the new seriously threatened Italian frontier. Archduke Eugene assumed overall command with General Dankl heading the Tyrolean front, General of the Cavalry Rohr Carinthia and General Boroević, commander of the Fifth Army, the Isonzo River front.

On May 20 preparations commenced to evacuate civilians from the potential war zones: 114,000, or one-third of the population, would be relocated to the Trentino, which also removed the risk of Italian espionage. By June the evacuation measures had been completed at all frontier areas although many people resisted leaving their homes.

The Italians signed a military convention with Russia on May 21. The new Entente allies had promised to launch offensives to bind Habsburg and German troops when Italy finally launched an offensive. The British operation never transpired and the Russians did not launch a major offensive until the next year, because of the unanticipated May 1915 Gorlice–Tarnow offensive that forced the major tsarist retreat.

By May 25 the German Alpine Corps commenced its railroad transport to the Italian front. On May 28, the Italians unleashed artillery barrages at the new primitive Habsburg defensive lines for the next six days, but by May 30 the few Italian excursions had been halted and an infantry brigade deployed to boost the frontier area defense.

Between the May 23, 1915 Italian declaration of war and November 1918, the Italians launched eleven major Isonzo River offensives against Austro-Hungarian forces. Conrad launched the May 1916 *Straf* (punishment) offensive and during late 1917 the Allies won an overwhelming Caporetto victory. The four 1915 Italian offensives proved futile, resulting in enormous Italian casualties for little territorial gain. The new battlefront encompassed disputed frontiers that extended from the Swiss frontier, to the Alpine Mountain foothills, then on to the Adriatic Sea, encompassing a 450-mile stretch. Large-scale Italian offensive operations eventually became feasible only in the Isonzo Valley. The Alpine Mountains, which jutted into northern Italy, provided a Habsburg salient (the Trentino) but this area quickly proved far too difficult to supply troops and wage major battles. Initial Italian efforts in the northern mountainous terrain gained nothing of significance, causing General Cadorna to shift his attention to the Isonzo Valley area.

Italian High Command initially did not anticipate significant Habsburg defensive resistance along the Isonzo River line, thus its troops could "walk to Vienna."

Then, on May 23, Italian Second Army units prepared a cautious advance into South Tyrol. Ten infantry regiments and supporting artillery, including heavy pieces, advanced toward the critical Doberdo Plateau against the twenty-four defending Habsburg *Landsturm* battalions. Hand-to-hand combat ensued on multiple sections of the front. On May 24, the first Italian patrols advanced, destroying bridges and traversed areas across the Isonzo River line to prepare to launch an offensive onto the barren rocky Carso Plateau. Two armies crossed the frontier to attempt to occupy Karfreit and establish positions at the Isonzo River line. The next day, after seizing Karfreit, vanguard units advanced toward the Habsburg bridgehead at Gorizia where fortified positions had been hurriedly constructed to protect the city. Habsburg troops piled up stones for protection against Italian artillery fire, because they could not dig into the rocky terrain. They suffered enormous casualties. Some constant factors that continued during the Eleventh Isonzo River battles included the Italian Army always attacking with superior numbers and armaments, particularly artillery. Most attacks were preceded by multihour artillery barrages, followed by brutal assaults and counterattacks that ended in deadly hand-to-hand combat. On May 24, attacks targeted Sagrado, while the Italians unleashed artillery barrages along the entire front for three days.

By May 25, Italian patrols repeatedly crossed the Isonzo River to the barren, mostly rocky, but important, Bainsizza Plateau, to then attempt to advance to Gorizia to establish positions on the Carso Plateau before driving to their major objective, Trieste. On May 28, the Gorizia bridgehead was considered prepared for defensive action.[28]

On the first day of the war, the Habsburg Navy raided the Italian eastern coastline, particularly targeting railroad lines in an attempt to disrupt Italian mobilization measures. Meanwhile, Italian troops achieved minor victories during the first three weeks of the war as they repeatedly attempted to cross the Isonzo River to attain the Carso Plateau area. Once they established a foothold across the river, they planned to advance toward the critical Gorizia bridgehead, but first had to capture the three major mountain peaks that protected that city from attack. Called the three saints, Mt. Sabatino was north of the city, Mt. San Michele to the south and Mt. San Gabriel to the west. Habsburg defensive forces had increased to twenty-seven and a half infantry battalions, thirty-nine *Standesschützen* and eight *Kaiserschützen* detachments, one and a half cavalry squadrons and twenty mobile artillery batteries consisting of seventy-five guns. Those troop numbers signified that only 110 infantrymen defended every kilometer of the front, but by May 25 only small Italian units had successfully advanced to the frontier ridges west of the Isonzo River. The next day some troops reached the Tyrolean frontier, but did not cross it.

Between May 31 and June 1 three Italian Second Army infantry divisions, several Alpine battalions and artillery batteries crossed the Isonzo River and

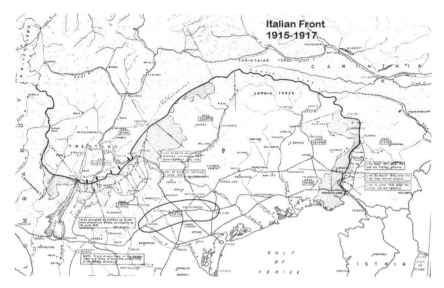

Map 7   *1915–1917 Italian Front*
Map courtesy of the United States Military Academy Department of History

advanced toward Habsburg Mrzli Vrh defensive positions along that mountain range. At first, they encountered no significant Habsburg resistance, then
Italian attacking troops were hurled back. On May 26, Italian artillery fired
barrages against various targets in the Tyrol, and launched minor assaults
along the roads to Carinthia and Karfreit. It also launched several small unit
advances toward the Gorizia bridgehead and the right flank area of the key
Mt. Sabatino defensive positions. On the next day strong Italian columns
moved toward Gorizia and Plava defensive positions across the Isonzo
River. The heaviest Italian artillery fire targeted Mt. Sabatino and the
approaches to Gorizia including the high ground at Plava. On May 29, the
fire from Habsburg mortar batteries halted the Italian assault at Mt. Sabatino
with heavy losses, thus Gorizia momentarily remained secure. By May
30 all Italian offensive endeavors had been halted, while it became obvious
that Italian artillery commanders could not locate Habsburg defensive
positions.[29]

During the next two days, the Italians launched four unsuccessful attempts
to seize Mt. Sabatino, one of the key defensive positions protecting Gorizia,
and just a few miles from the key Italian objective, Trieste. When these efforts
failed, they prepared to attack along the Carso Plateau toward Podgora, and

Mts. Sabatino and Santo. Italian troops took twelve days to reach the thin extended Habsburg defensive lines, then crossed the Isonzo River at Plava intending to unleash a decisive assault against Gorizia. General Cadorna also launched a flanking attack over the Bainsizza Plateau where only makeshift Habsburg defensive positions had been prepared because of the extreme terrain difficulties. Italian troops also attacked Habsburg positions on Mt. Krn in the Mrzli Vrh area.

The 450-kilometer-long Habsburg front, as mentioned, was defended mostly by inadequately trained soldiers. Combat-experienced troops were desperately required to defend the eighty-kilometer front that extended from Mt. Krn to the Adriatic Sea. The anticipated major Italian offensive direction was defended by only six Habsburg infantry divisions redeployed from the Balkan front (XV and XVI Corps) and a few *Landsturm* sections. These Habsburg units and those transferred from the Russian front suffered from combat fatigue. Approximately sixty battalions composed of South Slavic soldiers (Slovenes, Croats, Bosnians and Dalmatians) comprised the Habsburg Fifth Army. Only three divisions had combat experience, but South Slavic troops defended against a hated enemy attempting to conquer their homeland. There were also twenty-five thousand volunteers from German Alpine regions between Carinthia and Tyrol.[30]

Of the initial twenty-four understrength defending infantry battalions only eight consisted of first-line units; the remaining consisted of March and *Landsturm* troops, supported by obsolete field cannons and two modern 30.5-cm guns. Artillery units possessed few shells, had no indirect fire training and their guns lacked recoil mechanisms. The initial defensive positions, established ten to twenty kilometers from the frontier, extended from the Carso Plateau at Podgora and Mt. Sabatino to Gorizia with insufficient manpower to halt the superior Italian troop numbers.[31]

During the early phases of the war, Habsburg defensive positions had to be dug into dense rock formations, an impossible task, thus the troops had little if any protection from enemy artillery fire. The Italian Army problems provided critical advantage to the Austro-Hungarian Army. The month of Italian military inactivity provided the Habsburg units crucial time to deploy troops and prepare defensive positions.

When Habsburg VII Corps troops arrived on the front, they became part of the 225,000 infantry troop contingents. The Italians' 2,000 mobile artillery pieces provided them a significant numerical advantage in that category, but they initially lacked adequate numbers of machine guns and aircraft.

In early June Italian attempts to advance along the entire front collapsed. By June 4 the Italians had advanced only a few hundred paces. General Cadorna commenced a yearlong self-deception that additional heavy-artillery units and shells would provide the impetus for the eagerly sought Italian victory. From late May to late June 1915 battles continued in the Krn and Flitsch areas, but by June 8–9 had been halted. Italian commanders became frustrated by the lack of progress against such a numerically inferior enemy. Battle erupted on June 17 in the critical Plava area, where Habsburg troops had deployed forward toward the frontier. Significant difficulties immediately confronted both combatants, including terrible sanitary conditions on the treacherous rocky mountain terrain, unfavorable communication conditions, the excessive width of Habsburg defensive unit front lines, the lack of sufficient technical troop units, inadequate water supplies and generally irregular logistical service that endured throughout the years of conflict.

The critical lack of drinkable water and the few means to provide it to the mountain front lines created a major problem never completely resolved. Rainwater could not be drunk, because it was often contaminated by corpses and debris. A serious outbreak of cholera worsened the situation as the increasing number of dead, wounded and sick troops forced into close proximity seriously exacerbated the situation in the oppressive summer heat. Winter introduced cold weather problems.

The two key Habsburg fortresses on the Asiago Plateau, Folgaria and Lavarone, had been constructed with the mission to support the launching of a major offensive into Italy if war erupted. They did not possess adequate armor protection but were situated within Italian cannon range. Early in the conflict the Italian Army unleased multiple days of artillery barrages against the two bulwarks, causing extensive damage. Habsburg troops quickly repossessed some key positions they had abandoned because of the Italian inactivity.

General Boroević feverishly prepared Fifth Army defensive lines behind the Isonzo River extending to the bloody Krn–Mrzli Vrh ridges and Tolmein bridgehead to protect the key port at Trieste. Habsburg troops' early defensive victories against vastly superior enemy numbers, however, came at heavy human cost.

Battle raged between Plava and the Adriatic Sea during June 5–22. Italian corps attacked the Doberdo Plateau; another attempted to seize Gorizia while launching a secondary effort against Mt. Sabatino. The Italians also targeted Habsburg positions at Mt. Kuk, to enable the Italian forces to cross the eastern Isonzo River bank. Defending Habsburg troops, particularly at the Tolmein bridgehead, sustained heavy casualties mainly from enemy artillery fire. On June 8, following additional artillery bombardment, Italian infantry attacked the weakly held Habsburg defensive positions. After capturing Monfalcone, the victorious troops advanced while the VI Corps attempted to seize Gorizia. Two battalions stormed Hill 383, a critical position that extended one kilometer east of Plava and fourteen miles downstream from Mt. Krn, but were halted by defensive artillery firepower.

On June 9 Italian forces crossed the Isonzo River above Sagrado, halting their attack at the edge of the Carso Plateau after encountering heavy defensive machine-gun and rifle fire. Vicious battle soon ensued on the Doberdo Plateau and Mt. Sabatino, but as long as Habsburg forces occupied the highest Carso terrain, it proved extremely difficult for the Italians to launch a successful major attack along the coastline to seize their ultimate objective, Trieste.

Italian Second Army then received the mission to attack the Gorizia bridge-head, Third Army the Carso Plateau, while by June 10, Habsburg Fifth Army forces had increased to seventy-six and a half battalions, four cavalry squadrons and seventy-five artillery batteries, but remained seriously outnumbered by the enemy. Two Italian armies composed of 240 battalions, 40 cavalry squadrons and 188 artillery batteries opposed Hapsburg Fifth Army. The failure to seize the initial military objectives resulted in General Cadorna attempting to seize the high terrain to force a crossing of the middle Isonzo River between Plava and the mouth of the Vipacco Valley. Italian II Corps troops crossed the river at Plava and, after a heavy-artillery bombardment, attacked Hill 383. Attacks continued against Plava positions defended by Infantry Regiment 22, consisting of crack Dalmatian (South Slavic) troops. Inevitably, these hotly contested battles ended in bloody hand-to-hand combat with the troops using every conceivable weapon possible. The Italians renewed their frenzied attempts to occupy Hill 383 on June 11 to create a bridgehead between the key Gorizia and the Tolmein positions. Over a thousand Italian corpses covered the small area between the Isonzo River and Hill 383. Italian artillery batteries continued to target Habsburg defensive positions until June 17, when seven infantry divisions crossed the Isonzo River to attack the beleaguered Infantry Regiment 22.

Waves of Italian soldiers rushed into that regiment's defensive machine-gun fire, while assaults continued against other important Habsburg defensive positions on the Isonzo River front – the Carso Plateau, Gorizia, Tolmein bridgehead and the leading edge of Plava. Sustaining enormous casualties, Italian infantry finally overran bloody Hill 383, which would not be recon-quered until the 1917 Tenth Isonzo battle. Meanwhile, often underreported, casualty numbers mounted for both sides.

By mid-June, while Habsburg troops had improved their defensive pos-itions, Italian attacks continually targeted Sagrado and Krn. The Italians commenced launching small but significant battles that nevertheless failed to pierce Habsburg lines. Attacks were halted in the Tyrol and Carinthia on June 14 and 15, while on June 15 the Italians launched two strong attacks at the bridge at Sagardo. Attacks to seize Plava continued on June 16 and 17, including night assaults, terminating in the customary bloody hand-to-hand combat during each encounter.

When Habsburg troops repulsed the numerically superior enemy troops early in 1915, they rapidly gained confidence and felt superiority to their foe, perhaps too much. Between June 11–14 and 16–17 heavy battle erupted again at Plava, the Italians seizing its forward positions. The fighting at Hill 383 persisted with renewed Italian attacks but without either side being able to utilize artillery support because of the close proximity of the combatants. Habsburg Infantry Regiment 22 ultimately had to retreat because of overpowering enemy troop numbers, after earlier preventing an Italian breakthrough at this critical location. The attacking Italian infantry formations advanced in ten-man-deep rows, replacing their casualties, then resuming the assaults. As battle raged the hand-to-hand struggles produced additional casualties.

Initially, the Italians enjoyed the advantage of favorable roads and interior lines, but the remote Alpine heights region they originally selected to attack quickly became inaccessible, because of weather and terrain conditions, although battle raged on the most important harsh mountain peaks. This eventually forced General Cadorna to choose the more favorable Isonzo River region terrain to launch his offensives.

On June 20 the Italians crossed the Isonzo River, four divisions attacking Sagrado alone, the ultimate objective the Gorizia bridgehead and low hills at Podgora and Mt. Sabatino. On June 22 twenty-four-hour attacks ensued against Gorizia and the Doberdo Plateau. On June 23 the first major Italian offensive effort, the first Isonzo River offensive, targeted the Carso Plateau, Mts. San Michele and Sabatino that protected Gorizia. Although enjoying a six-fold numerical advantage the Italians failed to capture Gorizia. Their meager territorial gains measured only several hundred meters. The Italians sacrificed fifteen thousand troops, the defenders ten thousand.

Italian formations advanced cautiously because of the lack of intelligence information. General Cadorna attempted to destroy Habsburg defensive positions with week-long massive artillery barrages, particularly targeting the Plava and Mt. Krn positions, then launched massed offensives. Second Army objectives became to conquer Mrzli Vrh while attempting to extend the bridgehead at Plava. Third Army would attack the edge of the Carso Plateau.

During mid- to late June Italian offensive efforts continued. On June 21 Cadorna ordered a general offensive launched against Gorizia and Trieste, but the month of mostly Italian military inactivity had provided the army sufficient time to prepare adequate defensive positions and deploy new troops.

Italian Second Army attacked toward Gorizia with 160 infantry battalions supported by 136 artillery batteries. Four divisions attempted to seize the hills protecting Gorizia and secure the west bank of the Isonzo River, then seize the city. Troops attempted to secure the Plava bridgehead and attack southward toward Mt. Santo.

Third Army attacked the western edge of the Carso Plateau, then seized terrain that overlooked Gorizia. The army's main mission became to conquer

Mt. San Michele, the highest mountain in the area, while attempts to capture the several hills on the southern flank of the Carso Plateau progressed.

Habsburg Fifth Army numbers were one-third those of the attacking Italian troops and only three-fifths its artillery numbers. The army possessed no reserve formations while the Italians had a plentiful supply. The main defending force at the Gorizia bridgehead, the 58. Infantry Division, consisted of Dalmatian mountain formations. That division repulsed the enemy's multiple efforts because of good commanders and favorable defensible terrain. It protected a seven-mile stretch extending from Mt. Santo to the Vipacco Valley, but its specific mission entailed the defense of the strategic half-mile stretch along the western Isonzo River bank that included two major hills, Podgora and Oslavia, where major bloody battles ensued.

Between June 20 and 23 new Italian assaults launched with fresh units. On June 22 attacks targeted Gorizia protecting the Doberdo Plateau. During June 21–23, Italian artillery barrages intensified against the Gorizia bridgehead and surrounding areas including Plava and the Doberdo Plateau. XVI Corps defended the area. The major Italian effort encompassed one division attacking the defenders at Plava eight times. Further attempts during the next two days achieved nothing.

Between June 23 and July 7 eighty Italian assaults were launched preceded by heavy-artillery barrages and culminating in close combat. Both sides deployed reinforcements and often launched night counterattacks, attempting to regain any surrendered terrain.

The Italian Second Army's overwhelming assaults against the positions protecting the Gorizia bridgehead could only hope to succeed if it seized Mts. Sabatino and Podgora to the northwest. Sustaining enormous casualties during the first Isonzo offensive, Italian troops gained mere meters of territory. After forty-eight hours of intense artillery barrages on June 24, many defensive positions had been destroyed and the few surviving troops were near collapse, lacking both manpower and the means to maintain a solid defensive front. Italian troops attacked Hill 383 eight times, but failed. At Mt. San Michele, eighty thousand Italian soldiers attacked twenty-five Habsburg defenders, when Boroević possessed only eight thousand reserve troops.[32] On June 23 Italian artillery targeted Sagrado, attempting to gain a foothold on sprawling Mt. San Michele.

On June 25, weakened defending forces sustained additional severe casualties at Podgora and Monfalcone. They eventually had to retreat to secondary positions because of the deadly Italian artillery barrages. Many Habsburg troops lacked mountain training, particularly VII Corps deployed in the Krn region. That important area had to be defended at all costs to prevent a serious military crisis.

During the night to June 30, the first major Italian effort commenced at the edge of the Carso Plateau. Italian Second and Third Army assaults continued along a broad front between June 29 and July 6, supported by superior artillery fire. Three Third Army corps, the main attacking force (130,000 troops supported by 500 artillery pieces) attacked the forward Carso high flatland positions on the Doberdo Plateau. Habsburg troops fortunately received desperately needed reinforcements in the most threatened area. The Habsburg 57. Infantry Division, reinforced with five mountain brigades, participated in the bloody battle.[33]

The First Isonzo River offensive occurred during a period of extreme heat, more unbearable for the troops because the unreliable supply of water. Conditions became so desperate that some soldiers drank their own urine.[34]

Italian heavy-artillery barrages targeting the Carso Plateau made it obvious that the Italians' major objective was to seize Trieste, their second to conquer the Gorizia bridgehead and Hill 383 at Plava. Hungarian Infantry Regiment 76 delayed an Italian crossing of the Isonzo River for two weeks. The battle on the Carso Plateau extended eighteen kilometers along rocky mountain terrain at the upper terrain depression extending from Hermada southward and Mt. San Michele to the north. The Doberdo Plateau lay in between. The front extended through the northern portion of Mt. San Michele northward through the Gorizia basin, across the Isonzo River south of the city, then to Podgora and Mt. Sabatino. A rocky slope about eleven kilometers long at Podgora protected the Gorizia bridgehead. A defensive line also extended from the Isonzo River to Mt. Santo, a precipitous stretch along the Isonzo Valley through Mt. Kuk and Hill 383 by Plava.

To the east lay the Bainsizza Plateau, a rugged rocky wasteland, but a strategic location where soldiers could only establish a few effective defensive positions in the inhospitable rocky terrain. That brutal terrain could not accommodate large numbers of troops, nor easily facilitate the critical transportation of water, ammunition and other vital supplies. Troops struggled against nature, encountering enormous engineering problems preparing defensive positions on the Carso Plateau (Mts. Sabatino and Santo, the central Doberdo Plateau and Hermada).

The multiple minor encounters during the first month of the war produced heavy casualties: Habsburg Fifth Army almost fifty thousand troops, the Italians forty-two thousand. During July 3–6 Italian infantry advanced in torrential rain across the muddy terrain against Mrzli Vrh and from Sagrado toward Mt. San Michele. Defending the Carso Plateau positions resulted in casualties dramatically increasing.

Italian Third Army renewed its attack on the Carso Plateau, causing Habsburg troop numbers to drop rapidly. Troops suffered combat fatigue and psychological damage from the solid week of heavy artillery barrages. No reserve units existed to replace the serious losses while troops were ordered to defend the positions to their death. Every inch of terrain had to be contested.

The Carso Plateau and Gorizia bridgehead were attacked twenty-two times, one assault following another hurled against the most vital Habsburg defensive positions. Overnight, eight Italian divisions attacked Podgora defensive positions.

Cadorna continued to hurl strong forces against Podgora and ten-night attacks against Gorizia and Mt. Krn, some with overwhelming numerical superiority. Dynamite and boring machines constructed second defensive line positions on Mt. San Michele. The Italians achieved meager territorial gains by July 7, measuring a few hundred meters. This raised Habsburg troop morale significantly as the first Isonzo offensive terminated. Sick and wounded soldiers could not be removed from the battlefield because of incessant battle and artillery barrages. Sick and dead intermingled with healthy troops. Body parts were scattered over the battlefield because of the constant artillery fire. Screams of the wounded could not be heard through the enormous artillery shell explosions.

On July 17, barely two weeks after the first offensive terminated, the second Isonzo offensive commenced. Second and Third armies again targeted positions at Gorizia, Mt. San Michele and the Tolmein bridgehead, but only attained limited success on Mt. San Michele and north of the Doberdo Plateau. The next day, following strong hurricane-artillery barrages against the western edge of the Carso Plateau, the Italians launched human-wave assaults, successfully piercing defensive positions on Mt. San Michele, simultaneously launching an assault against Mt. Sabatino, the Habsburg right flank bridgehead. Attacks continued until August 3. Italian artillery fire reduced defensive positions to rubble. Italian Third Army attacked the southern pillar of Mt. San Michele where the major battle resulted in extreme casualties. Between July 18 and 20 attacking troops temporarily seized the Mt. San Michele peak. Cholera and typhus began to take their toll on both sides of the front.

On July 19 massed Italian troop columns advanced after thirty hours of intensive heavy-artillery preparation into defensive crossfire, producing multiple piles of corpses at Podgora. Battle at Oslavia and toward the Doberdo Plateau continued. Overpowering Italian artillery fire forced evacuation of multiple defensive positions and lack of ammunition of further multiple positions.

Morning enemy attacks against Mt. Sabatino and Oslavia collapsed in rivers of blood, although artillery barrages left no living Habsburg troops in some positions. Three Italian brigades repeatedly assaulted Habsburg positions at Podgora with bayonet charges. Troops brandished every conceivable weapon in these brutal and bloody exchanges, particularly clubs. On July 22 Italian forces finally seized the bridgehead at Podgora, but the next day counterattacks forced them to retreat, abandoning thousands of corpses on the battlefield. Meanwhile, incessant attacks against the southern edge of the

Carso Plateau produced enormous losses for both armies. Critically necessary Habsburg reinforcements finally arrived, including some *Kaiserjäger* troops redeployed from the Russian front. The Second Isonzo battle, contrary to the first, ended gradually on August 10. Every day witnessed consistent small but violent clashes.

During the four-week Second Isonzo battle Habsburg Fifth Army suffered almost forty-seven thousand casualties, the attackers forty-two thousand. The Italian Army began to receive weapons from Entente allies, and the Italian home armaments industry began to increase production. Italian tactics continued to hurl one human-wave assault after another. Battle conditions remained horrendous; troops suffered terribly from summer heat as the severe shortage of water supplies steadily worsened. Soldiers dying from cholera intermingled with the sick and wounded. Surviving Alpine soldiers now defended their homeland. Many had perished on the Galician plains during 1914 and in the Carpathian Mountain Winter War.

Italian Second Army continued its assaults on Gorizia and the Tolmein bridgehead supported by more accurate heavy-caliber guns. The lack of metal helmets, combined with Italian heavy-artillery barrages into the rocky terrain, produced many head wounds from flying and splintering rocks. The dense rock formations continued to prevent Habsburg troops from being fully entrenched. Without sufficient cover, troops suffered terribly from the hellish exploding shells. Bodies were shredded multiple times and strewn over the surviving troops. During the incessant Italian artillery fire, many Habsburg units were annihilated. The most severe battle occurred at the Carso Plateau, while supporting attacks targeted the Gorizia bridgehead area.

Honvéd VII Corps troops redeployed to Mt. San Michele, bringing cholera with them from the Carpathian Mountains fronts. Positions changed hands multiple times before battle terminated on August 3. Sporadic firefights continued along the entire front throughout August and September. In the interim, Entente leadership requested that an Italian offensive be launched during September to occur simultaneously with the projected Western front offensive operations.

On the Russian front during July, Central Power forces advanced rapidly during the Gorlice–Tarnow offensive. Major territory was conquered, but the Russian Army had not been destroyed. During the second half of July, Habsburg troops sustained 40 percent casualties from the deadly Italian artillery barrages. Troops feverishly improved their defensive positions and constructed solid second-line positions, particularly on the Doberdo Plateau, where six to seven Italian division mass formations attacked but achieved no significant results.

On August 21 Italian massed attacks targeted Habsburg positions on Mt. Krn, the Tolmein bridgehead, but specifically the edge of the Doberdo Plateau.

These feverish attacks resulted partially as a response to the Italian parliament convening during December, Cadorna seeking a major victory for domestic consumption.

In early September 1915, French General Joffre pressured the Italian High Command to renew its offensive efforts to support Entente Western front operations. Initially Cadorna balked, but eventually agreed to launch a third Isonzo River offensive, but stalled a month later because of ammunition shortages and the necessary time to train troops to replace the many battle casualties.

On October 18 Italian hurricane-artillery barrages introduced the Third Isonzo Offensive that continued until November 4. Two-thirds of the Italian Army attempted to seize its key objective, the Gorizia bridgehead. The battle reached its highest intensity between November 1 and 4, but achieved only minor Italian success at the cost of sixty-seven thousand casualties, almost a quarter of the troops involved. Austro-Hungarian casualties reached forty-one thousand. Cholera and typhus spread through both combatants' ranks.

Between October 18 and 20 little was achieved attempting to conquer Mt. Sabatino. Heavy artillery blasted Habsburg positions at Mt. Krn, the Doberdo Plateau and Mt. San Michele with increasing intensity, while mass attacks targeted Mrzli Vrh and the Tolmein bridgehead. The Italians launched multiple attacks during the Central Power invasion of Serbia on October 7, 1915. The successful Serbian campaign released strong forces to deploy on other fronts. Falkenhayn concentrated on planning for his 1916 Verdun campaign, Conrad his *Straf* offensive. Although Italian artillery fire intensified daily, inclement weather conditions lessened its effects. Italian offensive operations extended further than during earlier campaigns, but still concentrated on the heights dominating Gorizia extending from the Tolmein bridgehead to the sea.[35] On October 20 Italian troops attempted to cross the Isonzo River in the Vipacco Valley area, then on October 21, they unleashed a powerful night attack on the entire front. The attack produced particularly bitter battle on the Doberdo Plateau. Four days later the Italians paused to reorganize their units and replenish their depleted ranks and ammunition. On the next day, after bloody battle, they captured the western corner of Mt. San Michele, but a counterattack forced them to evacuate it. They, meanwhile, enlarged their bridgehead at Plava and achieved some progress on the Carso Plateau, reaching the area below the crests of Mts. San Michele and San Martino (defensive lines to protect the Gorizia bridgehead had been established at the Isonzo River as well as Podgora and Mt. Sabatino, the bastion of that portion of the front).

Cadorna launched his third Isonzo River offensive convinced that Habsburg troops were exhausted, depleted and incapable of halting another major attack. The main objective of the third and fourth Isonzo offensives remained Gorizia. Italian Second Army attempted to outflank Gorizia from the direction of Plava, Third Army the Mt. San Michele area. Twenty-four infantry divisions with over 300,000 troops supported by 180 heavy and 1,300 light artillery pieces fought in the campaign.

The Fourth Isonzo River offensive almost immediately followed termination of the Third, continuing until mid-December 1915. Again, the Italians achieved no major territorial gains and got bogged down because of their horrendous casualties and winter weather conditions. Entente leadership increasingly became contemptuous because of the lackluster Italian battlefield achievements. Italian civilians also became demoralized by the acceleration of casualty numbers, but lack of concrete results.

Cadorna finally introduced a new tactic of holding fresh reserve battalions directly behind the lead attack units. He launched assaults three to five times a day until December 15. The main objective remained capturing the Gorizia bridgehead, but now included the city and the high mountain terrain between Mt. Sabatino and Podgora. Battle also erupted again during early December on the Doberdo Plateau. Inclement weather conditions stymied aerial reconnaissance missions between November 10 and 30. Most battle terminated on December 11. The rest of the month proved fairly quiet, but the constant Italian artillery fire reduced the city of Gorizia to rubble.

On November 29 all further Italian attempts to cross the Isonzo River had been defeated. The Italians launched persistent attacks against Podgora between November 21 and 29 but achieved no particular success as their infantry forces merely sustained enormous losses.

Between November 11 and 16 the Italian Third Army attacked the Doberdo Plateau. Italian artillery bombarded the defensive front then unleashed strong frontal attacks during stormy weather conditions. For forty-seven days, Italian troops stormed Mt. Sabatino fifteen times, Podgora forty, Oslavia thirty times.

Most battle activity wound down by November 18–30, with inclement weather conditions negatively affecting artillery accuracy.

Russian and Serbian war theater events were not influenced by the Italian offensives. Italy fought a war of attrition to bleed the Austro-Hungarian Army dry. Conrad realized that his army could not absorb such enormous losses much longer, and if attrition warfare continued there could be almost no hope of achieving a Habsburg victory. During the four 1915 Isonzo offensives, the greatly outnumbered defending troops' success against incredible numerical odds spared Austria-Hungary from military defeat. Its surviving soldiers received much-needed respite from major battle as winter approached.

Earlier, during January 1915, when General Falkenhayn suggested that an Allied campaign be launched against Serbia instead of Conrad's projected Carpathian Mountain Winter War offensive, Conrad replied that such a campaign was out of the question, specifically because the Russians continued to attack and advance through the Carpathian Mountain ridges. When Falkenhayn raised the question of an Allied invasion of Serbia, the military situation remained critical.[36] A Serbian campaign would require eight to ten

Habsburg infantry divisions but German units would have to replace Habsburg Eastern front troops, because Conrad could not provide such large troop numbers, due to the losses sustained during the Carpathian Mountain Winter War, Gorlice–Tarnow and Rovno offensive campaigns. Conrad emphasized that Bulgarian participation in a Balkan campaign would be essential and that the Russian Carpathian Mountain threat to break onto the Hungarian plains and Transylvania had become extremely critical.[37]

Falkenhayn continued to pressure Conrad to launch an offensive against Serbia to relieve the Turkish ally because of increasing concern relative to the lack of armaments and ability to continue in the war. The increased German pressure partially resulted from the threat of Italy entering the war against Austria-Hungary. Conrad continued to pressure Falkenhayn to reinforce his forces. During March 1915, the British-French Dardanelles campaign commenced at Gallipoli, as the Carpathian Mountain offensive produced only Habsburg disaster. German diplomatic and military leaders urged Habsburg diplomats to soften their approach to Italy, particularly relative to territorial concessions. Negotiations to maintain Italian neutrality commenced early in 1915.

In the meantime, Foreign Minister Burian had replaced Berchtold in early 1915. He was never convinced that the Russian campaign could be completed soon, and urged launching the Balkan campaign, but the diplomatic situation relative to Italy remained critical. If Italy entered the war, a Serbian campaign would become impossible.

During early summer 1915 Falkenhayn renewed his request for a joint Balkan military campaign, encouraged by the early Gorlice–Tarnow victories and the Entente April failures at Gallipoli. German pressure increased enormously after the Entente Gallipoli campaign to invade Serbia.

Conrad calculated that ten infantry divisions would have to be redeployed from the Eastern front to counter Italy if it declared war, but Falkenhayn reassured him that it would take the Italians at least a month to become a real military threat. Thus, a rapid attack could be launched against Serbia and accomplished by July 1, before Italy became a serious military problem.[38] Then Allied forces could counter the new foe. Conrad insisted that if Bulgaria did not join the campaign it could not be launched. The Carpathian Mountain front remained threatened, which raised the question of a Romanian invasion of Transylvania.[39]

In January 1915, when General Falkenhayn suggested that an Allied campaign be launched against Serbia instead of Conrad's suggested Carpathian Mountain offensive, Conrad emphasized that Russian pressure of the Carpathian Mountain ridges remained critical.[40]

During July German High Command began to seriously plan for a Balkan campaign, because by the end of the month, tsarist troops had to initiate a major retreat. General Falkenhayn emphasized that a Serbian campaign had to be launched at the latest by September, thus within four to six weeks, to provide sufficient time to complete the Polish front operations. The Bulgarians had to harvest their crops, while it could be assumed that Romania would not intervene because of the Gorlice–Tarnow successes. On the Western front, no major offensives had been launched after the first half of June, but a threat of a renewed French Champagne offensive remained.

At the end of August, the Bulgarians negotiated a military agreement with German High Command to participate in a Serbian campaign. The successful Polish campaign influenced the decision, while only the Central Powers could provide the territory Bulgaria lost during the 1913 Second Balkan War.

On September 6, 1915, the German and Austro-Hungarian Supreme Commands agreed to each provide six divisions for the campaign to commence within thirty days of the treaty signing. An invasion would eliminate South Slavic agitation and military threat. It would also open contact with Turkey and the Danube River for supplying supplies to the isolated ally.

However, the failed Rovno campaign resulted in the assigned six Habsburg infantry divisions being unavailable for a Serbian campaign. German troops replaced some of the designated units.

Habsburg troops deployed in Bosnia-Herzegovina would prevent Montenegrin troops from intervening in the operation. However, troop numbers had been greatly reduced to redeploy forces to the Italian front. The Serbian campaign included simultaneous assaults launched from the northern and eastern frontier areas to prevent them from utilizing their interior lines to advantage. Bulgarian forces invaded Macedonia to sever the rail link to the Salonika Army in Greece.

The invasion of Serbia could counter the three embarrassing 1914 Balkan front defeats, and prevent neutral countries from intervening in the war. This was the first time the Central Powers possessed a numerical superiority over their opponents.[41] The campaign was only feasible if the Germans provided massive troop contingents, while the threat existed of Germany extending its power into the Balkan Peninsula.

The Balkan front remained quiescent for most of 1915, partially because of the heavy casualties the Serbian Army sustained during the 1914 campaigns. The troops also suffered from an appalling typhus epidemic that killed at least a hundred thousand people, particularly during winter and spring 1915. The army also lacked adequate stores of artillery shells and it could not sustain major casualties.

The command question for the operation represented one of prestige for Conrad and the Habsburg Army. The Bulgarian High Command, however, refused to serve under Habsburg command, its mistrust dating back to the lack of support from Vienna support during the 1913 Balkan War and its 1914 military defeats. The Bulgarians determined to participate because of the successful Gorlice–Tarnow offensive, but also the failure of the first fourth Italian

Isonzo River offensives that resulted in Falkenhayn and Conrad agreeing to the September 6, 1915 Central Power treaty. Meanwhile, on September 21 Entente forces launched major offensives. The British failed to achieve success as heavy rainfall commenced, transforming the battlefield into a veritable marsh.

Preinvasion aerial reconnaissance located every bridge crossing the Danube, Sava and Drina Rivers while railroads deployed the numerically superior invasion force. Solid strategy and command also had a major effect on the campaign outcome. The invasion would not be launched in the disastrous 1914 campaign direction. The major invasion targeted Belgrade. The Bulgarian First Army would seize Nis; its Second Army would advance into the Vardar Valley to destroy the railroad connection to Salonica and protect First Army's flank. Logistical problems rapidly arose in the unfavorable attack areas terrain. The campaign timing proved critical because of the impending notorious Cossava storm conditions. The weather remained suitable just long enough for the commencement of the offensive. Delaying the invasion timing could have been disastrous. The two-month campaign commenced on difficult terrain, often unfavorable climatic conditions and against a battle-hardened enemy defending its own country.

The length of the vital Morava-Vardar trench presented the invaders the potential to launch a flank attack to the east, while the main Serbian armies attempted to defend their northern front. Unexpectedly high winds and rain soon created problems for the advancing troops. Even after the Cossava storm subsided, pontoon bridges had to be rebuilt, but the incessant rainfall made it difficult to launch large troop formations to defeat the Serbians' northern flank forces and cut off supplies and reinforcements to the remaining units.

The Central Power mission was to destroy the Serbian Army. Invading forces had to overcome natural defensive positions along the Danube and Save rivers to be crossed. The main force, Habsburg Third Army, crossed the rivers to Belgrade; its ultimate mission to seize Kragajevac. German Eleventh Army crossed the Danube River at three different locations, while to the south a weak Habsburg force, XIX Corps, advanced from Bosnia across the Drina River. That corps, after successfully crossing the river, became bound by Serbian forces so it could not assist other attacking troops to complete the envelopment of Serbian forces nor reach the Morava Valley.

Third Army's immediate mission, having crossed the river and captured Belgrade, became to seize the mountain positions south and southeast of the capital, and construct a bridge and secondary crossings, particularly at Zigeuner Island, as quickly as possible. Because the riverbank was higher on the Serbian side, the enemy could observe military activity and prepare for an invasion across the water (the Danube and Sava River terrain was unfavorable for an invasion). Terrain north of the Sava was swampy and difficult to traverse, while marshy wetlands lay north of the Danube River.

In September 1915 it was determined that a combined division consisting of about twenty infantry battalions and its artillery would invade the city. Secrecy was critical; the troops not learning of their mission until the last possible minute. Two attack groups, the Habsburg VIII Corps and the German XXII Reserve Corps, crossed the Danube and seized the largest Zigeuner Island on the Sava River. They then approached Belgrade from the west.

On October 5 artillery barrages protected the troops forcing passage across the river barriers. The next day Habsburg units crossed the Danube River into Belgrade, while the main German force, XXII Reserve Corps, invaded from the west. Serbian forces abandoned their capital. On October 7 Serbian resistance tightened, but within a week the invaders advanced again. On October 8 the Habsburg Third Army attacked across the Sava River, while the next day the German Eleventh Army also crossed the Danube River.

Austro-Hungarian Third and German Eleventh armies invaded Serbia on October 6, 1915; Bulgarian forces on October 11. The first day entailed preparatory artillery fire to protect the troops attempting to cross the river. On the night of October 5–6 camouflaged enemy artillery units commenced defensive firing during limited visibility. Then on October 7 Central Power troops crossed pontoon bridges during light rain conditions to invade Belgrade.

During the night of October 6–7 fourteen infantry companies crossed the Danube River, but sustained heavy losses. Overwhelming defensive troop and artillery fire provided strong resistance in the swampy terrain, momentarily halting the invasion. Meanwhile, German XXII Reserve Corps troops crossed the water and landed on Zigeuner Island under difficult circumstances. Six infantry companies reached the island because the Serbians had not destroyed the bridge to it. They sustained multiple losses while many boats were sunk by machine-gun fire and hand grenades followed by bitter fighting on the shore-line. Crossing attempts had to be halted at daybreak, because so many boats and pontoons had been destroyed and many sappers killed or wounded. On October 7, as Serbian resistance intensified, only one-third of the transporting ships remained serviceable, the remainder either sunk or severely damaged.

During the night assault troops became exhausted attempting to cross the river and ran out of ammunition repelling repeated Serbian attacks. Then, during the night of October 7–8, thirteen and a half additional infantry companies landed on the opposite river banks, but meanwhile the Danube River water level rose, threatening the German Eleventh Army troops that had just landed. Bitter hand-to-hand combat ensued on October 8 at Zigeuner Island. Danube River monitor fire support helped to finally force a Serbian retreat.

Much of Belgrade was captured by October 9, as Serbian troops retreated to the south and southeast heights from the city. They continued their stiff resistance and launched counterattacks to halt the invaders. During the night of October 9, troops, without artillery or supply trains, crossed the river during the inclement weather conditions. Then the Sava River level rose and immersed Zigeuner Island, necessitating the construction of a bridge over the island.

The Bulgarian Second Army swept into Macedonia on October 11, as Serbian forces continued to retreat. By mid-November the defending forces faced annihilation, while on October 12 after additional Central Power troops crossed the river the notorious Cossava weather system (heavy rain and high winds) negatively impacted the operation. Meanwhile, Serbian reinforcements and supplies could only be transported on the single-track railroad that traversed the Vardar trench. Eventually, Central Power forces seized the railroad and cut off Serbian access to it.

Many Serbian troops survived because they did not fight pitched battles with advancing Central Power forces; their outnumbered military forces retreated south and southwest toward Kosovo. Heavy snow accumulations slowed movement, commencing on November 17.

By mid-October, the invading armies encountered unfavorable terrain conditions, winter cold temperatures and extremely difficult road conditions accompanied by the disastrous loss of horses as during in the 1914 campaigns. It proved difficult to establish a functional supply system over the Danube and Sava Rivers. The terrain difficulties and inclement weather helped prevent Central Power units from enveloping Serbian forces by October 22. Advancing troops achieved only slow forward progress. In particular, the Bulgarian effort proved disappointing, enabling many Serbian troops to escape.

Toward the end of October, a major portion of the Habsburg Third Army advanced with difficulty toward Kraljevo and the German Eleventh Army the western Morava Valley. On November 1 Eleventh Army forces took Kragajevac, encountering no serious resistance. Then between November 5 and 8 Habsburg Third Army VIII Corps crossed the Morava River. After slow progress because of destroyed bridges, the pursuit of retreating Serbian forces commenced.

After Bulgarian troops captured Nis on November 5 Serbian counterattacks halted further progress. Habsburg troops also failed to keep pace with the German advances as the terrain forced time-consuming offensive efforts. The failure of Habsburg and Bulgarian units to match German efforts proved costly. Attempts to encircle the retreating Serbian troops terminated at the end of the month. Serbian delaying rearguard actions, the difficult terrain features and inclement weather conditions greatly assisted the Serbian retreat. The limited number of poorly maintained roads enabled Serbian forces to continually harass advancing Central Power troops. The inclement weather conditions also severely curtailed effective German air reconnaissance efforts until weather conditions improved in November.

Meanwhile, Entente troops advanced from the Salonika front toward southern Serbia to assist the retreating forces, but Bulgarian forces prevented the attempts to intervene. The Salonica operation to assist the Serbians failed because it lacked sufficient troop numbers, thus Bulgarian Second Army had no trouble halting its progress. When the Serbians surrendered Kragajevac, their important fortress and arsenal position, they retreated to the central area of the country, then to Montenegro and mountainous Albania.

Conrad sought a complete victory, wanting to continue operations to eliminate the threat from Salonika. Falkenhayn refused, insisting that it would expose his troops to hunger and disease, and he required as many German forces as possible to counter an Entente Western front offensive. Eight infantry divisions redeployed to Hungary commencing on November 6 before final victory had been attained. On the next day advancing forces reached the key Serbian position at Arangjelovac, while other forces advanced toward Valjevo.

By November 6 the German Eleventh Army had reached the western Morava region and the Bulgarian First Army had attained Nis, which severed the Serbians' main supply route. The German XXII Reserve Corps forced its way to Kraljevo. Elsewhere, Habsburg units reached Visegrad where they repulsed a strong Montenegrin attack before it could advance to occupy the Lim area.

Conrad immediately demanded to quickly extend the Serbian campaign because the enemy had not been defeated, but during mid-November Falkenhayn removed the mentioned eight infantry divisions. Falkenhayn claimed that the withdrawn troops were no longer necessary for the campaign.

Serbian forces were not encircled at Kragajevac and Kosovo because the Central Power left flank XIX Corps 62. Infantry Division attack proved too weak, while the Habsburg attack out of Bosnia had practically no effect on the campaign. Serbian left flank positions were never threatened. The Serbians counterattacked Bulgarian forces, but Bulgarian offensive efforts proved too ineffectual, allowing Serbian troops to escape envelopment.

The Central Power troops had marched and fought without any breaks, desperately requiring rehabilitation and rest. As battle continued during the winter months many had not been issued winter equipment or even uniforms. Supplying food, equipment and other necessities proved particularly difficult. Railroads were sparse and the troops were 130 kilometers from their major railroad depot. Wagons constantly sank up to their axles in mud and slime.

During early 1916 Central Power Conrad–Falkenhayn personal relations collapsed, when Habsburg forces invaded Montenegro then Albania. The two commanders accused each other of violating their agreements on Balkan and Italian policies and severed relations for months. Falkenhayn became engrossed in his Verdun strategy as Conrad prepared for his 1916 *Straf* offensive against Italy. Falkenhayn refused to support Conrad's proposed Italian offensive, and kept him in the dark about his plans for his Verdun offensive.

On November 13, Central Powers forces conquered the Morava–Maritza trench. The Serbian Army now suffered from a serious lack of ammunition and supplies as much had been consumed, captured or abandoned. Exhausted Serbian troops had surrendered their main railroad supply artery, the single railroad line leading to the Morava–Vardar trench, which forced their retreat into rugged, and now snow-covered, mountain terrain.[42]

By mid-November the desperate Serbs faced annihilation, continuing their retreat through late December into early January. During February 1916, surviving troops were shipped to Corfu from the Adriatic coast then, in early autumn, to Salonica in Greece. The Serbian Army suffered over 150,000 casualties, which included 90,000 killed or wounded and 74,000 captured, and lost about 600 artillery pieces.[43]

A new Serbian Army would be created on the Salonica front, destined to free Serbia, and be part of the victorious September 1918 Balkan front victory. For now, the Salonica Army suffered mostly from disease that killed many soldiers.

The Serbian victory now allowed transport of military supplies to the Turkish ally. The Central Powers now dominated the Balkan Peninsula. Only Romania remained as a potential adversary. Many of the victorious troops could be redeployed elsewhere.

Thus, 1915 ended on a positive note for the Central Powers, but the seeds had been sown for disaster in 1916 commencing with the abrupt ending of Conrad–Falkenhayn relations. Habsburg replacement troops could not duplicate the troops' battle effectiveness. Disastrously, the Central Powers did not coordinate their strategy for 1916, as we will now investigate.

1916

During 1916, Austria-Hungary suffered through four bloody Isonzo River attrition battles, the failure of Conrad's *Straf* offensive, the disastrous Brusilov offensive and war with Romania at the end of the year. Battle intensified everywhere and both alliance systems again launched major offensives against strong enemy defensive lines, producing further stalemate and millions of casualties.[1] The Russians sustained almost two million casualties from the Brusilov offensive and Lake Naroch disaster. All armies became far less effective on the battlefield, and war weariness became an increasingly critical factor on all battle and home fronts. Manpower sources rapidly dwindled, heralding the approach of *Matérielschlacht* in 1917 as weapons production accelerated.

The Dual Monarchy fought another three-front war during the year, when Romania entered the conflict on August 27, 1916. Massive battlefield losses and the multiple disastrous battles brought the Habsburg state close to exhaustion. By autumn 1916, Dual Monarchy economic resources had begun to rapidly decline, while the army increasingly suffered severe supply shortages. After the Brusilov offensive debacle, Austria-Hungary, now the obviously much weaker component in the alliance, became increasingly dependent upon Germany for economic aid and military assistance. The 1916 blood battles of Verdun, the Somme and the Brusilov offensive brought economic warfare glaringly to the forefront as Britain further tightened the blockade noose. After the Battle of Verdun, Germany reverted to a defensive stance, while the largest naval battle of the war was fought at Jutland. This stalemated naval battle provided the background for the commencement of unlimited German submarine warfare in 1917, with its dire consequences for the Central Powers.

In Austria-Hungary, another poor harvest fueled intense food riots and a tightening coal supply situation. Decreased food rations negatively affected workers' productivity, while prices rose sixfold during the year. Inflation slipped out of control, accompanied by increasing distress and misery, while both Germany and the Dual Monarchy suffered from crop failures that exasperated the critical shortage of food for both. The lower grain yields resulted from late-summer cold weather, not battle. The situation worsened because so many farmers had been drafted into the armed forces and horses sequestered. Women, children and the elderly now cultivated the soil.

Growing crops became more difficult because nitrates had to be used for ammunition production rather than soil cultivation, therefore yields declined. Acreage also declined for food production.

The scarcity of food worsened and further rationing became necessary during the summer, while food shortages fueled the war weariness. Increasingly, it became evident that the Habsburg central government could not alleviate the economic distress or nationality issues resulting in a lack of confidence in it and growing friction with the various nationalities. Riots erupted in Bohemia, while strikes and serious disturbances proliferated. In Vienna, there were widespread demonstrations and riots. Popular unrest became a normal occurrence, fed by the cited war weariness, inflation and accelerating political unrest.

Exacerbating the situation, by mid-1916 the Habsburg transportation system began to collapse. The lack of coal for locomotives, steadily diminishing available railroad cars plus insufficient and poorly trained railroad personnel assured that the transportation system increasingly declined. This negatively affected the already worsening economic situation. Food and other necessary civilian commodities could not be transported to the starving people in cities. Raw materials became increasingly scarcer for industry because the few available supplies could not be delivered. The lack of adequate personnel and railroad maintenance aggravated the problem. The production of locomotives remained steady during 1916 and into 1917, but could not maintain steady commodity delivery to the cities, further inciting civil unrest and hardship.

Coal for civilian consumption became scarce as much of it was earmarked for military and industrial use. Winter witnessed multiple strikes and disturbances because of the lack of heat and resulted in increased civilian suffering. So many miners being drafted led to inexperienced personnel replacing them, which resulted in lowered productivity.

The death of Emperor Franz Joseph in late November had an enormous psychological effect on the Dual Monarchy's population, because he had symbolized unity for seven decades. His replacement, nephew Karl, was unprepared to rule. Emperor Karl proved too easily influenced by other people, particularly his wife, Zita, but he realized that his country desperately required peace. His failed attempts at establishing peace resulted in a major scandal with the publication of his notorious Sixtus Affair letter.[2] When the Sixtus crises exploded, Emperor Karl had to travel to German military headquarters at Spa aware that German leaders no longer trusted him. The affair proved fatal for the Dual Monarchy because, with the 1917 Russian revolutionary events, it resulted in the Entente Powers' decision to support the evolution of new states of Czechoslovakia, Poland and a South Slavic entity following spring 1918. This resulted from the Dual Monarchy's perceived dependency on Germany as witnessed by Emperor Karl having to pay penance to German High Command at its headquarters in Spa on May 12, 1918.

Emperor Karl also realized that his domains were near the end of their resources and the army was demonstrating signs of collapse, particularly after the devastating summer Brusilov offensive disaster. He also realized and hated the fact that Austria-Hungary had become the junior partner to Germany. During late 1916, however, the Habsburg Army replaced the previous year's horrific losses and actually significantly increased manpower numbers to almost five million troops. However, it also had become overwhelmingly obvious that the Entente Powers possessed far superior troop numbers and far vaster materiel resources and industrial power, which eventually changed the tide of battle against the Central Powers.

On October 6, 1916, a Habsburg Ministerial Council meeting discussed the worsening economic situation and created a food office within the Ministry of the Interior. This, however, failed to achieve efficiency in governmental action and, on November 13, an Austrian officer became responsible for providing food for the civilian population but the organization lacked any real power. Attempts were made to expand land cultivation and the search accelerated for substitute (*Ersatz*) materials for the limited supplies of such commodities as coffee, or those that could no longer be obtained. Meanwhile, friction increased between the Austrian and Hungarian governments over the worsening food situation as starvation increasingly threatened Austria. The Hungarians shipped grain to Germany, but withheld it from the Austrian half of the empire, causing much friction between the empire's two halves. The dualism system produced much unnecessary friction and wasted productivity that did not bode well for the Dual Monarchy.

On the Italian front, the Habsburg Army suffered its worst defeat during the Sixth Isonzo River battle, having to surrender its important symbol of resistance, the Gorizia bridgehead. This placed the Italians closer to their major objective, Trieste. The Seventh through Ninth Isonzo battles, though short in duration, produced enormous Italian casualties for little territorial gain. On the other hand, the late 1916 Central Powers' crushing victory over Romania insured enough grain and oil supplies to help keep them in the war although their economic situations continued to worsen. Negatively, the Hindenburg program, introduced at the end of the year, worsened the economic situation as the Entente blockade prevented the importing of necessary strategic materials, particularly nitrates, while the Dual Monarchy's transportation system commenced its decline. Habsburg industry could not meet the challenge introduced by the German program.

Manpower shortages became a major problem, however, predictably leading to the use of prisoners of war in industry, agriculture and at the front for manual labor. Their productivity fell far below the norm. Widespread illness, war weariness and mounting political instability resulted in the resignation of the Austrian minister president during October 1916.

During December 1915, the Russians launched an attack against Austro-Hungarian right flank positions in the Bukovina close to the Romanian frontier. A tsarist army group advanced into the area between the Dniester and Pruth Rivers attempting to capture the capital city of Czernovitz. A second group attacked across the Strypa River attempting to force Habsburg troops to

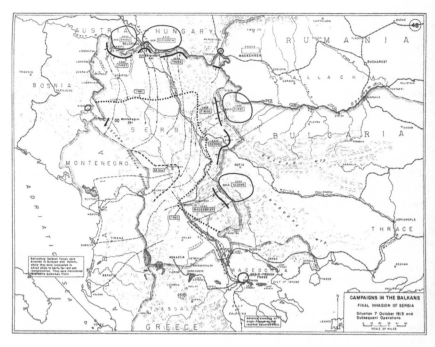

Map 8   *1915 Serbia campaign*
Map courtesy of the United States Military Academy Department of History

retreat northward. The tsarist offensive commenced on December 27, 1915 following the most intense artillery barrage ever witnessed on the Eastern front.[3] In the interim the Habsburg Army had somewhat recovered from its bloodletting during the Carpathian Mountain Winter War, Gorlice–Tarnow and Rovno campaigns.

Habsburg intelligence sources learned of the transfer of tsarist forces before the attack commenced, thus Habsburg Supreme Command immediately transferred troops to reinforce threatened positions. The initial Russian attack was followed by a series of thrusts in the Strypa River region between December 27, 1915 and January 30, 1916, tsarist forces attempting to turn the extreme Habsburg right flank position. They failed: Habsburg forces inflicted seventy thousand casualties on Russian forces, their victory resulting from superior tactics, among other factors.

Habsburg leadership proved effective during the battles; artillery was effectively utilized, while the troops also fought well. Reserve formations were inserted into battle at appropriate times, while the Russians wasted time transporting reinforcements to the front and lacked artillery–infantry cooperation and effective reconnaissance results. Habsburg field commanders assumed that their tactics, so successful during the December 1915 and January 1916 battles, had proven satisfactory for the future. Those tactics would be tested within half a year and failed completely. German experiences in the March 1916 battle of Lake Naroch, to be discussed later, helped convince high-level Habsburg commanders that their defensive positions constructed over many months and tactics could halt any future major Russian attacks.

The late 1915 and early 1916 tsarist campaigns failed because roads became impassable and saturated terrain proved unconducive for conducting such an operation. The Russian logistical system also collapsed to the extent that Russian Seventh Army troops almost starved to death. The inadequately planned tsarist offensives resulted in excessive casualties. The two participating armies had orders not to assist each other until one of them achieved a decisive victory.

The Russians also lacked sufficient heavy-artillery pieces, and the available batteries failed to support the infantry albeit unleashing long barrages, many shells landing on unoccupied Habsburg positions. Tsarist attacks also commenced too distant from Habsburg defensive lines, allowing the defenders to unleash massive and effective counterfire. Tsarist artillery had not been properly registered and no effective reconnaissance conducted.

These late 1915 and early 1916 battles are critical in understanding the success of the 1916 Brusilov offensive. Significantly, General Brusilov learned from the multiple tsarist mistakes while Habsburg leadership was grossly misled by its victory, becoming overconfident in its defensive tactics for future battle. A very costly error resulted from artillery batteries being deployed too close to the front lines, because this tactic had proven so successful earlier. A tragic result; many were destroyed during the initial tsarist hurricane-artillery barrages.

By the March 1916 battle at Lake Naroch the Russians had achieved a five-to-one ratio in troop numbers and increased their artillery battery numbers and shells in that region. The tsarist Lake Naroch operation attempted to relieve German pressure on Verdun on the Western front, as Germany's Eastern front had been bared of troops for that battle. The main Russian Lake Naroch objective was to envelop German right flank positions toward Kovel, a major strategic railroad junction. The marshy, forested terrain, however, proved unsuitable for such a large-scale operation. Simultaneously, diversionary actions attempted to bind German reserve troops on other fronts to prevent them from intervening in the Lake Naroch military operation. German intelligence, however, detected Russian intentions, partly as a result of successful air reconnaissance missions.

On March 15, 1916, Russian artillery unleashed the greatest artillery barrages to date on the Eastern front. However, the tsarist commander repeated the recent mistakes made on the Austro-Hungarian front by attacking during inclement weather conditions – winter snow and rainfall over a far too extensive battlefront. On March 17, a sudden thaw set in accompanied by dense fog, which reduced Russian observation and mission support efforts. On the next day, 350,000 tsarist First and Second Army troops attacked 75,000 well-entrenched heavily armed German Tenth Army troops. In the meantime, temperatures had risen and the attack frontage transformed into a sea of mud, seriously inhibiting forward movement. German machine guns annihilated rows of tightly packed, advancing tsarist soldiers. As a macabre result, dead soldiers appeared to be standing upright in the mud while corpses piled up before the German machine-gun nests and many attacking troops became caught in German artillery and machine-gun crossfire. The tsarist forces suffered 115,000 casualties and the Germans 20,000.[4] On April 4, a Russian attempt to seize Riga failed, resulting in another major tsarist military setback. If that offensive had succeeded, it would have forced the Germans to withdraw their Eastern front lines to avoid being outflanked. The Lake Naroch operation drew no German troops from the Verdun battle.

To senior Russian field commanders, if 350,000 troops and 1,000 artillery pieces firing enormous quantities of shells could not defeat the Germans, then that task had become almost impossible. Tsarist military leadership remained passive on the Northern front until the summer Brusilov offensive. In the interim, General Conrad deployed six additional combat-experienced divisions as well as separate combat-experienced battalions and fifteen heavy-artillery batteries to the Italian front for his May 1916 *Straf* operation, to be discussed shortly.

Other contemporaneous military events included the April British and French Gallipoli campaign and tsarist-Turkish summer battle in the Trans-Caucasus region and, of course, the major "blood battle" encounters at Verdun and the Somme that lasted nine and six months respectively.

During an April 14 conference at Mogilev, Entente military leaders attempted to coordinate their 1916 operations. Russian leaders determined to target Germany, although some generals opposed the decision because of the Lake Naroch disaster. Russian military leaders intended to assist the Italians who had appealed for immediate military assistance, threatened by the Habsburg *Straf* offensive and the French at Verdun. The newly appointed tsarist Southwest front commander, General Brusilov, who replaced General Ivanov during March 1916, surprisingly announced that he intended to launch an offensive to pin down Habsburg forces to prevent their reserve forces from being redeployed to his attack areas. This operation would support the planned major tsarist attack against Germany. Brusilov learned that he would not receive additional reinforcements, artillery or ammunition, thus he would only have a 132,000-troop advantage over his opponent.[5]

Between April 18 and 20, 1916, General Brusilov issued directives to his four army commanders outlining his June plans to launch an offensive along the entire 450-kilometer front extending from the Styr River to the Romanian frontier. He instructed army commanders to select one specific fifteen-to-twenty-kilometer section of their respective front to launch their offensive operation. This would avoid enfilade enemy artillery fire on the attacking troops. This could neutralize the opposing Habsburg forces, possibly diverting reserve formations to that front. It would assist the prioritized Russian offensive against Germany, originally planned for June, later delayed until July. It also reputedly would release pressure on the Somme, Verdun and Italian fronts.

On June 3, the Russian chief of the General Staff questioned General Brusilov's proposed offensive, insisting that his plans be postponed until a concentrated attack could be planned. Brusilov replied that his troops were prepared to launch the operation, his artillery already in position, thus he could not delay it.[6] The offensive commenced on June 4.

In the meantime, the Russians increased the intensity of their artillery barrages against Habsburg defensive positions, as tsarist soldiers sapped closer to Habsburg positions, particularly the Fourth and Seventh armies. Habsburg artillery batteries proved incapable of countering the enemy artillery because of the lack of shells; heavy-artillery pieces and shells had been deployed to the *Straf* offensive operation against *Erbfeind* Italy. Therefore, Habsburg artillery units, sparing their limited shells, could fire only a few rounds each day against enemy troops sapping toward their lines, but to no major effect. Habsburg troops observed Russian soldiers inch ever closer to their defensive positions, in some locations to within sixty yards or less.

Although aware that the Russians would soon launch an offensive, Habsburg defenders proved sorely unprepared for the magnitude of the impending shock action. Habsburg army and corps daily logbooks confirm that Russian troops relentlessly sapped closer to their defensive positions, and conducted other obvious preoffensive activities.[7]

General Brusilov planned to have his soldiers very close to enemy lines when they launched their attacks following the unleashing of enormous preparatory artillery barrages.[8] This would minimize the time between the supporting artillery barrages and the initial assault. Infantry advances commenced from only yards from Habsburg defensive lines, leaving only moments for the defenders to react to the mass attacks after absorbing intense hurricane-artillery barrages that trapped them in their partially underground defensive structures.[9]

General Brusilov's forty infantry and fifteen cavalry divisions attacked thirty-eight Habsburg infantry and eleven cavalry units. The Russian advantage in troop numbers amounted to only 132,000 soldiers (600,000 vs. 500,000 troops). The main Russian advantage resulted from massing assault units at the ordered twenty-kilometer-wide attack positions, outnumbering those defenders on the army fronts. Brusilov, unlike his contemporary Russian

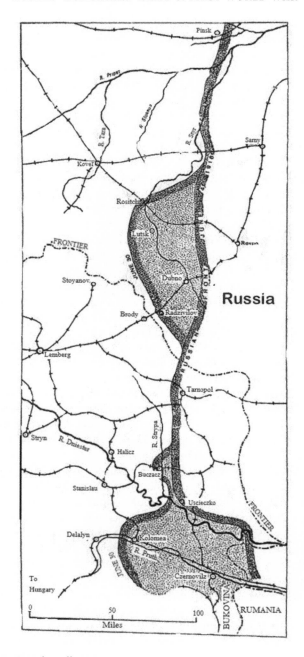

Map 9   *1916 Brusilov offensive*

generals, analyzed the tsarist military mistakes committed at Lake Naroch, the 1904–1905 Russo-Japanese War and in the Bukovina (Habsburg front) during December 1915 and January 1916. He also studied the French sapping actions during the recent Western front Champagne battle. Brusilov massed superior artillery units for his offensive effort, whereas Conrad, as we have learned, had redeployed fifteen of his heavy-artillery batteries and enormous amounts of shells to the Italian front for the May *Straf* offensive, seriously weakening his Eastern front artillery strength.

General Brusilov also demanded that the preoffensive artillery *Trommelfeuer* destroy all Habsburg barbed-wire emplacements and forward trenches. Artillery and infantry cooperation proved critical as four simultaneous offensives would be launched so the enemy could not effectively redeploy its reserve forces, or counter the multiple assaults, as so often had occurred in the past. Infantry assaults must be supported by continuous artillery barrages to provide cover for the attacking troops, while destroying Habsburg forward positions. If successful, neighboring enemy positions would be also forced to retreat. Tsarist troops sapped forward so Habsburg defenders did not have time to mass reinforcements at their threatened positions as during the December 1915 and early 1916 battles.

Tsarist commanders, also contrary to normal practice, deployed reserve units immediately behind the front attack lines so they could be rapidly deployed as a concentrated force. Simultaneously, communication trenches were dug to rear echelon positions so troops could swiftly advance toward the targeted Habsburg front lines.

General Brusilov ordered aerial reconnaissance photographs be taken of Habsburg positions, particularly of artillery battery locations. The resulting maps, combined with information gathered from prisoners of war and deserters, provided an accurate overview of Habsburg defensive positions. Models of the positions were constructed in rear echelon areas for troops to practice assaulting multiple times. Large defensive structures (*Fuchslöcher*) constructed partially underground trapped Habsburg units in their positions during the initial assault. Tsarist artillery units also practiced firing concentrated barrages at these structures. If Brusilov's four armies simultaneously attacked their specific objective areas, he calculated that Habsburg commanders could not deploy their reinforcements, or reserve formations, rapidly enough to effectively assist the suddenly endangered positions. A few days before the offensive launch, shock troops and artillery batteries were shifted to the front lines during the night to ensure complete surprise when the offensive commenced. In addition to releasing misinformation about his intentions, General Brusilov left one gun from each artillery battery in their original positions to deceive the enemy into thinking the tsarist situation remained stationary. He perceived that short, concentrated artillery barrages, earlier so effective in Western front battles and at Gorlice–Tarnow, would produce success.

Tsarist intelligence reports indicated that General Conrad had redeployed six of his best combat divisions and multiple heavy-artillery batteries to the Italian front, and that the Germans had redirected significant troop units to the Western front for the Verdun campaign. To Russian advantage, General Falkenhayn did not believe the Russians had the capability of launching a major offensive action because of the previous year's Gorlice–Tarnow campaign defeat. Both Central Power commanders transferred significant troop numbers to other fronts without informing each other. Most Habsburg units remaining on the Russian front lacked experienced and capable officers; some regiments contained only one career officer for each unit.[10] Yet, May and early June unit status reports to higher commanders proclaimed that Habsburg defensive positions could ward off any enemy attacks, erroneously retaining the belief that the earlier December 1915 and early 1916 Bukovina battles had provided a successful model for defensive actions against any tsarist offensive military effort. The soon-to-be-imploded Habsburg Fourth Army had recently been inspected by the army group commander, who reported it was prepared.

The mission of tsarist first-wave infantry assault troops armed with hand grenades was to break through the enemy front trenches then neutralize artillery pieces that the initial tsarist artillery bombardment had not destroyed. The second assault wave followed two hundred paces behind the initial attack units to overpower the second Habsburg trench line. A third wave advanced armed with machine guns to expand the forced gaps in the enemy lines, while a fourth wave secured the flanks of those gaps.

At 4:30 a.m. on June 4, 1916 tsarist artillery barrages, unprecedented in their ferocity, commenced on the Eastern front. This was followed on the second day by *Trommelfeuer*. Coordinated artillery fire included light-artillery batteries receiving target information from attacking frontline infantry officers, ensuring close artillery–infantry cooperation. Artillery units had clearly defined missions. Concentrated hurricane-artillery barrages destroyed Habsburg barbed-wire emplacements and machine-gun positions. As the infantry advanced, supporting light artillery shifted from counter battery fire to destroy the enemy's heavy-artillery units once within range. Russian heavy-artillery units would destroy enemy communications lines then refocus fire onto the Habsburg frontline positions. All artillery functions occurred within a ten- to twelve-minute span. Heavy-artillery barrages prevented reserve units from being deployed into the front lines during the immediate attack. Habsburg artillery units failed to counter the intense initial tsarist barrages. The few defending reserve formations were inserted into the front lines piecemeal, thus counterattacks failed to halt the onslaught, with the concomitant enormous loss of life.

Russian troops assaulted the three Habsburg defensive positions spaced between fifty and a hundred meters apart, each protected by three belts of barbed-wire emplacements designated to allow heavy defensive artillery and machine-gun fire against any attacking troops. The defenders' rear echelon positions consisted of huge concrete reinforced dugouts that had been constructed to provide infantry protection from enemy artillery fire. Following earlier experience, Habsburg artillery had been deployed generally no further than three kilometers behind the first trench lines. The forward trenches also contained concrete reinforced dugouts from which machine-gun fire could be concentrated on any attacking enemy forces. The forward trench positions, three to four meters deep, had been reinforced to reputedly withstand enemy artillery fire of up to 18-cm caliber. Additionally, special positions housed observers in concrete reinforced positions from which to direct defensive artillery fire if attacked. However, only the very forward frontline positions had been constructed by summer 1916, although extensive work on improving the positions had occurred.

The night before the offensive commenced, General Conrad celebrated the birthday party of the nominal commander of the Austro-Hungarian Army, Archduke Friedrich, in a rear echelon area, and thus failed to see the translated tsarist order for the launching of the offensive at 4 a.m. on June 4. Once the assault commenced Habsburg corps commanders panicked, or misrepresented or misunderstood the full extent of the ensuing crisis on their fronts. This produced disaster, particularly for the Habsburg Fourth and Seventh armies during the initial hours of the offensive. The Russian Ninth Army struck Habsburg Seventh Army on a narrow three and a half-kilometer-wide frontage, smashing through the defending infantry division on the southern Dniester River bank. On June 10, the attack expanded to a twenty-kilometer front successfully penetrating six to twelve kilometers. Seventh Army was split apart, forcing it to retreat under the threat of being outflanked. By June 13 tsarist forces had advanced fifty kilometers. Seventh Army sustained a hundred thousand casualties within two weeks.

Once tsarist artillery had systematically destroyed the front Habsburg trench lines, it zeroed in on the second hundred-meter lines and adjoining communication trenches then extended its fire to reserve formation assembly areas. Rapidly advancing Russian troops completely surprised the defenders, leaving them no time to react effectively. The few available Habsburg reserve units were hurled into battle piecemeal, being pulverized. They proved completely ineffective and became mere cannon fodder.[11]

The initial Russian artillery barrages reduced Habsburg defensive positions to rubble. Smoke and sand filled the air, rendering the breaches of the defenders' rifles inoperable and hindering observation. Explosive gas paralyzed the troops. This resulted in the rapid loss of positions thought impregnable, leading to lack of faith in the Habsburg officer corps and their defensive positions.

The Russians attacked seemingly out of nowhere; they crossed the damaged barbed-wire obstacles and dashed forward in mass waves. The defenders, having no time to react effectively, surrendered in large numbers. Habsburg artillery pieces emplaced close to the front lines were destroyed in the opening artillery barrages. Lacking the necessary artillery support and possessing inadequate troop numbers, more than half of the defending soldiers became casualties. The immediate tsarist tactical success threw the Habsburg Army into total disarray, while dismantling Fourth and Seventh armies. Conrad remained five hundred kilometers from the action.

Retreats commenced almost immediately, Fourth Army's entire front. No order had countermanded the retrograde movement. Chaos continued at this major point of the tsarist front.

The Brusilov offensive resulted in more than one million Russian casualties and disastrous Habsburg losses of 750,000, or over one-half of the troops on that front, compounded by the severe negative psychological shock effect on both troops and officers. The first line of barbed wire and trenches was surrendered within two hours of the offensive launch. There was no Habsburg artillery cooperation during the initial assault, nor was heavy-artillery support available.

During June, 140,000 Habsburg replacement troops were transferred to the front, but proved inadequate to replace the 300,000 casualties sustained by then. By July 29, the official Habsburg battle losses numbered 6,750 officers and 319,500 soldiers.[12] Within the initial twenty-four hours, Fourth Army sacrificed 54 percent of its troop stands, Seventh Army 68 percent. Fourth Army numbered 117,800 troops on the first offensive day; four days later only 35,000 troops remained, or 70 percent losses. Counting reinforcements, or reserve troops, hurled into battle, the army's loss reached 89,700 soldiers.[13] Some examples of individual division casualty numbers are that, on June 4, the 70. Honvéd Infantry Division numbered 14,000 soldiers, but by June 8, only 4,000 remained. In the interim, March replacement troops replaced some of the losses, but by June 20, division numbers averaged only about 3,600 troops. Another example is that the 2. Infantry Division had 13,100 soldiers on the first day of the offensive, and four days later only 1,500, even after 3,000 replacement troops had been deployed to the unit. Many units had been annihilated.

Tsarist Eighth Army launched the most significant offensive action along major railroad lines toward Lutsk, a major Habsburg supply and transportation hub. When Lutsk fell the army pressed on to the Styr River line within days, where Habsburg troops proved incapable of maintaining their positions. During the initial assault, the attacking 148 battalions countered 53 defending units.

Russian forces achieved their surprising and most significant rapid victory at Lutsk, while launching a second pincer movement between the Dniester and

Pruth Rivers. They calculated that their rapid battlefield success would sway Romania to ally with them to destroy the Austro-Hungarian Army. Attacking troops planned to hurl the Habsburg Seventh Army right flank positions far rearward, diverting attention from the main Russian Eighth Army attack at Lutsk.

In ten days, the Russians drove a wedge ninety kilometers wide and sixty kilometers deep around the area of Okna. In the process, the victorious tsarist soldiers captured 233,600 prisoners of war and 52 artillery pieces. Brusilov, however, committed a major tactical error, when rather than breaking through the Habsburg lines to roll up their flank positions, he turned his attention to seizing the capital Czernovitz (Bukovina) for its political effect upon Romania. He paused his operation after the first week to rest his troops, to consolidate their positions and receive reinforcements rather than continuing the offensive.

The Russians forced Habsburg troops to retreat behind the Strypa River, threatening neighboring South Army's flank positions north of the embattled Habsburg Seventh Army, also deployed along the river. The Russian Ninth Army failure to immediately extend its successful breakthrough operation saved Habsburg Seventh Army from total annihilation. On June 18 Habsburg troops retreated into the Carpathian Mountains. In the meantime, four reinforcing tsarist corps arrived on the attack front, which allowed the Russians to launch another offensive, this time at Kovel, a major strategic transportation center. After tsarist forces advanced thirty kilometers, four German divisions were deployed to plug the gaps in the Habsburg lines. Many retreating Habsburg troops drowned in the Styr River or were killed by artillery fire. The demoralized troops could not defend the river line. Units became intermingled as panic and exhaustion spread.

The sudden and unanticipated defeat on the Russian front, as General Conrad's Italian *Straf* operation had already stalled, forced him on June 5 to frantically appeal to General Falkenhayn for German reinforcements. The Germans, however, had become entangled in their major offensive at Verdun, while already on June 24 artillery bombardments announced the July 1 commencement of the British Somme campaign. The Germans nevertheless eventually deployed sufficient reinforcements to halt the tsarist flood to again rescue the Habsburg Army. Initially, General Falkenhayn declared that German troops would be redeployed to the Habsburg front only if the Russians transferred troops from their northern (German) front where they outnumbered German forces by at least three to one. This assured that no troops would be immediately forthcoming. However, at a Conrad–Falkenhayn Berlin meeting on June 8, Conrad agreed to redeploy two infantry divisions from the Italian front to the Russian.

Meanwhile, the unrelenting Russian offensive forced Conrad's Fourth Army to retreat from the Lutsk area where it was overrun. Division headquarters were often located too distantly from the battlefield to be able to react rapidly enough to the immediate circumstances. Entire regiments surrendered en masse to tsarist forces.

Fourth Army units initially retreated thirty kilometers, their front decimated, losing thousands of troops and officers, artillery pieces, machine guns and untold war supplies. The army's losses proved so severe that its various corps troop numbers had become the equivalent of an infantry division.

A thoroughly disgusted General Falkenhayn hurriedly transferred German troops from the Western front to Rovno, the major railroad center located between the northern and southwestern Russian fronts. This became the next major target of Brusilov's offensive efforts after the fall of Lutsk. Generals Conrad and Falkenhayn discussed plans to launch a counterattack toward Lutsk along both sides of the Kovel–Rovno railroad line with seven and a half divisions. Such action had to be postponed until the arrival of heavy-artillery batteries to support the operation.

Habsburg First Army received orders to counterattack, but tsarist assaults against it and Second Army forced First Army to retreat. On June 10–11 alone a Russian assault created a thirty-five to forty-five-kilometer breach between the reeling Fourth Army and suddenly threatened First Army.

The tsarist Ninth Army advanced into the Bukovina along the Dniester River line. The Habsburg Seventh Army retreat was halted by its 48. Infantry Division. The Ninth Army offensive threatened the Habsburg Army eastern flank positions in Eastern Galicia and the Bukovina. The tsarist Eleventh Army also launched a demonstrative attack toward Tarnopol and Lemberg to disrupt that major railroad junction area. Thirty-two battalions attacked fifteen Habsburg units. Meanwhile, General Brusilov halted his advance fearing that a flank attack would be launched from the adjoining German front. Conrad had to redeploy several infantry divisions from the Italian *Straf* offensive front to the Russian because of the Brusilov offensive success.

Between June 16 and 17 German forces launched a counterattack. They could not pierce tsarist lines, but halted the Russians' advance toward Kovel. The Russians halted their operation for several days, to rest tsarist troops and replenish supplies.[14] A Russian attack, launched on June 16, took tsarist troops across the Pruth River, but it was not until July that the Russians pushed Habsburg forces against the Carpathian Mountains, again threatening an invasion of Hungary. The tsarist Ninth Army attack, meanwhile, separated Habsburg Seventh Army units at the Dniester River front. On June 9, after a day of battle, Russian forces broke through Habsburg lines and drove the defeated troops across the river. Only a lack of sufficient reserve troop numbers prevented the attackers from exploiting their initial victories south of the river, and they were also hampered by major supply difficulties because of the treacherous terrain. Russian pressure on this front continued throughout the latter part of June. With the Habsburg Seventh Army collapse, too few Austro-Hungarian troops were available to halt the Russian steamroller on that portion of the front, thus the Germans redeployed four divisions to that hard-pressed Habsburg flank area.

The Russians regrouped to launch a major offensive between June 24 and 27. When Habsburg Seventh Army troops retreated to the west, it exposed South Army's rear echelon and flank positions to attack. Thus, Seventh Army had to alter its retreat direction under continued enemy pressure, leading to the army's collapse. The army consisted of reliable Hungarian and Croatian troops.

The Habsburg Seventh Army suffered at least a hundred thousand casualties within two weeks. That army's mission, even after its unanticipated rapid disintegration, remained to defend the southern Bukovina area, the Habsburg extreme right flank position. The army also had to prevent a tsarist invasion of Hungarian territory through the Carpathian Mountains, which could encourage Romania to declare war. Tsarist forces, meanwhile, suffered three hundred thousand casualties during the month.

On June 28 Brusilov launched a new offensive, at Baranovichi, advancing over marshy terrain. The operation was preceded by a two-day artillery bombardment, but shells striking soft terrain did not have full effect. In the meantime, the Germans had time to reinforce their threatened positions.

On the northern German-Russian front, on July 1 tsarist General Evert, possessing both vast numerical troop superiority, as well as artillery and shells, launched his offensive partially to force Habsburg troops to retreat behind the Sereth River. Fortunately for the Habsburg military situation, the Russians postponed the offensive numerous times. When it ultimately commenced, it immediately collapsed because of heavy casualties. Tsarist troops had become exhausted from the constant battle on the muddy front that also negatively affected timely transfer of reinforcements. General Brusilov soon reverted to his old tactics, producing excessive tsarist casualties with his multiple frontal attacks. His tendency to often halt offensive actions provided the Central Powers invaluable time to reinforce their positions.

The Russians recruited new troops after July 24 to launch a new major offensive. On July 1 the Somme offensive had been launched to release pressure off the French at Verdun as the Germans simultaneously frantically shifted troops from the embattled Western front to the collapsing Habsburg Eastern front. Fifteen infantry and three cavalry divisions eventually tightened the ally's reeling front lines.

On July 2 Russian artillery barrages introduced a tsarist assault at Baranovichi, the only sector on the entire German front between the Baltic Sea and Pripjet Marshes occupied by Habsburg troops. The attack, on a small eight-kilometer front, halted almost immediately. Additional Russian attacks served as diversionary actions.

During July, the Russians launched a major offensive against the critical Central Power defensive position at the Stokhod River line, which formed the base of the Styr salient along that river. On July 14, General Evert canceled a further German front offensive and, by July 19, Brusilov formations had been hurled back eighteen kilometers, sustaining enormous casualties. Until July 20 five Russian armies attempted to force the strategic Stokhod River line. Wave after wave of tsarist troops assaulted their formidable objective, creating one of the greatest Central Power crises during the entire campaign. When tsarist forces attempted to outflank German positions south of Kovel, their Garde Corps suffered 80 percent losses.

Elsewhere, the tsarist Ninth and Seventh armies advanced toward the Hungarian plains south of the Dniester River, but hastily deployed German reinforcements to this newly endangered position foiled the efforts. The Germans eventually wrested control of almost all Central Power Eastern front command positions, while preventing the implosion of the Habsburg Army. German forces eventually neutralized Brusilov's attacks, as his armies began running short of artillery shells and other battlefield necessities.

During the second half of July the Russians launched a major attack at Kovel, while the battle at Baranovichi terminated. The Central Power military situation, however, remained critical, thus they launched counterattacks to halt the persistent tsarist assaults, but the Russians maintained the initiative, sustaining over half a million casualties.

The tsarist Third, Special and Eighth armies attacked toward Kovel on July 19, and then on July 25 five divisions reinforced the assault, the Eleventh Army initiating a separate assault. On July 28 Brusilov offensive operations entered a new desperate phase, when troops were again hurled against the Stokhod lines. Elite Garde, Third and Eighth Army troops attacked the strong Central Power defensive positions, while the Seventh, Ninth and Eleventh armies bound Habsburg troops on the other fronts.

On July 29 sustained Russian pressure forced the Allies to retreat behind the Stokhod lines, while serious battle continued until August 11, producing further battered Habsburg troop and materiel losses. Even with multiple waves of twenty-deep soldier columns attacking, the Russians failed to pierce stubborn German resistance, at the cost of massive casualties and equipment.

Tsarist troops also attempted to capture the capital city of Galicia, Lemberg. The defending Habsburg Second Army retreated on July 28 and on August 4 and 14. Fighting also reerupted on the Dniester front as both antagonists launched offensives. Battle continued on the Carpathian Mountain front during the second half of August, with tsarist soldiers conquering an almost fifty-kilometer-deep area, resulting from Habsburg defeats north and south of the Dniester River. On August 27 Romania declared war against Austria-Hungary, extending the Eastern front by over two hundred kilometers and forcing the Russians to deploy over twenty divisions to the new front to assist their new

Balkan ally. German, Austro-Hungarian and Bulgarian troops eventually ended this threat by rapidly attacking the poorly prepared enemy, hurling back a Romanian invasion of Transylvania and conquering much of Romania.

Several subsequent Brusilov offensives were launched, but tsarist Seventh and Eleventh armies terminated their offensives. The loss of professional officers, noncommissioned officers and troops on both sides proved devastating.

General Conrad had to accept German military command extended over much of his front on September 6, 1916, because the Germans had again rescued the Habsburg Army from potential disaster. The excessive casualties of General Brusilov's forces provided one of the key factors in the outbreak of the first Russian Revolution during February–March 1917. The 1916 campaign became a significant turning point for both Austria-Hungary and tsarist Russia.

The offensive, accounting for the nearly two million casualties on both sides, produced the greatest Entente victory of the war. It conquered more enemy territory than any other Allied victory and threatened to force Austria-Hungary out of the war again. Brusilov's strategy lost effectiveness when repeated attacks at different intervals allowed the defenders to prepare for them. Most trained tsarist troops were sacrificed, leaving raw recruits. In addition to obvious military effects, political facets also proved extremely significant. The offensive relieved some pressure off the German attack on Verdun, and assisted the British Somme campaign launched on July 1. Yet, the Germans transferred eighteen divisions to the imperiled Habsburg front. There has been historiographical argument that the Brusilov offensive also saved Italy from the Habsburg *Straf* offensive, but that operation had been effectively halted before the commencement of the Brusilov campaign.

Russia regained all the territory it had surrendered during the 1915 Gorlice–Tarnow offensive, and again deployed troops on the Carpathian Mountain foothills. On some sections of the front Russian troops drove Habsburg forces back almost 160 kilometers. Only the rapid intervention of reinforcing German troops prevented the collapse of the Austro-Hungarian front and utter defeat of its army.

Turning to the Italian front, the French appealed for Italian military assistance because of the German Verdun offensive unleashed during February 1916. The Italians launched half-hearted attacks during the Fifth Isonzo offensive, which lacked any significant objectives. Their forces attacked the Gorizia and Tolmein bridgeheads in a series of local military actions that commenced on March 9, 1916 and lasted for eight days. Limited attacks proceeded against the Carso Plateau and the west bank of the Isonzo River, opposite Gorizia. Terrain and inclement weather conditions (flooding, snowstorms and poor visibility) reduced the accuracy of artillery fire during the battle. The series of probing incursions always terminated with the customary hand-to-hand combat with clubs, stones and any other available weapon.

To avoid mountain snowstorms, General Cadorna prepared his troops weeks in advance to launch a spring offensive. His forces enjoyed a vast numerical superiority of 150 battalions to the Habsburg's 100 and an even greater advantage in artillery: 1,400 versus 467 guns. They unleashed assaults against Mrzli Vrh, the Tolmein bridgehead and specifically Habsburg positions on northern Podgora.

On February 20, 1916, Italian artillery commenced firing barrages against the northern Carso Plateau. On February 25, it targeted Mt. San Michele, then the infantry launched an offensive. Early Italian gains were quickly squandered when Habsburg troops counterattacked. General Boroević withdrew his troops from forward front lines before the Italians commenced their forty-hour artillery barrage, which greatly damaged forward Habsburg trench positions, but did not cause major casualty numbers.

On March 11 Italian artillery again commenced firing after a long battle pause, which continued until March 13 during pouring rain conditions. The attempt to cross the Isonzo River at the mouth of the Vippach Valley was stymied by Habsburg artillery fire. An advance toward Mt. San Michele led to intensive battle through the night of March 14. On March 19 Habsburg forces launched a counterattack, regaining some lost high terrain. During battle pauses both combatants feverishly repaired and improved their positions for the next clash of arms.

Then on March 30 Italian forces achieved some success; however, on April 26 Habsburg forces reconquered any surrendered terrain. Battle continued until June, although much of April and May proved deceivingly quiet. During April Habsburg VII Corps 17. Infantry Division sustained 17 percent casualties during May, 20 percent as losses mounted for the numerically inferior Habsburg defenders.[15]

Italy was a secondary war theater to General Falkenhayn, thus his unreceptiveness to Conrad's repeated requests for German participation regarding the launching of the May 1916 *Straf* offensive. Falkenhayn instead focused attention on planning for the Verdun campaign.

A mortal Italian threat to the Mt. San Michele positions was neutralized by the actions of one Hungarian rifle company during skirmishes on that front. In preparing for the first Habsburg major (*Straf*) Southwest front offensive, troops encountered serious obstacles because of the difficult Alpine mountain terrain and lack of suitable roads for troop and supply transport. Conrad planned to achieve a strategic victory by launching an offensive from the Trentino mountain front by attacking from South Tyrol, to sever Italian Isonzo River supply lines and cripple the Italian war effort, exacting revenge against the perfidious ally. The planned tactical surprise was to prevent the threat of a breakthrough on the Isonzo River front. It would also bind large numbers of enemy troops and, if the offensive progressed thirty kilometers, it would threaten the Italian Isonzo River rear echelon positions and railroads. It would also gain the initiative and significantly shorten the front lines.

Multiple Italian field fortifications had to be overcome to gain control of both sides of the Asiago Plateau. On the Dolomite Mountain front, snow masses three to five meters deep and avalanches posed a constant threat. Only three mountain roads could transport heavy-artillery batteries, especially 42-cm Howitzers, to the Folgaria and Lavarone plateaus. Troops had to constantly shovel snow, while air reconnaissance proved difficult because low clouds, snowstorms and poor visibility negatively affected artillery fire accuracy. Shell explosions often were diluted by deep snow masses.

General Boroević learned of Conrad's plans on March 3, just prior to the Italians unleashing their Fifth Isonzo offensive. Habsburg Supreme Command planned the decisive breakthrough of Italian lines with its Eleventh Army. Fifth Army had to transfer four of its best divisions (seventy thousand troops) and some heavy-artillery batteries to the Tyrolean mountain front for the *Straf* offensive, seriously weakening the Isonzo River front and presenting a deadly threat if the Italians should attack Fifth Army. This unfortunately occurred.

Conrad planned to unleash a powerful two-army offensive. Strong artillery would support the operation. Then, on May 10, came a fatal change in the plans – a corps would now attack into the Val Sugana, weakening the mass for the main attack and extending the attack frontage.[16]

Third Army attack forces, recently transferred from the dormant Serbian front, with the Habsburg Eleventh Army (250 battalions and over 1,000 artillery pieces) finally unleashed the offensive on May 15. Multiple units contained veteran mountain soldiers, including III Corps with Slovene and German Alpine troops. XX Corps, commanded by Archduke Eugene, consisted of two divisions of Tyrolean and upper Austrian regiments, accustomed to treacherous mountain terrain.

The *Straf* expedition's objective was the city of Padua, forty-five miles behind the Italian lines and only twenty miles from the Adriatic coastline. Railroad supply lines to the Italian Isonzo River forces were situated in this area. To reach Padua, the troops had to traverse very difficult mountain terrain to force an enemy retreat.

On May 15, with clear weather, a thousand Habsburg artillery pieces commenced firing barrages on a twenty-mile front. Italian First Army failed to offer serious resistance, so, by the end of the first battle day, Habsburg troops had advanced up to five miles in some locations. For several days units advanced at a steady pace, although delayed by the rugged terrain. General Cadorna began transferring multiple forces from the Isonzo River front to the Asiago Plateau front, creating a new Italian Fifth Army consisting of eight divisions and numerous Alpine and Bersaglieri battalions in addition to dozens of artillery batteries. By the end of May (in just twelve days) almost half a million Italian soldiers had been transferred to the threatened front when, nevertheless, additional territory fell to the attackers.[17]

Thirty thousand Italian prisoners of war and over four hundred artillery pieces were captured. Ninety-four Habsburg battalions from other fronts participated in the offensive endeavor.[18]

In December 1915, Habsburg Supreme Command had shifted its focus to the Italian war theater, primarily because the Eastern front held little promise of success. Conrad believed that front prevented potential offensive possibilities against hated Italy. The Bukovina defensive victories on December 20, 1915 and January 26, 1916 increased Conrad's self-confidence and drew his attention from the Eastern front to the perfidious former ally. Habsburg troops, meanwhile, concentrated on improving defensive positions at the expense of offensive training in the tsarist theater. Conrad redeployed six combat-experienced divisions and fifteen heavy-artillery batteries with a large complement of shells to the Southwest front. Habsburg heavy-artillery gun and shell numbers drastically shrank on the Russian front. Veteran soldiers were replaced by recruits, who spent much time constructing defensive positions.

On December 12, 1915 Conrad discussed his proposed offensive plan against Italy with Falkenhayn requesting four infantry divisions and one-third of the necessary artillery, to launch his Italian campaign. At the same time Conrad expected the Russians to launch an offensive in the Vistula–Bug River area. He realized that the tsarist army remained a major threat even after the Gorlice–Tarnow operation. He intended his Italian operation to succeed before the Russians launched the anticipated attack. General Falkenhayn refused to support the request, because he did not believe that such an offensive would knock Italy out of the war. Thus, the proposed operation would not have the necessary twenty-five infantry divisions and enormous amount of artillery necessary to achieve a decisive victory.

At a January 7, 1916 Ministerial Council meeting Conrad and Hungarian Minster President Tisza agreed to launch a military campaign to defeat Italy to maintain the Dual Monarchy's vital Adriatic east coast.[19] General Falkenhayn suggested that Habsburg forces maintain a defensive stance against Italy, and any excess troop numbers be deployed against Russia. Conrad's revenge campaign would harm the common war effort in the long run. Habsburg soldiers' conditions remained desolate, as the physical standards for recruits were lowered. Insufficient food rations at training centers resulted in no rigorous physical exercise. Training personnel invariably proved of inferior caliber, thus troops were inadequately prepared for the front. Reserve officers outnumbered professional comrades by a ratio of five or six to one, seriously lowering frontline fighting effectiveness.

During early 1916 Conrad transferred troops from the Russian, Balkan and Isonzo fronts for the Italian *Straf* offensive to be launched out of the Tyrol. Significantly, the Isonzo front had to be protected against any potential threat of an Italian breakthrough during the *Straf* offensive. Removal of troops for the new offensive severely strained General Boroević's Fifth Army, resulting in the Isonzo Army lacking sufficient troop numbers to launch a counterattack if necessary, because of the lack of troop numbers and reserve forces. III Corps and additional troops and artillery batteries deployed to the Tyrolean front.

Unfortunately, the Germans also removed numerous units from the tsarist front for their Verdun campaign, without informing Conrad, because of the personal antipathy that had developed between the two generals at the end of 1915. Falkenhayn charged Conrad with breaking agreements when Habsburg troops invaded Albania and conquered Montenegro during January 1916. Personal contact elapsed until early 1916.

General Falkenhayn harbored sound reasons for opposition to Conrad's proposed operation. He did not want to remove any German troops from the Western front Verdun cauldron and absolutely did not wish to declare war against Italy. He also feared that German troops would be bound on the Italian front as they had been on the Eastern to be sacrificed for Habsburg interests. He also deeply mistrusted Habsburg military abilities, particularly of field commanders, because of continued lackluster battlefield performances.

The *Straf* offensive, intended to be a surprise operation, represented a high-stakes gamble to knock Italy out of the war. The ultimately unsuccessful operation drained the Habsburg Army of needed manpower, resulting in the successful Italian Sixth Isonzo counterattack at Gorizia and success of the Russian front Brusilov offensive.

Two basic assumptions for success included possessing adequate troop numbers and their ability to complete the operation. Regardless, the Russian front had to be secure at all costs. Tragically, a decisive Italian front victory could only succeed with German assistance. The lack of cooperation resulted in the offensive being launched in South Tyrol, but not also on the Isonzo River front. Attack troops encountered extreme inclement weather conditions, which required enormous troop exertion. The several weather-related delays in launching the offensive also ensured that there would be no surprise. The lack of reinforcements and sufficient reserve troop numbers to follow up any battlefield successes also became factors. The earliest reinforcements could not arrive until May 21, much too late to affect the outcome of the campaign.

A significant prerequisite for operational success was ensuring that adequate enemy soldiers were bound on the Isonzo front. The *Straf* offensive would be launched from the Tyrol because no other terrain or attack direction held much chance for success considering the number of available troops. The dense Italian railroad networks gave the enemy the ability to rapidly redeploy troops to counter an Isonzo front attack. Another critical factor was that there were three separate command centers; no unified headquarters existed. Habsburg Supreme Command headquarters was seven hundred kilometers from the battlefield.

General Conrad's original operational preplanning consisted of drawing six pencil marks on a piece of paper designating the intended attack direction.

However, as so often, Conrad ignored the fact that the troops would have to maneuver through inhospitable and difficult mountain terrain. No reconnaissance of the attack front was planned.

Tragically, the directive for the offensive contained insufficient details for the attack.[20] Conrad conveniently ignored the extreme winter climatic conditions.

The designated attack units proved inadequately equipped, insufficiently fed and poorly commanded. Conrad, again overestimating his forces' capabilities, did not visit the operational front. Many soldiers had not received mountain training. Habsburg Supreme Command's R (Russia) Group, in the interim, had repeatedly warned against weakening troop numbers on the Eastern front, particularly at the end of May after intercepted tsarist radio messages indicated the Russians' intention to launch an offensive soon.

The rugged Tyrolean mountain terrain seriously delayed all movement, and retarded logistical support, because of the few poorly maintained serpentine roads that curled through the rugged wooded mountainous terrain. The scarcity of railroad transportation signified that the Habsburg military could not sustain the necessary human and materiel delivery to the front. The Italians, to the contrary, possessed multiple railroad lines enabling rapid transport of supplies and reinforcements, presenting them an enormous advantage.

Multiple Italian field fortifications had to be overcome, to secure the terrain along both sides of the Asiago Plateau to enable troops to invade the Italian plains. Weather conditions became particularly important between February and May when mountain snowfall was heaviest. Blocked roads and unfavorable conditions also delayed the transport and positioning of vitally necessary artillery pieces. Avalanches, an ever-present danger to soldiers, buried thousands.[21] Conrad also seriously underestimated the extent of Italian resistance, while the few available troop reserve formations were deployed too far from the front to add impulse to any achieved attack momentum.

General Falkenhayn warned Conrad that the delays in launching the offensive should negate the operation, but Conrad insisted that preparations could not be halted because artillery had already been placed in position. At the end of April Conrad altered the operational plans, with the heavyweight of the assault now shifting to Eleventh Army's right flank units. On May 3, 1916, Falkenhayn again requested that Conrad cancel his planned offensive.[22] On the Italian side General Cadorna had prepared to launch an offensive weeks before the end of Alpine mountain snowstorms. A valid question was whether the Habsburg Army possessed the capability to launch a major offensive after the severe bloodletting of the Carpathian Mountain Winter fiasco, the Gorlice–Tarnow and Rovno offensives then the late 1915 Serbian campaign. Commencing in early February 1916, Conrad redeployed troops and artillery from the Eastern to the Italian front, severely weakening the tsarist front.[23]

During mid-April major amounts of snow accumulated in the mountains, delaying the offensive launch, but General Cadorna did not believe intelligence reports that indicated that Habsburg forces would soon launch an offensive. Cadorna considered that his defensive positions could repulse any attack, but when he inspected positions in early May, he discovered that the First Army commander had disobeyed repeated orders to prepare extensive defensive positions. Only the first two inadequately organized lines were occupied by troops.

On May 14 a Habsburg demonstration operation was launched on the Carso Plateau to deceive the enemy of the actual major objective, while the Isonzo front remained quiescent. When the main operation commenced the next day the Italian First Army failed to halt the attack; by the end of the day Habsburg troops had advanced up to five miles. Habsburg forces had achieved early tactical, but not operational, surprise. During the next twelve days, as attacking formations advanced, General Cadorna rapidly transferred multiple Isonzo River forces to the threatened Tyrolean front.

Inexplicably, the initial plans were altered. To obtain victory Habsburg forces required a relative numerical troop superiority, which rapidly dissipated when the attacking troops ran out of reinforcements. Additional troops became vital, but none existed. Habsburg logistical and troop movement delays enabled Italian reserve formations to be rushed to the endangered front, quickly reversing the numerical troop ratio to Italian favor.

The first operational phase transpired between May 15 and 20, when by May 19 the offensive had faltered. By May 18 one designated group had not launched its attack while some units reached the designated ridgeline. When XX Corps failed to advance on May 20 Habsburg troops required a pause of several days to transport heavy-artillery pieces over the mountain terrain to support the new front. In the meantime, the Italians reinforced and improved their defenses, committing four infantry divisions to the new Italian Fifth Army.[24] Meanwhile, Conrad had inserted his last reserves into battle.

On May 20 the heavyweight of the offensive was altered as Conrad launched the second wave of assaults on the edge of the Asiago Plateau. Meanwhile, the Italians had reinforced their front with the mentioned four infantry divisions. On May 23 inconsequential battle occurred.

Between May 25 and 28 Habsburg troops captured Asiero and Asiago in the center of the front. The third and final offensive stage commenced on May 31, but almost immediately stalled. Meanwhile, Italian leaders requested that Russia launch an offensive to relieve the pressure on their troops, but by June 1 Italian resistance had stiffened considerably. An Italian counterattack denied further Habsburg success and ended the offensive.

The Russians responded to their ally's plea by launching the Brusilov offensive on June 4, 1916, quickly overwhelming defending Austro-Hungarian troops and rapidly forcing a headlong retreat. On June 6 General

Falkenhayn pressured Conrad to redeploy two divisions to the Russian front because of the overwhelming tsarist successes against Habsburg Fourth and Seventh armies. The Italian counterattack on June 10 forced a Habsburg retreat as troop units had to be redeployed to the Russian front. On June 16, when four divisions had to be rushed to the Russian front, a full retreat commenced, continuing on June 25 to more favorable defensive positions. Italian troops could not pursue the defeated enemy, because of troop exhaustion. Italian losses reached 148,000, those of the Habsburgs 89,000 including 26,000 prisoners of war.

Habsburg forces had been halted at the edge of the twelve-mile-wide Asiago plateau divided by high mountain terrain just before entrance to the Italian plains. On June 21 General Cadorna prepared to launch an Italian counter-offensive to coincide with the Brusilov campaign. Fighting on the Italian front settled into a steady pattern, while disciplinary problems and desertions increased within Italian Army ranks.

The Isonzo front had to be held at all costs, but, with the *Straf* operation, that front's resources had been strained to the limit. Insufficient troop numbers remained to defend against an attack. The units, transferred to the Tyrolean front, could not be redeployed to the threatened Isonzo front because of the Brusilov offensive victories. This immediately produced a catastrophe. Worse, all available hinterland *Ersatz* troops, equipment and materiel had to also be rushed to stem the Eastern front disaster. The fate of the Isonzo front now hung in the balance.

The Sixth Isonzo battle followed the year of bloody stalemates, resulting in major Habsburg retreat and defeat. During the campaign the Habsburgs launched their first gas attack on this front (the first poison gas attacks on Italian positions. The phosgene gas struck two Italian divisions on Mt. San Michele, which sustained 7,000 casualties and 2,600 dead. The attacking Habsburg troops gained no territory, but after the episode the Italians took no prisoners of war.). General Cadorna had been preparing to launch an attack against Mts. Sabatino and San Michele since February 1916, when Conrad launched his *Straf* operation on May 15, 1916. The Italians utilized twenty-two divisions for the Sixth Isonzo battle, adding new artillery models. They would be attacking the 58. Infantry Division containing only eleven battalions, half of which consisted of *Landsturm* troops on a front extending from Mt. Sabatino to the Vipacco Valley. Italian brigades attacked Habsburg battalions, indicating Italian numerical advantage.

On June 16 Cadorna ordered Third Army to attack the fortified Gorizia bridgehead positions in two stages. During the first, Third Army had the mission to capture the heights of Mt. Sabatino and Oslavia. The second phase would be launched on the Carso Plateau in the Mt. San Michele sector. A total of 300,000 Italian soldiers were eventually transported by rail to the front. The

Italians disseminated false information to confuse the Habsburg defenders, making it appear that the attack would be elsewhere.

Third Army attacked Mt. Sabatino and the Gorizia bridgehead with four first-line divisions and two second echelon on a five-mile front. Seventy-seven battalions attacked Mt. San Michele, nineteen battalions the central Carso Plateau. Two divisions (thirty-five battalions) attacked Habsburg southern Carso Plateau positions.

The defending Habsburg Fifth Army, weakened from transferring some of its best units to the *Straf* offensive, had only 110 battalions to counter the Italian attack. Some troops deployed between Tolmein and Plava and nine battalions between Mt. Sabatino and the southern slopes of Podgora. During the Sixth Isonzo offensive Italian Third Army's 200-plus battalions attacked Fifth Army's 58. Infantry Division's 18,000 troops, one-half territorial militia. Fifth Army possessed no reinforcements because any available troops had to be hurriedly redeployed to halt the Brusilov offensive.

The Sixth Isonzo River battle developed into the most successful Italian offensive to date. General Cadorna concentrated 250 battalions and 1,250 artillery pieces into the seven-kilometer-wide front at Gorizia. Habsburg defenders consisted of only seventy-eight battalions.

On August 4 the Italians commenced an enormous artillery barrage extending from Tolmein in the north to the Adriatic coast. The heaviest targeted the Gorizia bridgehead. The intense artillery fire blinded the defenders in dense clouds of dust and smoke unlike ever before. When telephone lines were interrupted infantry had no contact with headquarters or artillery units, and soon ran out of ammunition.

The eight Habsburg infantry divisions lacked sufficient troop numbers to provide an adequate defense. Minuscule reserve units were available and there was a serious shortage of artillery shells, especially for heavy-caliber guns. Many batteries had been transferred to Tyrol, then to the Brusilov front. Fifth Army, caught by surprise, enabled Italian forces to conquer Mts. Sabatino and San Michele within hours. This forced the surrender of the Gorizia bridgehead and the Doberdo Plateau. Only the timely arrival of three divisions and artillery reinforcements from the Tyrolean front enabled the Habsburg troops to hold their second defensive line. Two divisions had to be transferred back from the threatened Russian front to stem the tide.

The attackers enjoyed a more than two-to-one troop number superiority. After thirty-six hours of brutal battle the seriously depleted Habsburg defenders had to evacuate the Gorizia bridgehead and retreat to avoid annihilation. Only five thousand of the eighteen thousand defending Habsburg troops escaped the carnage. Gorizia had no strategic significance, but provided Italy its first significant victory, with the success giving encouragement for capturing Trieste. Gorizia became the first Habsburg city to be captured by the Italians.

By the morning of August 8, 58. Infantry Division faced a crisis situation, when it had exhausted its artillery shells and lacked troop numbers. The surviving Gorizia garrison retreated east of the city to defend a new eight-mile front on high terrain. Troops were hurriedly reformed into thirteen understrength battalions, but they were a motley assortment of troops.

When Habsburg troops retreated from the Gorizia bridgehead, they also had to surrender the western half of the Doberdo Plateau because further defense had become meaningless. Defensive positions that had required a year to build in the rocks and caves had to be abandoned.

The consistent overwhelming Italian artillery fire caused enormous casualties, but the Italians themselves sustained such losses that they could not immediately resume offensive operations. The victory silenced some of General Cadorna's critics, who had decried his many defeats and the huge casualty numbers. Cadorna continued to launch Italian offensives on limited fronts preceded by massive concentrations of artillery fire.

On the same day, August 8, Italian Second Army received orders to attack Plava then the key Mts. Kuk and Vodice to assist the advance against the Mts. Santo–San Gabriel line. Italian artillery targeted while troops enveloped Mt. San Michele, annihilating multiple Hungarian defensive units.

Before Italian troops launched a bayonet attack against Mt. San Michele, their artillery fire killed many defending troops and destroyed multiple positions, allowing Third Army to conquer Gorizia.[25] With the loss of Mt. San Michele, Italians targeted the critical Doberdo Plateau, raising the threat of an advance into the Vipacco Valley on the eastern Carso Plateau only twenty miles from Trieste. General Boroević ordered the evacuation of most of his positions on the Carso Plateau to strengthen the Gorizia bridgehead area. He requested at least three reinforcing infantry divisions, but because of the Brusilov offensive none could be provided.

The Italians launched eighteen regiments on a massed narrow front. Reserve formations deployed directly behind them totaled one hundred battalions that pursued the retreating Habsburg defenders to their new positions. To Italian advantage, their artillery could continue firing without having to be moved forward because of the short distance to the front. The battle consumed huge quantities of Habsburg shells and guns, a major disadvantage during the next several days. The obvious Italian target became the Vipacco Valley, and Trieste. Remaining Habsburg defenders had to retreat from Mt. San Michele during the night of August 10. The next day the Italians extended their attack into the Vipacco Valley along a thirty-kilometer battlefront. Habsburg defenders still could not receive reinforcements as General Boroević's mission became to defend Trieste.

Intense battle continued along the entire front through August 14 but senseless incessant Italian bloody attacks achieved no success. On August 15 General Cadorna ordered new attacks be launched against Habsburg positions north of Gorizia, consisting of four divisions that attacked on a multimile front. Italian VI Corps troops were slaughtered, and ultimately forced to retreat. Multiple Italian regiments disappeared conquering Habsburg positions.

Cadorna suspended the Sixth Isonzo offensive on August 16, although his troops enjoyed a ten-to-one numerical advantage. The campaign had been costly for the Italians.[26] The bloody encounters on the Carso Plateau and Gorizia equaled the attrition battles at Verdun, Flanders and other Western front battlefields. Cadorna's troops had failed to achieve a strategic break-through, but had nevertheless brought close the collapse of the Austro-Hungarian Army.

The bloody battles defending the Gorizia bridgehead created an honorable chapter for the old Imperial Army. General Cadorna would launch three additional Isonzo offensives during the year.

Cadorna listed three objectives for his Seventh Isonzo offensive following the successful Sixth campaign. The first entailed breaking through the Vipacco River front, the second to capture the hills east of Gorizia and the third to seize the Carso Plateau.[27] The Italian Third Army, made up of twelve infantry divisions, attacked on a seven-mile front with a three-to-one manpower advantage and four-to-one in artillery pieces. The attack originally had to be delayed because of unrelenting rainfall that flooded trenches. The ultimate objective remained to seize Trieste after occupying the Vipacco Valley.

Italian artillery fire, intensified with heavier-caliber guns, on September 9 targeted Habsburg supply depots and reserve unit positions. On September 13 the artillery barrages increased to enormous destructive *Trommelfeuer*, while Italian Caproni bombers participated in the battle. The final phase commenced on September 14 when artillery barrages saturated the entire front, extending from the Vipacco River to the Adriatic Sea. The nine-hour artillery barrage destroyed Habsburg communication points, supply depots and all roads leading to the front area. It also annihilated many Habsburg soldiers while destroying their defensive lines. Surviving troops proved far too weak to withstand another major attack. The Italian Third Army advanced two kilometers, sustaining eighteen thousand casualties. But on September 15 Italian Third Army's superior troop numbers were stunned by small detachments of Habsburg defenders repulsing entire Italian division attacks, often launching effective counterattacks after the enemy had gained some terrain. The next day provided the most intense combat of the entire campaign when Third Army hurled three army corps against enemy lines, but achieved only minimal results. Italian corpses lay strewn across the plateau.

Elsewhere, at Mt. Rombon the Italian Second Army attempted to break through Habsburg defensive lines, to seize Flitsch, which prevented it from seizing the upper Isonzo River terrain. In one battle mass Italian attacks were halted by one Bosnian regiment in a hail of machine-gun fire and one 175-mm artillery piece that fired point-blank into the attacking Italian soldier ranks. A Bosnian counterattack drove the Italians back with severe losses.

On September 17 Third Army again attempted to conquer the Carso Plateau, but after seventy-two hours of constant battle had achieved nothing. The battle terminated in four days, Third Army having conquered some small positions, but nothing noteworthy militarily. The Habsburgs lost over half of their troops during the battle, but halted the major Italian offensive. Third Army regrouped to launch the Eighth Isonzo battle.

The Eighth battle also produced heavy Italian losses for minimal gains, causing troop morale to plummet.[28] Eighteen Italian divisions attacked on a ten-mile front; General Cadorna assumed that his numerical and material superiority would defeat the weakened Habsburg units still recovering from the Seventh Isonzo battle.

Between the two battles, General Boroević's first priority remained to reestablish his main defensive line, where eight thousand laborers worked around the clock to repair damaged positions and prepare a third defensive line. Boroević anticipated an imminent Italian attack, but could anticipate receiving no reinforcements because Romania declared war on August 27, 1916. The Russian threat remained a greater danger than the Italian, thus the Isonzo front received lowest priority for reinforcements. Boroević thus had the hopeless mission to halt the far superior numerical enemy with his inadequate forces.

A week-long Italian artillery barrage commenced on October 3, steadily increasing in intensity. On October 6 rainfall and thick fog conditions halted artillery activity. On October 7, intensive artillery fire continued for forty-eight hours, saturating the entire Habsburg front, destroying many trenches, machine-gun positions and supply lines and causing many casualties.

The Eighth Isonzo battle commenced on October 9 with "annihilation" artillery fire from over a thousand artillery pieces targeting the Carso Plateau. The following day artillery fire swept the entire front from Gorizia to the Adriatic coast, further devastating Habsburg defensive lines and forcing further retreat. On the northern Carso front four reinforced Italian divisions attacked Habsburg VII Corps positions, immediately forcing the half-strength defenders to retreat. On the central Carso Plateau three Italian divisions captured territory along the entire front. As so often occurred, one Habsburg infantry company counter-attacked an entire Italian corps and forced its troops to retreat.[29] Similar unit sacrificial counterattacks often saved the entire Habsburg front from collapse.

On October 11 Italian artillery fire resumed along the entire Carso Plateau extending to the Adriatic Sea. Six Italian divisions again attacked VII Corps positions. Meanwhile, Fifth Army regained some lost territory, but sustained enormous casualties.[30] Italian Third Army troops became exhausted from their constant assaults and concomitant losses.

On October 12 repeated Italian attacks produced only further defeat, so Cadorna finally halted his efforts. The mass attacks on the ten-kilometer Vipacco front repeatedly ended in vicious hand-to-hand combat. The Italians suffered sixty thousand casualties but now controlled two-thirds of the Carso Plateau. They had finally penetrated Habsburg defensive lines; the question became how long the battered and exhausted Habsburg troops could maintain their positions.

On October 16 General Boroević notified Conrad that Fifth Army had been seriously weakened because of the severe losses and with no possibility of receiving reinforcements. Each division, excluding during major Italian offensive operations, required two thousand replacement troops a month. The attrition battles were taking a deadly toll. The Habsburg Army had lost a hundred thousand soldiers in eight weeks and possessed almost no replacement troops. Inclement weather conditions delayed launching the Ninth Isonzo offensive until November 1.[31] The continued major battle on the north and central Carso Plateau spread over a vast front produced small Italian gain, but conquered more territory than the earlier two operations. The two efforts failed to rupture Habsburg defensive lines. Heavy snow fell as troop morale suffered on both sides.

The Italians outnumbered their foes by 221 battalions to 91. It was even worse for artillery pieces: The Italians possessed 1,350 versus 543 for the defenders.[32] On October 25 Italian artillery barrages enveloped the entire Carso Plateau, but terminated at noon because of dense fog and rain. The next day, October 26, artillery fire recommenced, continuing for several days, targeting major Habsburg headquarters. Defending artillery could not disrupt the enemy barrages, thus infantry trenches stretching from Mt. Santo to the Adriatic Sea were reduced to rubble, many Habsburg defenders buried in the debris.

Habsburg soldiers endured the persistent deadly and psychologically devastating artillery barrages through October 31. Then, on November 1, the Italians opened "annihilation" artillery barrages before their Second and Third armies launched offensives. In the ensuing operation several brigades attacked a single Habsburg defending unit. One Italian division assault occurred on a quarter-mile front, ten Italian soldiers covering every foot of the front, but Habsburg defenders repulsed the attacks in rivers of blood.

On November 2, Habsburg VII Corps troops recaptured ten major positions, but the situation of VII Corps remained critical as enemy artillery fire nearly annihilated the entire unit, forcing a bloody night retreat.

On November 3 the Italians attacked VII Corps' second defensive line, but no Habsburg reserve units existed anywhere on the entire Isonzo front. The seriously weakened 58. Infantry Division resisted all Italian efforts to progress far past Gorizia. The Italians had advanced two miles closer to Trieste on a four and a half-mile front during Carso Plateau battles. Only fourteen more miles remained to attain their ultimate objective, but Italian front fighting ended for the year.

Early on August 27, 1916 Romanian troops invaded the Dual Monarchy.[33] Romania had been allied to the Austro-Hungarian monarchy in the Triple Alliance since 1883. Its military mission had entailed covering the Habsburg extreme right flank positions during a War Case "Russia" to bind the Russian Fifth and Kiev armies. Then during the 1913 Second Balkan War Romania allied with Austria-Hungary's archenemy Serbia against Bulgaria, a potential Habsburg ally. It became increasingly possible that Romania might not support the alliance in the future, particularly in a Balkan Peninsula war. Three million Romanians lived in the Hungarian province of Transylvania. Although pressured multiple times, Hungarian Minister President Tisza refused to grant concessions to the Romanians in that province, because it would negatively affect the Hungarian Magyarization policy and political dominance. German military and diplomatic leaders consistently pressured Vienna to compromise to prevent Romania from entering the war against them, at a minimum to be kept neutral in an armed conflict. However, the Entente could offer Bucharest the Habsburg irredenta territory they craved: Transylvania, the Bukovina and the Banat.

Frantic diplomatic activity occurred between Vienna and Bucharest throughout the July 1914 crisis, Vienna pressuring Romania to fulfill its alliance agreements. Then, on August 1, 1914, the Romanian Crown Council declared its neutrality, because Hohenzollern King Carol realized that the Romanian people opposed war against Serbia. During fall 1914 the Russians made their first proposals attempting to win Romania to the Entente. On July 31 the Russian government promised it Transylvania for just maintaining a neutral stance, which removed possible Romanian participation in the war to gain the province. However, the Russians had surrendered any leverage in further diplomatic negotiations.

Romanian leaders, however, realized they had to ally with Russia to obtain their irredentist territory. On October 2, 1914 the Romanian prime minister signed a benevolent neutrality pact with Russia to receive Transylvania after the war. Then during May 1915 an agreement stipulated that Bucharest would receive Transylvania, the Bukovina and Banat if it joined the Entente. King Carol died on October 4, with his nephew Ferdinand, who favored the Entente, taking the throne. Ferdinand and his prime minister awaited favorable battlefield results to enter the war at the pertinent moment to achieve cheap territorial gain.

The two 1914 Galician Lemberg battles and three Serbian defeats tempted Romania to intervene in the war, but German victories at Tannenberg and Lodz prevented it. The 1915 Carpathian Mountain Winter War again tempted Romania to declare war on Austria-Hungary, but the Gorlice–Tarnow campaign caused Romanian leaders to await a conclusive tsarist battlefield victory before committing to enter the conflict.

Romania signed a treaty with the Entente on August 17, but Minister Bratianu claimed that Vienna had nothing to fear from his country. However, on August 22, Romanian troops began to deploy at the Hungarian frontier. Romania declared war on August 27, 1916, believing that the Brusilov offensive and Somme campaigns presented them the best opportunity to seize Transylvania. The Russians again were pressing the Habsburg troops against the Carpathian Mountains. Possessing a small industrial base, Romanian troops were armed only with obsolete weapons except for some modern artillery. However, they possessed few heavy-artillery pieces and airplanes and were not prepared for the warfare that had evolved since 1914.

In late August 1916 a rapid three-army Romanian invasion of Transylvania was resisted by only two Habsburg infantry divisions, reservists, militia and gendarmes, a total of thirty thousand defending forces. The grossly outnumbered Habsburg troops received significant aid from radio intercept and aerial reconnaissance, often learning of Romanian intentions. The Habsburg military mission became to delay the invaders until sufficient forces could be deployed. The invasion caused panic in Hungary, because Transylvania was virtually undefended, and it was feared that the huge Romanian population might revolt against Habsburg political rule.

The thirteen Romanian divisions that rapidly invaded the Carpathian Mountains marched on foot or rode horseback once they crossed the frontier because of the lack of railroad lines. The Carpathian Mountain terrain favored the invading troops launching converging attacks, but the limited narrow passes channeled military advance into specific directions and presented the threat of flanking attacks.

The advance into Transylvania had the objective to eliminate that province as a Habsburg salient before Romanian troops could march into central Hungary. The invading troops enjoyed the advantage of interior lines into the Carpathian Mountains.

General Falkenhayn, replaced as German chief of the General Staff because he did not anticipate Romania declaring war until at least after its harvest, now commanded the newly created Ninth Army that eventually repelled the invaders out of Transylvania, commencing already in September 1916. His forces briefly checked the Romanian troops in October then pressed through the major Carpathian Mountain ranges, crossed several major rivers and captured Bucharest, destroying three Romanian armies in the process. Instead of the anticipated rapid victory over Austro-Hungarian forces, Romania lost the rich resources of Wallachia and retreated from Transylvania and most of the Dobruja during November after multiple attacks into Romania. The remaining

Romanian troops retreating from the Carpathian Mountains defended the Danube River line and Dobruja at the Bulgarian frontier. The Romanian advantage of vastly superior troop numbers was neutralized by Central Power military experience and superior training.

The timing of Romania's declaration of war proved unfortunate; the Central Powers were under siege everywhere, particularly on the Western front. Romanian leaders had stretched their negotiations with the Entente Powers to absolutely ensure that they would obtain an easy victory. The timing of the declaration of war proved disastrous as the country unexpectedly had to fight a two-front campaign. Germany's armed forces had been bound at Verdun, the Somme and Austria-Hungary and Germany with the Brusilov offensive. Two years into the war, following major bloody Western front battles and sweeping, but indecisive, victories on the Eastern front, the war had settled into a stalemate. Entente leaders optimistically anticipated that Romanian declaration of war would result in a rapid victory over the Habsburg opponent. They, however, seriously misjudged the situation relative to the Brusilov offensive, to their severe disadvantage.

Central Power troops enjoyed the major advantage of combat experience, while the Romanian Army had not kept pace with the latest military developments. Its officer corps proved largely inept, many troops were inadequately trained and the army lacked sufficient supplies and equipment to sustain a serious campaign.

When the war commenced Romanian High Command deployed insufficient troop units to protect the Danube River line and the Dobruja.[34] The mobilization required excessive time because of the poor Romanian railroad and road systems vital for logistical support. Nevertheless, the northernmost mobilized First Army crossed the Hungarian frontier during the first night of the war and secured the Carpathian Mountain passes in its area. When Romanian troops invaded Transylvania they sacrificed their advantage of interior lines and created immense logistical difficulties the further they advanced from their supply depots. Meanwhile, within three weeks of the Romanian declaration of war, the German Army assembled two hundred thousand troops, half of which deployed into the Carpathian Mountains to counter the Romanian invasion.

Eighty percent of the army, 350,000 Romanian troops, invaded the Hungarian province. The overwhelming numerical superiority ensured some easy early victories. The numerically weak defensive forces could not provide serious resistance against the overwhelming enemy numbers, thus they quickly retreated from the frontier area. However, early mountain snowfall stalled the Romanian offensive over the rugged terrain, also seriously worsening supply problems.

Three invading armies advanced on three axis lines over mountain terrain that extended over 150 miles, preventing effective cooperation between the three groups. Logistics proved a major disadvantage. The lack of sufficient railroads, poorly constructed roads and inclement weather conditions brought the campaign to a halt. Only one Romanian cavalry and five infantry divisions remained at the other southern front to defend against a potential Bulgarian invasion and the Danube River line being crossed.

By the end of the month, Romanian troops nevertheless had conquered a broad swath of territory eight miles deep, encountering little resistance. However, a Central Powers thrust into the Dobruja Province in southern Romania forced the transfer of troops from the Carpathian Mountain front to defend the Danube River line from the invaders. Romanian troop deployments were separated along the 320-kilometer front, a severe disadvantage.

Central Power aerial reconnaissance identified Romanian positions and arrival of Russian forces and supplies. Once reinforcements deployed to the Transylvanian front they hurled Romanian troops out of that province, then proceeded to neutralize the southern Russian flank position threat. Romanian commanders committed critical tactical errors that neutralized any early advantages. For example, they failed to sever the critical railroad lines leading from Hungary into Transylvania, and invaded Habsburg territory, ignoring the potential threat from Bulgaria.

The eventual crushing Central Power victory over Romanian and allied Russian forces resulted from superior intelligence operations, vastly superior artillery (particularly heavy guns) and their troops' maneuverability. Exceptional operational planning and timing, organizational skills and superior strategy overcame difficult terrain conditions. Combat experience, superior leadership and speed also proved critical as Central Power assaults kept Romanian troops off balance, preventing them from establishing effective defensible lines or deploying in a timely fashion.

Romania had been promised a supporting offensive launched from the Salonica Greek front intended to quickly bind the Bulgarian Army if that country declared war, but those units failed to prevent Central Power offensive operations on the Danube River line. The promise of significant tsarist military support also never materialized, partially because of the many Russian troops still committed to the Brusilov offensive. The Entente Salonica Army, fourteen Anglo-French and two Serbian divisions, failed to prevent the Bulgarian invasion. German General Mackensen assembled ten divisions that neutralized any Entente forces advancing from the Salonica front and then invaded the Dobruja.

The Romanian Army sustained almost three-quarters casualties of the 750,000 troops mobilized during the campaign. A total of 335,706 soldiers died, 120,000 were wounded and almost 100,000 became prisoners of war or were listed as missing in action. Such losses proportionally surpassed any other nation in the war. By 1918, only six Romanian divisions of the original twenty-three remained, and they lost most of their artillery, machine guns and small arms.

On September 1 Bulgaria declared war on Romania, while General Mackensen's ten infantry divisions, consisting of German and Bulgarian troops, immediately invaded the Dobruja to capture Constanta. They rapidly drove defending Romanian troops back to the Cernavodă–Constanta railroad junction. Excellent air reconnaissance and Habsburg radio intercepts enabled Central Power troops to destroy two Romanian divisions, then drive remaining defenders toward the critical Constanta railroad line. To Romania's disadvantage it had deployed only one army, of second-line and poorly equipped troops to protect the Dobruja. That province's defense rested primarily on the expectation of Russian military support to defend the Danube frontier.

On September 2 German forces rapidly crossed the frontier overrunning Romanian defensive lines, providing the Central Powers with a major military advantage; the advance isolated the major Romanian fortress of Tutrakan, the reputed Romanian Verdun. Situated on the Danube River east bank, it protected the frontier from a potential Bulgarian invasion. The fortifications consisted of three defensive lines and fifteen earthworks. German troops were rapidly transferred to the Romanian theater on 1,500 trains from the Western front. In the Transylvanian mountain theater Habsburg troops continued retreating, drawing the invading forces deeper into the mountains where they would be attacked by General Falkenhayn's German Ninth Army.

On September 3, the major fighting occurred west of Fortress Tutrakan, while on September 4 the Russian commander ignored orders to deploy forces to the Fortress Tutrakan area, because he realized they could not arrive in a timely manner. As Romanian reinforcements began to redeploy to the Danube River line, German heavy-artillery fire silenced the defending fortress guns, badly damaging many. The final major citadel defensive positions capitulated, with only five thousand of the original forty thousand defending troops escaping across the Danube River.

Bulgarian troops ceased their offensive efforts by mid-September, enabling the Romanians to establish a strong defensive line to protect the vital railroad line between the Black Sea port of Constanta and Cernavodă, including the last railroad bridge across the Danube River. This vital area became a high German bombing priority against Romanian and Russian troop units.

Central Power forces captured Fortress Tutrakan on September 6, which forced the Romanian General Staff to alter its original strategy. The serious military defeat on the southern front near Bucharest made it impossible to continue the invasion of Transylvania with the bulk of the Romanian Army. The Romanian military had to immediately transfer three divisions to the threatened southern front, which terminated its Transylvanian offensive in mid-September. The limited number of available railroad lines to transfer troops from one theater to another made the altering of the strategy by the Romanian General Staff a disastrous choice.

Constanta became the next German objective. A Romanian counterattack failed despite its far superior troop numbers. Constanta fell on October 22, Central Power troops advancing into the Dobruja.

Romanian reconnaissance aircraft failed to discover the Germans' deployment of arriving forces. Then, on September 21, Falkenhayn's Ninth Army launched a counterattack on the Transylvanian front, producing a series of local victories. On September 22 advancing German Ninth and Habsburg First Army forces launched a major offensive to attempt to outflank enemy positions. The Romanian military remained unaware of the threat developing at the Danube River front.

Meanwhile, German troops traversed the rugged Carpathian Mountain terrain with extended strenuous marches, the troops transporting their own food, water and all military supplies with them. They soon halted the Romanians south of Hermannstadt. On September 25, Ninth Army attacked Romanian flank and rear positions, severing any remaining Romanian supply lines. This substantial German victory forced Romanian troops into a rapid disorderly retreat.

On October 3 Habsburg Danube fleet monitors provided fire support for advancing Central Power troops. General Falkenhayn now targeted the Romanian Second Army flank. Any Romanian counterattacks were halted mainly by effective German artillery fire.

Differences of opinion between German military and diplomatic leadership over Allied policy toward Romania became evident. Thus, no definitive policy evolved relative to Romania.

On October 9, seriously threatened Romanian troops retreated into Moldavia, abandoning the critical railroad crossing at Kronstadt. After Central Power forces received heavy-artillery reinforcements, their right flank units advanced. Defending Romanian troops had to establish positions across too vast an area to defend their Carpathian Mountain positions against attack.

Reinforcement and additional heavy-artillery pieces in mid-October enabled the offensive to be extended. General Falkenhayn's attempt to join forces with Mackensen to encircle Romanian forces suffered because of the severe supply conditions, effect of the weather conditions and the attacking troops' lack of mountain training. Falkenhayn's Ninth Army forces advanced toward Bucharest from the north and west, only briefly encountering strong enemy resistance.

On October 19, General Mackensen's forces rapidly overwhelmed and routed the main Romanian Army near Constanta, the only Black Sea port and terminus of the single railroad line extending from the sea to Bucharest.[35] Once Constanta fell on October 23 the Russians could no longer support the Romanians. Constant aerial bombing prevented Russian reinforcements from assisting the reeling Romanian troops. Once the Dobruja had been conquered,

Falkenhayn's Ninth Army advanced into the Romanian heartland toward its capital, Bucharest. At the end of the month zeppelins bombed the city; Transylvania was reconquered by the end of the month.

As the Romanian left flank position crumbled, their strong forces defending the central frontier passes retreated to avoid encirclement. Many defending units disintegrated, and large numbers of peasant conscripts deserted. On November 2 large numbers of Mackensen's forces crossed the Danube River supported by Danube River monitor fire. On November 10 Falkenhayn launched a five-division attack, delayed only by tenacious Romanian resistance. Nevertheless, the Romanian defensive positions were crushed after an attack launched on a wide front produced a breakthrough. German cavalry forces entered the Danube Plain on a wide front. General Falkenhayn's troops then traversed the Transylvanian mountains on the Northern front as winter snow commenced, then descended into the level Wallachian terrain.

On November 23 a German and Bulgarian division crossed the Danube River and formed a bridgehead. By November 25 most Central Power troops had crossed the Danube River. Then, on November 26, Mackensen's and Falkenhayn's troops joined forces to advance to Bucharest. General Mackensen's troops pushed Russian and Romanian forces out of the northern half of the Dobruja, while Falkenhayn's recaptured the Carpathian Mountain region.

Of the original twenty-six Romanian infantry divisions, six had disintegrate and two had been captured, leaving only ninety thousand Romanian soldiers, most of whom withdrew into Moldavia, the last natural barrier to Bucharest, on November 22.

The Romanian military debacle forced General Brusilov to scale down his successful offensive, because he was forced to redeploy multiple units to the Romania theater. Since the Romanian Army now lacked many equipment necessities, the Russians provided it with a hundred thousand Habsburg rifles, twenty-five million rounds of ammunition, a large number of machine guns and other critical supplies.[36]

On December 3 the Romanian retreat commenced to Bucharest, but when the main Romanian assault group collapsed, the army possessed no means to defend the capital, thus it was evacuated.

The Central Power advance was hindered only by snow and frost conditions, while mountain roads into the valley areas had become a morass of mud, wagons and guns sinking to their axles.

As Bucharest fell on December 5 and the Ploesti oil fields a few days later, the Romanian Army retreated to the northwest corner of the country, crossing the Sereth River to regroup its forces. Entering Moldavia, German forces pushed into the central passes, advancing unopposed against fleeing Romanian troops, until a new front was established.

By mid-December the Romanian First and Second armies had literally disintegrated. As the German offensive terminated, the remnants of the two defeated armies established new defensive positions. Almost all of Romania had been occupied and most of its army destroyed.

During January 1917 inclement winter weather conditions halted all operations on the Sereth River and Carpathian Mountain passes, while Romania surrendered the Dobruja and Wallachia.

During May 1918, the Romanian government signed the Treaty of Bucharest because of the Russian Revolutions and resulting loss of Russian military support. The surrender removed any major threat to Habsburg Balkan flank positions, thus also to the Hungarian Plains, and opened communication lines to Turkey. The country suffered enormous casualties and lost an equal number as prisoners of war.

The Treaty of Bucharest marked the zenith of German expansion in the First World War. The harsh treaty and the March 3, 1918 Brest-Litovsk Treaty with Bolshevik Russia later had a major effect on the Versailles peace settlement negotiators. The Treaty of Bucharest made Romania an economic appendage of Germany. The delay in peace negotiations and the necessity of occupation troops meant additional troops were not available for the 1918 German Western front offensive. The treaty extended the Central Powers' sway in the Balkan Peninsula to the Black Sea by 250 miles.

The major impact of the Romanian campaign produced as much economic as military effect. The Central Powers gained control of much-needed oil and grain that enabled them to remain in the war for two additional years. Berlin received a ninety-year lease on the country's grain and oil. The grain proved significant, maintaining the German and Habsburg fighting forces and helping to feed the starving Central Power civilian population. Conquering Wallachia in 1917 alone helped extend the war another year. Vienna, meanwhile, became more dependent on Berlin. General Brusilov had to terminate his offensive as Romania quickly transformed from a reputed asset to a serious liability. The victory over Romania also negatively affected the German December 1916 to January 1917 peace movement. The German High Command assumed an increasingly hard-line stance relative to territorial acquisitions and belief in further military conquest potential. The Romanian campaign achieved the important German mission of opening the single rail line to Turkey to provide supplies to keep that ally in the war. It also stabilized the Eastern front after the crisis, but German strategic plans for 1916 had failed. A key to the Central Powers' victory was the excellent use of Hungarian railroads. Between August 1916 and January 1917, 2,082 Hungarian trains traveled to the front, an average of 15 daily during the crucial buildup for the campaign. During September, the average daily train number was 22. However, Romania reentered the war toward its climax.

Thus, 1916 brought Austria-Hungary to the brink of catastrophe, devastated by the Brusilov offensive. Rescued again by their German ally, Romanian armed forces were crushed. But at what cost? The Germans took command of much of the Eastern front and, as in the 1915 Serbian and Gorlice–Tarnow campaign, took command of the Romanian operation.

Meanwhile, the Dual Monarchy economic situation had worsened. Another poor harvest, tightened rationing and the collapse of the transportation system increasingly negatively affected the hinterland. Turmoil and war weariness enveloped Habsburg society.

8

1917

The year 1917 witnessed major crises across Europe, which produced a turning point in the war. The Western front endured several more large-scale offensives, which produced enormous casualties and repeated the strategic and tactical mistakes of the past two years.[1] All belligerents suffered significant war weariness and loss of civilian and military morale, while Central Power people grew increasingly restive because of the effects of the tightening Entente naval blockade most effective during 1917–1918. This produced mounting pressure on food supplies in both Austria-Hungary and Germany, as civil disturbances increased and food shortages worsened. The spring harvest provided temporary relief, but the crisis returned in the fall.

Agricultural supplies declined to between 40 and 80 percent of prewar production. This resulted in food riots that accelerated particularly in early 1918. Acreage declined precipitously. Deficiencies in metal increased drastically in the Dual Monarchy, negatively affecting ammunition and weapon production. Coal production also decreased enormously. Strikes were commonplace.

The German Army remained on the defensive on the Western and Eastern fronts during the first half of 1917, until the summer Kerensky offensive, while its troops remained bound on the Western front with the bloody Verdun and Somme attrition battles. By the end of the year, there appeared to be no end in sight to the war. Western Entente armies commenced preparations for the anticipated major German spring 1918 offensive to defeat France and England before American troops arrived in large numbers on the continent. The best German troops received storm trooper training, while a million soldiers in forty-four infantry divisions had been redeployed from the Eastern front because of the collapse of the Russian Army, resulting from the two Russian Revolutions and summer Kerensky offensive defeat.

However, all warring countries began to emphasize defensive postures, a result of the rapid decrease in manpower and rapidly accelerating morale problems among the military and civilian populace. Discontent proliferated with the all-encompassing war weariness. It soon became clear that

Matérielschlacht (materiel supremacy) would determine the outcome of the war as the year progressed. For Austria-Hungary, the casualties resulting from the 1915 Carpathian Winter War, Gorlice–Tarnow, Rovno and the 1916 Brusilov offensive proved disastrous. The Central Government failed to alleviate the rapidly expanding civil and military problems.

In early 1917, half of the Austro-Hungarian Army remained deployed on the Southwest front where all Habsburg nationalities fought well, particularly Slavic soldiers who did not relish fighting their ethnic Russian and Serbian brothers on the other fronts. Slavic troops hated the Italians, because they realized Italy sought to conquer their homelands. However, the Tenth and Eleventh Isonzo battles placed the Habsburg Army in a catastrophic situation. German troops launched the Caporetto offensive on October 24 with Habsburg troops to retrieve the Allied military situation as on numerous earlier occasions.

Russian and Austro-Hungarian homefront conditions steadily worsened. Both suffered food, fuel and raw materials shortages, exacerbated by their military's insatiable desire for manpower and materiel. Economic conditions continued to decline, producing a major black market in both countries, where the lower-middle and urban classes suffered the most. Women waited long hours to purchase substandard goods if any became available. The combination of drastic domestic hardship and battlefield casualties dampened the sense of patriotism and loyalty that had sustained both empires during the first two years of war. The Russian and Austro-Hungarian transportation systems continued to collapse, reducing the supply of food, coal and fuel transport to cities. The lack of effective central government action relative to the food situation exacerbated homefront suffering. Habsburg government mismanagement, even after the Austrian parliament, or *Reichsrat*, reconvened, further exasperated the dwindling food supplies. Emperor Franz Joseph's death in November 1916, at eighty-six years of age, became widely viewed as a major turning point in Austro-Hungarian history. His nephew, Karl, replaced him, although never trained to become emperor. Karl proved indecisive, choosing ineffective advisors and replacing all of Franz Joseph's officials as well as Conrad's Habsburg Supreme Command. His rapid coronation as King of Hungary effectively postponed any chance of reform and reorganization, to ultimately prove fatal in 1918.

On the Habsburg home front, war weariness, famine and troop desertions accelerated throughout the year. Rations dropped to almost half the normal consumption level, while mortality rates rose for young and old alike. Escalation of labor and industry problems also increased the cost of domestic goods, worsening inflation, while production declined because of the lack of raw materials. Estimates reached as high as seven hundred thousand citizens having died directly or indirectly from starvation in 1917. By October, conditions had seriously worsened and troop desertions had become epidemic.

Coal, oil and bread remained in short supply, while strikes regularly erupted. The number of work stoppages increased and sabotage plagued industrial production. Protests and strikes coalesced with political problems and created doubts as to whether the war could be won. Such factors were exacerbated by labor shortages and reduced production and strained labor relations. Plant shutdowns or producing at a much lower capacity worsened because railroad production of train cars dropped 50 percent. As the war increasingly evolved into *Matérielschlacht*, skilled laborers began returning to industry when released from the armed forces. With declining food supplies and decreasing industrial production, Habsburg citizens could only hope for a German Western front military victory during spring 1918 as their hardship worsened.

As battlefield casualties continued to mount, soldiers and civilians began to question the human toll of the war. Habsburg troops and civilians alike suffered from food shortages, leaving them exhausted and malnourished. Simultaneously, equipment and materiel supplies continued to shrink, partly a result of the Entente blockade and the paralysis of Habsburg industry. Repeated battlefield defeats resulted in the desertion of increasingly large numbers of troops, not to the enemy but to the hinterland.

While antiwar dissent increased, the *Reichsrat* reconvened in 1917, having been prorogued in March 1914 because of ethnic turmoil – Czech and South Slav propaganda and dissension. This inflamed the Dual Monarchy ethnic situation. Severe weather conditions produced another poor harvest as the people increasingly grew desperate, fearing the approach of winter and its consequences.

German military and economic aid continued to prove indispensable to the Habsburg Monarchy's military survival, but the 1916 Verdun, Somme and Brusilov offensives seriously weakened both armies. Because the Central Powers assumed a defensive stance on both fronts, the Entente Powers seized the strategic initiative as their steadily increasing numerical and materiel advantages became increasingly evident. The Germans, however, remained prepared to seize any opportunity that might arise on the Eastern front. The Russian Revolutions appeared to be a godsend to Vienna as Eastern front guns fell silent, allowing the Habsburg Supreme Command to redeploy multiple infantry divisions to the Italian front where its troops had suffered enormous casualties during the earlier numerous Isonzo River attrition battles. The Tenth and Eleventh Isonzo battles bled the Habsburg defenders dry. Fear of an Allied collapse resulted in Germany providing seven infantry divisions to spearhead the October Caporetto offensive.

Increasing lack of food and heat during the winter months resulting from the shortages of coal, fuel and food also produced escalating civilian agitation and apathy. This was exacerbated by the worsening transportation difficulties, which resulted from insufficient supplies of coal and oil, forcing railroad traffic to significantly decrease, compounding the Dual Monarchy's problems. Coal became an increasingly rare commodity, while Habsburg railroad tracks steadily deteriorated. Locomotives, train cars and railroad tracks required maintenance, while repairs could not be performed because of the lack of workers, food and parts.

The military situation, however, proved relatively favorable for the Central Powers during early summer 1917. On the Western front the battle at Arras was followed by the Champagne and Aisne River campaigns during April and May, where German forces won resounding defensive victories. During March, before the French launched their disastrous Nivelle offensive, German troops retreated to create shorter front lines and free formations to prepare the new Hindenburg defensive line. A partial explanation for the failure of the early 1917 Entente Western front offensives was that Russia did not launch its usual supportive effort because of its February/March revolution. The Eastern front settled into half war and half unsettled peace. Then in March the Germans attacked the key tsarist position on the Stokhod River line, surprisingly seizing the right bank of the strategic waterway. The unanticipated light Russian resistance indicated to the German High Command that the demise of the Russian Army had commenced.

The success of the German offensive against Russian Stokhod River positions on March 21 and 22 caused tsarist General Alexseev to reevaluate his plans to maintain a defensive stance until June 1917. Alexseev believed that the Russian Army must be prepared to launch an offensive, but effective Bolshevik propaganda demanded peace without annexations or war indemnities. Such propaganda had a major effect on Russian soldiers as many believed that this signified that they no longer had to fight or die. By late March the Russian High Command determined that launching a major offensive had to wait until July at the earliest.

The first Russian Revolution provided some relief for the Central Powers, but on March 15 increased Russian military activity commenced with the preparation of multiple new positions. Serious problems had occurred in St. Petersburg with the revolution, but one could not yet estimate their effect on the former tsarist military establishment. Serious street fighting and disorders erupted, accompanied by multiple strikes and factories being destroyed in that city.

The Eastern front, therefore, remained static during spring 1917, the opposing armies defending their positions extending from Riga in the north, Minsk to the west, stretching along the eastern Carpathian Mountain slopes to the Black Sea halfway between Constanta and Odessa. The massive 1916 Brusilov offensive casualties negatively affected Russian troop morale as evidence increased of dissatisfaction escalating in Russian Army ranks, while troop desertions escalated.

The German High Command determined not to launch a major offensive operation, particularly after the first Russian Revolution, to prevent a nationalistic response against the Germans during the escalating domestic and political turmoil. The German Army transported Nicolai Lenin to Russia in a sealed train to encourage further revolution, because his Bolshevik party was the only one demanding immediate peace. The German government spent vast amounts of money attempting to destabilize the Russian provisional government to assist the Bolsheviks in seizing power.

During mid-March 1917, following the revolution, the tsarist officer corps commenced a purge, which negatively affected the army's possibility of launching an offensive soon. Order had to be restored in army ranks as well as strengthening and disciplining rear echelon troops. The General Staff, however, determined that it must await the full effects of the March revolution before commencing any major offensive action.

On the Italian front, the Tenth Isonzo battle failed to achieve General Cadorna's objective of conquering Trieste, and the Italians required time before they could launch their next offensive operation, the Eleventh Isonzo battle. In the Balkans the Romanian Army was being reorganized, while the Albanian front remained quiet. On the Macedonian front a Salonika offensive had failed to defeat the Bulgarians but no major military activity occurred on the Balkan front during 1917.[2] Between March 11 and 17, an offensive failed at Monistar, and between May 5 and 19 at Vardar against the Bulgarians. On February 1, 1917, the Germans unleashed their fateful unrestricted submarine warfare that brought the United States into the war on April 6.

After the German Stokhod military action, the Central Powers released propaganda leaflets and their troops fraternized with Russian soldiers as many of those increasingly deserted the ranks. Political activism and indiscipline increased within Russian Army ranks. Late in March, General Brusilov determined to launch an offensive, but continuing troop morale problems forced its delay. Then on June 4 Brusilov replaced Alexseev in the army hierarchy.

On March 26 Entente military leaders requested that the Russians soon launch an offensive, but General Alexseev, still chief of the General Staff, realized that because of the recent revolutionary events the Russian Army could not launch a major offensive operation. He determined that one could not be launched before May 1, 1917, when weather conditions would have improved. Therefore, he signed a directive ordering commanders to commence preparations for it.

On May 12, some Central Power front commanders invited their Russian counterparts to negotiate an armistice, while until the end of the month troops fraternized along the entire front. On May 18 Alexander Kerensky became war minister. Believing that Russia must remain active in the war, he attempted to prepare the army to launch an offensive. The army, however, remained in disarray, while declining railroad capacity further complicated its logistical matters. Late supply deliveries to the front resulted in food shortages becoming endemic. Furthermore, Russian industry could not produce the necessary equipment to properly prepare the army for a major offensive operation, although it possessed sufficient artillery pieces and shells.

The major Russian Army problem remained the lack of discipline and general war weariness, particularly following the bloody 1916 Brusilov offensive. Given the poor condition of Russian forces on the German fronts, War Minister Kerensky determined to launch an offensive in East Galicia against the weakened Austro-Hungarian foe. The proposed offensive operation did not remain secret for long. Central Power military leaders noticed the increased tsarist aerial and artillery activity as early as April particularly through aerial reconnaissance. In addition, Russian prisoners of war reported that Kerensky had visited the front lines during May, encouraging the troops to prepare for a major offensive operation. As Russian High Command carried out redeployment efforts to replace troops not completely loyal to the provisional government, it became increasingly obvious to Central Power command that the anticipated offensive would be launched in the Zborov and Brzezany areas south of the Dniester River near Stanislau.

The intensive Central Power propaganda efforts terminated at the beginning of June. By then, Russian military activity opposite the Habsburg South Army's front positions had raised the possibility of an attack being launched in the near future. Nighttime Russian activity included the redeployment of several units, including the VII Corps at Kolomea and the XXXIV and II Corps to the south Dniester River area, which increased the possibility of an attack on Habsburg Third Army positions in the Stanislau area.

Austro-Hungarian units occupied the southwest Eastern front positions, where the main Kerensky offensive struck in late June 1917. Habsburg Second Army deployed north of Lemberg, while South Army, consisting of four German, three Habsburg and one Turkish division occupied positions opposite Brzezany just south of Lemberg. The Third Army defended north of the Dniester River, the Seventh Army south of Kalusz.

Habsburg South Army command prepared for an anticipated attack by twenty-three to twenty-five enemy divisions. Russian military and political leadership realized that if the projected offensive failed, it could prove disastrous for the provisional government. During the winter of 1916 eleven new Russian infantry divisions had been formed, and all divisions except Garde units had been reduced from sixteen battalions to twelve through army reorganization in January 1917. The extra four battalions helped to create sixty-two new infantry divisions by March, though problems arose supplying the new divisions with suitable complements of artillery. Russian High Command accumulated vital supplies and trained the new troop formations for the pending operation. *Stavka* correctly anticipated that the Western Entente allies would also launch offensives to support their effort. But the key event that intervened was the internal turmoil caused by the initial Russian Revolution.

The Russian High Command was also reorganized because of the revolution and, within a week, two *Stavka* and six army front commanders were cashiered. During the next three months, dozens of division and corps commanders were replaced. Further purges during the summer completed the cleansing of the officer corps. The Russian German front commander, General Ruzskii, also lost his position. The command purge naturally produced significant unrest in the ranks, while providing further excuse to delay launching a major offensive.

During the latter half of June, the Russians accelerated preparations to launch their major offensive, transferring four corps to the Habsburg Second Army southern flank area. This made it appear that they intended to attack between Tarnopol and Zborov. By the end of the month, deserters and decoded Russian radio messages made it clear that they intended to attack Habsburg South Army at Zloczov.

The decision to launch the July 1917 Kerensky offensive was determined at a December 1916 meeting at Mohilev, but, as detailed, the Russian Army had to be reorganized following the 1916 Brusilov offensive. Only minor military operations would be launched on the German front to bind the troops there. The offensive would maintain the initiative, but most of the troops were not Russian, but Finnish, Siberian and other nationalities, significantly also a Czech Legion brigade.

The demoralization and indiscipline within the army ranks caused Kerensky to determine that the army had to wait at least three to four months before new units could be trained to serve as reinforcements for present frontline troops. This in turn forced a revision of plans for launching the Kerensky offensive; a major operation could not be launched before July 1, 1917. War Minister Kerensky had to justify the further delay in Russian military activity to his Entente allies.

The main tsarist attack would strike on the Habsburg front, with secondary attacks to be launched simultaneously. The attacking troops represented a major advantage in troop and artillery numbers. The strategic objective became to seize the provincial capital of Galicia, Lemberg, and to break through Habsburg defensive positions in East Galicia. The immediate objective became the oil fields near Drohobyoz. The first attack phase required the reconquering of the western bank of the Zlota Lipa River, then to drive northwest through Zloczov–Gliniany. Russian Eleventh and Seventh Army flank forces would attack into the region near the railroad Zborov–Krasne.

Secondary attacks would be launched on neighboring fronts to bind Central Power troops there.

By the end of May, Habsburg command leadership anticipated an enemy attack because of the increased enemy military activity, particularly in the Stanislau area. The critical question remained as to whether the Russian infantry would actually fight, because of the recent revolutionary experiences and Kerensky's visits to the Russian front.

During early June, Habsburg Third and Second Army commanders did not anticipate an immediate enemy attack, but the South Army command did because of increased enemy activities on its front. During the first half of June, strong Russian forces began to deploy against South and Second Army's southern flank positions. Behind the Russian front four corps had been transferred to this region, soon followed by one infantry and two cavalry corps from the south Dniester River front.

Increased enemy artillery activity in the Stanislau area also raised the possibility of action there. Meanwhile, Central Power preparations continued for the anticipated enemy attack. Although a Russian offensive was anticipated during the second half of June, it did not transpire. The German General Staff surmised that this resulted from the Russians' necessity to restock their artillery shell supplies. Meanwhile, Habsburg Second Army reconnaissance missions indicated that multiple enemy corps were massing before their front lines.

Habsburg Supreme Command anticipated that the main offensive would be launched toward Tarnopol and Zborov against 33. Infantry Division, but that attack might camouflage where the main assault would commence. Around June 20 the first serious indications of a major operation became evident, but the question remained as to whether Russian infantry would actually fight.

The Russians might also attack Habsburg Third Army positions in the Stanislau area, while on the South Army front ten Central Power divisions were now opposed by almost twenty-five enemy units, which appeared to be preparing to attack. South Army command felt confident that its troops could repel an enemy effort if they received additional artillery formations, particularly heavy guns with sufficient shell supplies. Habsburg artillery units fired light field artillery barrages against the anticipated enemy assembly areas.

The offensive was launched on a 65-kilometer front with 31 infantry divisions and 800 light-, 158 middle- and 370 heavy-artillery pieces. The major attack was launched on the Russian Eleventh Army south flank along both sides of Zborov and Kuniuchy. The attacking forces included Third Army consisting of five corps and reserve formations. Seventh Army's five corps (XLI, VII, XXX, IV and XXI) would attack through Brzezany with the II Garde Corps in reserve. Russian forces deployed between June 25 and 29.

A two-day artillery bombardment preceded the July 1 offensive, but contrary to *Stavka* plans Eleventh and Seventh armies' operations did not commence simultaneously. The Eleventh Army attack against Habsburg Second Army was launched first, the Seventh Army effort twenty-four hours later against the South Army. This resulted in separate battles fought at Zborov and Brzezany, on the same terrain as the 1916 Brusilov campaign, but with significantly larger troop numbers.

During June 1917, Central Power military planners prepared what they considered suitable countermeasures against the Russian operation for when it was unleashed. The Allies anticipated it to be launched between Group Böhm-Ermolli and South Army positions. The major effort was anticipated in the area of Zloczov so a powerful counteroffensive was planned to be launched in that area toward Tarnopol, its left flank forces protected by the Sereth River.

As the Kerensky offensive launching date approached, conditions on the Russian and Austro-Hungarian home fronts and front lines had steadily worsened. Both suffered from severe food, fuel and raw material shortages, while troop exhaustion proliferated through the ranks and civilians and soldiers alike received inadequate sustenance (as well as insufficient military equipment and material supplies). Both witnessed an insatiable demand for more manpower. Black market activity assumed increasing significance, while industrial strikes and food riots reached epidemic proportions. The accelerating domestic hardship and continuing battlefield casualties negatively affected patriotic loyalty toward both empires that existed during the first years of the war. Steadily increasing war weariness and worsening economic hardships plummeted morale even further. For Austria-Hungary this partially resulted from the tightening effects of the British blockade; for Russia the Central Power blockade of the Black Sea, both of which produced enormous internal suffering. Such negative factors produced increasing dissatisfaction in the Dual Monarchy from the Czechs, Poles and South Slavs and in Russian society in general. Increasing starvation conditions in cities did not bode well for both incompetent governments.

On the Western Front, the Nivelle offensive had failed miserably and reputed "mutinies" had broken out in many French combat units that resulted in the French command halting major offensive efforts. In Russia, General Brusilov replaced General Alexseev as chief of the General Staff because he supported Kerensky's concept of launching an offensive.

Habsburg Army Group Böhm-Ermolli's troops were deployed against the Russian Eleventh and Seventh armies. The Russian Eleventh Army deployed eleven infantry divisions at the front, six infantry and one cavalry division in reserve, as well as possibly two to three additional divisions. The Russian Seventh Army deployed seventeen infantry divisions in its front lines; eight infantry and two cavalry divisions served as a reserve force. Forty-two to forty-seven Russian infantry divisions ultimately deployed against Habsburg Army Group Böhm-Ermolli. The Army Group consisted of only twenty-four infantry and two cavalry divisions, presenting the Russians a very significant numerical advantage. The Army Group also benefited from airplanes for initial aerial superiority.

The planned German counterattack against a Russian offensive assumed that all enemy assault troops would have already been committed to the battle. German troops would strike enemy flank positions after the enemy reserve formations had been committed to the battle. German command would rapidly railroad deploy six to seven infantry plus one cavalry division and two field artillery regiments from the Western front for the counteroffensive effort. Surprise would ensure battle success, therefore participating troops would not be informed, or receive details, about the mission. General Conrad approved the German plan and ordered eighteen heavy and thirteen howitzer batteries from other Habsburg units to be redeployed to Army Group Böhm-Ermolli. This activity occurred concurrently with the Italian front Eleventh Isonzo battle.

On June 27, German *Oberost* command released orders to launch a counterattack against any potential enemy offensive extending from the areas of Zloczov to Tarnopol, the operational objective being to attain the line Tarnopol–Czernovitz (capital city of the Bukovina). In the interim Army Group Böhm-Ermolli received orders to launch an offensive before any major enemy action occurred. The preemptive Habsburg attack would consist of three infantry divisions on its left flank at the Sereth River. The main attack objective was Zloczov with a secondary assault to be launched over the Zlota Gora. That attack objective involved decisively neutralizing any enemy threat against the Habsburg northern flank positions.

The Habsburg preemptive attack echelon units deployed in a relatively small area at 33. Infantry Division positions, where the potential attack was assumed. Strong reserve units stood poised to follow the attacking units. The key factor involved the Habsburg assault columns breaking through the Russian front to roll up their flank positions then to pursue the anticipated retreating enemy troops. It was determined that at least seven divisions had to be deployed for the main effort, while a secondary force consisting of three infantry divisions and thirty heavy-artillery batteries advanced along the Sereth River toward Tarnopol. A recurring problem entailed the regular supplying of food for infantry troops and feed for cavalry horses.

Meanwhile, the Russian Eleventh Army had anchored its right flank positions near Zloczov, Seventh Army in the center-front area at Brzezany, while Eighth Army deployed south of the Dniester River to launch a flanking maneuver toward Kalusz.

The Russian Eleventh Army finally unleashed its attack on July 1, Seventh Army a day later. This created major problems for both armies later and weakened the attack effect. Thus, separate battles erupted at Zborov and Brzezany. Russian Seventh Army's eighteen divisions attacked South Army right flank positions at Zloczov, where only four infantry divisions defended the front lines with two divisions in reserve. Initially, the defending troops had only one infantry regiment from two divisions as a reserve unit.

Five Habsburg infantry divisions received the brunt of Russian Eleventh Army's eight attacking divisions, which struck the Habsburg XX Corps deployed on the South Army northern flank sector at Zloczov. Meanwhile, the designated German counterattack troops included the XXIII Reserve Corps (five to six infantry divisions), the 16. Reserve Division and one cavalry division.[3] Russian forces launched their offensive before the Habsburg Second Army front initiated their own operation, as five German infantry divisions and artillery batteries soon had to be deployed behind Army Group Böhm-Ermolli to halt its ensuing retreat.

On July 1, the heaviest Eastern front artillery barrages to date targeted the Zloczov area where Czech troops defended the front lines. Massed Russian forces attacked Habsburg Second Army's IX Corps and a portion of the South Army. The Russian Seventh Army stormed positions at Brzezany, Eleventh Army Zborov. Russian artillery bombardments commenced at 4 a.m. then rose in intensity. The offensive came as no surprise to the troops defending Brzezany and Koniuchy, because Russian deserters had alerted the defenders of the approaching operation.

Habsburg defensive artillery fire failed to halt the mass Russian attack that struck Koniuchy at 9 a.m. Habsburg Infantry Regiment 81's lines quickly ruptured, while strong enemy forces advanced toward 19. Infantry Division's southern flank Zborov positions. That division contained many Czech soldiers.

Russian troop numerical superiority and lack of Habsburg reserve forces resulted in an Infantry Regiment 75 (19. Infantry Division) defeat and several-kilometer retreat, sustaining severe losses.[4] Ultimately, Habsburg Infantry Regiments 35 and 75 troops halted the enemy advance, but at great human cost. When the grossly outnumbered predominantly Czech regiments could not be reinforced, the attacking Russian Czech Legion brigade, composed of many former Habsburg soldiers, renewed its attack the next day, again penetrating Infantry Regiment 35 lines to disastrous effect even though all reserve units had been hurled into the battle. Habsburg 19. Infantry Division, ordered to hold its first-line positions at any cost, had its units cut off and surrounded, which bared the flank of the neighboring *Honvéd* Infantry Regiment 32, resulting in multiple casualties to that unit.

After Russian units broke through the Koniuchy defensive lines they fanned out and captured numerous prisoners of war as they advanced. The several-kilometer-wide gap in Habsburg defensive lines assisted the enemy's significant progress. German forces were rushed to the threatened front and eventually succeeded in halting Russian progress. When fresh troops arrived on July 2 the enemy advance was partially halted at the third defense line kilometers rearwards. A major enemy breakthrough was thus thwarted. The rapidly deployed German reserve forces prevented major Russian territorial gains and worse military defeat. German command continued to prepare its planned counterattack originally scheduled for July 12.

In the meantime, Russian Eleventh Army's six infantry divisions achieved early and significant success against Habsburg Second Army's X Corps, forcing it to retreat to Zloczov. Russian Seventh Army forces pushed South Army troops rearward almost thirty miles. Many Habsburg troops simply threw down their weapons and fled, while thousands surrendered. Enemy units seized major stocks of war supplies from the retreating troops, but lacked sufficient reserve units to follow up their success and rapidly outpaced their supply lines. This caused the offensive to initially falter then halt. Russian troop discipline also began to suffer, partially because of the enormous casualties.

The critical Habsburg military situation forced the Germans to immediately deploy two and a half divisions originally designated for the counterattack force. These German reinforcements rapidly reversed the increasingly unfavorable Habsburg military situation, partially because of their excellent interior lines and vastly superior railroad network. On July 2, *Oberost* dispatched a division to Zloczov to reestablish the situation at that endangered area, while the Russian Eleventh and Seventh armies' 240 infantry battalions assaulted 83 Habsburg units.[5]

On the same day, the few surviving Infantry Regiments 35 and 75 troops, with some reinforcements, halted the Russian attack at the third Habsburg defensive line, preventing a major enemy breakthrough.[6] Both regiments sustained severe casualties, mostly reported as "missing in action," during their rapid retreat. IX Corps troop stand dropped from sixteen thousand to seven thousand, while two of its shattered divisions were replaced by the few available German troops. The Kerensky offensive with the notorious Czech versus Czech battle emphasized the seriousness of the growing nationality problem for the Austro-Hungarian Army. Meanwhile, German divisions designated for the Central Power counteroffensive continued to replace defeated and retreating Habsburg troops.

After the first Russian Revolution the famous Czech brigade, comprised mostly of Russian Czechs and some former Habsburg prisoners of war, was one of the few units that remained loyal to the tsarist government during spring 1917. It spearheaded the Russian attack against Habsburg defensive positions manned mainly by Czech troops near Zborov. Lacking sufficient reserve troop numbers, defending Habsburg forces could not launch a counteroffensive, thus were forced to retreat from their first trench line positions, creating a disastrous military situation on that front sector.

A lingering question that involved whether Russian Czech brigade troops contacted Infantry Regiment 35 and 75 Czech soldiers before they attacked them has been answered in a recent book.[7] Some senior Habsburg officers accused those Czech troops of not resisting the enemy attack. Habsburg Supreme Command demanded an investigation, which proved difficult because most of the participating troops were dead or had become prisoners of war.

Conrad, naturally prejudiced against them, was convinced that Czech soldiers caused the ensuing military debacle. However, the initial charges concerning their unreliability had to be revised when German soldiers and Russian prisoners of war reported that both regiments had fulfilled their duties. The Russian attacks against Infantry Regiment 35 succeeded because of vastly superior troop numbers, the lack of Habsburg reserve formations and local commanders' multiple tactical errors.

Unavoidable traffic delays caused by terrible road conditions became a significant factor in the delay in launching the Central Power counterattack. The first transports of four reinforcing German divisions finally arrived from the Western front to rectify the unfavorable Habsburg situation.

On July 4, the Russians also launched a powerful attack against South Army, successfully repulsed by July 6–7. Again, on July 6 and 7, three Russian divisions repeatedly attacked the Habsburg Third Army 33. Infantry Division at Zloczov, forcing it to retreat over thirty miles in ten days beyond Kalusz. German troops originally designated to launch the counterattack at Zloczov, as related, had to be diverted to halt the Habsburg retrograde movement.

Russian forces on July 8 broke through the Habsburg Third Army front at Stanislau, forcing a general retreat. Again, German reserve divisions had to be quickly deployed to alleviate the situation. The Russians conquered additional territory on July 9, which required further reinforcements to be dispatched to buttress the wavering Habsburg Third Army front lines. Nevertheless, the enemy succeeded in breaking through the positions and hurling the defenders rearward. On July 11, Habsburg forces surrendered their positions at Kalusz, twenty-five kilometers behind the front. This represented the greatest extent of the Russian effort on that portion of the front.

Pouring rain on July 12 caused the Sereth and Strypa Rivers to overflow and flood roadways, delaying launching the German counterattack from July 12 to July 16. It also required additional time to deploy heavy-artillery batteries and shells, thus the counteraction had to be delayed again on July 16 because of the continuing Third Army critical situation.

Meanwhile, the twelve-day offensive terminated, hampered by the lack of food, inclement weather conditions and rapid defeat. Troops from most units suddenly refused to obey orders. The German counterattack was finally launched on a twelve-mile front on July 19 against Russian flank positions rather than a frontal assault. An intense artillery bombardment preceded the operation. Opposing Russian formations quickly disintegrated as demoralization rapidly swept through the ranks. Russian soldiers deserted in droves as

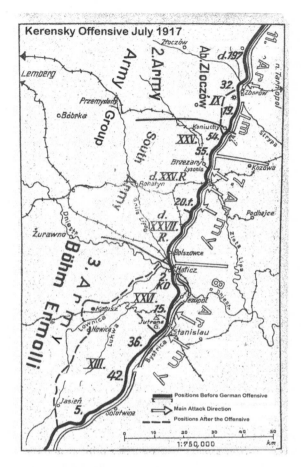

Map 10   *1917 Kerensky offensive*

troop discipline collapsed. Some units mutinied, while most soldiers simply refused to obey orders. On the first counterattack operational day, German troops advanced nine miles; their attack east of Zloczov toward the Sereth River proved a complete success following a brief intense artillery barrage. The five German and single Habsburg division improvised forces rapidly destroyed hastily prepared enemy positions.

The surprised Russian troops, which General Brusilov intended to use to launch a counterattack, retreated to the south and southeast. Favorable weather conditions assisted the success of the German counterattack. On July 20, Russian troops disappeared, retreating twenty-one kilometers, which resulted in the offensive pursuit of the defeated enemy. Roads became filled with fleeing Russian troops. The retreat extended almost two hundred kilometers from Kalusz.

On July 21 Russian units retreated so rapidly that they could not be attacked by pursing Allied troops. The Russian Eleventh Army was basically decimated. Then the Central Power advance direction shifted to the north. Tarnopol and other cities surrendered, resulting in an Eleventh Army rapid retreat forty-five kilometers behind the front lines without significant defensive resistance. All 1916 Brusilov offensive territorial gains were recaptured as well as additional land loss. On July 21 Eleventh Army received orders to attack, but did not, instead retreating. Each day witnessed further Russian retrograde movements.

On July 22, Russian troops continued their retreat movement on the entire front between the Dniester and Pruth Rivers as their front collapsed. Third and South armies pursued the Russian forces until July 25 when they retreated to south of the Carpathian Mountains. On the mountain front, Habsburg Archduke Joseph's left flank army formations could only slowly advance because Russian forces occupied more favorable defensive terrain. Central Power troops were exhausted, thus on July 23 only localized battles erupted.

After the capture of Tarnopol on July 25 Russian forces could not halt the victorious Austro-Hungarian and German forces, because their positions had become untenable. Thus, Seventh and parts of Eighth Army retreated behind the Zbrucz River. Central Power troops finally attained the Zloczov area.

On July 28, the Russians, though stiffening resistance, continued to retreat. Habsburg South Army advanced without encountering enemy opposition; however, the successful offensive would soon have to be terminated, because the troops had outdistanced their railroads, negatively affecting steady supply of ammunition, equipment and reinforcements.[8] Heavy battle erupted along the entire front on July 31, when a strong Russian attack against the Habsburg Third Army's XIII Corps was repelled.

During early August, Russian formations retreated from Galicia and the Bukovina, while German forces prepared to launch an offensive on the north German front at Riga close to the Russian capital of St. Petersburg. Czernovitz, Bukovina's capital city, surrendered on August 3, as the entire Russian front collapsed. Troop discipline evaporated as some soldiers shot their officers and most refused to continue to fight. The counteroffensive operation, however, had to be halted at the Galician frontier because of insufficient resources to successfully continue the action. Once Czernovitz fell, the campaign had practically ended by August 5.

The Kerensky offensive military disaster occurred early July in Petrograd when the Bolsheviks attempted to seize control from the provisional government. Kerensky responded by arresting many Bolshevik leaders, while Lenin fled to Finland. Their putsch attempt proved premature.

It had become obvious that there were no vital objectives for further offensive efforts as the Russians surrendered more territory than recaptured during the Brusilov offensive. This included vital cities, geographical targets or natural resources that would force Russia out of the war. Thus, conquered positions such as Stanislau, captured at great cost during the 1916 Brusilov offensive, were abandoned without any serious resistance.

Recent research has revealed that the alleged general unreliability of Czech soldiers in the Habsburg Army was largely a myth. Prejudice against Czech soldiers commenced before the war, when some General Staff officers harbored disparaging views of all Slavic troops in general, but specifically the Czechs. This eventually had a major negative effect on Slavic and non-Slavic Habsburg nationality political struggles, which intensified in 1917, resulting in the destruction of the Austro-Hungarian Empire one year later.

General Staff officers often deliberately blamed battlefield defeats, resulting from their own faulty leadership, onto specific national units, such as Czech Infantry Regiments 28 and 36 during the Carpathian Winter War and the 21. *Landwehr* Infantry Division at Cer Mountain in Serbia during the first 1914 Balkan campaign. Despite the charges that large numbers of Czech troops willingly deserted to the enemy, no proof has been produced that an entire regiment or battalion actually changed sides. Lack of such evidence did not halt nationalistic propaganda and postwar historiography, particularly in Austria and Czechoslovakia, where historical sources (in both) insisted that Czech soldiers had no desire to fight for the Dual Monarchy.[9]

Until 1918, when many Habsburg troops actually did desert, they rarely did so for nationalistic reasons. Many merely returned home not surrendering to the enemy because they were usually driven by starvation, seeking to avoid combat, or because of mounting concern for their families' welfare. The Austro-Hungarian Army was hardly unique in this respect, as the Russian Army witnessed many troop desertions as well. Nevertheless, suspected nationalist sympathies for the enemy provided an easy excuse to cover up various battlefield setbacks. Following the war, Austrian and German writers openly charged that Slavic people and soldiers failed to loyally perform their duties and conspired with the enemy, which made ultimate Central Power defeat inevitable.[10] Many postwar books and memoirs encouraged the legend of the reputed general unreliability of Czech soldiers. Perhaps predictably, the claims ignored the numerous predominantly Czech units that received commendations for bravery after halting a Russian counterattack during the Kerensky offensive and the numerous accounts of Czech bravery on the Italian front throughout the war.

Conrad specifically blamed Czech units for a number of military debacles, and the General Staff and *Reichsrat* launched an anti-Czech campaign in 1917 to investigate the reputed failure of Second Army Czech regiments to provide "proper" resistance to Russian attacks at the battle of Zborov. By the time the War Ministry attempted to directly address the accusations, Viennese newspapers had printed the story, which generated further derisive controversy.

Ironically, the Austro-Hungarian and German governments' suspicion of Czech loyalties greatly aided the cause of Czechoslovakian nationalists. Exiled Czech politicians exploited reports of Czech desertions to demand an independent Czech state and for Entente Powers to approve formation of a national Czech Army, drawn from the ranks of their prisoners of war, to fight on the Allied side. Such efforts finally convinced the English, French and United States governments to demand the reconstruction of the Austro-Hungarian monarchy into new national units to help end the war. When Austria-Hungary clung to the German alliance in 1918, although earlier Entente leaders did not intend to break up the Dual Monarchy, their policy reversed to the severe disadvantage of Austria-Hungary as its adherence to the alliance ultimately helped to lead to its downfall.

On the Italian front before spring 1917 General Cadorna commenced planning for the Tenth Isonzo battle. He intended to launch strong left flank forces against the Bainsizza Plateau, while his Third Army right flank forces attempted to achieve a breakthrough on the southern Carso Plateau, their ultimate goal, to conquer Trieste. The first phase of the operation encompassed attacking the western edge of the Bainsizza Plateau extending from Plava to Mts. Santo and San Gabriel north of the key objective Gorizia. Second Army actions had the intention to mislead General Boroević as to the location of the main offensive.

Three Italian divisions advanced toward the critical Hermada position to capture the open road to Gorizia as the main assault. As a result of the first 1917 Russian Revolution Italy had become the greatest military threat to Austria-Hungary. Inclement weather conditions (rainfall) assisted Italian offensive efforts by camouflaging the preparation measures. The Tenth Isonzo offensive encompassed the entire front, but then separated into individual battles targeting the weakest Habsburg defensive positions. The battle extended over a much larger frontage than the earlier ones and produced far more casualties.

Meanwhile, the Austro-Hungarian military situation remained bleak on that front during 1917. The Habsburg Fifth Army achieved an impressive and unanticipated recovery against the numerically superior Italian forces in 1916. Its troops still defended the Isonzo River line, had survived the 1916 Eastern front Brusilov offensive and had decisively defeated (with major German assistance) a Romanian invasion of Transylvania in late August. However, the Entente blockade increasingly worsened the escalating Habsburg shortage of food, weapons, ammunition and spare parts. Most importantly, Habsburg troop numbers had declined precipitously, a result of the enormous casualties sustained on the front.

Aware in late April that the Italians intended to launch another offensive soon, the Habsburg Army commenced preparations to defend against the renewed onslaught. Fifth Army had attained record strength, with eighteen infantry divisions including reserve formations, an additional five divisions since the last Isonzo battle. The army now consisted of 215 infantry battalions, 1,470 artillery pieces and 434 mortars; however, it also suffered from grave weaknesses. Most infantry units remained understrength and artillery batteries only possessed a limited supply of artillery shells. Fifth Army could now survive a brief battle, but not a series of attrition actions, as occurred on the Carso Plateau between September and November 1917. The Habsburg Army possessed limited staying power, thus it had to defeat attacking Italian units rapidly to preclude potential disaster.

Habsburg Supreme Command anticipated that the main Italian effort would be launched south of the Carso Plateau region, where it had consistently occurred during the previous autumn. In early May the Isonzo River front remained relatively quiet partially because of the consistent rainy and foggy weather conditions, which obscured the Italian transit of guns and supplies to the front lines. Radio traffic also remained desultory until the weather began to improve by the second week of the month, while deserters provided information on the anticipated Italian offensive to Habsburg interrogators.

On April 19 the Italians released preliminary orders to launch an offensive on a front extending from the Tolmein bridgehead to Gorizia toward the Vipacco Valley and strategic Hermada positions. In the meantime, Habsburg troops received new equipment and training, some troops learning storm trooper tactics.

On April 19 and 20 Habsburg divisions halted attacks between Mts. Santo and San Gabriel. With good artillery support they halted the attacks at Vodice and Mt. San Gabriel although battle there continued. Italian Third Army attacked Vipacco Valley positions but was halted despite huge amounts of Italian gas and granite shells being expended. Both sides sustained bloody losses as major Italian attacks failed to conquer Mt. San Gabriel.

As often occurred the Italians failed to expand on initial successes and persistently lacked effective unit coordination. They also misused their vast numerical superiority and often inserted reinforcements tardily. The Habsburg Army had meanwhile increased its number of battalions by sixty. Italian artillery launched prolonged deadly barrages against defending positions as the Italians attempted to seize the Bainsizza Plateau.

The entire Adriatic coastline became enflamed, the Italian fleet even participating in the bombardments until Habsburg coastal artillery forced the warships away. The Italians unleashed destructive fire from Plava to the coastline on a fifty-kilometer front. Italian troops then crossed the Isonzo River at multiple locations, continuing to unleash massive artillery barrages against enemy defensive positions. Repeated attacks were launched, but when Habsburg XXIV Corps could not halt the attack it created a highly critical situation.

The Italian artillery barrages that commenced on May 12 were the heaviest to date on this front. The Italians employed over 2,100 artillery pieces, almost 1,000 mortars and 4,000 machine guns, targets extending from the northern portion of the Bainsizza Plateau, northeast of Gorizia, to the Adriatic Sea thirty miles to the south. On May 12 and 13 Italian artillery fire killed and maimed thousands of Habsburg troops, destroyed hundreds of trenches, machine-gun nests, supply dumps and command posts.

Cadorna's military objective during the first phase of the Tenth Isonzo offensive encompassed enlarging the Plava bridgehead, then attacking the Hermada positions on the Carso Plateau and securing a foothold and flank positions on the Bainsizza Plateau. That required conquering Mts. Kuk, Vodice, Santo and San Gabriel. After launching a diversionary attack Second Army would deploy its forces toward the Gorizia bridgehead.

Italian Third Army unleashed massive artillery barrages, commencing battle that stretched from the Tolmein bridgehead south. Italian troops attacked in simultaneous waves from north of Plava and Zagora to mountainous Kuk and Vodice. Italian artillery focused on Habsburg XVII Corps positions while Italian Second Army deployed at the key bases of Gorizia, Mts. San Gabriel and Santo. The heaviest attack would initially be east of Gorizia to enable Italian troops to advance to the Vipacco Valley. Then they would attack the high terrain east of Plava and Zagora to advance to Kuk and Vodice.[11]

The Italians initially had to secure their flank positions on the Bainsizza Plateau before attacking the Habsburg mountain defensive positions. Their highest priority, where earlier Italian attacks had only gained a foothold while sacrificing several infantry divisions, became to smash through Habsburg lines at the Plava bridgehead.

At noon on May 14 following a forty-hour artillery bombardment an offensive commenced at the upper Bainsizza Plateau area at Hill 383 that extended to the Adriatic Sea. Fifth Army defenders received orders to defend their positions to the last man as the intense barrages tore the troops and their positions to pieces. It became impossible to deliver reinforcements and sorely needed ammunition. Artillery fire intensified against VII Corps positions. Tremendous artillery bombardments continued both day and night, the Italians unleashing major assaults at Zagora and Mts. Santo and San Gabriel. Storm attacks targeted beyond Gorizia and its defending 58. Infantry Division. Italian Caproni bombers stuck Habsburg artillery positions without resistance.

The Italian forces attacking Hill 383 consisted of five regiments of fifteen battalions. After twenty-three months of intense battle, "bloody 383" finally fell to the Italians. Within three hours 1,521 defenders became casualties. The Italian Army had attained its first objective; its next would be a mile downstream from Hill 383, the village of Zagora defended by Croats and Serbian troops. Again, General Boroević demanded that the troops defend their positions to the death. The closest of the three saints was now Mt. Santo (Holy Mountain) where the summit was literally blown off during multiple artillery attacks. Other targets included Zagora and Mts. Santo and San Gabriel.

Five columns of Italian soldiers attacked the northeastern spur of Mt. Kuk positions, until the defenders ran out of ammunition. Habsburg troops also absorbed enormous losses including from friendly artillery fire. Italian artillery fire destroyed hundreds of trenches, machine-gun nests, ammunition depots and command posts. If the Habsburg troops advanced beyond the Bainsizza Plateau there were few natural defensive positions for them to establish.

Most Habsburg troops had become casualties within forty-eight hours, which severely affected troop morale. Italian attention turned to Vodice to concentrate efforts on the western edge of the Bainsizza Plateau, principally Mt. Santo and Vodice, then the base of Mt. San Gabriel, the ultimate objective. Meanwhile, the Italians replenished their depleted ranks with recruits and unleashed massed high-explosive artillery fire and deadly crossfire against Habsburg positions. The eventual loss of the Vodice position represented a serious military setback and psychological blow for the defending troops. The Italian High Command correctly sensed that the defending troops were close to complete collapse, thus they continued their attacks, but their efforts were often halted by defensive artillery fire.

Italian artillery barrages literally annihilated the Croatian defenders on Mt. Santo, the savage battle comparable to the earlier bloodbaths at Mts. Sabatino and San Michele. Italian VI and VII Corps initially attempted to break through the defensive lines east of Gorizia, launching eleven brigades into the area between Mt. San Gabriel and the Vipacco Valley, but that effort failed. The 58. Habsburg Infantry Division defended Mt. San Gabriel, greatly assisted by effective defensive artillery support. Meanwhile, Italian Third Army launched attacks to finally capture territory beyond Gorizia. Italian forces also attempted to conquer the entire Bainsizza Plateau after seizing Hill 383 and much of the Plava position. Caproni bombers continued to machine-gun and bomb Habsburg artillery positions without any countereffect.

On the next day, May 15, the Italians continued their attacks, launching three divisions at the Plava bridgehead. Mass attacks against Mt. San Gabriel also targeted Mt. Kuk. Within hours nearly all Habsburg defenders had become casualties. The bloody battle at Zagora annihilated two battalions of Infantry Regiment 22, killing 2,034 soldiers. Hand-to-hand battle erupted at Mt. Kuk and the Vodice area. The Habsburgs' Vodice line, ordered to be held at any price, signified death for its defenders. Unfortunate soldiers of the XVII Corps suffered under merciless artillery fire that cut off any retreat routes. Italian troops also sustained major casualties during the two-day battle.

On May 16 the attackers regrouped their forces then hurled five brigades against the Habsburg positions at Mts. Kuk and Vodice, the keys to capturing Mt. Santo. The exhausted defending troops had received no food or water for three days, yet successfully defended their positions until May 17, when their ammunition ran out. On May 18 the Italians turned their attention to the new defensive positions, protecting the land bridge to Mt. San Gabriel. They continued to concentrate overwhelming attacks at the western edge of the Bainsizza Plateau. Their depleted ranks had been refilled by new recruits. Defending troops on Vodice did not surrender an inch of territory on May 18, while during the night of May 19–20 the Habsburgs inserted forty-eight additional artillery pieces into the defensive Bainsizza Plateau positions. The attacking troops sustained up to 60 percent losses of their troop numbers, while reaching the crest of Mt. Santo. They were, however, driven off as constant battle continued against the Habsburg XVII Corps.

To May 20 multiple mass attacks continued against various portions of the Gorizia defensive area. The Italian secondary attack mission continued to be to convince General Boroević to redeploy his reserves from the Carso Plateau, the main Italian objective. Artillery fire preceded massed infantry attacks northeast of Gorizia, but each was driven back by heavy defensive artillery fire that caused enormous casualties. But the enemy ploy succeeded; it drew General Boroević's attention from the main offensive launched on the southern Carso Plateau. During the battle, 7. Infantry Division dropped from 6,900 troops to 1,700 within forty-eight hours. Two days of battle followed, slowly de-escalating, so that by May 26 only minor skirmishes occurred. Many Habsburg troops sacrificed their lives defending their positions.

Habsburg VII and XXII corps troops were hurled back and, possessing few reserve troops, their situation rapidly became hopeless. During the first offensive assault, seventeen brigades initially attacked, fourteen following in the second echelon. As during earlier operations, smoke and dust camouflaged the assault movements, resulting in the Habsburg forward trenches almost immediately being overrun, which signified the loss of half of the southern Carso positions. The Italian Third Army also made impressive gains further south where the defenders protected the approaches to Trieste.

The Habsburg Isonzo Army had so far surrendered Hill 383, Mt. Kuk and the summit of Vodice but its soldiers still maintained a portion of Mt. Santo. The weary defenders, possessing no reserve forces, witnessed their numbers declining rapidly. The remaining troops could only hope to survive until reinforcing divisions arrived from the Russian front in a few weeks.

Inclement weather conditions delayed the offensive on the Carso Plateau until May 23. In the interim General Boroević deployed sorely required reinforcements. Nevertheless, the aggressing forces advanced one and a quarter kilometers, capturing three Habsburg defensive lines. The Italian Third Army success was impressive compared to Western front warfare achievements. The defending Habsburg XVII Corps sustained twelve thousand casualties, two-thirds of which died, raising the total losses on the Habsburg front to thirty thousand. Several regiments were annihilated. Repeated Italian storm attacks continued toward the Vipacco Valley, while two-thirds of the Italian troops became casualties. Habsburg VII Corps repelled all bloody assaults. Casualty numbers represented two times as many as in any earlier Isonzo River battles.

Thus ended the northern phase of the Tenth Isonzo battle, introducing a short pause. The more decisive second phase commenced on the Carso Plateau, when on May 23 the Italian Third Army assaulted all enemy positions extending to the Adriatic Sea, supported by the most powerful artillery bombardment ever witnessed on the Isonzo River front.[12] A total of 1,250 artillery pieces and nearly 600 mortars blasted the eleven-mile Carso front. An Italian artillery piece was emplaced every thirty feet. Hundreds of thousands of shells were fired each hour, a total of one million, which signified that twenty shells struck every foot of the front. The impact proved devastating, far worse than ever before. Habsburg communications were disrupted and supply routes destroyed. The six defending divisions were thrown into disarray, as few reserves were available to replace the mounting losses. The situation appeared hopeless for the Habsburg defenders.

Bloody day and night battles ensued along the southern Carso Plateau front on May 24 and 25, but the murderous skirmishes only bled both forces white and destroyed any troop morale. All troops became exhausted after such devastating battle. By dawn on May 27 the Carso Plateau fighting had terminated, the offensive operation ending on May 28. By May 27 forty-one Italian Isonzo front regiments had sustained more than 50 percent casualties since May 13, which accelerated defeatism and resignation within their ranks. Cadorna blamed his exhausted troops for the lack of battlefield success.

Meanwhile, the senseless battle of Oritaga commenced on the northern Asiago Plateau. The 1916 *Straf* offensive had enabled Habsburg troops to seize the Asiero and Asiago Heights, which General Cadorna considered a serious threat. Thus, a week after the Tenth Isonzo battle terminated he launched an attack to push Habsburg troops back on that plateau. This produced bloody battle that resulted in no Italian gain but the loss of twenty-five thousand soldiers. The battle had no strategic or tactical goals that could be achieved.

On June 18 inclement weather conditions including wind, rainfall and fog affected battlefield conditions.[13] Massed frontal assault troops presented excellent targets against the Oritaga mountain summit. On the next day, June 19, friendly fire again killed many troops. Aerial warfare also raged as Italian troops absorbed increasingly heavy losses. The enormous casualties were comparable to any of the Isonzo River battles. Italian commanders did not heed terrain, weather conditions or topography in launching their offensive efforts. The senseless attack was canceled on June 20.

In the interim General Boroević received two reinforcing divisions from the Russian front to help replace the enormous losses. Then, on June 3, a Habsburg counterattack utilizing new tactics along a three-mile front on the

Carso Plateau produced a resounding success as the Italian Army exhibited increasing signs of exhaustion and defeatism. Thus, unexpectedly, Habsburg troops retook the original frontline positions, driving the Italian defenders from Hermada. The Italians had gained hardly two kilometers before the front finally quietened down.

Habsburg troops had miraculously accomplished another major reversal of fortune, but their situation remained cloudy. The result of the greatest Italian offensive to date nearly annihilated Boroević's Isonzo Army. Battle losses had been appalling, the defenders sustaining a nearly 60 percent casualty rate, most sustained within the first days of battle. In addition, the Habsburg Isonzo Army lost 23,400 soldiers as prisoners of war, with total casualties reaching 75,000. The Isonzo Army nearly collapsed under the strain of the massive Italian offensive, while the material losses seriously strained already scarce Habsburg resources. Habsburg forces could not afford to fight such attrition battles, both in human and economic terms. One more major Italian attack could pierce the Habsburg defensive lines.

The Italians had achieved their second greatest territorial gain of all the Isonzo offensives. Their 159,000 casualties included 36,000 dead, 96,000 wounded and 27,000 captured, or a 25 percent loss rate. The Italians began the battle with 280,000 troops, supported by 2,200 guns and 1,000 mortars. Italian troop morale again reached crisis levels, including widespread disillusionment and disaffection. The significant result of the battle was the seizure of an Italian foothold on the Eastern Isonzo River bank, from which further assaults could be initiated, but General Cadorna had anticipated winning a decisive victory.

This offensive lasted longer than the previous Isonzo campaigns, but the Italians failed to achieve their decisive victory. Intervening factors included Russian weakness and the collapse of the Western front offensives earlier in the year. Casualties far exceeded previous Isonzo River battles. Prisoner-of-war troop numbers equaled that of three full infantry divisions.

The majority of Habsburg casualties resulted from artillery fire as the number of Italian artillery pieces had increased significantly after each campaign. The Italians suffered severe losses, but, sustaining enormous losses, the Habsburgs had won a great defensive victory although their numbers dropped from 165,000 to 76,300 troops (7,300 dead, 45,000 wounded and 23,400 became prisoners of war).

Following the Tenth Isonzo battle, Cadorna transferred troops from the northern Trentino front to the Isonzo River battle area. After transferring twelve infantry divisions from the Alpine front he deployed fifty-one infantry divisions between the Tolmein bridgehead and Adriatic Sea on a sixty-kilometer front. The Eleventh Isonzo offensive commenced after three months of stockpiling sufficient artillery shells for the operation.

The focus of the offensive became the Bainsizza Plateau in the area between Gorizia and the Tolmein bridgehead along the middle Isonzo River. If Italian forces successfully conquered the Bainsizza Plateau their troops could shift southward toward Mts. Santo and San Gabriel, the protective mountain terrain behind Gorizia.

The Italians possessed an overwhelming advantage in firepower and manpower. Fifty-one infantry divisions countered twenty Habsburg and 5,200 artillery pieces were countered by 2,000 Habsburg guns. The attacking Second Army's mission became to eliminate the critical Tolmein bridgehead over the Isonzo River and capture the Bainsizza Plateau. Third Army must pierce Habsburg lines on the Carso Plateau.

By the end of the vicious campaign Italian forces threatened to break through Habsburg front lines. However, during this phase they sacrificed two opportunities that would have made a decisive difference in the outcome of the battles. Deficient leadership allowed pauses in both cases that Habsburg forces could use to recover and prepare new defensive positions.

Preceding the Eleventh Isonzo battle, Italian artillery barrages extended from Mrzli Vrh to the Adriatic Sea. The Italians attempted to build bridges over the Isonzo River under Habsburg artillery fire, producing heavy losses. For the approaching battle the Italians utilized 4,000 artillery pieces versus the Habsburg 1,434 and 1,700 mortars against 112 Habsburg. To Habsburg disadvantage 30 percent of their guns proved inoperable.[14]

During early summer 1917 Italian lines extended above the Asiago Plateau and basically ran north–south from the Brenta to the Assa Valley facing Austrian positions entrenched along the line of some two-thousand-meter-high mountains. The Eleventh Isonzo offensive was designed to achieve a favorable position to attack the Val Sugana Valley after the Austrian counterattack was launched on Mt. Hermada between June 4 and 10 during appalling weather. The effort was immediately repulsed except on the northern flank of XX Corps, where it terminated the next day because of the inclement weather conditions. A Habsburg counterattack renewed on June 18 achieved little, but sacrificed twenty-four thousand men.[15]

Cadorna sought to preserve the initiative and coordinate operations with the British and French on the Western front, where the British launched their Passchendaele offensive, the French their fateful Nivelle endeavor and the Russian's Kerensky July campaign. Locally, the Italian offensive attempted to create a stronger defensive front resting on the Bainsizza Plateau as northern and southern bulwarks linked by the Gorizia basin. Third Army's battle to seize Trieste received support from 1,800 guns and 1,882 mortars.

Third Army attacked the Comen Heights and key Hermada positions and Second Army the Bainsizza Plateau; the Italians successfully advanced twelve kilometers. The Second Army commander extended his front as far north as Mrzli Vrh, the mass of troops targeting the Tolmein bridgehead.[16]

The Italian offensive extended along a seventy-kilometer front, assuming gigantic proportions, with Italian artillery firing every caliber weapon to destroy connecting Habsburg trenches and telephone lines. On August 18 annihilating artillery fire targeted Habsburg positions extending from Plava to the Adriatic Sea coast.

Habsburg artillery counterfire could not neutralize the ensuing enemy hurricane barrages, then Italian troops attacked the southwest portion of the Bainsizza Plateau and seized the terrain to the northwest. Defending Habsburg XXIV Corps troops possessed little resistance capability after their earlier bloody encounters. Yet the major Italian attacks failed along that forty-kilometer front.

The ultimate Italian objective became to conquer Mt. San Gabriel. On August 19 and 20 Habsburg defenders repulsed the enemy attacks between Mts. Santo and San Gabriel largely resulting from excellent Habsburg artillery support. As battle raged through the night Habsburg units counterattacked at Vodice and Mt. San Gabriel. In the interim the Italian Third Army attacked Habsburg Vipacco Valley positions, but were repulsed in spite of heavy Italian artillery support. Then, the Habsburg XXIV Corps could not halt the attacks, creating a highly critical situation.

As so often occurred on this front the Italians did not continue their initial successes partially because of lack of coordination between attacking units. Thus, they failed to utilize their great numerical superiority as well as deploying reinforcements too late to affect the outcome of battle.

Italian airstrikes supported Italian operations on the thirty-six-kilometer-long front on August 19 and 20. Attacks launched between Mts. Santo and San Gabriel were hurled back. When the Italian VI Corps attacked Habsburg Mt. Santo bloody losses ensured that the troops could no longer launch major offensive operations.

On August 20 the situation at the Habsburg XV and XXIV Corps inner flanks steadily worsened as heavy Italian artillery fire concentrated on the Bainsizza Plateau. Habsburg forces could not launch a counterattack against the massed enemy artillery fire, which Habsburg artillery could not neutralize.

On August 21 Habsburg troops retreated, surrendering the northwestern portion of the Bainsizza Plateau but establishing new defensive lines about a mile from the Isonzo River. They could not halt the attacking troops because they lacked reserve formations. Thus, the situation on the Carso Plateau became increasingly critical because of the massive uninterrupted Italian storm attacks. Yet four attacking corps failed to achieve significant progress.

The initial attack had commenced on August 19, then on August 20 two infantry divisions crossed the Isonzo River against Mrzli Vrh, the ensuing battle raging until August 22 as XXIV Corps' defensive resistance steadily weakened against the persistent Italian assaults. The enemy forces then pressed south with massed troop formations, when Habsburg artillery fire again could not halt them. Seven Italian divisions launched an attack. But Habsburg defenders could not expect any reinforcements. The Italian offensive specifically targeted the southern portion of Mt. Santo, which threatened to pierce the Habsburg defensive lines along the entire front. Retreat appeared to be the only possible alternative until reinforcements could be provided.

Elsewhere, Italian Second Army suffered enormous losses and failed to advance even after launching several efforts against Vodice. Battle also commenced at Hermada, the key position defending Gorizia and Trieste. Further north the Italian operation proved unsuccessful against the Tolmein bridgehead partly because of effective Habsburg artillery fire and heavy-machine-gun crossfire. Habsburg 17. Infantry Division halted mass attacks, terminating in hand-to-hand combat. Battle continued for the fourth day with Italian VII Corps fighting at the Vipacco Valley where hand-to-hand combat added enormous losses. The Italians threatened to pierce the Habsburg defensive lines along the entire front. A Habsburg retreat appeared to be the only possible alternative.

On August 23, XXIV Corps troops, as a result of desperate battle, had to retreat. On August 24 the troops reached the line defending Mt. St. Gabriel to await the arrival of reinforcements anticipated by August 29. The Italians concentrated their efforts in capturing their main objective, Trieste.[17] Following retrograde movement battered Habsburg troops' prepared new defensive positions. During the night of August 26, the Italians launched their next serious attempt to smash the tenuous Habsburg defensive lines. The next several days witnessed successive storm attacks, but the defenders maintained their positions although sustaining horrendous casualties. The hard-pressed Habsburg defensive troops also maintained their positions in the area north of Mts. Santo to Saint Gabriel, which ultimately forced the Italians to terminate their offensive efforts.

Habsburg Supreme Command now considered the possibility of launching a military offensive at Karfreit on the northern sector of the front to relieve the overpowering enemy pressure on the Isonzo River sector. The Habsburg key remained the defense of Mt. San Gabriel. As Habsburg troops continued to protect their few remaining positions on the Bainsizza Plateau, they consistently lacked adequate troop numbers, reserve formations and reinforcements, while war supplies dwindled. The troops increasingly lacked the necessary equipment to conduct effective defensive operations.

In multiple front areas Italian troops outnumbered the defenders by as many as four to one. They also enjoyed the advantage of possessing far more artillery pieces, trench mortars and aircraft. During all the Isonzo River battles the soldiers suffered from the horrendous battlefield conditions, even when there was no combat. During the summer the heat became unbearable, and disease, particularly malaria, spread rapidly through the ranks. Water remained scarce particularly when enemy artillery destroyed the pipelines that supplied it. Then autumn rains commenced to continue endlessly.

On the mountain front the conditions in the many caves proved horrendous. Dead and wounded soldiers, gas, dust and smoke, as well as the stench of corpses, made living conditions unbearable. Suicide became a viable option. Soldiers feared mostly enemy artillery barrages. If they survived the massive bombardments, they rejoiced that the worst was seemingly past, but then came the bloody hand-to-hand combat when Italian troops continued to attack. Transportation, a vital element on the home, as well as the battle front, became the essential provider of reinforcement (*Ersatz*) troops, equipment, food and other necessities. The massive military utilization of railroad lines competed with commercial traffic to the home front, which already suffered terribly from the Entente blockade. The Homeland economic and domestic situation continued to worsen, even though the future overwhelming Caporetto victory represented a major military achievement. The operation negatively affected food and supply delivery to the hinterland. The worsening railroad conditions presented major problems, while many locomotives required repair; the railway tracks and railroad cars had been overused. Thus, even if food or materiel became available, it often could not be transported to the cities.

A report revealed the increasingly problematic transportation situation. The available 105,000 covered rail wagons, between 60 and 70 percent of those available, supported the later Caporetto offensive operations, but negatively impacted the transport of food and vitally necessary goods to the home front, representing a critical decline in the transfer of vitally necessary goods.[18] The situation worsened because not only did normal supplies and food have to be transported during autumn, but attention had to be focused on the problem of transporting food during the winter. Huge quantities of food, such as potatoes, which rotted or froze during autumn and winter weather, had to be shipped to the starving populations of the cities. Also, heating material such as coal became more scarce.

The Dual Monarchy appeared to be rapidly approaching its breaking point as food, equipment and other vital items had almost become exhausted. People prayed for peace, particularly during 1917 and after the February 1918 Ukrainian "Bread Peace." It was anticipated that the Bread Peace would increase the possibility of cities receiving more grain. The worsening economic climate also negatively affected the military situation. Earlier, on February 17, General Boroević had dispatched a report to Habsburg Supreme Command concerning the serious situation resulting from the disruptions of food supplies to the army. Boroević emphasized that increasing hunger in the ranks produced a loss of discipline as the troops increasingly suffered from overwhelming exhaustion. Even the higher commanders and field officers began to give in to despair. General Boroević demanded rapid action be taken.

As the domestic situation continually worsened it incensed the various nationalities and ethnic disgruntlement awakened. Strikes and the spread of radical political ideas partially resulted from the lack of strong governmental leadership and the increasing scarcity of vital material necessities. The turmoil on the home front could no longer be kept secret from frontline soldiers, who became increasingly concerned for their families' welfare at home.

During early September at Mt. San Gabriel, the southern pillar of the Austrian defensive system dominating the Vipacco Valley and protecting Gorizia, the Italians launched counterattacks west of Hermada, recovering some lost terrain. In two years fighting on the Carso Plateau seven miles of terrain had been lost, costing over forty-three thousand Italian casualties including nineteen thousand dead. The Habsburgs suffered thirty-five thousand casualties with ten thousand dead. Between May to the end of September there were four hundred thousand casualties, but at the same time between a quarter and a half-million soldiers reported to sick call. The severely weakened Habsburg forces not only had to abandon their well-constructed defensive position but also lost an enormous amount of equipment.

Then in mid-August Italy launched its Eleventh Isonzo offensive, finally capturing its objective, the Bainsizza Plateau, and advancing toward Mt. San Gabriel, named "the mountain of death" because of the bloody fighting that occurred there. The Habsburg troops maintained the strategic position, but the casualties had been severe for both sides, exceeding all previous battles. Italian command continued launching attacks for a month. Of the 143,000 Italian casualties, 40,000 died; the Habsburg's 110,000 casualties included 10,000 dead. The Eleventh Isonzo River offensive attempted to finally capture Trieste that had already produced hundreds of thousands of Italian deaths from the multiple offensive operations. The Italians, however, could afford the horrendous losses; the Austro-Hungarians could not.

On August 29, General Cadorna terminated the Second and Third armies' offensive efforts. Then, during September and early October 1917, the Central Powers deployed forces to launch a major counterattack, the German High Command again fearing the collapse of the Austro-Hungarian Army. Habsburg Fifth Army became designated the First and Second Isonzo armies, their deployment area extending from Trieste into the Isonzo River Valley. The newly created German Fourteenth Army commanded by General Below would initiate the new offensive effort. The requisitioning of trains to transport soldiers and supplies resulted in the blocking of the distribution of food and other goods to the civilian population as winter approached, as related, thus many towns and city civilians were left starving and without fuel.

The Eleventh Isonzo River battle represented the largest and bloodiest of the Isonzo River slugfests. Habsburg defensive efforts, however, repelled the attackers, thus the Italians failed to capture their major objective of Trieste. They had won a significant victory on the Bainsizza Plateau, advancing six miles on an eleven-mile front, which for the First World War represented a major success. The Italians attempted for two years to obtain this success, but their armies remained far from driving the enemy out of the Isonzo Valley and finally conquering Trieste. Third Army advanced less than seven miles on the Carso Plateau, or one-third of the distance to Trieste.

Cadorna's attrition strategy had achieved battle success, but at the cost of the cited horrendous casualties. Enormous troop numbers were sacrificed in the Eleventh Isonzo battle. Fatefully, Italian troops paused at what some military historians considered the moment that could have produced a significant victory; not the first time this had transpired. After eleven efforts the Italian casualty list cited 460,000 dead and 960,000 wounded soldiers.

In less than a month the Italians had sacrificed 300,000 soldiers: 160,000 between August 18 and September 13. Of these 40,000 were dead, 180,000 were wounded and many were missing. In attempting to achieve victory General Cadorna's casualties far outpaced the April French Nivelle offensive numbers. Italian soldiers' morale dropped to new depths. Of the Austro-Hungarian 110,000 losses roughly 15,000 died, 45,000 were wounded, 30,000 were missing and 20,000 were seriously ill. The number of missing soldiers equaled the troop numbers of three infantry divisions. Habsburg forces also lost enormous amounts of equipment, including one-third of their artillery pieces being destroyed or captured.

The major question was whether Austria-Hungary could maintain its front much longer. Another major attack could finally shatter Habsburg lines. The next campaign could determine the fate of the entire Italian campaign. That served as the background for the successful Central Power October Caporetto offensive campaign.

For thirty months Italian forces had attacked eleven times in the Isonzo River battles, but barely gained ten kilometers. By the end of the latest battle Cadorna anticipated that the front would remain quiescent until spring 1918. He predicted this conclusion because winter would arrive soon and the Austro-Hungarian forces had never launched an offensive over the Isonzo River. October also brought constant rain. The main factor was that the Austro-Hungarian Army was reeling from the Eleventh Isonzo battle.

The German planners had only five to six weeks to deploy 40,000 troops with half a million artillery shells transported in 2,400 convoys over difficult mountain terrain. The inclement weather conditions camouflaged their massive concentration, but made it even more difficult to traverse the few and poorly constructed mountain roads.

During 1917, the Italian front situation dramatically altered. During the Tenth and Eleventh Isonzo battles the Italians had attempted to extend their forward lines fighting extremely bloody attrition campaigns. The attackers could sustain such horrendous losses but defending Habsburg forces had been bled almost to death. During the latter campaign the timely arrival of two German infantry divisions ultimately rescued the desperate Habsburg military situation. Habsburg Fifth Army troop morale had collapsed, having sustained catastrophic losses and the awareness that the army could expect no reinforcements because none existed. Fortunately for Austria-Hungary the Russian Revolutions occurred, which allowed troops to be transferred to the Italian front and eventually the overwhelmingly victorious Caporetto campaign could be launched. The June–July 1917 Kerensky offensive military situation negatively affected Austro-Hungarian military problems.

During August, Emperor Karl requested that the German ally provide troop units to launch a relieving offensive against the Italians after only requesting artillery units because this was the Habsburg battle. On August 29 General Ludendorff rebuffed the approach; he intended to complete the Russian and Romanian military campaigns. The battle of Riga on the northern Russian front also commenced on September 1, while battle still raged twenty miles north and northwest of Bucharest, where German troops attempted to drive Romanian and Russian forces over the Sereth River into Moldavia. The Germans also simultaneously fought in the Flanders area. Nevertheless, a German delegation traveled to the Isonzo River front to investigate the possibility of launching an effective relieving offensive because of the Habsburg Army's catastrophic situation.

On September 1 Emperor Wilhelm notified Karl that six German divisions from the strategic reserve would be deployed to the Italian front after the completion of the Kerensky offensive, the ongoing Riga battle and the outcome of the Flanders battle. Wilhelm emphasized that if the Riga operation proved successful and weather conditions permitted, German troops soon could be redeployed to the Italian front to launch an offensive. The German delegation had recommended that a successful Allied Isonzo River offensive was possible. Wilhelm then announced that he could not immediately transport the troops because of the ongoing Flanders battle, and that the German General Staff recommended emphasis be placed on the campaign in Romania to obtain a surrender.

By September 5 the battle of Riga had proven a resounding success. The German High Command could deploy the designated six infantry divisions.[19] On September 8, a German general visited the Italian front to further investigate the possibility of launching the campaign. In the meantime, a message to Habsburg Supreme Command confirmed that there would be an offensive. General Ludendorff felt that he must support the Habsburg ally to prevent its defeat, and Turkey and Bulgaria being severed from contact with Germany. Thus, an agreement evolved that seven German divisions and twelve artillery batteries of four guns each would be deployed to the Italian front. A new Fourteenth Army with heavy artillery and strong air power would power the Austro-Hungarian offensive effort.

Five days later the operational commanders accepted the plans for the new campaign. On September 12 Archduke Eugene's two Isonzo armies and German troops received the mission to hurl the enemy back from the present front and drive it to the Tagliamento River. The German Fourteenth Army would launch the main attack from the critical Tolmein bridgehead.

Preparations commenced for the operation, initially the transporting of heavy-attack artillery and one million shells over the treacherous mountain terrain to be followed by assault troops. The mountain terrain often required eight days to transport one heavy-artillery piece to its prearranged emplacement position. The extensive offensive preparations had to be completed during appalling weather and terrain conditions.

The Central Powers eventually amassed the greatest number of artillery pieces ever deployed on this front for the operation. Their forces also provided a three-to-one numerical supremacy in troop numbers at the specific attack locations. All preparations transpired in secrecy; the soldiers not being informed of their mission until the very last minute. During constant inclement weather conditions supplies arrived, but often stymying logistical efforts. Climatic conditions also prevented Italian aerial reconnaissance efforts, while no flights were conducted far to the north, a major Central Power advantage.

Italian intelligence sources received indications of the approaching offensive, but Cadorna felt confident that the lateness of the year would prevent launching a major enemy offensive operation. Thus, he ignored intelligence reports that indicated that multiple Habsburg infantry divisions had been shifted from the Russian to the Southwest front. Cadorna feared a future attack would be launched on the Trentino rather than the Isonzo front. Then, on October 9, Italian intelligence sources calculated that seventeen Habsburg infantry divisions and an unknown number of German troops had transferred to their front. Again, Cadorna basically ignored the warning, anticipating that if such an attack occurred it would commence on the Bainsizza Plateau or at the crest of Mt. Santo and the Vodice region.

To Central Power advantage, various Italian Army front commanders had failed to implement necessary precautionary defensive measures, as Cadorna had ordered. Cadorna, aware of the presence of German troops, remained self-confident of the strength of Italian defensive positions and of his troops' ability to halt an attack. He realized the advantage of superior and shorter Italian interior railroad lines; thus, Italian forces could reputedly rapidly overcome any potential threat. However, Italian High Command had no conception of the potential effects of German poison gas shells, which ultimately proved critical in overpowering Italian resistance during early battle.

The Italians enjoyed aerial superiority after 1916 partly because the French provided Nieuport 17 airplanes, which Habsburg aircraft could not effectively counter. Also, Caproni bombers appeared regularly over Habsburg lines. The enemy aerial superiority resulted in the fact that no Habsburg reconnaissance missions could be flown over Italian territory until the Germans transferred large numbers of their aircraft to the Italian front for the looming Caporetto campaign. The Germans concentrated their greatest air power during the entire war for this operation. They deployed eight aircraft companies and three fighter unit reconnaissance sections, as well as a bomber squadron. The

German Albatros DIII successfully prevented Italian reconnaissance over Habsburg territory before the launching of the offensive. However, a disadvantage was that the reconnaissance flights did not extend to the northern Tagliamento River, one of the main offensive objectives. Habsburg forces did not receive a Flik company in that area until November 15, which was far too late to assist during the initial operation.

As early as October 17 Habsburg deserters informed their Italian captors that there would be a major Habsburg offensive launched between Plezzo and the Tolmein bridgehead. This became obvious because of increased troop numbers deployed opposite the Italian lines, particularly at the Italian Second Army left flank positions in the Tolmein bridge area. Two days later accurate intelligence reports predicted an imminent Central Power offensive strike with seven German divisions supported by a thousand artillery pieces, but Cadorna still believed that a major campaign would not be launched this late in the year and definitely not in the Julian Alps region. On October 20, a Czech deserter revealed to his Italian interrogators that an offensive would be launched within two days, but inclement weather conditions delayed that launch until October 24. On October 21, two Romanian officers presented the Italians with the actual attack plan.

The major attack was launched on the weakest Italian front section at the strategic Tolmein bridgehead. Two factors proved of immense significance from the very beginning – the German use of gas shells and the accompanying new storm trooper infiltration tactics. The bulk of the new German Fourteenth Army deployed around Tolmein. Its first objective encompassed a five-kilometer-wide mountainous section near Flitsch. A pincher assault would be launched to the north, along a valley leading to the slopes of Mt. Rombon and the high ridges west at Mt. Krn toward Caporetto where Italian defensive positions had not been solidly established.

On the southern pincher terrain area three German and one Habsburg division attacked from the Tolmein bridgehead spearheading to the west. On the right flank the 50. Infantry Division attacked Mrzli Vrh then advanced into the valley to assist the German 12. Infantry Division as they both attempted to capture Caporetto. German Fourteenth Army then moved south from its newly captured ridges. General Boroević's initial mission entailed holding Italian troops on the Bainsizza and Carso Plateaus then attacking the Italian Second Army.

During the first operation day, October 24, Central Powers troops smashed enemy defensive positions at Plezzo and Tolmein, overwhelming two Italian corps. Habsburg I Corps rapidly captured Flitsch, advancing to the third Italian defensive position and then to the Carso Plateau and Karfreit. Italian troops on the eastern bank of the Isonzo River were forced to retreat, resulting in the capture of a large number of prisoners of war. Large gaps in the defensive lines could not be sealed, resulting in rapid Italian retreats from the Bainsizza Plateau to Mt. Santo.

General Cadorna finally became aware of the impending danger from the major offensive, but too late to take effective counteraction. The Italian High Command, once aware of an imminent attack, still did not believe it could occur on the rugged Tolmein–Flitsch terrain under the inclement weather conditions. Cadorna, confident that his forces could repulse an attack, did not anticipate a Habsburg offensive before 1918.

As the offensive launch date rapidly approached, on October 22 the Isonzo River flooded, the result of three weeks of heavy rainfall that caused bridges to collapse. The following day the Italian Second Army commander realized that his troops faced an attack, but his mountain-gun tubes could not be pressed downward to fire into the valleys, providing the attacking troops a major advantage. The German advance through the valley utilized the foggy and rainy conditions, which totally surprised the defending Italian troops. Habsburg troops had traditionally advanced through mountains not valleys; the Germans chose valleys. Traversing the crest of the Julian Alps to prepare for the offensive in the unfavorable weather conditions was an amazing feat; troops had marched fifteen straight hours to their deployment positions.

On October 23 fresh snow covered the key Habsburg Mt. Rombon positions, troops freezing in their positions. For some reason Central Power supportive artillery fire did not include the significant Mt. Rombon attack area. Habsburg troops therefore suffered under horrendous conditions on that mountain, sustaining severe losses from direct Italian machine-gun and artillery fire. The heavy casualties demoralized the troops.

Compared to the Western front preoffensive artillery fire, barrages lasted several days or longer. The Germans unleashed brief intensive artillery fire against Italian defensive positions, which included thousands of gas shells. German Fourteenth Army broke through the Tolmein bridgehead positions and reconquered the Bainsizza Plateau and Gorizia where Italian Third Army defended. The unfolding offensive threatened the flank and rear of northern Italian troop locations, which forced their rapid retreat, severing their food and supply connections.

On October 24 at 2 a.m., a thousand-gun artillery barrage hurled thousands of phosgene and chlorine gas shells against known Italian artillery battery locations, communications centers and forward trenches along the twenty-five-mile front extending from Mt. Rombon to Gorizia. The barrages continued until 4:30 a.m. At 6 a.m., destructive artillery fire commenced after the two-hour interlude, this time with high explosive shells and, an hour later at 7 a.m., trench mortars joined the murderous hellfire. The lethal barrages quickly demobilized defending Italian troops when the storm trooper attack commenced at 8 a.m. supported by rolling artillery barrages at the Tolmein–Krn ridges and at Mrzli Vrh. Weather conditions alternated between light to heavy rainstorms, flooding the valleys with waist-high snow in the mountain elevations. Mist shrouded the valleys when the offensive commenced, thus visibility proved very limited, providing the attackers an enormous advantage. The main assault encountered very little resistance, because the defending soldiers had been neutralized by the gas shells and intense artillery barrages. During the first twenty-four hours thirty thousand prisoners of war were captured and the most difficult defensive positions overcome. Italian troops had to retreat across the Isonzo River, Central Power troops reaching their rear echelon lines because of weak defensive opposition, thus opening a breach in the lines.

With minor Italian resistance encountered at the Tolmein bridgehead, a fifteen-mile gap opened into the Italian lines on the thirty-two-kilometer multi-objective attack front. Defending troops literally vanished, many fleeing from the battlefront. By nightfall, some Central Powers troops had reached the west bank of the Isonzo River as Italian troops retreated to the southwest to their defensive network on the lower right Isonzo River. Italian artillery batteries did not support their troops on the first attack day because those battery commanders that survived had awaited orders that were never received.

Meanwhile, on the Bainsizza Plateau, the Habsburg Second Isonzo Army failed to make rapid progress, but by evening the defenders realized that they could no longer hold their indefensible positions. The Italian Second Army completely imploded, a chaotic retreat ensuing. General Cadorna ordered that a new defensive line be established at Mt. Maggiore, sixteen miles north of his present Udine headquarters. He also ordered that a defensive line be prepared at the Tagliamento River as his Third and Fourth armies conducted an orderly retrograde movement.

Central Power forces reconquered the Bainsizza Plateau and Gorizia on the Western Carso Plateau, the Caporetto offensive operation, now threatening the northern Italian troop fortifications. Their garrisons rapidly retreated. Simultaneously, Habsburg troops launched an offensive on the Dolomite Mountain front. This forced the Italians to retreat on this front as well, surrendering one-half of their occupied Alpine territory. The front lines changed more in twenty days than in the previous two years, the battle occurring about the same time as the Western front Ypres, or Passchendaele, campaign.

During the second operation day, October 25, weather conditions improved, enabling the attacking troops to achieve steady progress opening major gaps into and rapidly overrunning enemy lines. The advance now precluded the benefit of heavy-artillery support as Central Power guns could not keep pace with the rapidly advancing troops. The hastily prepared Italian defensive line at Mt. Maggiore was quickly threatened. Meanwhile, General Cadorna also issued the order to prepare to retreat behind the Tagliamento River, but delayed sending it for thirty-six hours even though Italian Bainsizza Plateau positions had become untenable. Cadorna piecemeal and haphazardly hurled his few available reserve units into nonvital locations against the advancing German Fourteenth Army.[20] Italian air reconnaissance efforts failed to locate the attackers' strength and intentions, partially because they had never dispatched missions north toward Tolmein, not anticipating a serious threat from that area. In addition, German aerial superiority prevented effective Italian reconnaissance efforts. No major battle had occurred previously in that region; thus, the vast majority of Italian forces had been concentrated south on the Isonzo front. The major objective of the Caporetto operation became to hurl Italian troops out of the Doberdo basin and threaten enemy positions in South Tyrol then, if successful, advance from the mountain front onto the Italian Plains to knock Italy out of the war.[21]

When Italian defensive positions rapidly crumbled breakthroughs occurred along the entire front; the first Central Power objective had been obtained. With the Italians' defensive lines collapsed, their troop morale evaporated and their will to resist vanished. Italian Second Army defenses had quickly shattered, creating chaos as the German Fourteenth Amy broke through its lines at Tolmein, and Rombon. The attack fanned out from the Mt. Krn area.[22] It also forced the Italian northern flank Fourth Army Group to retreat in the Dolomite Mountains to avoid encirclement, a result of the Second Army debacle. Fourth Army established defensive lines on the linchpin of the major Italian northern position, Mt. Grappa. By the end of the second battle day Central Power forces controlled the Isonzo River north of the Tolmein bridgehead and were threatening the Italian Isonzo front positions. Italian headquarters having become paralyzed into inaction also negatively affected the Italian Third Army situation.

Some Italian divisions fought well, but because the majority of troops had been deployed on the front lines and heavy-artillery pieces emplaced too close to the front, the defenders did not receive artillery support when attacked. When Central Powers troops advanced to the Tagliamento River it removed any chance of the Italians conquering their main objective, Trieste. If Central Power troops broke through the Italian front lines at any single location, the entire front would collapse, whereas on the Western and Eastern fronts such a breakthrough would not cause such a disaster. A major Central Power problem arose almost immediately, that of supplying ammunition and basic supplies to the rapidly advancing attack troops. As a result of previous disastrous battlefield casualties, Habsburg commanders could not deploy large troop numbers or provide adequate artillery shells or other necessary equipment and supplies to defeat the Italians without German assistance. Again, the Habsburgs' powerful ally had prevented a crippling defeat. The German Fourteenth Army received unanticipated assistance when the enemy inserted its reserve units poorly, and the successful storm trooper tactics ensured that the defenders did not have time to organize any strong resistance. Captain

Erwin Rommel of Second World War fame captured 9,000 prisoners of war within two days with 150 men. His losses were six dead and thirty wounded.

During early morning hours the tremendous breaches through the Italian lines were rapidly expanded, the Italians forced to retreat from conquered territory from the past twenty-seven months. The German Fourteenth Army now controlled the entire Isonzo triangle and the chain of mountains that dominated the Italian Plains extending to the upper Tagliamento River.

On October 26, the third attack day, Central Power forces continued to advance toward Mt. Maggiore. The Italian Second Army troops received orders to defend their positions to the last man extending from Mt. Maggiore to Kuk and Mt. San Gabriel. The Habsburg Second Isonzo Army forced an Italian retreat over the Isonzo River near Plava and on the Bainsizza Plateau, then pursued the retreating troops to Vodice and Mt. San Gabriel. The First Isonzo Amy reported that enemy troops were withdrawing from the Gorizia front, creating chaos throughout Italian rear echelon areas. Italian troops in their haste destroyed enormous quantities of supplies and equipment, but huge amounts were captured as the confused troop masses retreated. Advancing Central Power troops encountered destroyed bridges, vehicles and many thousands of refugees fleeing the battle area. As troop discipline evaporated, the demoralized Italian troops pillaged their own villages for days. As the route of Italian troops continued, General Cadorna continued to make poor command decisions.

Following the breakthrough of the Mt. Maggiore defensive line, General Cadorna rapidly transferred his headquarters to Treviso. In the meantime, his Second Army had been decimated, eight divisions almost destroyed. Its troops panicked as General Cadorna ordered his defeated soldiers to retreat to the Tagliamento River line. Meanwhile, Allied aerial combat surpassed any previous campaigns. The Central Powers commanders also received excellent intelligence from decoded enemy transmissions, in other words, of enemy destruction of equipment and supplies, but Fourteenth Army had to halt its successful progress to await delivery of ammunition, particularly artillery shells.

On October 27, the retreating Third and Second Italian armies were ordered to defend the few Tagliamento River bridges. The river remained flooded as driving rain continued throughout the night. Italian command, paralyzed into inaction and confusion, panicked, resulting in a hasty retreat movement but panic occurred everywhere, assisted by the fact that there had been no retreat plans prepared. Meanwhile, German troops seized the few remaining Julian Alps positions, dooming the remains of the Italian Second Army. Fighting in the Mt. Rombon area proved especially vicious and bloody. Italian Third Army's retreat during a downpour continued until October

28 as the German Fourteenth Army reached to within six kilometers of Cadorna's headquarters.

On October 28, when the Italian Udine and Gorizia positions capitulated with heavy defending troop losses, it forced their retreat to the western bank of the Tagliamento River and threatened to encircle three Italian corps. As a result of the inclement weather conditions, heavy artillery and supply trains continued to lag behind, advancing Central Power troops. Italian Second Army left flank positions collapsed, as Third Army began to retreat, suffering bitter defeat after initially successfully repulsing Habsburg attacks on the Bainsizza Plateau. Positions conquered earlier with such enormous bloodshed were surrendered to Habsburg forces, including Gorizia, Plava, Podgora, Oslavia and Mts. Santo, Sabatino and San Michele, all earlier scenes of incredible misery for the troops involved during the past years.

Central Power commanders determined to continue the offensive beyond the Tagliamento River, once German Fourteenth Army arrived there. In the pursuit action, German troops captured sixty thousand prisoners of war and enormous amounts of food and alcohol, slowing down the advance. The German Fourteenth and Habsburg Second Isonzo armies established strong positions on Italian soil. Cadorna, as usual, blamed his troops for the continuing retreat movement.

Central Power forces captured some Tagliamento River bridges before they could be destroyed, their success proving far greater than anticipated. Enormous numbers of Italian deserters, their vehicles and artillery fled the chaos. Three Italian Second Army corps initially became isolated then destroyed. Retreating Italian soldiers were harassed by strafing aircraft. Central Power troops continued to receive little artillery support, because the units could not keep their rapid pace. By midnight all Italian troops had crossed the river, but they had been allowed to escape. German High Command ordered the advance to continue as rapidly as possible to prevent the Italians from preparing new defensive positions.

On October 30 Central Power troops encountered no resistance when they reached the Tagliamento River line in force, nor when they crossed the river. They had advanced thirty miles from the Isonzo River front as they raced to seize Tagliamento River bridges before they could be destroyed by the retreating enemy troops. Italian troops ultimately deserted their Tagliamento positions, retreating thirty miles to the Piave River. During the next two days both sides prepared for a major attempt to cross that river. While Austro-German troops could not maintain their supply efforts, retreating Italian formations encountered every form of hindrance strewn along the roads. Habsburg troops reached the only partially destroyed bridge at Cornini, to their great advantage.

Heavy rain remained a significant factor as it prevented Central Power formations from rapidly crossing the Tagliamento River because of the general muddy morass that also negatively affected communication efforts. Within eleven days the advancing Central Power forces had shortened the Italian front lines by 140 kilometers. Meanwhile, the rapid approach of winter weather conditions placed enormous time pressure on the advancing Allied troops. Many Italian wagons continued to bog down in the mud and had to be abandoned along the roads. The last major Central Power offensive launched against Mt. Grappa failed, an attempt to push beyond the Asiago Plateau to attain the Venetian Plains. Battle continued at that location until the end of the year. Strong Italian resistance lines, meanwhile, were eventually erected at the Piave River.

During the evening of October 31, the Italians transferred troops across the Tagliamento River but could not halt Central Power troops crossing that waterway until the night of November 2–3. Meanwhile, the flooding river reached its highest level then receded, which helped Central Power troop efforts, but flooding delayed the troops from crossing the river.

On November 1, as Central Power troops approached the undestroyed Cornini Bridge over the Tagliamento River, the Italians prepared to retreat to the next major waterway, the Piave River. On November 2 the attacking Allied troops broke out onto the Italian Plains. This could have been a disaster for the Italian Army, but General Boroević's Habsburg troops remained stationary, reputedly because of the lack of pontoon bridges. The Italians retreated so rapidly they could not destroy much of their equipment. General Cadorna failed to release the order to retreat to the Piave River until November 4; by then Central Power forces had crossed the Tagliamento River.

The advancing Central Powers Northern front troops proceeded southward along the west bank of the Tagliamento River. Five Central Power corps waited for the bridges to be repaired, the troops having been ordered to advance as rapidly as possible. On November 3 Fourteenth Army launched an offensive in the Trentino to capture Mt. Grappa.

The Habsburg 55. Infantry Division crossed the Tagliamento River on November 3 as the British and French began to redeploy troops and equipment to the Italian front to halt the disastrous Italian retreat. The Italians established a new defensive line between the Piave River and northern Mt. Grappa while the Central Powers halted their advance because of their accelerating supply problems and lack of artillery support. The Italians had lost over a quarter of a million prisoners of war and 2,300 artillery pieces. Numerous Italian units surrendered without a fight. British and French leaders demanded that General Cadorna be replaced after King Victor Emmanuel formally requested military assistance from the Entente. General Armando Diaz became the new chief of the Italian General Staff. He received three major missions, the most obvious being to halt the Central Power invasion, then the task of rebuilding the badly defeated Italian Army and then, alternately, winning the war.

Between November 5 and 11, the Italian Fourth Army eastern flank positions became exposed as remaining Second Army units hurriedly retreated to the Piave River. Italian troop morale, which had already suffered during the Eleventh Isonzo battle, continued to deteriorate. Many Italian artillery pieces were captured; thus, the retreating troops did have that support.

The lack of reserve troops for insertion at threatened locations became a major factor in the Italian defeat. The massive Mt. Grappa became the main Italian defensive position on the new Northern front. General Cadorna reinforced positions there with fifty battalions or around fifty thousand troops. The Italian positions at Montello and Mt. Grappa now gained significance; they would be further fortified, although already strengthened during the 1916 *Straf* offensive. The route of the Italian Second Army had been so great that the Fourth and Third Army Corps troops had to defend the seventy-five-kilometer Tagliamento River front. Meanwhile, General Cadorna feared that Conrad could also launch an offensive from the Trentino that could trap his troops on the Venetian Plains.

On November 6 Italian Second Army unit remnants continued to withdraw under heavy enemy pressure, exposing the important Belluna basin to enemy advantage. The German Fourteenth Army attacked Italian positions along the mountain system as enemy troops continued their retreat toward Belluna and the Piave River.

Meanwhile, the Italian Fourth Army continued its retreat on November 7 without pressure on its northern flank, while further south Third Army crossed the Piave River. News also arrived that Anglo-French troops had reached that area. The Habsburg XVII Corps had to be deployed on Mt. Grappa to protect one flank. On November 8 heavy rains persisted as flooding streams and rivers became raging masses. Italian Third Army forces slowly arrived at the Piave River right bank. Some Fourth Army troops occupied the key Montello mountain position.

During the second week of November the Italians made a defensive stand on the mile-wide Piave River, which flowed from the Dolomite mountains across the coastal plains reaching the Adriatic Sea approximately twenty miles northeast of Venice. The river represented the last defensive obstacle before Venice; thus, the Central Power advance had to be halted before northeastern Italy had been conquered. Italian Fourth Army defended Mt. Grappa for six weeks with its forty-seven infantry and four engineering battalions. German Fourteenth Army, meanwhile, attacked in a north–south direction through its deep valleys.

Central Power armies had the almost impossible mission of attempting to cross the Piave River before winter weather arrived. It required several weeks for supply trains to finally reach the waterway. In the interim the attacking troops received inadequate food, equipment and supplies. General Ludendorff unexpectedly began to redeploy troops from the Italian front.

The Caporetto operation had unexpectedly produced an unprecedented catastrophe for the Italians. By November 20 they had sustained almost eight hundred thousand casualties and lost three hundred thousand prisoners of war, while as many as four hundred thousand soldiers deserted the army. Central Power losses totaled thirty thousand troops while the number of Italian infantry divisions had sunk from sixty-five to thirty-three.

The British and French rapidly deployed eleven divisions to the Piave River and Asiago Plateau fronts to prevent the complete collapse of the Italian Army. The British provided five divisions, the French six, while new Italian formations were quickly recruited to replace the enormous casualties. The German storm trooper tactics had proven very successful earlier during the battles of Riga and the 1917 Kerensky offensive. The specially equipped assault troops advanced along the entire front, punching deep holes into rear echelon areas, isolating Italian frontline troops while disrupting communications and reaching the enemy's rear areas before the defenders could deploy their reserves.

Italian newspaper columns were replete with defeatist and pacifist messages, which negatively affected the retreating demoralized Italian troops. Meanwhile, General Ludendorff removed German troops in preparation for the 1918 Western front offensive, which greatly infuriated Habsburg Supreme Command. General Diaz cautiously rebuilt Italian troop morale and strength, while restricting his operations to occasional raids and avoiding launching major offensives.

By November 9 the significant provinces of Udine and Belluna, as well as portions of three others, had been occupied by Central Power troops. On November 10 Fourteenth Army troops and Habsburg Conrad Group forces attacked on the Asiago Plateau, attempting to weaken the Italian defenses on the northern Piave River front. Most Italian divisions had lost their artillery, while Italian Fourth Army, when it retreated on both banks of the Piave River, had its troops strafed by German airplanes, causing panic in the ranks.

Fourteenth Army and Boroević's Isonzo Army were ordered to cross the Piave River on November 11, a most difficult task. Meanwhile, major battle ignited on Mt. Grappa where the Italians had established strong defensive positions. All Piave bridges had been destroyed by November 12 as the German Fourteenth Army turned its attention to Mt. Tomba on November 13, hoping to gain access to the Piave Valley to the east. Italian forces established their new Piave River defensive positions as British and French troops began to arrive to reinforce them. On November 14 Central Power forces again assaulted the Grappa Massif with four infantry divisions, but failed to penetrate Italian lines. By November 15 extremely cold temperatures resulted in troops freezing to death in the trenches. Attacks continued against the Mt. Grappa positions.

Battle continued without pause as Central Powers troops continued to attempt to break through the Italian lines. Ferocious battle continued for control of the western pillar of the Mt. Grappa summit defenses, but Italian lines ultimately held. Artillery fire on November 17 killed or destroyed everything within range for both combatants.

General Conrad's troops attacking Mt. Grappa had to halt their efforts because they no longer received the necessary supplies and equipment to continue battle and the troops were totally exhausted. Meanwhile, the Germans had already begun removing their troops to transfer them to the Western front. Central Powers troops had advanced 150 kilometers, shortening the Italian front by almost two-thirds. In addition to the severe casualties sustained by the defeated Italian Army, Central Powers troops captured hundreds of wagons loaded with technical material, over seven thousand train cars and automobiles as well as much other valuable equipment.

On December 3 Central Power troops terminated their efforts, while the next day British forces counterattacked at Montello, the French at Mt. Tomba. Central Power troops had sustained seventy thousand casualties, probably as many as one-fourth dead.

The new German storm trooper tactics proved to be a major factor in the success of the Caporetto offensive, enabling the specially trained troops to successfully infiltrate Italian lines, utilizing speed and brutal force to create chaos in rear echelon areas. The offensive had evolved so rapidly that Italian leadership could not react rapidly enough to counter its threats, and became paralyzed. By the time Italian High Command realized the actual military situation it was too late to react effectively. Uncoordinated actions produced thousands of Italian soldiers' deaths.

The Caporetto campaign was conducted in two separate theaters of operation, on the Italian Plains and on the mountainous terrain in the Mt. Grappa area. Central Power planners realized that very limited time existed to achieve success because of the rapidly approaching winter weather. On the Italian side Cadorna proved indecisive and lacking in energy, an example being the thirty-six-hour interlude during which he did not order his troops to retreat to the Tagliamento River. Also significant, the Italian Army was primed to launch another offensive, thus was caught completely by surprise as it usually was the one to launch the offensives on that front. Reserve troops were poorly utilized, while Cadorna spent the first nineteen days during October on leave to write his memoirs.

The first day of the offensive quickly provided excellent results; Central Power troops crashed through the Italian defensive lines and soon terrorized

Italian rear echelon areas. The rapid opening of the half-mile breach on the Isonzo River bank against the Italian defensive lines provided the opportunity to advance to Caporetto. Surprise was greatly aided by German aerial supremacy, which allowed reconnaissance missions and prevented the Italians from implementing them.

The Caporetto campaign became the most successful operation during the entire war, decimating the Italian Army. British and French troops had to be rapidly deployed to that front to halt the Central Power advance. What would 1918 bring? Only half of Italy's 65 infantry divisions had survived intact, but as mentioned half of its artillery lost over 3,100 pieces.

1918

During the fateful year 1918 economic conditions worsened considerably in the Dual Monarchy, as the empire approached complete economic collapse. This fed into the accelerating war weariness, despair, increasing pressure for peace and severe shortage of food.[1] The central government's finances had become so disastrous that German capital was required to keep it functioning. The obvious incapacity of the central government to feed the people, improve their conditions and resolve ethnic conflict led to the non-German and non-Magyar peoples revolting, ultimately producing catastrophe. The question of another winter without sufficient food or fuel increased the pressure to terminate the war. During the winter of 1917–1918, because of lack of fuel, raw materials and ammunition, the war industry also collapsed. The production of artillery pieces and shells dropped to half that in the first six months of 1917. Another major concern arose – manpower and equipment resources had been expended, thus adequate reserve troop numbers were no longer available. This was in addition to the worsening food situation aggravated again in January, resulting in civilian disturbances, but military forces controlled the situation during January and February. Fewer pigs and cattle further reduced the already diminishing capacity to provide meat and milk to the army and civilians. The military now received half the flour it required. Meanwhile, ethnic turmoil exacerbated the accelerating social and political conflicts as they fatefully intermixed. Confidence in both the central government and Emperor Karl rapidly evaporated. Only in 1918 after a winter season of starvation did the army commence serious indications of implosion.

Yet as the year 1918 commenced the Austro-Hungarian monarchy appeared to be in a much more favorable military position than earlier. Russia had dropped out of the war because of its revolutions and the July 1917 Kerensky offensive defeat. Serbia had been occupied in late 1915, and by the end of 1917 the Central Powers controlled almost the entire Balkan Peninsula. In addition, the Italian Army had been soundly defeated at the battle of Caporetto, although it continued to contest Habsburg forces in the Slavic areas of Croatia, Slovenia, Dalmatia and Istria.

Austria-Hungary, as mentioned, was not prepared for long-term economic or industrial warfare, which also severely and progressively aggravated the nationality question. In Hungary the Magyarization policy alienated the Slovaks, Croatians, Slovenes, Serbians and Romanians. The ensuing economic problems, combined with nationality issues, ultimately destroyed the empire during late 1918. That economic and social issues had become linked to the war became obvious when Polish, Czech and South Slav deputies in the *Reichsrat* demanded major changes in the government structure during early 1918, and the masses became involved in politics because of starvation, inflation and war weariness. The Dual Monarchy government suffered escalating weakness after 1916, while the probability of eventual military defeat accelerated the various newly formed national councils' pressure as they pushed toward independence.

Fuel supplies also increasingly became scarce, while famine spread into multiple areas as the shortage of raw materials and commodities, particularly coal, became critical. The horrendous conditions were compounded by the collapse of the Dual Monarchy's transportation system. Industrial production also slackened from lack of fuel and raw materials and the railroads' declining capabilities. Respect for the government had disappeared because of its inefficiency, corruption and failure to resolve the ethnic and economic issues. The state had lost the respect of the various nationalities and exhausted frontline troops. The army and civilians competed for the dwindling supplies of food that created friction from all political levels. Food riots in Vienna exacerbated earlier national and ethnic problems. Health conditions also steadily worsened as Spanish flu cases became prevalent during the spring and summer of 1918. The real epidemic, however, struck in autumn. Shortages of doctors, even hospital beds, worsened health conditions. Cases of tuberculosis doubled between 1914 and 1918. The accelerating decline of central government authority and failure to alleviate the overall economic situation for the cold and starving people of Vienna and the empire become glaringly obvious.

The South Slavic problem escalated when worsening conditions in Slovenia continued to be ignored by the central government and South Slav opinion swung against Vienna. This change spread from Slovenia to Croatia, Dalmatia and Bosnia-Herzegovina. Meanwhile, Germany continued to provide money, raw materials and military assistance to its weaker alliance partner.

The increasing army and civilian material and personal depravation, combined with the constant lack of food, accelerating homefront starvation, particularly in cities, produced general disaffection with the central government. Currency inflation and rising prices continued to diminish people's buying power. Disease also had become rampant; the second deadly flu epidemic suddenly struck, while malaria became a major problem on the Isonzo and Albanian fronts, severely lessening troop battle effectiveness. Entente Western front victories, commencing in July, lowered troop and civilian morale, while the viral Spanish flu epidemic destroyed it further. On the Piave River front hundreds of soldiers reported daily to sick call, while troops and equipment became increasingly difficult to acquire or repair. By May 1918 only 946,000 combat troops remained available. Until summer the army was strong enough to swiftly suppress all internal revolts, but increasing agitation persisted. Only one-fourth of the soldiers actually served on the Italian front. The expanding Entente superiority in troop numbers, food and equipment became increasingly evident to Central Power troops. During the first quarter of the year two hundred thousand Hungarian soldiers deserted and starvation enveloped Galicia. Disastrously declining troop numbers could not be replaced. During the first half of 1918 attention focused on the Western front where the Germans attempted to win the war before large numbers of American troops could be deployed on the battlefield. Habsburg civilians accepted that their fate depended upon these battles. During winter 1917–1918, one million German troops redeployed from the Eastern to the Western front to prepare for their major spring offensive. The Habsburg Army, meanwhile, suffered grave internal problems, partly because of the situation created by returning prisoners of war from Russia. These former soldiers did not want to serve in combat again and many brought Bolshevik propaganda back with them. Many also deserted to home. More than half a million soldiers disappeared from early 1918 until the June 1918 offensive. The individual soldier's concern for his family's welfare became an increasingly significant factor. The former prisoners of war became horrified to learn of their families' poverty and exhaustion. Between March and July another half a million soldiers also contracted the Spanish flu during its first deadly phase.

The 1918 harvest fell well below that of 1917, itself a disastrous year, and food supplies proved insufficient to alleviate the desperate food situation except temporarily. Hunger riots erupted throughout Austria as famine conditions worsened. The impending winter season and effects of the second round of Spanish flu destroyed any remaining civilian or army morale. The agriculture sector continued to deteriorate at a rapid rate because of the lack of nitrates, the many male farm workers drafted into the army and animals requisitioned into military service. Utter despair set in. The food crisis increasingly and negatively affected both the army and the hinterland. This was partially blamed on the weak central government. The Russian front no longer produced major concern while food was requisitioned for the eight Habsburg infantry and four cavalry divisions stationed there. However, on the Italian front the lack of food became critical as plundering and the seizing of crops extended into 1918. By the beginning of January 1918, no adequate food supplies remained in Italy to feed the Habsburg Army. None could be brought from the home front to make up the difference. Already by mid-January the Dual Monarchy food crisis had worsened, but reached a boiling point during March, extending into May.

The worsening supply effort for the army was accompanied with food becoming quantitatively and qualitatively inferior and distasteful to the troops.

They ate dried vegetables, potatoes and other ersatz materials to make bread. Warm coffee water had to be used to make the food edible, because it lacked any taste. Army and civilians competed for the shrinking supplies of food; the army winning resulted in increasing anti-military feelings among the general population.

Meat supplies for the troops had been reduced by one-third whereas on the battlefront when no meat was delivered slaughtered horses provided the protein. On a bad day frontline troops received 500 grams of barley; March formations received significantly less if they even received any. Individual divisions between January and the end of March 1918 might receive only 725 grams of bread per soldier, often made from corn or poor-quality potatoes difficult to digest. Fresh vegetables were not available; after March the potato harvest was of inferior quality.

During the final war year, the Habsburg multinational society fragmented into its various ethnic subdivisions as the army also began to implode. Ethnic animosities worsened in various regiments, while combat-experienced officers continued to become casualties, being replaced by far less qualified reserve officers who also proved more susceptible to ethnic influences. Some provincial bureaucratic officials began to prioritize ethnic interests and provincial agencies over imperial concerns.[2] Emperor Karl had realized for some time that the fate of both his empire and dynasty depended upon achieving peace at the earliest possible date and that his army had begun to disintegrate. His foreign policy problems, however, continued to proliferate, and he could not break the fateful German connection. Internally, the German National Party was created relative to occurrences in Czechoslovakia.

When US President Wilson announced his Fourteen Points program in a speech on January 8, 1918 his Point 10 of "autonomous development" did not necessarily signify independence for the various nationalities of the Austro-Hungarian monarchy. The president advocated a constitutionalized federal rule, not its dissolution at this point. Meanwhile, Emperor Karl demanded peace feelers be initiated as soon as possible; the resulting tragedy a consequence of his method of attempting to achieve it, as the Sixtus Affair demonstrated.

During January 1918 the tightening rationing measures led to an extended series of strikes commencing on January 14. These protests against the worsening food situation rapidly spread throughout the Dual Monarchy. This quickly increased political pressure as the government proved unable to alleviate the worsening food crisis. Hunger and malnutrition conditions worsened. Seven hundred thousand workers of all nationalities went on strike for days, further fragmenting the multiethnic society while demonstrating the people's unrelenting war weariness and strong desire for immediate peace. The accelerating unrest appeared to introduce revolutionary currents as the common people became increasingly concerned about the lack of progress with the Brest-Litovsk peace negotiations. This unleashed mass spontaneous strikes that eventually resulted in the ultimate collapse of the Dual Monarchy. It also had significant effects on the army as soon a series of mutinies occurred, commencing in early February at Cattaro. The serious scarcity of food supplies during winter 1916 hastened the physical and psychological decline of the working class as it became increasingly exhausted and suffered from malnutrition. Strikes commenced during the hunger winter of 1916–1917. January 1918 introduced lasting wild mass strikes and hunger riots; the spontaneous revolts encouraged the furthering of radicalism. Sabotage, passive resistance and political action also affected the Dual Monarchy's social order as prisoners of war, women and children joined the ranks of the working class in the factories. Citizens began to demand their rights be addressed.

Striking workers, originally in the arms industry, presented four main demands, the most obvious to alleviate the disastrous food situation, the second that the Brest-Litovsk peace negotiations not be delayed because of German demands for increased territorial acquisitions in the East, thus continuing the war. Also, the militarization of industry had to be terminated. Strike activity soon extended into Hungary because of food requisitioning and hunger. It became critical to halt revolutionary activities and end strikes before they spiraled out of control. On January 16 further unrest erupted in Krakow and by January 19 the number of strikers had increased. Reports indicated that the strike movement had begun to take on a revolutionary character. The turmoil caught Social Democratic party leaders by surprise.

The unrest in Hungary required military units to be dispatched there by January 14. The first serious uprisings occurred in Galicia on the same day. This resulted from expectations of peace being established at Brest-Litovsk, as well as the transfer of food from the Galician province to Austrian cities instead of Warsaw. Plans commenced to create a separate Polish Army.

On January 13 Social Democratic leaders met in Vienna to discuss their position regarding the unanticipated strike movements. The threat of fomenting revolution caused their leader Victor Adler to support moderation, which became the key to Social Democratic strategy. Party leaders encouraged the workers to strive toward developing a more democratic government. A precipitating cause of the strikes was the persistent food shortages, particularly in the Austrian industrial areas, and the seemingly endless Brest-Litovsk peace negotiations. Five Social Democratic meetings followed relating to the peace negotiations as the situation became increasingly explosive.

The food situation continued to deteriorate and became even more critical in Vienna partly because grain could not be shipped from Romania on the frozen Danube River. Serious trouble commenced in Vienna on January 17 when the flour quota was again slashed after a particularly cold winter. The lack of progress of the Brest-Litovsk negotiations also had an effect. Trouble occurred in Vienna and the industrial area in Niederösterreich on

January 20. One day later, strikes erupted in Wiener Neustadt at the Daimler Motor Works and then extended to Trieste. They then spread to Budapest and beyond. On January 16 newspapers printed Social Democratic demands that added a political dimension to public pressure to end the war and to establish peace without asking for territorial acquisitions. The right to self-determination was also demanded. The strikes, becoming serious in Vienna, continued to spread as demands for peace accelerated.

Workers in Wiener Neustadt, where there was a high concentration of radical workers and non-German laborers, went on strike. Wiener Neustadt workers produced the most radical demands in the Dual Monarchy. They claimed they would not return to work until rations had been restored. Word of the strike spread throughout the surrounding areas. During the next week or so the economic demands suddenly transformed into political demands as workers continued to refuse to return to work.

The Wiener Neustadt delegation to the *Reichsrat* presented two demands, the first that the government increase the flour ration and the second that the delegates pledge that peace be achieved at the Brest-Litovsk negotiation. Social Democratic political leadership remained passive. Riots spread to the non-German parts of Austria and food riots erupted in Krakow, while the food situation in the monarchy's coastal areas had become catastrophic. Trieste could only be fed by grain shipped from the Pola naval base.

By evening January 16, the strike movement had expanded substantially in most of Vienna following the Daimler Works action, while the Viennese newspaper the *Arbeiter Zeitung* featured the now revolutionary workers' manifesto on its front page. Obtaining peace and ending the war without annexations at the Brest-Litovsk negotiations became the major demand of the workers' revolutionary movements. The Wiener Neustadt manifesto presented more radical elements than the Social Democratic Party anticipated. Left-leaning groups utilized the opportunity to involve the masses, which shook Social Democratic leadership into activity.

As the situation became more radicalized and conditions continued to deteriorate, Vienna city leaders requested military assistance to squelch the civil disorders during the first half of 1918. Troops soon deployed, but additional demonstrations erupted relative to the same issues. As the situation continued to deteriorate the major question became completion of the Brest-Litovsk peace treaty and assuring the delivery of food items to Austro-Hungarian cities. The steadily worsening food situation caused common people to become increasingly concerned with the Brest-Litovsk peace negotiations and the possibility of receiving grain supplies from Eastern Europe to feed the starving people, particularly from the Ukraine. The "Bread Peace" concluded with the weak Ukrainian government appeared to be a godsend for the starving Habsburg people who desperately sought new food supplies as the harvest again fell below necessity. It was also thought that the acquisition of food would prevent the outbreak of revolution and potential catastrophe.

On January 17 *Arbeiter Zeitung* published the Social Democratic leadership manifesto, which included demands that the ongoing peace talks not be affected by German territorial demands. It also demanded that the government reorganize the Habsburg food ministry and end the hated militarization of industry. There had been enough suffering – the war should be ended as quickly as possible.

Social Democratic leaders, attempting to regain control of the workers' movement, suggested that Habsburg political leaders initiate negotiations with local authorities in an attempt to prevent radical agitators from seizing control of the unleashed popular mass movement. They demanded that the flour ration not be lowered, and that the Brest-Litovsk peace treaty be resolved as quickly as possible, so food could be delivered from Russia and the Ukraine to neutralize the effects of the Entente naval blockade and poor harvests. Meanwhile, Habsburg Supreme Command redeployed two infantry regiments to Vienna from the Eastern front. The situation in the city appeared to be spinning out of control. New worker assemblies emphasized umbrage about the slow pace of the Brest-Litovsk peace negotiations. Officials reported that the Austrian food supply could last only until March 1. As a result of these factors, the Habsburg delegation at the peace negotiations was seriously compromised, to obvious German advantage. The drawn-out negotiations revealed the Habsburg junior role relative to Germany.

Krakow became the third major urban center to experience turbulence, joining Vienna and Trieste. On January 16 bakeries in Vienna were looted, causing most to close the next day. Rioters demanded peace and political self-determination. The Vienna riots intensified when the flour ration was reduced on January 17.[3] On January 17 and 18, a hundred thousand workers went on strike in Vienna, the disturbance expanding into the Alpine regions thus halting military production. On January 18 further demonstrations and strikes occurred, when no bread supplies were available. Disturbances continued on January 20, but Social Democratic representatives, following negotiations with government officials, succeeded in ending the strikes in Vienna and Budapest. Elsewhere, outrage at the sluggish progress of the Brest-Litovsk negotiations intensified following German General Hoffmann's inflammatory speech on January 12.[4] Meanwhile, the expanding strike movement linked more closely to peace negotiations as war weariness overwhelmed the starving people.

In Budapest unrest again commenced on January 18, developing into a general strike on the following day. On January 19 Social Democrat leaders demanded peace, expanded individual rights and expanded food supplies. On January 19 and 20 the demonstrations widened as 113,000 workers halted work in Niederösterreich alone. This resulted in gendarmes, police officers and machine-gun sections being deployed. Military units transferred into the hinterland, removing them from the Italian battlefront.

Habsburg Foreign Minister Czernin, negotiating at Brest-Litovsk, claimed that the German demand for territorial expansion would not delay the peace negotiations. When the rioting subsided in Vienna workers had not won a decisive victory, so unrest continued. During January 15,000 workers struck at the Skoda plants in Pilsen, Bohemia, then spread to other Czech industrial cities, including Prague. On January 22, a general strike of 50,000 workers soon increased to 150,000 demanding self-determination. The lack of food and increasing inflationary conditions incensed anger and produced ethnic disturbances.

The Vienna military situation was unfavorable when the strikes commenced, as only three thousand troops were garrisoned in the city. On January 16 a request to strengthen the garrison to secure the inner city resulted in additional troops being alerted. Similar events occurred in Bohemia. By January 17 troops deployed in Prague, Pilsen and Krakow. The appearance of combat troops made a profound psychological impression on strikers. Removing so many troops to quell the January riots and later additional units seriously weakened Italian front troop numbers.

Only about seventy-five thousand army troops were available to curb the strike activity in the entire empire, and those soldiers' availability became determined by the length of their training. Thus, only forty-one thousand troops became available for deployment. On January 15, Wiener Neustadt officials, fearing sabotage, contacted military authorities to request troops. Troops also had to be deployed in Galicia. In Hungary sixty military assistance (Assistenz) units of a hundred men each were deployed. During January 19 and 20 further units deployed into the hinterland, halting the strikes at least for the time being.

Delivering coal to the cities during the cold winter weather became problematic, because of accelerating transportation problems and the priority to deliver to the military. Coal distribution quickly became a major problem, particularly during cold weather spells, compounded by the deteriorating railroad situation. Lack of coal was blamed on disorganized industry, the lack of sufficient workers, strikes, insufficient sustenance for the workers and the mounting transportation difficulties. The increasing lack of raw materials and the worsening transportation problems including lessened production of train cars lowered railroad capacity. Even the army's needs could not be fulfilled.

The shortage of vital raw materials for the armaments industry had quickly become a critical problem. Habsburg industry had proven unprepared for the war and unable to maintain the war effort, collapsing by 1918. Shortages of weapons, ammunition and equipment became decisive during winter 1917–1918.

Thirty-five thousand railroad workers were drafted in 1914, creating an increased workload for those still employed. New inexperienced workers lowered the transport efficiency. The cost of living and inflation worsened each year as the price of food increased.[5] Rapidly printing paper money by 1918 devalued currency value fifteen-fold. The dearth of locomotives had a major effect on delivering food, raw materials and troops to the front and Homeland. During 1914, the Dual Monarchy possessed twelve thousand locomotives, increasing to fourteen thousand. By the end of the war only nine to ten thousand remained available, while during winter months 50 percent required repairs. Thus, sufficient amounts of food and ammunition could not be delivered to the army. Although fifty to sixty locomotives were produced each month, it proved inadequate because warfare had extended the railroad lines through Russia, the Ukraine, Romania, Serbia and Italy, vastly extending wear and tear on all equipment and rails.

A major problem for Austria-Hungary resulted from the dualistic system, which produced duplication of multiple efforts that lowered productivity, partly a result of major differences between the agricultural and industrial strengths of the two halves of the Dual Monarchy. Serious coordination problems evolved as multiple agencies became responsible for the same projects. This rankled ordinary citizens, particularly when Hungary did not increase its food allotments to Austria as starvation increased in its cities.

Events occurred in rapid succession in February, including initially a naval uprising in Cattaro, the unrest soon spreading to *Ersatz* army units then, after the March 3, 1918 Brest-Litovsk Treaty signing, the return of hundreds of thousands of prisoners of war and the resulting unrest among them. This produced accelerating economic and social problems that aggravated festering nationality issues. During February additional demonstrations erupted, particularly in Bohemia and Moravia; the people demanding improved living conditions. Austria-Hungary had survived three and a half years of war, suffered numerous battlefield defeats and absorbed horrendous causalities. Now the hinterland raised unresolvable problems because of the worsening economic situation, war weariness and overwhelming desire for peace. The masses increasingly opposed the war effort.

On February 1 at Cattaro, a major naval base on the south Dalmatian coast, four thousand sailors revolted because of their abysmal living and working conditions, the lack of sufficient food, inferior quality of available supplies and mistreatment by officers.[6] Loyal army and navy units quickly crushed the uprising, nevertheless, it indicated that military units were now willing to protest. Unrest in army rear echelon areas soon erupted, thus the Cattaro incident unfortunately proved not be an isolated incident. Fortuitously, during the first half of 1918 the Italian front remained basically uneventful.

Mass protests continued during February, making them more dangerous because some governmental officials, the mainstay of the regime, now participated in them. The March 3, 1918 Brest-Litovsk Treaty terms also terminated fifty years of Polish government support, because the area of Cholm in the eastern Ukraine was ceded to the Ruthenians.[7] This unleashed an immediate Polish backlash. Domestic matters increasingly became significant as turmoil accelerated. Meanwhile, the Entente Powers supported the creation of a free Poland, encapsulated in Point 13 of Wilson's Fourteen Points. Galicia became ungovernable in February as ethnic violence exploded, accompanied by further loss of trust in government authority, particularly in Krakow, which later resulted in revolution and the recreation of a Polish state. The meaningless verbal discussions between Bolshevik leaders and Central Power negotiators at Brest-Litovsk caused Foreign Minister Czernin to separately negotiate with Ukrainian delegates because of the possibility of obtaining grain supplies. The process accelerated when Bolshevik soldiers seized the Ukrainian capital the day before the signature of the peace treaty, the first of the war with a noncombatant entity.

On February 2 a peace treaty signed with the newly created Ukrainian Peoples' Government (the *Rada*) allowed the Germans to establish hegemony in Central and Eastern Europe. On February 18, the treaty resulted in one million German troops, and far fewer Dual Monarchy participants, conquering the Baltic States (Latvia, Estonia, Lithuania, consisting of nonethnic Russians) and the Ukraine, which forced the Bolsheviks to sign the Brest-Litovsk Treaty on March 3, 1918. The treaty allowed the transfer of fifty-three Habsburg infantry divisions and assorted reserve units to the Italian front, but that transfer cut both ways. As the units redeployed, the soon-released Russian Habsburg prisoners of war returned home, many with Bolshevik propaganda. The treaty greatly decreased troop numbers stationed in Russia, but some thirty German divisions, consisting of older and younger troops, remained to garrison the conquered territories. Article XIII of the treaty released more than two million prisoners of war, the vast majority Austro-Hungarian. Russian prisoners, however, were not released until the end of 1918, to keep them in the Habsburg work force (many on the Italian front, others in the interior).

On February 11, after canteens and food depots had been raided, the first *Assistenz* units arrived in Hungary, while difficulties erupted in March formation ranks. After the revolt of six March companies in Albania (*Schützen Regiment 1*) an investigation revealed that the troops had not received promised leave time and were reacting to the effects of the Russian Revolution. Such activities displayed anti-patriotic and anti-Habsburg inclinations.

On February 19 the Habsburg minister president claimed that his government did not want to intervene in the Ukraine, but home starvation conditions forced it to. The main Habsburg military mission became to secure the railroad lines to ensure safe food transport back to Austria-Hungary. This extended the Habsburg rail network thousands of miles to Odessa, while the general transportation system continued to deteriorate. Inadequate troop numbers for the mission resulted in its failure. One Habsburg soldier was deployed every six square kilometers. The sparseness of troop numbers and lack of means to transport any grain to railroad stations insured its nondelivery.

As Central Power troops advanced to Odessa, the Bolsheviks had ten thousand sailors, the Black Sea fleet and fifty thousand workers to potentially defend the city. On March 12 Bolshevik forces surprisingly abandoned Odessa as within fourteen days the railroad lines to the city had been secured. Emperor Karl claimed that the Ukraine operation was an invited incursion, not a conquering military operation. Eventually seven Habsburg infantry and three cavalry divisions deployed to this front.

The increasing misery resulting from the drastically worsening Austro-Hungarian food situation had forced Vienna to also join German troops advancing into Eastern Europe. Habsburg troops entered the Ukraine because its central government could not feed its people until the next harvest and incorrectly assumed that the Ukrainian grain would provide sustenance, feeding the starving Dual Monarchy population. An ancillary effect of the Ukrainian invasion was that Romania finally negotiated a peace treaty because of the collapse of the Russian Eastern front, and due to the Russian Revolutions. The Treaty of Bucharest had been delayed by bickering over the economic terms.

Via the peace treaty Germany received a ninety-nine-year lease on Romania's oil and grain supplies. The Habsburg Empire was forced out of Romania without obtaining compensation elsewhere. In the meantime, the "hopeless supply situation" worsened because of Ukrainian farmers' opposition and the lack of transport means to deliver available grain supplies to railroad terminals.

As skeleton Habsburg forces and March brigades deployed to the Ukraine, the Italian front required every soldier it could receive. During March the Habsburg Army finally established its own propaganda organization, copying the German model, attempting to counter war weariness, effective Bolshevik and Entente propaganda and to buttress troop morale. The program produced too little, too late, lacking even necessary administrative personnel to ensure its effectiveness. In the meantime, the mentioned enemy propaganda increasingly affected war-weary soldiers and civilians.

Significantly, Russia's exit from the war negatively affected the Entente Powers' position relative to the Dual Monarchy. Their leaders began to reconsider maintaining Austria-Hungary in some form. They eventually supported the various national independence movements because of the results of the Sixtus Affair and May German Spa headquarters meeting, as we shall see.

On March 21 the Germans launched Operation Michael, their initial 1918 Western front spring offensive, intended to defeat Entente forces before American troops could deploy in Europe in large numbers. The offensive successively recaptured the territory lost during the 1916 Somme campaign, but lacked sufficient troop numbers to exploit its impressive initial successes.

World, particularly European, attention became fixated on the Western front battles. At the same time the initial command was issued for launching a Habsburg June offensive on the Italian front, resulting from increasing pressure from the Germans for a relieving operation to support their Western front effort. The Habsburg Army lacked necessary equipment and artillery shells for a successful operation. Starving troops had to improvise much of the preparations for the separate hundred-kilometer two-front attack areas. Troops lacked numerical superiority on both the Piave River and Tyrolean Mountain attack fronts, because Emperor Karl could not establish a single operational command structure or demand a mass operation on one of the separated fronts to obtain a victory.

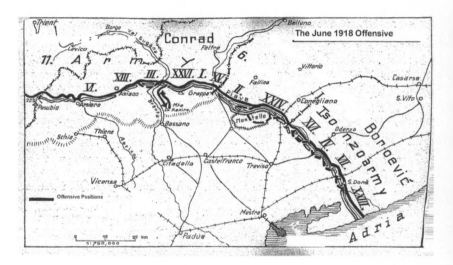

Map 11   *June 15, 1918 offensive*

Food scarcity obviously had a major effect on the morale and well-being of the Austro-Hungarian civilian population. For example, August 1917 calculations determined the amount of grain necessary to feed the Habsburg military and civilian population, but less would be harvested. Hungary had a surplus. The central government negotiated additional grain deliveries from Poland, Serbia, Germany and Romania, the amounts far short of necessary requirements. Adequate supplies lasted during January and February, but famine again loomed in April. Twenty barges carrying Romanian grain on the Danube River destined for Germany were confiscated to feed the starving Viennese population, where bread rations had been further reduced from 500 to 283 grams commencing mid-April to June 30.

The return of the hundreds of thousands of prisoners of war from Russia after the signing of the Brest-Litovsk Treaty required the construction of large military camps, hospitals and barracks and the supply of clothing, food and medical attention to the returnees. Many had died from epidemics during captivity. The enormous number of former prisoners overwhelmed the attempts to provide for them, but the government could not afford to properly administer the situation.[8] Over 400,000 had perished in Russia, while one-third served in captivity in the Ukraine. Between early 1918 and mid-October some 670,000 returned to the Dual Monarchy.

Many prisoners of war were corrupted by Bolshevik propaganda. They received a medical examination, were deloused and served an incubation period or were quarantined for fourteen days, in an attempt to prevent serious outbreaks of disease. They got four weeks' vacation time, then spent weeks in special camps, receiving inadequate food rations and shoddy uniforms. Then they received orders to be deployed to the front lines in replacement units. Most were not in suitable physical condition to return to the ranks while their arrival back home further aggravated the existing food emergency. Learning of their families' terrible conditions in the hinterland caused enormous concern, thus when they finally received leave, many did not return to duty, while others poisoned their units with Bolshevik propaganda, inevitably destroying unit cohesion.

Many mutinied when notified they would be returned to combat duty if they had not been too radicalized by Bolshevik propaganda. When assigned to March replacement units for deployment to the front, they created problems in rear echelon areas where they encouraged troop mutinies. Initially, such actions created only small spontaneous outbursts, but because of their enormous numbers the actions quickly evolved into major confrontations as conditions steadily worsened.

In the internment camps few officers spoke the troops' language and unfavorably impressed the returning soldiers by treating many as traitors. They immediately felt isolated and initially had no knowledge of the worsening conditions at home.

Between April 1 and 4, 1918 the unprecedented Congress of Oppressed Nationalities met in Rome convened by the Italian government with representatives from the Czech, Polish and Yugoslavia political committees and from Transylvania. The participants, obviously many from the Dual Monarchy, appealed to the Entente Powers to support their attempts at emancipation from Habsburg domination. A "Pact of Rome" momentarily produced an Italian, Polish and South Slav pledge to mutually support those countries' national unity efforts against Austria-Hungary and a formal announcement of Czech and South Slav national aspirations and the borders to be established on the basis of national determination. This encouraged Serbian, Croatian and Slovenian exiled leaders to form a Yugoslav Committee to foster the collapse of the Dual Monarchy, and the creation of an independent South Slav state. Delegates demanded economic and political independence. The meeting's significant propaganda effect spread through Habsburg lands, encouraging ethnic resentment and rebellion, while President Wilson's January Fourteen Points speech further fanned the flames.

Habsburg Supreme Command requested German assistance to alleviate the deteriorating food crisis, and the army attempted to extract more food supplies from Galicia, leading to starvation conditions there causing extreme reactions. On April 6 the United States declared war on Germany not Austria-Hungary, while on April 2 the Italian government recognized the Czech National Committee as a government in exile and authorized the formation of a Czech Army Corps from the prisoners of war. During the month the second German offensive was launched. April also witnessed multiple unanticipated revolts and strikes as unrest spread across the Dual Monarchy. This resulted in further radicalism and increasingly civilian population passive resistance. The people's loss of patience with the army receiving priority for food and goods unleashed increasing antagonism toward the military. Meanwhile, the Habsburg social structure was significantly affected by the appearance of women, children and Russian prisoners of war entering the workforce.

In early May additional demonstrations erupted across the Dual Monarchy because of the increasing food scarcity and the unfavorable Western front situation. No coal was available for steel production, drastically terminating weapon production. Many army units lacked full artillery complements because only one-third of the necessary horses survived to transport the guns. Locomotives and train cars required constant repair because of poor maintenance practices, the lack of replacement parts and proper lubrication materials, as well as the continuing track deterioration. It became increasingly difficult to transport supplies and troops to the front and food and coal to city dwellers.

The unfortunate Sixtus Affair became a major factor in the dissolution of the Austro-Hungarian monarchy. It partially emanated from the uneasy relationship between Foreign Minister Czernin and Emperor Karl, who sometimes determined imperial policy without notifying his minister. Czernin became increasingly sensitive until the Sixtus Affair exploded, initiated by a Karl letter to the French government proposing peace conditions by accepting, among other matters, the condition that France receive Alsace-Lorraine to end the war. Czernin, unaware of the letter, alleged that French Prime Minister Clemenceau had initiated peace feelers toward Austria-Hungary. Karl initially told Czernin that he had not dispatched such a letter. Czernin then released a communiqué insisting that no peace offering had been initiated to France. Unfortunately, an angry Clemenceau publicized the actual letter in newspapers, which created a major, embarrassing and ultimately fateful problem for the emperor.

The March 23, 1917 letter was nominally addressed to Prince Sixtus of the Bourbon Parma family. Sixtus was the elder brother of Emperor Zita. The letter's intended audience was French President Poincaré and the other Entente leaders in an attempt to initiate Habsburg peace feelers. On March 31 Sixtus delivered the letter to President Poincaré, which led to French discussions and attempts to separate Austria-Hungary from Germany. The possibility of a separate peace with Vienna had the negative effect of delaying Entente recognition of the various Habsburg nationalist movements until Entente leaders determined that Vienna could and would not terminate the German alliance after the May 12, 1918 Allies meeting at the German military headquarters in Spa.

The uproar and outcome of the affair destroyed the moral authority of the emperor and his foreign minister. Czernin resigned and Karl traveled to Spa. This finally convinced Entente leaders to encourage the various Austro-Hungarian nationalities to strive to end the war. This reversed their earlier position, destroying any Entente goodwill toward Vienna. The Dual Monarchy had sealed its fate by tightening its alliance with Germany at Spa.

The Sixtus Affair also significantly discredited both the emperor and Czernin in the eyes of the German Austrians and Hungarians, previously the dynasty's strongest supporters; it destroyed their loyalty and resulted in lost moral support from the Dual Monarchy's people. A major negative factor was that the Sixtus Affair and May Spa meeting destroyed what little creditability the emperor maintained with the various Slavic peoples. Many formerly loyal Habsburg citizens now favored a drastic change in the government. The handwriting was on the wall. The tightening of the Habsburg association with the Germans also dismayed many Habsburg officers and many others.[9] Karl suffered extreme humiliation at the May Spa Canossa meeting and, accused of duplicity and treachery by his ally, fatefully became more dependent upon the German alliance. Seeking peace, nevertheless, the emperor's methods led to his failure.

Czernin was replaced as foreign minister by Burian, mainly resulting from the embarrassing Sixtus Affair. In addition to now representing a military liability to the German ally, the emperor had also committed a serious act of treachery. This presented the foundation for the commercial and military agreements signed by both German and Austro-Hungarian sovereigns and their chief ministers. The Spa agreement extended the existing alliance into a long-term political and military alliance, and sought for the gradual creation of a customs union, but nothing concrete emerged from it.

The Spa agreements were never ratified, because they depended upon mutual agreement relative to the Polish question, which never transpired. The meeting encouraged Entente leaders to support Czech and South Slav exiles' demands for the dissolution of the Austro-Hungarian monarchy. Several nationalities began to openly demand the dissolution of the Dual Monarchy. Adherence to the German alliance signified that the Habsburg central government could not resolve the perpetual nationality problem; in fact the German alliance became a prop to not realistically confront that potentially deadly issue.

A directive from US Secretary of State Lansing on May 29 indicated that the United States supported the Czech, Slovak and South Slavic peoples' goal of independence, which greatly encouraged and accelerated their subsequent revolutionary activities. The German High Command also increased its pressure on General Arz to launch an offensive against Italy to support its Western front efforts.

During the month serious revolts erupted in Hungary as unrest continued throughout the Dual Monarchy. Additional *Assistenz* troops had to be deployed to several locations during the summer months. The fateful food dilemma made the situation catastrophic.

Between May 20 and June 6, the third German offensive phase transpired in the Aisne River region as rapt attention remained riveted on the Western front. On the Homeland front mutinies began to increase in number. On May 12 *Ersatz* troops of Slovene Infantry Regiment 17 revolted in Judenberg, others at the end of the month at Rumburg. Rebellious troops were isolated and disciplined, while 133,000 went AWOL. Starvation and famine conditions continued to spiral out of control as agitation in army units began to multiply.

As the Habsburg situation steadily worsened in June, particularly in the hinterland, a German deputation arrived in Vienna on June 23 to negotiate providing essential food deliveries. Two days later it announced that during the second half of July 1,700 wagons of grain would be delivered to the Dual Monarchy from the Ukraine, Romania and Germany, and 750 during the first half. Habsburg leaders threatened their German associates that if they did not receive sufficient food supplies, Vienna would have to seek peace. Mutiny broke out in a Slovene army unit, a harbinger of further fateful events to occur soon.

By the end of June over five hundred thousand prisoners of war had returned from Russia. General Slavic dissatisfaction increased, as did civilian opposition to continuing the war. This partially resulted from the continued currency inflation and slackening industrial output because of the scarcity of fuel, raw materials and the steadily deteriorating railroad situation. The fate of the army accelerated with the launching of the inadequately planned offensive operation on June 15. By May starving troops performed some duties with difficulty, while some they simply could not do. An attempt was made to provide the designated attack troops more rations, but supply problems prevented this from happening.

The Habsburg Army launched its ill-fated offensive operations – one along a fifty-kilometer Piave River front; the other along a forty-kilometer mountain front. Famine was widespread at both fronts. The troops were generally poorly commanded and ill-equipped. Troop desertions multiplied. Disastrously, there would be no massed assault against a single objective, because the operation encompassed too broad a front, and insufficient troops were dispersed to obtain success. Failure to attack in mass against one objective produced failure. Gas shells, critical for operational success, remained of inferior quality and the artillery support proved totally inadequate. Conrad's mountain offensive collapsed within twenty-four hours largely because of supply problems and difficult mountain maneuvering. General Boroević launched his Piave River attacks on the extreme flanks, Montello in the north and the south mouth of the Piave River. Italian troops, alerted to the forthcoming attack, withdrew from their forward positions so initial Habsburg artillery barrages proved ineffective.[10] Defending troops burst from the forested terrain and decimated General Conrad's advancing units, causing the demoralized Habsburg troops to retreat. The sudden termination of the Asiago campaign allowed the rapid transfer of Italian troops to the Piave River front. Significantly, Conrad's forces attacked British and French troops not Italian ones. Boroević's offensive also lacked mass, consisting of several separate attacks.

On June 1 Habsburg troops numbered 1,430,000; one month later they had dropped to 1,280,000. As the numbers decreased, the Italian Army had recovered from the Caporetto fiasco and its ranks had refilled with trained recruits. Its reequipped troops received support from eleven British and French divisions, multiple Allied artillery batteries and other vital military equipment. The Habsburg Army increasingly suffered from the results of the rapid economic decline and the central government no longer providing the moral or material support that the army or society required. The army deployed seven infantry divisions in the hinterland to preserve order following the January 1918 and later disturbances. Additional units maintained home-front tranquility, though many were not returned to the front for the June offensive fiasco nor forthcoming October battle debacle.

The offensive initially had to be delayed because of inclement weather and terrain conditions. The mountain campaign naturally proved far more difficult than the Piave River operation, because of the difficult high terrain, inadequate roads and few overtaxed railroad lines required to transport the necessary food and equipment for the operation. On the eve of the offensive, the army's food supplies could only last for a few days. Troops quickly expended their supplies on the mountain front while some heavy-artillery batteries lacked shells. General Arz and Emperor Karl could not be reached at critical times because they often were not at headquarters, and thus failed to provide vitally necessary leadership resulting from lack of communication between three command centers. This factor also later negatively affected armistice negotiations. Habsburg Supreme Command leadership completely failed, partially because the Baden command headquarters was too distant from the battlefield. Enormous confusion also resulted from having forfeited surprise for the offensive.

The enemy was fully prepared for the attack, partially due to Italian espionage. The Italians withdrew their troops from their front lines, as mentioned, while the inadequate preparatory artillery barrages caused only minor damage to the empty enemy front lines, but inadvertently created excellent defensive positions for enemy machine-gun emplacements. The superior Italian artillery fire was not neutralized, its opening barrages striking Habsburg troop assembly areas. The offensive result also revealed the lack of critical artillery–infantry cooperation as well as effective artillery observers, to great enemy advantage. In addition, Habsburg artillery lacked shells and critical gas shells malfunctioned. The Italians also employed the major advantage of vast aerial superiority.[11]

The military failure created pressure for the resignation of Chief of the General Staff Arz. Arz offered to resign several times, but Karl refused his requests. By now, the army had lost faith in both the emperor and Arz. Karl was blamed amid the uproar because of the unanticipated disastrous military debacle, following the earlier 1917 Caporetto campaign, as was his wife Zita. Karl received increasing criticism following the fateful May 1918 Spa meeting. His taking command of the armed forces proved to be a fatal mistake. His notorious amnesty declarations for political detainees, particularly Czechoslovakian ones, and the persistent hunger and increasing turmoil caused public opinion to turn against both emperor and Habsburg Supreme Command. Their prestige never recovered as revolutionary activities began to accelerate. Angered Hungarian officials demanded an investigation into the disastrous June offensive failure. Conrad became the scapegoat and was at long last relieved of command.

The Italians possessed quantitative and qualitative aircraft advantage, ensuring aerial superiority over the battlefield throughout the offensive. Their aircraft bombed and destroyed Habsburg pontoon bridges constructed across the Piave River and killed many pioneering troops.[12] Habsburg forces lacked both sufficient aircraft numbers and pilots and could not counter Caproni bomber attacks. Planes dropped propaganda broadsheets as far as Vienna. The Habsburg air arm lost two-thirds of its aircraft during the doomed action. Habsburg air activity proved far more active on the Italian front than either the Russian or Balkan.

During his mountain offensive Conrad employed ineffective infantry tactics in the heavily wooded mountain terrain, attempting to break onto the Italian plains as he had during the 1916 *Straf* campaign. The Italians inflicted multiple Habsburg casualties and within two days Habsburg troops ran low on supplies and had to retreat.[13] The offensive rapidly halted on that front, allowing the Italians to quickly transfer troops to the Piave River front.

The Habsburg Army lacked necessary supplies, equipment, food stores and manpower to launch the offensive with any chance of success. In addition, weapons and equipment were in short supply, often obsolete, and some ammunition faulty, particularly gas shells. Conrad's troops attacked in unfamiliar snow-covered mountain terrain, while on the Piave River front, the Italians'

far superior interior railroad network enabled them to rapidly rush reinforcements to any threatened area. Habsburg forces possessed only two mountain rail
lines on Conrad's front. After brief initial Piave River front success, the attack
troops quickly bogged down, the troops exhausted from malnutrition, inclement
weather conditions and well-entrenched Italian positions that unleashed murderous crossfire against attacking formations. During the first operational day
Italian resistance stiffened, while friendly artillery fire did not adequately support advancing troops. Enemy artillery dominated the battlefield.[14] Some troops
reached the Italian third-line defensive positions, but then were counterattacked.
The soldiers were already weakened by hunger and illness, including dysentery,
malaria and the Spanish flu pandemic on the Isonzo River front. They also
suffered from the rapidly deteriorating materiel situation, which had become
hopeless. Reserves were deployed on the first offensive day, none remaining in
two days. Within seventy-two hours the offensive clearly had failed. By mid-
summer the war had obviously been lost.

The continuing loss of horses, because of lack of fodder and proper care,
also negatively affected the operation. Between 1917 and 1918 the number of
military animals decreased from 1.16 million to 460,000, severely hindering
the maneuverability of artillery pieces, shells, equipment and supplies.
Meanwhile, because of the constant rain, the Piave River's rapid currents
and rising flood waters created a major obstacle to establishing the required
pontoon bridges for the offensive. Some river areas tripled in width from the
flooding. The 143,000 casualties destroyed the last reliable Habsburg Army
strength and accelerated the army's rapid demise. The military infrastructure
began to collapse and war-weary disillusioned civilians, many of whom had
anticipated another Caporetto- style victory, vehemently demanded peace.
Disturbances continued during troop transfers to the front. Restive nationalities lost their last vestige of faith in the Habsburg cause as revolutionary ardor
escalated and troop desertions accelerated. In Vienna anger and despair
produced mass rioting. War weariness and the overwhelming desire for peace
had become universal.[15] The fatal June offensive coincided with the continuing hunger crisis in Austrian cities, forcing many people into the countryside
to plunder fields for food. Strikes broke out in Vienna; during the second half
of the month the rioters demanding an end to the conflict.

In hindsight, several factors mitigated against launching the disastrous
offensive. Inclement weather and terrain conditions neutralized gas shells.
When front unit commanders requested a short delay in launching the
operation, Habsburg Supreme Command announced that it was too late
because attack preparations had progressed too far. Eleventh Army troops
possessed only a few days' ration supplies; the situation was compounded by
the difficult Asiago Plateau mountain supply and transportation conditions.
The situation was also negatively affected by the necessity to feed 1.3 million
Italian and Russian prisoners of war.

Other significant negative factors included the widening cleft between the army and the general population, due in part to the army receiving a perceived oversupply of food. The retreat to its original positions also had a terrible effect on troop morale. Italian troop numerical superiority and vast aerial supremacy also affected it.

Conrad's mountain artillery units reported one-third of their guns inoperable. On the Piave River theater Italian artillery barrages targeted the Habsburg offensive assembly areas, creating many casualties. In addition to Piave River flooding destroying many pontoon bridges, Italian airplanes drove off Habsburg aircraft and bombed the bridges.

Despicably, the undernourished "Hunger Offensive" troops lacked weapons, food (Sixth Army troops on average weighed barely 120 pounds) and adequate artillery support because of the shortage of shells and poor-quality gas shells. Artillery units became immobile because so few, undernourished, horses remained. Mortar shells often failed to explode, resulting from the decline and quality of industrial production, lack of raw materials and deteriorating transportation system.

Some nationalities began to openly voice their demands. Regretfully, the government continued to prove incapable of resolving the fatal nationality problem, because many of the multiple nationalities' demands would negatively affect the basic structure of the Dual Monarchy, thus basically no serious action was attempted to appease the various ethnic groups.[16] The Hungarians also refused to allow any alteration in their national structure. Meanwhile, negotiations with Berlin concerning the fate of Poland produced stalemate, while the Entente Powers could offer much more to the Poles.

On June 19 alarming reports of serious homefront strikes were released. Starving industrial workers had become far less productive so the army could no longer anticipate adequate assistance from the hinterland, especially because of the failing railroad situation.

The troops' rapidly deteriorating physical and moral condition ensured that they could not launch another major offensive effort as the Habsburg military situation rapidly declined. Advancing malnutrition made troops susceptible to disease such as malaria and typhus, compounded by the sudden Spanish flu epidemic, which seriously curtailed troop effectiveness. On the Piave River front, 800 soldiers a day reported to sick call, and by August 37,000 reported because of the summer epidemics. Meanwhile, 550,000 soldiers had deserted the ranks since 1917, while infantry company numbers had dropped to less than half.[17]

Overutilized railroad lines rapidly deteriorated, the situation becoming increasingly critical when locomotives and cars sat idle lacking fuel and necessary repair work. Railroad capacity had declined at a rapid rate. Mistrust increased against Habsburg generals, and dangerously against the emperor and his wife. The enlarging dangerous gap between Habsburg leadership and people continued to fester and grow. Meanwhile, mutual exhaustion resulted in no major battles on the Italian front during late summer and fall 1918.

The Italians recaptured the military initiative by launching attacks, while between July 1 and the end of September, Habsburg front troop numbers declined from 650,000 to 400,000, resulting chiefly from desertion and disease, which produced far greater casualty numbers than combat losses. General Diaz resisted Entente military leadership pressure to launch an offensive, claiming that Italian troops were exhausted from the earlier battle. July and August also introduced Habsburg famine days, resulting in starvation in some areas, and destroying the little remaining Habsburg morale.

On July 2, at a German Crown Council Meeting at the Spa military headquarters, the German generals jettisoned the proposed Habsburg plan to create a Polish state that included Galicia and the Russian portion of that entity. German military command intended to annex extensive Polish frontier strips for strategic advantage (partly railroads). Interallied friction continued over the vexing Polish question that was never resolved. During the second half of July, Italian artillery fire primarily targeted the western and southern Tyrol areas, while the emperor granted his infamous amnesty to political prisoners, mostly Czechs. The Germans claimed that disloyal prisoners (in particular Czech political activists) had been exonerated, and reacted negatively to the move, causing further opposition to the Habsburgs.

Between July 16 and 18 Italian small offensive endeavors against Habsburg III and XIII Corps continued. On July 20 battle erupted on the Asiago Plateau. Air battles occurred along the entire Piave River front, while incessant Italian Caproni bomber attacks harassed the battle-weary Habsburg troops. After mid-July almost the entire front witnessed regular battle.

As the military situation rapidly deteriorated it became more difficult to ensure that food supplies reached the front. Reinforcements to the Italian front had to undergo four to five weeks of additional training before they could be inserted into the front lines, because Eastern front troops proved unprepared for the brutal, physically exhaustive mountain warfare. The Italian front battles equaled the Western front battles in intensity and slaughter.

General Boroević consistently requested additional food supplies for his troops, emphasizing the critical situation, because without sufficient nourishment the troops rapidly became exhausted and more prone to panic. Already during February the troops had been undernourished for weeks, causing them to lose faith in their officers, which did not bode well for the army.

On the Western front, a massive Entente counterattack commenced on July 18, followed by the Amiens offensive resulting in the German August 8 army "black day" that finally shattered Habsburg belief in the German Army's invincibility. There followed the Entente hundred-day campaign. Meanwhile, the Italians launched a successful offensive against Habsburg troops in Albania. Western front defeats signified the Germans could not win the war, producing feelings of utter helplessness in the Dual Monarchy.

Incredibly, following the devastating June 15 failed offensive, Habsburg Supreme Command planned to potentially launch another major operation during fall 1918. Thirteen divisions, eight in the first wave, would attack between the Brenta and the Piave Rivers, supported by four thousand artillery pieces. The operation would require at least three months' preparation, but the army lacked sufficient equipment, manpower and artillery to launch an operation let alone provide sufficient food supplies. Hindenburg and Ludendorff increased pressure to redeploy Habsburg divisions to the Western front as promised earlier. German troops could no longer assist Habsburg forces on their embattled front.[18] The Central Powers were no longer in position to strike a decisive blow.

During the last August 13 and 14 Spa summit meeting, General Arz informed his counterparts that the Habsburg Army must suppress serious political unrest at home, while troops, materiel and reinforcements could no longer be transported to the Albanian or Adriatic Sea fronts. He further claimed that Austria-Hungary could not continue the war beyond the end of the year, thus peace must be negotiated as soon as feasible before the domestic situation worsened further. German leaders apparently did not realize how desperate the Habsburg situation had become. Central Power leaders also discussed the question of a truce, revealing for the first time that German leaders considered accepting peace based on the status quo.

General Arz had accepted that the army's fate depended upon Germany winning the war on the Western front, but that obviously would not happen. As the meeting adjourned, news arrived that the British government had recognized the Czech national council in Paris. This inflamed already deep-seated Habsburg Slavic dissatisfaction and opposition to the war as national antagonisms and pessimism continued to escalate. No strong leader headed the crumbling government to master the situation.

It became increasingly apparent that the Entente possessed an overwhelming military superiority in manpower and materiel. Habsburg field commanders became apathetic, accepting that any further human sacrifice would be useless. Troop desertions accelerated.[19] A majority of civil servants, including high-ranking government officials, began cooperating with the various evolving national councils, signaling further Habsburg central government demise. A facet of the November 1918 bloodless Austrian revolution resulted from Habsburg civil servants serving the newly created states. Meanwhile, German Christian Socialist Party members hesitated to prepare to separate Austria from the Dual Monarchy, but demanded the German right to self-determination, the first serious indication that the Habsburg government faced significant trouble.

Bohemian, South Slav and Galician railroad officials, indicating the national turmoil and prerevolution activities, began to block military or food delivery railroad traffic to Austria. The distressed German Austrian industrial mountain region situation had become unsustainable, with widespread starvation. Famine conditions became prevalent by early September in Galicia, Hungary and Bohemia, but more so in Vienna.[20]

By late September, domestic disturbances reached dangerous levels as people realized that Entente war aims now included the destruction of the Habsburg monarchy along ethnic lines. Labor unrest in war industries resulted in serious strikes and demonstrations, partially a result of further draconian rationing measures, and the increasing shortages of raw materials and commodity goods. Supplying basic items became almost impossible as inflation increasingly savaged civilian buying power. Women lined up for hours in queues to obtain bread and other necessities, often returning home empty-handed. Many were widows or cared for physically or mentally handicapped husbands.

English troops attacked Habsburg positions on the Asiago Plateau, while Habsburg Supreme Command redeployed two weakened divisions to the Western front. This signified that Boroević's forces would not secure further reinforcements. On August 18, General Arz released his last formal assessment of the Austro-Hungarian Army situation, questioning the Dual Monarchy's long-term survivability. Increasing concerns about the major disturbances and inner homefront chaos caused Emperor Karl to convene periodic meetings with his top military commanders. During the initial September 7 conclave, major discussions involved ensuring that supplies continued to flow to the field armies and how to stem the increasing troop desertions.[21]

Habsburg leaders consistently pleaded for German assistance for their critical food needs. German officials initially refused to assist, but then promised to provide thousands of wagons of grain. In return, Germany would receive all food supplies emanating from the Ukraine. The Germans eventually delivered some desperately required supplies, but only enough to satisfy minimal army needs. Feeding the army through summer 1918 became problematic because the national railroad system had collapsed and food supplies had dwindled further. Troops ate dried vegetables instead of meat and grain.

The rapidly deteriorating overall situation led to an August 12 Ministerial Council meeting to discuss the matter. Various government officials supported granting concessions to the nationalities, but as usual nothing noteworthy transpired. Chaos erupted in Galicia, particularly Krakow, a result of the worsening economic conditions. Although starvation intensified in Galicia, additional food was confiscated to be transported to alleviate suffering in Vienna.

The Habsburg Army and diminishing civilian food deliveries also resulted in desperate requests for more meat and grain deliveries from Hungary, which had solely fed the army since 1916. Hungarian Minister President Tisza initially refused to comply with the pleas, but eventually agreed to increase grain shipments to Austria. The misuse of food supplies was a common occurrence among the armies. Although sufficient amounts were delivered, much did not reach the trenches, but fed rear echelon troops.

The month of September heralded fatal events for the Central Powers. On September 3 the United States recognized the Czech national council in Paris as a de facto legitimate government, because of Czech Legion military feats in Russia. Emperor Karl attempted to establish peace talks based on President Wilson's Fourteen Points, and belatedly introduced some long-overdue political reforms for Austria; however, in the interim the Entente position had hardened relative to possible armistice terms. On September 4 the Vienna government attempted to initiate peace negotiations, but the Entente Powers rejected the proposal, because they sought a Central Power surrender not a negotiated settlement.

Meanwhile, insufficient and substandard food and poor-quality clothing, if available, produced sickness in army ranks. As one soldier lamented, "we are not heroes we are beggars."[22] The Habsburg Army recorded its manpower strength at two and a half million soldiers but half were unaccounted for. Manpower shortages continued: Of the Isonzo Army's fifteen divisions, seven claimed to be one-third filled, only three reported full strength while the other five had two-thirds their stand.

Entente forces continued to force German retreats during September, recapturing the territory they had surrendered during the spring offensives. On September 11, Emperor Karl convened his second meeting with senior military officers; the main discussions encompassed the critical necessity to train more field officers to replace the excessive battle casualties, as well as seeking a solution to the worsening problem of troop desertions. Most defecting soldiers returned home rather than to the enemy. During the month, approximate troop desertion numbers equaled the equivalent of twenty infantry divisions.[23] Two factors dominated, overwhelming Entente military superiority and soldiers' concerns for their families. The critical shortages of food and goods raised the question of whether the Dual Monarchy could survive through another winter.

When the September 14 peace appeal was rejected (Count Burian defied his German ally to initiate it), the Habsburg destiny would be determined on the battlefield. The next day Emperor Karl publicly appealed to President Wilson to accept an armistice. Then on September 17 disturbing reports emphasized the sparse availability of *Ersatz* formations, as well as the deficit of 225,000 replacement troops during the month alone.

Karl convened his third meeting with senior officers on September 30 to discuss the number of combat troops deployed in the hinterland and again to institute more effective measures to prevent troop desertions.[24] Knowledge that Habsburg Supreme Command sought an armistice produced paralysis in Habsburg Army ranks as soldiers questioned why they should risk their lives when the war could soon end. Habsburg Supreme Command concentrated on maintaining the army intact regardless of battlefield events. The long-simmering national and revolutionary activity finally exploded in Hungary, while the Habsburg central government continued to unsuccessfully resolve the crises exacerbating the situation.

An Entente offensive launched on the Salonica front (Greece) broke through Bulgarian defensive lines on September 14–15 at Dobro Polje, spear-headed by Serbian troops, that resulted in a rapid Bulgarian surrender in late September. The Bulgarian surrender came as a complete surprise to Habsburg Supreme Command. It also signaled the fate of both the Austro-Hungarian and German armies, because not only were there no troops to deploy on the collapsed front, but even if there were, the railroads could not have trans-ported them as the entire national system was collapsing. Bulgarian civilians and soldiers had been suffering from many of the same debilitating economic conditions that existed in Austria-Hungary. War weariness, starvation diets and low troop morale predominated, and a sense of futility resulted in a high rate of Bulgarian troop desertions. Then local unit mutinies rapidly trans-formed into insurrections, forcing the signing of the armistice within a month. The collapse of the Bulgarian front initiated the process of Habsburg defeat that terminated at the battle of Vittorio Veneto by baring the southern Habsburg flank in the Balkans. On September 20, the Serbian front collapsed, leading to the mutiny of Hungarian, Polish and Czech units on the Galician front and frantic attempts to rapidly restore a crumbling Balkan theater defensive, to prevent an invasion of Hungary, where no major military forces were deployed. The Habsburgs had to sign a peace treaty before Hungary faced invasion, but the failure led to further disaster.

Habsburg troops had to maintain the occupation of Serbia as long as possible, for economic as well as military purposes. When the Serbian front collapsed, Central Power troops could not close the ensuing gaping holes in the front lines because the declining railroad system disallowed the rapid deployment of troops to that area.[25] It required an estimated thirty days to establish an adequate Balkan defensive line. Only porous positions could be established on the Danube and Sava River lines as Habsburg troops slowly retreated toward Hungary. Slavic troops increasingly deserted their units, causing the South Slav problem to explode and Hungarian troops to demand to return home to defend their homeland against invasion. Serbian forces entered Belgrade on November 1.

By September 21 the Salonica Army had successfully separated the Bulgarian First and Second armies. The Bulgarian General Staff demanded that six German divisions be transferred immediately as reinforcements as promised by the alliance treaty. On September 24 the Bulgarians frantically reported that they now must have ten reinforcing divisions to maintain their lines, otherwise the situation would become catastrophic. Their allies could not do it because it would have required thousands of trains to redeploy that many troops on the small capacity rail lines from the Romanian and Ukrainian fronts. On September 25 the Salonica Army entered Bulgarian territory. The Bulgarians repeated their request for reinforcing troops as the extremely critical situation threatened the collapse of the entire Macedonian front.[26] At a September 1918 Habsburg Crown Council meeting it was determined to establish defensive measures in the Serbian theater, then peace initiatives would be introduced. Meanwhile, various nationalities pressed their separatist tendencies because of a lack of firm leadership everywhere.[27] An ominous leadership paralysis became increasingly obvious. Meanwhile, the loyalty of *Assistenz* troops deployed in the hinterland came into question.

On September 28 the Bulgarian minister president requested an armistice; hostilities terminated on September 30. Bulgaria became the first Central Power ally to surrender. The armistice conditions included Bulgarian troops having to evacuate Serbian and Greek soil and immediately demobilizing. A secret clause would enable Entente forces to traverse through Bulgaria, thus as with the later Habsburg surrender, it represented a capitulation. The collapse of the Bulgarian front helped persuade the German government to seek peace terms on the basis of President Wilson's Fourteen Points.

On October 4 the Serbian Army advanced on a broad front toward Nis between the Drina and Danube Rivers to invade northern Serbia. Habsburg and German troops had to defend the Danube River line to prevent an invasion of southern Austrian provinces, but unfortunately had neither the necessary forces nor the requisite three to four weeks to transfer troops to the endangered front.

The Bulgarian capitulation provided strategic and political advantage to the Entente. It ruptured the Serbian front, which could not be adequately defended, threatening southern Austria, Hungary, Turkey, Serbia and Albania with invasion. There were no military units in southern Hungary to halt Entente troops approaching the frontier from Serbia or Romania. It also endangered the transit of food and oil supplies from Romania. Turkey soon demanded an armistice. These occurrences provided the background to the October 4 Emperor Karl note to President Wilson as South Slav politicians increased their radical demands. This was a decisive moment in the war.

The omnipresent war weariness, critical food crisis and fuel shortages increasingly thrust economic and national issues to the forefront, negatively affecting frontline soldiers' morale because of their growing concern for their families. News of the German Meuse–Argonne defeat followed by the hundred-day Entente offensive campaign that continued until September 28 destroyed the severely depleted Habsburg morale, as troop strengths continued to rapidly dwindle through desertion, disease and battlefield casualties.

The anti-war socialist Friedrich Adler, son of Social Democrat Party leader Victor Adler, assassinated Minister President Sturgkh on October 24, symptomatic of the accelerating Austrian political turmoil. Adler's action represented an abortive attempt to alter the political deadlock paralyzing Austria, because Sturgkh represented the oppressive central government to many. His death and the earlier demise of Emperor Franz Joseph removed constraints to radical activity. Adler received jail time, but later Emperor Karl pardoned him.

In early October 1918 further draconian rationing measures exacerbated an already critical situation because of the rapidly dwindling supplies of every type of necessity. In Vienna only enough flour and raw materials existed to last until November. Strikes, food riots, protests, demonstrations and civil unrest evolved into massive upheavals as inflation continued to destroy the already decimated civilian buying power. By the end of the month the rising turmoil had reached epidemic proportions.

During the latter two weeks of the month, the Habsburg Army disintegrated, while national revolutions erupted across the home front. Cases of insubordination increased in army training camps. On October 1 Habsburg troops had to retreat from Albania, while multiple *Landwehr* and *Honvéd* units were to counter the accelerating internal strife. In Germany on October 3 Generals Hindenburg and Ludendorff demanded an immediate armistice as Ludendorff surprisingly declared that the war had been lost. This shocked the public, because newspapers had only reported continued battlefield victories, while troops remained deployed in multiple countries outside of Germany. On October 2 the Habsburg joint cabinet meeting with the emperor determined to seek an armistice under the increasing domestic pressure. This resulted in the October 4 request for peace on the basis of Wilson's Fourteen Points.[28] This introduced an exchange of notes between President Wilson (not including the Entente powers) and the Central Powers between October 10 and 23 as well as enhanced anticipation in Vienna. President Wilson replied on October 8 to an earlier communication that resulted in a proposed request for an armistice that was introduced in the Habsburg *Reichsrat*. The American president also relayed messages on October 14 and 23. The German government responded on October 12, 20 and 27. On the domestic front the German Austrian nationalists accepted the German Social Democratic proposal for self-determination on October 4. The Christian Socialists also accepted it on principle.

The October 4 peace offer based on the Fourteen Points created great alarm at Habsburg Supreme Command headquarters because the proposal stirred up revolutionary emotions in the army on the eve of the Italian offensive against the Dual Monarchy. The lack of a rapid US response from President Wilson to the Habsburg peace proposals caused enormous concern in Vienna. The Wilson reply proved deadly for the Dual Monarchy. In the meantime, various nationalities became increasingly restive and more active, particularly after the decisive German Western front defeats. The German setbacks created the opportunity to attempt to achieve independence from the hated Habsburg central government.

On October 5 frenzied demonstrations erupted in the Dual Monarchy because of rumors that an armistice had been concluded. Emperor Karl conferred with multiple national party leaders, attempting to organize a cabinet to establish a federal Austrian state. Czech leaders indicated that they would only accept their own independent government, which destroyed any chance of Karl forming a coalition ministry of nationalities. Between October 5 and 11 the Czechs, then South Slavic leaders, formed a national council at Zagreb to defend the South Slavic movement as well as the creation of a Polish national council. On October 6 South Slavic leaders convened the national summit meeting at Agram (Zagreb) to prepare the creation of a unified Yugoslavia, while Czech and Slovak delegates met in Prague. Both began to function as de facto national governments distancing from the central government. This increased the threat of simultaneous, national revolutions. Habsburg Army ethnic cohesion began to further crumble as the armistice question produced increasing paralysis in the ranks.[29] Arz demanded the creation of an armistice commission on October 5 but released no instructions for it, while Habsburg Supreme Command concentrated on maintaining the army as a viable military force regardless of future circumstances.[30] General Arz and Emperor Karl would determine the proper time, but would not introduce significant peace talks while their troops occupied vast areas of Italian territory.

On October 7 Galician Poles declared their independence and Polish soldiers began to disarm loyalist troops. Hungary announced its separation from Austria and also denounced the German alliance. Meanwhile, President Wilson's October 8 diplomatic reply to the German peace request stipulated that Austria-Hungary must evacuate all occupied Allied territory before he transmitted a diplomatic communiqué to Vienna. German troops must also immediately evacuate Belgium and France. The German government affirmed it would evacuate Entente territory if peace would be based on Wilson's Fourteen Points. On October 9 the South Slavs (Slovenes, Serbians and Croatians) and Czechs met to assist each other in establishing national governments. Turmoil continued in the hinterland as the military situation worsened. The multiple Dual Monarchy problems could not be resolved at this late hour.

The increasingly chaotic situation raised the question of how to provide food to the starving Viennese population.[31] Soldiers continued to desert their ranks to return home. Habsburg front lines could only be defended if some immediate and/or radical action brought order in the hinterland, which unfortunately did not occur. In the interim, Karl informed political leaders that he intended to create a federal state although he also encountered difficulty finding a new foreign minister.[32]

On October 11, as the Austrian and Hungarian minister presidents (Hussark and Wekerle) resigned their positions, turmoil accelerated and panic began to take hold. Italian and French troops launched a diversionary attack on the Asiago Plateau, targeting Mt. Grappa, the keystone of the Habsburg northern front defensive system. But the major Entente offensive would be launched between the Brenta and Piave Rivers two weeks later. The diversionary effort failed, but by October 14 Italian, British and French troops prepared to launch the long-anticipated offensive to end the war.

On October 12, German Austrian Social Democratic deputies constituted themselves as a provisional national assembly and claimed the formation of an Austrian state. They were the first political party to withdraw from the *Reichsrat* and thus the empire ended. The Hungarian-Romanian minority established a National Assembly that demanded self-determination for Transylvania and separation from the Dual Monarchy (Romania received Transylvania in the Treaty of Trianon on June 4, 1920). The Italian government determined to secure the territories promised in the 1915 Treaty of London, thus their final offensive served primarily as a last-minute land grab.

The Habsburg Army's fighting capabilities declined rapidly as independence movements in Galicia, Czech and South Slav regions reached fever pitch. Various national military units became increasingly mutinous, while sickness and casualty attrition caused troop numbers to continue to decline precipitously. The second Wilson reply to the Habsburg peace offer shattered any misconceived ideas.[33] President Wilson had raised his demands.

A coordinated general strike erupted in Bohemia on October 14 as efforts continued to install a functioning, fledging provisional Czech government. Food shipments to Vienna and the army were halted. On October 14 and 17 exiled Czech leaders Masaryk and Benes announced the birth of the Czech Republic. On October 15 Habsburg Supreme Command ordered the evacuation of troops from Russia and the Ukraine, terminating the possibility of any further grain delivery from there for its starving people. Polish *Reichsrat* deputies declared themselves divorced from the Habsburg state.

During the next two weeks, conditions steadily worsened as the army began to disintegrate and strikes and national independence movements gained strength. The escalating economic, social and political unrest and revolutionary activities occurring in the army's rear echelon areas had a devastating effect on the psyche and morale of frontline troops, compounded by their overwhelming exhaustion, malnutrition and war weariness. Habsburg battle effectiveness and troop discipline continued to collapse. At the same time, Emperor Karl's promises to Polish leaders and continuing South Slav agitation created an increasingly confusing domestic situation.

Initially, only rumors of the worsening homefront conditions reached front-line troops. Then, the formerly *kaisertreu* Hungarian Minister President Tisza gave his infamous "the war is lost" speech in Budapest, which created a firestorm amongst *Honvéd* troops, as well as negatively affecting Habsburg morale.[34] This helped accelerate the far advanced process of disintegration throughout the Dual Monarchy. By mid-October the Habsburg central government obviously had lost control of the situation. A general strike erupted in Galicia, as its railroads passed into Polish hands, rapidly curtailing traffic to Austria.

Karl's Manifesto of October 16, approved by the *Kronrat* (Crown Council), purported to transform Austria into a federal state after his two failed peace proposals, represented a desperate last-minute attempt to resolve the empire's internal and external problems and pacify President Wilson. It was obvious that neither the army nor general population could survive the winter. The Manifesto, which specifically targeted the Czechs and South Slavs, received no popular support. The common people's main concern remained the shortage of food and their economic plight. Then the French government recognized the Czech provisional government. Emperor Karl intended for the Manifesto to save his dynasty. Minorities (not in Hungary) had to organize national councils from *Reichsrat* deputies to facilitate the process of federalization. Hungary's refusal to accept the Manifesto destroyed the *Ausgleich*, the agreement to create the Austro-Hungarian Empire following Austria's defeat to Prussia in 1866. The only thing left for the Hungarians was the personal union, with Karl remaining as king. Romanian and Slovakian leaders pressed for immediate self-determination as the South Slavs' situation was basically ignored. Various areas increasingly came under the jurisdiction of evolving national councils. The Manifesto, containing no specific details, became one of the final nails in the Dual Monarchy's coffin. The document appeared to concede to the Czech, Polish and South Slavic National Committees the right to create their own national councils and accelerated the formation of independent states and national governments. The government lost control of the situation. *Reichsrat* deputies opened the floodgates to the separate independence movements well underway. The Manifesto destroyed the foundation of the central governmental, while it received an overall unfavorable reaction from the citizenry, particularly the various national leaders. The Manifesto alerted the public to the desperation that the situation had created. A few days later, as battlefield defeat loomed, the emperor released the Habsburg officer corps from their oath of allegiance to the dynasty, destroying any remaining army morale. The oath was the last and strongest bond binding the army together. Officers quickly joined their newly created states' armies, terminating their allegiance to the empire.

Czech and South Slavic leaders, particularly Slovenes, widely interpreting they were free, rushed to create their own national governments and refused to cooperate with Karl's efforts, accelerating internal dissolution and the formation of independent national governments. Magyar leaders erroneously calculated that by being represented separately in future peace negotiations they could maintain their present territory, but the new revolutionary situation opened the door for all ethnic independence tendencies, including the Magyar Slavic peoples.[35] When Hungarian leaders declared the *Ausgleich* dissolved, Romanian and Slovak leaders asserted their right of self-determination, although the Slovenes, Serbians and Croatians briefly remained relatively quiescent.

In response to President Wilson's reply to the earlier request for an armistice, General Arz ordered the evacuation of the Venetian Plain on October 17. This ordinarily would require three months to accomplish and result in the loss of enormous quantities of supplies and equipment. Increasingly disconcerting events continued as the military leadership sought an armistice, fearing anarchy would erupt in the ranks of the starving and poorly maintained troops.

On October 18 South Slav leaders declared themselves the sole arbiters of their future. A Ruthenian national council convened in Lemberg while Romanian leaders did so in Czernovitz. Neither the Austrian Germans nor Hungarians had faith in Emperor Karl because of his indecisiveness and failed leadership.[36] The Czech national council in Paris published its Declaration of Independence on October 18, creating a Czech-Slovak provisional government on October 19, partly because of Thomas Masaryk's concern over the effects of Karl's Manifesto. Habsburg claims in Bohemia and Moravia were summarily negated, as the Czech and South Slav national councils refused to negotiate with the central government before a peace conference convened. Nationalist leaders believed that they could gain nothing negotiating with Viennese officials, because they demanded complete independence. In Czech and South Slavic territories, authorities continued to halt the railroad movement of troops and food supplies, particularly to Vienna. A Czech blockade of food shipments gravely hurt the starving Vienna populous. Meanwhile, revolutionary events erupted in Budapest.

On October 20 General Staff officers were dispatched to Prague, Krakow, Villach and Agram to plea to the new national councils to cooperate to prevent potential anarchy and destruction of the army before demobilization. The turmoil aggravated the troops, a result of two factors, the Manifesto and commencements of the creation of national armies. Military leadership feared anarchy would erupt in German territories as returning troops robbed, pillaged, burned, raped and plundered.[37] During the next two days several units either mutinied or refused to be deployed into the front lines. As the army began to implode, the developing new national governments instructed their troops to return to their homeland. Soon half the army either rebelled or marched from the front.

The army suffered as shortages of every conceivable item continued. Artillery pieces continued to fail at an alarming rate, troops became increasingly unreliable in combat, reserve units refused to deploy and others mutinied. On the Serbian front, troops continued a slow retreat to the Sava–Danube River line. Reinforcements, now increasingly difficult to marshal, could not be redeployed rapidly enough, partially because of the almost complete railroad collapse that set off a chain reaction.

In an attempt to end the war, the emperor appointed Julius Andrassy to replace Foreign Minister Burian four days after President Wilson's reply to Karl's peace proposals. The emperor now believed that the German alliance must be terminated for the monarchy to survive as revolutionary events erupted in all major Habsburg cities. The emperor resisted senior army generals' pleas, particularly General Boroević's, to deploy troops to intervene in the internal crisis. In Budapest the parliament voted for constitutional changes and demanded that all formal ties to Austria be severed. To attempt to maintain peace in the interior an additional 207½ infantry companies and 8 field artillery battalions provided support. This raised the total number to 315 units, but their effectiveness and loyalty increasingly became questionable.

On October 21, President Wilson responded to the earlier Habsburg peace note exclaiming that significant events forced him to jettison his previous position to Austria-Hungary. The USA recognized Czechoslovakia as a belligerent nation, its national council now constituting a de facto government. Wilson again demanded that Vienna accept Southern Slav aspirations for independence. His acknowledgment of the Czechoslovakian national council and the future South Slav state finalized the demise of the Habsburg monarchy and hastened the collapse of central authority. South Slav, Polish and Czechoslovakian authorities organized their own national armies.

As revolutionary activities increased, German *Reichsrat* deputies proclaimed the creation of a new Austrian state encompassing the German-speaking areas of the former empire. They declared themselves a provisional national assembly until a constituent assembly could be elected. They included the predominantly German-speaking areas of Bohemia and what became the Sudetenland, which represented the first formal break from the Austrian portion of the empire. The final Lammasch ministry considered its responsibility to be to liquidate the monarchy as peacefully as possible.

Further demonstrations erupted in Prague and Krakow, while in Budapest the new Karolyi-dominated parliament ordered all Hungarian soldiers to return home without regard to the military situation on the Italian front to defend the Balkan frontier. War Minister Linder's November 1 decree initially applied to only Hungarian troops in rear echelon areas.[38] Events developed rapidly in Budapest. Karolyi and his Social Democrat supporters formed a national council on October 23. A student revolt erupted on October 24 and a portion of a mob forced the doors of the Hungarian parliament. On October 27 the large crowds that surrounded the parliament building created the nucleus of the Magyar revolution. Violence resulted in the parliament being suspended and the Hungarian minister president resigning. Then, on October 30, revolutionary officers and troops swore loyalty to the new Hungarian state. On October 31 Emperor Karl appointed Karolyi minister president, having accepted the revolutionary Hungarian situation. On October 22 Karl had dispatched Archduke Joseph, a popular Hungarian general, to Budapest to calm the situation, but it proved too late to achieve any positive results. The tensions in the capital continued. Croatians, Slovaks and Romanians revolted against the despised Magyars, while incessantly negative news arrived from the front.

On the Italian mountain front the 27. and 38. *Honvéd* Infantry Divisions then three infantry and one cavalry division refused to fight. When the news spread through army ranks that the 27. *Honvéd* division was going to march home Slavic soldiers began to refuse to obey orders. Karl notified Wilhelm that he must seek an armistice within twenty-four hours.

The Habsburg government resigned. On the front twenty-one of fifty-one infantry divisions refused to obey orders, while most Magyar troops began to desert the front lines. This provided indications of serious problems from escalating troop disobedience. As the Habsburg home front also collapsed major battle erupted on the Italian mountain theater as the Italians attempted to gain a stronger bargaining position at a peace conference.

The Habsburg central government remained paralyzed as anti-dynastic agitation accelerated. Croatian, Czech, Hungarian and Romanian soldiers deserted their posts, signaling open revolt. South Slavic troops refused to continue fighting, preferring to defend their new homelands. Karl formed his last official government under former college professor Heinrich Lammasch. Thereupon Lammasch notified President Wilson that Vienna accepted that the various nationalities could seek their own destiny within the Dual Monarchy, particularly the Czechs and South Slavs.[39] Vienna initially would accept any peace terms as long as the army retained its honor and did not have to capitulate, but as a result of grievous leadership mistakes the armistice negotiations resulted in capitulation.

In the meantime, British troops raided Habsburg positions on the Papadopoli Island in the Piave River, a vital jumping-off point for the looming major Italian offensive across the river. Entente and Bolshevik propaganda increasingly influenced Habsburg citizens and troops. Karl's approval of Hungarian soldiers returning home inflamed Slavic troops. The collapse of the army accelerated on October 22 when multiple regiments mutinied, troops deserted and demonstrations erupted in the hinterland. Increasingly negative news arrived from the Balkan front, while Habsburg Supreme Command efforts to isolate soldiers from news of the escalating turmoil and economic conditions on the home front failed. Slavic troops joined Hungarian units that refused to continue fighting, as serious rebellions, troop desertions and mutinies escalated.[40] Emperor Karl belatedly issued a message appealing to soldiers to remain loyal to the Habsburg cause and fulfill their duty.

The long-anticipated Italian offensive commenced on October 24, the date chosen to erase memory of the disastrous Caporetto battle a year earlier. The offensive caught Habsburg Supreme Command by complete surprise because its intelligence service failed. Six divisions attacked Habsburg positions at Mt. Grappa. Troop numbers rapidly declined, although the remaining soldiers fought fiercely for several days, driven mainly by the instinct to survive. Both sides sustained significant casualties.[41] Although mutinies immediately occurred, most units initially held their lines. Commanders discovered that they had no replacement troops.

The Italian offensive objective was to split Habsburg Fifth and Sixth armies apart. This would threaten the positions on the Asiago Plateau and Mt. Grappa. The operation commenced on Mt. Grappa.

Most soldiers, deciding they had suffered enough, disappeared, even members of the elite Viennese *Edelweiss* 3. Infantry Division on October 29. Troops refused to replace the Hungarian troops leaving the front lines, signaling open revolt in the army. Demoralized officers became paralyzed as the situation rapidly degenerated. Disease ranging from malaria, dysentery and Spanish flu struck down the starving Habsburg soldiers.

On October 25, the Italians extended their offensive to the key Belluno Group on the Piave River front. Following heavy-artillery barrages between the Brenta and Piave Rivers, the Fourth and Sixth Italian armies launched a diversionary attack on a twenty-two-kilometer front. Italian Fourth Army units assaulted mountain peaks from both sides of critical Mt. Grappa. Following intensive battle Italian forces conquered key positions on the Belluno Group front.

Troops quickly realized that they could not defend their positions much longer, because there were no reserve units and severe causalities took an enormous toll on remaining troop numbers. Multiple battalions had sunk to company strength with no officers. Habsburg Supreme Command and the war minister demanded an immediate armistice to prevent an army collapse. Within the next few days three Czech and three Croatian divisions as well as thirteen regiments mutinied, creating chaos.[42]

The military situation had deteriorated so seriously that a Habsburg Supreme Command delegation traveled to the front lines to attempt to persuade the remaining troops to defend their positions until an armistice could be concluded; however, en masse mutinies and desertions had become the order of the day. Remaining units could no longer repel a major Italian attack. Karl informed Wilhelm that he would have to seek an armistice.

Artillery fire briefly camouflaged that portions of the Habsburg front had disintegrated. Italian High Command did not immediately recognize the extent of the chaos behind enemy lines.

The main Italian attack proceeded on October 26; an overpowering assault against the Habsburg Papadopoli bridgehead drove the enemy's forces across the river. Most troops refused to obey orders. Another Italian attack opened access to the Belluno basin, seriously weakening that key defensive line. During brutal battle some units defending the river front collapsed when their situation became hopeless. Entire divisions refused to man their front lines and marched to rear echelon areas, accelerating the army's disintegration. Habsburg troops fought for ninety-six hours without rest or reinforcements. Mutinies now coincided with the multiple Piave front disturbances.

National antagonisms exploded meanwhile on the home front as Hungarian troops returned. This return opened a Pandora's box. Croatian Infantry Regiment 79 occupied Fiume, indicating increased separatist nationalist military activity. Vienna would now accept all Entente armistice conditions.

On the next day defender resistance slackened considerably. Casualties again proved costly as ammunition supplies were depleted. Early on October 27 three Italian armies, supported by strong artillery fire, crossed the Piave River, and Habsburg troops could not seriously resist the assault. Many troops refused to fight or simply deserted their units. Only a few reserve formations continued to defend the critical Brenta and Piave River lines.

Between October 26 and 27 at least thirteen divisions began to implode as many troops marched to rear echelon areas, while most remaining Hungarian troops refused to obey orders. The battle between the Brenta and Piave Rivers had been exceedingly bloody. In the second phase Italian troops advanced into the Belluno basin and against both sides of Mt. Grappa, then to the Vittoria Vento area to neutralize the Eleventh Army on the Asiago front. Habsburg forces were catastrophically low in troop numbers, ammunition and all military necessities. All hopes faded; resistance was broken. Simultaneously, revolutionary events erupted throughout the Dual Monarchy, which had an increasingly negative effect on soldier morale.

Why should any soldier risk his life if the war could end soon? Karl finally authorized General Viktor Edler Weber to seek an armistice (an armistice commission had been established in early October). A peace offer was transmitted to Washington, DC requesting an immediate armistice on the basis of the October 18 diplomatic note.

Army Group Belluno, despite critical loss of men and ammunition, reconquered terrain lost three days earlier, but at heavy human cost. Regiments now numbered only 50–300 men, instead of the normal 4,400. The army group survived destruction only because Italian troops halted their advance because of exhaustion, losing 35,000 troops in the process.

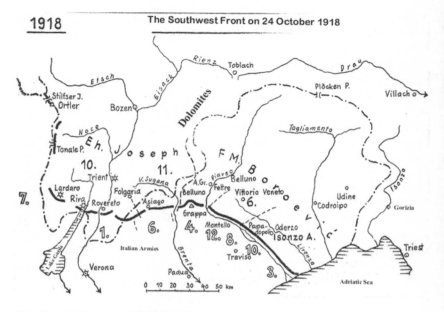

Map 12   *October 24, 1918 Italian Front*

The major fighting in the mountains terminated within twenty-four hours, allowing the Italians to turn their main attention to the Piave River front as during the earlier 1916 *Straf* offensive. With the end of mountain fighting, a dangerous series of events transpired. The Piave front began to collapse, prohibiting the redeployment of Hungarian troops from that battlefield as well. Some Hungarian units simply began marching home. In the meantime, a scheduled counterattack had to be canceled because of mutinies or soldiers' refusal to obey orders.

On October 28 a major demonstration in Budapest was followed by a general strike and demands for an immediate armistice and acceptance of President Wilson's conditions for peace. Reports from the Tyrol warned of catastrophe and anarchy if an armistice was not immediately forthcoming. A Czech national council, after a bloodless popular revolt in Prague, proclaimed a Czechoslovakian nation and assumed the administration of Bohemia and Moravia.

Also on October 28, General Weber received instructions that any armistice must avoid capitulation; emphasis must be the army's honor. An enormous disadvantage of the Habsburg negotiation team was that it often did not receive timely correspondence from Habsburg Supreme Command or the emperor.

The next day the order to prepare material for destruction and initial retreat contingency plans was prepared. Most troops rushed from the front, except German formations. By evening Sixth Army had disintegrated, unable to defend its front. A contiguous front no longer existed between the Isonzo Army and Army Group Belluno. Retreat had to be ordered before the troops were surrounded.

Five divisions pierced the lines between Army Belluno Group and Sixth Army on October 29. A retreat ensued. The troops regrouped at the 1917 Caporetto line, but the retrograde action could not be halted as mutinies, revolts and desertions accelerated. The army disintegrated between October 28 and 31, the background to the creation of new national states.

On the same day Foreign Minister Andrassy dispatched a note to President Wilson as General Arz dispatched the armistice commission to the front because field commanders now accepted that further struggle was purposeless. As the general rapid retreat continued on October 29, many additional units mutinied as reports of plundering of food and supply depots accelerated. The Italians unleashed heavy-artillery fire on a fifty-kilometer front. Meanwhile, many wounded soldiers succumbed to their wounds before they could be removed from the battlefield. As troops rapidly abandoned their positions the wounded were forgotten. On the Piave River front Italian troops, led by English forces, broke through Habsburg lines and created a bridgehead six miles deep and twelve miles wide on Papadopoli Island.[43] Arz informed German High Command that he required an immediate armistice, as the grossly overburdened army logistical system rapidly collapsed. A Slovak national council endorsed a union with the Czechs on October 29, as workers and soldiers in Budapest filled the streets, ending the Hungarian revolution. Hungarian leaders proclaimed a republic on October 31. The Croatians also declared their independence and established a national council in Zagreb.

General Weber dispatched Captain Ruggera to the front lines at Roverto in the early morning hours with a letter to be delivered to the Italian High Command, which requested negotiations for an armistice. When no reply was received Habsburg Supreme Command broadcast it in a radio message from the Pola naval station.

At 10 p.m. a reply arrived refusing negotiations because Captain Ruggera was not authorized to represent Habsburg Supreme Command. The answer also proclaimed that the Italians had no intention of halting their combat operations. They would only accept General Weber as chief negotiator. Further delays allowed the Italians to strengthen their position for the postwar peace.

Frantic Habsburg military leaders attempted to save at least a portion of the army and maintain the present borders, but Italian troops were already breaking through their front lines. Habsburg Supreme Command had delayed too long to sue for peace and the Italians no longer had incentive to accept an immediate armistice. There were no strong military formations at the Serbian frontier so Hungarian leaders frantically sought troops to defend the Serbian and Romanian borders particularly when Romania threatened to reenter the war. The withdrawal of Magyar troops divided and then destroyed the remaining remnants of the *k.u.k.* Army unity. An armistice had become critical because of homefront conditions as well. It became evident that the government had lost control of the situation, although initiating multiple ineffective attempts to calm the increasing revolutionary activities. The Social Democratic Party prevented a destructive revolution in Austria during late 1918 and in 1919, as will be revealed in Chapter 10. On October 30 Habsburg Supreme Command reported that the army could no longer maintain order.

By October 30 the military situation was beyond rectification. Vienna witnessed violent mass daily demonstrations, increasingly supported by large numbers of soldiers opposing the social and political system, resulting in military defeat and social revolution occurring simultaneously. The Piave River front collapse steadily pushed the front toward the mountain theater. When the Isonzo Army's northern flank joined the ensuing retreat movement it would force troops in the Tyrol to also withdraw. Starving troops plundered and burned military depots and destroyed civilian property. Some retreating troops fought with military police and guard units. Rear echelon areas were in utter disarray. The mountain front collapsed by November 1, thus neither the army nor Dual Monarchy existed any longer.[44]

Following major demonstrations and a general strike, the revolutionary government formed in Budapest, while separate Slovak, Croat and Slovenian states were proclaimed. In Germany, the sailors at Wilhelmshaven Naval Base revolted. The insurrection resulted partially from the sailors' terrible living conditions, resembling the February 1918 Habsburg Cattaro naval incident. The German military defeat on the Western front enabled the various Dual Monarchy nationalities to finally secede from the monarchy.

Chaos continued. Troops stormed trains, grabbing any available seat. Hundreds riding on top of locomotives and train cars lost their lives traveling through tunnels and over bridges. Troop commanders ordered retreat movements without enemy provocation. The Dual Monarchy faced the immediate chaos of hundreds of thousands of troops rapidly returning home.

Czech-German agitation continued in Bohemia. Emperor Karl appointed Karolyi Hungarian minister president on October 31, 1918 in a final attempt to preserve the constitutional link with that neighbor. The new coalition government received strong support from soldiers and officers. The government denounced the 1867 *Ausgleich* agreement, declaring Hungarian independence. On the same day, following demonstrations in the capital, soldiers murdered Tisza at his home. On October 30 a separate German Austrian government was formed with the Social Democrat Karl Renner, the first chancellor.

The Italians claimed a major victory at Vittorio Veneto, which severed Habsburg troops on the southern Italian front from those in northern Tyrol. The "victory" came against a disintegrating army. The new Hungarian government immediately encountered serious problems. It had to negotiate a favorable peace treaty, while organizing a new government capable of governing. The nationality problem had to be quickly resolved, as did the division of peasants' land, while raising the overall standard of living. A further major problem involved the integration of former Russian prisoners of war into economic and political life.

On October 30 an Allied Paris conference discussed Vienna's armistice request. On the same day Turkey signed the Mudros Armistice. removing it from the war. At 6 p.m. General Weber and Lt. Colonel Karl Schneller crossed Italian front lines. Weber wanted to immediately commence negotiations, but was informed that the Italian officers were not authorized to accept his request. Italian stalling tactics had started. Habsburg tardiness in seeking an armistice resulted partially from time needed to negotiate with the German ally, as well as the creation of national councils for the new states, the military collapse and strong opposition to the German treaty.

Entente leaders had convened meetings relative to a potential armistice on October 7, 12 and 15, with the decisive one determining final conditions on October 30. This included a possible invasion of Germany.

As new governments and armies prepared to establish seven separate states, soldiers rushed home, looting and adding new support for the evolving revolutionary events. Habsburg Supreme Command attempted to halt the intensifying riots and plundering, specifically in the Habsburg Alpine lands.

The Habsburg armistice commission was notified on October 31 that the armistice conditions would be communicated. Matters progressed slowly because Italian command was in no hurry to negotiate a treaty. In the interim its troops entered Trent and Trieste before an armistice could be negotiated. By 4 p.m. the Austrian commission was driven to Villa Giusti. General Diaz received notification that the Allied command conditions had been defined (in French) and that the text demanded unconditional surrender. Battle continued almost without pause.

The situation continued to deteriorate rapidly because of accelerating chaos, which resulted in Arz requesting that national councils send deputations to the front lines to intercede in the chaotic retreat. Habsburg Command was questioned over whether the Alpine passes could be defended by Habsburg troops, causing the Germans to fear for the safety of Bavaria.[45] Habsburg Command also lost control of its military forces in the hinterland.[46]

Four German and additional divisions would defend the Alps along the main mountain heights because of the increased Entente threat to the German southern Bavarian flank. Then Minister President Lammasch raised the question of terminating the German alliance treaty.

In Vienna, the government remained impotent as rioting erupted throughout the city and public buildings were occupied. The Dual Monarchy continued to implode, but somehow some soldiers representing all nationalities continued to fight on a few sectors of the front, although the Dual Monarchy was in absolute turmoil. Thousands died mostly in isolated battle, when their homeland no longer existed.

Military academy cadets protected Emperor Karl and his family in Schönbrunn Palace until his departure to Switzerland. In Slovenia and other southern Slavic areas, the green cadre forces of army deserters controlled large areas armed with machine guns and artillery pieces hidden in forests and living off the countryside. This lawlessness in South Slavic territories was crushed at the end of the war by invading Serbian troops, a major factor in Croatians and Slovenes accepting a united Yugoslavia.

The Habsburg people suffered sheer exhaustion, hunger and war weariness during 1918 as the army sustained its final defeat. Food and industrial production problems seemed hopeless, particularly in Vienna. The Austro-Hungarian Empire ended, its remnants creating new states. The Italian front war ended on November 4. In Chapter 10 we examine events concerning the collapse of the Dual Monarchy during November then the Versailles peace treaty and its effect as well as the newly created nations. Meanwhile, by the end of October the newly established government worked in unison with the old regime administrators, particularly the diplomatic corps.

10

November 1918 and Results

When the First World War reputedly terminated on November 11, 1918, chaos, violence, warfare and revolution continued in Central and Eastern Europe particularly with the Russian Civil War of 1918–1922.[1] The frontiers of the seven new countries resulting from the collapse of the Austro-Hungarian monarchy left porous frontier areas, many of which witnessed revolution, civil and regular warfare, wars of independence and ethnic conflicts for multiple years. Thus, the Versailles peace treaty did not restore stability and prosperity in Central and Eastern Europe, but instead produced conflicting interests and ethnic turmoil as well as chaos and violence because the frontiers often had been imprecisely improvised. England and France had been too weakened by the war to strongly control the events in Central and Eastern Europe, but utilized the Allied "winners" Czechoslovakia, Yugoslavia and Romania to become the Little Entente to represent their interests in this area of the continent.

Economic conditions in these parts of Europe worsened as inflation exploded throughout the entire region, negatively affecting the various currencies. The winter season merely worsened the situation. The economies remained basically agrarian, except for Czechoslovakia and Austria, once frontiers had been established. The newly created entities had the major problem of absorbing millions of soldiers and refugees returning to their territories, which increased the further social and economic dislocation and violence.

Returning to November 1918, Entente armistice terms arrived on November 1. Emperor Karl attempted to avoid signing the document until the new national governments convened, hoping that they would accept them, particularly the German Austrian and South Slavic. He tried to have them assume the burden of signing the document. However, he received no reply from Laibach or Agram (the South Slavic capitals) and the new civilian Austrian government refused to sign the document. In the meantime, non-Slavic troops attempted to retreat from the Piave River line but were briefly restrained by South Slavic officials. In Serbia native troops reoccupied Belgrade. As a result of the many earlier events both Emperor Karl and the Habsburg imperial government had lost the confidence of its citizens already before October 1918.

On November 1, 1918 the new Hungarian war minister Linder demanded that all Hungarian soldiers return to the Homeland to defend against a Serbian invasion. General Arz delayed transmission of that message to the various fronts until the next day. Thus began the disintegration of the Austro-Hungarian Army.

Following the armistice, the new Magyar leader Karolyi proclaimed a democratic Hungarian republic on November 16, 1918 and served as president between January and March 1919. He lost the Hungarian people's confidence when the various nationalities (Croats, Slovenes, Romanians and Slovaks) declared their independence and the Paris peacemakers carved out Hungarian territory for them. Support also dwindled because the Hungarian economy and transportation system had collapsed and not recovered, so Karolyi resigned on March 20, 1919. In the interlude the Entente gave the Habsburg leadership until midnight November 3 to accept the armistice conditions or it would resume offensive operations. Finally, at 11:30 p.m. Emperor Karl accepted the conditions, although he protested Point 4 concerning Entente troops having free movement through Austria-Hungary, a vital military threat to Germany.

On November 1 the Italian armistice delegation finally arrived at 10 a.m. to negotiate, but dragged its feet. The major Italian representative, General Pietro Badoglio, proclaimed that the negotiations could not commence, because the interallied council in Versailles was still preparing the armistice terms, which would not be delivered before November 2. The Italian delegation also claimed that a cease-fire could only be negotiated with fully accredited Habsburg Supreme Command representatives. The delegates refused to allow Captain Ruggera to act as an intermediary; they would only accept General Weber as the accredited negotiator.[2] Hostilities would not be halted until all armistice conditions had been met.

The Habsburg representatives sought to negotiate an immediate armistice to maintain their army and their frontiers intact. The Italian negotiators, to the contrary, were in no hurry to finalize an armistice because their troops had broken through Habsburg front lines. Every delay strengthened Italy's position at the Paris peace negotiations. Habsburg Supreme Command had delayed too long to seek a cease-fire, not realizing that its army had already commenced its implosion much earlier than anticipated.

Armistice conditions approved by Lloyd George and Clemenceau in Paris were telephoned to Italian Supreme Command during the morning of October 31. The terms were repeated to the Habsburg Armistice Commission members. Meanwhile, General Weber's group had received permission to cross the Italian front lines, and then was escorted by automobile to arrive at 8 p.m. at Villa Giusti. There the group learned that the Italian negotiation committee would not arrive until the next day and that there would not be any concessions on armistice terms. All conditions had to be accepted. The only alternative – continuing the war – was an impossibility for the Habsburg Army. An answer was demanded by November 3. Any request for alterations would be tantamount to a refusal to accept the armistice agreement.

The "informal" cease-fire terms included the immediate suspension of hostilities, complete demobilization and rapid withdrawal of all troops from the battle front. Austria could retain twenty infantry divisions in the postwar period. In addition, it required the immediate evacuation of all territory by Habsburg troops to the Brenner Pass in Tyrol, the specific time to be specified later. Armistice points 2 and 4 produced the most serious Habsburg reaction, allowing Entente troops occupation rights, which included the right for the troops to march through Austria-Hungary to the Germany frontier. This produced enormous consternation for the Habsburg command structure because it impinged on the honor of the army. It amounted to a capitulation. Habsburg Supreme Command had to determine whether to accept the terms, because General Weber would not accept authorization to sign the treaty in its present format.

Habsburg Chief of the General Staff General Arz claimed to be stunned by the severity of the document. The Italian terms, not an armistice, demanded complete surrender and capitulation. The Habsburg Army, in the process of dissolution, had no bargaining power regarding the cease-fire terms. Captain Ruggera and Lt. Colonel Schneller departed to Trent, where they reported directly to Habsburg Supreme Command and delivered a dispatch from the chief negotiator General Weber. Colonel Schneller also teletyped the Habsburg chief of operations on the Italian front that an answer to the capitulation terms was demanded by November 3 and requested instructions how to respond to the document terms.[3] On the same day Emperor Karl announced that the Habsburg officer corps could swear allegiance to the newly formed national armies. This terminated their bond to the Imperial Army and destroyed the remaining remnants of the "*Alt Armee.*" Soldiers faced the moral dilemma of either remaining in the Habsburg Army or joining the newly created national armies. Before the armistice was signed Czechs, Slovaks and South Slavs had begun formation of their own armies. During the first days of November, there was even a German Austrian Army being prepared.[4]

During the first week in November Emperor Karl resisted pressure to abdicate. He reputedly renounced his right to serve in any new Austrian government, but that still signified the possibility of his reestablishing monarchial government in Austria, as well as Hungary. By November 2 the Habsburg Army had ceased to exist as its units had lost national cohesion and its troops had long lost any faith in a chance of victory, thus many troops and units rapidly stopped active duty. The military situation had become irredeemable and plundering and devastation had become universal (i.e., depots stormed and robbed). Tons of equipment were burned or abandoned. In the hinterland hunger and misery prevailed. Order could not be restored.

Tens of thousands of starving, exhausted troops lay down along retreat routes, surrendering to the Italians and becoming prisoners of war. Often this resulted from the troops' horrendous physical condition, their designated retreat routes, the speed of their retreat movements and their specific locations on November 3 and 4. The new German Austrian National Assembly demanded that Emperor Karl sign the armistice agreement, but he did not want to accept that odium. The emperor would not accept lone responsibility, so it became a question of whether the newly created states would, because by October 30–31 the various national assemblies had assumed power. Meanwhile, as the armistice date approached, chaos continued unabated. During the night of November 2, pressure for an armistice from the frontline commanders became overwhelming, raising the demand to sign immediately or face the threat of increasing anarchy. Every half-hour phone calls were attempted to Habsburg Supreme Command to inquire whether the armistice should be signed, but no response came. Emperor Karl, who desperately sought an armistice, learned of its conditions in the morning and later that British troops had invaded Habsburg territory. As the military front collapsed a Crown Council meeting convened at 9:15 and 11:30 p.m. In the interim the military front had imploded. At 11:30 p.m. on November 2 the Habsburg Italian front chief of operations, Major General Waldstätten, received instructions to order General Weber to sign the armistice terms, but he must strongly protest Point 4. Having no choice, General Weber had to sign the agreement because the army could no longer defend its front lines. General Weber was informed that he must immediately accept all armistice conditions because of the chaos enveloping the interior of the Dual Monarchy.[5] Most Hungarian troops not in combat had begun to desert the front, creating enormous confusion. The removal of those troops basically destroyed the Austro-Hungarian Army. The few railroad lines and roads available to transport those troops home caused delays in every other form of military transportation. German troops were deployed to defend the Brenner Pass on November 6. As Italian units crossed the Tagliamento River, Habsburg troops surrendered the Asiago Mountain frontier.

A second wave of Habsburg troops began to congregate at the railroad stations at Udine, Gorizia and Trieste on November 2. Two days later, more than half a million soldiers of all nationalities created massive turmoil attempting to return home. By November 6, trains were transporting hundreds of thousands of troops homeward from the various railroad loading stations. Italian and Russian prisoners of war filled the trains returning to the stations in Italy and Eastern Europe.

Some soldiers threw their weapons away; others were disarmed when they arrived in Czechoslovakia, Slovenia and other South Slavic areas. However, not all troops were disarmed. Some hid pistols in their uniforms. Tons of war equipment were abandoned on the retreat roads and hundreds of artillery pieces deserted. The greatest concern for the retreating soldiers was to return home, affected by the increasing worry for their families on the home front, many close to starvation.

Emperor Karl frantically convened a meeting of parliamentary leaders on November 2 in an attempt to have them accept the cease-fire terms. When they refused, the emperor and Habsburg Supreme Commander General Arz had to determine whether to accept the terms. Lt. Colonel Schneller of the armistice team emphasized to both that speed was of the essence as hundreds of thousands of armed troops continued to attempt to return home by rail as rapidly as possible. The Sixth Army could no longer defend its Isonzo River line. The critical Army Group Belluno began to retreat, but that quickly turned into a rout because its retrograde movement could not be halted.

The Habsburg Army's disastrous situation and the revolutionary events occurring in the hinterland placed the emperor in a situation that he could not control, particularly once the army had collapsed. The Italians refused to cease their military advance before the armistice terms had been accepted. General Diaz announced again that the Entente governments demanded that the cease-fire terms be accepted before midnight November 3. No modification of the terms would be accepted. If Emperor Karl did not accept the terms, the war would continue; thus he had no choice but to accept the ultimatum.

General Weber, as mentioned, received the order to accept the cease-fire regardless of any terms. Demarcation lines for the new frontiers on that front generally followed the 1915 Treaty of London agreement. The first cease-fire term demanded the immediate secession of hostilities. Regretfully, General Arz did not carefully consider the consequences of his precipitate action to announce the armistice and halting of military action on November 3, when during the night at 2 a.m. he dispatched orders before any document had been signed to army commanders to immediately terminate hostilities. He evidently interpreted the "immediate" termination of hostilities to signify Italian acceptance of the armistice, a fateful misjudgment because there was no cease-fire. A more prudent General Arz should have announced the imminent signing of the armistice agreement, but delayed transmittal of the actual final command until the official documents had been signed. The Habsburg cease-fire order fatefully proved premature. General Arz's misunderstanding resulted in many troops suffering a horrible fate, hundreds of thousands becoming prisoners of war of which thirty thousand died in captivity in Italian prisoner-of-war camps unprepared for the huge influx of soldiers. Only a few minutes after General Arz's initial communication relative to a cease-fire had been transmitted, he made the frantic effort to retract it. Thus at 2:15 a.m. he relayed a second message attempting to annul the first order. He probably reasoned that if necessary, he could cancel the order, but his original message had already been transmitted to frontline Habsburg Army forces. Army Group Commander Tyrol immediately replied that he had already forwarded the original order to his commanders. The Eleventh Army chief of staff announced that the cancellation of the original notice would produce utter chaos amongst his troops.[6] The Isonzo and Sixth armies still held firm at the Tagliamento River.

A partial timeline for the cease-fire events included at 11:18 p.m. the presentation of the final armistice conditions. At 1:20 a.m. Lt. Colonel Schneller was ordered to accept the demand to evacuate all territories still occupied by Austro-Hungarian troops. A horrified General Weber protested when he learned on November 3 that Italian units would not receive orders to halt fighting during the next twenty-four hours but on November 4 at 3 p.m. He attempted to inform Habsburg Supreme Command of the new development, but his efforts failed because of the communication difficulties, or lack of response, a common occurrence throughout the process. Yet, on the Balkan front, which possessed much worse communication connections, fighting halted within six hours of notification of the armistice. All armies then received the warning that the hostilities would not be terminated until November 4.

Shortly after the treaty was signed at 3:20 p.m. Italian troops moved into their ultimate objective, Trieste. Habsburg Supreme Command accepted the cease-fire, contemplating, as suggested, that it would take effect on November 3. However, General Badoglio, after looking at his watch (it was 3:20 p.m.), announced that the cease-fire would not become official until November 4 at 3 p.m. During the next twenty-one hours Austro-Hungarian Army troops would either be captured or continue attempting to reach home. Schneller wired the armistice terms to Habsburg Supreme Command, then returned to Trent to make his ordered telephone contact at 5 a.m. The defeated Habsburg troops were physically weakened from sickness, exhaustion, malnutrition and the fall weather conditions. General Arz dispersed new orders, revoking his earlier message, adding to the confused atmosphere.

Meanwhile, the most destructive factor for the Habsburg Army was, as mentioned, when the pacifist Hungarian war minister Bela Linder on November 1 ordered Hungarian soldiers to return to their homeland to defend it from imminent invasion from the Balkan theater. That threat resulted from Bulgaria surrendering, exposing the southern Hungary frontier. Habsburg Supreme Command had no alternative but to accept the first overly hasty order to halt fighting and accept the consequences. At 3 a.m., Emperor Karl resigned as commander-in-chief of Habsburg forces and appointed General Arz to the post to escape the responsibility for the armistice, as stated. Karl, however, did not abdicate his throne, but General Arz would not sign the armistice.[7] The emperor then appointed General Kövess, commander of the Habsburg Balkan front, as the new chief of the Austro-Hungarian General Staff, to create the illusion that Kövess, not Karl, would sign the treaty. General Kövess, however, remained there, attempting to establish a viable defensive front against the Salonica forces advancing from Serbia, thus he was not available to make any major decisions. Meanwhile, General Weber received permission to submit the armistice papers, although he had learned to his extreme dismay that the Italians demanded the twenty-four hours to cease hostilities. The resulting Italian military "victory" at Vittorio Veneto defeated an army and empire that no longer existed. Chaos reigned as troops retreated as rapidly as possible. In addition to plundering, troops forced all trains to travel north toward the Homeland. Almost four hundred thousand Habsburg soldiers became prisoners of war. The German and Hungarian prisoners would not be released until the signing of the 1919 St. Germain Treaty. Slavic troops, however, had a far more rapid release, Czechs in particular.

General Weber had attempted on numerous occasions to contact Habsburg Supreme Command to appraise it of the circumstances, but received no reply. A major factor in the failed Austro-Hungarian attempts to achieve a rapid cease-fire resulted from the fateful lack of communication between the negotiators and Habsburg leaders. An example is that at 6 p.m. General Weber learned of a raging battle in the Adigo Valley (key to an Italian advance to the Brenner Pass). Habsburg officers were dispatched to Trent, but because of the battles they could not travel further. They had to utilize a wireless station at Pola, but could not telegraph Habsburg command because of the lack of direct transmission to Vienna. Telegraph messages had to be relayed through other locations such as Budapest. Several messages arrived much too late, three between three and eight hours later than transmitted.

General Weber signed the armistice, although making reservations relative to articles 2 and 4. He informed General Badoglio that a Habsburg cease-fire order had gone into effect and requested that Italian Supreme Command halt the fighting. General Badoglio announced, as stated, at 3:20 p.m. that hostilities would end at 3 p.m. November 4. Weber signed the agreement at 3:20 p.m. At 6 p.m. the protocol of the armistice and maps were delivered. At 11 p.m., General Arz, just learning of the twenty-four-hour delay for the armistice, protested to General Diaz. Diaz replied that the agreement had been signed by duly appointed Habsburg Armistice Commission members and that a twenty-four-hour interval was unavoidable in order to inform all Italian land and sea commands.

The Italians' claim that it would require twenty-four hours to notify all their troops provided them sufficient time to achieve their reputed Vittorio Veneto military victory. The Italians, however, did not have sufficient camps to contain the four hundred thousand captured prisoners of war, nor could they adequately feed them. The Italians utilized the prisoners of war for additional leverage at the peace negotiations. Troops from sixteen infantry and three cavalry divisions were captured during the twenty-four-hour interlude, while Italian troops advanced to Trent, Trieste and the Brenner Pass.

General Arz, Emperor Karl and the Habsburg Italian front chief of operations, Major General Waldstätten, unfortunately mishandled the armistice terribly, just as they had done during the fatal June 15, 1918 offensive. They mistakenly believed that the Habsburg Army could continue to operate, thus they delayed commencing armistice negotiations until the army had begun to implode, retreat and face imminent disaster. Thus, the hasty cease-fire order demonstrated the lack of effective leadership and sound judgment that produced disastrous results.

The armistice negotiations progressed through three phases. The first witnessed Italian delaying tactics between October 28 and 31, which allowed the Italian High Command time to conduct the final Vittorio Veneto offensive against Habsburg forces. The second phase incorporated reputed communication technical difficulties with contact to Emperor Karl and General Arz, which delayed critical responses, resulting in a loss of thirty-five hours. The third and fateful phase involved the overhasty Habsburg November 3 cease-fire order, because of "misinterpretation" of treaty terms. This created a chaotic situation during the twenty-one hours between 7 p.m. November 3 to 3 p.m. November 4. Hungry, starving and sick troops retreated through cold temperatures as many simply collapsed along the long retreat routes, becoming prisoners of war.

Italian troops advanced as some Austro-Hungarian units disintegrated and the hinterland supply and rearward services completely collapsed. Troops retreated from the Piave River front, but Tenth Army units momentarily maintained their Tyrolian mountain lines. Eleventh Army soldiers eventually had to retreat, but the South Slavic revolution negatively affected their circumstances as local officials halted railroad traffic to the front. Chaos reigned, relative to railroad transport. Further battle obviously would only produce more bloodshed. Meanwhile, frontline ethnic troop units refused to fight, but the lack of roads and railroad connections made it difficult for them to reach home.

On November 3, as Habsburg soldiers waved white flags, Italian forces announced that peace could not be established until November 4 as their units continued to pursue the retreating troops. Once the final Habsburg retreat commenced on November 3, the Isonzo Army proved somewhat successful in its subsequent withdrawal. Eleventh Army mountain troops encountered much more difficult conditions as Italian patrols pursued retreating soldiers with cavalry, regular troops and armored cars, capturing many hapless, exhausted and ill Habsburg troops. Individual soldiers and entire units often offered no resistance. Officers, to avoid further bloodshed, surrendered their units, believing that captivity would only endure for a few days, a terrible and unfortunate miscalculation.[8] Armed troops, particularly Hungarian, were not halted by enemy troops. The worst troop conditions occurred during the retreat from the Tyrol, as eastern flank forces sustained severe casualties.[9] A troop unit's fate depended upon several factors such as (in addition to earlier cited ones) the speed of the Italian advance, the troops' physical condition and whether they maintained unit cohesion.

Mountain roads quickly became jammed with fleeing troops, while Italian troops entered Trieste and Trent without resistance. Plundering activities accelerated behind the front lines. Only an immediate cease-fire appeared capable of relieving the chaotic military situation. Mutinying troops plundered Eleventh Army magazines as far as the Innsbruck railroad station. The critical question became whether German Austrian troops could defend the language frontier against Italian invasion when so few troops, lacking sufficient artillery pieces, remained south of the Brenner Pass. Only armed troops could potentially prevent anarchy and further devastation. Attempts continued to maintain railroad traffic during the mass evacuations. Massive turmoil ensued with over half a million troops rushing to the hinterland.

At the November 3 armistice signing Sixth and Isonzo armies still maintained their defensive positions on much of the Piave River line, although some Entente troops had crossed the River. Tenth Army briefly maintained its mountain front lines near the Brenner Pass, but Eleventh Army formations, as stated, had collapsed, retreating units blocking the roads between the Tagliamento River and Tenth Army. Italian troops seized southern Tyrolean territory when their advance could not be halted.

Some units plundered, murdered, raped and looted. In rear echelon areas, the newly forming South Slavic and Czech governments seized military depots and railroads, and harried and hindered retreating non-Slavic soldiers. South Slavic and Czech militias often blocked soldiers' efforts to return home, preventing them from entering villages and towns as they trudged homeward. Pandemonium reigned along the return roads and railways. Adriatic Coast defensive positions had been abandoned early; thus, Trieste was occupied without opposition. The Czech blockade of food shipments to Vienna created a critical situation for the city, which continued long after the armistice.

Although the cease-fire order had been transmitted to the front many troops did not know or comprehend the rapidly unraveling circumstances, nor did English or Italian division commanders have knowledge of the armistice. Retreating soldiers encountered roadblocks with Italian machine-gun positions, resulting in many discarding their weapons and being captured. Hundreds of artillery pieces were abandoned. Armed troops simply marched through Italian lines. Chaos, mutinies and retreat movements intertwined. In Vienna confusion reigned. Habsburg, Czech, Russian, Romanian and Italian prisoners of war were released within a few weeks, creating pandemonium. Italian troops secured the southern Tyrolean railroads, road junctions and military depots to take possession of the province. A question remains as to whether the troops had been allowed to be captured, because of the fear of the hunger and chaos conditions in northern Tyrol and the enormous problems of feeding and transporting the massive troop numbers with the threat of violence with so many hundreds of thousands of potentially armed soldiers returning home.

The tragic prisoners-of-war fate resulted because the Italians proved completely unprepared for the huge numbers of soldiers that filled the few poorly equipped prisoner-of-war camps.[10] A total of thirty thousand, mostly German troops, ultimately starved to death or perished from the effects of weather and disease. The Austrian people blamed the army command for the disaster, so immediately after the war the Austrian National Assembly investigated its reputed degree of responsibility for the tragedy. It found little proof of charges against specific individual commanders, as did later postwar military investigations, but these inquiries occurred in a turmoil-filled postwar period. Officers often had their rank, battle ribbons and other emblems torn from their uniforms on the streets and local populations often robbed soldiers of their valuables. They were slandered by newspapers for some time, but then the situation changed.

Hundreds of wagons and thousands of horses were abandoned to die along the retreat roads. Then, on November 1, Emperor Karl bequeathed the Habsburg fleet to the Kingdom of the Serbs, Croats and Slovenes, which infuriated Italian military leadership. The Italians seized the ships from the Yugoslavs, and sank the Habsburg flagship *Veritas Unitas* in its harbor. The valuable Adriatic possessions were lost, while Italy and Yugoslavia immediately became competitors for the coastal terrain, seeking dominance in the Adriatic Sea area.

Habsburg Supreme Command officers remained in their Baden headquarters for several days, but when enlisted personnel refused to obey their orders and deserted, many also fled. Officers took refuge in the Vienna war archive building, while the Austrian war minister prepared demobilization plans that never went into effect, because the armed forces fragmented along ethnic lines began to report to their new national state armies. Czechs, Poles, Hungarians, even Austro-Germans denounced the dynastic government. Emperor Karl never released a formal farewell to his troops, but drafted a never-published proclamation on November 11; military and political fragmentation followed. Threats of revolution emanated from marauding soldiers as the hated Habsburg leadership was overthrown. Chaotic conditions reigned throughout Central Europe.

On November 3 French troops occupied portions of Transylvania, preventing a Hungarian attempt to create a federation with that province, while the Czechs received permission to occupy Slovakia. In Austria the Communist Party was founded and a German Austrian political entity came into existence, and with it the necessity for a military force, because of threats from its hostile neighbors. In early 1919 the successor states received authorization to occupy Hungarian territory, so Czech and Romanian troops invaded to seize or protect the territories they claimed. The Austrian people became overcome with feelings of hopelessness, despair and depression, particularly after learning the early June 2 hurriedly prepared peace terms. They viewed the St. Germain peace treaty as a *Diktat*, as they discovered unfriendly surrounding neighbors blockaded their country from critically necessary food and raw materials. Meanwhile, Spanish flu claimed lives throughout much of Vienna – encouraging revolutionary activity that spread during early November as the masses became ever more desperate because of their economic plight.

On November 5 Entente forces crossed the Sava River and primarily Serbian and Romanian troops occupied large portions of southern Hungary territory. The occupation of these territories commenced before the Versailles peace treaty had been signed, thus it was a direct violation of the November 3 Belgrade military convention signed with Hungarian officials that negated such action.[11] The most pressing problem for the new Austrian and Hungarian governments remained to establish independent states and receive international recognition, which it was believed erroneously would improve possibilities for a modified peace. These attempts were blocked by their new and hostile neighbors.

On November 6, troops rushing home threatened to create serious social problems, because there were not sufficient troops to defend against potential armed soldier activities. Troops had abandoned, stolen or burned enormous quantities of food, weapons and equipment. Ammunition dumps and magazines were left unguarded in Vienna as troops returned home and Hungarian *Assistenz* troops departed. The city garrison had become unreliable; at one point only four loyal infantry companies remained at its disposal. The problem became the arrival of trains loaded with half-starved and rebellious armed soldiers, leading to daily shootings. On the next day, November 7, Hungarian leaders, attempting to secure their frontier and maintain their territory, officially withdrew from the Dual Monarchy and disarmed and disbanded its military formations. Before the year ended Czech and Romanian troops had already occupied significant swaths of Hungarian territory. Further north, trouble erupted between the Czechs and Germans in the Sudetenland region, when the Czechs proclaimed their complete independence from Habsburg rule. The lingering Czech-German problem festered until the 1938 Munich Crisis.

Several Bavarian battalions deployed to the Brenner Pass on November 8 to defend the mountain invasion route to their territory, but when revolution broke out at home they immediately withdrew. The royal family, residing in Schönbrunn Palace, raised the serious question of their security because the situation could rapidly deteriorate due to the thousands of armed soldiers roaming the streets of Vienna, particularly the revolutionary Red Guards, former prisoners of war in Russia deployed in the notorious 41. Battalion. Viennese police worried about potential looting and a proletarian uprising. Armed soldiers defending Emperor Karl and his family dispersed. Until the royal family departed from the palace it had been protected by two hundred War Academy cadets. Karl soon emigrated to Switzerland.

The November 9 German revolution affected the general atmosphere in Austria as the last troops crossed the Brenner Pass. Emperor Wilhelm abdicated in Germany and civilian Friedrich Ebert became the leader of the government, that news arriving in Vienna on November 11. On November 10 the emperor fled Berlin, while Austrian provisional republican government leaders warned Emperor Karl that they might not be able to provide him security unless he abdicated, which he refused to do. He released a purposely vague statement, without abdicating. Social Democratic Party leaders demanded that Karl leave Vienna so they could establish a republic. In April 1919 the Habsburg Exclusion Act nullified all political and property claims of the former ruling family. Karl refused to accept it. Romania reentered the war on November 10, 1918 to ensure possession of Transylvania. Authority had disappeared in that province as armed bands and violence consumed the entire area, thus Romanian troops occupied the province. During August/ November 1919 Romanian troops also occupied Budapest. The Romanians did not sign the Belgrade military convention with Hungary that delineated territorial demarcation lines for that country. More significantly, it did not prevent their invasion of Hungary.

At 11:11 a.m. on November 11 the armistice took effect, which focused attention on commencing peace treaty negotiations. Peacemakers in Paris were too weak to enforce their terms in Eastern Europe so they utilized their new allies, Czechoslovakia, Romania and Poland – the Little Entente – to act on their behalf. Eastern Europe did not receive procedural precedence in the initial peace negotiations. Peace treaties with Austria, Hungary and Bulgaria contained the League of Nations covenant and war guilt and reparation clauses (the latter never enforced because the Austrians could not pay them). What transpired in Central European countries would be determined by revolutions and local militias or armies by the end of 1918. In Austria the unexpected death of Social Democratic leader Victor Adler allowed Otto Bauer to emerge as the leading Social Democrat to then become the Austrian foreign minister. Adler and his followers ensured that peace and discipline in Vienna were preserved by restraining proletarian extremist demands for revolution and by organizing *Volkswehr* military units to maintain order.[12]

On November 11 Emperor Karl accepted that German Austrians had established a government. The next day a revolutionary German provisional national assembly was proclaimed, creating a new republic and state, in an attempt to prevent anarchy. Many of the starving and poorly clad returned troops in Vienna discarded their weapons, shouting "give [us] bread, we are tired of being slaughtered." Horses were killed in the streets for food, and larceny and crime became a commonality. On November 12 Emperor Karl signed a proclamation renouncing his authority in the new Austrian state affairs, but did not formally abdicate when he departed Schönbrunn Palace with British protection. Karl's family departed for Switzerland on March 24,

1919. The sudden threat of a putsch in Vienna emanated from intellectuals and former prisoners of war. Masses congregated in inner Vienna. Shots were fired after which the panicked crowd disappeared. The gathering protested the lack of available food supplies for the starving population. The preceding Austrian revolution produced a social movement led by the masses that were controlled by the Social Democratic Party, but with a large number of former military personnel of all ranks. Soldier councils evolved. Two days later the Vienna parliament building was stormed during a meeting demanding the abdication of Karl, resulting in chaos and looting.[13] The capital shut down, with the citizen *Volkswehr* army maintaining order and peace. Such revolutionary activity worried the peace negotiators and eventually became a factor in the Inter-Allied Commission results.

On November 13, Hungarian leaders signed a new armistice seeking better peace terms, and Victor Adler's funeral took place in Vienna. Earlier in the month Adler had admitted that the new Austrian state was powerless, having no means of defending itself. A November 13 chief of the General Staff report investigating the collapse of the Austro-Hungarian Army concluded that the troops had endured inadequate food and clothing for far too long and that they had suffered extended war weariness. The soldiers specifically desired to return home safely. Homesickness had been reinforced by rumors emanating from hinterland newspaper articles that graphically described the worsening internal conditions. This increasingly agitated Habsburg frontline troops because of their increasing concern for loved ones at home, which negatively affected troop morale and fighting spirit. It also had an enormous effect on the implosion of the Austro-Hungarian Army. On November 14 Hungarian Minister President Karolyi dispatched a letter to President Wilson requesting that his country's territorial integrity should be maintained, insisting that foreign troops should not occupy Hungary. He also described the terrible economic situation, explaining that the country had no coal supplies because neighboring countries had invaded its territory and seized its last mines. He emphasized that the new government was attempting to eradicate the autocratic past and create a democracy, but its people faced imminent starvation.

The Hungarian People's Republic was proclaimed on November 16, but the largest Hungarian minorities, the Slovaks and Romanians, had no representation in the new government. Hungary and Austria faced comparable domestic concerns, each accused of being a major instigator of the war. Both encountered multiple obstacles establishing and then maintaining a liberal democratic administration and domestic order.

During late November the Romanian Army invaded Transylvania, and in early December the Hungarians were ordered to withdraw their invading troops from Slovakia. The November 3 Belgrade Convention had been broken in favor of Czechoslovakia.[14] On December 3 the Czechs received authorization to occupy Slovakia.

At the end of December Serbian troops crossed the Drina River that had been established as the line of demarcation by the November 3 Belgrade Convention. The Hungarian government protested the Serbian action, because the invading troops seized the country's last coal mines. The Austrian government appealed to the Versailles Treaty negotiators, as did Germany, emphasizing that a new civilian government embraced Wilson's Fourteen Points and disinherited the Habsburg past. The peacemakers, while fearing a potential Bolshevik revolution, were resolved to prevent a rapid recovery of German power, thus the Austrian attempt at an *Anschluss* with that country failed, mainly at French instigation. Economic weakness also caused the desire for *Anschluss* based on President Wilson's self-determination principle.

The Austro-Hungarian Empire of fifty-plus million inhabitants disappeared with the Russian, Turkish and German empires. The Habsburg Empire collapsed before the Versailles Treaty negotiations commenced.[15] The St. Germain peace treaty with the severely truncated Austria and Trianon with Hungary officially recognized the destruction of the Dual Monarchy. Both treaties created multiple problems that quickly manifested themselves. The majority of the former Habsburg Empire became portions of the newly created Poland, Yugoslavia, Czechoslovakia and a greatly enlarged Romania, altering multiple Central and Eastern European frontiers. None of these new entities originally possessed strong governments or military security. A small area became German Austria, half of its population residing in the capital city of Vienna. It was born a poor nation, a "rump state," with no means to support itself, and isolated from its new hostile neighboring states. Instead of ten million German-speaking people, and despite the Versailles Treaty emphasis on self-determination, only six and a half million became citizens of the new country. This was because South Tyrol, Bohemia, Moravia, Galicia, Bukovina, Banat and lower Austria became parts of other national entities. The new land-bound Austria surrendered its maritime provinces to the new Kingdom of Serbs, Croats and Slovenes. Its existence was threatened as its frontiers remained unsecure. Its strategic location, however, included important railroads and roads astride the Danube River. Austrian citizens, shocked by the harshness of the St. Germain peace treaty, predicted a very bleak future, and became disillusioned with their new perilous situation and wary of their hostile neighbors. The war produced a psychologically and economically uncertain future, which depressed the citizenry and left people feeling helpless. The population continued to suffer from severe food shortages and a lack of heating, proper clothing and other necessities. The American Beveridge report on the conditions concluded that without immediate relief German Austria could socially collapse. Other alarming communication confirmed this.

The Dual Monarchy's demise destroyed the centuries-old Central European economic structure, while new neighboring states refused to supply drastically needed food and raw materials to German Austria. Moreover, the country lacked funds to purchase food or other vital necessities for its people. Ultimately, the Versailles peacemakers, fearing the spread of Bolshevism from Hungary into Austria on the heels of the Bela Kun communist episode, and a potential communist uprising, supplied some relief aid to the impoverished people. The Entente blockade was lifted on March 9, 1919, enabling more food to be transported to Austria. The country received a thirty-million-dollar credit allotment. On March 19 it was announced that elections for a new Austrian government would be conducted during fall 1919. The Social Democratic, Christian Socialist and other political parties formed a left-leaning new government coalition, governing until 1921. Meanwhile, demobilized soldiers had to be fed and any threat they might pose had to be neutralized. A communist uprising was crushed in June 1919 with relative ease, as alarming reports reached Versailles of continuing extensive unemployment, lack of essential food supplies, starving children and long soup kitchen lines. The state could not provide food and necessities, lacking means to do so, while most people could not afford adequate food or other essentials, facing potential starvation. The situation rapidly became drastic. The Paris peacemakers finally recognized the quandary created by Austria's neighbors' voracious territorial demands and their false claims of self-determination. They also recognized the terrible economic situation and suffering of the citizenry, which created future problems in Central and Eastern Europe. The newly created states of Czechoslovakia, Yugoslavia, Poland and Romania were comprised of at least 30 percent of other ethnic peoples.

The Austrian revolution included the swiftly crushed communist attempts to seize power in Vienna during April and June 1919, but economic dislocation and civilian suffering continued to threaten the stabilization of the state. The Social Democratic Party succeeded in controlling the masses' revolutionary tendencies and, with Friedrich Adler's leadership, guaranteed the loyalty of the *Volkswehr* militia to that political party. Originally the *Volkswehr* units did not prove reliable in maintaining peace, partially a result of the quality of some of the volunteers. Many were returning soldiers and undesirable citizens.

The Austrian social revolution terminated once the Entente announced its peace demands, which influenced the Constituent National Assemblies' ratification of the St. Germain peace treaty. The coalition government ended the revolution without excessive bloodshed. However, "Red Vienna" faced a threat from the Alpine mountain regions and outer provinces. Farmers often refused to transport food to the capital, because of resentment created by wartime crop and animal requisitions and against the central government. Mass demonstrations in Vienna rapidly developed into mobs demanding the establishment of a republic and end of Habsburg rule. The Vienna parliament building street became filled with demonstrators who demanded the emperor's abdication on October 30. Looting continued the next day. Many soldiers joined the political upheaval, assuming prominent roles in the revolutionary movements in both

Vienna and Budapest. The Vienna garrison initially displayed no discipline or reliability, briefly endangering the young state. A newly formed Red Guard composed of former Russian prisoners of war became the infamous 41. Battalion. The catastrophic food situation also affected multiple cities besides Vienna. The many unemployed included the millions of returning soldiers, invalids and former prisoners of war. The returning prisoners of war and refugees aggravated the prevalent starvation conditions. Many soldiers could not adjust to civilian life, and the many invalids aggravated the situation.

During the first half of 1919, attempted coups to overthrow the government caused enormous problems in both Austria and Hungary. The effects of the Kapp Putsch in Germany on March 13, 1920 included a shift to the right for many citizens and produced further social excess in Vienna. Conservative groups raised private paramilitary formations. A struggle for control of a new Austrian Army caused competition, particularly between the Social Democratic and Christian Socialist parties. The Social Democrats attempted to control the new *Reichswehr*, while Christian Socialists established a strong Vienna police force. During 1919 and 1920 Austria continued to suffer from high unemployment, continuing drastic food shortages in the cities, serious crime and inflation. The 1920s witnessed more violence with riots, attempted putsches, armed street fighting, paramilitary activity and continual uncertainty. National revolutions and other conflict continued at the various frontiers. In 1919 conflicts erupted in areas where none had previously occurred, as ethnic tensions easily exploded into violent confrontations. March 1919 revolutionary occurrences in Hungary influenced German Austrian Communist Party members to act. Almost daily huge demonstrations, arson and rioting erupted, participants demanding to arm the proletariat. Disturbingly even *Volkswehr*, the new military units, appeared to join the agitators. The Hungarian ambassador to Austria and German Austrian Communist Party leaders collaborated as intensive Bolshevik propaganda and communist agitators were smuggled into Austria. Revolutionary activity heated up in Vienna following the declaration of the short-lived Soviet Republic in Munich, Germany (April 7, 1919) while during May the new Hungarian Red Army reconquered much of Slovakia. Developments in Austria became critical for the success of the Bela Kun communist regime. The Hungarians desperately required weapons and ammunition, and Austria possessed large quantities of both following disarmament and still possessed factories to continue production. Weapon and ammunition smuggling rapidly commenced across the Austrian frontier into Hungary, Czechoslovakia and Poland. The new Inter-Allied Commission failed to fulfill its objective to destroy weapons and dismantle paramilitary forces and private armies, for reasons to be discussed. Unemployment in Vienna rose to over 130,000 people as industry lacked necessary raw materials for industrial production.

On April 12–13, 1919 spontaneous demonstrations erupted in Vienna because of the persistent lack of sufficient food supplies and due to the domestic unrest that had been encouraged by the founding of the Hungarian Soviet Republic and Soviet regime in Munich. Six people were killed and fifty-six seriously wounded. Communist placards posted in industrial areas encouraged Austrian workers to join Russia and Hungary by establishing a communist government. The brief communist putsch attempt encouraged by the Hungarian Kun administration, however, dissipated. Several hundred destitute people, *Heimkehr* and invalids stormed the Vienna parliament building on April 14, setting a fire, but they were eventually repulsed by police and volunteer militia forces. A newly elected Vienna District Workers Council unanimously voted to oppose communist attempts to create a Soviet state.

Nevertheless, on April 17, 1919 a large crowd consisting mostly of unemployed workers, invalids and returning soldiers again stormed the Austrian parliament building. The rioters broke windows and erected barricades and entrenchments. Defensive fire wounded many demonstrators. *Volkswehr* units restored order when the police could not disperse the demonstrators.

The April events created an Entente reaction, threatening to interrupt desperately needed food deliveries. The April turmoil resulted in counter-revolutionary activities as peasants in the countryside, supported by the Entente commission, countered Social Democratic efforts to have *Reichswehr* troops implanted into a new army. Several country provinces created their own military formations in opposition to Social Democratic Red Vienna.

On May 14, the Austrian delegation arrived in Paris to discover that peace terms had not been established. Upon their arrival, the delegates found themselves essentially imprisoned and treated like outcasts. On May 30, a hurriedly prepared draft treaty was presented but minus several vital clauses, particularly relating to Italy, finances and the army. The final draft of the Austrian peace treaty was delayed because of Italian and Yugoslavian territorial claims. The completed draft containing 381 articles was presented on July 20, with the reaction to it to be submitted by August 6. On June 20, 1919, Austrian leaders submitted their proposed revisions. On September 2, the Austrian delegation received orders to sign the final treaty within five days. On September 6 Chancellor Karl Renner presented the document to the Austrian National Assembly, which evoked shocked and strong emotional responses. After multiple protests were elucidated, the treaty was finally accepted. Most of the opposition related to the loss of the former Habsburg crown lands, in other words South Tyrol, and the fact that German Austria was not sufficiently protected and economically impossible to sustain. Austria had become a much poorer Switzerland. On September 10 Renner and the National Assembly members signed the peace treaty at 11 a.m. It took effect on July 16, 1920, creating German Austria.

Did the peacekeepers understand the many Central and Eastern European problems? What knowledge did they have of the geography, economics and political history of the area? In the interim, Otto Bauer, who championed the push for *Anschluss* with Germany, retired from office, so the Austrian representatives received a time extension to submit their August 6 reply. The detailed formal rebuttal to the treaty emphasized that the economic and financial burden would ruin the country. Paris treaty commissioners' reports described the deplorable conditions in Vienna. Factories had closed due to a lack of fuel, inflation was rampant, soup kitchen lines were long and 125,000 people remained unemployed. The quality of food continued to deteriorate. Communist agitation continued after the June 15 putsch attempt. July 20 street demonstrations resulted in a general strike on July 21. Then the Bela Kun regime collapsed in Hungary and he and his followers fled to Vienna.

On June 6, 1919 communist agitators planned massive protests that produced general strikes, the activities greatly influenced by the rampant inflation, lack of food and temporary Hungarian military success against the Czech and Romanian invaders of that country's territories. Demands to support the Hungarian government resulted in attempts to establish an Austrian communist government.

A call for mass action commenced on June 13. A major question for the central government became which *Volkswehr* units would support the government against a potential communist putsch attempt. On June 14, during the evening, multiple communist leaders meeting to plan an uprising the next day were arrested.

Ten to twelve thousand demonstrators, the vast majority under the age of twenty-one, marched to the prison demanding that their leaders be released. Violence again produced multiple casualties. *Volkswehr* troops prevented the attempted communist putsch, occupying strategic positions and surrounding the Red Guard 41. Battalion barracks, preventing it from interfering in the street demonstrations and coup attempt. A communist dictatorship had been prevented at the cost of twenty dead, fifty seriously and thirty lightly wounded. Crushing the putsch attempt created increased confidence in the coalition government and the very effective police chief, Schober.

The Treaty of Versailles' terms proved disastrous for the regions comprising the former Austro-Hungarian Empire. Seven new countries appeared before the Paris peace negotiations convened, but violence quickly erupted everywhere. Between 1917 and 1921 enormous turmoil appeared everywhere in Central and Eastern Europe, including wars of independence, civil wars, revolutions and multiple ethnic conflicts. Two major factors influenced these events – the Russian Revolutions and the situation resulting from the implosion of the Austro-Hungarian monarchy. The creation of new nation-states quickly produced border disputes, armed conflicts and violence as a result of the various conflicting territorial claims. Rapidly organized militias and paramilitary forces added to the violence over territorial aggrandizement. Ethnic violence erupted in the Balkan Peninsula, Hungary, Czechoslovakia, the

Ukraine and the Baltic states. The victorious Entente Powers could not police the Versailles Treaty, but increasingly meddled diplomatically and politically, even economically, to influence the territorial disputes in Central Europe. Within a week after the St. Germain Treaty was released, sympathy strikes for the Russian and Hungarian proletariat erupted. On July 20–21 general strikes broke out in various areas of Austria, but eventually subsided. A major problem resulted from Inter-Allied Commission attempts to establish an Austrian Army, to end political struggles and disarm the evolving paramilitary forces. The treaty created a small thirty-thousand-man professional army.

In the prewar era Austria-Hungary had proven self-sufficient relative to basic foodstuffs. Significant amounts had to be imported only during poor harvest seasons. Between 1913 and 1917 agricultural products and services declined 40 percent. Acreage in Austria was halved, mainly because of Russian conquest of Galicia, but remained stable in Hungary during the war years. Bread grains such as wheat dropped to 38 percent and rye 44 percent of earlier amounts.

During the war, the Dual Monarchy never established a national food agency with sufficient executive power. Even the joint food commission established by Emperor Karl in early 1917 lacked power. Starvation affected Vienna, but eventually other regional and local areas. Some farmers under-reported their harvests, hoarded them or sold them in the black market, which formed a secret economy. The central government offices could not resolve the problem of uneven food distribution because of corruption or incompetence. This lack of efficiency led to social upheaval, riots and the masses becoming involved in disruptive and revolutionary activities because of war weariness, inflation and lack of faith in the central government.

The individual consumption of bread grains decreased steadily throughout the war compared to the prewar era. Rationing of basic foods was established almost immediately; some examples include bread grain in 1915, coffee, fats and other items in 1916, potatoes in 1917 and finally meat in 1918. For example, Vienna workers' intake of calories from the prewar level dropped 71 percent for non-self-supporters and 55 percent for heavy labor. *Ersatz* materials, both organic and synthetic, extended food quantities, but only worsened the quality of food. Excessive numbers of livestock and pigs had to be slaughtered because they were seen as competing with humans for the rare food resources.

The destruction of Galician farmland that produced one-third of the cereal crops was lost to Russian invasions during 1914–1915. Much land was devastated by battle. The entire agricultural sector suffered from persistent labor shortage, lack of animal power and scarcity of fertilizers that instead were utilized in the gunpowder industry.

Prisoners of war provided some replacement labor for the unemployment caused by the army drafts, but proved less than 50 percent as proficient.

Vienna continued to be dependent upon Hungary for food, but the delivery to Austria between 1913 and 1917 declined sharply. Livestock numbers declined by two-thirds. Romania and the Ukraine provided substantial amounts of grain for food during 1916–1917, but could not match demand.

On August 10, 1919, mass demonstrations erupted again in Vienna and, on August 13, ten thousand *Volkswehr* troops marched to parliament, but the Communist Party had lost much of its influence over the masses. During 1919 the Austrian domestic situation steadily worsened while the country's viability became dependent upon agreements with its surrounding states and Entente financial assistance, but the common policy of the surrounding states encompassed the containment of Hungary and preventing a Habsburg restoration. The Little Entente (Czechoslovakia, Romania and Yugoslavia) fit into the newly French alliance system, replacing Russia as an Eastern Europe ally. It obviously could not replace a Great Power like Russia, but could help influence Entente policies in Central Europe.

The end of 1919 question of political, economic and geographical survival being a major issue for Austria, Karl Renner attempted to end its isolation by negotiating treaties, particularly with Czechoslovakia and Italy. In December 1919 the Austrian government reversed political direction in an attempt to normalize relations with both the victorious powers and hostile neighbors. Vienna also sought economic cooperation from its neighbors, but initially two problems proved difficult to resolve: Carinthia with Yugoslavia and Burgenland with Hungary.

Negotiations, initiated in Prague, produced a secret treaty between Austria and the Czech nation on January 10–12, 1920. The central item involved the maintenance and defense of the St. Germain peace treaty. Both countries agreed to oppose a Habsburg restoration and would finally cooperate economically. Both opposed the Hungarian counterrevolution occurring at that time. The treaty had to be kept secret because the Christian Socialist and *Grossdeutsch* parties would have voted against it. Significantly, the treaty broke Austria's encirclement by hostile countries. For a short time during 1918–1919, Vienna had had no contact with its hostile neighbors, but in 1919 food and production problems and Austria's weakness forced it to alter its stance.

However, a conflict erupted in Czechoslovakia between Czech and Germans citizens, the latter claiming administrative leadership in what became the Sudetenland territory, a large German enclave in the new state. The Czechs claimed their historical Bohemian and Moravian provinces, but some Austrian government officials sought unsuccessfully to incorporate the German districts of Bohemia and the Sudetenland into Austria. Through the 1920s, Austria suffered one crisis after another until Adolf Hitler invaded the beleaguered country to achieve the 1938 *Anschluss*.

On April 21, 1919 a newly created Hungarian Red Army deployed along a 250-kilometer front. Romanians invaded Hungary between April 30 and May

2, reaching the Tisza River frontier line. On April 27 Czechoslovakian troops also crossed the Hungarian frontier, but defending troops quickly contained that invasion. Romanian troops occupied Budapest on August 4.

On May 2, 1919 the Hungarian government proclaimed a general mobilization to assist organizing the new Red Army more rapidly. At the end of the month Hungarian troops defeated the Czech invaders then turned to counter the Romanian invasion threat. By June 6 Red Army troops had broken Czechoslovakian resistance and, by June 10, driven their troops back a hundred kilometers. The Entente Powers intervened, demanding the withdrawal of Hungarian troops from Czech territory (Slovakia). Their intervention encouraged neighboring hostile states to seize Hungarian territory.

On July 27, 1919, Romanian troops crossed the Tisza River and advanced toward Budapest, sealing the fate of the Hungarian Soviet Republic. Invading units occupied major Hungarian industrial and agricultural areas after encircling the country on three sides. The Red Army was seriously outnumbered, while on the home front the economic situation had not improved, causing a backlash against the communist regime that ultimately led to its demise.

The Hungarian government dispatched multiple complaints and appeals to the Paris peacemakers about the invasions of their truncated country. This finally resulted in the formation of an Entente commission to investigate the ravaged country's political and economic conditions. The government reported numerous armistice violations, while Serbian, Romanian and Ukrainian troops occupied significant tracts of Hungarian territory, approved by the Paris victors. This deprived Hungary of invaluable raw materials and crippled its already small industry, raising unemployment numbers and producing the threat of increased Bolshevik influence. Industrial and commercial life collapsed. The Budapest government also encountered difficulties distributing food to its starving citizens, and the lack of coal forced factories to close, leaving homes unheated. The domestic situation consistently worsened partially because Hungary was excluded from foreign aid programs, and its neighbors refused to provide it assistance. Similar earlier circumstances helped force the Karolyi republican government to resign on March 20, 1919, but it also resulted from the Entente representative Vyx demanding that Hungarian troops withdraw to predetermined demarcation lines deep within Hungary. Karolyi resigned as minister president and the communist Bela Kun seized power without a gunshot being fired.

Some Austrian leaders attempted to achieve an *Anschluss* with Germany, considering it critical for the truncated and isolated country to survive and based on President Wilson's principle of self-determination. On November 1 the official position became to seek union with Germany, arguing that German Austria could not survive economically by itself indefinitely. The effort was partially influenced by Social Democratic Party realization of countryside opposition to Red Vienna. On November 12 the provisional assembly passed a resolution supporting the union and subsequently initiated negotiations with Germany to achieve that goal. The German government, however, refused to negotiate because it understood the negative implications for its Paris peace negotiations position. The French vehemently opposed the *Anschluss*, while establishing an Austrian peace treaty became a secondary Versailles agenda item because the peace negotiators' initial main concern was to establish peace terms with Germany and other major issues.

Versailles subcommittees convened for four months between January and June 1919. They continued to meet in October into the night, negotiating the various peace treaties. The major victorious powers refused to sacrifice their own interests, even to President Wilson's Fourteen Points. The discredited previous European diplomatic balance of power concept was replaced by a collective security system epitomized by the League of Nations. While Lloyd George and Clemenceau possessed strong mandates from the home electorate, President Woodrow Wilson's Democrats lost control of Congress and, as a result, the United States did not ratify the Versailles Treaty nor the League of Nations, a fateful turn of events for Europe and the world.

When the Adriatic Sea question came to the forefront, nationalism became a prevailing factor in the ensuing events. The Entente Treaty of London terms with Italy had already been accepted at Versailles. President Wilson found the Italian claims in the Adriatic region to be unacceptable, demanding a "natural border at the Alpine line" – his advisers regarded his position as disastrous for the future. Italy supported Austria's position relative to Carinthia, countering South Slavic efforts to incorporate the province into what became Yugoslavia during 1919.

When Paris peacemakers tackled major territorial adjustments, it related chiefly to the former Dual Monarchy, emphasizing establishment of Yugoslavian and Czechoslovakian frontiers, a reborn Poland and a greatly enlarged Romania. Only the sensitive issue dealing with Italy and the possession of the Tyrol received immediate attention for Austria. Most former Habsburg Empire territory disappeared from the map, meanwhile the plight of Austria was overlooked. Soon the Italians and Yugoslavs clashed over their claims to Habsburg territory on the Adriatic coast and the port of Trieste. Grievous Versailles Treaty decisions placed almost 250,000 German-speaking South Tyroleans in Italy and three million Germans in Bohemia, Moravia and the Sudetenland in Czechoslovakia. These actions contradicted President Wilson's self-determination principle.

Versailles peacemakers eventually conducted numerous acrimonious debates relative to the newly created Austrian nation after it received major blame for the outbreak of the world war. That former Austro-Hungarian diplomatic officials became the new German Austrian state representatives caused confusion in Paris and stoked the blame that Austria caused the war.

When the war ended national antagonisms and inner ethnic competition and violence erupted at frontiers and spread into multiple areas; some never had such trouble in the past. These included southern Carinthia, western Hungary, eastern Galicia and southern Slovakia. As new national states emerged from the Austro-Hungarian Empire, creating armed forces became a major factor during the early postwar turmoil. Militias also rapidly appeared that produced violence such as the 1919–1920 "White Terror" in Hungary when as many as five thousand people might have been killed. In Yugoslavia political stability was obtained by suppressing groups that opposed the Serbian-led government, initially the Croat Peasant Party and the Communist Party in 1921. A major effect of the lost war and erupting turmoil, including the collapse of governments, was associated with the unprecedented human misery and a lack of respect for human life and dignity that resulted in violence. This created the background for the emergence of militias and paramilitary formations.

During summer 1919, violence erupted in Germany, Austria and Hungary. Plundering and anarchistic activities threatened the new Austrian government, particularly from Bolshevik elements. The unrest expanded as hundreds of thousands of people continued to starve and became unemployed, while currency became almost worthless. The victorious Allies, haunted by the threat of a Bolshevik revolution, determined to contain any such activity, particularly in Hungary.

The *Kronen* also collapsed by over 300 percent, creating runaway inflation during summer 1922 that threatened complete Austrian collapse. Neighboring states refused to assist German Austria. In particular, Czechoslovakia refused to ease Austria's problems. Bordering countries defended their own national interests as hatred continued against the former Habsburg power center. The Austrian central government dispatched multiple notes to Versailles concerning the escalating military threat of foreign invasion at its Yugoslav frontier.

On October 17, 1919 the Yugoslav parliament claimed possession of the province of Carinthia, its troops invading it. Austria sought support from France or Italy, the major postwar antagonists in Southeastern Europe. The Italians and Yugoslavians attempted to establish supremacy in the Adriatic Sea region, while the French protected the South Slavic state against Rome. Italy supported Austria because of their common interest in preventing the South Slavic state from seizing territory, particularly southern Carinthia and Styria. During May 1919 Yugoslav troops invaded Carinthia, seizing Klagenfurt. The Paris Council of Four ordered the invaders to leave. On May 12 the Paris Council of Ten announced the calling of two plebiscites in Carinthia. They encompassed the northern region occupied mostly by Slovenians, the southern half by Germans. Heavy fighting had occurred there at the end of May and during early June when Yugoslav troops occupied Klagenfurt. On June 20 the Paris Supreme Council adopted conditions for the two plebiscites to be administered in the disputed territories. Voting in southern Carinthia favored Austria on October 20, and Yugoslavian troops finally departed the disputed territory after an Allied ultimatum.[16]

Added to this was the fact that only a minimum amount of food existed to provide meat, fat and bread to the people because almost all of it had disappeared. Vienna had a large population but could not feed itself. It also suffered from the enormous deficits that grew quickly. Inflation also made its mark until it reached over 1,000 percent.

Divisions also arose between Vienna and the traditional borderlands, which seriously affected Austria's economic isolation. During 1918 food and production problems appeared hopeless in the capital, as the outlying provinces sometimes did not provide food supplies to Red Vienna partly due to resentment because of continuing crop requisitions after the war. During winter 1918–1919 railroads and trams could not run on schedule and industrial production proved hardly one-third of 1913, compounding unemployment that had risen to over a hundred thousand workers. By September 1920 industry was running at 25 percent capacity, because of a lack of coal. Iron and steel production remained at 10 percent of 1913 levels.

The Versailles peace treaty ratification process occurred during a period of much unrest, economic disruption and chaos in the new German Austria and Hungary. Economic hardship intensified with the continuation of the Entente blockade after the war ended. Compounding the situation, severe winter weather struck as the financial situation steadily worsened. Food and raw materials could not be purchased from neighboring countries, and there was no coal or power for factories.

The Hungarian Trianon Peace Treaty was belatedly ratified on June 4, 1920, because of the brief postwar Bela Kun communist upheaval. By its terms, Hungary lost two-thirds of its population (well over three million subjects) and two-thirds of its territory. The harshest Versailles Treaty left three million Hungarians under foreign rule in contradiction to Wilsonian self-determination. A third of a million Hungarians immigrated back to their homeland. The government had to pay reparations and, like neighboring German Austria, lost its former economic markets and sources of raw materials. The country of eight million people had been transformed into an agricultural entity. Hungary, not surprisingly, became a revisionist power during the early interwar period under former Admiral Horthy, the admiral without a navy, who became its dictator. The country entered the Fascist Italy and Nazi German orbit during the 1930s through its extensive economic ties with Berlin, but also as a revisionist power attempting to regain its lost First World War territories. It succeeded for a few years during the Second World War, but had to surrender those gains after the conflict.

During tumultuous November 1918, the Karolyi government encountered opposition from both right- and left-wing political parties because the Hungarian economy had collapsed.[17] The government's continued problems stemmed largely from continuing starvation as the population experienced no improvement in its economic condition. Then the country endured

Czechoslovakian and Romanian invasion. Ceding Transylvania to Romania, according to the Versailles Treaty, severed Hungarian access to the Adriatic Sea. When Minister President Karolyi's support disintegrated, many Hungarians initially accepted a short-lived communist revolution as a solution to their multiple problems. Following a one-week interim government after Karolyi resigned, the victorious powers demanded the withdrawal of Hungarian Red Army troops from a wide swath of their former territory. The Paris War Council authorized Czechoslovakia, Romania and Yugoslavia to occupy former Hungarian lands, but the invading troops advanced beyond the designated demarcation lines.

The first Magyar attempt at establishing a republic failed with Karolyi's demise and the resulting Bela Kun 133-day communist regime. Minister President Karolyi had demanded Hungarian independence from the Dual Monarchy and the *Ausgleich*; thus, he had hoped to negotiate a separate more favorable peace treaty with the Entente to retain historical Hungarian lands. However, his abrupt breaking of the union with Austria also sealed the Habsburg fate. Karolyi's Western-oriented policy failed and Hungary did lose much former territory.

On February 2, a communist-inspired demonstration turned violent in Budapest. In addition to the external military threat, unemployment accelerated and starvation conditions continued unabated. Then, on March 20, 1919, the French dispatched the Vyx twenty-four-hour ultimatum, demanding the withdrawal of Hungarian armed forces behind the demarcation lines established by the peace treaty, stipulating a thirty-six-hour response time. Hungarian forces evacuated extensive territory in the neutral zone between Hungary and Romania. This led to Karolyi's resignation, particularly after his desired Wilsonian peace treaty was rejected, but more immediately because of the Vyx ultimatum. This encouraged a communist coup.

On March 21 a proclamation in Budapest entitled "To All" called for the establishment of a Soviet Republic under communist hegemony. A rapidly formed Red Army initially successfully fought Romanian and Czech forces in an attempt to maintain the former Hungarian frontiers. Hungarian Red Army troops captured much of Slovakia, but it had to be surrendered because of Entente demands destroying Red Army troop morale.

The newly established Hungarian Bela Kun communist government appealed to the Austrian Social Democrat Party for an alliance and to establish an Austrian Soviet Republic on March 22, 1919. When that approach failed, Kun sought to organize a putsch in the Austrian capital to establish a communist regime. On March 31 the French government condemned the peace conference treatment of Hungary, which resulted in the dispatch of the General Smuts mission to Hungary that produced the Belgrade military convention on December 3.

The Hungarian Bela Kun regime became the only successful European communist revolution outside of Soviet Russia. Kun became a tsarist prisoner of war following the 1916 Brusilov offensive. Following his captivity, Kun founded the Hungarian Communist Party on December 20, 1918. The surprise proclamation of the Hungarian Soviet Republic startled Versailles peacemakers, who feared a Bolshevik foothold in Central Europe. Kun's domestic policies produced chaos and further disruption to the agricultural sector, seriously aggravating the dangerous food shortages. His policies alienated nearly every sector of society, particularly the farmers, who resented the continuing requisitioning of crops. He maintained power with the assistance of the Red Army and Bolshevik terrorist methods. Failure to control inflation, alleviate food shortages and blatant government corruption led to his demise.

Kun had attempted to achieve a too rapid transformation of Hungary's extremely precarious economic situation. Then, during June 1919, French forces invaded Hungary. On August 1 Kun fled to Austria and later died during Stalin's 1937 purges. Kun's primary threat emanated from neighbors that had already gained substantial Hungarian territory under the terms of the Versailles Treaty.[18]

Another factor, on July 20, was that a successful Red Army offensive was halted by Romanian troops that forced Hungarian troops to retreat from the liberated areas. The Red Army disintegrated. On August 4 Romanian troops entered Budapest and two days later a small counterrevolutionary group overthrew the communist government. From mid-August a national army was established. Political issues, chaos and morale loss from foreign invasions divided the "People's Army" over political issues. No communist revolutions elsewhere supported Kun's regime, particularly in Austria.

Transylvania, Habsburg territory since the eleventh century, had been promised to Romania under the terms of the 1916 Treaty of Bucharest with the Entente Powers. During early 1918 authority had vanished in the province as armed violence erupted. Hungarians constituted only some 25 percent of that province's population. By the Versailles peace treaty Romania doubled in size, receiving the Bukovina, south Banat and Transylvania. Romanian troops looted the areas once they occupied them. Then Romanian and Czechoslovakian troops invaded Hungary, ostensibly to crush the Bela Kun communist regime, prompting Kun to initially successfully invoke Hungarian patriotism to resist the invaders. The Paris peacemakers meanwhile had been momentarily distracted by the Italian-Austrian territorial boundary question over South Tyrol while still concerned with the peace treaty with Germany. On August 4, 1919, Romanian troops entered Budapest and installed a counterrevolutionary government, while Romanian and Yugoslav troops invaded other portions of the country, remaining until late 1919. During November the Versailles peacemakers ordered the invading forces to withdraw from designated Hungarian territory, which they did slowly.

Counterrevolutionary activity commenced in the countryside with former army officers planning a coup to place Admiral Horthy into power. Then a

"White Terror" was unleashed against the communist "Red Terror" and other enemies of the new conservative regime through the latter half of 1919 and early 1920. Thousands reputedly perished during this period of extreme political unrest. In mid-November, in a symbolic show of power, Admiral Horthy entered Budapest riding a white horse. Hungarian Burgenland, compatible with self-determination, a source for food for Austria and to Paris peacemakers necessary to protect Vienna from a Bolshevik-style revolution, became part of Austria.

During the early postwar period, revolutionary turmoil and violence drastically transformed the former Austro-Hungarian monarchy. This partially resulted from the contrast of the Western front's trench warfare and the more extensive Eastern front that made military maneuvering far more fluid. This exposed millions of civilians to military action, brutality and death. Troops accustomed to the battlefield slaughter and civilian casualties became radicalized when they returned home. They brought extreme violence (perpetual massacres, killing of prisoners of war and combat) home with them. The military defeat of Russia, Austria-Hungary and Germany prepared the creation of states from the Dual Monarchy. Soldiers returning to their new homelands no longer respected the rules of warfare.

Much instability marked the interwar period, particularly from real or reputed external threats. New national leadership made multiple promises to co-nationals, but never intended to fulfill them, for example Czech unfulfilled promises to the Slovaks. Persistent outside intervention produced instability in the new states, accompanied by misery and lawlessness. This created the conditions for the population movements, border conflicts and extreme territorial claims from Czechoslovakia, Romania, the Ukraine and Poland. This resulted in them creating their own ethnic armies.[19] Disputes over frontiers and self-defense measures became serious because of the easy supply of weapons, particularly in Austria with its intact weapons factories.

Ethnic issues remained a lingering problem, because they had never been resolved. Self-determination proved impossible to be effectively established in Central and Eastern Europe with its rich intermix of nationalities, opening multiple frontiers to constant violence during the early prewar period. An additional significant factor was that masses of refugees returned to their homelands, which caused disruption and violence when various ethnic groups sought advancement of their own national development in their new homeland. Leadership believed that such ethnic activity created a threat to the state's sovereignty, resulting in anger and disappointment for many inhabitants. It also angered national minority groups when their specific aspirations remained unfulfilled at the end of the war. This produced much of the summer 1919 violence.

An additional factor resulted from wartime economic exploitation of conquered territories such as Galicia, Serbia and Romania. The unstable European economies and domestic politics suffered from the extreme continuing economic conditions, particularly in Germany, Austria and Hungary and in the other Central and Eastern European states.[20] The St. Germain Treaty created a homogeneous but economically unsustainable Austrian state of 6.5 million people. The surrounding successor states opposed restoring Austrian, Hungarian or Habsburg domination; instead sought to bolster their own industrial bases by raising trade barriers against their neighbors. Austrian and Hungarian factories were severed from their raw material sources and markets, creating immediate severe economic dislocation. The dire situation propelled prevailing Austrian sentiment toward *Anschluss* with Germany. The successor states remained basically agricultural entities except for Czechoslovakia, which possessed a strong industrial foundation. The combination of economic collapse and general exhaustion was profoundly worsened by the two outbreaks of Spanish flu that produced high mortality rates. To many people, the treaty represented a diktat, a hated signal of defeat.

The Austrian desperate economic situation caused Allied policy to assist the rump state in recovering from the war. On August 20, Allied representatives claimed that at least thirty thousand unauthorized rifles were in Vienna barracks and thousands were in the provinces.[21] Domestically, many problems arose resulting from the interpolitical struggles and suspicions that concentrated on the question of creating the new Austrian Army from the ranks of the *Reichswehr* and police force. The Social Democrats hoped to control the new *Reichswehr*, which resulted in the Christian Socialist and *Grossdeutsch* parties creating their own militias.

When the Inter-Allied Commission arrived in Vienna it produced great tension and mistrust between it and the new government. In addition to creating a new federal army, the commission had the mission to confiscate excess weaponry and war materiel. Following the attempted communist putsches in April and May 1919 paramilitary activity flourished. Political groups feared that the other parties would obtain military advantage.

During spring 1921 right- and left-wing groups openly armed themselves so that by summer the existence of paramilitary units had become serious. The situation worsened during 1922. This and the fear of the spread of Bolshevism led the Entente Powers to acquiesce in their attempts to disarm Austrian citizens and paramilitary groups. The victorious powers could only punish Austria if they placed economic sanctions on it, but that country obviously suffered from extreme poverty, starvation conditions and economic instability. Thus, the Austrian Republic remained plagued with paramilitary forces and armed individuals, which led to the bloody 1927 encounter and 1934 Civil War.

The new Austrian government encountered formidable obstacles. The disastrous economic situation included a crippled financial system that desperately required reform. The government also had to adopt a constitution and feed its starving population.

The St. Germain Treaty dictated that the Austrian Army consist of thirty thousand long-term volunteers. Austria, Hungary and Bulgaria would have limited armed forces, the new Entente-friendly powers Czechoslovakia, Poland and Yugoslavia would not.

During the interwar years, Czechoslovakia, Poland and Romania contained a large 30 percent Magyar and German minority population. Italian territory contained 240,000 Germans; millions of Germans were in the Sudetenland, Bohemia and Moravia. These minority populations mocked Wilson's Point 10, which stipulated self-determination for the former Dual Monarchy peoples, an impossible task!

During the 1920s, the Little Entente of Romania, Czechoslovakia and Yugoslavia prevented a Habsburg restoration and a Hungarian Versailles peace revision. The alliance replaced Russia as a French partner. These small countries could not equal Russian power but they completed the Cordon Sanitaire to block the spread of Bolshevism extending into Central Europe during the interwar years.

Czechoslovakia officially received Ruthenian territory in the 1919 St. Germain Treaty, creating a multinational state in which the Czechs became a minority in their own country. The major problem evolved with the Sudetenland Germans who eventually created enormous turmoil in the post-war period. Adolf Hitler utilized that situation to initiate the 1938 Munich crises that played such a major role in the outbreak of the Second World War. Ignoring the emphasis on self-determination, the French supported the incorporation of the Sudetenland into the new Czech-Slovak state as it provided a natural defense line against a potential German invasion.

The 1920 Treaty of Rapallo extended the Italian eastern frontier until it encompassed the Julian Alps and Carso Plateau, which was administered with an iron fist.[22] Many Italians felt they had lost the peace, a myth that lingered long after the war. Sustaining one million casualties, Italy received South Tyrol from Austria, extending its frontier to the strategic Brenner Pass, a major deviation from Wilson's self-determination. Italy also received Gorizia, Istria and the port of Trieste, but Wilson refused to have it also receive Dalmatia. The turbulent immediate postwar internal conditions facilitated the rise of Benito Mussolini. In the immediate interwar years, Italy and Yugoslavia competed for Adriatic Sea possessions. Vienna received Italian support when Versailles peacekeepers ordered the plebiscites held in Carinthia after it was invaded by Yugoslav troops. The apparent threat from Italian and German influence in late 1918 helped drive the Slovenes and Croats into the Serbian orbit and the creation of the South Slavic state. Serbian troops' crushing of the green cadres in Croatia and Slovenia also greatly influenced the creation of the future Yugoslavia, including the social divisions between city and countryside.

On Easter Sunday 1921, Karl, traveling incognito by railroad, attempted to reclaim the Hungarian throne, but he failed because of massive resistance and Little Entente opposition. Karl later waited for what he felt was a suitable time to attempt to regain the crown. After secret preparations on March 25, 1921, again traveling incognito, the former emperor arrived in Hungary hoping that Admiral Horthy would relinquish his power as regent. Horthy did not, claiming that a restoration would immediately result in Little Entente military intervention. By April Karl returned to his exile home in Switzerland.

All Austrian political parties opposed a Habsburg restoration. Unlike Hungary there was not a separate political party that supported Karl. On April 3, 1919 an Austrian law outlawed the Habsburg family, but in Hungary the downfall of the Karolyi Republic, communist Kun government and counterrevolution created enough turmoil for Karl to initiate his attempts.

Karl flew with Zita into Western Hungary from Switzerland after months of preparation to attempt to gain the kingship. They flew on October 20, providing complete surprise, but this also prevented serious planning such as railroad transport for the troops supporting Karl. The next day Karl and his rapidly assembled troops attempted to reach Budapest by train, but progress proved slow. Admiral Horthy gained time to deploy loyal troops on October 23. There was initially a standoff but then government troops forced a small skirmish, which ended the attempt.

The Czechs and Yugoslavs ordered a partial mobilization – a major overreaction – initiated partly because the French had been involved in the fiasco. In German Austria a second attempt had almost no influence, because Karl lacked armed support. The unfortunate Karl was banished to Madeira where he died of the flu at the age of thirty-five during April 1922.

Poland again became an independent nation, having disappeared from the European map in 1799. It became one of the most difficult problems for the Versailles peace negotiators because of its numerous postwar conflicts with Czechoslovakia, while Polish troops halted the Red Army advance into Western Europe during the 1920 Soviet-Polish War. The Poles simultaneously participated in four conflicts with Germany relative to Silesia, Czechoslovakia and Teschen, the Ukraine over Galicia and the Soviet Union, resulting in the 1920 war. Seizing Russian territory with its largely non-Polish citizens produced extreme Russian resentment. In 1939 the Russians invaded eastern Poland soon after in conjunction with the German advance into the western portion as the Second World War commenced.

A Versailles peace condition, totally unacceptable to all Germans, was Poland receiving the Polish Corridor thus extending its territory to the North Sea and port of Danzig. This bisected Prussian territory and severed East Prussia from Germany. All Germans regarded this as one of the most egregious terms of the peace treaty.

The Kingdom of the Serbs, Croats and Slovenes (including Bosnia-Herzegovina) became Yugoslavia in 1929. Its internal weakness lay in the various religions (Catholic, Greek Orthodox and Muslim), languages and economic problems that plagued the new entity during the interwar period. The Yugoslav parliament claimed Carinthia then invaded it. A plebiscite held during October 1920 placed Carinthia in Austria; only then did Yugoslavian troops exit the disputed territory. The Slavic peoples in Yugoslavia were controlled by the Serbian Army and Great Serbian government, never receiving the assurances they had been promised before unification.

A truly turbulent period in Central and Eastern European history ended between 1917 and 1921, favoring left-wing political parties. At the same time there was an increase in right-wing insurgency that resulted in the rise of fascism. That had a major effect after the First World War in this part of Europe with the collapse of Germany, Russia and the centuries-old Habsburg monarchy. Another World War resulted.

~

Conclusion

The initial 1914 battles in the First World War portended the end of the Austro-Hungarian monarchy when the Habsburg Army suffered devastating defeats on both the Russian and Balkan fronts. This crippled the army within a month and a half of the outbreak of the war when it surrendered much of Galicia, with its critical food, oil and potential military recruits. Hungary was threatened with invasion through the Carpathian Mountains and from the Fortress Krakow flank. The army had suffered disastrous defeat with the loss of dead, wounded and missing professional and noncommissioned officers and soldiers. In September 1914 increasingly inadequately commanded and trained soldiers were hurled into battle as cannon fodder. Thus, as early as September 1914, no later than December, the Habsburg Army had become a militia force. Inadequately trained reserve officers, far inferior to the professional officers, replaced the casualties. A new (but less effective) armed force had to be created due to the loss of the officers and troops.

Austria-Hungary suffered enormous economic difficulties throughout the war, instigated by the Entente blockade, which cut off raw materials for its industry and food supplies for its citizens. An already crippled industry faltered then collapsed in 1918. As food sources became scarcer, yearly harvests proved devastating, seriously compounding the situation. Refugees fleeing the Russians from Galicia into the Austrian heartland during 1914 and 1915 exacerbated the nationality issue. Eleven major nationalities coexisted at different levels of development. Some had no history, others had neighboring countries with irredentist claims for Habsburg territory. Government failure to alleviate the worsening economic situation and multiple battlefield defeats with their enormous casualties soon exacerbated the seething nationality issues that simmered just below the surface. Germany provided raw materials, food, military equipment and hundreds of millions of Deutschmarks to the Dual Monarchy, as the Entente superior troop numbers and industrial might received tremendous support from worldwide colonies, slowly overpowering the Central Powers in late 1918.

The Dual Monarchy became increasingly dependent upon the German military to survive. German troops rescued the Habsburg Army at the end of the August/September 1914 Russian campaign, during the 1915 Carpathian

Mountain Winter War, the Gorlice–Tarnow and Rovno campaigns, the 1916 Brusilov offensive and the 1917 Kerensky and Caporetto ones. As a result of German success Austria-Hungary rapidly found itself the junior partner in the alliance. Germany repeatedly had to forgo Western front offensive plans, having to deploy troops to the Eastern front to save its faltering ally. Emperor Franz Joseph died in November 1916. His successor, Emperor Karl, unprepared for the position, attempted to negotiate a separate peace, but this was nullified by the unfortunate Sixtus Affair. The emperor served his Canossa at the embarrassing May 12 Spa meeting with German military leadership, which in turn fatefully affected the Entente stance toward Austria-Hungary. Following the Spa meeting, the British and French determined to terminate efforts at seeking a separate peace with Austria-Hungary. The Dual Monarchy, defeated on the battlefield, broke into separate national entities. Its fate was sealed largely because of its German alliance ties.

Conrad's belief in the cult of the offensive resulted in the lack of training for retrograde movement in 1914. This proved fateful during the disastrous 1914 150-kilometer retreat following the devastating Russian military victories. The progressive destruction of the army, briefly lessened during mid-war, resulted from obsolete tactics, lack of artillery–infantry cooperation, inferior artillery and lack of combined arms coordination. The tsarist and Italian armies possessed overwhelming superiority in troop numbers and artillery. The Habsburg Army had to be recreated several times during the war, increasingly becoming a *Miliz*, or a militia force. The Entente blockade negatively affected the army, as each year it became increasingly more difficult to obtain food, raw materials, equipment and rations for the troops, as well as fulfill civilian requirements. By October 1918 civilian suffering had become drastic, with army battlefield defeats, ethnic tensions at home and on the army front and rear echelon areas producing the conditions that led to the collapse of the monarchy. Significantly, soldiers made up a large element of revolutionary forces in Vienna and Budapest in 1918.

Conrad displayed major weaknesses throughout the war. Tragically, he never learned his army's capabilities, continually launching large offensive operations in which his troops could never achieve success. He also underestimated the enormous effect of Russian and Italian artillery and numerical superiority, and did not realize that Russia and Serbia had gained invaluable combat experience during the Russo-Japanese and Balkan Wars. He repeatedly ordered offensive operations that turned his troops into cannon fodder. He ordered the invasion of Serbia in July 1914 before deploying major troop numbers against the far more dangerous Russian opponent. Instead of the forty infantry divisions reputedly promised to General Moltke during the prewar period to launch an invasion into Russia, far fewer opposed the numerically superior tsarist army. This resulted in the disastrous Lemberg defeats, worsened by the three humiliating 1914 Serbian campaign results. The

German military required Austro-Hungarian forces to initially bind as many Russian troops as possible to enable the Schlieffen Plan invasion of France. Conrad nevertheless initially invaded Serbia, assuming he had a two-week window of opportunity because of his erroneous belief in a slow tsarist mobilization. The July 1 *Rückverlegung* caused enormous supply and transportation difficulties prior to initial battle, while troops lacked proper equipment, adequate training and firepower. The German Army, to the contrary, won the initial 1914 defensive battles in East Prussia, while Habsburg forces suffered the fatal Lemberg battles. Then came the bloody fall battles and 1915 Carpathian Mountain Winter War offensive disaster in an unsuccessful attempt to attract neutrals to the Central Powers or at least prevent them from joining the Entente. Troops continued to sustain battlefield defeats while many did not receive mountain training for the Carpathian, Romanian and Serbian campaigns. They also suffered from inferior command leadership.

Something that gravely hampered the Central Powers was the absence of a unified command structure, not rectified until September 1916 because of the Habsburg Brusilov offensive fiasco. Allied problems arose from the prewar Conrad–Moltke correspondence when they each misled the other as to their actual intentions and details relative to mobilization plans. Both encouraged their counterpart to take initial military action that supported their efforts. With the 1914 Lemberg battles' destruction of the prewar Habsburg Army Conrad nevertheless launched his 1915 Carpathian Mountain Winter War offensive with new recruits, its horrendous results including Italy entering the war on May 23, 1915. German assistance produced the greatest Central Power victory of the war; the summer Gorlice–Tarnow offensive as well as the fall 1915 Serbian, 1916 Romanian and 1917 Kerensky and Caporetto campaigns had German commanders.

Additional problems resulted from frayed relationships between Conrad and Falkenhayn, then between Hindenburg, Ludendorff and Conrad. Upon Emperor Franz Joseph's death in late November 1916, his successor Emperor Karl proved as equally unprepared as Tsar Nicholas of Russia to command the armed forces. Karl replaced Habsburg Supreme Command leadership, as well as Franz Joseph's diplomats and administrators.

The Austrian-Hungarian and German 1879 alliance encountered a vastly different situation in July and August 1914. In the interim both had developed divergent strategic interests while intending to expand their influence in the Balkan Peninsula. The alliance, defensive under Otto Bismarck, morphed into a dangerous offensive strategy in 1914.

The German Army never evaluated the Habsburg armed forces, a major error, leaving them unaware of its multiple weaknesses. The 1914 assassination of Archduke Franz Ferdinand caused Austro-Hungarian leaders to launch a local war against Serbia to protect and maintain the sinking Habsburg Balkan prestige. Germany would prevent Russia from intervening during the invasion, which obviously failed.

Czech and other Slavic troops were accused of treasonous activity during the 1914 Serbian campaign, while the Czech-German prewar turmoil continued as a major domestic factor throughout the war. Internal and external forces combined to haunt Habsburg leaders. In 1918, starvation and drastic economic conditions together with battlefield defeats and the failure of the central government to alleviate food shortages, as well as the nationality question, coalesced to cause the empire's collapse. Obsolete military equipment, declining weapon output, disease, war weariness and enormous casualties helped to destroy the entire edifice.

Habsburg naval forces were overwhelmed once Italy declared war on the Dual Monarchy in 1915 and were joined by Entente ships. During war naval forces conducted hit-and-run tactics. The only significant naval successes resulted from German submarine warfare. The first day of the Italian war, May 23, 1915, the Habsburg fleet performed its only full-fledged combat activity during the war, attempting to interrupt the new enemy's mobilization measures along its central coast. The other major naval effort occurred in the Otranto Straits during 1917.

The era after the Versailles Treaty witnessed chaos, violence, revolution and armed conflicts. Austria and Hungary became pariahs to their neighbors while the Austrian people continued to face starvation and lack of natural resources, retarding Habsburg industry. Ultimately, Karl Renner negotiated treaties with Czechoslovakia, Romania and Italy in 1920, ending Austria's isolation. With Italian assistance the Carinthian crisis was resolved with Yugoslavia. Thereafter, multiple meetings did not achieve significant economic relief for Vienna. Then, during 1922, a treaty assisted Austria's perpetual financial difficulties.

On September 22, 1922, the Geneva October 4 protocol provided Austria 150 million golden Kronen. A large amount would remove earlier debts; the remainder would cover budget deficits for the next two years.

Habsburg military weaknesses, glaringly evident during the war's opening campaigns, continued throughout the conflict. The problem of inadequate logistical support against Russia, Serbia and Italy was never resolved. The situation progressively worsened as the conflict continued. At the outbreak of the war general enthusiasm permeated the Dual Monarchy, but enormous casualties and military defeats ended that.

In the early years of the war South Slavic (Croat and Slovene) loyalty remained with the Habsburg state, but worsening economic conditions ignored by the central government in South Slavic territories and later wartime concerns of Italian and German threats to Slavic interests transformed that loyalty toward the South Slav national movement. The nationality issue and ethnic problems appeared early in the war, but did not become fatal until

October 1918, with the collapse of the army, the perpetual economic woes resulting in increasingly drastic rationing conditions in the hinterland. As the military front began to collapse anarchy erupted in the rear echelon areas where reserve units (*Ersatz*) troops began to mutiny. Troops plundered depots and commandeered trains, which commenced the implosion of the army. By the end of 1918 many officers and soldiers had become political activists, which signaled the breakdown of military discipline and performance. They became major participants in the revolutionary activities in Vienna, Budapest and other Austro-Hungarian cities.

By October 31, 1918 mass demonstrations resulted in the proclaimation of an Austrian republic, terminating hundreds of years of Habsburg rule. Large mobs produced the almost bloodless Austrian revolution during looting and plundering and then the critical question arose of how to manage demobilized soldiers and former prisoners of war, when one could not count on military forces maintaining peace at home during the early prewar period. After the two 1919 attempted communist coups were rapidly crushed, a German Austrian republic was established. In the interim, Social Democrats attempted to create an army, the *Volkswehr*, that it supported. The other coalition party, the Christian Socialists, preferred a strong police force. The creation of paramilitary forces plagued the young republic, a situation not resolved by an interallied disarmament group.

The nationality question took a serious setback with the 1867 *Ausgleich*. Before and throughout the war the central government initiated no major steps to alleviate the worsening economic and ethnic problems. The most serious nationality conflict had evolved between the Czechs and Germans in Bohemia and Moravia, a major factor before and during the war. The Czech-German clashes in the *Reichsrat* led to its proroguing in 1914 until 1917 when Karl reinstated it. The nationality problem immediately exploded as Czech, South Slavic and other nationalities utilized the resurrected political platform to exacerbate ethnic confrontations, demanding some form of self-governance for them. The 1867 *Ausgleich* blocked Czech demands for national recognition of their *Staatsrecht*, while in Hungary the Magyarization policy stymied Croats, Slovenes, Serbs and Romanians from receiving political rights. The conflict between Poles and Ruthenians exploded with the March 3, 1918 Brest-Litovsk treaty that gave the Ruthenians the territory around Cholm, raising violent Polish opposition that introduced a long struggle between the two Slavic opponents.

New revolutionary conditions included contested territorial boundaries, revolutions and frontier militia and armed band encounters, in attempts to establish permanent territorial boundaries. Many demobilized soldiers joined the newly formed national armies, militias and armed groups.

During the immediate pre–Second World War period, the fledgling Austrian republic faced multiple critical problems. The most pressing was the horrendous economic situation: widespread starvation, accelerating unemployment, factory closings and an undernourished, sickly population. The threat of an attempted communist putsch lasted until summer 1919, fueled by the short-lived communist regime in Munich and Bela Kun episode in Hungary.

A constitution had to be prepared, the peace treaty signed and ratified, a police force created and an army formed to protect against potential outside threats. The republic found itself surrounded by hostile neighbors that refused to provide raw materials and food. Continued economic distress and civilian suffering threatened the stabilization of the truncated German Austrian state, but the Social Democrat Party succeeded in controlling the Vienna masses' revolutionary activities. Friedrich Adler's leadership created a loyal *Volkswehr* to maintain peace and protect the new unstable country, while the original people's militia proved unreliable for maintaining peace for the new republic.

In early November 1918 only four infantry companies remained loyal to the Vienna coalition government, while major ammunition depots and magazines had been left unguarded. The threat of violence escalated with each train that arrived crammed with half-starved mutinous soldiers brutalized by the war and often still armed. Violence and plundering plagued all of society, particularly in the cities.

Summer 1919 witnessed major revolutionary upheaval in Central Europe. The newly created governments proved unable to curb the violence and chaos, much of which had not occurred in specific areas during the war. The cities in particular witnessed serious turmoil as the disastrous food situation and rationing endured until 1920 and beyond. Between 1918 and 1921 many people were unemployed and in starvation conditions.

Austrian and Hungarian attempts to receive international recognition and rebuild their economically devastated territories were sabotaged for years. The Little Entente of Czechoslovakia, Romania and Yugoslavia opposed a Habsburg restoration and recovery of the former imperial lands. Their troops invaded Hungary to extend their national frontiers during 1919 with Entente approval.

The Austrian social revolution terminated with the St. Germain peace treaty. A coalition government successfully ended the Austrian revolution peacefully. However, "Red" Vienna faced opposition from conservative Alpine mountain provinces.

The Social Democratic, Christian Socialist and German Nationalist party coalition endured tensions until 1921, particularly concerning the security issue. The Social Democrats created the *Volkswehr* paramilitary group, and hoped that the troops would become part of the national army. Christian Socialists preferred a strong police force, while paramilitary forces proliferated in the country.

The Interallied Commission attempted to remove military equipment and weapons and disarm the citizenry because Vienna had been the center of the former empire's military complex. Enormous amounts of weapons and ammunition remained readily available. Although the Interallied Commission had the mission to disarm the people, surplus weapons and ammunition were traded to Czechoslovakia, Poland and Romania in exchange for critically needed food and raw materials. The Allies could not apply economic sanctions to force disarmament because the small and poor country was in terrible economic shape – the people suffered widespread starvation and disease. Ultimately, disarmament clauses could not be enforced.

The troubled interwar period in Central and Eastern Europe produced the conditions and settings for subsequent events that led to the fascist era. One can blame the demise of the Habsburg monarchy and its territories on its centuries-old dominant position in Central Europe, resulting from the First World War. The Dual Monarchy was not prepared to wage and survive the ordeal. Central Europe progressed from left-leaning to right-wing governments after the 1920 German failed Kapp Putsch. That commenced the background events for the Second World War. The war that destroyed the Austro-Hungarian monarchy did not resolve the issues that caused it. The war and the Versailles Treaty created the background to further catastrophic events.

NOTES

Introduction

1 For the most thorough coverage of Austria-Hungary during the entire war: Manfried Rauchensteiner, *Der Tod des Doppeladlers: Österreich-Ungarn und der Erste Weltkrieg*, Graz, Vienna and Cologne: Verlag Styria, 1993. For the prewar Habsburg Army, see: Günther Kronenbitter, *"Krieg im Frieden": Die Führung der k. u.k. Armee und die Grossmachtpolitik Österreich-Ungarns 1906–1914*, Munich: R. Oldenbourg Verlag, 2003 and his multiple articles in English and German; James S. Lucas, *Austro-Hungarian Infantry, 1914–1918*, London: Almark, 1973. For the "official" articles on the major battles during the war: Gunther E. Rothenberg, *The Army of Francis Joseph*, West Lafayette, IN: Purdue University Press, 1976; Max Schwarte, *Der große Krieg, 1914–1918, vol. V: Der österreichisch-ungarische Krieg*, Leipzig: Barth in Ausgl., 1922. For the very influential highest-ranking German general in Habsburg Supreme Command headquarters and an important source: August Cramon, *Unser Österreichisch-Ungarischer Bundesgenosse im Weltkriege*, Berlin: E. S. Mittler & Sohn, 1920. Also: Anton Pitreich, *Der Österreich-ungarische Bundesgenosse im Sperrfeuer*, Klagenfurt: Arthur Killitsch, 1930; Wilhelm Czermak, *In deinem Lager war Österreich: Die österreichisch-ungarische Armee, wie man sie nicht kannte*, Breslau, W. G. Korn, 1938; Arthur J. May, *The Hapsburg Monarchy 1867–1914*, Cambridge, MA: Harvard University Press, 1960 and *The Passing of the Habsburg Monarchy*, 2 vols., Philadelphia: University of Pennsylvania Press, 1966. Chapter 9 surveys the significant events of 1918 and Chapter 10 discusses the collapse of the Dual Monarchy and the creation of the German-Austrian Republic and its tragic beginning surrounded by hostile neighbors, its people starving, its industry idle because of the lack of raw materials, violence – partially from returning armed soldiers and former prisoners of war – having to sign a *Diktat* peace and form a new government.

2 Nationalism: Adam Wandruszka and Peter Urbanitsch, *Die Habsburgermonarchie, 1848–1918, vol. III: Die Volker des Reiches*, Vienna: Verlag der Österreichischen Akademie der Wissenschaften, 1980; Robert Kann, *Multinational Empire: Nationalism and National Reform in the Habsburg Monarchy, 1848–1918*, 2 vols., New York: Octagon Books, 1970. A more recent account for Austria-Hungary: Aviel Roshwald, *Ethnic Nationalism and the Fall of Empires: Central Europe, the Middle East and Russia, 1914–1923*, London: Routledge, 2001. For a detailed refutation of alleged Czech soldier desertion during the war: Richard Lein, *Das militärische Verhalten der Tschechen im Ersten Weltkrieg*, Dissertation, University of Vienna, 2009 and subsequent book. For articles: Solomon Wank, "Foreign Policy

and the Nationality Problem in Austria-Hungary, 1867–1914," *Austrian History Yearbook*, vol. 3, 1967, pp. 37–56; Rudolf Kiszling, "Das Nationalitätproblem in Habsburg Wehrmacht, 1848–1918," *Der Donauraum*, vol. 4, 1959, pp. 82–92; Kurt Peball, "Um das Erbe: Zu Nationalitätenpolitik des k.u.k. Armeeoberkommandos während der Jahr 1914 bis 1917," *Österreichische Militärische Zeitschrift* (Special Issue), 1967.

3 Economics: Max-Stephan Schulze, "Austria-Hungary's Economy in World War I," in Stephen Broadberry and Mark Harrison, eds., *The Economics of World War I*, Cambridge: Cambridge University Press, 2005, pp. 77–111; Robert J. Wegs, *Die österreichische Kriegswirtschaft 1914–1918*, Vienna: Schendl, 1979; *Austrian Economic Mobilization during World War I with Particular Emphasis on Heavy Industry*. Dissertation. University of Vienna, 1970 and "Transportation: The Achilles Heel of the Habsburg War Effort," in Robert A. Kann, Béla K. Király and Paula S. Fichtner, eds., *The Habsburg Empire in World War I: Essays on the Intellectual, Military, Political and Economic Aspects of the Habsburg War Effort*. New York: Eastern European Quarterly, 1977, pp. 121–135. Other worthwhile sources: Gustav Gratz and Richard Schüller, *Der Wirtschaftliche Zusammenbruch Österreich-Ungarns: Die Tragödie der Erschöpfung*, Vienna, Hölden-Pichler-Tempsky, A. G., 1930; David F. Good, *The Economic Rise of the Habsburg Empire, 1750–1914*, Berkeley: University of California Press, 1984; Herbert Matis, ed., *The Economic Development of Austria since 1870*, Northampton: Edward Elgar Publishing, 1994.

4 The Habsburg dynasty was established in 1278. In 1526 King Louis II of Hungary and Bohemia died without a son. Following the historic battle of Mohacs, 1526, the Habsburgs inherited his two crowns. During the sixteenth and seventeenth centuries the Habsburgs protected Central Europe from the Turkish invasion danger and the Protestant Reformation. Marie Theresa (r. 1740–1780) and her son Joseph (r. 1780–1790) centralized the Habsburg administration system and made the German language the official one. Following the French Revolution and Napoleonic seizure of power in 1806, the Holy Roman Empire became the Austrian Empire. Following the loss of the war of 1859 with France and Piedmont the Habsburgs lost possession of Venetia. In the Treaty of Prague, the Habsburgs were excluded from the Holy Roman Empire German territories.

5 During the war the Serbian government pursued a nationalistic program; its leaders opposed sharing power with the other South Slavs. Without Entente recognition, Serbian troops occupied the Habsburg South Slavic territories and eradicated the green cadre scourge in the countryside pushing the other South Slavic peoples toward incorporation in a Serb-led Yugoslavia.

6 Bosnia, in particular, contained a majority Serbian population.

7 Poland had disappeared from the map of Europe after Russia, the Holy Roman Empire and Prussia divided its territories in 1772, 1795 and 1799. In 1910 the Poles represented 17.8 percent of the population, mostly in Galicia.

8 For detailed information on the critical joint command questions, see the multiple articles by Günther Kronenbitter such as: "The German and Austro-Hungarian General Staffs and Their Reflections on an 'Impossible' War," in Holger Afflerbach and David Stevenson, eds., *An Improbable War: The Outbreak of World War I and European Political Culture before 1914*, New York: Berghahn Books, 2007, pp. 149–158; "Von Schweinehunden und Waffenbrüdern: Der Koalitionskrieg der

Mittelmächte 1914/15 zwischen Sachzwang und Ressentiment," in Gerhard Gross, ed., *Der vergessene Front – der Osten 1914–15: Ereignis, Wirkung, Nachwirkung,* Paderborn: Schöningh, 2006, pp. 157–186. Also valuable: Gerald E. Silberstein, *The Troubled Alliance: German-Austrian Relations, 1914–1917,* Lexington: The University Press of Kentucky, 1970; Rudolf Jeřábek, *Die Brussilowoffensive 1916: Ein Wendepunkt der Koalitionskriegführung der Mittelmächte,* Dissertation, University of Vienna, 1982.

9 Navy: Paul G. Halpern, *The Battle of The Otranto Straits: Controlling the Gateway to the Adriatic in WWI,* Bloomington: Indiana University Press, 2004 and *The Naval War in the Mediterranean, 1914–1918,* Annapolis, MD: Naval Institute Press, 1987; Anthony E. Sokol, *The Imperial and Royal Austro-Hungarian Navy,* Annapolis, MD: US Naval Institute, 1968; Lawrence Sondhaus, *The Naval Policy of Austria-Hungary 1867–1918: Navalism, Industrial Development and the Politics of Dualism,* West Lafayette, IN: Purdue University Press, 1994. Airforce: John H. Morrow, *German Air Power in World War I,* Lincoln: University of Nebraska Press, 1982; Reinhard Karl Boromäus Desoyne, *Die k.u.k. Luftfarhtruppe – Die Entstehung, die Aufbau und die Organisation der österreichisch-ungarischen Heeresluftwaffe 1912–1918,* Hamburg: Diplomica Verlag GmbH, 1999; Sebastian Rosenboom, *Im Einsatz über der "vergessenen Front": Der Luftkrieg an der Ostfront im Ersten Weltkrieg,* Potsdam: Verlag Militärgeschichtliches Forschungsamt, 2013.

Chapter 1

1 For a thorough background on the Habsburg Army, consult Walter Wagner, "Die k.(u.) k. Armee – Gliederung und Aufgabentellung," in Adam Wandruszka and Peter Urbanitsch, eds., *Die Habsburgermonarchie 1848–1918, vol. V: Die bewaffnete Macht,* Vienna: Verlag der Österreichischen Akademie der Wissenschaften, 1987, pp. 142–633; Maximillian Ehnl, "Die österreichisch-ungarische Landmacht nach Aufbau, Gliederung, Friedensgarnison, Einteilung und nationaler Zusammensetzung im Sommer 1914," in *Ergänzungsheft 9 zu Österreich-Ungarns letzter Krieg,* Vienna: Militärwissenschaftliche Mitteilungen, 1934, pp. 1–21; Fritz Franek, "Entwicklung der österreichische-ungarische Wehrmacht in den ersten zwei Kriegsjahren," in *Ergänzungsheft 5 zu Österreich-Ungarns letzter Krieg,* Vienna: Militärwissenschaftliche Mitteilungen, 1935. For the prewar developments of the Habsburg Army, read Kronenbitter, *"Krieg im Frieden";* James S. Lucas, *Fighting Troops of the Austro-Hungarian Army 1868–1914,* New York: Hippocrene Books, 1987 and *Austro-Hungarian Infantry.* See Rothenberg, *Army of Francis Joseph.*

2 Rothenberg, *Army of Francis Joseph;* Rudolph Hecht, *Fragen zur Heeresergänzung der gesamten Bewaffneten Macht Österreich-Ungarns während des ersten Weltkrieges,* Dissertation, University of Vienna, 1969.

3 Hecht, *Fragen zur Heeresgänzung;* see Rothenberg, *Army of Francis Joseph;* Lucas, *Austro-Hungarian Infantry.*

4 Norman Stone, "Army and Society in the Habsburg Monarchy, 1900–1914," *Past & Present* , vol. 33, no.1, 1966, pp. 95–111.

5 Hecht, *Fragen zur Heeresgänzung;* Lucas, *Austro-Hungarian Infantry.*

6 KAN *(Kriegsarchivnachläße),* B/726, Robert Nowak, No. 8: *Die Klammer des Reiches: Das Verhalten der elf Nationalitäten Österreich-Ungarn in der k.u.k. Wehrmacht 1914–1918.*

7 Ibid.; Hecht, *Fragen zur Heersgänzung*; Rothenberg, *Army of Francis Joseph*.
8 Zbyněk A. B. Zeman, *The Break-Up of the Habsburg Empire, 1914–1918*, London: Oxford University Press, 1961. Multiple factors such as disease, lack of food, years of battlefield defeats, the disastrous June 1918 offensive and weather conditions produced the background circumstances for the collapse of the Habsburg Army in October 1918. The lack of effective professional officers and noncommissioned officers, and inadequate supply services became additional factors.
9 Franz Conrad von Hötzendorf, *Aus meiner Dienstzeit, 1906–1918*, 5 vols., Vienna: Rikola Verlag, 1921–1925.
10 Hecht, *Fragen zur Heeresgänzung*.
11 Emil Ratzenhofer, "Verlust Kalkül für den Karpatenwinter 1915," in *Ergänzungsheft 1 zu Österreich-Ungarns letzter Krieg*, Vienna: Militärwissenschaftliche Mitteilungen, 1930, p. 35.
12 Hecht, *Fragen zur Heeresgänzung*; Conrad, *Dienszeit*, I; *KAN*, B/203, Otto Berndt, No. 3.
13 *ÖULK (Österreich-Ungarns letzter Krieg)*, I, p. 26; Hecht, *Fragen zur Heeregänzung*.
14 Various sources.
15 See, for example, *KAN*, B/600, G. M. Anton von Lehar.
16 Rauchensteiner, *Tod des Doppeladlers*.
17 Standardized repeating rifles became available between 1889 and 1905 and more modern artillery between 1895 and 1908.
18 Fritz Franek, "Probleme der Organisation im ersten Kriegsjahre," in *Ergänzungsheft 5 zu Österreich-Ungarns letzter Krieg*, Vienna: Militärwissenschaftliche Mitteilungen, 1935. See Rauchensteiner, *Tod des Doppeladlers*.
19 István Deák, *Beyond Nationalism: A Social and Political History of the Habsburg Officer Corps 1848–1918*, Oxford: Oxford University Press, 1990; *KAN*, B/700, Hans Mailáth-Pokorny, No. 12.
20 See *KA NFA (Kriegsarchiv Neue Feld Akten)*, 3. Op. Armee Kdo., fasz. 42; *KAN*, B/62, Alexander von Krobatin; A. Pitreich, *Bundesgenosse im Sperrfeuer*, pp. 78–79; Alfred Krauss, *Der Ursachen unserer Niederlage: Erinnerungen und Urteile aus dem Weltkrieg*, Munich: J. F. Lehmann, 1921.
21 *KAN*, B/700, Mailáth-Pokorny, No. 12; *KAN*, B/203, Berndt, No. 3, et al.
22 Norman Stone, *The Eastern Front 1914–1917*, New York: Charles Scribner's Sons, 1975.
23 Ibid.; Lawrence Sondhaus, *Franz Conrad von Hötzendorf: Architect of the Apocalypse*, Leiden: Brill, 2000.
24 Sondhaus, *Franz Conrad von Hötzendorf*.

Chapter 2

1 Conrad, *Dienstzeit*, III, p. 670. For the July crisis, Samuel R. Williamson, Jr., *Austria-Hungary and the Origins of the First World War*, New York: St. Martins, 1991, is excellent.
2 Gina Hötzendorf, *Mein Leben mit Conrad von Hötzendorf: Sein geistiges Vermächtnis*, Leipzig: Grethlein & Co. Nachf., 1935, p. 57.
3 Conrad, *Dienstzeit*, IV.
4 Matscheko served as a senior section leader and chief of Count Berchtold's Foreign Ministry Division.

5 *ÖUA* (*Österreich-Ungarns Aussenpolitik*), VIII, pp. 277–278.

6 Williamson, *Austria-Hungary and the Origins*, p. 68.

7 Rauchensteiner,*Tod des Doppeladlers*, p. 68.

8 The *Rückverlegung* was ordered officially on July 13; Conrad, *Dienstzeit*, V, p. 71; *ÖULK*, I, p. 414; *KAM* (*Kriegsarchiv Manuskript*), fasz. A103, *Eisenbahn Aufmarsch 1914*, Kalman Kéri.

9 Rauchensteiner, *Tod des Doppeladlers*.

10 *ÖUA*, VIII, No. 9995; *KAN*, B/5, Julius von Preanfeld Lustig-Prean; Conrad, *Dienstzeit*, III, p. 789.

11 *ÖUA*, VIII, No. 9984; *DD* (*Die deutschen Dokumente*), I, No. 13; Hugo Hantsch, *Leopold Graf Berchtold*, vol. II, Vienna: Verlag Styria, 1963, pp. 568, 571, 682.

12 *DD*, I, No. 7.

13 *ÖUA*, VIII, No. 9984; No. 13; Conrad, *Dienstzeit*, IV, pp. 36–37; Hantsch, *Berchtold*, II, pp. 568, 571.

14 *DD*, I, No. 74; Luigi Albertini, *The Origins of the War of 1914*, 3 vols., London: Oxford University Press, 1952–1957.

15 Rauchensteiner, *Tod des Doppeladlers*, pp. 71, 152; Samuel R. Williamson, Jr., "Confrontation with Serbia: The Consequences of Vienna's Failure to Achieve Surprise in July 1914," *Mitteilungen des Österreichischen Staatsarchivs*, vol. 43, 1993, pp. 173–174.

16 Conrad, *Dienstzeit*, IV, pp. 36–37.

17 *ÖUA*, VIII, No. 10076.

18 *HHSTA:PA* (*Haus-, Hof- u. Staatsarchiv-Politisches Archiv*), I, fasz. 496, Präs No. 4529; *ÖUA*, VIII, Nos. 10058, 10901; *DD*, I, Nos. 15, 18; Hantsch, *Berchtold*, II, pp. 572–576; Risto Ropponen, *Die Kraft Russlands: Wie beurteilte die politische und militärische Führung der europäischen Grossmächte in der Zeit von 1905 bis 1914 die Kraft Russlands?*, Helsinki: Akateeminen Kirjakauppa in Komm, 1968, pp. 263–264.

19 During the 1912–1913 Balkan War Crisis, particularly during October 1913, when Vienna had seen its position weakened.

20 Conrad, *Dienstzeit*, IV, pp. 52ff.

21 See Graydon A. Tunstall, "The Habsburg Command Conspiracy: The Austrian Falsification of Historiography on the Outbreak of World War I," *Austrian History Yearbook*, vol. 27, 1996, pp. 181–198 for further information on the falsification of Austrian documents at the outbreak of war.

22 Conrad, *Dienstzeit*, IV, pp. 51, 53–54, 57; *ÖUA*, VIII, pp. 141–150.

23 *ÖULK*, VIII, No. 10118.

24 Max von Pitreich, *1914: Die Militärischen Probleme unseres Kriegbeginnes: Ideen, Gründe und Zusammenhänge*, Vienna: Selbstverlag, 1934, p. 124; Conrad, *Dienstzeit*, IV.

25 The notes of this meeting are in *ÖUA*, VIII, pp. 447–448.

26 Conrad, *Dienstzeit*, IV, p. 80.

27 *ÖUA*, VIII, No. 10393.

28 *ÖUA*, VIII, No. 10393; Conrad, *Dienstzeit*, IV, pp. 54–55, 87–92; Imanuel Geiss, *Julikrise und Kriegsausbruch 1914: Eine Dokumentensammlung*, 2 vols., Hannover: Verlag für Literatur und Zeitgeschehen, 1963, p. 139; M. von Pitreich, *1914*, p. 15.

29 *KAAOK* (*Kriegsarchiv Armeeoberkommando*), EBB (Eisenbahnbüro), fasz. 4119; *KAM*, fasz. A103, Kéri.

30 Rauchensteiner, *Tod des Doppeladlers*, fn, p. 566.

31 Second, Fifth and Sixth armies or eight corps (including fourteen mountain brigades, three cavalry divisions, eight *Landsturm* brigades, six March brigades, eight *Honvéd* regiments and seven *Landwehr* regiments).
32 Williamson, *Austria-Hungary and the Origins*.
33 Sergei Dobrorolski, *Die Mobilmachung der Russischen Armee, 1914*, Berlin: Deutsche Verlagsgesellschaft für Politik und Geschichte, 1922, p. 19.
34 *DD*, I, No. 370.
35 Conrad, *Dienstzeit*, IV, pp. 123–133; *DD*, I, No. 216.
36 *DD*, I, Nos. 219, 281; II, No. 281; Conrad, *Dienstzeit*, IV, p. 133; Albertini, *Origins*, II, p. 472.
37 *DD*, I, Nos. 155, 219; II, No. 342; Graf A. Pourtalès, *Meine letzten Verhandlungen und Dokumente*, Berlin: Gesellschaft für Politik und Geschichte, 1927, 27, Nos. 11, 53.
38 Conrad, *Dienstzeit*, IV, p. 137; *ÖULK*, I, p. 19; *KAM*, fasz. A103, Kéri.
39 Hans von Zwehl, *Erich von Falkenhayn, General der Infanterie: Eine biographische Studie*, Berlin: E. S. Mittler & Sohn, 1926, p. 574. Bethmann Hollweg had to consider the Social Democratic *Reichstag* party position.
40 *KAAOK*, EBB; Conrad, *Dienstzeit*, IV, p. 142; Dobrorolski, *Mobilmachung*, p. 23.
41 Conrad, *Dienstzeit*, IV, pp. 150–152; *ÖULK*, I, p. 15; *ÖUA*, VIII, No. 11002.
42 Conrad, *Dienstzeit*, IV, pp. 151–152; Geiss, *Julikrise*, II, pp. 355 and 759.
43 Conrad, *Dienstzeit*, IV, p. 155.
44 *KAAOK*, *R. Gruppe*, fasz. 495; Conrad, *Dienstzeit*, IV, p. 152; *ÖUA*, VIII, No. 11033.
45 *KAAOK*, EBB, fasz. 4118; *KAM*, fasz. A103, Kéri.
46 *ÖUA*, VIII, No. 10876; Conrad, *Dienstzeit*, IV, pp. 143, 147–148.
47 *ÖUA*, VIII, No. 11179; *DD*, II, No. 349; III, Nos. 487, 535, 536; Pourtalès, *Verhandlungen*.
48 *DD*, II, No. 473; III, Nos. 513, 575; IV; Anhang IV; Pourtalès, *Verhandlungen*.
49 *ÖUA*, VIII, pp. 11, 130.
50 *DD*, II, No. 479; Conrad, *Dienstzeit*, IV, p. 152; *RAWK* (*Reicharchiv der Weltkrieg*), I, p. 35; Albertini, *Origins*, II, p. 679. The telegram was dispatched at 1:45 p.m. and arrived at 4:10 p.m.
51 *ÖUA*, III, No. 1119; *DD*, IV, No. 825; Conrad, *Dienstzeit*, IV, p. 151.
52 *ÖUA*, VIII, No. 1118; *DD*, I, No. 482; III, Nos. 502, 503; *RAWK*, II.
53 *ÖUA*, VIII, Nos. 10937, 11093; *DD*, II, No. 424; Conrad, *Dienstzeit*, IV, p. 147.
54 *ÖUA*, VIII, No. 11125; *DD*, III, Nos. 503, 601; Conrad, *Dienstzeit*, IV, pp. 156, 160–161; *RAWK*, II, p. 29.
55 *KAAOK*, *R. Gruppe*, fasz. 495; Conrad, *Dienstzeit*, IV; Albertini, *Origins*, III, p. 47.
56 Conrad, *Dienstzeit*, IV, p. 155; *RAWK*, I, p. 33.
57 *KAAOK*, *R. Gruppe*, fasz. 496; Conrad, *Dienstzeit*, IV, pp. 155–156.

Chapter 3

1 For the campaigns in Galacia see N. Stone, *Eastern Front*; Holger H. Herwig, *The First World War: Germany and Austria-Hungary 1914–1918*, New York: Arnold, 1997; Rauchensteiner, *Tod des Doppeladlers*; Graydon A. Tunstall, *Planning for War against Russia and Serbia: Austro-Hungarian and German Military Strategies 1871–1914*, New York: Columbia University Press, 1993; Geoffrey Wawro, *A Mad Catastrophe: The Outbreak of World War I and the Collapse of the Habsburg*

Empire, New York: Basic Books, 2014; *ÖULK*, I and III; *RAWK*, II. Also, Alexander Watson, *Ring of Steel: Germany and Austria-Hungary in World War I*, New York: Basic Books, 2014; Prit Buttar, *Collision of Empires: The War on the Eastern Front in 1914*, New York: Osprey Publishing, 2016; Winston Churchill, *The Unknown War: The Eastern Front*, New York: Charles Scribner's Sons, 1931.

2 In particular, James Lyon, *Serbia and the Balkan Front, 1914: The Outbreak of the Great War*, New York: Bloomsbury Academic, 2015; Andej Mitrovic, *Serbia's Great War 1914–1918*, Lafayette, IN: Purdue University Press, 2007.

3 Conrad, *Dienstzeit*, V, pp. 222, 877; *ÖULK*, I, p. 168.

4 Bruce W. Menning, *Bayonets before Bullets: The Imperial Russian Army, 1861–1914*, Bloomington: Indiana University Press, 1992, pp. 136–137.

5 Kronenbitter, *"Krieg im Frieden,"* pp. 446–447, et al.

6 *ÖULK*, I, pp. 170–171; Conrad, *Dienstzeit*, IV.

7 Menning, *Bayonets before Bullets*.

8 Hew Strachan, *The First World War, vol. I: To Arms*, Oxford: Oxford University Press, 2001, p. 349.

9 Five infantry divisions, including the 38. and 20. Honvéd divisions, as well as the 40. *Landsturm* Brigade, part of the 12. March Brigade, then the 43. Infantry Brigade to be followed by the 43. Infantry Division.

10 German intelligence reports indicated that ten to eleven Russian corps had invaded East Prussia. Additionally, five further enemy corps could be directed against either of the Allies, while seven to eight tsarist reserve divisions had been deployed against Germany and nine to ten against the Dual Monarchy.

11 No solid defense could be prepared during early September, so the solution became to retreat to the Vereszyca River twenty-five kilometers to the west, particularly since Third Army no longer functioned as a viable unit. Movement in rear echelons proved exceedingly difficult because of blocked roads, refugees and panic.

12 The bulk of Fourth Army troops began to reverse front toward Rava Russka, a railroad junction fifty kilometers northeast of Lemberg.

13 *KAAOK*, fasz. 496 and 6180; Conrad, *Dienstzeit*, IV, p. 626; *ÖULK*, I, p. 273.

14 *ÖULK*, I, p. 273; *RAWK*, II, p. 340; M. von Pitreich, *1914*, p. 208.

15 VI Corps had been one of the few effective Third Army infantry elements. General Boroević immediately undertook the difficult task of restoring confidence and discipline in the army ranks. He would also prove effective in the 1915 Carpathian Winter War offensive campaign and then most significantly as the defensive leader on the Italian front from 1915 until 1918.

16 Graydon A. Tunstall, *Written in Blood: The Battle for Fortress Przemyśl in WWI*, Bloomington: Indiana University Press, 2016 and Franz Forstner, *Przemyśl: Österreich-Ungarns bedeutendste Festung*, Vienna: Österreichische Bundesverlag, 1987.

17 The Habsburgs established an incredible decoding system aided by Hermann Pokorny who constantly broke Russian codes, providing invaluable information that kept Austria-Hungary in the war although suffering defeat after defeat. He continually alerted Habsburg Supreme Command to enemy intentions that prevented even worse battlefield disasters than occurred.

18 Conrad, *Dienstzeit*, IV, pp. 487, 874; V, pp. 38, 256; Fritz Fellner, ed., *Schicksalsjahre Österreichs 1908–1919: Das politische Tagebuch Joseph Redlichs*, 2 vols., Graz and Cologne: Hermann Böhlaus Nachf., 1954, I, pp. 273, 279.

19 Conrad, *Dienstzeit*, IV.

20 Conrad, *Dienstzeit*, IV, p. 814.

Chapter 4

1 Lyon, *Serbia and the Balkan Front*; Jonathan E. Gumz, *The Resurrection and Collapse of Empire of Habsburg Serbia, 1914-1918*, New York: Cambridge University Press, 2014; Gunther E. Rothenberg, "The Austro-Hungarian Campaign against Serbia," *The Journal of Military History*, vol. 53, no. 2, 1989, pp. 127-146; John R. Schindler, "Disaster on the Drina: The Austro-Hungarian Army in Serbia, 1914," *War in History*, vol. 9, no. 2, 2002, pp. 159-195.

2 Lyon, *Serbia and the Balkan Front*.

3 Conrad, *Dienstzeit*, IV, p. 300; M. von Pitreich, *1914*.

4 *ÖULK*, I, p. 34.

5 *KAAOK*, Op. Büro, fasz. 607, Cramon.

6 IV, IX, VII Corps, 107. *Landsturm* Brigade and seven March brigades consisted of 135,000 troops supported by 300 artillery pieces.

7 The Second Army included IV, VII and IX Corps, Sixth Army, the XIII, XV and XVI Corps. Conrad, *Dienstzeit*, IV, p. 302.

8 This anticipated a Serbian army of 312,000 in six first-line divisions (96,000), six second-line providing 76,000 and a third line of 100,000 soldiers.

9 The Second Army consisted of IV, VII and IX Corps; the Fifth Army VIII and XIII Corps; the Sixth Army included the XV and XVI Corps, supported by five *Landwehr*, three cavalry divisions, as well as five *Landsturm* brigades, six March brigades and eight *Honvéd* regiments.

10 There were fourteen mountain brigades, three cavalry divisions, eight *Landsturm* brigades, six March brigades, eight *Honvéd* regiments and five separate infantry and two *Landwehr* regiments.

11 *KAN*, B/509, Karl Schneller, *Tagebücher*.

12 *Landwehr* divisions had fewer officers and NCOs than regular army units, while most troops were reservists with little if any military training and physically unprepared for combat situations.

13 This represented one of his negative traits that continued throughout the war.

14 Fifth Army had 89 battalions and 2,050 cannons against the Serbian Second Army's 54 battalions and 123 cannons, while Sixth Army's 125 battalions and 165 artillery pieces opposed the Serbian Third Army's 64 battalions and 88 cannons.

15 *ÖULK*, I, pp. 605-610.

16 Lyon, *Serbia and the Balkan Front*, pp. 292, 293.

17 Lyon, *Serbia and the Balkan Front*, pp. 180, 181.

18 N. Stone, *Eastern Front*, p. 347.

19 *KAN*, fasz. 405, *Balkankampf*, No. 3, pp. 122-123, 137, 141.

20 Wawro, *A Mad Catastrophe*, p. 322.

21 *ÖULK*, VII, pp. 715-716.

22 *ÖULK*, I, pp. 442-443.

23 *ÖULK*, VII, p. 762.

Chapter 5

1 For the October through December 1914 campaign Conrad, *Dienstzeit*; *ÖULK*, II; *RAWK*; M. von Pitreich, *1914*; Rauchensteiner, *Tod des Doppeladlers*; N. Stone, *Eastern Front*; Herwig, *The First World War*; Wawro, *A Mad Catastrophe*; David Stone, *The Russian Army in the Great War: The Eastern Front, 1914-1917*,

Lawrence: University Press of Kansas, 2015; Churchill, *The Unknown War*. For the question of the conduct of Czech soldiers, see Richard Lein, *Pflichterfüllung oder Hochverrat: Die tschechischen Soldaten Österreich-Ungarns im Ersten Weltkrieg*, Vienna; Lit, 2011.

2   General Aleksei A. Brusilov, *A Soldier's Notebook 1914–1918*, Westport, CT: Greenwood Press, 1930, p. 80; *KAN*, B/1041, Karl Bornemann; *KA* Ms 1. Wkg, *Rußland, 1914*, No. 19: *Festung Przemyśl*. On Fortress Przemyśl see Tunstall, *Written in Blood*; Forstner, *Przemyśl*. For this chapter Conrad, *Dienstzeit*; *ÖULK*; *RAWK*; N. Stone, *Eastern Front*; Rauchensteiner, *Tod des Doppeladlers*; Herwig, *The First World War*; D. Stone, *The Russian Army in the Great War*.

3   General Max Hoffmann, *War Diaries and Other Papers*, 2 vols., Eric Sutton, trans., London: M. Secker, 1929, I, p. 49; see *ÖULK*, I; *RAWK*, V for details.

4   *KAN*, B/1137, No. 2: Hermann Kusmanek, *Przemyśl*; *KA MKSM* (*Militär Kanzlei Seiner Majestät*), fasz. 100, Op. No. 1956; *KA* Ms 1. Wkg, *Rußland, 1914*, No. 19: *Festung Przemyśl*; BWA, TGY 99, Pamperl, *Chronicle*; Tunstall, *Written in Blood*; Forstner, *Przemyśl*.

5   Conrad, *Dienstzeit*, V, pp. 39–41; *KAAOK*, Op. No. 2821.

6   *KA* Ms 1. Wkg, *Rußland, 1914*, No. 19: *Festung Przemyśl*; *KAN*, B/1137, No. 2: Kusmanek, *Festung Przemyśl*; *KAN*, B/1041, Bornemann; Forstner, *Przemyśl*; *KA* Ms 1. Wkg, *Rußland, 1914*, No. 6. The 65. Reserve Infantry Division served as a reserve force. 3. *Schutzen* Brigade and the 58., 60., 69., 78. and 82. Reserve Infantry Divisions launched the attacks. *ÖULK*, I, p. 381.
More than 7½ infantry divisions, 3 rifle brigades and additional supporting units, totaling 117 battalions, 24 cavalry squadrons and 483 artillery pieces, participated in the initial tsarist attacks.

7   *KA* Ms 1. Wkg, *Rußland, 1914*, No. 19: *Festung Przemyśl*; Forstner, *Przemyśl*, p. 171; Hermann Heiden, *Bollwerk am San: Schicksal der Festung Przemyśl*, Oldenburg: Gerhard Stalling, 1940, p. 134; Bruno Wolfgang, *Przemyśl 1914–1915*, Vienna: Österreichischer Wirtschaftsverlag, 1935.

8   *KA MKSM*, Separat fasz. 100, Res. No. 1956, 69-6/3; *KAN*, B/1137, No. 2: Kusmanek, *Festung Przemyśl*; *KA* Ms 1. Wkg, *Rußland, 1914*, No. 19: *Festung Przemyśl*. See Conrad, *Dienstzeit*, V, pp. 56, 61; *ÖULK*, I; Forstner, *Przemyśl*, pp. 197–198; *KAAOK*, *Übersetzung Nordost*, No. 28: A. M. Zajonstschowskij, *Von Lodz bis Gorlice Jänner-März 1915*.

9   *KAAOK Übersetzung Nordost*, No. 14: Tscherkassow, *Sturm, Oktober 1914*.

10 Heiden, *Bollwerk am San*, p. 153; *KAAOK*, Op. No. 2992.

11 *KAN*, B/1137, No. 2: Kusmanek, *Przemyśl*; *KA* Ms 1. Wkg, *Rußland, 1914*, No. 19: *Festung Przemyśl*.

12 Conrad, *Dienstzeit*, V, pp. 352, 367, 370, 381; Herwig, *The First World War*.

13 The Second Army units still deployed in the Carpathian Mountains included VII Corps (17. and 34. Infantry Divisions), the 20. and 38. *Honvéd* Infantry Divisions, the 103. *Landsturm* Infantry Brigade and the 1., 2. and 17. *Landsturm* Territorial Brigades, as well as the 1., 5. and 8. Cavalry Divisions.

14 A. Pitreich, *Bundesgenosse im Sperrfeuer*, p. 5; Conrad, *Dienstzeit*, V.

15 *KAN*, B/1137, No. 2: Kusmanek, *Przemyśl*; *KA* Ms 1. Wkg, *Rußland, 1914*, No. 19: *Festung Przemyśl*; *ÖULK*, II; Forstner, *Przemyśl*; see *KAAOK*, fasz. 523, *Festung Przemyśl*, AOK Op. No. 7960 (December 3), p. 207.

16 Lodz was a major.

17 Fortress Krakow blocked tsarist forces from invading Austrian and German provinces (Carpathian Mountains and Silesia).
18 *KAAOK*, Op. Büro, fasz. 14, k.u.k. Infantry Regiment 74, III Corps, No. 10, reserve, AOK Op. No. 5761.
19 It proved to be a catastrophe that almost all M 80 15-cm howitzer and field cannon M 75/96 9-cm guns had to stop firing during December. Field cannon M 05 8-cm shells had to be reserved for enemy attacks. During the first siege large numbers of short-range shells were utilized against the tsarist storm attacks, then long-range shells and field artillery for the numerous garrison sorties.
20 For the fortress saga, see Tunstall, *Written in Blood* and Forstner, *Przemyśl*.
21 *ÖULK*, I, pp. 814–815; Conrad, *Dienstzeit*, V, p. 682. Intercepted messages revealed that the Russian VIII Corps was moving toward Neu Sandec in the gap between the Habsburg Third and Fourth armies, particularly the right flank Group Roth. Reinforcements were desperately needed to secure Fourth Army's south flank at Neu Sandec.
22 Their exchanges can be found in *KAAOK*, fasz. 512, *Rußland*, Conrad–Falkenhayn, *Korrespondenz*.
23 For further details, see Tunstall, *Written in Blood*; Forstner, *Przemyśl*.
24 Conrad, *Dienstzeit*, V, p. 791; *ÖULK*, I, pp. 791, 805; *KAN*, B/509, Schneller, *Tagebücher*.
25 *ÖULK*, II; *KAN*, B/509, Schneller, *Tagebücher*. III Corps numbers represented two-thirds of a full infantry division.
26 The troop numbers within the fortress were 131,000 with an additional 21,000 horses and 30,000 civilians. Most of the fortress garrison numbers and food supply calculations, however, were based on the prewar figure of 85,000 soldiers and 3,700 horses, not the actual number during the war.
27 Second Army units had been redeployed from the Carpathian Mountain theater to the German during November to fill the 180-kilometer gap in the lines and defend industrial Silesia.
28 For further details see Tunstall, *Written in Blood*; Forstner, *Przemyśl*.

Chapter 6

1 *ÖULK*; *RAWK*; Rauchensteiner, *Tod des Doppeladlers*; Herwig, *The First World War*; Brusilov, *A Soldier's Notebook*. For the Carpathian Winter War campaign see Graydon A. Tunstall, *Blood on the Snow: The Carpathian Winter War of 1915*, Lawrence: University Press of Kansas, 2010 and *Written in Blood*. Also, Forstner, *Przemyśl*. For Italy, John R. Schindler, *Isonzo: The Forgotten Sacrifice of the Great War*, Westport, CT: Praeger, 2001 and Mark Thompson, *The White War: Life and Death on the Italian Front, 1915–1919*, London: Faber & Faber, 2008. For the 1915 Serbian campaign, Richard L. DiNardo, *Invasion: The Conquest of Serbia, 1915*, Santa Barbara, CA: Praeger, 2015.
2 Tunstall, *Blood on the Snow*.
3 Comparable to the German troop positions on the Western front.
4 *KAN*, B/577, Karl Freiherr von Pflanzer-Baltin, *Tagebücher*.
5 *KAN*, B/13, Rudolf Kundmann, *Tagebücher*; only six thousand casualties resulted from battle.
6 See Tunstall, *Blood on the Snow*, for a refutation that the fortress completely ran out of food.

7 For the battle of Gorlice–Tarnov, see *ÖULK*, II; *RAWK*, VII and Richard DiNardo, *Breakthrough: The Gorlice-Tarnow Campaign, 1915*, Santa Barbara, CA: Praeger, 2010.

8 Hermann Wendt, *Der italienische Kriegsschauplatz in europäischen Konflikten: Seine Bedeutung für die Kriegführung an Frankreichs Nordostgrenze*, Berlin: Junker und Dunnhaupt Verlag, 1936, No. 46, pp. 432–433, Op. No. 769 Ib; *KAAOK*, fasz. 512, *Rußland*, Conrad–Falkenhayn, *Korrespondenz*, AOK Op. No. 9763.

9 Multiple factors favored the Gorlice campaign plans, including the favorable terrain, that there would initially be no major river as an obstacle and that the German troops were proven combat veterans with excellent training and morale. The attacking troops would have enormous numerical advantage in the number of artillery pieces and troops for local superiority at the initial attack objectives. The numerical troop advantage became 375,000 versus 219,000 tsarist Third Army positions.

10 *KA* Ms 1. Wkg, Ms. Luftfahrte Archiv, No. 13: Erich Kahlen, *Die FLIK 10*.

11 *KAAOK*, fasz. 512, *Rußland*, Conrad–Falkenhayn, *Korrespondenz*, Falkenhayn to Conrad.

12 Alfred Knox, *With the Russian Army, 1914–1917*, London: Hutchinson & Co., 1921.

13 *KAAOK*, fasz. 512, *Rußland*, Conrad–Falkenhayn, *Korrespondenz*, Op. No. 9763, No. 777 Ib; No. 777 Ib, 750 Ib; fasz. 607, Cramon–Falkenhayn 1/6; N. Stone, *Eastern Front*, p. 138.

14 *KAAOK*, fasz. 512, *Rußland*, Conrad–Falkenhayn, *Korrespondenz*.

15 *KAAOK*, fasz. 512, *Rußland*, Conrad–Falkenhayn, *Korrespondenz*, AOK Op. Nos. 9991, 9970, Falkenhayn Op. No. 1054r.

16 *KA*, Luftfahrte, Kahlen, *Die FLIK 10*.

17 Gina Conrad, *Leben mit Conrad*, p. 138.

18 *KAAOK*, fasz. 561, *Italien*, Conrad–Falkenhayn, *Korrespondenz*, enclosed in AOK Op. No. 10323, Op. No. 1138r; fasz. 560, *Italien*, Conrad–Falkenhayn, *Korrespondenz*, enclosed in AOK Op. No. 10138.

19 *KA*, Luftfahrte, Kahlen, *Die FLIK 10*.

20 *KAAOK*, fasz. 560, *Italien*, Conrad–Falkenhayn, *Korrespondenz*, AOK Op. No. 10170.

21 Jaroslau was one of the earlier bridgeheads defending the approaches to Fortress Premyśl during September 1914.

22 *KAN*, B/13, Kundmann, *Tagebücher*; only six thousand casualties resulted from battle.

23 Rauchensteiner, *Tod des Doppeladlers*; *ÖULK* and *RAWK*.

24 Rauchensteiner, *Tod des Doppeladlers*, p. 454.

25 *KAAOK*, fasz. 560, *Italien*, Conrad–Falkenhayn, *Korrespondenz*, AOK Op. No. 11170, re Op. 2076r. 20768.

26 *KAAOK*, fasz. 561, *Italien*, Conrad–Falkenhayn, *Korrespondenz*, AOK Op. Nos. 6509 zu Op. No. 6509.

27 *KAN*, B/13, Kundmann, *Tagebücher*.

28 Conrad originally planned to evacuate Gorizia and Trieste, but the slow Italian deployment allowed the Habsburg military to commence construction of bridge-heads at Tolmein and Gorizia.

29 See Schindler, *Isonzo* for details.

30 Gorizia was defended by Dalmatian troops (58. Infantry Division) and Mt. San Gabriel by Slovenes.

31 The Habsburg units consisted of 560 battalions, 48 Finance Guard and mobile *Miliz* units, 510 artillery batteries and 35 cavalry units; Fritz Weber, *Das Ende der alten Armee*, Salzburg: Verlag das Bergland-Buch, 1959.

32 Weber, *Das Ende der alten Armee*.

33 Georg Veith, "Die Isonzoverteidigung," in *Ergänzungsheft 3 zu Österreich-Ungarns letzter Krieg*, Vienna: Militärwissenschaftliche Mitteilungen, 1932, pp. 1–42.

34 Weber, *Das Ende der alten Armee*, p. 55.

35 As we have learned, Carso Plateau consisted of barren, rocky terrain while the Gorizian front is characterized by of hills of limestone.

36 DiNardo, *Invasion*.

37 *KAAOK*, fasz. 560, *Balkan*, Conrad–Falkenhayn, *Korrespondenz*, AOK Op. No. 2076.

38 *KAAOK*, fasz. 551, *Balkan*, Conrad–Falkenhayn, *Korrespondenz*, AOK Op. No. 1355 (5/19); Carl Mühlmann, *Oberste Heeresleitung und Balkan im Weltkrieg 1914–1918*, Berlin: Wilhelm Limpert, 1942, pp. 107–108. For the campaign see DiNardo, *Invasion*.

39 *KAAOK*, fasz. 560, *Italien*, Conrad–Falkenhayn, *Korrespondenz*, AOK Op. No. 2076.

40 DiNardo, *Invasion*.

41 The Central Powers had 350 infantry battalions with 1,300 artillery pieces against 275 Serbian battalions and only 654 artillery pieces, or 330,000 troops against 192,000.

42 All ammunition, other supplies and reinforcements had to be transported over this key railroad.

43 *ÖULK*, III, p. 336.

Chapter 7

1 Key sources for 1916 include *ÖULK*; *RAWK*; Rauchensteiner, *Tod des Doppeladlers*; Herwig, *The First World War*; N. Stone, *Eastern Front*. For the Brusilov offensive, the most comprehensive is Jeřábek, *Die Brussilowoffensive*; Timothy Dowling, *The Brusilov Offensive*, Bloomington: Indiana University Press, 2008. For Italy, see Schindler, *Isonzo*; Thompson, *The White War*; Gerhard Artl, *Die österrechische-ungarische Südtiroloffensive 1916*, Vienna: Österreichischer Bundesverlag, 1983; and Hans Jürgen Pantenius, *Der Angriffsgedanke gegen Italien bei Conrad von Hötzendorf: Ein Beitrag zur Koalitionskriegsführung im ersten Weltkrieg*, 2 vols., Vienna: Böhlau Verlag, 1984. For Romania, Glenn E. Torrey, *The Romanian Battlefront in World War I*, Lawrence: University Press of Kansas, 2011 and *Romania and World War I: A Collection of Studies*, Iaşi: The Center for Romanian Studies, 1998; Silberstein, *The Troubled Alliance*. Also, A. Pitreich, *Bundesgenosse im Sperrfeuer* and Cramon, *Unser Bundesgenosse im Weltkriege*.

2 The Sixtus Affair involved Emperor Karl sending a letter to the French government stating that he sought peace and would accept France receiving Alsace-Lorraine from his ally Germany.

3 See *ÖULK*, IV; N. Stone, *Eastern Front*; Dowling, *Brusilov Offensive*; Jeřábek, *Die Brussilowoffensive* for basic information on this and the summer Brusilov offensive.

Jeřábek's work is incredibly detailed and should be translated into English in an abbreviated version.

4 *ÖULK*, IV; *RAWK*, X; Jeřábek, *Die Brussilowoffensive*, pp. 232, 236; Dowling, *Brusilov Offensive*.

5 *ÖULK*, IV; Dowling, *Brusilov Offensive*; Jeřábek, *Die Brussilowoffensive*.

6 Brusilov, *A Soldier's Notebook*, pp. 213–216; *ÖULK*, IV; Jeřábek, *Die Brussilowoffensive*; Dowling, *Brusilov Offensive*.

7 *KA NFA*, 4. Op. Armee Kdo., fasz. 166, *Tagebücher* 1916–1917, multiple entries; *KAAOK*, fasz. 819, *Evidenz der eigener Situation*.

8 The Russians had 1,700 light-, 168 heavy- and many medium-artillery pieces, achieving superiority on specific attack fronts. The mission of tsarist light-artillery pieces was to blow breaches in the Habsburg barbed wire; large guns were utilized to obliterate frontline trenches and silence Habsburg artillery. Meanwhile, airplanes with radios directed the artillery fire.

9 *ÖULK*, IV; Jeřábek, *Die Brussilowoffensive*; Dowling, *Brusilov Offensive*.

10 One *Landsturm* division replaced the combat units. Troops on the Eastern front for the most part consisted of untried recruits. While a great deal of construction occurred, little was accomplished on rearward defensive positions; A. Pitreich, *Bundesgenosse im Sperrfeuer*, p. 274.

11 *KAAOK*, fasz. 475; see Jeřábek, *Die Brussilowoffensive*; *KAN*, B/13, Kundmann, *Tagebücher*.

12 Dowling, *Brusilov Offensive*; Jeřábek, *Die Brussilowoffensive*.

13 Jeřábek, *Die Brussilowoffensive*; *KAN*, B/13, Kundmann, *Tagebücher*.

14 N. Stone, *Eastern Front*, p. 250.

15 Schindler, *Isonzo*, pp. 203–205.

16 In particular, besides *ÖULK*, see Pantenius, *Die Angriffsgedanke Conrad*; Artl, *Die österreichisch-ungarische Südtiroloffensive 1916*.

17 *ÖULK*, IV, pp. 253–358.

18 Pantenius, *Der Angriffsgedanke Conrad*, p. 642.

19 *RAWK*, X, p. 571; *KAAOK*, fasz. 551, *Italien*, Conrad–Falkenhayn, *Korrespondenz*, Falkenhayn–Conrad, AOK Op. No. 19974.

20 Pantenius, *Der Angriffsgedanke Conrad*, p. 1051.

21 *ÖULK*, IV, pp. 194–195; Herwig, *The First World War*, p. 206; Kurt Peball, "Führungsfragen der österreichisch-ungarischen Südtiroloffensive im Jahre 1916," *Mitteilungen des österreichischen Staatsarchivs*, vol. 31, 1978, pp. 418–433.

22 *RAWK*, X, p. 460.

23 *KAAOK*, fasz. 514, Op. Nos. 2620, 2622; *ÖULK*, IV, pp. 184–185.

24 Fifth Army was composed of 179,000 men, divided into four corps each with two divisions, or a total of eight divisions.

25 By evening the city and local suburbs had been evacuated and the most noted bridge blown up, while the approximately three thousand surviving troops retreated to the new defensive positions on the high ground east of Gorizia.

26 Gaetano V. Cavallaro, *The Beginning of Futility: Diplomatic, Political, Military and Naval Events on the Austro-Italian Front in the First World War 1914–1917*, vol. 1 [self-published], 2009.

27 *ÖULK*, V, pp. 631–639.

28 *ÖULK*, V, pp. 660–663.

29 Schindler, *Isonzo*, pp. 184–185.

30 There were twenty-four thousand troops killed, wounded or missing, as well as forty-one artillery guns, the most losses suffered by the Italians in one day of battle.
31 *ÖULK*, V, pp. 663–675, November 1–4.
32 Schindler, *Isonzo*, p. 187.
33 In particular, Torrey, *The Romanian Battlefront in World War I*.
34 The Dobruja went to Romania from Bulgaria after the 1913 Second Balkan War.
35 Bridges at Constanta crossed the Danube River to Cernavodă, the only span across the Danube between there and Belgrade.
36 Torrey, *The Romanian Battlefront in World War I*.

Chapter 8

1 For reference, *ÖULK, RAWK* and Rauchensteiner, *Tod des Doppeladlers*; Herwig, *The First World War*; A. Pitreich, *Bundesgenosse im Sperrfeur*; Hans Löwenfeld-Russ, *Die Regelung der Volksernährung im Kriege*, Vienna: Hölder-Pichler-Tempsky A. G., 1926 and *Im Kampfe gegen den Hunger: Aus den Erinnerungen des Staatssekretärs für Volksernährung, 1918–1920*, Munich: R. Oldenbourg Verlag, 1986; General Ottokar Pragenau von Landwehr, *Hunger: Die Erschöpfungsjahre der Mittelmächte 1917–1918*, Zurich: Amalthea-Verlag, 1931; Vasja Klavora, *Monte San Gabriele, Die Isonzofront 1917*, Vienna: Verlag Hermagoras/Mohorjeva, 1998; Borislav Chernev, *Twilight of Empire: The Brest-Litovsk Conference and the Remaking of East-Central Europe, 1917–1918*, Toronto: University of Toronto Press, 2017.
2 Falkenhayn described Salonika as the "greatest internment camp in the world."
3 Ms 1. Wkg, *Rußland, 1917*, No. 11: Kiszling.
4 *ÖULK*, VI, pp. 229–230.
5 The Russians captured 300 officers, 18,000 troops and 26 artillery pieces. Russian Eighth Army troops pierced Habsburg Third Army lines, capturing 131 officers, 7,000 troops and nearly 50 guns.
6 Lein, *Pflichterfüllung der Hochverrat*.
7 Ibid., pp. 265–317.
8 Ms 1. Wkg, *Rußland, 1917*, No. 10: *Überblick über die Operationen in Galizien im Juli 1917*.
9 N. Stone, *Eastern Front*, p. 127; Zeman, *Break-Up of the Habsburg Empire*, pp. 70, 142; Edmund von Glaise-Horstenau, *Die Katastrophe: Die Zertrümmerung Österreich-Ungarns und das Werden der Nachfolgerstaaten*, Vienna: Amalthea-Verlag, 1929, p. 64.
10 Carl Freiherr von Bardolff, *Soldat im alten Österreich: Erinnerungen aus meinem Leben*, Jena: E. Diederichs Verlag, 1943; Glaise, *Katastrophe*, p. 64, but particularly Lein, *Pflichterfüllung der Hochverrat*.
11 Second Army consisted of forty-six battalions and five hundred artillery pieces against the Habsburg XVII Corps, outnumbering the Habsburgs by three to one. Vodice protected the approach to the Bainsizza Plateau.
12 The Italians gained no territory, losing 159,000 casualties to the Habsburgs' 80,000. During this first phase of battle the Italian objective was not achieved, although Italian artillery fired over a million shells.
13 *ÖULK*, VI, pp. 193–196.
14 *ÖULK*, VI, pp. 456, 497.

15 Schindler, *Isonzo*, p. 223.
16 Rauchensteiner, *Tod des Doppeladlers*, fn, p. 225.
17 A. Pitreich, *Bundesgenosse im Sperrfeur*, p. 413.
18 *KAAOK*, AOK Op. Geh, 1917, p. 421.
19 This would be the third time that the Germans deployed their strategic reserve divisions during 1917 to achieve military victory. The first time occurred during the Kerensky offensive, the second Riga, the third the overwhelming Caporetto success.
20 The Italian Army, usually the aggressors, were not prepared for defensive warfare and were in no position to counter the revolutionary Central Power tactics.
21 Rauchensteiner, *Tod des Doppeladlers*, p. 78.
22 Thompson, *White War*, p. 302.

Chapter 9

1 For the fateful year 1918 see Edmund von Glaise-Horstenau, *The Collapse of the Austro-Hungarian Empire*, New York: E. P. Dutton, 1930 and *Katastrophe*; Hugo Kerchnawe, *Der Zusammenbruch der österreichisch-ungarischen Wehrmacht*, Munich: J. F. Lehmann, 1921; *ÖULK*, VIII; *KAN*, B/509, Schneller, *Tagebücher* for details. Also valuable: Rauchensteiner, *Tod des Doppeladlers*; Zeman, *Break-Up of the Habsburg Empire*; Leo Valiani, *The End of Austria-Hungary*, New York: Alfred A. Knopf, 1973; Ludwig Jedlika, *Vom alten zum neuen Österreich*, St. Polten: Niederösterreichisches Pressehaus Druck- und Verlags GmbH, 1975; Peter Broucek, *Karl I, (IV): Der politische Weg des letzten Herrschers der Donaumonarchie*, Vienna: Böhlau Verlag, 1977.
2 See Kerchnawe, *Der Zusammenbruch* for details on the military operations and nationality issues.
3 On January 17 flour rations were reduced from 300 to 225 grams and to non-providers from 200 to 165. This came after the rations had been severely cut in mid-1917 and the food situation had severely worsened. Outside grain supplies had been drastically reduced. This raised the serious question as to how much more suffering the people could endure.
4 General Hoffmann was the chief German negotiator at Brest-Litovsk.
5 It increased 600 percent during the war.
6 The Cattaro revolt represented the first major event concerning the military establishment. Negotiations commenced as land military units prepared to intervene, particularly artillery. An ultimatum to the sailors began the return to normalcy. Only the major instigators were executed.
7 The Central Powers treaty with the Ukraine promised the delivery of one million tons of grain to Austria-Hungary and Germany within six months. Meanwhile, the province of Cholm, promised earlier to Poland, now in a secret clause, would create an autonomous province for the Ukrainians in Galicia. The treaty would become null and void if the grain was not delivered.
8 The number of returning prisoners of war continued; an estimated 54,200 officers and 2,050,000 soldiers. *ÖULK*, VII, p. 43. By the end of April 360,000 had returned, by the end of June it was 517,000, end of July, 522,255, September 4, 623,068 and by October 31, 664,500. *ÖULK*, VII, p. 45.
9 *Varia*.
10 Veith, "Die Isonzoverteidigung."

11 *KAN*, B/54, Anton Ritter von Pitreich, pp. 116–122.

12 Reputedly Italian aircraft shot down eighty-six Habsburg aircraft, while the British claimed to have destroyed sixty-one. Anti-aircraft fire also claimed additional victims. Habsburg sources claimed that they lost only thirty-one aircraft, while shooting down forty-three Italian planes.

13 A most significant problem for the Habsburg Army throughout the war and during the June 15 offensive was the high casualty rates of officers. In 1914 there were 25,000 officers deployed, by 1918, 20,000 had become casualties. A total of 5,000 were dead, 2,000 sick or wounded and 4,000 had become invalids or could not serve. Another 3,000 were missing in action, while 6,000 had become prisoners of war. During January 1918 there were only 12,000 officers at the front, only a quarter of those necessary.

14 A. Pitreich, *Bundesgenosse im Sperrfeuer*, p. 325; *ÖULK*, VI.

15 See Maureen Healy, *Vienna and the Fall of the Habsburg Empire: Total War and Everyday Life in World War I*, Cambridge: Cambridge University Press, 2004, for wartime conditions in Vienna.

16 *Varia.*

17 Rauchensteiner, *Tod des Doppeladlers*, p. 538.

18 During July, the Habsburg Supreme Command had promised to send four to six divisions. The unfavorable situation on the Italian front removed any possibility of fulfilling the pledge. On July 18 the Second Battle of the Marne occurred.

19 *KAN*, B/151, Theodor Ritter von Zeynek, p. 209.

20 Löwenfeld-Russ, *Im Kampf gegen den Hunger*, p. 110.

21 Hecht, *Fragen zur Heeresergänzung*, pp. 387–388.

22 *ÖULK*, VII, p. 662.

23 Hecht, *Fragen zur Heeresergänzung*, p. 388.

24 AOK Op. No. 148284; Sondhaus, *Conrad*, p. 390.

25 During the month, five thousand railcars were removed from service, 21 percent of the total.

26 Bulgaria, at war since 1912 and the 1912–1913 Balkan Wars, witnessed the home front becoming war weary. The army and people were exhausted and the German ally seized the rich farmlands of the Dobruja. Thus, by summer 1918, the lack of food and basic necessities produced serious demoralization and growing antagonism toward the country's German ally.

27 Graf Stephan Burian, *Drei Jahre: Aus der Zeit meiner Amtsführung im Kriege*, Berlin: Verlag von Ullstein, 1923, p. 397.

28 The hopelessness of the present situation evoked the Austro-Hungarian decision that the country could not continue the brutal war for much longer. The participants also sought to seek peace based on Wilson's Fourteen Points program.

29 May, *The Passing of the Habsburg Monarchy* presents a very readable account of these events.

30 *ÖULK*, VI, p. 579, et al.

31 Löwenfeld-Russ, *Im Kampf gegen den Hunger*.

32 Glaise-Horstenau, *Katastrophe*, p. 441.

33 David Stevenson, *The First World War and International Politics*, Oxford: Oxford University Press, 1988, p. 226.

34 Glaise-Horstenau, *Katastrophe*, p. 444; Rauchensteiner, *Tod des Doppeladlers*; et al.

35 Glaise-Horstenau, *Katastrophe*, p. 443.

36 His failed leadership included the Sixtus Affair, amnesty to political prisoners, altering the Supreme Command's entire structure and having commanded the fateful and disastrous June 1918 offensive.

37 Glaise-Horstenau, *Katastrophe*, p. 240.

38 Ibid., p. 240.

39 Glaise-Horstenau, *The Collapse of the Austro-Hungarian Empire*, pp. 228, 231–231; Rauchensteiner, *Tod des Doppeladlers*, pp. 1041ff.

40 *ÖULK*, VII, p. 600.

41 A mountain artillery battery behind the Italian front, and Infantry Regiment 25 mutinied, resulting in the Hungarian 27. and 38. Infantry Divisions abandoning their front lines. Also, unrest in the 21. *Landwehr* Infantry Division resulted.

42 In particular, the 3., 5., 13., 26., 29., 42., 43., 57. Infantry Divisions. See Arthur Arz von Straussenburg, *Zur Geschichte des Grossen Krieges, 1914–1918*, Vienna: Rikola Verlag, 1924 for a full breakdown.

43 Eleven British and French divisions supported the Italians against the Habsburg armies in late 1917. This helped to halt the disastrous Italian Caporetto battle.

44 Constantin Schneider, *Die Kriegserinnerungen, 1914–1919*, Vienna: Böhlau Verlag, 2003, for a participant's description of the misery of the retreat.

45 See *KA* Ms 1. Wkg *Italien, 1918*, No. 19: *Der Waffenstillstand 1918* and *KAN*, B/509, Schneller, *Tagebücher* for the details.

46 Kerchnawe, *Der Zusammenbruch*, pp. 118–119.

Chapter 10

1 Erika Weinzierl and Kurt Skalnik, *Österreich 1918–1938, vol. 1: Geschichte der Ersten Republic*, Vienna: Verlag Styria, 1983; Robert Gerwarth, *The Vanquished: Why the First World War Failed to End*, New York: Farrar, Straus and Giroux, 2016; Robert Gerwarth and John Horne, eds., *War in Peace: Paramilitary Violence after the Great War*, Oxford: Oxford University Press, 2012; Jedlika, *Vom alten zum neuen Österreich*; Günter Bischof, Fritz Plasser and Peter Berger, eds., *From Empire to Republic: Post-World War I Austria* (Austrian Studies, 19), New Orleans, LA: University of New Orleans Press, 2010; Joseph S. Roucek, "The Problems Connected with the Departure of Karl the Last from Central Europe," *East European Quarterly*, vol. XV, 1982, pp. 453–468; Helmut Konrad and Wolfgang Maderthaner, eds., *Das Werden der Ersten Republik: ... Der Rest ist Österreich*, 2 vols., Vienna: Carl Gerold's Sohn Verlagsbuchhandlung, 2008.

2 *Der Waffenstillstand*, p. 8; Jedlika, *Vom alten zum neuen Österreich*.

3 *Der Waffenstillstand*, pp. 11–12; Arz, *Zur Geschichte des Grossen Krieges, 1914–1918*.

4 On September 29 it was determined to establish an armistice commission. On October 5 territorial issues were discussed.

5 When the French text arrived at midnight on November 2, General Weber was unaware of any time limit to sign the armistice. At 6 p.m. the representatives of the two commissions met again. The full text was in French. It basically followed General Badoglio's telephone version.

6 *Der Waffenstillstand*, pp. 26–28; see Arz, *Zur Geschichte des Grossen Krieges, 1914–1918* for an explanation of his actions.

7 Rauchensteiner, *Tod des Doppeladlers*, pp. 122, 124, et al.

8 Of the 400,000 prisoners of war, 300,000 had been captured in the last twenty-four hours offering up no resistance. One-third were German Austrians, 83,000 Czech-Slovaks, 61,000 South Slavs, 40,000 Poles, 32,000 Ukrainians, 25,000 Romanians and 7,000 were Italians.

9 Glaise-Horstenau, Katastrophe, p. 300.

10 Troops from sixteen infantry and three cavalry divisions as well as four corps commanders surrendered to advancing Italian forces.

11 The Belgrade Convention granted the Entente powers the right to occupy strategic Hungarian positions.

12 In Austria the Communist Party was founded and a German Austrian country came into existence followed by a call for some type of military force. For an interesting description of the surrender and the men becoming prisoners of war, see Schneider, Die Kriegserinnerungen, 1914–1919, pp. 606–618.

13 November 11, 1918 brought peace to Western Europe, but not to Central or Southeastern Europe, as civil wars and multiple ethnic confrontations occurred. Löwenfeld-Russ, Die Regelung der Volksernährung im Kriege.

14 The lack of action by the Paris peacemakers provided the opportunity to Hungary's neighbors to invade and occupy territory.

15 The Ottoman Empire became Turkey after a successful nationalist war against an invading Greek army. Mustapha Kamal repulsed the attempt to seize Smyrna and other former Turkish territories. The Turkish military victory over Greece produced the only revised Versailles settlement.

16 The key factors during this period encompassed the loss of South Tyrol to Italy and the unresolved issue of the boundaries of Kärntner (= Carinthia) as well as the Sudetenland, Czechoslovakia and the frontier with Yugoslavia.

17 The country suffered from rising unemployment, starvation conditions and inflation. On October 31 Karolyi had been appointed minister president then on November 16 a Democratic Hungarian Republic was proclaimed. Karolyi served as president of the republic between January and March 1918.

18 Hungary lost Transylvania, the Bukovina and the eastern Banat to Romania; Slovakia and Carpathian Russian territories to Czechoslovakia; and Croatia, Slovenia, Bosnia and Herzegovina to the Kingdom of the Serbs, Croats and Slovenians. Three million Hungarians became citizens of Czechoslovakia, Romania and Yugoslavia.

19 The apex of revolutionary activity transpired in early 1919. For two years national revolutions and armed conflicts raged along the borderland. The war had unleashed radicalism everywhere.

20 Alexander V. Prusin, The Lands between: Conflict in the East European Borderlands, 1870–1992, Oxford: Oxford University Press, 2010.

21 Gerhard Botz, Gewalt in der Politik: Attentate, Zusammenstöße, Putschversuche, Unruhen in Österreich 1918 bis 1938, Munich: Wilhelm Fink Verlag, 1983, p. 177.

22 The new territory entrapped 300,000 Slovenes, 200,000 Croats and 250,000 German-speaking people. Italian numbers equaled 650,000 but the Italians were a very unpopular minority. Italy would lose these territories as well as others after the Second World War. Thompson, White War, pp. 381–382.

BIBLIOGRAPHY

Unpublished Documents

Haus-, Hof- u. Staatsarchiv, Politisches Archiv

Politsche Archiv I

fasz. 496–500, 506–507, 512–516

Politsche Archiv XII

fasz. 357, 365, 424–425, 440–450

War Archives: Vienna (*Kriegsarchiv*)

Conrad–Falkenhayn

fasz. 512   *Rußland*, Conrad–Falkenhayn, *Korrespondenz*

fasz. 551   *Balkan*, Conrad–Falkenhayn, *Korrespondenz*

fasz. 560   *Italien*, Conrad–Falkenhayn, *Korrespondenz*

fasz. 561   *Italien*, Conrad–Falkenhayn, *Korrespondenz*

k.u.k. Operations Abteilung "R" Gruppe: 1914–1917

fasz. 475–476

fasz. 495–496

fasz. 514

fasz. 515–522

fasz. 523

fasz. 607   Falkenhayn–Cramon

Verbindungsoffiziere (*VO*)

fasz. 6180

Evidenz der eigenen Situation

fasz. 819

Evidenz der feindlichen Situation

Archiv Conrad

A-6, 7   varia

B-7   varia

B-12   Kundmann, *Tagebuch* vom 23. Juli–31. Dezember
B-13   Kundmann, *Tagebuch* vom 1/1 1915–4/XI 1916

Armeeoberkommando (AOK)

AOK Tagebücher
Eisenbahnbüro
Neue Feld Akten
1. Op. Armee Kdo.
2. Op. Armee Kdo.
3. Op. Armee Kdo.
4. Op. Armee Kdo
7. Op. Armee Kdo 1915 (Group Pflanzer-Baltin)

Luftfahrte Archiv

Ms 13   Eric Kahlen, *Die FLIK 10*
Ms 40   Improvisationen zur Bekämpfung von Luftfahrzeugen in der Festung Przemyśl 1914/1915, Generalmajor Hans Schwab
Ms 61   Meine Luftpost Reise Wien-Kiew, Major Tanner
Ms 72   Als Flieger in Przemyśl, Oberst Feldpilot Nikolaus Wagner Edler von Florheim
Ms 77   Letzter Flug aus Przemyśl, Roman Grutschnig

Militär Kanzlei Seiner Majestät (MKSM)

Separate fasz. 78/77   *Korrespondenz* Conrad–Bolfras 1914, 1915
Separate fasz. 79/42   *Korrespondenz* Conrad–Bolfras 1914, 1915
Separate fasz. 79/53
Separate fasz. 84
Separate fasz. 100 res. varia

Militär Kanzlei Franz Ferdinand

fasz. 194
fasz. 202

Nachläße

B/3   Viktor Dankl
B/4   Svetozar Boroević
B/5   Julius von Preanfeld Lustig-Prean
B/13   Rudolf Kundmann, *Tagebücher*
B/16   Ferdinand Marterer, Frh.u. Ritt.v
B/20   Ing. Waldemar Stuckheil
B/23   Karl Mayern
B/45   Georg Veith
B/54   Anton Ritter von Pitreich

B/60   Alfred Krauss
B/62   Alexander von Krobatin
B/75   Arthur Freiherr Bolfras von Ahnenberg
B/133   Rudolf Brougier
B/151   Theodor Ritter von Zeynek
B/190   Egon von Peharnis Lauppert
B/198   Max von Bacsany Csicerics
B/203   Otto Berndt
B/509   Karl Schneller, *Tagebücher*
B/544   Gottlieb Kralowetz von Hohenrecht
          Karpatenkrieg-X. Korps-Manuskript
B/557   Karl Freiherr von Pflanzer-Baltin, *Tagebücher*
B/589   Max Pitreich
B/600   G. M. Anton von Lehar
B/700   Hans Mailáth-Pokorny
B/726   Robert Nowak
          No. 8: *Die Klammer des Reiches: Das Verhalten der elf Nationalitäten
          Österreich-Ungarn in der k.u.k. Wehrmacht 1914–1918*
B/800   Rudolf Kiszling
          Die k.u.k. 2. Armee vom 10 November 1914 bis zum Jahresschluss
B/892   Hans von Seecht
B/1000   Hermann Kövess
B/1024   Johann Ritter von Galatai
B/1041   Karl Bornemann
B/1063   No. 6: Auskünfte über Eisenbahn technische Fragen
B/1137   No. 2: Hermann Kusmanek, *Przemyśl*

Manuskripte

Allgemeine

A4   *Werdigang und Untergang*, George Veith
A103   *Eisenbahn Aufmarsch 1914*, Kalman Kéri

Manuskripte 1. Weltkrieg 1914: Rußland

No. 1   *Entschlüsse und wichtige Befehle des k.u.k. AOK vom Kriegsausbruch R bis zur
          Aufnahme der allgemeinen Offensive gegen Russland im August 1914*
No. 6   *Die ersten Operationen der russischen Armee im Jahre 1914*
No. 9   *Kämpfe der 3. Armee östlich Lemberg bis zum Rückzug an die Wereszczyca*
No. 11   *Rechtfertigungsschrift des G.d.K. Brudermann*
No. 17   *Die Schlacht an der Weichsel, Kämpfe am San und Schlacht bei Chyrow*
No. 18   *Die Feldzüge von Krakau, die Schlachten bei Lodz, Limanowa–Lapanow und
          bei Jaslo*

No. 19   *Festung Przemyśl*

No. 45   *Die Schlacht von Limanowa–Lapanow*

No. 46   *Die Schlacht bei Limanowa–Lapanow*

No. 51   *Unser Feldzug 1914 gegen Russland*

No. 52   *Der Winterfeldzug in Polen und Galizien. 18/12. 1914–Anfang Jänner 1915*

No. 53   *Limanowa-Tätigkeit des k.u.k. 4. Armeekommandos vor und während der Schlacht*

No. 56   *Die k.u.k. 2. Armee in der Karpathenschlacht 1914/1915*

No. 58   *Der Feldzug von Limanowa–Lapanow v. Dezember 1914*

No. 60   *Der Kampf um Przemyśl 1914/1915*

No. 62   *Przemyśl 1914/1915*

No. 103   *Eisenbahn Aufmarsch 1914*

Manuskripte 1. Weltkrieg 1915: Rußland

No. 1   *Die k.u.k. 2. Armee in der Karpatenschlacht 1914/15*

No. 2   *Die Karpaten-Schlacht Mitte Jänner bis Ende April 1915*

No. 3   *Kriegserinnerungen aus den Karpathenkämpfen von März 1915*

No. 5   *Die westliche Flügelgruppe der 7. Armee in Karpaten*

No. 6   *Der Winterfeldzug in Polen und Galizien. 18/12. 1914-Anfang Jänner 1915.*

No. 11   *Der Feldzug von Rovno*

No. 21   *Die Erstürmung des Gürtelhauptwerkes Pralkowce (Przemyśl)*

No. 24   *Die Kämpfe um den Brückenkopf von Zaleszczyky im Frühjahr 1915 und dessen Einnahme am 8. Mai*

No. 25   *Die Schlacht um die Sanlinie, 14.5–3.6.1915*

No. 26   *Zur Vorgeschichte der deutschen Südarmee*

No. 32   *Die Winterschlacht in den Karpathen 1915*

No. 34   *Die Offensive der Armeegruppe Pflanzer-Baltin über die Ostkarpathen im Winter 1915*

No. 35   *Sommerfeldzug 1915 in Ostgalizien und der Feldzug von Rowno*

No. 36   *Die deutsche Südarmee von Anfang Januar bis Juli 1915*

Manuskripte 1. Weltkrieg 1916: Rußland

No. 1   *Die Neujahrsschlacht 1915/1916*

No. 2   *Die Kriegführung in Russland und Ostgalizien in den Jahren 1916 und 1917: Militärpolitische Übersicht*

No. 5   *Der Feldzug von Luck im Sommer 1916*

No. 12   *Die Krise der 7. Armee nach der Schlacht bei Okna v. 4.–10. Juni 1916. – Wodurch wurde sie verursacht?*

Manuskripte 1. Weltkrieg 1917: Rußland

No. 3   Der Sommerfeldzug in Ostgalizien 1917
No. 10   Überblick über die Operationen in Galizien im Juli 1917
No. 11   Kiszling
No. 12   Die Schlacht bei Zborow vom 29. Juni–2. Juli 1917

Manuskripte 1. Weltkrieg 1918: Rußland

No. 1   Der österreich-ungarische Vormarsch in die Ukraine

Manuskripte 1. Weltkrieg: Balkan

No. 15   Der Herbstfeldzug 1914 gegen Serbien und Montenegro. 1. Teil: Anfang
         September–15. November 1914
No. 23   Die Oberste Heeresleitung und der Balkan (1914) Feldakten, AOK Akten
No. 405 Balkankampf

Manuskripte 1. Weltkrieg 1917: Italien

No. 11   Die 11. Isonzoschlacht
No. 12   Die 12. Isonzoschlacht
No. 27   Der Durchbruch von Tolmein 1917

Manuskripte 1. Weltkrieg 1918: Italien

No. 14   Die k.u.k. Piaveschlacht
No. 16   Die Piaveforcierung und die Erstürmung des Montello
No. 19   Der Waffenstillstand 1918

Übersetzung Nordost

No. 2   Strategische Skizzen des Krieges der Jahre 1914–1918.
         Periode vom 12. (25.) Nov. 1914–15. (28) Feb. 1915
No. 3   Unser Verlust von Galizien im Jahre 1915. M Bontsch-Brujewitsch
No. 8   Das militärische Ubereinkommen Rußlands
No. 10   Strategische Studie über den Weltkrieg, 1914–1918 (14 Sept. bis 20
         Nov. 1914). G. Korolkow
No. 14   Tscherkassow, Sturm, Oktober 1914
No. 28   A. M. Zajonstschowskij, Von Lodz bis Gorlice Jänner-März 1915

War Archive Budapest (BWA)

Auszug aus dem Berichte über die Aktion im III Verteidigung Bezirk. Während der Einschliessung. GdI Karl Waitzendorfer
Stuckheil Manuskript – *Festung Przemyśl*
TGY 2819 II 143 Armee Gruppe Szurmay
TGY 2819 II 143, Poeffel Papers
TGY 99 Pamperl, *Chronicle*

Published Documents and Official Collections

Published Documents

Austria

Österreich-Ungarns Aussenpolitik von der Bosnischen Krise 1908 bis zum Kriegsausbruch 1914: Diplomatischen Aktenstücke der Österreichish-Ungarisch Ministeriums des Äussern, ed. Ludwig Bittner, 9 vols., Vienna: Österreicher Bundnis Verlag, 1930.

Germany

Die deutschen Dokumente zum Kriegsausbruch, ed. Karl Kautsky, 4 vols., Charlottenberg: Verlags Gesellschaft für Politik, 1919.

Official Military Histories

Austria

Österreich-Ungarns letzter Krieg 1914–1928, vols. I–VIII, Bundesministerium für Heereswesen und vom Kriegsarchiv, Vienna: Militärwissenschaftliche Mitteilungen, 1931–1938. (OULK)

Germany

Der Weltkrieg 1914 bis 1918, 14 vols., *Die militärischen Operationen zu Lande,* Berlin: E. S. Mittler & Sohn, 1927–1944. (*RAWK*)

Monographs

Afflerbach, Holger, *Falkenhayn, Politisches Denken und Handeln im Kaiserreich,* Munich: R. Oldenbourg Verlag, 1994.
Afflerbach, Holger and David Stevenson, eds., *An Improbable War: The Outbreak of World War I and European Political Culture before 1914,* New York: Berghahn Books, 2007.
  Auf Messers Schneide: Wie das Deutsche Reich den Ersten Weltkrieg verlor, Munich: C. H. Beck, 2018.

Albertini, Luigi, *The Origins of the War of 1914*, 3 vols., London: Oxford University Press, 1952–1957.

Angelow, Jürgen, ed., *Der Erste Weltkrieg auf dem Balkan: Perspektiven der Fasschung*, Berlin: Be.bra wissenschaft Verlag, 2011.

Artl, Gerhard, *Die österreichisch-ungarische Südtiroloffensive 1916*, Vienna: Österreichischer Bundesverlag, 1983.

Arz von Straussenburg, Arthur, *Zur Geschichte des Grossen Krieges, 1914–1918*, Vienna: Rikola Verlag, 1924.

Kampf und Sturz der Mittelmächte, Vienna: J. Günther, 1935.

Asprey, Robert B., *The German High Command at War: Hindenburg and Ludendorff Conduct World War I*, New York: William Morrow and Co., 1991.

Auffenberg-Komarów, Moritz, *Aus Österreich-Ungarns Teilnahme am Weltkriege*, Berlin: Ullstein & Co., 1920.

Aus Österreichs Höhe und Niedergang: Eine Lebensschilderung, Munich: Drei Masken Verlag, 1921.

Aull, Otto, *Das K.K. Landsturm-Regiment St. Pölten, Nr. 21* [pamphlet], Wiener Neustadt, 1935.

Bachinger, Bernhard and Wolfram Dornik, eds., *Jenseits des Schützengrabens: Der Erste Weltkrieg im Osten – Erfahrung – Wahrnehmung – Kontext*, Vienna: Studien Verlag, 2013.

Banac, Ivo, *The National Question in Yugoslavia: Origins, History, Politics*, Ithaca, NY: Cornell University Press, 1984.

Bardolff, Carl Freiherr von, *Soldat im alten Österreich: Erinnerungen aus meinem Leben*, Jena: E. Diederichs Verlag, 1943.

Barkley, Karen and Mark von Hagen, eds., *After Empire: Multiethnic Societies and Nation-Building – The Soviet Union and the Russian, Ottoman, and Habsburg Empires*, Boulder, CO: Westview Press, 1997.

Barrett, Michael B., *Prelude to Blitzkrieg: The 1916 Austro-German Campaign in Romania*, Bloomington: Indiana University Press, 2013.

Bauer, Ernest, *Der Löwe vom Isonzo: Feldmarschal Svetozar Boroević de Bojne*, Graz: Verlag Styria, 1986.

Bauerkamper, Arnd and Elise Julien, eds., *Durchhalten!: Krieg und Gesellschaft im Vergleich 1914–1918*, Göttingen: Vandenhoeck & Ruprecht, 2010.

Beck, Ludwig and Hans Speidel, eds., *Studien*, Stuttgart: K. F. Koehler, 1955.

Beckenbaugh, Lisa, *Treaty of Versailles: A Primary Document Analysis*, Santa Barbara, CA: ABC-CLIO, 2018.

Bihl, Wolf-Dieter, *Österreich-Ungarn und die Friedensschlüsse von Brest-Litovsk*, Vienna: Böhlau, 1970.

Bischof, Günter, Fritz Plasser and Peter Berger, eds., *From Empire to Republic: Post-World War I Austria* (Austrian Studies, 19), New Orleans, LA: University of New Orleans Press, 2010.

Böhler, Jochen, Wlodzimierz Borodziej and Joachim von Puttkamer, eds., *Legacies of Violence: Eastern Europe's First World War*, Munich: Oldenbourg Verlag, 2014.

Bossi-Fedrigotti, Anton Graf, *Die Kaiserjäger im Ersten Weltkrieg*, Graz: Ares Verlag, 2009.

Botz, Gerhard, *Gewalt in der Politik: Attentate, Zusammenstöße, Putschversuche, Unruhen in Österreich 1918 bis 1938*, Munich: Wilhelm Fink Verlag, 1983.

Boyer, John W., *Culture and Political Crises in Vienna: Christian Socialism in Power, 1897–1918*, Chicago: University of Chicago Press, 1995.

Bridge, Francis R., *The Habsburg Monarchy among the Great Powers, 1815–1918*, New York: Berg, 1990.

Broadbury, Stephen and Mark Harrison, *The Economics of World War I*, Cambridge: Cambridge University Press, 2005.

Broucek, Peter, *Ein General in Zwielicht: Die Erinnerungen Edmund Glaise von Horstenau*, vol. 1, Vienna, Cologne and Graz: Veröffentlichungen der Kommission für neuere Geschichte Österreichs, 1980.

Karl I. (IV): Der politische Wege des letzten Herrschers der Donaumonarchie, Vienna: Böhlau Verlag, 1997.

Brusilov, General Aleksei A., *A Soldier's Notebook 1914–1918*, Westport, CT: Greenwood Press, 1930.

Burian, Graf Stephan, *Drei Jahre: Aus der Zeit meiner Amtsführung im Kriege*, Berlin: Verlag von Ullstein, 1923.

Buttar, Prit, *Collision of Empires: The War on the Eastern Front in 1914*, New York: Osprey Publishing, 2016.

Germany Ascendant: The Eastern Front 1915, New York: Osprey Publishing, 2017.

Russia's Last Gasp: The Eastern Front 1916–17, New York: Osprey Publishing, 2017.

The Splintered Empires: The Eastern Front 1917–1921, New York: Osprey Publishing, 2017.

Carsten, Francis Ludwig, *Die Erste Österreichische Republik im Spiegel zeitgenössischer Quellen*, Vienna: Böhlau Verlag, 1988.

Cavallaro, Gaetano V., *The Beginning of Futility: Diplomatic, Political, Military and Naval Events on the Austro-Italian Front in the First World War 1914–1917*, vol. 1 [self-published], 2009.

Cecil, Hugh and Liddle, Peter, *Facing Armageddon: The First World War Experience*, London: Cooper, 1996.

Chernev, Borislav, *Twilight of Empire: The Brest-Litovsk Conference and the Remaking of East-Central Europe, 1917–1918*, Toronto: University of Toronto Press, 2017.

Churchill, Winston, *The Unknown War: The Eastern Front*, New York: Charles Scribner's Sons, 1931.

Conrad von Hötzendorf, Franz, *Aus meiner Dienstzeit, 1906–1918*, 5 vols., Vienna: Rikola Verlag, 1921–1925.

Private Aufzeichnungen: Erste Veröffentilchung aus Paperiern des k.u.k. Generalstabs-Chefs, Kurt Peball, ed., Vienna and Munich: Amalthea-Verlag, 1977.

Conrad von Hötzendorf, Gina, *Mein Leben mit Conrad von Hötzendorf: Sein geistiges Vermächtnis*, Leipzig: Grethlein & Co. Nachf., 1935.

Contemporary European History, vol. 19, no. 3, *Aftershocks: Violence in Dissolving Empires after the First World War*, [online]: Cambridge University Press, 2010.

Conze, Werner, *Polnische Nation und deutsche Politik im ersten Weltkrieg*, Cologne and Graz: Böhlau Verlag, 1958.

Cormons, Ernst U., *Schicksale und Schatten: Eine österreichische Autobiographie*, Salzburg: O. Müller Verlag, 1951.

Cornwall, Mark, ed., *The Last Years of Austria-Hungary: Essays in Political and Military History 1908–1918*, Exeter: University of Exeter Press, 1990.

The Undermining of Austria-Hungary: The Battle for Hearts and Minds, New York: St. Martin's Press, 2000.

Cramon, August, *Unser Österreichisch-Ungarischer Bundesgenosse im Weltkriege*, Berlin: E. S. Mittler & Sohn, 1920.

Cramon, August and Paul von Fleck, *Deutschlands Schicksalsbund mit Österreich-Ungarn: Von Conrad von Hötzendorf zu Kaiser Karl*, Berlin: Verlag für Kulturpolitik, 1932.

Czermak, Wilhelm, *In deinem Lager war Österreich: Die österreichisch-ungarische Armee, wie man sie nicht kannte*, Breslau: W. G. Korn, 1938.

Czernin von und zu Chudenitz, Ottokar, *In the World War*, New York: Harper & Collins, 1920.

Danilov, General Jury N., *Rußland in Weltkriege 1914–1915*, Jena: Verlag Frommann, 1925.

Deák, István, *Beyond Nationalism: A Social and Political History of the Habsburg Officer Corps 1848–1918*, Oxford: Oxford University Press, 1990.

de Bussy, Carvel [trans.], *Count Stephen Tisza, Prime Minister of Hungary: Letters (1914–1916)*, New York: Peter Lang, 1991.

Dennis, Peter and Jeffrey Grey, *Entangling Alliances: Coalition Warfare in the Twentieth Century – The 2005 Chief of Army Military History Conference*, Canberra: Australian History Military Publications, 2005.

Desoyne, Reinhard Karl Boromäus, *Die k.u.k. Luftfarhtruppe: Die Entstehung, die Aufbau und die Organisation der österreichisch-ungarischen Heeresluftwaffe 1912–1918*, Hamburg: Diplomica Verlag GmbH, 1999.

DiNardo, Richard L., *Breakthrough: The Gorlice-Tarnov Campaign, 1915*, Santa Barbara, CA: Praeger, 2010.

Invasion: The Conquest of Serbia, 1915, Santa Barbara, CA: Praeger, 2015.

Djokić, Dejan and James Ker-Lindsay, eds., *New Perspectives on Yugoslavia: Key Issues and Controversies*, New York: Routledge, 2011.

Dobiasch, Sepp, *Kaiserjäger im Osten: Karpaten-Tarnow-Gorlice 1915*, Graz: Leykam-Verlag, 1934.

Dobrorolski, Sergei, *Die Mobilmachung der Russischen Armee, 1914*, Berlin: Deutsche Verlagsgesellschaft für Politik und Geschichte, 1922.

Dockrill, Michael, *The Paris Peace Conference 1919: Peace without Victory?*, Basingstoke: Palgrave, 2001.

Doppelbauer, Wolfgang, *Zum Elend noch die Schande: Das altösterreichische Offizierkorps am Beginn der Republik*, Vienna: Österreichischer Bundesverlag, 1988.

Dotterweich, Volker, *Mythen und Legenden in der Geschichte*, Munich: Ernst Vögel, 2004.

Dowling, Timothy, *The Brusilov Offensive*, Bloomington: Indiana University Press, 2008.

Duppler, Jörg and Gerhard P. Gross, *Kriegsende 1918: Ereignis, Wirkung, Nachwirkung*, Munich: R. Oldenbourg Verlag, 1999.

Ehnl, Maximillian, "Die österreichisch-ungarische Landmacht nach Aufbau, Gliederung, Friedensgarnison, Einteilung und nationaler Zusammensetzung im Sommer 1914," in *Ergänzungsheft 9 zu Österreich-Ungarns letzter Krieg*, Vienna: Militärwissenschaftliche Mitteilungen, 1934, pp. 1–21.

Ehrenstein, Leopold, *Der Fall der Festung Przemyśl*, Bratislava: Vilmek, 1935.

Falkenhayn, Erich von, *Der Feldzug der 9. Armee gegen die Rumänien und Russen, 1916/17*, 2 vols., Berlin: E. S. Mittler & Sohn, 1921.

General Headquarters 1914–1916 and Its Critical Decisions, London: Hutchinson, 1919.

The German General Staff and Its Decisions, 1914–1916, New York: Dodd, Mead and Co., 1920.

Die Oberste Heeresleitung 1914–1916 in ihren wichtigsten Entschliessungen, Berlin: E. S. Mittler & Sohn, 1920.

Feldl, Peter, *Das verspielte Reich: Die letzten Tage Osterreich-Ungarns*, Vienna: Paul Zsolnay Verlag, 1968.

Fellner, Fritz, ed., *Schicksalsjahre Österreichs 1908–1919: Das politische Tagebuch Joseph Redlichs*, 2 vols., Graz and Cologne: Hermann Böhlaus Nachf., 1954.

Fiala, Peter, *Die letzte Offensive Altösterreichs: Führungsprobleme und Führerverantwortlichkeit bei der öst.-ung. Offensive in Venetien, Juni 1918*, Boppard: H. Boldt, 1967.

Flotow, Ludwig and Erwin Matsch, *November 1918 auf dem Ballhausplatz: Erinnerungen Ludwigs Freiherrn von Flotow, des letzten Chefs des Österreichisch-Ungarischen Auswärtigen Dienstes 1895–1920*, Vienna: Böhlau, 1982.

Forstner, Franz, *Przemyśl: Österreich-Ungarns bedeutendste Festung*, Vienna: Österreichische Bundesverlag, 1987.

Francois, Hermann, *Gorlice, 1915: der Karpatendurchbruch und die Befreiung von Galizien*, Leipzig: K. F. Koehler, 1922.

Freytag-Loringhoven, Freiherr von, *Menschen und Dinge*, Berlin: E. S. Mittler & Sohn, 1923.

Führ, Christoph, *Das K.u.K. Armeeoberkommando und die Innenpolitik in Österreich, 1914–1917*, Graz, Vienna and Cologne: Hermann Böhlaus Nachf., 1968.

Funder, Friedrich, *Vom Gestern ins Heute: Aus dem Kaiserreich in die Republik*, Vienna and Munich: Verlag Herold, 1971.

Galáltai, József, *Hungary in the First World War*, Eva Gruz and Judit Pakoly, trans., Budapest: Akadémiai Kiadó, 1989.

Die österreichisch-ungarische Monarchie und der Weltkrieg, Budapest: Akadémiai Kiadó, 1979.

Geiss, Imanuel, *Julikrise und Kriegsausbruch 1914: Eine Dokumentensammlung*, 2 vols., Hannover: Verlag für Literatur und Zeitgeschehen, 1963.

Gellert, Georg, *Der Kampf in Feindesland: Erzählung aus dem Völkerkriege 1914/15*, Berlin: Verlag Jugendhort, 1915.

Gerwarth, Robert, *The Vanquished: Why the First World War Failed to End*, New York: Farrar, Straus and Giroux, 2016.

Gerwarth, Robert and Erez Manela, eds., *Empires at War, 1911–1923*, Oxford: Oxford University Press, 2014.

Gerwarth, Robert and John Horne, eds., *War in Peace: Paramilitary Violence after the Great War*, Oxford: Oxford University Press, 2012.

Glaise-Horstenau, Edmund von, *The Collapse of the Austro-Hungarian Empire*, New York: E. P. Dutton, 1930.

Franz Joseph's Weggefährte, Vienna: Amalthea-Verlag, 1930.

Ein General im Zwielicht: Die Erinnerungen Edmund Glaise von Horstenau, vol. I, Peter Broucek, ed., Vienna: Böhlau Verlag, 1980.

Die Katastrophe: Die Zertrümmerung Österreich-Ungarns und das Werden der Nachfolgerstaaten, Vienna: Amalthea-Verlag, 1929.

Glatz, Ferenc and Ralph Melville, eds., *Gesellschaft, Politik und Verwaltung in die Habsburgermonarchie 1830–1918*, Wiesbaden: Franz Steiner Verlag, 1987.

Golovin, Nicholas N., *The Russian Army in the World War*, New Haven, CT: Yale University Press, 1931.

The Russian Campaign of 1914: The Beginning of the War and Operations in East Prussia, A. G. S. Muntz, trans., Carlisle, PA: The Command and General Staff School Press, 1933.

Gomoll, Wilhelm Conrad, *Im Kampf gegen Rußland und Serbien*, Leipzig: A. Brockhaus, 1916.

Gonda, Imre, *Verfall der Kaiserreiche in Mitteleuropa: Der Zweibund in den letzten Kriegsjahren (1916–1918)*, Budapest: Akadémiai Kiadó, 1977.

Good, David F., *The Economic Rise of the Habsburg Empire, 1750–1914*, Berkeley: University of California Press, 1984.

Gottsmann, Andreas, ed., *Karl I. (IV.): Der Erste Weltkrieg und das Ende der Donaumonarchie*, Vienna: ÖAH, 2007.

Gratz, Gustav and Richard Schüller, *Der wirtschaftliche Zusammenbruch Österreich-Ungarns: Die Tragödie der Erschöpfung*, Vienna: Hölder-Pichler-Tempsky A. G., 1930.

Gross, Gerhard P., ed., *Die vergessene Front: Der Osten 1914/15 – Ereignis Wirkung, Nachwirkung*, Paderborn: Schöningh, 2006.

Grosz, Peter, George Haddow and Peter Schiemer, *Austro-Hungarian Army Aircraft of World War One*, Mountain View, CA: Flying Machine Press, 1993.

Gumz, Jonathan E., *The Resurrection and Collapse of Empire in Habsburg Serbia, 1914–1918*, New York: Cambridge University Press, 2014.

Hagan, Mark von, *War in a European Borderland: Occupation and Occupation Plans in Galicia and Ukraine, 1914–1918*, Seattle: Herbert J. Ellison Center for Russian, East European, and Central Asian Studies, 2007.

Halpern, Paul G. *The Battle of the Otranto Straights: Controlling the Gateway to the Adriatic in WWI*, Bloomington: Indiana University Press, 2004.

The Naval War in the Mediterranean, 1914–1918, Annapolis, MD: Naval Institute Press, 1987.

Hamilton, Richard and Holger Herwig, eds., *War Planning 1914*, Cambridge: Cambridge University Press, 2004.

Hantsch, Hugo, *Leopold Graf Berchtold*, 2 vols., Vienna: Verlag Styria, 1963.

Healy, Maureen, *Vienna and the Fall of the Habsburg Empire: Total War and Everyday Life in World War I*, Cambridge: Cambridge University Press, 2004.

Heiden, Hermann, *Bollwerk am San: Schicksal der Festung Przemyśl*, Oldenburg: Gerhard Stalling, 1940.

Herwig, Holger H., *The First World War: Germany and Austria-Hungary 1914–1918*, New York: Arnold, 1997.

Hindenburg, Paul von, *Aus meinem Leben*, Leipzig: Hirzel, 1920.

Out of My Life, F. Holt, trans., London: Cassell, 1920.

Höbelt, Lothar, *"Stehen oder Fallen?": Österreichische Politik im Ersten Weltkrieg*, Vienna: Böhlau Verlag, 2015.

Höbelt, Lothar and Thomas G. Otte, *A Living Anachronism? European Diplomacy and the Habsburg Monarchy: Festschrift für Francis Roy Bridge zum 70. Geburtstag*, Vienna: Böhlau Verlag, 2010.

Hoffmann, General Max, *Der Krieg der versäumten Gelegenheiten*, Munich: Verlag für Kulturpolitik, 1924.

The War of Lost Opportunities, A. Charnot, trans., London; K. Paul, French Trubner & Co., 1924.

War Diaries and Other Papers, 2 vols., Eric Sutton, trans., London: M. Secker, 1929.

Horne, John, ed., *State, Society and Mobilization in Europe during the First World War*, Cambridge: Cambridge University Press, 2009.

Hornykiewicz, Theophiul, ed., *Ereignisse in der Ukraine 1914–1922*, vol. IV, Philadelphia, PA: W. K. Lypynsky East European Research Institute, 1966.

Horsetzky, General Ernst, *Die vier letzten Kriegswochen*, Vienna: K. Harbauer, 1920.

Horst, Taitl, *Die Österreichisch-Ungarischen Kriegsgefangenen in feindlichen Lagern 1914–1921*, vol. 1, Dornbirn: Im Selbstverlag Dornbirn, 1992.

Hoyer, Helmuth, *Kaiser Karl I. und Feldmarschall Conrad von Hötzendorf: Ein Beitrag zur Militärpolitik Kaiser Karls*, Vienna: Notring, 1972.

Janssen, Karl Heinz, *Der Kanzler und der General: Die Fuhrungskrise um Bethmann-Hollweg und Falkenhayn (1914–1916)*, Göttingen: Musterschmidt Verlag, 1967.

Jászi, Oscar, *The Dissolution of the Habsburg Monarchy*, 1929. Reprint: Chicago: University of Chicago Press, 1961.

Jedlika, Ludwig, *Vom alten zum neuen Österreich*, St. Pölten: Niederösterreichisches Pressehaus Druck- und Verlags GmbH, 1975.

Jerábeck, Rudolf, *Potiorek: General im Schatten von Sarajevo*, Graz: Verlag Styria, 1991.

Johnson, Douglas Wilson, *Topography and Strategy in the War*, New York: Henry Holt & Co., 1917.

Josef, Feldmarschall Erzherzog, *A Világháború amilyennek én láttam*, Budapest: Ungarische Akademie der Wissenschaften, 1926–1931.

Kaebisch, Generalleutnant Ernst, *Streitfragen des Weltkrieges, 1914–1918*, Stuttgart: Bergers Literarisches Bureau, 1924.

Kann, Robert A., *Erzherzog Franz Ferdinand Studien*, Vienna: Verlag für Geschichte und Politik, 1976.

The Habsburg Empire: A Study in Integration and Disintegration, New York: Frederick A. Praeger, 1957.

A History of the Habsburg Empire 1526–1918, Berkeley: University of California Press, 1974.

Kaiser Franz Joseph und der Ausbruch des Weltkrieges, Vienna, Cologne and Graz: Hermann Böhlaus Nachf., 1971.

Multinational Empire: Nationalism and National Reform in the Habsburg Monarchy, 1848–1918, 2 vols., New York: Octagon Books, 1970.

Die Sixtus Affäre und die geheimen Friedensverhandlungen Österreich-Ungarns im Ersten Weltkrieg, Vienna: Verlag für Geschichte und Politik, 1966.

Kann, Robert A., Béla K. Király and Paula S. Fichtner, eds., *The Habsburg Empire in World War I: Essays on the Intellectual, Military, Political and Economic Aspects of the Habsburg War Effort*, New York: East European Quarterly, 1977.

Keimel, Reinhard, *Österreichs Luftfahrzeuge: Geschichte der Luftfahrt von den Anfängen bis Ende 1918*, Graz: H. Weishaupt, 1981.

Kerchnawe, Hugo, *Der Zusammenbruch der österreichisch-ungarischen Wehrmacht*, Munich: J. F. Lehmann, 1921.

Kerchnawe, Hugo and Ernst Ottenschläger, *Ehrenbuch unserer Artillerie: Österreichs Artillerie im Weltkrieg, 1914–1918*, Stockerau: Engelbert Hlavka, 1925.

Kerchnawe, Hugo, Rudolf Mitzka, Felix Sobotka, Hermann Leidl and Alfred Krauss, *Die Militärverwaltung in den von den Österreichisch-ungarischen Truppen besetzen Gebieten*, Vienna: Hölder-Pichler-Tempsky A. G., 1928.

Kerekes, Lajos, *Von St. Germain bis Genf: Österreich und seine Nachbarn, 1918–1922*, Vienna: Hermann Böhlaus Nachf., 1979.

Király, Béla and Nandor Dreisinger, eds., *East Central European Society in World War I*, Boulder, CO: Social Science Monographs, 1985.

Kiszling, Rudolf, *Die Hohe Führung der Heere Habsburg im Ersten Weltkrieg*, Vienna: Bundesministerium für Landesverteidigung, Büro für Wehrpolitik, 1984.

Österreich-Ungarns Anteil am ersten Weltkrieg, Graz: Stiasny Verlag, 1958.

Klavora, Vasja, *Monte San Gabriele: Die Isonzofront 1917*, Vienna: Verlag Hermagoras/Mohorjeva, 1998.

Kneussel, Paul, *Przemyśl Mai–Juni 1915*, Munich: Selbstverl, 1925.

Knox, Alfred, *With the Russian Army, 1914–1917*, London: Hutchinson & Co., 1921.

Komjáthy, Miklós, ed., *Protokolle des Gemeinsamen Ministerrates der Oesterreichisch-Ungarischen Monarchie, 1914–1918*, Budapest: Akadémiai Kiadó, 1966.

Komlos, John, ed., *The Habsburg Monarchy as a Customs Union: Economic Development in the Habsburg Monarchy in the Nineteenth Century*, Princeton, NJ: Princeton University Press, 1983.

Konrad, Helmut and Wolfgang Maderthaner, eds., *Das Werden der Ersten Republik: ... Der Rest ist Österreich*, 2 vols., Vienna: Carl Gerold's Sohn Verlagsbuchhandlung, 2008.

Kraft, Heinz, *Staatsräson und Kriegsführung im kaiserlichen Deutschland 1914–1916: Der Gegensatz zwischen dem Generalstabschef von Falkenhayn und dem Oberbefehlshaber Ost im Rahmen des Bündniskrieges der Mittelmächte*, Göttingen, Frankfurt and Zurich: Musterschmidt Verlag, 1980.

Krauss, Alfred, *Theorie und Praxis in der Kriegskunst*, Munich: Lehmann, 1935.

Die Ursachen unserer Niederlage: Erinnerungen und Urteile aus dem Weltkrieg, Munich: J. F. Lehmann, 1921.

Kronenbitter, Günther, *"Krieg im Frieden": Die Führung der k.u.k. Armee und die Grossmachtpolitik Österreich-Ungarns 1906–1914*, Munich: R. Oldenbourg Verlag, 2003.

Kuprian, Hermann J. W. and Oswarld Überegger, *Der Erste Weltkrieg im Alpenraum*, Innsbruck: Universitätsverlag Wagner, 2006.

Kurek, Julian W. and Marcus Kurek, *Artyleria Twierdzy Przemyśl*, Przemyśl: Drukarnia San Set, 2002.

Landwehr, General Ottokar Pragenau von, *Hunger: Die Erschöpfungsjahre der Mittelmächte 1917–1918*, Zurich: Amalthea-Verlag, 1931.

Lehar, Anton, *Erinnerungen: Gegenrevolution u. Restaurationsversuche in Ungarn 1918– 1921*, Munich: R. Oldenbourg Verlag, 1973.

Lein, Richard, *Pflichterfüllung oder Hochverrat: Die tschechischen Soldaten Österreich-Ungarns im Ersten Weltkrieg*, Vienna: Lit, 2011.

Leonhard, Jorn, *Pandora's Box: A History of the First World War*, Patrick Camiller, trans., Cambridge, MA: The Belknap Press of Harvard University Press, 2018.

Leonhard, Jörn and Ulrike von Hirschhausen, eds., *Comparing Empires: Encounters and Transfers in the Long Nineteenth Century*, Göttingen: Vandenhoeck & Ruprecht, 2010.

Lincoln, W. Bruce, *Passage through Armageddon: The Russians in War and Revolution 1914–1918*, New York: Simon & Schuster, 1986.

Löwenfeld-Russ, Hans, *Im Kampf gegen den Hunger: Aus den Errinerungen des Staatssekretärs für Volksernährung, 1918–1920*, Munich: R. Oldenbourg Verlag, 1986.

Die Regelung der Volksernährung im Kriege, Vienna: Hölder-Pichler-Tempsky A. G., 1926.

Lucas, James S., *Austro-Hungarian Infantry, 1914–1918*, London: Almark, 1973.

Fighting Troops of the Austro-Hungarian Army 1868–1914, New York: Hippocrene Books, 1987.

Ludendorff, General Erich von, *Meine Kriegserinnerungen 1914–1918*, Berlin: E. S. Mittler & Sohn, 1921.

Lützow, Heinrich von Graf, *Im diplomatischen Dienst der K.u.K. Monarchie*, Munich: R. Oldenbourg Verlag, 1971.

Lyon, James, *Serbia and the Balkan Front, 1914: The Outbreak of the Great War*, New York: Bloomsbury Academic, 2015.

Macdonald, John with Željko Cimprić, *Caporetto and the Isonzo Campaign: The Italian Front 1915–1918*, Barnsley: Pen & Sword, 2018.

Mackensen, August von, *Briefe und Aufzeichnungen des Generalfeldmarschalls aus Krieg und Frieden*, Leipzig: Bibliographisches Institut A. G., 1938.

Mathes, Kurt, *Die 9. Armee im Weichselfeldzug, 1914*, Berlin: Junker & Dunnhaupt, 1936.

Matsch, Erwin, *November 1918 auf dem Ballhausplatz: Erinnerungen Ludwigs Freiherrn von Flotow des Letzen Chefs des Osterreichish-Ungarischen Auswärtigen Dienstes 1895–1920*, Vienna: Hermann Böhlaus Nachf., 1982.

Matis, Herbert, ed., *The Economic Development of Austria since 1870*, Northampton: Edward Elgar Publishing, 1994.

Max, Ludwig, *Neuzeitliche Festungen: Von der Ringfestung zur befestigten Zone*, Berlin: E. S. Mittler & Sohn, 1938.

May, Arthur J., *The Habsburg Monarchy 1867–1914*, Cambridge, MA: Harvard University Press, 1960.

The Passing of the Habsburg Monarchy, 2 vols., Philadelphia: University of Pennsylvania Press, 1966.

May, Ernest R., ed., *Knowing One's Enemies: Intelligence Assessment before the Two World Wars*, Princeton, NJ: Princeton University Press, 1984.

Mazohl-Wallnig, Brigitte, Hermann J. W. Kuprian and Gunda Barth-Scalmani, *Ein Krieg zwei Schützengräben: Österreich-Italien und der Erste Weltkrieg in den Dolomiten 1915–1918*, Bozen: Verlagsanstalt Athesia, 2005.

Meckling, Ingeborg, *Die Aussenpolitik des Grafen Czernin*, Vienna: Verlag für Geschichte und Politik, 1969.

Meier-Welcker, Hans, *Seeckt*, Frankfurt: Bernard & Graefe, 1967.

Menning, Bruce W., *Bayonets before Bullets: The Imperial Russian Army, 1861–1914*, Bloomington: Indiana University Press, 1992.

Michaelsburg, J. V., *Im belagerten Przemyśl: Tagebuchblätter aus grosser Zeit*, Leipzig: C. F. Amelangs Verlag, 1915.

Millett, Allan R. and Williamson Murray, eds., *Military Effectiveness*, vol. 1, Boston: Allen & Unwin, 1988.

Mitrovic, Andej, *Serbia's Great War 1914–1918*, Lafayette, IN: Purdue University Press, 2007.

Mommsen, Hans, Dušan Kováč and Jiri Malir, *Der Erste Weltkrieg und die Beziehungen zwischen Tschechen, Slowaken und Deutschen*, Essen: Klartext Verlag, 2001.

Monticone, Alberto, *Deutschland und die Neutralität Italiens 1914–1915*, Wiesbaden: Steiner, 1982.

Moritz, Verena and Hannes Leidinger, *Oberst Redl: Der Spionagefall, der Skandal, die Fakten*, Vienna: Residenz Verlag, 2012.

Morrow, John H., *German Air Power in World War I*, Lincoln: University of Nebraska Press, 1982.

Mühlmann, Carl, *Oberste Heeresleitung und Balkan im Weltkrieg 1914–1918*, Berlin: Wilhelm Limpert, 1942.

Muller, Martin, *Vernichtunge und Koalitionskreigfuhrung: Das Deutsche Reiche und Österreich-Ungarn in der offensive, 1917/18*, Graz: Verlag Leopold Stocker, 2003.

Neck, Rudolf, *Österreich im Jahre 1918: Berichte und Dokumente*, Vienna: Verlag für Geschichte und Politik, 1968.

O'Connor, Martin, *Air Aces of the Austro-Hungarian Empire 1914–1918*, Mesa: Champlin Fighter Museum Press, 1986.

Ortner, M. Christian, *Storm Troops: Austro-Hungarian Assault Units and Commandos in the First World War: Tactics, Organization, Uniforms and Equipment*, Vienna: Verlag Militaria, 2005.

Pantenius, Hans Jürgen, *Der Angriffsgedanke gegen Italien bei Conrad von Hötzendorf: Ein Betrag zur Koalitionskriegsführung im ersten Weltkrieg*, 2 vols., Vienna: Böhlau Verlag, 1984.

Partsch, Joseph, *Die Kriegschauplätze, vol. III: Der östliche Kriegsschauplatz*, Leipzig and Berlin: Verlag von B. G. Teubner, 1916.

Pastor, Peter, ed., *Revolutions and Interventions in Hungary and Its Neighbor States, 1918–1919*, Boulder, CO: Social Science Monographs, 1988.

Pastor, Peter and Graydon A. Tunstall, eds., *Essays on World War I*, Boulder, CO: Social Science Monographs, 2012.

Payk, Marcus M., *Frieden durch Recht?: Der Aufstieg des modernen Völkerrechts und der Friedensschluss nach dem Ersten Weltkrieg*, Berlin: De Gruyter Oldenbourg, 2018.

Payk, Marcus M. and Roberta Pergher, *Beyond Versailles: Sovereignty, Legitimacy, and the Formation of New Polities after the Great War*, Bloomington: Indiana University Press, 2019.

Petho, Albert, *Agenten für den Doppeladler: Österreich-Ungarns Geheimer Dienst im Wettkrieg*, Graz: Stocker, 1998.

Pitreich, Anton, *Der Österreich-ungarische Bundesgenosse im Sperrfeuer*, Klagenfurt: Arthur Killitsch, 1930.

Pitreich, Max von, *1914: Die Militärischen Probleme unseres Kriegsbeginnes: Ideen, Gründe und Zusammenhänge*, Vienna: Selbstverlag, 1934.

Lemberg, 1914, Vienna: Verlag von Adolf Holzhausens Nachfolger Universitätsbuchdrucker, 1929.

Plaschka, Richard Georg, *Cattaro-Prag: Revolte und Revolution – Kriegsmarine und Heer Österreich-Ungarns im Feuer der Aufstandsbewegungen vom 1. Februar und 28. Oktober 1918*, Graz and Cologne: Hermann Böhlaus Nachf., 1963.

Plaschka, Richard G., Horst Haselsteiner and Arnold Suppan, *Innere Front: Militärassistenz, Widerstand und Umsturz in der Donaumonarchie 1918*, vols. 1–2, Vienna: Verlag für Geschichte und Politik, 1974.

Plaschka, Richard G. and Karlheinz Mack, eds., *Die Auflösung des Habsburgerreiches: Zusammenbruch und Neuorientierung im Donauraum*, Vienna: Verlag für Geschichte und Politik, 1970.

Polzer-Hoditz, Arthur Graf, *Kaiser Karl: Aus der Geheimmappe seiner Kabinettchefs*, Zurich, Leipzig and Vienna: Amalthea-Verlag, 1929.

Popel', Nikolaï Kirillovich, *Panzer greifen an*, Berlin: Deutscher Militärverlag, 1968.

Pourtalès, Graf A., *Meine letzten Verhandlungen und Dokumente*, Berlin: Gesellschaft für Politik und Geschichte, 1927.

Prusin, Alexander V., *The Lands between: Conflict in the East European Borderlands, 1870–1992*, Oxford: Oxford University Press, 2010.

Rauchensteiner, Manfried, *Der Erste Weltkrieg und das Ende der Habsburgermonarchie 1914–1918*, Vienna: Böhlau Verlag, 2014.

Der Tod des Doppeladlers: Österreich-Ungarn und der Erste Weltkrieg, Graz, Vienna and Cologne: Verlag Styria, 1993.

Waffentreue, Die 12: Isonzoschlacht 1917, Vienna: Österreichischen Staatsarchiv, 2007.

Rebolt, Genieoberst Jules, *Die Festungskämpfe im Weltkriege*, Zurich: Herausgebersellschaft für militärische Bautechnik, 1938.

Redlich, Josef, *Austrian War Government*, New Haven, CT: Yale University Press, 1929.

Österreichische Regierung und Verwaltung im Weltkrieg, Vienna: Hölder-Pichler-Tempsky A. G., 1925.

Schicksalsjahre Österreichs, 1908–1919: Das politische Tagebuch Josef Redlichs, Fritz Fellner, ed., 2 vols., Graz: Böhlau, 1953–1954.

Rees, Louis H., *The Czechs during World War I*, Boulder, CO: East European Monographs, 1992.

Regele, Oskar, *Feldmarschall Conrad: Auftrag und Erfüllung, 1906–1918*, Vienna: Verlag Herold, 1955.

Gericht über Habsburg Wehrmacht: Letzte Siege und Untergang unter dem Armeeoberkommando Kaiser Karls 1. Generaloberst Arz von Straussenburg, Vienna and Munich: Verlag Herold, 1968.

Ritchie, Robertson and Edward Timms, eds., *The Habsburg Legacy: National Identity in Historical Perspective* (Austrian Studies, 5), Edinburgh: Edinburgh University Press, 1995.

Ritter, Gerhard, *Staatskunst und Kriegshandwerk*, vols. 3 and 4, Munich: R. Oldenbourg Verlag, 1964–1968.

Ronge, Max, *Kriegs-und Industriespionage: Zwölf Jahre Kundschaftsdienst*, Zurich: Amalthea-Verlag, 1930.

Ropponen, Risto, *Die Kraft Russlands: Wie beurteilte die politische und militärische Führung der europäischen Grossmächte in der Zeit von 1905 bis 1914 die Kraft Russlands*, Helsinki: Akateeminen Kirjakauppa in Komm, 1968.

Rosenboom, Sebastian, *Im Einsatz über die "vergessene Front": Die Luftkrieg on der Ostfront im Ersten Weltkrieg*, Potsdam: Verlag Militärgeschichtliches Forschungsamt, 2013.

Roshwald, Aviel, *Ethnic Nationalism and the Fall of Empires: Central Europe, Russia and the Middle East, 1914–1923*, London: Routledge, 2001.

Roth, Josef, *Die Schlacht von Limanowa-Lapanow 1914*, Vienna: Kinderfreund, 1928.

Rothenberg, Gunther, *The Army of Francis Joseph*, West Lafayette, IN: Purdue University Press, 1976.

Rutherford, Ward, *The Russian Army in World War I*, London: Gordon Cremonesi, 1975.

Schaumann, Walther, *Isonzo, 1915–1917: Krieg ohne Wiederkehr*, Bassano del Grappa: Ghedina & Tassotti, 1993.

Schenk, Gerhard, *Przemyśl 1914–1915: Monographia über eine historischen Ereígnís*, Vienna: Verlag Polbschanosky, 2003.

Schindler, John R., *Isonzo: The Forgotten Sacrifice of the Great War*, Westport, CT: Praeger, 2001.

Schneider, Constantin, *Die Kriegserinnerungen, 1914–1919*, Vienna: Böhlau Verlag, 2003.

Schubert, Peter, *Piave 1918: Österreich-Ungarns letzte Schlacht*, Klagenfurt, Ljubljana and Vienna: Hermagoras/Mohorjeva, 2000.

Schwarte, Max, *Der große Krieg 1914–1918, vol. V: Der österreichisch-ungarische Krieg*, Leipzig: Barth in Ausgl., 1922.

Schwartz, Engelbrecht, *Frauen in Przemyśl Festung, 1914–1915*, Leipzig: Darnstadt, 1936.

Seeckt, Hans von, *Aus meinem Leben 1866–1917*, Leipzig: V. Hafe & Koehler Verlag, 1938.

Shanafelt, Gary W., *The Secret Enemy: Austria-Hungary and the German Alliance 1914–1918*, New York: Columbia University Press, 1985.

Sharp, Alan and Conan Fischer, eds., *After the Versailles Peace Treaty: Enforcement, Compliance, Contested Identifies*, London: Routledge, 2008.

Showalter, Dennis E., *Tannenberg: Clash of Empires*, Hamden, CN: Archon Books, 1991.

Silberstein, Gerald E., *The Troubled Alliance: German-Austrian Relations, 1914–1917*, Lexington: The University Press of Kentucky, 1970.

Singer, Ladislaus, *Ottokar Graf Czernin*, Graz, Vienna and Cologne: Verlag Styria, 1965.

Singer, Roland, *Karpatenschlachten: Der Erste und Zweite Weltkrieg am oberen Karpatenbogen*, Berlin: Pro Business, 2012.

Sokal, Hans, *Österreich-Ungarns Seekrieg*, 2 vols., Graz: Akademische Druck und Verlagsanstalt, 1967.

Sokol, Anthony E., *The Imperial and Royal Austro-Hungarian Navy*, Annapolis, MD: US Naval Institute, 1968.

Sondhaus, Lawrence, *Franz Conrad von Hötzendorf: Architect of the Apocalypse*, Leiden: Brill, 2000.

The Naval Policy of Austria-Hungary 1867–1918: Navalism, Industrial Development and the Politics of Dualism, West Lafayette, IN: Purdue University Press, 1994.

Stevenson, David, *1917: War, Peace, and Revolution*, Oxford: Oxford University Press, 2017.

The First World War and International Politics, Oxford: Oxford University Press, 1988.

Stone, David, *The Russian Army in the Great War: The Eastern Front, 1914–1917*, Lawrence: University Press of Kansas, 2015.

Stone, Norman, *The Eastern Front 1914–1917*, New York: Charles Scribner's Sons, 1975.

Strachan, Hew, *European Armies and the Conduct of War*, London: Allen & Unwin, 1983.

The First World War, vol. I: To Arms, Oxford: Oxford University Press, 2001.

Straube, Wolfgang Berhard, *Przemyśl 1914–15*, Vienna: Payer, 1936.

Strohn, Matthas, ed., *1918: Winning the War*, New York: Osprey, 2018.

Stuckheil, Franz, *Drugie oblezenie Twierdzy Przemyśl*, Wydawnictwo Fort: Tomasz Idzikowski, 2006.

Stürgkh, Josef Graf, *Im deutschen Grossen Hauptquartier*, Leipzig: Paul List Verlag, 1921.

Politische und militärische Erinnerungen, Leipzig: Paul List Verlag, 1922.

Szabo, Laslo, *A nagy temeto Przemyśl ostrema 1914–1915*, Budapest: Kossuth, 1982.

Szende, Zoltán, *Die Ungarn im Zusammenbruch 1918: Feldherr, Hinterland*, Oldenburg: Schulze, 1931.

Taitl, Horst, *Kriegsgefangen: Österreich und Ungarns als Gefangene der Entente 1914–1921*, vol. 1, Dornbinn: H. Taitl, 1992.

Taslauanu, Octavian C., *With the Austrian Army in Galicia*, London: Skeffington, 1915.

Tauber, Joachim, ed., *Über den Weltkrieg hinaus: Kriegserfahrungen in Ostmitteleuropa, 1914–1921* (Nordost-Archiv 17), Lüneburg: Nordost-Inst., 2009.

Thompson, Mark, *The White War: Life and Death on the Italian Front, 1915–1919*, London: Faber & Faber, 2008.

Thum, Gregor, *Traumland Osten: Deutsche Bilder vom ostlichen Europa im 20 Jahrhundert*, Göttingen: Vandenhoeck & Ruprecht, 2006.

Tisza, Count Stephen, *Briefe, 1914–1918*, Oskar Werthheimer, ed., 2 vols., Berlin: Reimer Hobing, 1928.

Torrey, Glenn E., *Romania and World War I: A Collection of Studies*, Iași: The Center for Romanian Studies, 1998.

The Romanian Battlefront in World War I, Lawrence: University Press of Kansas, 2011.

Tranmer, Keith, *Przemyśl 1914–1915: Militär und Philatelie, 204, a*, Vienna: Arbeitsgemeinschaft Militaria Austriaca Philatelia im Heeres-Briefmarken-Sammler-Verein, 2003.

Tunstall, Graydon A., *Blood on the Snow: The Carpathian Winter War of 1915*, Lawrence: University Press of Kansas, 2010.

Planning for War against Russia and Serbia: Austro-Hungarian and German Military Strategies, 1871–1914, New York: Columbia University Press, 1993.

Written in Blood: The Battle for Fortress Przemzÿl in WWI, Bloomington: Indiana University Press, 2016.

Überegger, Oswald, ed., *Zwischen Nation und Region: Weltkriegsforschung im interregionalen Vergleich Ergebnisse und Perspektiven*, Innsbruck: Universitatverlag Wagner, 2004.

Urbanski von Ostrymiecz, August, *Conrad von Hötzendorf: Soldat und Mensch – Dargestellt von seinem Mitarbeiter Feldmarschalleutnant August*, Vienna: Ulrich Mosers Verlag, 1938.

Urbas, Emanuel, *Schicksale und Schatten: Eine österreichische Autobiographie*, Salzburg: O. Müller, 1951.

Valiani, Leo, *The End of Austria-Hungary*, New York: Alfred A. Knopf, 1973.

Vermes, Gabor, *István Tisza: The Liberal Vision and Conservative Statecraft of a Magyar Nationalist*, Boulder, CO: East European Monographs, 1985.

Vít, Jan, *Wspomnienia z mojego pobytu w Przemyślu podczas rosyjskiego oblezenia, 1914–1915*, Ladislav Hofbauer and Jerzy Husar, trans., Przemyśl: Poludniowo-Wschodni Instytut Naukowy, 1995.

Volgyes, Ivan, ed., *Hungary in Revolution, 1918–19*, Lincoln: University of Nebraska Press, 1971.

Völker, Rudolf, *Przemyśl: Sieg und Untergang der Festung am San*, Vienna: Tyrolia, 1927.

Wandruszka, Adam and Peter Urbanitsch, *Die Habsburgermonarchie 1848–1918, vol. III/1: Die Volker des Reiches*, Vienna: Verlag der Österreichischen Akademie der Wissenschaften, 1980.

Die Habsburgermonarchie, 1848–1918, vol. III/2: Die Volker des Reiches, Vienna: Verlag der Österreichischen Akademie der Wissenschaften, 1980.

Die Habsburgermonarchie, 1848–1918, vol. V: Die bewaffnete Macht, Vienna: Verlag der Österreichischen Akademie der Wissenschaften, 1987.

Wandruszka, Adam, Richard Plaschka and Adam Drabek, eds., *Die Donaumonarchie und die südslawische Frage von 1848 bis 1918*, Vienna: Verlag der Wissenschaften, 1978.

Watson, Alexander, *Ring of Steel: Germany and Austria-Hungary in World War I*, New York: Basic Books, 2014.

Wawro, Geoffrey, *A Mad Catastrophe: The Outbreak of World War I and the Collapse of the Habsburg Empire*, New York: Basic Books, 2014.

Weber, Fritz, *Das Ende der alten Armee*, Salzburg: Verlag das Bergland-Buch, 1959.

Wegs, Robert J., *Die österreichische Kriegswirtschaft 1914–1918*, Vienna: Schendl, 1979.

Weindling, Paul J., *Epidemics and Genocide in Eastern Europe, 1890–1945*, Oxford: Oxford University Press, 2000.

Weinzierl, Erika and Kurt Skalaink, *Österreich 1918–1939, vol. 1: Geschichte der Ersten Republike*, Graz: Verlag Styria, 1983.

Wendt, Hermann, *Der italienische Kriegsschauplatz in europäischen Konflikten: Seine Bedeutung für die Kriegführung an Frankreichs Nordostgrenze*, Berlin: Junker und Dunnhaupt Verlag, 1936.

Werkmann, Freiherr Karl von, *Deutschland als Verbündeter*, Berlin: Verlag für Kulturpolitik, 1931.

Wieslaw, Baczkowski, *Samoloty bombowe I wajny sivatowej*, Warsaw: Wydawnictwa Komunikacji I Lacznosci, 1986.

Williamson, Samuel R., Jr., *Austria-Hungary and the Origins of the First World War*, New York: St. Martin's Press, 1991.

July 1914: Soldiers, Statesmen and the Coming of the Great War – A Brief Documentary History, Boston: St. Martin's Press, 2003.

Williamson, Samuel R., Jr. and Peter Pastor, eds., *Essay on World War I: Origins and Prisoners of War*, New York: Columbia University Press, 1983.

Wisshaupt, Ernst, *Die 52. Landwehrinfantriebrigade im Weltkriege 1914–1918*, Reichenberg: Heimat Söhne im Weltkrieg, 1928.

Die Tiroler Kaiserjäger im Weltkriege 1914–1918, Vienna: Verlagsanstalt Amon Fran Göth, 1935.

Wolfgang, Bruno, *Przemyśl 1914–1915*, Vienna: Österreichischer Wirtschaftsverlag, 1935.

Zametica, John, *Folly and Malice: The Habsburg Empire, the Balkans and the Start of World War One*, London: Shepheard-Walwyn Ltd, 2017.

Zeiler, Thomas W. and David K. Ekbladh, *Beyond 1917: The United States and the Global Legacies of the Great War*, Oxford: Oxford University Press, 2017.

Zeman, Zbyněk A. B., *The Break-Up of the Habsburg Empire, 1914–1918*, London: Oxford University Press, 1961.

Zwehl, Hans von, *Erich von Falkenhayn, General der Infanterie: Eine biographische Studie*, Berlin: E. S. Mittler & Sohn, 1926.

Selected Articles

Afflerbach, Holger, "The Eastern Front," in Jay Winter, ed., *The Cambridge History of the First World War, vol. 1: Global War*, Cambridge: Cambridge University Press, 2014, pp. 234–265.

"The Topos of Improbable War in 1914," in Holger Afflerbach and David Stevenson, eds., *An Improbable War: The Outbreak of World War I and European Political Culture before 1914*, New York: Berghahn Books, 2007, pp. 161–182.

Allmayer-Beck, Johann Christoph, "AOK und 'Armeefrage' im Jahre 1918," *Österreichische militärische Zeitschrift*, vol. 6, 1968, pp. 430–435.

Angelis, Maximilian, "Flieger im Gebirge," *Militärwissenschaftliche und-technische Mitteilungen*, vol. 60, 1927, pp. 517–522.

Baanbor, Jan and Józef Dobrowolski, "Przemyśl und Verdun-entscheidende Festungen im ersten Weltkrieg," in *Fortyfikacja Europejskim Dziedzictwem Kultury*, vol. X [pamphlet], Krakow: Towarzystwo Przyjaciol Fortyfiksciji.

Barang, Robert, "Primäre (Wundnaht) bei Schussverletzungen speziell des Gehirnes," *Wiener Klinische Wochenschrift*, vol. 20, 1915, pp. 524–529.

Barany, George, "Ungarns Verwaltung: 1848–1918," in Adam Wandruszka and Peter Urbanitsch, eds., *Die Habsburgermonarchie 1848–1918, vol. II: Verwaltung und Rechtswesen*, Vienna: Verlag der Österreichischen Akademie der Wissenschaften, 1975, pp. 304–368.

Barth-Scalmani, Gunda, "Memory-Landscapes of the First World War: The Southwestern Front in Present-Day Italy, Austria and Slovenia," in Günter Bischof, Fritz Plasser and Peter Berger, eds., *From Empire to Republic: Post World War I Austria* (Austrian Studies, 19), New Orleans, LA: University of New Orleans Press, 2010, pp. 222–253.

Berend, Iván T. and György Ránki, "Ungarns wirtschaftliche Entwicklung 1849–1918," in Adam Wandruszka and Peter Urbanitsch, eds., *Die Habsburgermonarchie 1848–1918, vol. 1: Die wirtschaftliche Entwicklung*, Vienna: Verlag der Österreichischen Akademie der Wissenschaften, 1973, pp. 462–527.

Bergien, Rüdiger, "Vorspiel des 'Vernichtungskrieges'? Die Ostfront des Ersten Weltkriegs und das Kontinuitätsproblem," in Gerhard Gross, ed., *Der vergessene Front – der Osten 1914–15: Ereignis, Wirkung, Nachwirkung*, Paderborn: Schöningh, 2006, pp. 29–34.

Bihl, Wolf-Dieter, "Die Ruthenen," in Adam Wandruszka and Peter Urbanitsch, eds., *Die Habsburgermonarchie 1848–1918, vol. III/1: Die Völker des Reiches*, Vienna: Verlag der Österreichischen Akademie der Wissenschaften, 1980, pp. 555–584.

"Der Weg zum Zusammenbruch Österreich Ungarn unter Karl I (IV)," in Erika Weinzierl and Kurt Skalnik, eds., *Österreich, 1918–1938: Geschichte der Ersten Republik*, Vienna: Verlag Styria, 1983, pp. 27–54.

Böhler, Jochen, "Enduring Violence: The Postwar Struggles in East-Central Europe, 1917– 1921," *Journal of Contemporary History*, vol. 50, 2014, pp. 58–77.

Brait, Andrea, "Der Isonzoraum – Ein transnationaler Gedächtnisort für Österreichischer, Italiener und Slowenen," in Manfried Rachensteiner, ed., *Waffentreue: Die 12. Isonzoschlacht 1917*, Vienna: Österreichischen Staatsarchiv, 2007, pp. 115–130.

Brettner-Messler, Horst, "Die Balkanpolitik Conrad von Hötzendorf von seiner Wiederernennung zum Chef des Generalstabes bis zum Oktober-Ultimatum 1913," *MÖStA*, vol. 20, 1967, pp. 180–276.

"Die Militärischen Absprachen zwischen den Generalstäben Österreich-Ungarns und Italiens vom Dezember 1912 bis Juni 1914," *Mitteilungen des österreichischen Staatsarchivs*, vol. 23, 1970, pp. 225–249.

Broucek, Peter, "Die deutschen Bemühungen im Zweibund 1879 bis 1914: Ein Bericht über den Stand der Forschung," in *Bericht über den 15. Österreichischen Historikertag in Salzburg 15.–18. September 1981*, Vienna: Verband Österr.Geschichtsvereine, 1984, pp. 81–87.

"Heereswesen," in Erika Weinzierl and Kurt Skalnik, eds., *Österreich, 1918–1938: Geschichte der Ersten Republik*, Vienna: Verlag Styria, 1983, pp. 209–229.

"Taktische Erkenntnisse aus dem russisch-japanischen Krieg und deren Beachtung in Österreich-Ungarn," *Mitteilungen des österreichischen Staatsarchivs*, vol. 30, 1977, Ergänzungsband, pp. 191–220.

Cimprič, Željko, "The War in Upper Isonzo Valley on the Battlefield and in the Minda," in Stefan Karner and Philipp Lesiak, eds., *Erster Weltkrieg: Globaler Konflikt – lokale Folgen: Neu Perspektiven*, Innsbruck: Studien Verlag, 2014, pp. 123–146.

Cohen, Gary B., "Nationalist Politics and the Dynamic Monarchy, 1867–1917," *Central European History*, vol. 40, 2007, pp. 241–278.

Cole, Laurence, "Questions of Nationalization in the Habsburg Monarchy," in Nico Wouters and Laurence van Ypersele, eds., *Nations, Identities and the First World War: Shifting Loyalties to the Fatherland*, London: Bloomsburg Academic, 2018, pp. 115–134.

Collenberg, Ludwig von Rüdt, "Die Heeresleitung *und* der Oberbefehlshaber Ost in Sommerfeldzug 1915," *Wissen und Wehr* , 1932, pp. 291–296.

Cornwall, Mark, "Disintegration and Defeat: The Austro-Hungarian Revolution," in Mark Cornwall, ed., *The Last Years of Austria-Hungary: A Multinational Experiment in Early Twentieth-Century Europe*, Exeter: University of Exeter Press, 1990, pp. 213–220.

"The Great War and the Yugoslav Grassroots: Popular Mobilization in the Habsburg Monarchy 1914–1918," in Dejan Djokic and James Ker-Lindsay, eds., *New Perspectives on Yugoslavia: Key Issues and Controversies*, London: Routledge, 2011, pp. 27–45.

Deák, István, "The Decline and Fall of Habsburg Hungary, 1914–1918," in Iván Völgyes, ed., *Hungary in Revolution 1918–19: Nine Essays*, Lincoln: University of Nebraska Press, 1971, pp. 1–30.

"The Habsburg Empire," in Karen Barkey and Mark von Hagen, eds., *After Empire: Multiethnic Societies and Nation-Building – The Soviet Union and the Russian, Ottoman, and Habsburg Empires*, Boulder, CO: Westview Press, 1997, pp. 129–141.

Deak, John, "The Great War and the Forgotten Realm: The Habsburg Monarchy and the First World War," *The Journal of Modern History*, vol. 86, no. 2, 2014, pp. 336–380.

Demmer, Fritz, "Erfahrungen einer Chirurgengruppe in österreichisch-russichen Feldzuge 1915," *Wiener Medizinische Wochenschrifte*, no. 12 (1915), pp. 515–562; no. 14, pp. 591–598; no. 15, pp. 626–638.

Diehl, James M., "No More Peace: The Militarization of Politics," in Roger Chickering and Stig Forsters, eds., *The Shadow of Total War*, Cambridge: Cambridge University Press, 2009, pp. 97–112.

DiNardo, Richard L., "The Limits of Encirclement: The Invasion of Serbia, 1915," *The Historian*, vol. 78, issue 3, 2016, pp. 486–503.

"The Limits of Technology: The Invasion of Serbia, 1915," *Journal of Military History*, vol. 79, 2015, pp. 981–996.

DiNardo, Richard L. and Daniel Hughes, "Germany and Coalition Warfare in the World Wars: A Comparative Study," *War in History*, vol. 8, 2001, pp. 166–190.

Diószegi, István, "Die österreichisch-ungarische Monarchie in der internationalen Politik im letzten Drittel des 19 Jahrhunderts," in Gy Ember et al., eds., *Études Historiques Hongroises*, Budapest: Akadémiai Kiadó, 1970, pp. 364–395.

Djordjvic, Dimitrije, "Vojvoda Putnik, the Serbian High Command and Strategy in 1914," in Béla Király, Nandor Dreiszinger and Alfred Nofi, eds., *War and Society in East Central Europe, vol. 19: East Central European Society in World War I*, New York: Columbia University Press, 1985, pp. 569–589.

Dornik, Wolfram and Peter Lieb, "Misconceived Realpolitik in a Failing State: The Political and Economical Fiasco of the Central Powers in the Ukraine, 1918," *First World War Studies*, vol. 4, no. 1, 2013, pp. 111–124.

"Der überlagerte Krieg: Österreich-Ungarische Soldaten im Osten 1914–1918," in Stefan Karner and Philipp Lesiak, eds., *Erster Weltkrieg: Globaler Konflikt – lokale Folgen: Neu Perspektiven*, Innsbruck: Studien Verlag, 2014, pp. 95–104.

Engle, Jason, "'The Monstrous Front Will Devour Us All': The Austro-Hungarian Soldier Experience, 1914–1915," in Günter Bischof, Ferdinand Karlhofer and Samuel R. Williamson, eds., *1914: Austria-Hungary, the Origins, and the First Year of World War I* (Austrian Studies, 23), Innsbruck: Innsbruck University Press, 2014, pp. 145–166.

:tschmann, Wolfgang, "Österreich-Ungarn zwischen Engagement und Zurückhaltung k.u.k. Truppen an der Westfront," in Jörg Duppler and Gerhard P. Gross, eds., *Kriegsende 1918: Ereignis, Wirkung, Nachwirkung,* Munich: R. Oldenbourg Verlag, 1999, pp. 97–108.

"Die Südfront 1915–1918," in Klaus Eisterer and Rolf Steininger, eds., *Tirol und der Erste Weltkrieg,* Innsbruck: Österreichischer Studien Verlag, 1995, pp. 27–60.

:arkas, Márton, "The Military Collapse of the Austro-Hungarian Monarchy, October 24 to November 3, 1918," in Peter Pastor, ed., *Revolutions and Interventions in Hungary and Its Neighbor States 1918–1919,* Boulder, CO: Social Science Monographs, 1988, pp. 11–25.

"Die politische Erziehungsarbeit in des Armee am Ende des Erstens Weltkrieges," in Richard G. Plaschka and Karlheinz Mack, eds., *Die Auflösung des Habsburgerreiches: Zusammenbruch und Neuorientierung im Donauraum,* Vienna: Verlag für Geschichte und Politik, 1970, pp. 266–269.

:elberbauer, Franz, "Die 12. Isonzoschlacht: Der Operationsplan und seine Durchführung," in Manfried Rachensteiner, ed., *Waffentreue: Die 12. Isonzoschlacht 1917,* Vienna: Österreichischen Staatsarchiv, 2007, pp. 13–33.

:ellner, Fritz, "Der Vertrag von St. German," in Erika Weinzierl and Kurt Skalnik, eds., *Österreich, 1918–1938: Geschichte der Ersten Republik,* Vienna: Verlag Styria, 1983, pp. 85–106.

"Zwischen Kriegsbegeisterung und Resignation-ein Memorandum des Sektionschefs Graf Forgách vom Jänner 1915," in Heidrun Maschl and Brigitte Mazohl-Wallnig, eds., *Vom Dreibund zum Völkerbund: Studien zur Geschichte der internationalen Beziehungen 1882–1919,* Vienna: R. Oldenbourg Verlag, 1994, pp. 142–153.

:leischer, Obst. Rudolf, "Der Rückzug nach Przemyśl im Herbst 1914: Erinnerungen eines Truppenoffiziers," *Militärwissenschaftliche und-technische Mitteilungen,* vol. 55, 1924, pp. 18–26, 120–129.

:ranek, Fritz, "Entwicklung der österreichische-ungarische Wehrmacht in den ersten zwei Kriegsjahren," in *Ergänzungsheft 5 zu Österreich-Ungarns letzter Krieg,* Vienna: Militärwissenschaftliche Mitteilungen, 1935.

"Probleme der Organisation im ersten Kriegsjahre," in *Ergänzungsheft 5 zu Österreich-Ungarns letzter Krieg,* Vienna: Militärwissenschaftliche Mitteilungen, 1935.

:ussek, Alexander, "Ministerpräsident Karl Graf Stürgkh und die parlamentarische Frage," *Mitteilungen des Österreichischen Staatsarchivs,* vol. 17/18, 1965, pp. 337–358.

:aboi, Helén, "The Hungarian Revolutions and Austria," in Peter Pastor, ed., *Revolutions and Interventions in Hungary and Its Neighbor States, 1918–1919,* Boulder, CO: Social Science Monographs, 1988, pp. 201–210.

:alandauer, Jean, "Die mislungene Kampf das letzten Königs von Böhmen um die Rettung seines Thrones," in Andreas Gottsmann, ed., *Karl I. (IV): Der Erste*

Weltkrieg und das Ende der Donaumonarchie, Vienna: ÖAW, 2007, pp. 147–152.

Galáltai, Joszef, "István Tisza und der Erste Weltkrieg," *Annales Universitatis Scientiarum Budapestinensis, Sectio Historica*, vol. 5, 1963, pp. 185–205.

Gilewicz, Alesky, "Twierda Przemyśl w XIX I XX w (Boudowa, oblezenie, rola e I wojnie swiatowej)," *Rocznik Przemyśl: Towarzystwo przjaciól nauk w Przemyślu*, vol. XII, 1968, pp. 149–192.

Glaise-Horstenau, Edmund, "Flitsch-Tolmien, zum zehnten Jahrestage," *Militärwissenschaftliche und-technische Mitteilungen*, vol. 1, 1927, pp. 499–503.

"Der Verfolgung über den Tagliomento bis zum Piave," *Militärwissenschaftliche und-technische Mitteilungen*, vol. 1, 1927, pp. 515–524.

Golovin, Nicholas, "The Great Battle of Galicia (1914): A Study in Strategy," *The Slavonic Review*, vol. 5, 1926/1927, pp. 25–47.

Gonde, Irme, "Über das Verhältnis Deutschlands zur österreichisch-ungarischen Monarchie in den Kriegsjahren 1916 bis 1917," in Fritz Klein, ed., *Österreich-Ungarn in der Weltpolitik 1900 bis 1918*, Berlin: Akademie-Verlag, 1965.

Gross, Gerhard P., "Ein Nebenschauplatz: Die deutschen Operationen gegen Rumanien 1916," in Jürgen Angelow, ed., *Der Erste Weltkrieg auf dem Balkan Perspektiven der Forschung*, Berlin: be.bra Wissenschaft Verlag, 2011, pp. 143–158.

Halpern, Paul G., "Strategische Perspektiven im östlichen Mittelmeer," in Jürgen Angelow, ed., *Der Erste Weltkrieg auf dem Balkan: Perspektiven der Forschung*, Berlin: be.bra Wissenschaft Verlag, 2011, pp. 111–121.

Hämmerle, Christa, "Ein gescheitertes Experiment? Die Allgemeine Wehrpflicht in der multiethnischen Armee der Habsburgermonarchie," *Journal of Modern European History*, vol. 5, no. 2, 2007, pp. 222–243.

Handël-Mezetti, Rudolf, "Die erste Verteidigung des Grappa im November 1917," *Militärwissenschaftliche und-technische Mitteilungen*, vol. 9, 1927, pp. 515–524.

"Der Verfolgung über den Tagliomento bis zum Piave," *Militärwissenschaftliche und-technische Mitteilungen*, vol. 12, 1927, pp. 503–505.

Haslinger, Peter, "Austria-Hungary," in Robert Gerwarth and Erez Manela, eds., *Empires at War, 1911–1923*, Oxford: Oxford University Press, 2014, pp. 73–90.

Herwig, Holger, "Assymetrical Alliance: Austria-Hungary and Germany, 1891–1918," in Peter Dennis and Jeffrey Gray, eds., *Entangling Alliances: Coalition Warfare in the Twentieth Century*, Canberra: Australian Military History Publications, 2005, pp. 57–61.

"Disjointed Allies: Coalition Warfare in Berlin and Vienna," *Journal of Military History*, vol. 54, no. 3, 1990, pp. 265–280.

Hetés, Tibor, "Der militärische Zusammenbruch in Ungarn," in Richard G. Plaschka and Karlheinz Mack, eds., *Die Auflösung des Habsburgerreiches*,

Zusammenbruch und Neuorientierung im Donauraum, Munich: R. Oldenbourg Verlag, 1970.

Heumos, Peter, "'Kartoffeln her oder es gibt eine Revolution': Hungerkrawalle, Streiks und Massenproteste in den böhmischen Ländern 1914–1918," in Hans Mommsen, Dušan Kováč and Jiri Malir, eds., *Der Erste Weltkrieg und die Beziehungen zwischen Tschechen, Slowakei and Deutschen*, Essen: Klartext Verlag, 2001, pp. 293–305.

Hölbelt, Lothar, "Schlieffen, Beck, Potiorek und das Ende der gemeinsamen deutsch-österreichischen-ungarischen Aufmarchpläne im Osten," *Militärgeschichtliche Mitteilungen*, vol. 36, 1984, pp. 7–30.

"'So wir haben nicht einmal die Japaner angegriffen': Österreich-Ungarns Nordfront 1914/15," in Gerhard P. Gross, ed., *Der vergessene Front – der Osten 1914–15: Ereignis, Wirkung, Nachwirkung*, Paderborn: Schöningh, 2006, pp. 87–119.

Janssen, Karl Heinz, "Der Wechsel in der Obersten Heeresleitung 1916," *Vierteljahrshefte für Zeitgeschichte*, vol. 7, no. 4, 1959, pp. 337–371.

Jedlicka, Ludwig, "Der Kriegsbeginn und die ersten Ereignisse an der Südwestfront 1915 in den Tagebüchern des General Karl Schneller," in Heinrich Fichtenau and Erich Zöllner, eds., *Beiträge zur neueren Geschichte Österreichs*, Vienna: Hermann Böhlaus Nachf., 1974, pp. 454–468.

Jeřábek, Rudolf, "Die Ostfront," in Mark Cornwall, ed., *Die letzten Jahre der Donaumonarchie: Der erst Vielvölkerstaat im Europa des frühen 20. Jahrhunderts*, Essen: Magnus, 2006, pp. 155–173.

Kann, Robert A., "Count Ottokar Czernin and Archduke Francis Ferdinand," *Journal of Central European Affairs*, vol. 16, no. 2, 1956, pp. 117–145.

"The Social Prestige of the Officer Corps in the Habsburg Empire from the Eighteenth Century to 1918," in Béla Király and Gunther Rothenberg, eds., *War and Society in East Central Europe*, vol. 1, New York: Brooklyn College Press, 1979, pp. 113–137.

Keller, Tait, "The Mountains Roar: The Alps during the Great War," *Environmental History*, vol. 14, no. 2, 2009, pp. 253–270.

Kerchnawe, Hugo, "Der Karpatenfeldzüge 1914/15," *Militärwissenschaftliche und-technische Mitteilungen*, vol. 19, 1927, pp. 594–604.

"Die k.u.k. Militarverwaltung in Serbien," in Hugo Kerchnawe et al., eds., *Die Militärverwaltung in den von den Österreichisch-ungarischen Truppen besetzten Gebieten* (Carnegie Stiftung für internationalen Frieden), Vienna: Hölder-Pichler-Tempsky A. G., 1928, pp. 53–269.

Khristov, Khristo A., "Bulgaria, the Balkans and the Peace of 1918," in Peter Pastor, ed., *Revolutions and Interventions in Hungary and Its Neighbor States, 1918–1919*, Boulder, CO: Social Science Monographs, 1988, pp. 409–415.

Kipp, Jacob W., "Strategic Railroads and the Dilemmas of Modernization," in David Schimmelpenninck van der Oye and Bruce W. Menning, eds., *Reforming the Tsar's Army: Military Innovations in Imperial Russia from Peter the Great to Revolution*, Cambridge: Cambridge University Press, 2004, pp. 82–103.

Kiszling, Rudolf, "Feldmarschall Conrad von Hötzendorf," *Österreich in Geschichte und Literatur*, 1954, pp. 157–167.

"Generaloberst Freiherr von Kusmanek," *Militärwissenschaftliche und-technische Mitteilungen*, vol. 65, 1934, pp. 617–619.

"General von Seeckts Wirken im Österreich-Ungarn," *Österreich in Geschichte und Literatur*, 1968, pp. 271–276.

"Habsburg Wehrmacht in Spiegel des Nationalitäten Problems 1815–1918," in Theodor Mayer, ed., *Gedenkschrift für Harold Steinacher*, Munich: R. Oldenbourg Verlag, 1966, pp. 240–253.

"Der Krieg gegen Rumänien 1916," *Österreichische Militärische Zeitschrift*, vol. 2, 1966, pp. 465–471.

"Das Nationalitätenproblem in Habsburg Wehrmacht, 1848–1918," *Der Donauraum*, vol. 4, 1959, pp. 82–92.

Krauss, Alfred, "Die Besetzung der Ukraine 1918," in Hugo Kerchnawe et al., eds., *Die Militärverwaltung in den von den Österreichisch-ungarischen Truppen besetzten Gebieten* (Carnegie Stiftung für internationalen Frieden), Vienna: Hölder-Pichler-Tempsky A. G., 1928, pp. 359–390.

Kronenbitter, Günther, "Falsch verbunden? Die Militärallianz zwichen Österreich-Ungarn und Deutschland 1906–1914," *Österreichische Militärische Zeitschrift*, vol. 38, no. 6, 2000, pp. 743–754.

"The German and Austro-Hungarian General Staffs and Their Reflections on an 'Impossible' War," in Holger Afflerbach and David Stevenson, eds., *An Improbable War: The Outbreak of World War I and European Political Culture before 1914*, New York: Berghahn Books, 2007, pp. 149–158.

"Habsburgs Wehrmacht im Spiegel des Nationalitätenproblems 1815–1918," in Theodor Mayer, ed., *Gedenkschrift für Harold Steichacker*, Munich: R. Oldenbourg Verlag, 1966, pp. 240–253.

"Haus ohne Macht?" Erzherzog Franz Ferdinand (1863–1914) und die Krise der Habsburger Monarchie," in Wolfgang Weber, ed., *Der Fürst: Ideen und Wirklichkeiten in der europäischen Geschichte*, Cologne: Bölau, 1998, pp. 202–208.

"Krieg im Frieden: Die Führung der k.u.k. Armee und die Grossmachtpolitik Österreichs-Ungarns, 1906–1914," in Wilfred Loth, ed., *Studien zur Internationalem Geschichte*, vol. 13, Munich: R. Oldenbourg Verlag, 2003, pp. 579–595.

"Der Macht der Illusionen, Julikrise und Kriegsausbruch 1914 aus der Sicht des deutschen Militärattaches in Wien," *Militärgeschichtliche Mitteilungen*, vol. 57, 1998, pp. 519–550.

"Nur los lassen: Österreich-Ungarns und der Wille zum Krieg," in Johannes Burkhart, Josef Becker, Stig Förster and Günther Kronenbitter, eds., *Lange und kurze Wege in den Ersten Weltkrieg*, Munich: Vogel, 1996, pp. 159–187.

"Von Schweinehunden und Waffenbrüdern: Der Koalitionskrieg der Mittelmächte 1914/15 zwischen Sachzwang und Ressentiment," in

Gerhard P. Gross, ed., *Der vergessene Front – der Osten 1914–15: Ereignis, Wirkung, Nachwirkung*, Paderborn: Schöningh, 2006, pp. 157–186.

"Waffenbrüder: Der Koalitionskrieg der Mittelmächte 1914–1918 und das Selbstbild zweier Militäreliten," in Volker Dotterweich, ed., *Mythen und legenden in der Geschichte*, Munich: Ernst Vögel, 2004, pp. 157–186.

Kupiec-Weglinski, Jerry W., "The Siege of Przemyśl, 1914–1915," *American Philatelist*, June 2001, pp. 544–555.

Labanca, Nicola, "The Italian Front," in Jay Winter, ed., *The Cambridge History of the First World War, vol. 1: Global War*, Cambridge: Cambridge University Press, 2014, pp. 266–296.

Lagzi, Istvan, ed., *Wegrzy w Twierdzy Przemyskiej w latach 1914–1915*, Przemyśl: Wegierski Instytut Kuttury-Muzeum Narodowe Ziemi Przemyślu, 1985, pp. 12–25.

Langthaler, Ernst, "Dissolution before Dissolution: The Crisis of the Wartime Food Regime in Austria-Hungary," in Richard P. Tucker, Tait Keller, John R. McNeill and Martin Schmid, eds., *Environmental Histories of the First World War*, Cambridge: Cambridge University Press, 2018, pp. 38–61.

Lehmann, Conrad, "Conrad von Hötzendorf und die deutsche Oberste Heeresleitung im ersten Kriegshalbsjahr," *Archive für Politik und Geschichte*, vol. 1, 1926, pp. 521–566.

Leidl, Hermann, "Die Verwaltung des besetzten Gebiets Italiens (November 1917 bis October 1918," in Hugo Kerchnawe et al., eds., *Die Militärverwaltung in den von den Österreichisch-ungarischen Truppen besetzten Gebieten* (Carnegie Stiftung für internationalen Frieden), Vienna: Hölder-Pichler-Tempsky A. G., 1928, pp. 318–358.

Lein, Richard, "The Military Conduct of the Austro-Hungarian Czechs in the First World War," *The Historian*, vol. 76, issue 3, 2014, pp. 518–549.

Lenar, Jan, "Pamietnik z walk o Twierdze Przemyśl," *Architectura et Ars Militaris*, vol. 8, 2005.

Leslie, John, "The Antecedents of Austria-Hungary's War Aims: Policies and Policy-Makers in Vienna and Budapest before and during 1914," *Wiener Beiträge zur Geschichte des Neuzeit*, vol. 20, 1993, pp. 307–394.

"Österreich-Ungarn for dem Kriegsausbruch: Der Ballhausplatz aus der Sicht eines österreichisch-ungarischen Diplomaten," in Ralph Melville and Karl Otmar Aretin, eds., *Deutschland und Europa in der Neuzeit: Festschrift für Karl Otmar Freiherr von Aretin zum 65. Geburtstag*, Stuttgart: F. Steiner Verlag Wiesbaden, 1988, pp. 661–684.

Lipschutz, B., "Über sogenannte Blasenschwäche bei Soldaten (nach Beobachtungen in der Festung Przemyśl," *Wiener Klinische Wochenschrift 1915*, July 1915, pp. 948–951.

Lipták, Ľubomír, "Soldatenrevolten und die Spaltung der Nationalitäten in Ungarn 1918," in Hans Mommsen, Dušan Kováč and Jiri Malir, eds., *Der Erste Weltkrieg und die Beziehungen Zwischen Tschechen, Slowakey and Deutschen*, Essen: Klartext Verlag, 2001, pp. 287–292.

Litvan, György, "The Home Front during the Karolyi Regime," in Peter Pastor, ed., *Revolutions and Interventions in Hungary and Its Neighbor States, 1918-1919,* Boulder, CO: Social Science Monographs, 1988, pp. 123-130.

Lukan, Walter, "Die slowenische Politik und Kaiser Karl," in Andreas Gottsmann, *Karl I. (IV): Der Erste Weltkrieg und das Ende der Donaumonarchie,* Vienna: ÖAW, 2007, pp. 159-186.

Luvaas, Jay, "A Unique Army: The Common Experience," in Robert A. Kann, Béla K. Kiraly and Paula S. Fichter, eds., *The Habsburg Empire in World War I: Essays on the Intellectual, Military, Political and Economic Aspects of the Habsburg War Effort,* New York: East European Quarterly, 1977, pp. 87-103.

Lyon, James M. B., "A Peasant Mob: The Serbian Army in the Eve of the Great War," *The Journal of Military History,* vol. 61, no. 3, 1997, pp. 481-502.

Maderthaner, Wolfgang, "Die eigenartige Grösse der Beschränkung Österreichs Revolution im mitteleuropeaischen Spannungsfeld," in Helmut Konrad and Wolfgang Maderthaner, eds., *Das Werden der Ersten Republik: ... Der Rest ist Österreich,* vol. 1, Vienna: Carl Gerold's Sohn Verlagsbuchhandlung, pp. 187-206.

"Utopian Perspective and Political Restraint: The Austrian Revolution in the Context of Central European Conflicts," in Günter Bischof, Fritz Plasser and Peter Berger, eds., *From Empire to Republic: Post World War I Austria* (Austrian Studies, 19), New Orleans, LA: University of New Orleans Press, 2010, pp. 52-66.

Mamatey, Viktor S., "The Union of Czech Political Parties in the Reichsrat 1916-1918," in Robert A. Kann, Béla K. Király and Paula S. Fichtner, eds., *The Habsburg Empire in World War I: Essays on the Intellectual, Military, Political and Economic Aspects of the Habsburg War Effort,* New York: East European Quarterly, 1977, pp. 3-28.

Mayern, Obstlt, "Die Karpathenschlacht. Mitte Jänner bis Ende April 1915," *Militärwissenschaftliche und-technische Mitteilungen,* vol. 54, 1923, pp. 354-364.

Mazohl-Wallnig, Brigitte, Gunda Barth-Scalmani and Hermann J. W. Kuprian, "Ein Krieg zwei Schützengräben," *Ein Krieg zwei Schützengräben: Österreich-Italien und der Erste Weltkrieg in den Dolomiten 1915-1918,* Bozen: Verlagsanstalt Athesia, 2005, pp. 9-21.

Meier-Welcker, Hans, "Die Beurteilung der politischen Lage in Österreich-Ungarn durch Generalmajor von Seeckt im Sommer 1917," *Militärwissenschaftliche und-technische Mitteilungen,* vol. 68, 1937, pp. 87-104.

Menning, Bruce W., "The Offensive Revisited: Russian Preparation for Future Wars, 1906-1914," in David Schimmelpenninck van der Oye and Bruce W. Menning, eds., *Reforming the Tsar's Army: Military Innovations in Imperial Russia from Peter the Great to Revolution,* Cambridge: Cambridge University Press, 2004, pp. 215-231.

"War Planning and Initial Operations in the Russian Context," in Richard F. Hamilton and Holger H. Herwig, eds., *War Planning 1914*, Cambridge: Cambridge University Press, 2010, pp. 80–142.

Mitzka, Rudolph, "Die k.u.k. Militärverwaltung in Russich Polen," in Hugo Kerchnawe et al., eds., *Die Militärverwaltung in den von den Österreichisch-ungarischen Truppen besetzten Gebieten* (Carnegie Stiftung für internationalen Frieden), Vienna: Hölder-Pichler-Tempsky A. G., 1928, pp. 8–52.

Moritz, Verena, "Die Revolutionen in Russland und die Kriegsgegangenen des Zarenreiches in Österreich-Ungarns 1917–1918," in Stefan Karner and Philipp Lesiak, eds., *Erster Weltkrieg: Globaler Konflikt – lokale Folgen. Neu Perspektiven*, Innsbruck: Studien Verlag, 2014, pp. 187–208.

Musner, Lutz, "Im Schatten von Verdun: Die Kultur des Krieges am Isonzo," in Helmut Konrad and Wolfgang Maderthaner, eds., *Das Werden der Ersten Republik: ... Der Rest ist Österreich*, vol. 1, Vienna: Carl Gerold's Sohn Verlagsbuchhandlung, 2008, pp. 45–64.

Nachtigal, Reinhard, "The Repatriation and Reception of Returning Prisoners of War, 1918–22," *Immigrants & Minorities*, vol. 26, nos. 1/2, 2008, pp. 157–184.

Nagy, Zsuzsa L., "The Hungarian Democratic Republic and the Paris Peace Conferance, 1918–1919," in Peter Pastor, ed., *Revolutions and Interventions in Hungary and Its Neighbor States, 1918–1919*, Boulder, CO: Social Science Monographs, 1988, pp. 261–274.

Okey, Robin, "Austria and the South Slavs," in Ritchie Robertson and Edward Timms, eds., *The Habsburg Legacy: National Identity in Historical Perspective* (Austrian Studies, 5), Edinburgh: Edinburgh University Press, 1994, pp. 46–57.

Olejko, Andrzej, "Zapomniane lotnicze epizody z c.k. Przemyśla 1914–1915," *Roczik Przemyśki t.*, vol. XL, 2004, pp. 31–44.

Ortner, Christian, "Die Feldzüge gegen Serbien in den Jahren 1914 und 1915," in Jürgen Angelow, ed., *Der Erste Weltkrieg auf dem Balkan Perspektiven der Forschung*, Berlin: be.bra Wissenschaft Verlag, 2011, pp. 123–142.

Ortner, Christian M., "Austrian Troops for Mountain Warfare," in Hermann Hinterstoisser et al., eds.; Ian Mansfield, trans., *The Austrian Mountain Troops: History, Uniforms and Equipment of the Austrian Mountain Troops from 1906 to 1918*, Vienna: Verlag Militaria, 2006, pp. 23–26.

Palla, Luciana, "Kampf um die Dolomitentaler: Der Große Krieg im Grenzgebiet," in Brigitte Mazohl-Wallnig, Hermann J. W. Kuprian and Gunda Barth-Scalmani, eds., *Ein Krieg zwei Schützengräben: Österreich-Italien und der Erste Weltkrieg in den Dolomiten 1915–1918*, Bozen: Verlagsanstalt Athesia, 2005, pp. 341–361.

Pamperl, Robert, "Chirurgische Tatigkeit in der belagerten Festung Przemyśl," *Medizische Klinik*, no. 41, October 10, 1915, pp. 1126–1130.

450 BIBLIOGRAPHY

Pastor, Peter, "The French Military Mission in Hungary," in Peter Pastor, ed., Revolutions and Interventions in Hungary and Its Neighbor States, 1918–1919, Boulder, CO: Social Science Monographs, 1988, pp. 251–260.

Peball, Kurt, "Um das Erbe: Zu Nationalitätenpolitik des k.u.k. Armeeoberkommandoes während der Jahr 1914 bis 1917," Österreichische Militärische Zeitschrift (Special Issue), 1967.

"Der Feldzug gegen Serbien und Montenegro im Jahre 1914," Österreichische Militärische Zeitschrift (Special Issue), 1978.

"Führung und Taktikim Ruckblick: Die Südtiroloffensive 1916," Truppendienst, vol. 25, 1976, pp. 210–214.

"Führungsfragen der österreichisch-ungarischen Südtiroloffensive im Jahre 1916," Mitteilungen des österreichischen Staatsarchivs, vol. 31, 1978, pp. 418–433.

Pelinka, Anton, "Austrian Identity and the 'Standestaat,'" in Ritchie Robertson and Edward Timms, eds., The Habsburg Legacy: National Identity in Historical Perspective (Austrian Studies, 5), Edinburgh: Edinburgh University Press, 1994, pp. 169–177.

Pflug, Ottokar, "Die Entwicklung der Artillerieorganisation im Krieg 1914–1918," in Hugo Kerchnawe, ed., Ehrenbuch unserer Artillerie, vol. 1, Vienna: Reichsbunde der Artillerievereinigung gegen Österreichs, 1935, pp. 186–194.

Pichlík, Karel, "Der militärische Zusammenbruch der Mittelmächte im Jahre 1918," in Richard G. Plaschka and Karlheinz Mack, eds., Die Auflösung des Habsburgerreiches: Zusammenbruch und Neuorientierung im Donauraum, Vienna: Verlag für Geschichte und Politik, 1970, pp. 249–265.

Pitreich, Anton, "Die 12. Isonzoschlacht," in Max Schwarte, ed., Der grosse Krieg 1914–1918, vol. V: Der österreichische-ungarische Krieg, Leipzig: Barth in Ausgl., 1922, pp. 432–454.

"Die elfte Isonzoschlacht," in Max Schwarte, ed., Der grosse Krieg 1914–1918, vol. V: Der österreichische-ungarische Krieg, Leipzig: Barth in Ausgl., 1922, pp. 409–432.

"Der zehnte Isonzoschlacht," in Max Schwarte, ed., Der grosse Krieg 1914–1918, vol. V: Der österreichische-ungarische Krieg, Leipzig: Barth in Ausgl., 1922, pp. 469–477.

Plaschka, Richard G., "Contradicting Ideologies: The Pressure of Ideological Conflicts in the Austro-Hungarian Army of World War I," in Robert A. Kann, Béla K. Király and Paula S. Fichtner, eds., The Habsburg Empire in World War I: Essays on the Intellectual, Military, Political and Economic Aspects of the Habsburg War Effort, New York: East European Quarterly, 1977, pp. 108–115.

Potpeschnigg, Karl, "Vom galizischen Kriegschauplatz," Feldärtzliche Beilage zur Münchener Medizinische Wochenschrift, no. 14, January 26, 1915, pp. 136–139.

Ratzenhofer, Emil, "Die Aufmarsch hinter den Karpathen im Winter 1915," Militärgeschichtliche Mitteilungen, vol. 61, 1930, pp. 499–513.

"Truppentransport zu Kriegsbeginn," *Militärwissenschaftliche Mitteilungen*, vol. 10, 1929, pp. 231–244.

"Österreich-Ungarns Aufmarsche gegen Balkan und Russland: Einfluss der Aufmarshtechnik," *Österreichisch Wehrzeitung*, 39, 30, 41, 1927, pp. 2–3, 2–2.

"Verlust Kakül für den Karpatenwinter 1915," in *Ergänzungsheft 1 zu Österreich-Ungarns letzter Krieg*, Vienna: Militärwissenschaftliche Mitteilungen, 1930, pp. 1–23.

Rauchensteiner, Manfried, "Das neue Jahr machte bei uns einen traurigen Einzug. Das Ende des Grossen Krieges," in Helmut Konrad and Wolfgang Maderthaner, eds., *Das Werden der Ersten Republik: ... Der Rest ist Österreich*, vol. 1, Vienna: Carl Gerold's Sohn Verlagsbuchhandlung, pp. 21–44.

"Zum 'operativen Denken' in Österreich 1814–1914," *Österreichische Militärische Zeitschrift*, vol. 12, 1974, pp. 121–127, 207–211, 285–291, 379–384, 473–478.

Reiser, Rudolf, "Der Kampf um das Werk I/1 der Gruppe Siedliska am 7. Oktobre 1914," *Österreichische Wehrzeitung: Zeitschrift für Wehrfragen*, vol. 29, 1925, pp. 3–5.

Rendulic, Lothar, "Artillerieverwendung in Hochgebirge," *Militärwissenschaftliche und-technische Mitteilungen*, vol. 7, 1927, pp. 606–611.

"Die Montelloschlacht (June 1918): Ein Beispiel eisnes gewaltsamen Flussüberganges," *Militärwissenschaftliche und-technische Mitteilungen*, vol. 7, 1927, pp. 386–414.

Renzi, William A., "Italy's Neutrality and Entrance into the Great War: A Re-examination," *American Historical Review*, vol. 73, 1968, pp. 1414–1432.

Rosner, Willibald, "Die fortifikatorische Sicherung der Ostgrenze Südtirols," in Brigitte Mazohl-Wallnig, Hermann J. W. Kuprian and Gunda Barth-Scalmani, eds., *Ein Krieg zwei Schützengräben: Österreich-Italien und der Erste Weltkrieg in den Dolomiten 1915–1918*, Bozen: Verlagsanstalt Athesia, 2005, pp. 267–281.

Rothenberg, Gunther E., "The Austro-Hungarian Campaign against Serbia in 1914," *The Journal of Military History*, vol. 53, no. 2, 1989, pp. 127–146.

"The Habsburg Army in the First World War 1914–1918," in Robert A. Kann, Béla K. Király and Paula S. Fichtner, eds., *The Habsburg Empire in World War I: Essays on the Intellectual, Military, Political and Economic Aspects of the Habsburg War Effort*, New York: East European Quarterly, 1977, pp. 73–87.

Roucek, Joseph S., "The Problems Connected with the Departure of Karl the Last from Central Europe," *East European Quarterly*, vol. XV, 1982, pp. 453–468.

Rozanski, Jan, "Przemyśl w. I. Wojnie Swiatowy," *Muzeum ziemi Przemyskiej w Przemyslu*, Przemyśl, 1969.

"Tajemnice Twierdzy Przemyskiej," *Muzeum ziemi Przemyskiej w Przemyslu*, Przemyśl, 2000, pp. 62–132.

Rumpler, Helmut, "Kaiser Karl, die Friedenprojekte und das deutsch-österreichische Bundnis," in Andreas Gottsmann, ed., *Karl I. (IV): Der Erste Weltkrieg und das Ende der Donaumonarchie*, Vienna: ÖAW, 2007, pp. 269–284.

"Die Kriegsziele Österreich-Ungarns auf dem Balkan, 1916/1916," in Institut für österreichische Geschichtsforschung und the Wiener Katholischen Akademie, eds., *Österreich und Europa: Festgabe für Hugo Hantsch zum 70. Geburtstag*, Graz: Verlag Styria, 1965, pp. 465–482.

Schaefer, Theobald von, "Betrachtungen zum Bundniskrieg," *Wissen und Wehr*, 1938, pp. 373–392.

Schindler, John R., "Disaster on the Drina: The Austro-Hungarian Army in Serbia, 1914," *War in History*, vol. 9, no. 2, 2002, pp. 159–195.

"Steamrollered in Galicia: The Austro-Hungarian Army and the Brusilov Offensive," *War in History*, vol. 10, no. 1, 2002, pp. 27–59.

Schmetterer, Christoph, "Der Kaiser von Österreich als Oberster Kriegsherr, 1867–1918," *Journal of European History of Law*, vol. 4, 2013, pp. 10–18.

Schmidl, Erwin A., "From Paardeberg to Przemyśl: Austria-Hungary and the Lessons of the Anglo-Boer War, 1899–1902," in Jay Stone and Erwin A. Schmidl, eds., *The Boer War and Military Reforms*, Lanham, MD: University Press of America, 1988, pp. 89–155.

Schulze, Max-Stephan, "Austria-Hungary's Economy in World War I," in Steven Broadberry and Mark Harrison, eds., *The Economics of World War I*, Cambridge: Cambridge University Press, 2005, pp. 77–111.

Schwalb, Hans G. M., "Die Verteidigung vom Przemyśl 1914–15," *Mitteilungen über Gegenstücke des Artillerie und Geniewesens*, vol. 149, 1918, pp. 1373–1392.

Schwarzlitner, Chodwig, "Aufklärung und Beobachtungsdienst in Gebirge," *Militärwissenschaftliche und-technische Mitteilungen*, vol. 7, 1927, pp. 611–614.

Silberstein, Gerard E., "The High Command and Diplomacy in Austria-Hungary, 1914–1916," *The Journal of Modern History*, vol. 42, December 1970, pp. 586–605.

Sked, Alan, "Austria-Hungary and the First World War," *Historic Politique*, vol. 1, no. 2, 2014, pp. 16–49.

"Social Life and Legal Constraints: The Habsburg Army, 1890–1918," *The European Journal of Law and History*, vol. 3, 2012, pp. 11–32.

Sobotka, Feliz, "Der Anteil Österrich-Ungarns an die Militärverwaltung Rumeniens 1917–1918," in Hugo Kerchnawe et al., eds., *Die Militärverwaltung in den von den Österreichisch-ungarischen Truppen besetzten Gebieten* (Carnegie Stiftung für internationalen Frieden), Vienna: Hölder-Pichler-Tempsky A. G., 1928, pp. 305–317.

Steinitz, Edward, "Uber die Kampfe um das Grappamassiv," *Militärwissenschaftliche und-technische Mitteilungen*, vol. 7, 1927, pp. 501–515.

Steinrück, Heinz, "Das österreichisch-ungarische Donauflotille im Weltkriege," *Militärwissenschaftliche und-technische Mitteilungen*, vol. 1–2, 1928, pp. 5–18, 55–63.

Stone, Norman, "Army and Society in the Habsburg Monarchy, 1900–1914," *Past & Present*, vol. 33, no. 1, 1966, pp. 95–111.

"Austria-Hungary," in Ernest R. May, ed., *Knowing One's Enemies*, Princeton, NJ: Princeton University Press, 1988, pp. 37–61.

"Hungary and the Crisis of July 1914," *Journal of Contemporary History*, vol. 1, no. 3, 1966, pp. 153–170.

"Die Mobilmachung der österreichisch-ungarischen Armee 1914," *Militärgeschichtliche Mitteilungen*, vol. 16, no. 2, 1974, pp. 67–95.

"Moltke and Conrad: Relations between the Austro-Hungarian and German General Staffs, 1909–1914," in Paul M. Kennedy, ed., *War Plans of the Great Powers 1880–1914*, London: Allen & Unwin, 1970, pp. 224–232.

Stourzh, Gerald, "Ethnic Attribution in Late Imperial Austria: Good Intentions, Evil Consequences," in Ritchie Robertson and Edward Timms, eds., *The Habsburg Legacy: National Identity in Historical Perspective* (Austrian Studies, 5), Edinburgh: Edinburgh University Press, 1995, pp. 67–83.

Strachan, Hew, "Die Ostfront: Geopolitik, Geographie und Operationen," in Gerhard Gross, ed., *The Forgotten Front: The Eastern Theater of World War I*, Lexington: The University Press of Kentucky, 2018, pp. 11–26.

Stuckheil, Franz, "Die Festung Przemyśl in der Ausrüstungszeit. Provisorische Darstellung," *Militärwissenschaftliche und-technische Mitteilungen*, vol. 55, 1924, pp. 200–230.

"Die strategische Rolle Przemyśl auf dem östlichen Kriegschauplatz," *Militärwissenschaftliche und-technische Mitteilungen*, vol. 54, 1923, pp. 60–78, 132–146.

"Die zweite Einschliessung Festung Przemyśl II," *Militärwissenschaftliche und-technische Mitteilungen*, vol. 55, 1924, pp. 231–250.

"Die zweite Einschliessung der Festung Przemyśl III," *Militärwissenschaftliche und-technische Mitteilungen*, vol. 55, 1924, pp. 289–309, 395–417; vol. 56, 1925, pp. 110–133, 222–236, 346–367; vol. 57, 1926, pp. 162–173, 286–296, 405–410, 530–535.

Sweet, Paul R., "Germany, Austria-Hungary and Mitteleuropa: August 1915–April 1916," in Hugo Hantsch and Alexander Novotny, eds., *Festschrift für Heinrich Benedikt*, Vienna: Verlag Notring der Wissenschaftlichen Verbände Österreichs, 1957, pp. 190–191.

"Leaders and Policies: Germany in the Winter of 1914–1915," *Journal of Central European Affairs*, vol. 16, 1956/1957, pp. 229–252.

Timms, Edward, "Citizenship and 'Heimatrecht' after the Treaty of Saint-Germain," in Ritchie Robertson and Edward Timms, eds., *The Habsburg Legacy: National Identity in Historical Perspective* (Austrian Studies, 5), Edinburgh: Edinburgh University Press, 1994, pp. 158–168.

Torrey, Glenn R., "Indifference and Mistrust: Russian-Romanian Collaboration in the Campaign of 1916," *Journal of Military History*, vol. 57, no. 2, 1993, pp. 279–300.

"The Romanian Campaign of 1916: Its Impact on the Belligerents," *Slavic Review*, vol. 39, no. 1, 1980, pp. 27–43.

"The Romanian Intervention in Hungary, 1919," in Peter Pastor, ed., *Revolutions and Interventions in Hungary and Its Neighbor States, 1918–1919*, Boulder, CO: Social Science Monographs, 1988, pp. 301–320.

Troebst, Stefan, "Nationalismus und Gewalt im Osteuropa der Zwischenkriegszeit Terroristische Separatismen im Vergleich," *Bulgarian Historical Review*, vol. 24, no. 2, 1996, pp. 25–55.

Tunstall, Graydon A., "Austria-Hungary and the Brusilov Offensive of 1916," *The Historian*, vol. 70, no. 1, 2008, pp. 30–53.

"The Carpathian Winter War, 1915," in Peter Pastor and Graydon A. Tunstall, eds., *Essays on World War I*, New York: Columbia University Press, 2011, pp. 1–23.

"The Habsburg Command Conspiracy: The Austrian Falsification of Historiography on the Outbreak of World War I," *Austrian History Yearbook*, vol. 27, 1996, pp. 181–198.

"Die Karpatenschlachten 1915," *Truppendienst* (two-part series), vols. 2 and 3, 1990, pp. 132–137, 226–231.

Ullrich, Volker, "Entscheidung im Osten oder Sicherung der Dardanellen: Das Ringen um den Serbienfeldzug 1915," *Militärgeschichtliche Mitteilungen*, vol. 32, no. 2, 1982, pp. 45–63.

Veith, Georg, "Die Isonzoverteidigung," in *Ergänzungsheft 3 zu Österreich-Ungarns letzter Krieg*, Vienna: Militärwissenschaftliche Mitteilungen, 1932, pp. 1–42.

Vermes, Gabor, "Leap in the Dark: The Issue of Suffrage in Hungary during WWI," in Robert A. Kann, Béla K. Kiraly and Paula S. Fichter, eds., *The Habsburg Empire in World War I: Essays on the Intellectual, Military, Political and Economic Aspects of the Habsburg War Effort*, New York: Eastern European Quarterly, 1997, pp. 29–34.

Vermes, Ludwig, "Monte Priafora," *Ergänzungsheft 3 zu Österreich-Ungarns letzter Krieg*, Vienna: Militärwissenschaftliche Mitteilungen, 1932, pp. 43–64.

Verosta, Stephan, "Die österreichische Aussenpolitik 1918–1938 im europäischen Staatensystem 1914–1955," in Erika Weinzierl and Kurt Skalnik, eds., *Österreich, 1918–1938: Geschichte der Ersten Republik*, Vienna: Verlag Styria, 1983, pp. 107–146.

Vranesević, Branislav, "Die aussenpolitischen Beziehungen zwischen Serbien und der Habsburgermonarchie," in Adam Wandruszka and Peter Urbanitsch, eds., *Die Habsburgermonarchie, vol. VI/2: Die Habsburgmonarchie im System der internationalen Beziehungen*, Vienna: Verlag der Österreichischen Akademie der Wissenschaften, 1993, pp. 319–375.

Wagner, Walter, "Die k.(u.)k. Armee: Gliederung und Aufgabenstellung," in Adam Wandruszka and Peter Urbanitsch, eds., *Die Habsburgermonarchie 1848–1918, vol. V: Die bewaffnete Macht*, Vienna: Verlag der Österreichischen Akademie der Wissenschaften, 1987, pp. 142–633.

Wandysz, Piotr S., "East Central Europe 1918: War and Peace, Czechoslovakia and Poland," in Peter Pastor, ed., *Revolutions and Interventions in Hungary and Its Neighbor States, 1918–1919*, Boulder, CO: Social Science Monographs, 1988, pp. 397–408.

Wank, Solomon, "Foreign Policy and the Nationality Problem in Austria-Hungary, 1867–1914," *Austrian History Yearbook*, vol. 3, 1967, pp. 37–56.

"The Habsburg Empire," in Karen Barkey and Mark von Hagen, eds., *After Empire: Multiethnic Societies and Nation-Building: The Soviet Union and the Russian, Ottoman, and Habsburg Empires*, Boulder, CO: Westview Press, 1997, pp. 45–57.

"Some Reflections on Conrad von Hötzendorf and His Memoirs Based on Old and New Sources," *Austrian History Yearbook*, vol. 1, 1965, pp. 74–88.

Wargelin, Clifford F., "A High Price for Bread: The First Treaty of Brest-Litvosk and the Break-Up of Austria-Hungary, 1917–1918," *The International History Review*, vol. 19, no. 4, 1997, pp. 757–788.

Wegs, Robert J., "Transportation: The Achilles Heel of the Habsburg War Effort," in Robert A. Kann, Béla K. Király and Paula S. Fichtner, eds., *The Habsburg Empire in World War I: Essays on the Intellectual, Military, Political and Economic Aspects of the Habsburg War Effort*, New York: Eastern European Quarterly, 1977, pp. 121–135.

Wetzell, Georg, *Kritische Beiträge zur Geschichte des Weltkrieges; von Falkenhayn zu Hindenburg-Ludendorff: Der Wechsel in der deutschen Obersten Heeresleitung im Herbst 1916 und der rumänische Feldzug.*, (Beiheft z. 105 Jahrgang des *Militär Wochen Blattes*), Berlin: E. S. Mittler & Sohn, 1921.

Williamson, Samuel R., Jr., "Aggressive and Defensive Aims of Political Elites? Austro-Hungarian Policy in 1914," in Holger Afflerbach and David Stevenson, eds., *An Improbable War: The Outbreak of World War I and European Political Culture before 1914*, New York: Berghahn Books, 2007, pp. 61–75.

"Confrontation with Serbia: The Consequences of Vienna's Failure to Achieve Surprise in July 1914," *Mitteilungen des Österreichischen Staatsarchivs*, vol. 43, 1993, pp. 173–174.

"Leopold Count Berchtold: The Man Who Could Have Prevented the Great War," in Günter Bischof, Fritz Plasser and Peter Berger, eds., *From Empire to Republic: Post World War I Austria* (Austrian Studies, 19), New Orleans, LA: University of New Orleans Press, 2010, pp. 24–57.

Winsauer, Andrea, "Räder müssen Rollen: Die k.u.k Eisenbahnen im Ersten Weltkrieg und in der 12. Isonzoschlacht," in Manfried Rachensteiner, ed., *Waffentreue: Die 12. Isonzoschlacht 1917*, Vienna: Österreichischen Staatsarchiv, 2007, pp. 36–47.

Wirsching, Andreas, "'Augusterlebnis' 1914 und 'Dolchstoß' 1918: zwei Versionen derselben Legende?," in Volker Dotterweich, ed., *Mythen und Legenden in der Geschichte* (Schriften der Philosophischen Fakultäten der Universität Augsburg, 64: Historisch-sozialwissenschaftliche Reihe), Munich: Vögel, 2004, pp. 187–202.

Wróbel, Piotr, "The Seeds of Violence: The Brutalization of an East European Region, 1917–1921," *Journal of Modern European History*, vol. 1, no. 1 (Violence and Society after the First World War), 2003, pp. 125–149.

Wulff, Olaf Richard, "Die österreichisch-ungarische Donauflotille im Weltkriege, 1914–18," in *Dem Werke Österreich-Ungarns Seekreig, 1914–18*, Vienna: W. Braumüller, 1934.

Zechlin, Egmont, "Das schlesische Angebot und die italienische Kriegsgefahr 1915," *Geschichte in Wissenschaft und Unterricht*, vol. 14, 1963, pp. 533–556.

Zeidler, Miklos, "Charles IV's Attempted Returns to the Hungarian Throne," in Andreas Gottsmann, ed., *Karl I. (IV): Der Erste Weltkrieg und das Ende der Donaumonarchie*, Vienna: ÖAW, 2007, pp. 269–284.

Zükert, Martin, "Imperial War in the Age of Nationalism: The Habsburg Monarchy and the First World War," in Jörn Leonhard and Ulrike von Hirschhausen, eds., *Comparing Empires: Encounters and Transfers in the Long Nineteenth Century*, Göttingen: Vandenhoeck & Ruprecht, 2010, pp. 500–517.

Dissertations

Artl, Gerhard, *Die österreichisch-ungarische Südtiroloffensive 1916*, Dissertation, University of Vienna, 1983.

Dixon, Joe Clinton, *Defeat and Disarmament: A Study of Military Affairs in Austria, 1918– 1921*, Dissertation, University of Minnesota, 1980.

Hecht, Rudolph, *Fragen zur Heeresergänzung der Gestalten Bewaffneten Macht Österreich-Ungarns während des ersten Weltkrieges*, Dissertation, University of Vienna, 1969.

Hoffman, Edward F., *Feldmarschall Svetozar Boroević von Bojna: Österreich-Ungarns Kriegsfront an den Flussen, Isonzo and Piave*, Dissertation, University of Vienna, 1985.

Jeřábek, Rudolf, *Die Brussilowoffensive 1916: Ein Wendepunkt der Koalitionskriegführung der Mittelmächte*, Dissertation, University of Vienna, 1982.

Lein, Richard, *Das militärische Verhalten der Tschechen im Ersten Weltkrieg*, Dissertation, University of Vienna, 2009.

Mörz, Kurt, *Der österreichisch-ungarische Befestigungsbau 1866–1914*, Dissertation, University of Vienna, 1980.

Przybilovszki, Inge, *Die Rückverlegung der österreich-ungarischen Kriegsgefangen aus dem osten in den letzten Monaten der k.u.k. Monarchie*, Dissertation, University of Vienna, 1968.

Schmidt, Ulrike, *Die Beziehungen Österreich-Ungarns zu Rumänien vom 1. VIII 1914 bis zum Kriegseintritt Rumäniens*, Dissertation, University of Vienna, 1961.

Seyfert, Günter, *Die militärischen Beziehungen und Vereinbarungen zwischen dem deutschen und dem österreichischen Generalstab vor und bei Beginn des Weltkrieges*, Dissertation, University of Leipzig, 1934.

Wegs, Robert J., *Austrian Economic Mobilization during World War I with Particular Emphasis on Heavy Industry*, Dissertation, University of Vienna, 1970.

Zehnder, Ralph D., *Habsburg Preparations for Armageddon: Conrad von Hötzendorf and the Austro-Hungarian General Staff, 1906–1914*, Dissertation, Kansas State University, 1987.

INDEX

Lightning Source UK Ltd.
Milton Keynes UK
UKHW010749051121
393294UK00009B/330